TRANSFORMING
INTERRELIGIOUS RELATIONS

Transforming Interreligious Relations

Catholic Responses to Religious Pluralism in the United States

Leo D. Lefebure

ORBIS BOOKS

Maryknoll, New York 10545

ORBIS BOOKS
Maryknoll, New York 10545

Fathers and Brothers
MARYKNOLL.

Founded in 1970, Orbis Books endeavors to publish works that enlighten the mind, nourish the spirit, and challenge the conscience. The publishing arm of the Maryknoll Fathers and Brothers, Orbis seeks to explore the global dimensions of the Christian faith and mission, to invite dialogue with diverse cultures and religious traditions, and to serve the cause of reconciliation and peace. The books published reflect the views of their authors and do not represent the official position of the Maryknoll Society. To learn more about Orbis Books, please visit our website at www.orbisbooks.com.

Library of Congress Cataloging-in-Publication Data

Names: Lefebure, Leo D., 1952– author.
Title: Transforming interreligious relations : Catholic responses to
   religious pluralism in the United States / Leo D. Lefebure.
Description: Maryknoll, NY : Orbis Books, 2020. | Includes bibliographical
   references and index.
Identifiers: LCCN 2020011587 (print) | LCCN 2020011588 (ebook) |
   ISBN 9781626983939 (trade paperback) | ISBN 9781608338573 (ebook)
Subjects: LCSH: Catholic Church--Relations. | Multiculturalism—Religious
   aspects. | Religious pluralism.
Classification: LCC BX1407.M84 L44 2020 (print) | LCC BX1407.M84 (ebook)
   | DDC 261.2088/282—dc23
LC record available at https://lccn.loc.gov/2020011587
LC ebook record available at https://lccn.loc.gov/2020011588

To Stephen and Aidalyn Lefebure

CONTENTS

Part I
Being Catholic in the Multireligious Context of the United States

Part III
New Directions in Interreligious Dialogue
and Catholic Theology

ACKNOWLEDGMENTS

This work emerges from many years of involvement in interreligious conversations in the United States and around the world, and I am happy to acknowledge an incalculable debt of gratitude to all my partners in interreligious and ecumenical dialogues through the years. I would like to thank the members of the Jewish-Catholic Scholars Group of Metropolitan Chicago, as well as the members of the Jewish-Catholic Dialogue in Washington, DC, which I co-chaired for many years with my dear friend, the late Rabbi Joshua Haberman. I am grateful to all my partners in the Dialogues of Catholics and Muslims both in the Midwest and the Mid-Atlantic Regions, and also to my colleagues at the Prince Alwaleed bin Talal Center for Muslim-Christian Understanding and the Berkley Center for Religion, Peace, and World Affairs at Georgetown University for our collaboration.

I would like to thank the Istanbul Foundation for Religion and Culture and the Rumi Forum for Interfaith Dialogue and Intercultural Understanding for our many encounters. I thank the members of the Vaishnava-Christian Dialogue that meets each spring in the Washington, DC, area. I would also like to thank all those associated with Monastic Interreligious Dialogue, the Society for Buddhist-Christian Studies, Rissho Kosei-kai, the New York Buddhist-Catholic Dialogue, and the Faiths in the World Committee of the Catholic Association of Ecumenical and Interreligious Officers. I also thank all my colleagues at Georgetown University, Fordham University, the University of Saint Mary of the Lake, and the Council for a Parliament of the World's Religions. I owe a particular debt to the Trinity Long Room Hub Arts & Humanities Research Institute of Trinity College Dublin, where I spent an enjoyable time in spring 2019 and pursued research on this project.

I am very grateful to my colleagues Peter Phan and John Borelli and to Jill O'Brien, my editor at Orbis Books, for their careful reading of the manuscript and their invaluable comments, corrections, and recommendations. All errors remain my own. I would also like to thank all the persons around the world whom I have met in interreligious encounters and who have enriched my life greatly.

FOREWORD

Peter C. Phan

It is with immense pleasure and deep pride that I write the foreword to this book by Professor Leo Lefebure, my colleague and friend at Georgetown University. In fact, this book was conceived a couple of years ago as a joint work, with the number of its chapters evenly divided between the two of us. Unfortunately, in the meantime, I was bogged down by other pressing writing projects, and we decided that it would be better for Leo to write the book by himself.

In retrospect, it was a very wise decision, since it lends a unified voice to the book and allows it to appear, opportunely, at the very time when Americans urgently need a new vision to shape the future of their nation. While the book is not about American politics but about the ways the American Catholic Church has dealt with religious pluralism, the religious vision it conveys is one that, if and when diligently and persistently pursued, will bring healing and reconciliation to the deep divisions and hatred that are currently burning the body politic of the republic.

In this postfact and post-truth age, Lefebure describes, with unflinching honesty and historical accuracy, the ugly ditch that lies between the official rhetoric of human dignity and the inhuman behaviors of white Americans against Native Americans and black Africans brought to their lands through chattel slavery. There is another ditch, no less ugly and destructive, between the constitutional guarantee of religious freedom and the pervasive and systemic discriminations by American Protestants against first American Catholics (the "Papist Devils"), and then Jews, Muslims, and believers of various Asian religions. Race and religion are, in Theodore Vial's celebrated words, "conjoined twins," neither able to survive without the other. Consequently, the narrative of religions in America cannot be separated from the history of white supremacy that again and again rears its terrifying head and threatens to tear apart the fabric of equality, especially for racial and religious minorities.

Lefebure's account of religious diversity in America and the varied ways in which the American Catholic Church has related to other religions, though realistic, is filled with hope. Of course, like any other human institution, the American Catholic Church has its own fair share of darkness and sin in its treatment of the believers of other religions. But it also has moments of light and holiness, especially after Vatican II. The conciliar document *Nostra Aetate* on the relations of the Catholic Church with other religions and the papal teachings from St. John Paul II to Pope Francis on interreligious dialogue, not to mention episcopal conferences such as the Federation of Asian Bishops' Conferences, continue to serve as a sure guide on how American Catholics should behave toward the followers of other religions. Such behavior is guided by neither laissez-faire tolerance nor lazy syncretism. Rather it should welcome and embrace a religious pluralism in which each religion can learn from other religions, just as each can teach other religions how to love God with all one's heart and with all one's soul and with all one's mind and to love others as oneself.

With abundant gladness and joy we read Lefebure's hope-filled words: "Christian wayfarers today can welcome Jews, Muslims, Hindus, Buddhists, Sikhs, Jains, Daoists, practitioners of indigenous religions, and others as companions for the journey. While respecting the important differences between our traditions, we can hope that our journeys bring us close enough to each other that we are within the range of conversation. Interreligious partners and companions can give us hope and sustenance for the journey."

INTRODUCTION

Challenges and Opportunities of Catholic Theology and Religious Pluralism in American Society

The religious diversity of the United States of America offers many blessings and opportunities and also poses profound paradoxes and challenges for Christian theology. European American Christians have traditionally celebrated their history of respecting religious liberty and welcoming newcomers, and today Christian theologians from all backgrounds are actively developing new and promising relationships with followers of other religious traditions in America. Yet the history of Christian responses to religious diversity in the United States is complex and conflicted. Even though the First Amendment of the Constitution of the United States of America promises the free exercise of religion to all, enslaved African American Muslims were not generally allowed to practice Islam; and U.S. government officials repeatedly prohibited American Indians from performing their religious ceremonies. Much has changed in American Christian interreligious relations in the last seventy years, and today many American Christians enjoy cordial, respectful relations with their interreligious neighbors. Nonetheless, recent years have witnessed new expressions of religious animosity and bias against immigrants, Muslims, Jews, Sikhs, Hispanics, American Indians, and African Americans. Both the history and the present context of interreligious relations in the United States contain terrible tragedies as well as important breakthroughs, presenting Christians with both formidable challenges and distinctive opportunities.

A Diverse and Conflicted Heritage

To understand and address the challenges of the current situation, it is important to acknowledge that Catholics and other Christians in the United States inherit a complex, ambiguous, and often tragic history of relations with other religious traditions. Religious diversity was present in North America before the arrival of the first European Christians; the original inhabitants of the continent practiced a wide variety of religious traditions that permeated all of life and culture.[1]

---

[1] Sam D. Gill, *Native American Religions: An Introduction*, 2nd ed. (Belmont, CA: Wadsworth, 2005); Lee Irwin, ed., *Native American Spirituality: A Critical Reader* (Lincoln: University of Nebraska Press, 2000).

However, using the terminology of religion for American Indian practices can be misleading because the indigenous peoples did not identify one aspect of their lives as religious in contrast to other dimensions; it was usually Catholic and Protestant missionaries who initially made distinctions between certain activities of American Indians, such as dancing, that they deemed religious (and that were usually forbidden to Native Christians), and other activities, such as planting crops, that they assessed as economic or cultural and that were allowed to continue.[2]

Living with religious diversity challenged Christians in North America from the time of the first European settlements. Generation after generation, people arrived from many places around the world, bringing a wide variety of religious practices and beliefs. While many migrants came freely, many came in conditions of bonded labor; and millions of Africans were brought in bondage to suffer the horrors of chattel slavery. From the beginning, European Christians in North America have interpreted religious diversity in contradictory ways. Frequently there were conflicts, harsh judgments, and persecutions based on differences of religious belief and practice. Some early English settlers in New England set an ominous precedent by viewing the indigenous peoples as "heathens" or as the biblical "Amalekites." Interreligious encounters were recurrently marked by hostility and misunderstanding, even violence.

Given the long history of religious intolerance and animosity in Europe and the Mediterranean, it is not surprising that Christians in America faced turbulence in interreligious relations. What is remarkable is the emergence and development of alternative perspectives that sought to accept religious differences in the New World. In the seventeenth century Roger Williams challenged the intolerance of the Massachusetts Bay colonialists; sought harmonious relations with the indigenous peoples; and guaranteed "soul liberty," or religious freedom, in the new colony he founded in Rhode Island. This launched one of the most important American developments in living with religious diversity: the establishment of policies regarding religious freedom. Following the lead of Roger Williams in the seventeenth century, many Christians in North America advocated for religious freedom, and the First Amendment of the Constitution of the United States promises the free exercise of religion. In this climate Christians in the United States have often hoped for blessings of interreligious peace, freedom, harmony, understanding, and cooperation.

Nonetheless, the clash between hostility and generosity, intolerance and acceptance has shaped American interreligious relationships down to the present. From the colonial period to today, hopes for respectful interreligious relations have intertwined with conquests, oppression, and the construction of racial categories to justify domination. Religious and racial categorizations have entwined throughout

---

[2] Severin M. Fowles, *An Archeology of Doings: Secularism and the Study of Pueblo Religion* (Santa Fe, NM: School for Advanced Research Press, 2013); Tisa Wenger, *We Have a Religion: The 1920s Pueblo Indian Dance Controversy and American Religious Freedom* (Chapel Hill: University of North Carolina Press, 2009).

colonial and American history, with often poisonous results. Spanish and Portuguese thinkers pioneered modern racial categories to justify the enslavement and conquest of peoples in Africa, Asia, and the Americas.[3] During the latter part of the seventeenth century British Americans in Virginia developed racial categories for viewing people as "white," "black," and "red." Historian Alan Taylor describes the process of creating racial identities in colonial America:

> Over time, race loomed larger—primarily in British America—as the fundamental prism for rearranging the identities and the relative power of the many peoples in the colonial encounters. A racialized sorting of peoples by skin color into white, red, and black was primarily a product, rather than a precondition of colonization.[4]

British Protestants coming to North America developed a distinctive form of racialized slavery. The colonial rhetoric of liberty and equality served to unite lower-class whites with the landowning elite class against African Americans and American Indians. Early colonial racial and religious prejudices shaped the context for European American encounters with Muslims, Buddhists, and Hindus. As noted earlier, the majority of early Muslims who came to North America arrived enslaved, and most were not granted freedom to practice Islam. When Buddhists from China and Japan came in significant numbers, racial prejudice demonized them, leading to government actions against them. Religious and racial biases often reinforced each other in American and European life.[5] Theodore Vial has explored the academic context of how the modern concepts of race and religion were born together as "conjoined twins" in late eighteenth-century Europe. According to Vial, the modern notions of race and religion emerged together in the European Enlightenment as hierarchical rankings that privileged European Christians over other populations; perceptions of racial and religious identities intertwined to the extent that Vial finds that "the category of religion is always already a racialized category, even when race is not explicitly under discussion."[6] Vial stresses how strongly racial prejudices shaped the creation of the modern study of religion; and he finds that many contemporary American commentators continue to discuss religion as a racialized, hierarchical category, assuming that other societies and cultures, such as those in Africa, should make "progress" in order to become more like the United States.[7]

---

[3] Willie James Jennings, *The Christian Imagination: Theology and the Origins of Race* (New Haven, CT: Yale University Press, 2010).

[4] Alan Taylor, *American Colonies,* The Penguin History of the United States, ed. Eric Foner (New York: Penguin Books, 2001), xii.

[5] Tisa Wenger, *Religious Freedom: The Contested History of an American Ideal* (Chapel Hill: University of North Carolina Press, 2017).

[6] Theodore Vial, *Modern Religion, Modern Race* (Oxford: Oxford University Press, 2016), 1.

[7] Ibid., 221ff.

Religious, racial, and ethnic prejudices have long overlapped and reinforced each other in American life.[8] Racist views, combined with negative theological judgments about African, Asian, and American Indian religious practices, shaped prejudices against African Americans, Asian Americans, and American Indians. Modern racist biases against Jews reinforced traditional Christian accusations that all Jews of every generation were guilty for killing Jesus Christ.[9] From the late nineteenth century through the middle of the twentieth century, racist Jim Crow laws legislated discrimination against African Americans; and the criminal justice system generally turned a blind eye to crimes committed by white Americans against African Americans. The immigration laws of the 1920s sought to protect the white, Anglo-Saxon, Protestant character of American society by allowing Northern and Western Europeans to enter the United States in large numbers, and by establishing very limited quotas for persons from all other regions of the world. Tensions from religious and racial prejudice continue to challenge American society and Christian life and practice today. While many European American Christians have harbored religious prejudices, experiences in the United States prod them to learn to live together with followers of different religious traditions; over time the American experience of diversity has repeatedly transformed the religious traditions that come here.

Catholic Presence

Catholics were present from the beginning of European settlements in the Spanish- and French-ruled areas of North America. Catholics arrived in British North America at the founding of Maryland in 1634. While Maryland established religious liberty early in its history, this achievement was fragile and was revoked after the Glorious Revolution renewed distrust of Catholics in the British Empire. Catholics were often viewed as "Papist Devils" by Protestant colonialists, but nonetheless they would have a distinctive role to play in shaping American society, including interreligious relations.[10]

As the British American colonial society developed and eventually became the nation of the United States of America, the generous ideals of religious liberty and human equality collided with the brutal realities of enslavement and prejudice against religious minorities, including Catholics and Jews. Amid the tensions there emerged a new and distinctively American context of religious pluralism that privileged Protestants but that nonetheless allowed Catholics and Jews to develop and even to thrive. Catholics were a very small minority in the newly founded United

---

[8] Henry Goldschmidt and Elizabeth McAlister, eds., *Race, Nation, and Religion in the Americas* (Oxford: Oxford University Press, 2004).

[9] Jeremy Cohen, *Christ Killers: The Jews and the Passion from the Bible to the Big Screen* (Oxford: Oxford University Press, 2007), 136–42.

[10] Robert Emmett Curran, *Papist Devils: Catholics in British America, 1574–1783* (Washington, DC: Catholic University of America Press, 2014).

States of America. Charles Carroll was the sole Catholic to sign the Declaration of Independence. In 1776, the Continental Congress sent him and his cousin, John Carroll, together with Benjamin Franklin and Samuel Chase, on a mission to Canada to seek the support of French Catholics for the American Revolution.[11] Even though the mission did not succeed, the involvement of the two Carrolls demonstrated their support for the Revolutionary cause. John Carroll later became the first Catholic bishop in the United States and founded Georgetown Academy, which would become the first Catholic university, with an explicit openness to welcoming students of all religious traditions. Carroll had experienced prejudice and discrimination as a Catholic in a Protestant society, and he wanted his new school to offer an alternative path.[12]

In the late-nineteenth and early-twentieth centuries, large numbers of Catholics came to the United States, becoming in time the largest single Christian church. Even though they encountered much hostility and prejudice, a number of Catholic leaders participated with leaders of other traditions in the pioneering World Parliament of Religions in Chicago in 1893, which has been viewed as the dawn of the modern interreligious movement. The twentieth century, however, witnessed a terrible renewal of racial and religious prejudices from which Catholics were not immune. For example, the influential Catholic priest Charles Coughlin promoted viciously anti-Semitic accusations in his popular radio broadcasts of the 1930s and early 1940s until he was finally forced off the airwaves. Donald Warren has called Coughlin "the Father of Hate Radio," and Bradley W. Hart includes him among "Hitler's American Friends" because of his defense of Nazi policies against Jews.[13]

American Catholics had long shared with Jews the situation of being a suspected minority in a Protestant-dominated society. In the years following the Second World War, Catholics together with Jews were just entering into the mainstream of American society. Many Americans were coming to accept the interreligious triad of Protestant-Catholic-Jew as acceptable religious options, while other religious communities were usually either neglected or viewed with suspicion. Nonetheless, at midcentury many American Protestants continued to view Catholics with great suspicion, while Catholics debated whether persons outside the Catholic Church could be saved at all. In Boston, the Jesuit chaplain and editor, Leonard Feeney, vigorously insisted on a literal application of the traditional teaching that outside the Catholic Church there is no salvation until he was censured and silenced by Catholic authorities in 1953.[14] At the middle of the

---

[11] Ibid., 248–51.

[12] Robert Emmett Curran, *A History of Georgetown, Volume 1: From the Academy to University, 1789–1889* (Washington, DC: Georgetown University Press, 2010), 25–29.

[13] Donald I. Warren, *Radio Priest: Charles Coughlin, the Father of Hate Radio* (New York: Free Press, 1996); Bradley W. Hart, *Hitler's American Friends: The Third Reich's Supporters in the United States* (New York: Thomas Dunne Books, 2018), 68–95.

[14] Mark Massa, "On the Uses of Heresy: Leonard Feeney, Mary Douglas, and the Notre Dame Football Team," *Harvard Theological Review* 84, no. 3 (1991): 315–41.

century, a number of American Indian Catholics, including Nicholas Black Elk, continued to practice their Native religious traditions; but this dual religious observance received little attention from theologians and church leaders.[15]

During the years immediately following the Shoah, many American Catholics were still influenced by traditional prejudices against Jews; but a number of Catholic leaders felt the need for a radical change in Catholic-Jewish relations. To counter the age-old heritage of anti-Jewish animosity, a few Catholics in the United States, mostly immigrants from Germany with Jewish ancestry, launched efforts toward revising the traditional negative attitudes toward Jews and Judaism.[16] The transformation of Catholic relations with Jews would provide an important impetus for improving all other interreligious relationships and transforming the self-understanding of Catholics and many other Christians.

In the middle of the twentieth century, the Catholic Church generally remained aloof from Christian ecumenical ventures. Samuel Cardinal Stritch, Archbishop of Chicago, forbade Catholics from attending the meeting of the World Council of Churches in Evanston, Illinois, in 1954, though some Catholic journalists covered the event. During the 1950s, however, the attitudes and practices of Catholics and many other Christians in relation to other religious traditions began to move toward greater ecumenical and interreligious openness.

The Second Vatican Council profoundly and positively transformed Catholic attitudes and actions toward both other Christians and people from other religious traditions. Many Protestant communities in the United States went through similar transformations in these years. Since the Second Vatican Council, Catholics in the United States have actively participated in dialogues with Jews, Muslims, Hindus, and Buddhists, as well as efforts to understand American Indian religious traditions and their relation to Catholic practice. Many Catholic colleges and universities in the United States have centers for interreligious understanding. Catholics and many other Christians know followers of other religious traditions as neighbors, co-workers, friends, and family members. The transformation of Catholic responses to religious diversity in the United States is also closely linked to changes in racial relations, ethnic attitudes, and immigration law. Changes in racial relations and in immigration legislation in the 1960s contributed to improving Catholic responses to religious diversity.

Contemporary Context

Today, alongside the traditionally dominant traditions of American Protestant Christianity, virtually all the religious communities of the world find a

---

[15] Clyde Holler, *Black Elk's Religion: The Sun Dance and Lakota Catholicism* (Syracuse, NY: Syracuse University Press, 1995); Clyde Holler, ed., *The Black Elk Reader* (Syracuse, NY: Syracuse University Press, 2000).

[16] John Connelly, *From Enemy to Brother: The Revolution in Catholic Teaching on the Jews, 1933–1965* (Cambridge, MA: Harvard University Press, 2012).

home in the United States. Since the middle of the twentieth century, thanks to globalization and migration, the ethnic, cultural, and religious composition of the United States has grown increasingly diverse; and Americans have become more and more aware of the social and theological dimensions of living with different religious communities.[17] Since 1965, the United States of America has become, as Diana Eck and Robert Wuthnow have shown, one of the most religiously diverse nations in the world.[18]

While many celebrate interreligious diversity with openness and acceptance, not all Americans welcome religious differences. Suspicions and negative stereotypes about religious traditions continue to plague American life, and there have been expressions of prejudice and violent attacks on Jews, Muslims, Sikhs, Hindus, Buddhists, Hispanics, African Americans, and American Indians. Religious pluralism in the United States today is both praised and lamented; while some people praise religious diversity as one of the greatest strengths of the United States, others seek to restore a White Christian America on the basis of renewed religious, ethnic, and racial biases.[19] Catholics and other Christians in the United States today face renewed challenges and choices regarding religious diversity.

Today many American Catholics acknowledge the painful sins and crimes committed by earlier generations of Catholics who claimed to be serving the faith but who often mistreated indigenous peoples, enslaved Africans and African Americans, and harbored prejudices against immigrants from Asia, Latin America, Africa, and their descendants. The terrors of the Shoah provided a decisive impetus to Catholics and other Christians to improve relations with Jews, and numerous theologians have reflected on how to do Christian theology with integrity after the Holocaust.[20] American Christian theologians have devoted much less attention to the well-documented genocide carried out in California against American Indians between 1846 and 1873,[21] or to the repeated acts of ethnic cleansing of American

---

[17] Daniel G. Groody, "Crossing the Divide: Foundations of a Theology of Migration and Refugees," *Theological Studies* 70, no. 3 (2009): 638–67; Gioacchino Campese, "The Irruption of Migrants: Theology of Migration in the 21st Century," *Theological Studies* 73, no. 1 (2012): 3–32.

[18] Diana L. Eck, *A New Religious America: How a "Christian Country" Became the World's Most Religiously Diverse Nation* (San Francisco: HarperSanFrancisco, 2002); Robert Wuthnow, *America and the Challenges of Religious Diversity* (Princeton, NJ: Princeton University Press, 2005).

[19] Christian Picciolini, *White American Youth: My Descent into America's Most Violent Hate Movement—And How I Got Out* (New York: Hachette Books, 2017); Daryl Johnson, *Hateland: A Long, Hard Look at America's Extremist Heart* (Amherst, NY: Prometheus Books, 2019).

[20] John T. Pawlikowski, *The Challenge of the Holocaust for Christian Theology* (New York: Center for Studies on the Holocaust, 1978).

[21] Benjamin Madley, *An American Genocide: The United States and the California Indian Catastrophe, 1846–1873* (New Haven, CT: Yale University Press, 2016).

Indians across the United States,[22] or to the forced removal of young American Indians and their indoctrination in Christian schools where they were forbidden to speak their native languages.[23]

It has often been easier for European Americans to reflect on atrocities committed elsewhere than in their own land. In 1993, the United States Holocaust Memorial Museum opened its doors in Washington, DC, as a living memorial to the victims of the Holocaust. It was not until 2016 that the National Museum of African American History and Culture opened its doors in Washington, DC, telling the horrors of the Atlantic slave trade and slavery in the United States. Since 2004, the National Museum of American Indians on the National Mall in Washington, DC, honors the religious and cultural heritage of American Indians; but it does not communicate much information about the details of mistreatment of American Indians by European Americans. American Catholics today are increasingly coming to terms with the continuing effects of the history of oppression of American Indians, slavery, religious and racial discrimination, and hostility toward immigrants. For example, in the past few years, the community of Georgetown University, where I teach, is learning about and wrestling with its historical involvement in the enslavement and sale of African Americans, including the notorious sale of 272 enslaved persons in 1838.[24]

Since the middle of the twentieth century, many Catholics and other Christians in the United States have devoted much attention to improving interreligious relationships, ushering in an unprecedented situation of openness to religious pluralism. As Christians relate in new ways to Jews, Muslims, Hindus, Buddhists, and followers of other traditions, they not only come to a new awareness of the many dimensions of interreligious relationships; they also learn to recognize truth and holiness in other religious traditions, and to gain new insights into their own scriptures, traditions, practices, and beliefs. Each interreligious relationship presents a distinctive set of questions, challenges, gifts, and opportunities; and each relationship has implications for other interreligious relationships and for Christian identity.

Religious Diversity, Religious Pluralism

After centuries of largely negative attitudes toward other religious communities, many Americans today place a high value on religious pluralism, understood as the open acceptance of religious diversity, though this development is not without controversy. William R. Hutchison, a scholar of American religious history,

---

[22] Gary Clayton Anderson, *Ethnic Cleansing and the Indian: The Crime that Should Haunt America* (Norman: University of Oklahoma Press, 2014).

[23] David Wallace Adams, *Education for Extinction: American Indians and the Boarding School Experience, 1875–1928* (Lawrence: University Press of Kansas, 1995).

[24] *Report of the Working Group on Slavery, Memory, and Reconciliation to the President of Georgetown University* (Washington, DC: Georgetown University, 2016).

comments that in the United States of America today pluralism, "understood as the acceptance and encouragement of diversity, is a fighting word for participants in contemporary culture wars, and a key concept for those who write about them"; he explains that scholars often make a distinction between religious diversity and religious pluralism, that is, "the distinction between a fact or condition called diversity and an ideal or impulse for which the best term is *pluralism*."[25] Hutchison argues that religious pluralism in this sense developed in the United States only in the second half of the twentieth century as a belated acceptance of a situation already present: "I believe that Americans and their public policy are only now coming to terms, however grudgingly or opportunistically, with a radical diversification that came crashing in upon the young nation almost at the moment of its birth."[26]

Mary Boys, a Catholic theologian who has long taught at Union Theological Seminary in New York City and been active in Jewish-Christian relations, comments on the challenge of pluralism:

> Unlike tolerance, in which one resolves simply to live with difference, pluralism requires the pursuit of understanding. In distinction from relativism and syncretism, pluralism is built upon an encounter of commitments and a respect for difference that comes from extensive knowledge of one's tradition. . . . [P]luralism requires work and virtue.[27]

Religious pluralism is a far-reaching but not uncontested experience in American life today.[28]

Sociologist Peter Berger reflects on American religious pluralism in light of a shift in social scientific perceptions of religion in modern societies. Sociologists used to focus primarily on the secularization of the modern world, assuming that modernization would lead to the decline of religion. Now, Berger believes that

> pluralism, the co-existence of different worldviews and value systems in the same society, is *the* major change brought about by modernity for the place of religion both in the minds of individuals and in the institutional order. This may or may not be associated with secularization, but it is independent of it.[29]

---

[25] William R. Hutchison, *Religious Pluralism in America: The Contentious History of a Founding Ideal* (New Haven, CT: Yale University Press, 2003), 1, 4.

[26] Ibid., 4–5.

[27] Mary C. Boys, *Jewish-Christian Dialogue: One Woman's Experience* (New York: Paulist Press, 1997), 54–55.

[28] In this sense religious pluralism does not refer to the specific theological position of John Hick and others regarding parity of religions in offering salvation.

[29] Peter L. Berger, *The Many Altars of Modernity: Toward a Paradigm for Religion in a Pluralist Age* (Boston: Walter de Gruyter, 2014), ix.

Berger distinguishes three levels of pluralism: (1) involving religious perspectives in the minds of individuals and society; (2) between secular and religious perspectives; and (3) of different versions of modernity, including different relations between the secular and the religious.[30] Berger stresses the importance of "religious freedom in the context of a religiously neutral state," and grounds this not primarily in instrumental political considerations but in the fundamental human right to pursue one's sense of wonder and mystery wherever it may lead.[31]

Sociologist Robert Wuthnow stresses the major impact of relatively small religious minorities on the awareness of Americans:

> Although the share of the population that is Muslim, Hindu, or Buddhist is quite small, the impact of these groups on American culture is much larger. Millions of Americans who are Christians or Jews come in contact with Muslims, Hindus, and Buddhists through their work, their business dealings, and in their neighborhoods.[32]

But he notes a paradox in American discourse:

> In our public discourse about religion we seem to be a society of schizophrenics. On the one hand, we say casually that we are tolerant and have respect for people whose religious traditions happen to be different from our own. On the other hand, we continue to speak as if our nation is (or should be) a Christian nation, founded on Christian principles.[33]

In this context the acceptance or rejection of religious pluralism has become a contested issue in American society at large. Some welcome the growing religious and ethnic diversity, but others worry about the loss of traditional American Christian identity. The changing religious demographics of the United States increasingly challenge its claim to be a Christian nation, and not all are pleased. In 2016, Robert P. Jones, a scholar and commentator on American religion, published a dramatic obituary statement: "After a long life spanning nearly two hundred and forty years, White Christian America—a prominent cultural force in the nation's history—has died."[34] Jones observed contrasting responses: some Americans welcome the demise of White Christian America, and others are going through the painful stages of grief. However, not all Americans have accepted this announcement of death, and white supremacy has recently reemerged in public discourse.[35] Writing about religious pluralism in relation to current American

---

[30] Ibid., 78.

[31] Ibid., 92–93.

[32] Wuthnow, *America*, 228.

[33] Ibid., 6–7.

[34] Robert P. Jones, *The End of White Christian America* (New York: Simon & Schuster, 2016), 1.

[35] Picciolini, *White American Youth*.

political debates, *New York Times* columnist David Brooks defines and endorses pluralism in the American context as the conviction that "Human difference makes life richer and more interesting. We treasure members of all races and faiths for what they bring to the mosaic."[36] However, Brooks stresses the value of religious pluralism precisely because he sees it in danger in the current political climate.

The increase in tensions over American identity has fueled a polarization of opinion. Robert Putnam and David Campbell note, "Perhaps the most noticeable shift is how Americans have become polarized along religious lines. Americans are increasingly concentrated at opposite ends of the religious spectrum—the highly religious at one pole, and the avowedly secular at the other. The moderate religious middle is shrinking."[37] They also observe that if one ignores the heated rhetoric concerning religion in America and focuses on behavior, one sees a different picture, where

> the United States hardly seems like a house divided against itself. America peacefully combines a high degree of religious devotion with tremendous religious diversity—including growing ranks of the nonreligious. Americans have a high degree of tolerance for those of (most) other religions, including those without any religion in their lives.[38]

They pose a question and offer the beginning of a response: "*How can religious pluralism coexist with religious polarization?* The answer lies in the fact that, in America, religion is highly fluid. The conditions producing that fluidity are a signal feature of the nation's constitutional infrastructure."[39] Putnam and Campbell relate the acceptance of religious pluralism to the U.S. Constitution's refusal to establish a national religion: "More broadly, the absence of a state-run religious monopoly combined with a wide sphere of religious liberty has produced an ideal environment for a thriving religious ecosystem."[40] These tensions shape the context of American Catholic theology today, with all the promises and challenges facing the United States with regard to religious pluralism.

Pluralism in the United States at the present time involves not only external relationships among followers of different religious traditions; it also shapes a context where interreligious learning and borrowing is increasingly possible. Boundaries in relationships are important but fluid and often porous.[41] Religious

---

[36] David Brooks, "Marianne Williamson Knows How to Beat Trump," *New York Times,* August 2, 2019.

[37] Robert D. Putnam and David E. Campbell with the assistance of Shaylyn Romney Garrett, *American Grace: How Religion Divides and Unites Us* (New York: Simon & Schuster, 2010), 3.

[38] Ibid., 4.

[39] Ibid.

[40] Ibid.

[41] Michele Saracino, *Being about Borders: A Christian Anthropology of Difference* (Collegeville, MN: Liturgical Press, 2011).

traditions are not always homogeneous and external to each other but sometimes enter deeply into the lives and awareness of followers of other religious paths. The history of interreligious relationships includes repeated examples of borrowing and influence. Many Native American Catholics continue their indigenous religious practices while also participating in Catholic sacramental life; some Catholics engage in meditation practices derived from Buddhism or in yoga practice coming from Hinduism. Catholic theology in the United States today is shaped by the multifaceted social reality of numerous religious communities in close proximity to each other. American popular culture includes a wide array of religious images and symbols from different traditions that are often combined in new ways, and some persons experiment with multiple religious belonging.[42]

Structure of the Discussion

In light of recent Catholic activities in interreligious dialogue and with awareness of the work and teachings on interreligious dialogue of other Christian communities and the World Council of Churches, this book will explore Catholic involvement with other religious traditions in the history of the development of the United States and the significance of this experience of religious pluralism for Catholic theology.

Part I of this book will offer an overview of major developments in Catholic interreligious relationships, both in the context of changes in Catholic teachings and attitudes toward other religions and also in the multireligious context of the United States. Chapter 1 will survey the historic transformation of Catholic views and practices toward other religious traditions. We will note the long heritage of intolerance and animosity, and also the shift in the stance of Catholics and many other Christians regarding interreligious relations since the Second Vatican Council.

Chapter 2 will survey the development of Catholic responses to religious pluralism in North America in the context of the demographic, social, cultural, and religious landscape in the United States throughout its history and especially during the last half-century. Since the changes in immigration laws in the 1960s, American society has become more ethnically, culturally, and religiously diverse; and all major urban areas today are home to many religious traditions.

Part II of this book, which includes Chapters 3 through 7, will examine the historical development of particular interreligious relationships. Chapter 3 will examine Catholic engagement with American Indian religious traditions, with brief attention also to traditions of Africa. The first Christians to come to the areas that are now the United States of America were Spanish Catholics who encountered a variety of Native religions. Latin American and U.S. Hispanic Christian practice continue to bear the influence of these primal traditions, and in recent years

---

[42] Catherine Cornille, *Many Mansions? Multiple Religious Belonging and Christian Identity* (Maryknoll, NY: Orbis Books, 2002).

Hispanic Christians have reflected on the theological implications of this *mestizo* heritage. Enslaved Africans who were forcibly brought to North America carried with them the religious traditions of Africa, which flowed into the lives of African Americans and form an important part of their heritage. African American Christians have stressed the importance of this heritage.

Chapter 4 will explore the dynamics of Jewish-Catholic relationships in the United States, which have had a powerful impact on other interreligious relations. In the wake of the Second World War and the Shoah, many Christians went through a reassessment of their tradition's historically negative views of Jews and Judaism. Through numerous encounters, dialogues, and academic explorations, Christians and Jews in the United States came to know each other in new ways. For Christians, this process included major revisions in their interpretation not only of contemporary Jews and Judaism but also of Jesus, the early Christian community, and the development of Christianity in relation to Jews and Judaism. Because Christianity emerged from a Jewish matrix and because Jesus and his first followers were Jews, changes in this relationship have implications for every other Christian interreligious relationship.

There has been intense focus on Jewish-Christian relations in recent decades, but often these discussions have been somewhat isolated from the broader interreligious network of relationships. There is definitely an important place for specialized studies of each interreligious relationship. There is also a need for an overview of the ways in which the distinct dialogues have implications for each other and impact Christian thought and practice as a whole. The extensive discussions in Jewish-Christian relations have profoundly transformed how many Christians understand the Bible and the origin of Christianity; it is important to integrate the results of Jewish-Christian dialogue into the broader world of interreligious relations and into Christian theology as a whole.

Chapter 5 will turn to Muslim-Catholic relations in the United States, which face difficult challenges from Islamophobia but also present promising opportunities for the future. Relationships between Christians and Muslims were already developing in some organized Muslim-Christian dialogues in the final decades of the twentieth century. In many settings in the United States, Christians and Muslims enjoy cordial, respectful relationships. Nonetheless, for many Christians the current international context of conflict and violence reinforces traditionally negative views of Muslims and Islam.

Chapter 6 will explore Catholic relations with Hindus in the United States. The visit of noted theologian Howard Thurman and other African American leaders to Mahatma Gandhi in India in 1936 proved be to one of the most influential interreligious conversations in all of American history, since it prepared the way for the decisive influence of Gandhi's path of nonviolent resistance on Martin Luther King Jr. and other movements seeking social reform through nonviolent means. Hindu perspectives have influenced many Americans from Ralph Waldo Emerson and Henry David Thoreau to the present, and many American Christians have explored the practice and theory of yoga and have incorporated this into their Christian practice.

Chapter 7 will conclude the second part with a reflection on Buddhist-Catholic relationships in the United States. Many Christians have explored the practice of Buddhist meditation and found beneficial results. Buddhist perspectives and practices have been very influential on some leaders in the field of Christian spirituality. Monastic Interreligious Dialogue, an organization of Catholic monks and nuns that promotes interreligious exchange with monastics of other religious traditions, has held a number of encounters that have been milestones in the depth and quality of Buddhist-Christian exchange.

Part III will explore implications of changed interreligious relationships for Catholic theological reflection as a search for wisdom. Chapter 8 will examine some new ways that American Catholic thinkers have pursued theology as a quest for wisdom in light of religious pluralism.

One of the most important methodological questions for any religious tradition is the interpretation of its scripture; Chapter 9 will discuss the interreligious hermeneutical issues involved in Catholic biblical reflection. This chapter will propose that the biblical wisdom tradition offers important resources for reading the Bible in relation to other religious traditions.

Central to Christian faith are the activities of the Holy Spirit and Jesus Christ; early Christian leaders associated both the Spirit and Christ with the figure of personified Wisdom or Sophia. Chapter 10 will discuss the Holy Spirit in interreligious perspective as the universal presence of God affecting all human life.

Chapter 11 will focus on the significance of Jesus Christ as the incarnate Word and Wisdom of God in relation to other traditions.

Chapter 12 will explore how transformed interreligious relations impact Catholic ecclesial identity and what an interreligious wisdom community could look like.

Chapter 13 will conclude with reflections on Catholic spirituality in relation to interreligious relations. Traditional spiritual writers sought wisdom through the threefold path: the *via purgativa*, which turns away from sin and seeks to heal relationships; the *via illuminativa*, which seeks to see our neighbors and ourselves in a new and more accurate manner through dialogue with interreligious partners; and the *via unitiva*, which seeks to shape a healthy community of the world's religions based on respect for diversity.

The Epilogue will note the increasing convergence of interreligious conversations and concern for ecology and care for the earth.

A number of issues run through many of these interreligious relations. When crossing religious boundaries, we find at every stage both similarities and differences. Comparing religious traditions is frequently like looking at a Gestalt that can be viewed in different ways. Viewed from one perspective, traditions can appear so radically different that it seems impossible to have a genuine conversation; when seen from another perspective, however, the values of the same traditions can appear to be so similar that one wonders what difference the differences make. It is important to keep both perspectives in mind.

In multireligious contexts like the United States, the classic theological themes of sin, grace, freedom, transcendence, immanence, divine justice, and divine mercy find new resonances and applications in relation to either conflicting or analogous perspectives in other traditions. According to medieval Catholic theology, our condition in this world is that of *viatores,* wayfarers. The condition of a wayfarer is in-between, on the road toward a destination that is anticipated but not yet reached. Christians since the early centuries have made pilgrimages to sacred places, often as penitents seeking God's forgiveness for the sins of the past and praying for absolution and a new start toward a better future. Christian wayfarers today can welcome Jews, Muslims, Hindus, Buddhists, Sikhs, Jains, Daoists, practitioners of indigenous religions, and others as companions for the journey. While respecting the important differences between our traditions, we can hope that our journeys bring us close enough to each other that we are within the range of conversation. Interreligious partners and companions can give us hope and sustenance for the journey.

Part I

Being Catholic in the Multireligious Context of the United States

1

SHIFTING CATHOLIC PERSPECTIVES
ON RELIGIOUS DIVERSITY

For the most part Catholics and other Christians in colonial North America and the United States inherited from their earlier traditions very negative attitudes toward religious diversity. Indeed, in most places around the world prior to the mid-twentieth century, Catholics and other Christians generally approached other religious traditions with suspicion and negative judgments. The Catholic Church, like most other Christian communities, had a long, tragic relationship with virtually all of the world's other religious traditions, especially those religions with whom Christianity is most closely associated in history and belief: Judaism and Islam. Even though these three religions share many important beliefs and values, for centuries Christians had repeatedly vilified and demonized Jews and Muslims as allies of the Antichrist.[1] In the modern period European explorations and colonial empires brought Christians into increasing contact with Buddhists, Hindus, Daoists, Sikhs, Jains, and followers of indigenous traditions around the world; tragically Christians, including Catholics, frequently continued the age-old patterns of intolerance, defamation, and violence in new contexts.

In some settings prior to the mid-twentieth century, there were respectful interreligious conversations, and there were some Christians who seriously studied other religious traditions and who undertook bold initiatives to improve interreligious relations, but for the most part these efforts did not enjoy widespread publicity or the support of the highest levels of Christian church leadership. In the middle of the twentieth century Catholics and many other Christians went through a massive transformation of attitudes and actions regarding other religious traditions. To appreciate the broader context for understanding developments in the United States, this chapter will explore the international transformation of Christian theological attitudes and perspectives toward other religions, with a particular focus on the Catholic Church.

---

[1] Leo D. Lefebure, *True and Holy: Christian Scripture and Other Religions* (Maryknoll, NY: Orbis Books, 2014).

Historical Context of the Fifteenth and Sixteenth Centuries

The fifteenth century, when European Catholics first came to the Americas, was a time of bitter conflict between Muslims and Catholics in the Mediterranean world but also a moment when a few Catholic leaders formulated the ideal of respectful dialogue. In 1439, as Ottoman Turkish forces were threatening to capture Constantinople, Pope Eugene IV and the leaders of the Council of Florence made great efforts to heal the Great Schism with the Greek Orthodox Church; but in 1442 they also formally declared that all those who were not in the Catholic Church at the time of their death were destined to suffer eternal punishment in hell.[2]

Shortly after the fall of Constantinople in 1453, Nicholas of Cusa wrote a dialogue, *On the Peace of Faith* (*De Pace Fidei*), in an attempt to understand religious diversity.[3] In the dialogue the Word of God addresses a Chaldean, an Arab, an Indian, a Jew, a Persian, and representatives of other nations. The dialogue ends with the hope that people of every nation will come to recognize explicitly the one faith that they already implicitly share. Nicholas hopes that, given the oneness of faith, a plurality of rites and cults can flourish. He acknowledges that Jews and Muslims have understandable reasons for rejecting the Trinity, and he seeks to overcome these objections through his own explanation of the productive generativity of unity. As a Catholic, Nicholas assumes that all faith converges upon Jesus Christ, finding its fulfillment in him and that as mediator, Christ allows passage between God and humankind. In a time of widespread military conflict, Nicholas thus proposed a model of respectful interreligious dialogue known as *contraferentia*, hoping that interreligious partners could engage in serious theological conversation to discover a common faith.[4] However, his invitation was not widely heeded, and he accepted the earlier teaching of the Council of Florence concerning those outside the Catholic Church being damned. Juan de Segovia (ca. 1400–58), professor of theology at the University of Salamanca and a colleague of Nicholas of Cusa, also called for respectful dialogue with Muslims and took the initiative in organizing dialogues with a Muslim soldier and ambassador. He criticized Robert of Ketton's translation of the Qur'an for its inaccuracies; he sponsored a new translation of the Qur'an into Spanish and Latin, trusting that in an open, intellectual exchange, Christianity would emerge the victor.[5] These proposals for interreligious dialogue would not be widely implemented until the middle of the twentieth century.

---

[2] Council of Florence, "Decree to the Jacobites," 1442, in *Decrees of the Ecumenical Councils,* ed. Norman P. Tanner, vol. 1, *Nicaea I to Lateran V* (New York: Sheed & Ward/ Washington, DC: Georgetown University Press, 1990), 1:578.

[3] Nicholas of Cusa, *De Pace Fidei and Cribatio Alkorani: Translation and Analysis,* ed. and trans. Jasper Hopkins (Minneapolis: A. J. Banning Press, 1990).

[4] Nicholas of Cusa, *Unity and Reform: Selected Writings,* ed. Jay P. Dolan (Notre Dame, IN: University of Notre Dame Press, 1962); Nicholas of Cusa, *On Interreligious Harmony: Text Concordance and Translation of De Pace Fidei,* trans. and ed. James E. Biechler (Lewiston, NY: Edwin Mellen, 1993).

[5] Anne Marie Wolf, *Juan de Segovia and the Fight for Peace: Christians and Muslims in the Fifteenth Century* (Notre Dame, IN: University of Notre Dame Press, 2014).

After capturing Constantinople in 1453, Ottoman Turks threatened Christian-ruled areas in Europe throughout the sixteenth and seventeenth centuries, besieging Vienna in 1529 and again in 1683. Meanwhile, Spanish Catholics defeated the last Moorish rulers in the Iberian Peninsula in 1492 and continued to harbor a militant mentality toward perceived enemies of the Catholic faith, forcing Jews and later Muslims, to convert to Catholicism or depart or face execution.

The Protestant Reformation of the sixteenth century brought further tensions, including military combat, political oppositions, and theological condemnations. Many Protestants agreed with the principle of the Council of Florence that outside the true church there is no salvation, but they believed they were the true church and applied the prospect of eternal damnation to Catholics as well as to Jews and Muslims. At the beginning of the Protestant Reformation, Erasmus of Rotterdam championed an irenic, nondogmatic approach to Christian faith, but most other Christian leaders engaged in bitter doctrinal disputes, and soon there were bloody conflicts across the continent of Europe. Among Protestants, some of the Radical Reformers advocated religious liberty, but Catholics and Magisterial Protestants agreed in rejecting the proposals of Radical Reformers for religious tolerance and acceptance throughout society.[6] In time, some political rulers in Europe would begin to make accommodation for religious diversity, but gains were often fragile. King Henry IV granted religious liberty to French Protestants in the Edict of Nantes in France in 1598; but King Louis XIV later revoked this in 1685, prompting a number of Huguenots to flee France, seek safety in British North America, and settle in the colony of New York. The conflicts in Europe bequeathed a legacy of distrust to Christians in North America, and the theological disputes often increased in acrimony because of political events. Many of the leaders of the new United States would be mindful of the European history of religious conflict and would seek to protect the new nation from that troubled legacy.

The Troubled Relationship of Catholics with the Modern World

For many years the leaders of the Catholic Church in Europe firmly opposed the Protestant Reformation, religious liberty, and many aspects of the modern world. Most Catholic leaders in the sixteenth and seventeenth centuries opposed religious liberty, and the Spanish Inquisition fiercely pursued suspected heretics both in Europe and in New Spain.[7] This troubled history would have important repercussions for Catholics in the colonial era and in the United States, reinforcing negative Protestant perceptions of Catholic tyranny. Paul Blanshard wrote a

---

[6] Roland H. Bainton, *The Travail of Religious Liberty* (1951; reprint Eugene, OR: Wipf & Stock Publishers, 2008).

[7] Henry Kamen, *The Spanish Inquisition: A Historical Revision*, 4th ed. (New Haven, CT: Yale University Press, 2014); *The Inquisition in New Spain, 1536–1820: A Documentary History,* ed. and trans. John F. Chuchiak IV (Baltimore: Johns Hopkins University Press, 2012).

powerful polemic accusing Catholics of trying to undermine the American practice of separation of church and state.[8]

Not long after the American Revolution and the establishment of the United States of America with its constitutional guarantee of the free exercise of religion, the French Revolution posed a profoundly traumatic challenge to the Catholic Church on every level, from popes to bishops, from priests to religious communities and lay Catholics.[9] Even though some Catholics, like the Abbé Grégoire, supported the initial phases of the French Revolution, revolutionaries increasingly turned against the Catholic Church because of its entanglement in the *ancien régime*.[10] Historian Frank Coppa comments on the anticlerical assembly that convened in Paris in 1791: "Those who envisioned a human regeneration by universal revolution were anti-Catholic, and hoped to destroy the papacy as an obstacle to progress, toppling it from its privileged position among sovereignties."[11] In 1793 and 1794, the leaders of the French Revolution established the Worship of Reason and then the Worship of the Supreme Being in place of traditional Catholic devotion. In the revolutionary violence, many Catholics, including bishops, priests, members of religious congregations, and laypeople, were killed; many were uprooted; many were dispossessed; much church property was confiscated.[12] In the aftermath of the Revolution, Napoleon Bonaparte deliberately humiliated Pope Pius VI, who served as pontiff from 1775 to 1799, one of the most difficult periods in the entire history of the papacy. Napoleon's forces conquered the Papal States in 1796, and in 1798 French general Louis Berthier deposed Pius VI as head of the Papal States. Because the French were afraid that other forces might try to rescue him, they forced him to move first to northern Italy and then to France. As Frank Coppa explains, the director of the French Revolution, La Révellière-Lépeaux, "sought the destruction of the spiritual as well as the temporal power of the papacy, and the triumph of the Theophilanthropist church, based on the philosophic outlook of Voltaire and the English freethinkers."[13] In response, Pope Pius VI and his successors for many years saw the French Revolution as a conspiracy against the Catholic Church and a revolt against the order willed by God. Through the nineteenth and much of the twentieth century, the memories of the French Revolution and other attacks on Catholic people and institutions shaped the mentality of popes and many other

---

[8] Paul Blanshard, *American Freedom and Catholic Power* (Boston: Beacon Press, 1950).

[9] A. Aulard, *Christianity and the French Revolution,* trans. Lady Frazer (New York: Howard Fertig, 1966).

[10] Alyssa Goldstein Sepinwall, *The Abbé Grégoire and the French Revolution: The Making of Modern Universalism* (Berkeley: University of California Press, 2005).

[11] Frank J. Coppa, *The Papacy Confronts the Modern World* (Malabar, FL: Krieger, 2003), 4.

[12] John McManners, *The French Revolution and the Church* (New York: Harper Torch-books, 1969); Nigel Aston, *Religion and Revolution in France, 1780–1804* (Washington, DC: Catholic University of America Press, 2000).

[13] Frank J. Coppa, *The Modern Papacy since 1789* (London: Longman, 1998), 31.

European Catholic leaders. In light of this trauma nineteenth-century popes responded critically to the rhetoric of revolution, liberty, and equality.[14] Where the American Revolution offered Catholics the free exercise of their religion, the French Revolution presented a direct threat to traditional Catholic identity and power in Europe and to the very existence of the papacy.

After the fall of Napoleon, Catholic leaders were wary of modern European revolutionary movements, which had important ramifications for Catholics in the United States.[15] As the young United States was taking shape, Pope Leo XII, who was pope from 1823 to 1829, rejected religious tolerance, strengthened the practices of the Holy Office (the Inquisition) and the Index of Forbidden Books, and restricted Jews to ghettos and confiscated their property.[16]

Crucial to the problematic relationships with other religions and with modern Western culture was the traditional Catholic condemnation of religious liberty. For centuries the Catholic Church had insisted on the right of religious liberty for its followers when they were in a minority situation. However, it denied in principle any right to religious liberty for others. John Courtney Murray explained the traditional papal position in the nineteenth and early twentieth centuries:

> The theory of religious tolerance takes its start from the statement, considered to be axiomatic, that error has no rights, that only the truth has rights—and exclusive rights. . . . Catholicism, *per se* and in principle, should be established as the one "religion of the state," since it is the one true religion.[17]

Murray explained that papal policy held that other religions had no right to public existence, but in some circumstances, they might be tolerated: "Therefore error is to be suppressed whenever and wherever possible; intolerance is the rule. Error, however, may be tolerated when tolerance is necessary by reason of circumstances, that is, when intolerance is impossible; tolerance remains the exception."[18]

In his encyclical *Mirari Vos: On Liberalism and Religious Indifferentism*, issued in 1832, Pope Gregory XVI sharply condemned "indifferentism" (the view that people following other religious paths than that of the Catholic Church can be saved): "This perverse opinion is spread on all sides by the fraud of the wicked who claim that it is possible to obtain the eternal salvation of the soul by the profession of any

---

[14] Sheridan Gilley, "The Papacy," in *Cambridge History of Christianity,* vol. 8, *World Christianities, c. 1815–1914,* ed. Sheridan Gilley and Brian Stanley (Cambridge: Cambridge University Press, 2005), 8:13–29.

[15] Coppa, *Modern Papacy,* 50–153.

[16] Richard P. McBrien, *Lives of the Popes: The Pontiffs from St. Peter to John Paul II* (San Francisco: HarperSanFrancisco, 1997).

[17] John Courtney Murray, "Religious Freedom," in *Freedom and Man,* A Wisdom and Discovery Book, ed. John Courtney Murray (New York: P. J. Kenedy & Sons, 1965), 134.

[18] Ibid.

kind of religion, as long as morality is maintained."[19] Pope Gregory also condemned liberty of conscience in religion, which was guaranteed by the First Amendment of the U.S. Constitution: "This shameful font of indifferentism gives rise to that absurd and erroneous proposition which claims that liberty of conscience must be maintained for everyone."[20] He condemned the freedom of the press, which was also guaranteed by the First Amendment of the U.S. Constitution:

> Here We must include that harmful and never sufficiently denounced freedom to publish any writings whatever and disseminate them to the people, which some dare to demand and promote with so great a clamor. We are horrified to see what monstrous doctrines and prodigious errors are disseminated far and wide in countless books, pamphlets, and other writings which, though small in weight, are very great in malice.[21]

Because the encyclical rejected the free exercise of religion, freedom of conscience, and freedom of the press guaranteed by the U.S. Constitution, Samuel Morse drew the conclusion that Catholics could not be loyal citizens of the United States; Morse commented on the encyclical of Pope Gregory XVI: "We see clearly from *infallible authority* that the Catholic of the present day, wherever he may be, if he is true to the principles of his sect, cannot consistently tolerate liberty of conscience, or liberty of the press."[22] Because Pope Gregory sought the official establishment of the Catholic Church in every state, Morse drew the conclusion:

> Popery is more dangerous and more formidable than any power in the United States, on the ground that, through its *despotic organization,* it can *concentrate the efforts* for any purpose, with complete effect, and that organization being wholly under *foreign* control, it can have no real sympathy with any thing American.[23]

In a similar vein, prominent preacher Edward Beecher denounced the alleged papal conspiracy to take over the United States and reduce it to despotism:

> It has been seen that the Romish corporation places itself in such an attitude that it is practically the god of this world. It has an entire monopoly of the

---

[19] Pope Gregory XVI, *Mirari Vos: On Liberalism and Religious Indifferentism, Encyclical,"* August 15, 1832, #13. See also Owen Chadwick, *A History of the Popes, 1830–1914* (Oxford: Oxford University Press, 2003), 23–25.

[20] Pope Gregory XVI, *Mirari Vos,* #14.

[21] Ibid., #15.

[22] Samuel Finley Breese Morse, *Foreign Conspiracy against the Liberties of the United States: The Numbers of Brutus* (1835; reprint, New York: Arno Press, 1977), 42–43.

[23] Ibid., 119 (emphasis in the original text).

grace of God and of the word of God. God is invisible and inaccessible except through the mediation of this corporation.[24]

Beecher refused to regard Catholic bishops in the United States as American citizens:

I do not regard them as in any sense American citizens in heart, whatever they may be in profession. My reason is this: they are part and parcel of a great conspiracy which now exists to subvert the most important and fundamental principles of the constitution of these United States and of every particular state in this Union.[25]

In the *Syllabus of Errors*, issued in 1864, Pope Pius IX condemned the notion that the Pope should reconcile himself with progress, liberalism, and modern civilization. What Pius meant by "modern civilization" was the separation of church and state, freedom of conscience in religion, rebellion against legitimate princes, "the dissolving of monasteries, the institution of civil marriage, and the destruction of the social influence of the Church."[26] But many Protestants in the United States saw the statement as symbolic of a fundamentally antagonistic relationship between the Catholic Church and modern Western culture in general. To be sure, there were many aspects to Catholic relations with modern culture, but overall, the dominant tone and tendencies from the popes in the nineteenth century were inimical. In the early twentieth century Pope Pius X condemned a variety of forms of progressive Catholic thought under the rubric of Modernism. Most of those condemned denied that they held the positions being targeted, but the condemnations and the ensuing suspicions influenced much Catholic thought throughout the early and middle years of the twentieth century. This atmosphere did not encourage interreligious exploration and dialogue.

Catholic Developments in Interreligious Relations: Popes Benedict XV and John XXIII

On the international scene, Pope Pius X's condemnation of Modernism discouraged efforts to improve relations with other religious traditions. However, there soon appeared a harbinger of better relations between Catholics and other religious traditions in the pontificate of Benedict XV (1914–1922), sometimes called the unknown pope.[27] During the unprecedented violence of the First World War, Pope Benedict refused to take sides among the combatants and made a formal

---

[24] Edward Beecher, *Papal Conspiracy Exposed* (1855; reprint, New York: Arno Press, 1977), 212.

[25] Ibid., 399.

[26] Chadwick, *A History of the Popes*, 174.

[27] John F. Pollard, *Benedict XV: The Unknown Pope and the Pursuit of Peace* (New York: Continuum, 2005).

proposal for peace. He launched an unparalleled papal humanitarian initiative, caring for civilians and combatants of all nationalities and religions. Jews and Muslims took note and expressed gratitude. After the conflict had ended, Sultan Mehmet VI, the last sultan of the Ottoman Empire and the penultimate caliph of Sunni Islam, contributed funds to erect a statue in Istanbul in honor of Pope Benedict XV, with the inscription in French and Italian: "To the great Pope of the world's tragic hour, Benedict XV, the benefactor of all people without discrimination of nationality or religion."[28] Given the long history of Catholic-Muslim conflict, it is difficult to imagine any earlier Ottoman caliph donating funds to honor any Supreme Pontiff of the Roman Catholic Church. Pope Benedict XV gave a dramatic example on the world stage of what charity and benevolence could look like in practice.

The young Angelo Giuseppe Roncalli (1881–1963) served as a chaplain and stretcher bearer in the Italian Army during World War I, and he quietly took note of Pope Benedict's actions during this period of unprecedented violence. Throughout his life, Roncalli had a deep respect for persons of differing backgrounds, including persons of other religious traditions. From 1926 to 1936, Roncalli served as the Apostolic Visitor, the Holy See's official diplomatic representative, in Sofia, Bulgaria, where he became familiar with Bulgarian Orthodox Christians and Muslims. He served as the Apostolic Delegate to Turkey and Greece, living in Istanbul from 1936 to 1944, where he deepened his relations with Greek Orthodox Christian leaders and Muslims. In the courtyard of the Church of the Holy Spirit in Istanbul, Roncalli would have seen on a daily basis the statue of Benedict XV honoring his wartime generosity.[29] As the Apostolic Delegate in Istanbul amid the horrors of the Second World War, Roncalli followed the example of Benedict XV in an earlier time of horrific violence by seeking to relieve suffering wherever he could. In particular he supported efforts to protect Jews from the horrors of the Shoah (the Holocaust).

Roncalli was elected Pope John XXIII on October 28, 1958, just thirteen years after the end of the Second World War. The new pope remembered the example of Benedict XV in caring for all persons of whatever religion or nation; he recalled his audiences with each previous pope of the twentieth century and reportedly found Pope Benedict XV "the most sympathetic."[30] John XXIII powerfully prepared the way and set the tone for the developments at the Second Vatican Council. When he proposed on January 25, 1959, to convene an ecumenical council, he mentioned hopes for Christian ecumenical relations, but he did not originally intend to address interreligious relations. On June 5, 1960, he founded the Secretariat for Promoting

---

[28] Agnes de Dreuzy, *The Holy See and the Emergence of the Modern Middle East: Benedict XV's Diplomacy in Greater Syria (1914–1922)* (Washington, DC: Catholic University of American Press, 2016), 4.

[29] Peter Hebblethwaite, *John XXIII: Pope of the Century* (London: Continuum, 2000), 70.

[30] Ibid., 46.

Christian Unity and appointed Augustin Cardinal Bea, a German Jesuit scripture scholar, as its first president.[31]

A week later, on June 13, 1960, Pope John met the French Jewish historian Jules Isaac. Isaac had done an extensive study of the history of Christian contempt for Jews, and he told Pope John that the Jewish people knew his goodness and had great hopes for him.[32] Isaac presented Pope John with a request that the upcoming ecumenical council reverse the traditional negative teaching of the Catholic Church about the Jews, especially the charge that they were guilty of the death of Jesus Christ. At the end of the dialogue, Isaac asked Pope John if there was reason to hope, and the pope reportedly replied: "You have reason for more than hope."[33] According to Isaac's later recollection, Pope John commented that as soon as he saw Isaac enter the room for the audience, the pontiff saw that he should direct Cardinal Bea to examine the question of the Catholic Church's relations with the Jews.[34] At the suggestion of Pope John, Isaac met with Bea on June 15, 1960. Isaac's personal request moved Pope John to set in motion a process of reflection and discernment that would eventually lead to a statement on Catholic relations with Jews, thereby broadening the scope of planning for the Second Vatican Council to include Jewish-Catholic relations. In 1962, Pope John authorized Cardinal Bea to prepare a draft for a declaration on the relationship between the Catholic Church and the people of Israel. As discussions proceeded, the scope of the statement would eventually be expanded further to include other religions as well.

On December 25, 1961, Pope John issued the apostolic constitution, *Humanae Salutis,* which officially convoked the Second Vatican Council to begin on October 11, 1962. Pope John placed his call for the ecumenical council as a response to what he called "a crisis underway within society": "It is a question in fact of bringing the perennial life-giving energies of the Gospel to the modern world, a world that boasts of its technical and scientific conquests but also bears the effects

---

[31] Jerome-Michael Vereb, *"Because He Was a German!": Cardinal Bea and the Origins of Roman Catholic Engagement in the Ecumenical Movement* (Grand Rapids, MI: Eerdmans, 2006).

[32] Jules Isaac, *The Teaching of Contempt: Christian Roots of Anti-Semitism*, ed. Claire Huchet-Bishop (New York: Holt, Rinehart and Winston, 1964).

[33] Jules Isaac, "La Réception de Jules Isaac par Jean XXIII," *La Documentation Catholique* 65, no. 1528 (November 17, 1968): 2015–16; see also John M. Oesterreicher, "Declaration on the Relationship of the Church to Non-Christian Religions: Introduction and Commentary," in *Commentary on the Documents of Vatican II*, vol. 3, *Declaration on the Relationship of the Church to Non-Christian Religions; Dogmatic Constitution on Divine Revelation; Decree on the Apostolate of the Laity,* ed. Herbert Vorgrimler (New York: Herder and Herder, 1969), 3:2.

[34] Isaac, "Réception," 2015–16. See also John Borelli, *"Nostra Aetate*: Origin, History, and Vatican II Context," in *The Future of Interreligious Dialogue: A Multireligious Conversation on Nostra Aetate,"* ed. Charles L. Cohen, Paul F. Knitter, and Ulrich Rosenhagen (Maryknoll, NY: Orbis Books, 2017), 25.

of a temporal order that some have wanted to reorganize by excluding God."[35] Pope John hoped that the upcoming Council could help all humans seek better relations:

> And finally, to a world which is lost, confused, and anxious because of the constant threat of new frightful conflicts, the forthcoming Council is called to offer a possibility for all men of good will to turn their thoughts and proposals toward peace, a peace which can and must come above all from spiritual and supernatural realities.[36]

Pope John wanted to link the constant religious mission of the Catholic Church to the concrete situation of the contemporary world, seeking to be helpful in new and practical ways to all humans. He trusted that the light of Christ can illumine the concrete problems and crises of the human community. Pope John renewed this hope in his opening address to the Council, delivered on October 11. For their part, the Council Fathers issued a Message to Humanity on October 20, 1962, which explicitly accepted the agenda of Pope John, focusing especially on the challenge of building peace.

Pope John made a major contribution in the area of religious freedom, which played a major role in improving Catholic interreligious relations. In his final encyclical, *Pacem in Terris,* which was issued early in 1963 shortly before his death, Pope John reversed earlier Catholic teaching and clearly affirmed the right to religious freedom, making a crucial distinction between error and people who are in error. Pope John insisted that people who are in error in matters of religion or ethical standards are still human beings with personal dignity and rights.[37] This principle prepared the way for Pope Paul VI and the Second Vatican Council to affirm the right of all humans to religious freedom in *Dignitatis Humanae.*[38] *Pacem in Terris,* which was the first encyclical addressed to all people of good will, rather than just to Catholics, succeeded in reaching a broad audience. It is also the only encyclical to have been published in its entirety in both *Pravda* and the *New York Times,* and the only encyclical to be set to music, in the oratorio by Jewish composer Darius Milhaud.[39]

Pope Paul VI and the Second Vatican Council

For Catholics and also for many other Christians, the Second Vatican Council marked a decisive turning point in attitudes toward the modern world, religious liberty, and followers of other religious traditions.[40] The Council also

---

[35] Pope John XXIII, *Humanae Salutis,* December 25, 1961.

[36] Ibid.

[37] Pope John XXIII, *Pacem in Terris,* April 11, 1963, #158.

[38] Pope Paul VI, *Dignitatis Humanae,* December 7, 1965.

[39] Darius Milhaud, *Pacem in Terris: Symphonie Chorale* (Paris: Editions Salabert, 1963).

[40] John Borelli, "The Origins and Early Development of Interreligious Relations during the Century of the Church (1910–2010)," *U.S. Catholic Historian* 28, no. 2 (2010): 81–105.

had a major influence on Protestant attitudes toward Catholics and toward other religions.[41] During the often heated debates over a proposed declaration on relations with the Jewish people, some bishops argued the Church could not change its traditional teaching that Jews had completely broken off the covenant with God by rejecting Jesus and that their only hope for salvation lay in conversion to the Catholic Church. Despite the weight of traditional teachings, after the ravages of the Shoah, the large majority of bishops at Vatican II believed that it was imperative that the Catholic Church express a new attitude toward the Jewish community and seek more respectful relations. Most bishops recognized that centuries of Catholic anti-Jewish teaching and practice had fostered animosity and hatred toward the Jews in Germany as well as all across Europe and beyond; this recognition, combined with the painful awareness of massive, unjust suffering in the Shoah, motivated a search for new theological perspectives. In response to strong opposition from figures such as Cardinal Ignace Tappouni, the patriarch of Antioch in the Syrian rite, Archbishop Marcel Lefebvre, Superior General of the Congregation of the Holy Spirit, and Cardinal Ernesto Ruffini, the Archbishop of Palermo, many bishops, especially from Germany and the United States, insisted on the need for a clear condemnation of antisemitism and all forms of religious discrimination, from whatever source.[42] The Catholic Church's embrace of the right to religious freedom would be pivotal to Catholic engagements with pluralism in the United States.

In 1964, Pope Paul VI issued his first encyclical, *Ecclesiam Suam,* which set forth a vision of interreligious dialogue as an integral component of the program of his pontificate. In the encyclical, Pope Paul called Catholics to *metanoia,* a conversion of heart and mind in a spirit of charity and poverty; and he proposed the attitude necessary for dialogue:

> Confidence is also necessary; confidence not only in the power of one's own words, but also in the good will of both parties to the dialogue. Hence dialogue promotes intimacy and friendship on both sides. It unites them in a mutual adherence to the Good, and thus excludes all self-seeking. . . . In a dialogue conducted with this kind of foresight, truth is wedded to charity and understanding to love.[43]

---

[41] Jay Moses, Dirk Ficca, Nanette Sawyer, and Robert Cathey, with Jill Folan and Katie Rains, "Why Would Presbyterians Turn to a Catholic Document?," *Studies in Christian-Jewish Relations* 10, no. 2 (2015): 1–8, https://ejournals.bc.edu/index.php/scjr/article/view/9223/8281; Franklin Sherman, "Protestant Parallels to *Nostra Aetate,*" *Studies in Christian-Jewish Relations* 10, no. 2 (2015): 1–13, https://www.researchgate.net/publication/305079584_Protestant_Parallels_to_Nostra_Aetate.

[42] John W. O'Malley, *What Happened at Vatican II* (Cambridge, MA: Belknap Press, 2008), 223–26.

[43] Pope Paul VI, *Ecclesiam Suam,* August 6, 1964, ##81, 82.

Quietly reversing centuries of papal teaching and practice, Pope Paul expressed his hopes for interreligious dialogue, recognizing the goodness in other religions and the importance of working together (#108). Later that year *Lumen Gentium, The Dogmatic Constitution on the Church,*[44] explicitly included Jews and Muslims in God's salvific plan, affirming that Jews are "a people according to their election most dear because of their ancestors: for God never goes back on his gifts and his calling (see Rom 11:28–29)" and teaching also that "the plan of salvation also embraces those who acknowledge the Creator, and among these the Moslems are first; they profess to hold the faith of Abraham and along with us they worship the one merciful God who will judge humanity on the last day" (#16). These affirmations transformed traditional Catholic teaching and prepared the way for *Nostra Aetate*[45] the following year.

As discussions of a proposed statement concerning the Catholic Church's relationship with the Jewish people progressed, a number of Council fathers proposed broadening the scope of the document to include Muslims, Hindus, and Buddhists as well. The felt need for a new attitude toward the Jewish community had profound implications for the church's stance toward every other religious tradition.

Nostra Aetate begins by acknowledging that in the present age, the human community's ever closer contacts among nations call for new attention to other religions, especially consideration of "what human beings have in common and what draws them to live together their destiny" (#1).[46] The opening words in Latin, "*Nostra Aetate,*" mean "in our age" or "in our time."[47] They proclaim awareness that the present age is distinctive in its responsibilities to foster harmonious relations among religions. The council notes that there is a nearly universal religious sense of an unseen power at work in the universe and human life. Since all creation comes from God, is guided by God's providence, and returns to God, the Council looks in hope for a fundamental unity among the peoples of the world and calls for dialogue and collaboration to "recognize, preserve and foster the good things, spiritual and moral, as well as the socio-cultural values found among the followers of other religions. This is done through conversations and collaboration with them, carried out with prudence and love and in witness to the Christian faith and life" (#2). This statement sets the agenda for Catholic participation in interreligious relationships.

The Council notes various aspects of religious experience, mentioning Hinduism and Buddhism in particular, and then sets forth the fundamental prin-

---

[44] Pope Paul VI, *Lumen Gentium,* The Dogmatic Constitution on the Church, November 21, 1964.

[45] Pope Paul VI, *Nostra Aetate,* Declaration on the Relation of the Church to Non-Christian Religions, October 28, 1965.

[46] Thomas F. Stransky, "Translation of *Nostra Aetate,*" in *Nostra Aetate,* ed. Pim Valkenberg and Anthony Cirelli (Washington, DC: Catholic University of America Press, 2016), xix. Unless otherwise noted, translations of *Nostra Aetate* will be from Stransky's translation.

[47] Ibid., 4. Stransky translates "*nostra aetate*" as "in our time," but he acknowledges that the other translation, "in our age," is also possible.

ciple that "the church rejects nothing that is true and holy in these religions" (#2). By acknowledging truth and holiness in other traditions, the Council opened the door to viewing other religious traditions as recipients of divine manifestation and grace. Two months later *Gaudium et Spes, The Pastoral Constitution on the Church in the Modern World*,[48] would clearly teach that the Spirit of God is active throughout all human life, offering grace and salvation to all humans, whether they have explicitly followed the path of Jesus Christ or not (#22).

Nostra Aetate also reaches out to Muslims. Aware of the centuries of conflict between Muslims and Catholics, the Vatican Council expresses its respect for Muslims and praises their worship of the one God; their veneration of Abraham, Jesus, and Mary; their expectation of a day of judgment; and their practice of morality, prayer, almsgiving, and fasting. Passing over most earlier papal statements in silence, the Declaration cites a cordial letter from Pope Gregory VII to Al-Nasir, the Muslim ruler of Bijaya, in present-day Algeria in 1076.[49] In contrast to most conciliar documents that cite numerous earlier magisterial statements, *Nostra Aetate* refers to only this papal letter from the eleventh century, quietly reversing the attitude of most traditional teachings. Conscious of the history of past hostilities, the Council leaders did not want Catholic-Muslim relationships to be imprisoned in a cycle of recriminations; and so *Nostra Aetate* urges Muslims and Catholics alike "to forget the past, to make sincere efforts for mutual understanding, so as to work together for the preservation and fostering of social justice, moral welfare, and peace and freedom for all humankind" (#3).

Turning to the Jewish people, *Nostra Aetate* acknowledges the roots of the Catholic Church in the religion of ancient Israel. Implicitly discarding the long history of anti-Jewish, supersessionist teaching, the Council again cites Romans 11:28–29, recalling Paul's teaching that "God holds the Jews most dear for the sake of their Fathers; he does not repent of the gifts he makes or revoke the call he issues—such is the witness of the Apostle" (#4). Overturning centuries of Catholic teaching, the council rejects the charge that all Jews alive at the time of Jesus were responsible for his death, let alone Jews of later generations; the Declaration also states that the Catholic Church "decries hatreds, persecutions, and manifestations of anti-Semitism directed against Jews at any time and by anyone" (#4). While *Nostra Aetate* is very brief, it had a tremendous impact not only on Catholic relations with other

---

[48] Pope Paul VI, *Gaudium et Spes,* Pastoral Constitution on the Church in the Modern World, December 7, 1965.

[49] Gregory VII wrote: "Almighty God, who wishes that all should be saved and none lost, approves nothing in us so much as that after loving him one should love his fellow man, and that one should not do to others, what one does not want done to oneself. You and we owe this charity to ourselves especially because we believe in and confess one God, admittedly in a different way, and daily praise and venerate him, the Creator of the world and ruler of this world." See Pope John Paul II, "Message to the Faithful of Islam at the End of the Month of Ramadan, April 3, 1991," in *John Paul II and Interreligious Dialogue,* ed. Byron L. Sherwin and Harold Kasimow (Maryknoll, NY: Orbis Books, 1999), 66.

religions but also on other Christian communions, many of whom went through similar discernment in these years. Gregory Baum, who was of Jewish descent and who worked on the preparation of the Declaration, commented that the change in the Magisterium's teaching on the Jews was the greatest transformation of the ordinary magisterium that took place at the Second Vatican Council.[50]

The Declaration does not make any pronouncement on the degree to which other religions do or do not contribute to salvation. *Nostra Aetate* makes comments about Muslims but not about Islam as such. As Daniel Madigan points out,

> The Council thus avoids discussion of the issues of Muhammad, the Qur'an, the Shari'a, etc., in favour of a recognition of the positive elements in the life of the Muslim believer. It also avoids any mention of the characteristics of Rabbinic Judaism, focusing exclusively on aspects of the biblical People of God, and leaving unanswered the question of the ongoing covenantal life of the Jews.[51]

The Second Vatican Council profoundly transformed the landscape of Catholic relations with followers of other religious traditions. Nonetheless, like all ecumenical councils, it did not address all issues and thus left many questions for future consideration. In particular, *Nostra Aetate* did not clarify exactly what it meant by calling Catholics to "recognize, preserve and foster the good things, spiritual and moral, as well as the socio-cultural values found among the followers of other religions" (#2) or by stating that "the Catholic Church rejects nothing that is true and holy in these religions" (#2). The Second Vatican Council did not fully explain to what degree knowledge of God and saving grace come to people in and through the diverse religious traditions that they practice. *Nostra Aetate* describes aspects of the Hindu, Buddhist, Muslim, and Jewish traditions but does not express a complete Catholic position relating to the particular beliefs and practices of these communities. The ground-breaking initiatives of the Second Vatican Council have decisively shaped Catholic engagement with other religious traditions in the United States of America during the last half-century.[52]

---

[50] Gregory Baum, "The Social Context of American Catholic Theology," *Proceedings of the Catholic Theological Society of America* 41 (1986): 87.

[51] Daniel A. Madigan, "*Nostra Aetate* and the Questions It Chose to Leave Open," *Gregorianum* 87, no. 4 (2006): 783.

[52] On the significance of Vatican II for interreligious relations, see Leo D. Lefebure, "Is There Reason for Hope?: The Second Vatican Council and Catholic Interreligious Relations," in *The Long Shadow of Vatican II: Living Faith and Negotiating Authority since the Second Vatican Council*, ed. Lucas Van Rompay, Sam Miglarese, and David Morgan (Chapel Hill: University of North Carolina Press, 2015), 8–36; Gerald O'Collins, *The Second Vatican Council on Other Religions* (Oxford: Oxford University Press, 2013); *Never Revoked:* Nostra Aetate *as Ongoing Challenge for Jewish-Christian Dialogue*, ed. Marianne Moyaert and Didier Pollefeyt (Leuven, Belgium: Peeters; Grand Rapids, MI: Eerdmans, 2010).

*Gaudium et Spes: Pastoral Constitution on the
Church in the World of Today*

In the initial planning for the Second Vatican Council, there was no proposed document concerning relations of the Church with the global situation of the present time; indeed, there is no direct precedent for such a statement in the history of Catholic ecumenical councils. Traditionally, Catholic ecumenical councils had ruled on questions of doctrine and had established rules for Church order, but they had not offered lengthy interpretations of their age or sought a dialogue and collaboration with all people of good will.[53] The councils of the Catholic Church had never before admitted that the Church had made mistakes or been partly responsible for misunderstandings. The Catholic Church had never openly stated that it could learn from the world. Councils had not directly addressed issues such as poverty, social justice, and the development of many cultures in dialogue with all people of good will, including followers of other religious paths.

In the opening session in 1962, Cardinal Leo Jozef Suenens proposed a twofold mission for the Council regarding the Church *ad intra* and the Church *ad extra*; this developed into a proposal for a document on the Church in the Modern World. The method underlying the document is among its most important contributions to the Catholic Church's self-understanding. The Second Vatican Council accepted historical consciousness, the awareness that all of human life is in a constant process of development and change, including the Church and the understanding of the Gospel. This recognition opened the way to historical and literary critical studies of the Bible, to more nuanced discussions of the history of Church teaching, and to the need for interpreting the signs of the times in the present day. The Second Vatican Council changed the way the Church understands itself concretely in the world and the way the Church communicates with the world. This acceptance of historical consciousness would have particular importance for Catholics in the United States and for developing interreligious relationships.[54]

There is nothing in the history of Catholic Church councils that is quite like *Gaudium et Spes*.[55] Earlier councils had condemned heresies, clarified church teaching, and issued disciplinary rules for the order of the Church. But no council had issued a document like this one, addressed to all people of good will and devoted to "examining the signs of the times and interpreting them in the light of the gospel" (#4). The Council described humanity as being in "a new stage of its history in which fundamental and rapid changes are gradually extending to the

---

[53] Norman P. Tanner, *The Councils of the Church: A Short History* (New York: Herder and Herder, 2001); O'Malley, *What Happened at Vatican II*, 15–52.

[54] Mark S. Massa, *The American Catholic Revolution: How the Sixties Changed the Church Forever* (Oxford: Oxford University Press, 2010), 30, 31, 50–51.

[55] Vatican Council II, *Gaudium et Spes*, #42, in Vatican Council II, *The Conciliar and Postconciliar Documents*, vol. 1, rev. ed., ed. Austin Flannery (Northport, NY: Costello/Dublin, Ireland: Dominican Publications, 2004), 942.

whole globe" (#4). The Second Vatican Council was acutely aware that its age was different from earlier ages and it sought to make sense of this situation in dialogue with all people of good will. After reflecting on the challenging contemporary situation of humanity, *Gaudium et Spes* closes with a moving appeal to Catholics to work with all humans to shape a better world: "Since God our Father is the origin and destiny of all things, we are all called to be sisters and brothers. Therefore, in our common human and divine vocation we can and should work together without violence and deceit, and in true peace, to build the world" (#92).

Gaudium et Spes looks at the entire human community in relation to Christian revelation. It stresses the importance of respect and love, especially for those who are different from us, including even our enemies (#28). *Gaudium et Spes* calls for understanding and dialogue and accepts the distinction that Pope John XXIII had made: where the earlier Catholic position stressed that error has no rights, *Gaudium et Spes,* like Pope John, affirms that people in error do have rights (#28). On this basis, the Council condemns every form of discrimination, including those based on religious difference (#29). These affirmations were indispensable steps on the path toward better relations with followers of other religious traditions.

Gaudium et Spes declares that the Catholic Church is not bound to any one culture (##42, 53, 58) and that the Church has long drawn on the concepts and languages and philosophies of many cultures to present the Gospel (#44). *Gaudium et Spes* also publicly acknowledges for the first time in history that Catholics have often failed in their responsibilities toward members of other religions and cultures (#19). The Council noted the danger of traditional cultures being threatened by the increasing global exchanges between cultures (#56).

Religious Freedom

There were fierce debates during the Council concerning the proper teaching on religious liberty. Some argued that earlier papal teachings could not be changed. American Catholics, shaped by the history of the United States, played an important role, notably Francis Cardinal Spellman, the Archbishop of New York, Albert Cardinal Meyer, the Archbishop of Chicago, and John Courtney Murray, who argued for a convergence between aspects of the Catholic tradition and values of the United States.[56] Cardinal Meyer, who had earlier been a professor of Sacred Scripture and could speak fluent Latin, went through a dramatic personal transformation during the Council and brought a particular eloquence and passion in arguing for the affirmation of religious liberty and for the condemnation of antisemitism.[57]

---

[56] John Courtney Murray, *We Hold These Truths: Catholic Reflections on the American Proposition* (1960; Lanham, MD: Rowman & Littlefield Publishers, 2005); Barry Hudock, *Struggle, Condemnation, Vindication: John Courtney Murray's Journey toward Vatican II* (Collegeville, MN: Liturgical Press, 2015); Donald E. Pelotte, *John Courtney Murray: Theologian in Conflict* (New York: Paulist Press, 1976).

[57] Steven M. Avella, "'I Don't Think Any Council Father Could Go Back Home the

Both *Gaudium et Spes* and *Nostra Aetate* affirm the right of all humans to religious freedom, to worship God in accordance with their conscience; *Dignitatis Humanae, The Declaration on Religious Freedom,* develops this position at greater length. It repeats the traditional Catholic teaching that all humans have an obligation in conscience to seek the truth to the best of their ability, but it also develops the thought of Pope John XXIII in *Pacem in Terris* by affirming that people whom the Catholic Church views as being objectively in error nonetheless retain the right to pursue their conscience in religious matters. *Dignitatis Humanae* rejects any use of force in communicating the truth, insisting that

> the human person has a right to religious freedom. Such freedom consists in this, that all should have such immunity from coercion by individuals, or by groups, or by any human power, that no one should be forced to act against his conscience in religious matters, nor prevented from acting according to his conscience, whether in private or in public, whether alone or in association with others, within due limits. (#2)

The Declaration draws the further conclusion from this principle "that it is wrong for a civil power to use force or fear or other means to impose the acceptance or rejection of any religion, or to prevent anyone from entering or leaving a religious body" (#6). Like *Nostra Aetate, Dignitatis Humanae* is a very short declaration, but it had a tremendous impact on improving Catholic relations with other religious traditions. The affirmation of religious liberty brought Catholic teaching into accord with the First Amendment of the U.S. Constitution and had a particular resonance for Catholics in the United States.

Catholic responses to religious pluralism in the United States move within the new horizon opened up by the Second Vatican Council, and many Christians of other communities were profoundly affected by Catholic decisions and initiatives in interreligious relations. Another ground-breaking document, *Dei Verbum, Dogmatic Constitution on Divine Revelation,* encouraged biblical scholarship to study the original context and genres of biblical writings, which led to increasing collaboration between Catholic, Protestant, and Jewish biblical scholars and paved the way for biblical scholars to consider the Holy Qur'an in relation to the biblical texts.

Pope Paul VI and Interreligious Relations

In addition to promulgating the conciliar documents, Pope Paul VI took a number of important initiatives. In the span of one year, 1964, he traveled to the Holy Land in January, becoming the first pope since Peter to do so, meeting with Muslim leaders as well as the Greek Orthodox Ecumenical Patriarch Athenagoras. That spring he established the Secretariat for non-Christians, the first dicastery of

Same.' Albert G. Meyer and Preparing for Vatican II: A Case Study of Episcopal Transformation," *U.S. Catholic Historian* 30, no. 2 (2012): 25–37.

the Holy See dedicated to relations with people who are not Christian. In August he issued *Ecclesiam Suam* with the program of dialogue as central to his pontificate. In the fall he promulgated *Lumen Gentium,* which spoke favorably of Jews and Muslims being included in God's plan of salvation, together with followers of other religions. In December Pope Paul traveled to India for a Eucharistic Congress in Bombay (Mumbai), where he spoke to an interreligious assembly, quoting a passage from the Brihadaranyaka Upanishad as an Advent prayer.[58]

Pope John Paul II

Pope John Paul II developed the legacy of Vatican II regarding interreligious relations in important ways.[59] In April 1986 he became in all likelihood the first pope since Peter to visit the synagogue of Rome, where he commented that Judaism is not an external religion for Christians but is an intrinsic part of Christian faith.[60] He took important steps in developing relations with Muslims. The Holy Qur'an challenges Muslims to compete in virtue with followers of other religious paths: "So let your goals be everything good. Your destiny, everyone, is to God, Who will tell you about that wherein you differed" (Q 5:48).[61] In this spirit King Hassan II of Morocco invited Pope John Paul II to come and address thousands of young Muslims in Casablanca, Morocco, on August 19, 1985. No Muslim ruler in history had issued this type of invitation to a pope. Both the invitation and its acceptance are difficult to imagine apart from the transformation that Popes John XXIII and Paul VI and the Second Vatican Council had initiated in Catholic relations with other religions.[62]

Another dramatic encounter occurred the following year, in October 1986, at a time when the tensions of the Cold War were acute. At the time of the twenty-first anniversary of the promulgation of *Nostra Aetate,* Pope John Paul II invited religious leaders from a wide range of traditions to come to Assisi to pray for world peace. Jews and Muslims, Buddhists, Sikhs and Hindus, representatives of traditional African and Native American religions, Shintoists and Jains all participated. The pope noted that such diverse traditions could not make a common prayer together and added that Catholics can be present while others pray. In his remarks to the assembled leaders, Pope John Paul stressed both respect for the differences

---

[58] Pope Paul VI, "Address to the Members of Non-Christian Religions," *Journey to India,* December 3, 1964.

[59] Peter C. Phan, "John Paul II and Interreligious Dialogue: Reality and Promise," in *The Vision of John Paul II: Assessing His Thought and Influence,* ed. Gerard Mannion (Collegeville, MN: Liturgical Press, 2008), 235–57; *John Paul II and Interreligious Dialogue,* ed. Byron L. Sherwin and Harold Kasimow (Maryknoll, NY: Orbis Books, 1999).

[60] Pope John Paul II, "Address to the Jewish Community of Rome," April 13, 1964.

[61] *The Qur'an: A New Translation by Thomas Cleary* (Starlatch Press, 2004), 55.

[62] Pope John Paul II, "Address of His Holiness Pope John Paul II to Young Muslims," Morocco, August 19, 1985, 10.

among religious traditions and also the importance of affirming a common ground whence "to operate together in the solution of this dramatic challenge of our age: true peace or catastrophic war."[63]

John Paul II sought healing in relationships between Catholics and Muslims in spite of the conflicts in some areas. In the wake of the attacks of September 11, 2001, he clearly distinguished authentic Islam from the actions of the terrorists and was a leader in developing relations with Muslims. On May 6, 2001, he had become the first pope ever recorded to visit a mosque—the Umayyad Mosque in Damascus, which was built on an earlier Byzantine Christian church honoring the grave of St. John the Baptist.[64]

In 1990 Pope John Paul II issued *Redemptoris Missio: An Encyclical Letter on the Permanent Validity of the Church's Missionary Mandate*; some months later, in 1991 the Pontifical Council for Interreligious Dialogue and the Congregation for the Evangelization of Peoples jointly issued *Dialogue and Proclamation*. Both documents distinguish and relate the mission of the church to proclaim the Gospel and the imperative to improve interreligious relations.[65] In *Redemptoris Missio* John Paul II reaffirmed the teaching of Vatican II that through Jesus Christ, God offers salvation to all people, and he also acknowledged "participated forms of mediation of different kinds and degrees."[66] He set forth the principle: "In the light of the economy of salvation, the Church sees no conflict between proclaiming Christ and engaging in interreligious dialogue. . . . These two elements must maintain both their intimate connection and their distinctiveness" (#55). John Paul II also went beyond Vatican II by positively affirming that the Holy Spirit is actively at work in all cultures and in other religions, not only in individuals but also on a structural level (##28–29). In relation to the World Day of Prayer for Peace in Assisi, he affirmed that every genuine prayer from whatever tradition is inspired by the Holy Spirit.[67]

Structure of Interreligious Relationships

The 1991 document *Dialogue and Proclamation* proposes a fourfold structure for Catholic involvement in interreligious relationships that has been widely influential. Because followers of different religious paths dwell together on this

---

[63] Pope John Paul II, "The Challenge and the Possibility of Peace," *Origins* 16, no. 21 (November 6, 1986): 370.

[64] Pope John Paul II, "Address of the Holy Father," Meeting with the Muslims Leaders, Omayyad Great Mosque, Damascus, May 6, 2001.

[65] William R. Burrows, ed., *Redemption and Dialogue: Reading* Redemptoris Missio *and* Dialogue and Proclamation (1993; reprint, Eugene, OR: Wipf & Stock Publishers, 2009).

[66] Pope John Paul II, *Redemptoris Missio*, December 7, 1990, #5; Burrows, *Redemption and Dialogue*, 8.

[67] Pope John Paul II, "Address to Cardinals and the Roman Curia," December 22, 1986, 11; *Acta Apostolicae Sedis* 79 (1987): 1089.

planet, the all-embracing dialogue is the dialogue of life, addressing the challenge of how to dwell together as good neighbors. Within this horizon, the document distinguishes three further aspects, each related to the others and each overlapping the others. The dialogue of practical action for social justice reflects on the problems and challenges facing our communities and seeks common values as a basis for acting together to achieve goals of transforming society. The dialogue of theological exchange reflects on the beliefs and worldviews of different religious traditions, seeking points of contact and acknowledging areas of disagreement. The dialogue of sharing religious and spiritual experience reflects on the practices of prayer, ritual, monastic life, and meditation in different traditions, seeking mutual appreciation and enrichment.[68] None of these forms of dialogue proceed in isolation. One or another may be at the forefront of attention, but each hovers in the background of the others.

Dialogue and Proclamation recalls the teaching of Vatican II on the effects of God's grace and the action of the Holy Spirit in other religious traditions,[69] and it reflects on biblical texts that witness to the presence of God outside of Israel, such as the covenant with Noah, which Jews have traditionally seen as embracing all humankind and the entire earth:

> The Covenant with Noah, the man who "walked with God" (Gen 6:9), is symbolic of the divine intervention in the history of the nations. Non-Israelite figures of the Old Testament are seen in the New Testament as belonging to the one history of salvation. Abel, Enoch and Noah are proposed as models of faith (cf. Heb 11:4–7). They knew, adored and believed in the one true God who is identical with the God who revealed himself to Abraham and Moses. The Gentile High Priest Melchisedek blesses Abraham, the father of all believers (cf. Heb 7:1–17).[70]

As we have seen, in considering the covenant God made with the Jewish people, *Nostra Aetate* cites the Apostle Paul (Rom 11:28–29), teaching that the gifts and call of God are irrevocable (*sine poenitentia*) (#2). Pope John Paul II, inspired by *Nostra Aetate,* declared that the covenant God made with the Jewish people has never been revoked (*numquam revocata*).[71] In light of *Dialogue and Proclamation's* reference to the covenant with Noah, one can apply this principle of irrevocability also to the covenant with Noah, which God made with all peoples of the earth and which has similarly never been revoked.[72]

---

[68] *Dialogue and Proclamation,* May 19, 1991, #42; Burrows, *Redemption and Dialogue,* 104.

[69] *Dialogue and Proclamation* ##16–17; Burrows, *Redemption and Dialogue,* 98.

[70] *Dialogue and Proclamation* #19; Burrows, *Redemption and Dialogue,* 99.

[71] Pope John Paul II, "Speech to the Jewish Community of Mainz, West Germany," November 17, 1980.

[72] Peter C. Phan, "Reading *Nostra Aetate* in Reverse: A Different Way of Looking at the Relations among Religions," *Studies in Christian-Jewish Relations* 10, no. 2 (2015): 1–14.

Dialogue and Proclamation also notes the importance of the sapiential tradition of ancient Israel; the Israelite wisdom teachers respected the wisdom of their counterparts in Egypt and Mesopotamia and drew from these traditions: "In the Wisdom literature also, which bears witness to cultural exchanges between Israel and its neighbors, the action of God in the whole universe is clearly affirmed. It goes beyond the boundaries of the Chosen People to touch both the history of nations and the lives of individuals."[73] The biblical wisdom tradition is one of the important resources for developing interreligious relationships today.

Pope Benedict XVI

In September 2006, Pope Benedict XVI gave an address in Regensberg, Germany, in which he cited a medieval conversation reported between the Byzantine Emperor Manuel II Paleologus and an unnamed educated Persian in or about the year 1391. Benedict quoted a brusque remark of Manuel II: "Show me just what Mohammed brought that was new, and there you will find things only evil and inhuman, such as his command to spread by the sword the faith he preached."[74] Benedict went on to cite a Western scholar, Theodore Khoury, who claimed that Islam's view of the transcendence of God is so extreme that God's will is allegedly "not bound up with any of our categories, even that of rationality." Benedict cited Khoury quoting French scholar Arnaldez, who argues that a medieval Muslim scholar, Ibn Hazm, claimed that "God is not bound even by his own word, and that nothing would oblige him to reveal the truth to us. Were it God's will, we would even have to practice idolatry." Benedict also noted the claim of "some of the experts" that the Qur'anic command, "There is no compulsion in religions" (2:256) came from the early Meccan period, when Muhammadans were powerless and persecuted in Mecca. Benedict stated that Manuel II "also knew the instructions, developed later and recorded in the Qur'an, concerning holy war." This implied that the teaching against compulsion in religion is not as authoritative for Muslims as later Qur'anic teachings that allegedly refer to "holy war." Benedict then went on to praise the merger of Greek philosophy and biblical thought in the Catholic tradition and to criticize Franciscan theologians of the late Middle Ages who stressed the will of God in a way analogous to Benedict's view of Islam.

These remarks aroused a furor in the Muslim world, and many Muslim leaders protested. About a month later, thirty-eight Muslim scholars and leaders sent an "Open Letter to His Holiness Pope Benedict XVI," and this was endorsed by other Muslims later on.[75] In it they rejected the pope's dating of the command against

---

[73] *Dialogue and Proclamation* #20; Burrows, *Redemption and Dialogue*, 99.

[74] Benedict XVI, "Speech to Representatives of Science, University of Regensburg," September 12, 2006.

[75] "Open Letter to His Holiness Pope Benedict XVI by 38 Leading Muslim Scholars and Leaders," *Islamic Monthly,* October 4, 2006.

compulsion in religion to the early period of Muhammad's prophetic ministry. Instead, they dated this revelation to the Medinan period when Muslims were in power and when some wished to enforce Islam by the sword. The Qur'an forbade the use of violence to compel religious practice. The Qur'an and the Islamic tradition, they noted, have no teaching concerning holy war as such. Jihad means "struggle," and it can be in a holy cause. They reject the charge that Muhammad commanded that Islam be spread by the sword.

The Muslim scholars argued that Benedict's view of divine transcendence in Islam is "a simplification which can be misleading." They pointed out that Ibn Hazm, whom Benedict cites, by way of Khoury and Arnaldez, was a marginal figure belonging to the Zahiri School of Islamic law, which no one follows today. They suggested other figures as more central, such as Al-Ghazzali. They also suggested that Benedict's statement about God's Will not being bound up in any of our categories is also misleading. Benedict's dichotomy between reason and faith "does not exist in precisely the same form in Islamic thought."

Regarding the claim that Muhammad brought nothing new except what was "evil and inhuman, such as his alleged command to spread by the sword the faith he preached," the Muslim scholars note that Muhammad never claimed to bring something new. The Qur'an says, "Naught is said to thee (Muhammad) but what already was said to the Messengers before thee" (41:43). Regarding Khoury and Arnaldez, the Muslim scholars state that "Muslims have not to our knowledge endorsed *the* 'experts' you referred to, or recognized them as representing Muslims or their views."

Even though Pope Benedict did not publicly retract any of his remarks, he responded to the controversy by adding notes to the text of the speech when it was published on the Vatican website, distancing himself from the statement of Emperor Manuel II:

> In the Muslim world, this quotation has unfortunately been taken as an expression of my personal position, thus arousing understandable indignation. I hope that the reader of my text can see immediately that this sentence does not express my personal view of the Qur'an, for which I have the respect due to the holy book of a great religion. In quoting the text of the Emperor Manuel II, I intended solely to draw out the essential relationship between faith and reason. On this point I am in agreement with Manuel II, but without endorsing his polemic.[76]

On November 30, 2006, Pope Benedict traveled to Istanbul and visited the Sultan Ahmed Mosque, commonly known as the Blue Mosque. Accompanied by the Imam of the Blue Mosque and the Mufti of Istanbul, the pope visited the interior of the mosque with respect, and he stood alongside them for two minutes

---

[76] Benedict XVI, "Speech to Representatives of Science, University of Regensburg," September 12, 2006.

in silent meditation; many Muslims understood the pope to be praying alongside the imam and the mufti. This image brought a measure of healing to the relationship of Benedict to Muslims.

During the following year Pope Benedict's speech and the ensuing controversy elicited another response from Muslim leaders, which would be one of the most important and promising developments in the history of Muslim-Christian relations. In October 2007, 138 Muslim leaders from a wide variety of traditions and countries, in conjunction with a conference on "love in the Qur'an" at the Royal Aal al-Bayt Institute for Islamic Thought in Jordan, issued "A Common Word between Us and You," addressed not only to Pope Benedict XVI but also to a long list of Christian leaders from many different communities.[77] This statement, which has subsequently been endorsed by many, many other leaders, states,

> The future of the world depends on peace between Muslims and Christians. The basis for this peace and understanding already exists. It is part of the very foundational principles of both faiths: love of the One God, and love of neighbour. These principles are found over and over again in the sacred texts of Islam and Christianity. The Unity of God, the necessity of love for Him, and the necessity of love of the neighbour is thus the common ground between Islam and Christianity.

There have been international conferences to discuss "A Common Word" in many different locations, including the Vatican, Cambridge University, Yale University, and Georgetown University.[78] There is also an ongoing online forum for continuing discussions.[79]

In 2008, Pope Benedict spoke about interreligious relations to leaders from various religious traditions during his visit to Washington, DC. He praised interreligious collaboration and cooperation, as expressed in the American practice of holding interreligious services for the feast of Thanksgiving. He cited Alexis de Tocqueville on the benefits of freedom of worship in the United States. Without mentioning Pope Gregory XVI's condemnation of this freedom during the time of de Tocqueville, Pope Benedict stressed the importance of religious freedom, praised the American practice and hoped that others would take heart from the American experience of many becoming one. He stated that through interreligious dialogue both people and the society are enriched, and he stressed the vital importance of searching for truth in and through dialogue.[80]

---

[77] *A Common Word between Us and You* (Jordan: Royal Aal al-Bayt Institute for Islamic Thought, 2007).

[78] *A Common Word: Muslims and Christians on Loving God and Neighbor,* ed. Miroslav Volf, Ghazi bin Muhammad, and Melissa Yarrington (Grand Rapids, MI: Eerdmans, 2010).

[79] A Common Word; https://www.acommonword.com/.

[80] Benedict XVI, Speech to Representatives of Other Religions, John Paul II Cultural Center, Washington, DC, April 17, 2008.

Pope Benedict expressed a repeated concern for affirming religious liberty and renouncing religiously motivated violence. He also expressed a concern for dialogue with those who do not follow a religious path, inviting feminist philosopher Julia Kristeva to speak at the twenty-fifth anniversary of the Assisi Day of Prayer for World Peace; John Thavis described this encounter:

> Certainly, the pope and Kristeva offered quite different perspectives. For the pope, God is the key to every possible human solution to problems of peace and injustice. Kristeva never mentioned God and described the task of renewing culture solely in terms of human efforts. But they both appeared to agree that they need to talk to each other.[81]

Pope Benedict called this initiative an invitation to the Courtyard of the Gentiles.[82]

Pope Francis

From the time Jorge Bergoglio was young, he had a strong sense of the mercy of God reaching out personally to him. When Jesuit journalist Antonio Spadaro asked the newly elected Pope Francis to describe who he is, he paused, reflected, and responded, "I am a sinner whom the Lord has looked upon."[83] His experience of the mercy of God when he was young has decisively influenced Pope Francis's relations with followers of other religious traditions and with those who are not religious. In proclaiming a special Jubilee Year of Mercy, he affirmed, "Jesus Christ is the face of the Father's mercy. These words might well sum up the mystery of the Christian faith. Mercy has become living and visible in Jesus of Nazareth, reaching its culmination in him."[84] Publicly acknowledging his own weakness and sinfulness and entrusting his life to the mercy of God that he finds incarnate in Jesus Christ, Pope Francis issues an invitation to all people of good will to cooperate in relieving suffering and shaping a healthy community for all forms of life on this planet.

As Archbishop of Buenos Aires, Jorge Bergoglio came to know Rabbi Abraham Skorka. Through a series of conversations, the rabbi and the cardinal developed mutual understanding and friendship, and eventually they decided to share their reflections in a noteworthy book, *On Heaven and Earth*. This work offers a model of interreligious dialogue in which the speakers seek the true, the good, the

---

[81] John Thavis, "Philosopher and Atheist Julia Kristeva Addresses Assisi," *Catholic Near East Welfare Association News Service,* October 28, 2011.

[82] "Pope Benedict XVI's Message to Courtyard of the Gentiles," *Zenit,* March 26, 2011.

[83] Antonio Spadaro, "Interview with Pope Francis" (Vatican City: Libreria Editrice Vaticana, 2015).

[84] Pope Francis, *Misericordiae Vultus: Bull of Indiction of the Extraordinary Jubilee of Mercy,* April 11, 2015.

beautiful, and the holy. Bergoglio believes that in true dialogue, the participants are open to being transformed in the exchange because dialogue is not simply a defense of previously formulated positions. In introducing the conversations with his Jewish friend, he describes an image from the façade of the Cathedral of Buenos Aires that depicts Joseph and his brothers in Genesis: "Decades of misunderstandings converge in that embrace."[85] There is weeping at this reunion, and Joseph has to pose the question of whether his father still lives. It is a poignant image for Jewish-Christian relations because it evokes how closely we are related as siblings but also recalls the long years of estrangement and suspicion.

Bergoglio finds in this image an invitation to establish a "culture of encounter," and he offers a beautiful description of dialogue:

> Dialogue is born from a respectful attitude toward the other person, from a conviction that the other person has something good to say. It supposes that we can make room in our heart for their point of view, their opinion and their proposals. Dialogue entails a warm reception and not a preemptive condemnation. To dialogue, one must know how to lower the defenses, to open the doors of one's home and to offer warmth.[86]

In March 2013, when Jorge Cardinal Bergoglio was elected pope, he took the name of Francis in honor of Francis of Assisi, who is beloved by followers of many religious traditions. Pope Francis set forth the fundamental themes of his pontificate in his postsynodal apostolic exhortation, *Evangelii Gaudium*. Continuing the call of the Second Vatican Council to reach out to followers of all religious paths, Pope Francis strongly supports interreligious initiatives in the context of seeking peace and the flourishing of life for all: "An attitude of openness in truth and in love must characterize the dialogue with the followers of non-Christian religions. . . . Interreligious dialogue is a necessary condition for peace in the world, and so it is a duty for Christians as well as other religious communities."[87] In this exhortation Francis explains the hoped-for result of such an attitude of openness:

> In this way we learn to accept others and their different ways of living, thinking and speaking. We can then join one another in taking up the duty of serving justice and peace, which should become a basic principle of all our exchanges. A dialogue which seeks social peace and justice is in itself, beyond all merely practical considerations, an ethical commitment which brings about a new social situation. (#250)

---

[85] Jorge Mario Bergoglio and Abraham Skorka, *On Heaven and Earth: Pope Francis on Faith, Family, and the Church in the Twenty-First Century*, trans. Alejandro Bermudez and Howard Goodman, ed. in Spanish by Diego F. Rosemberg (New York: Image, 2013), xiii.

[86] Ibid., xiv.

[87] Pope Francis, *Evangelii Gaudium*, November 24, 2013, #250.

In 2015, Pope Francis responded to the call of the Second Vatican Council to interpret and address the signs of the times by discussing the current ecological challenge. In his encyclical *Laudato Si'*, Francis asserted that such a revolution must be informed by religious and ethical principles that go beyond the domain of empirical science.

> Any technical solution which science claims to offer will be powerless to solve the serious problems of our world if humanity loses its compass, if we lose sight of the great motivations which make it possible for us to live in harmony, to make sacrifices and to treat others well.[88]

Francis acknowledges that believers have not always been "faithful to the treasures of wisdom which we have been called to protect and preserve," but nonetheless he calls for a return to the sources of religious traditions in order to respond to current needs (*Laudato Si'*, #200). In this context, he places care for the earth at the center of the interreligious agenda and calls for renewed interreligious dialogue on ecological issues.

Decisively shaping Pope Francis's papal ministry is his commitment to building a culture of encounter based upon dialogue and the recognition of the goodness of diversity. Speaking to the representatives of civil society during his trip to Paraguay in July 2015, Pope Francis set forth a vision of dialogical engagement for the common good:

> Moreover, dialogue presupposes and demands that we seek a culture of encounter; an encounter which acknowledges that diversity is not only good, it is necessary. Uniformity nullifies us, it makes us robots. The richness of life is in diversity. For this reason, the point of departure cannot be, "I'm going to dialogue but he's wrong." No, no, we must not presume that the other person is wrong. I dialogue with my identity but I'm going to listen to what the other person has to say, how I can be enriched by the other, who makes me realize my mistakes, and see the contribution I can offer. It is a going out and a coming back, always with an open heart. If I presume that the other person is wrong, it's better to go home and not dialogue, would you not agree? Dialogue is for the common good and the common good is sought by starting from our differences, constantly leaving room for new alternatives. . . . Dialogue is about seeking the common good. Discuss, think, and discover together a better solution for everybody.[89]

In January 2016, Pope Francis released a video request for prayers on YouTube that noted the religious diversity of humans and ended with the hope "that sincere

---

[88] Pope Francis, *Praise Be to You: Laudato Si': On Care for Our Common Home* (Vatican City: Libreria Editrice Vaticana/San Francisco: Ignatius Press, 2015), #200.

[89] Pope Francis, Address to the Representatives of Civil Society, July 11, 2015.

dialogue among men and women of different faiths may produce fruits of peace and justice."[90]

Like his predecessors, Francis has affirmed religious liberty and denounced religiously motivated violence. Pope Francis has emphasized the mercy of God as a central theme of his pontificate, calling a year of mercy. Jesus Christ in the power of the Holy Spirit incarnates the mercy of God, which is offered to all people. The impact of the Second Vatican Council's invitation to Catholics to collaborate with all humans in building a world of respect, justice, and peace has been dramatic; this challenge echoes still.

World Council of Churches

Many other Christian communions have gone through analogous developments regarding interreligious relations during this period. The World Council of Churches, one of the most important international forums for Christian ecumenical reflection, has for many years convened meetings of Christians concerned about interreligious relations, with particular attention to dialogues with Muslims.[91] In 1971, the World Council of Churches opened a distinct section for interreligious dialogue; and in 2016, it issued *Called to Dialogue: Interreligious and Intra-Christian Dialogue in Ecumenical Conversation: A Practical Guide.*[92] The statement comments on the challenging situation for both interreligious and intra-Christian ecumenical dialogue: "The changing contexts for both intra-Christian and interreligious relations, namely the crisis in traditional expressions of ecumenism and the rise of religious extremism and fundamentalism across several religions, impinge on one another but also seem to undercut the efforts of both endeavours."[93] The authors identify common goals for both forms of dialogue: "the promise of diffusing tensions, addressing violence, fostering understanding and reconciliation and deepening the religious commitment and spirituality of those involved."[94] *Called to Dialogue* links interreligious relations to the action of God throughout creation, affirming,

> In interreligious dialogue, our purpose is to enter further into the mystery of what God is doing in the lives of people of other religions as part of the dialogue of salvation and so to come to a greater understanding and

---

[90] https://youtu.be/-6FfTxwTX34.

[91] Stuart E. Brown, compiler, *Meeting in Faith: Twenty Years of Christian-Muslim Conversations Sponsored by the World Council of Churches* (Geneva, Switzerland: WCC Publications, 1989).

[92] World Council of Churches, *Called to Dialogue: Interreligious and Intra-Christian Dialogue in Ecumenical Conversation: A Practical Guide* (Geneva, Switzerland: WCC Publications, 2015).

[93] Ibid., 3.

[94] Ibid.

honouring of one another which will build peace and community, through the God-wards transformation of humanity and the whole world.[95]

The document goes on to ground Christian participation in interreligious dialogue in God's self-manifestation in Jesus Christ:

> Our belief in God's manifestation through Christ's incarnation as the self-communication of a God who desires to be in communion with humanity as *logos* (John 1) and also as a self-emptying God (Philippians 2) who embraces vulnerability can be fruitful and act as a model in both intra-Christian and interreligious dialogue.[96]

The statement encourages the sharing of one's faith in an atmosphere of mutual respect and listening, but it cautions, "However, proselytism, by which we understand the deliberate use of dialogue as a means to convert the other, is not appropriate."[97] It goes on to assert the close relation to work for peace, justice, and ecology: "Interreligious dialogue is intrinsically connected to our commitment to justice and peace. . . The affirmation of the ultimate interconnectedness of all creation and humanity is foundational for interreligious dialogue, as we work with partners of other faiths for justice, peace and the integrity of all creation."[98] This statement of the World Council of Churches bears important similarities to the Vatican statements, *Mission and Dialogue* and *Dialogue and Proclamation*, which encourage dialogue partners to explore their experiences of prayer and contemplation in an atmosphere of respect, seeking mutual enrichment.[99]

Many have found their lives transformed by interreligious relations. Diana Eck, an American Protestant theologian, recounts her experience of working with a committee of the World Council of Churches pondering the relation of Christians to followers of other religious paths. Theologians from a variety of Christian traditions stated, "It is our Christian faith in God which challenges us to take seriously the whole realm of religious plurality. We see this not so much as an obstacle to be overcome, but rather as an opportunity for deepening our encounter with God and with our neighbors."[100] The theologians continued: "We find ourselves recognizing a need to move beyond a theology which confines salvation to the explicit personal commitment to Jesus Christ," and they went on to "affirm unequivocally that God the Holy Spirit has been at work in the life and

---

[95] Ibid., 15.

[96] Ibid., 16.

[97] Ibid., 17.

[98] Ibid., 18.

[99] Secretariat for Non-Christians, *Mission and Dialogue*, June 10, 1984; Pontifical Council for Interreligious Dialogue, *Dialogue and Proclamation*, May 19, 1991.

[100] Diana L. Eck, *Encountering God: A Spiritual Journey from Bozeman to Banaras* (Boston: Beacon Press, 1993), xi–xii.

traditions of peoples of other living faiths."[101] They concluded: "Our recognition of the mystery of salvation in men and women of other religious traditions shapes the concrete attitudes with which we Christians must approach them in interreligious dialogue."[102]

On June 28, 2011, the World Council of Churches, the Pontifical Council for Interreligious Dialogue, and the World Evangelical Association issued a joint statement, *Christian Witness in a Multi-Religious World: Recommendations for Conduct*.[103] The statement places mission at the heart of Christian life and offers recommendations for how witness can be appropriately shared in interreligious contexts through dialogue with people from various cultures. It strongly affirms religious freedom and rejects any form of coercion as a betrayal of the Gospel message. It calls for rejecting violence and renouncing false witness and commends mutual respect and solidarity with people from other religious traditions. The statement challenges Christians to deepen their own religious identity in and through the study of other religious traditions and through building healthy interreligious relationships.

---

[101] Ibid., xii.

[102] Ibid.

[103] World Council of Churches, the Pontifical Council for Interreligious Dialogue, and the World Evangelical Association, *Christian Witness in a Multi-Religious World: Recommendations for Conduct*, June 28, 2011.

2

RELIGIOUS DIVERSITY AND
MIGRATION IN THE UNITED STATES

Throughout American history, Catholic and other Christian responses to religious diversity and pluralism have intertwined intimately with the history of migrations, as wave after wave of immigrants have arrived from various locations around the world. The constantly changing demographic character of American society has shaped Christian responses to religious pluralism in different ways during different periods; theological interpretations of religious diversity, whether hostile or welcoming, always emerge from particular contexts of interreligious awareness. Increasingly, theologians are examining how migrations have shaped both the biblical heritage and the entire history of the Christian tradition, including the experience of Catholics in the United States.[1] The decisions of Americans to welcome or not to welcome new immigrants were closely linked to their attitudes toward religious pluralism and toward Catholics. On the one hand, many Americans have prided themselves on being a nation of religious liberty that welcomes immigrants; on the other hand, many other Americans have sought to defend a white Christian American identity and have been very wary of certain newcomers and their religious traditions.[2]

Controversy over who should be allowed to enter the United States continues at the present time. In August 2019, an assailant killed large numbers of shoppers in El Paso, Texas; the accused person had just earlier posted an online statement decrying an alleged Hispanic invasion of Texas. Immigration presents invaluable opportunities but also formidable challenges for living with religious and ethnic diversity. This chapter will examine the relation between migrations, demographics, and changing social attitudes in the United States with regard to religious diversity

---

[1] For an overview of migrations and the identity of the church, see Peter C. Phan, "Doing Ecclesiology in World Christianity: A Church of Migrants and a Migrant Church," *Offerings: A Journal of Christian Spirituality and Practical Theology* 11 (2018): 3–26; Peter C. Phan, "Church as the Sacrament of God the Migrant," *Religions* 10 (2017): 66–77; Peter C. Phan, "Deus Migrator-God the Migrant: Migration of Theology and Theology of Migration," *Theological Studies* 77, no. 4 (2016): 845–68.

[2] Joanna Michal Hoyt, *A Wary Welcome: The History of US Attitudes to Immigration* (London: SkinnyBottle, 2017).

and the role of religious identity in American life, with particular attention to Catholic experience.

Religious Tensions in the Colonial Period

The first Christians who came to North America were Spanish Catholics who explored Florida, the Atlantic coast, and the Chesapeake Bay in the early sixteenth century, and who later established settlements and churches in St. Augustine, Florida, in 1565, and in Santa Fe, New Mexico, in 1604. In 1570, along what today is known as the James River in present-day Virginia, Spanish Jesuits established a missionary settlement known as the Ajacán Mission; but this effort ended in 1571 when indigenous people killed the missionaries and captured a Spanish Catholic boy, Alonso de Olmos. Throughout the Spanish colonies in North America, the Catholic Church and the Spanish governing authorities together exercised control over major decisions affecting Catholic life. The Spanish monarchs received authority over the affairs of the Catholic Church in the Americas through the *Patronato Real* (Royal Patronage) granted by the Holy See in 1493, analogous to the *Padroado* that had been accorded to the Portuguese monarchs.

The form of Catholicism originally brought by the Spanish reflected the medieval period prior to the challenge of the Protestant Reformation and the response of the Council of Trent. Orlando Espín observes that for Iberian Catholics, "beliefs were expressed primarily in and through symbol and rite, through devotions and liturgical practices.... The teaching of the gospel did not usually occur through the spoken magisterial word, but through the symbolic, 'performative' word."[3] In this context the word *traditio* ("tradition") included both the scriptures and doctrinal definitions, as well as devotional practices that had developed on a popular level through the centuries.

Despite the chronic military conflicts and religious intolerance in the medieval Iberian Peninsula, there were some contexts where a culture of tolerance allowed for a complex intermingling of Jewish, Christian, and Muslim perspectives and practices. For example, Christians, Jews, and Muslims in eleventh-century Toledo (in central Spain) found themselves transformed and enriched by their mutual encounter.[4] Spanish Catholic missionaries in Florida and New Mexico continued this ambivalent and complex heritage, at times being harshly intolerant but at other times being open to accepting traditional Native American practices alongside of Spanish Catholic ones. While Spanish Catholic missionaries were generally not open to notions of tolerance or acceptance of religious diversity, nonetheless, in practice some priests allowed American Indians to engage in their traditional activ-

---

[3] Orlando Espín, *The Faith of the People: Theological Reflections on Popular Catholicism* (Maryknoll, NY: Orbis Books, 1997), 117, 119.

[4] Jerrilynn D. Dodds, María Rosa Menocal, and Abigail Krasner Balbale, *The Arts of Intimacy: Christians, Jews, and Muslims in the Making of Castilian Culture* (New Haven, CT: Yale University Press, 2008).

ities as well as Catholic rites. Since there was no systematic distinction between sacred and secular in American Indian life, it was often difficult for missionaries to distinguish what was to be deemed religiously objectionable and what was not. To a large degree, popular Hispanic Catholic piety developed on a grassroots level free from clerical interference and control.[5]

Beginning in the early seventeenth century, French missionaries preached to the American Indians in New France, consisting of present-day Canada, New York State, and the Midwest.[6] In the absence of soldiers, the French government did not offer protection to the first missionaries, and the French Jesuits often lived alone among the Indians. In 1633, Paul Le Jeune, the superior of the Jesuit mission, lived among the Montagnais Indians in New France; he viewed the Indian religious leader Carigonan as inspired by the devil and sought to discredit him. Nicholas Cushner interprets Le Jeune's experience as "a microcosm of Jesuit-Indian relations in New France. Conflict, struggle for power, opposing world views, misunderstanding, cultural chasms separating two worlds, were all present."[7] A number of Jesuit missionaries, including René Goupil, Jean de Brebeuf, and Pierre Marquette, died as martyrs to the faith.[8] In France the Catholic Church was closely linked to the French monarchs, who exercised authority over many matters of Church life. After the bitter French wars of religion in the sixteenth century, the Edict of Nantes of 1598 granted the French Huguenot community certain rights in France, but implementation varied under later monarchs. In 1685, King Louis XIV revoked the Edict entirely, launching a persecution in France and prompting many Huguenots to migrate to North America, especially New York City, New Rochelle, and New Paltz in present-day New York State.

The early Catholic explorers of North America shared what historian John Haines calls "the European Superiority Complex," a set of attitudes that viewed people in unknown lands outside of Europe as wild and savage, as living on a lower level than European Christians, indeed as barely human.[9] For example, many Catholic missionaries viewed the omnipresent dancing of the indigenous peoples with alarm. This prejudice precluded any notion of dialogue with equal partners. Nonetheless, on occasion, music provided a meeting place between different religions and cultures. In 1541, in present-day Arkansas the group led by Hernando

---

[5] Mark Francis, "Popular Piety and Liturgical Reform in a Hispanic Context," in *Dialogue Rejoined: Theology and Ministry in the United States Hispanic Reality,* ed. Ana María Pineda and Robert Schreiter (Collegeville, MN: Liturgical Press, 1995), 166.

[6] Nicholas P. Cushner, *Why Have You Come Here? The Jesuits and the First Evangelization of Native America* (Oxford: Oxford University Press, 2006), 149–69; Christopher Vecsey, *American Indian Catholics,* vol. 2, *The Paths of Kateri's Kin* (Notre Dame, IN: University of Notre Dame Press, 1997).

[7] Cushner, *Why Have You Come,* 155.

[8] Emma Anderson, *The Death and Afterlife of the North American Martyrs* (Cambridge, MA: Harvard University Press, 2013).

[9] John Haines, "The Earliest European Responses to Dancing in the Americas," *U.S. Catholic Historian* 30, no. 4 (2012): 3–4.

de Soto erected a new cross and sang a Gregorian chant, probably drawn from feasts of the Holy Cross and the Good Friday liturgy. The native Casqui people of that area also contributed their own music in an event that lasted four hours. Haines describes this as coming "close to a Native American and European musical merger."[10] The indigenous peoples were originally curious about the newcomers and their customs, including their music. However, by the 1530s, the European intent to conquer had become all too clear, the Native peoples began forcefully resisting the aggressive Catholic invaders, and cordial musical encounters became rarer. The Catholics, in turn, viewed the indigenous peoples very critically, usually in terms similar to traditional negative views of Muslims in Europe.[11]

In the British colonies of North America, religious conditions varied; the colonial settlers who came from England, Ireland, and Scotland were overwhelmingly Protestant, often from the church communities that dissented from the Church of England. Pilgrims came to New England in pursuit of religious liberty for themselves and freedom from the religious policies of the Stuart monarchy in England. Most, however, did not intend to grant religious liberty to those who disagreed with them, such as the Quakers, who trusted in the Inner Light of Christ, the direct movement of the Holy Spirit, and their own manner of interpreting the Bible. Quakers were very critical of formal external, institutional religion, whether the Church of England or in the Massachusetts Bay Colony.[12] The authorities of the Massachusetts Bay Colony hanged Mary Dyer in 1660 because she was a Quaker.[13]

From the beginning, Roger Williams challenged the Pilgrim leadership on a number of issues, vigorously affirming what he called "soul liberty."[14] After repeated church trials, he left the Massachusetts Bay Colony, purchased land from American Indians, and in 1636 founded the Colony of Rhode Island with Providence Plantations with religious liberty for all.[15] Rhode Island Christians would later welcome Jews, allowing them to establish the Touro Synagogue in Newport in 1763, the oldest continuous synagogue in the United States.[16]

American Indians followed a wide variety of religious practices, which displayed some widespread themes but no overall identity of structure or institution. Colonial Christian attitudes toward Indian religious life were generally, but not always, quite negative. Roger Williams was a major exception, expressing interest in and respect

---

[10] Ibid., 14.

[11] Ibid., 19–20.

[12] *Quaker Spirituality: Selected Writings,* ed. Douglas V. Steere (Mahwah, NJ: Paulist Press, 1984); Mark A. Noll, *A History of Christianity in the United States and Canada* (Grand Rapids, MI: Eerdmans, 1992), 65–68.

[13] Anthony Gill, *The Political Origins of Religious Liberty* (New York: Cambridge University Press, 2008), 60.

[14] Roger Williams, *On Religious Liberty: Selections from the Works of Roger Williams,* ed. James Calvin Davis (Cambridge, MA: Belknap Press, 2008).

[15] Edwin A. Gaustad, *Roger Williams* (Oxford: Oxford University Press, 2005).

[16] Jonathan D. Sarna, *American Judaism: A History* (New Haven, CT: Yale University Press, 2004), 17.

for Native religious perspectives and recording them in his pioneering work of cultural anthropology, *A Key into the Language of America*.[17] French Jesuit missionaries attempted to learn the languages, cultures, and religious practices of American Indians; in some cases they found acceptance and in others persecution.

In 1633 Cecil Calvert, the Second Baron Baltimore, founded Maryland Colony with religious tolerance for all Trinitarian Christians. Settlers arrived in 1634 at St. Mary's City, which some view as the birthplace of religious freedom in North America. The new colony offered refuge to Catholics, who came from England seeking religious liberty from the persecution of Catholics in England; but the majority of the inhabitants were Protestant.[18] English Catholicism at this time was strongly shaped by the struggle against Protestant Reformers and the culture of Northern Europe, in sharp contrast to the medieval, Iberian Catholicism of the Spanish colonies.[19]

Most Catholics in British America, like their Protestant counterparts, did not accept the intermingling of Catholic and indigenous traditions found in Spanish American practice. The form of Catholicism that emerged in British-ruled North America would influence most of the later European Catholic immigrants to the United States and would largely dominate Catholic life in the United States.[20] American Catholics usually view Baltimore as their first diocese, which dates from 1789; however, Catholics in Puerto Rico, which today is a territory of the United States, point out that the diocese of San Juan de Puerto Rico was established in 1511.

During the English Civil War in the 1640s, Protestants in Maryland rebelled against the Catholic Lord Baltimore and his brother, Governor Leonard Calvert, forcing the latter to flee to Virginia. The period from 1644 to 1646 would be remembered as "The Plundering Time," when Protestants plundered the property of Catholics. Leonard Calvert later returned and put down the rebellion with armed force. In the aftermath, in 1649, the Maryland Assembly passed the Toleration Act offering freedom of conscience to all Christians. However, in 1654, during the time of Puritan rule in England, this act was revoked. It was reinstated in 1657, when the Calverts returned to power, only to be revoked again in 1692, in the aftermath of the Glorious Revolution in England. Despite the checkered history of religious liberty in Maryland, other colonies approved measures granting religious tolerance, as in New Jersey in 1664, in Carolina in 1665, and in Pennsylvania in 1682.

Immediately south of Maryland, in Virginia, the Church of England became the established religion in 1619 under the supervision of the Bishop of London.

---

[17] Roger Williams, *A Key into the Language of America* (1643; reprint, Bedford, MA: Applewood Books, 1997).

[18] Cushner, *Why Have You Come,* 171–90.

[19] John W. O'Malley, *Trent and All That: Renaming Catholicism in the Early Modern Era* (Cambridge, MA: Harvard University Press, 2000).

[20] Allen Figueroa Deck, "At the Crossroads: North American and Hispanic," in *We Are a People! Initiatives in Hispanic American Theology,* ed. Roberto S. Goizueta (Minneapolis: Fortress Press, 1992), 4–5.

The English Act of Toleration of 1689 granted toleration to Dissenting Protestant communities, but not to Roman Catholics or Unitarians. In the eighteenth century, preachers from other Christian denominations found it difficult or impossible to obtain a license to conduct services in Virginia. James Madison witnessed the mistreatment of preachers from Dissenting Protestant churches, and, together with Thomas Jefferson and George Mason, became a supporter of religious freedom. The Virginia General Assembly approved the Statute for Religious Freedom in 1786.

During the eighteenth century, there was increasing acceptance of religious diversity, culminating in the First Amendment of the U.S. Constitution, which guaranteed the free exercise of religion and forbade the establishment of any one religion by the federal government. Even though the ideal of religious liberty was affirmed in the U.S. Constitution, white Protestants nonetheless dominated American society, with ramifications to the present day. From the beginning, American Indians and African Americans, as well as Asians who came to America later on, suffered from prejudicial attitudes, discriminatory practices, and often from violent oppression.

The Great Awakening

One of the most important Christian movements of the colonial era was the Christian revival movement known as the Great Awakening, which began in western Massachusetts in the 1730s and rapidly spread across the colonies, becoming the first major event to link the colonies to each other.[21] The vivid preaching of Jonathan Edwards and George Whitefield inspired numerous people to entrust themselves to God's grace and mercy in Jesus Christ. One effect of the Awakening was to stress the importance of personal experience of guilt and redemption, leading to a distrust of hierarchies and established churches. The preachers stressed that all humans are sinners in need of a divine redemption that cannot in any way be earned or merited. Isaac Backus went through an experience of conversion and became an influential preacher, articulating a basis for religious liberty as involving both the right of self-definition and equal recognition.[22]

The Great Awakening marked the first time that significant numbers of African Americans and American Indians accepted Christianity. Like Christian indigenous peoples in the Southwest, these new followers of Jesus Christ retained aspects of their traditional African or Native beliefs and practices in their lives as Christians; scholars debate the degree to which the earlier traditions persisted, but it is clear that there was a certain amount of continuity.[23] Many have seen the Great

---

[21] Thomas S. Kidd, *The Great Awakening: The Roots of Evangelical Christianity in Colonial America* (New Haven, CT: Yale University Press, 2007); John Howard Smith, *The First Great Awakening: Redefining Religion in British America, 1725–1775* (Madison, NJ: Fairleigh Dickinson University Press /Lanham, MD: Rowman & Littlefield Publishers, 2015).

[22] Chris Beneke, *Beyond Toleration: The Religious Origins of American Pluralism* (Oxford: Oxford University Press, 2006), 141.

[23] Linford D. Fisher, *The Indian Great Awakening: Religion and the Shaping of Native*

Awakening as preparing the way for the American Revolution, with its critique of British corruption, and as setting a tone for later evangelical Christianity, with its stress on personal experience.

Religious Diversity in the
Early Republic of the United States

At the time of the American Revolution, Catholics and Jews constituted a very small minority of the population of the United States. Estimates vary, but there may have been about 40,000 Catholics in the United States in 1790; another estimate is that there were 30,000 Catholics amid a population of three million Protestants.[24] A number of the leaders of the American Revolution were influenced by Deism, but the majority of Americans were Protestants who were viewed as Nonconformists or Dissenters in Great Britain. Roger Finke and Rodney Stark estimate that in 1776, Congregationalists constituted 20.4 percent of all religious adherents in the United States, Presbyterians 19 percent, and Baptists 16.9 percent. Episcopalians counted for only 15.7 percent, while Roman Catholics constituted 1.8 percent.[25] In a speech delivered on March 22, 1775, Edmund Burke emphasized to the British Parliament that American colonists were largely dissenters from the Anglican establishment; for centuries they had insisted on God-given rights of conscience in resisting religious establishments. Burke pointed out that "the dissenting interests have sprung up in direct opposition to all the ordinary powers of the world, and could justify that opposition only on a strong claim to natural liberty."[26] Burke related their dissenting Protestant heritage of insisting on liberty to their rebellion against British rule and recommended that the Parliament seek reconciliation with them.[27] Overwhelmingly, the British colonies and the early United States formed a predominantly Protestant world, with some very influential Deists as well.[28] Many Protestants distrusted and feared Catholics as allies of a foreign power, and

---

Culture in Early America (Oxford: Oxford University Press, 2012); Albert J. Raboteau, *Slave Religion: The "Invisible Institution" in the Antebellum South* (Oxford: Oxford University Press, 2004).

[24] James M. O'Toole, *The Faithful: A History of Catholics in America* (Cambridge, MA: Belknap Press of Harvard University Press, 2008), 43; the second estimate is from Christine Mary Athans, "Courtesy, Confrontation, Cooperation: Jewish-Christian/Catholic Relations in the United States," *Studies in Christian Jewish Relations* 5, no. 1 (2010): 2.

[25] Roger Finke and Rodney Stark, "How the Upstart Sects Won America: 1776–1850," *Journal for the Scientific Study of Religion* 28, no. 1 (1989): 31; see also Noll, *History of Christianity,* 153.

[26] Edmund Burke, "Speech on Conciliation with the Colonies," in Edmund Burke, *The Portable Burke,* ed. Isaac Kramnick (New York: Penguin Books, 1999), 262.

[27] Thomas S. Kidd, *God of Liberty: A Religious History of the American Revolution* (New York: Basic Books, 2010), 75.

[28] David L. Holmes, *The Faiths of the Founding Fathers* (Oxford: Oxford University Press, 2006).

many believed there was a Catholic conspiracy to overthrow Protestantism and any republican government.[29] Despite the strong anti-Catholic bias in American society, there were Catholics who participated prominently in the American Revolution, such as Charles Carroll of Carrollton, who signed the Declaration of Independence; but he was the only Catholic to do so. The participation of Catholics in the Revolution, as well as the vital assistance of Catholic France in the war, helped to improve the image of Catholics more generally in society, and Chris Beneke writes of "a pronounced transformation in public discourse on Catholicism" as a result.[30]

Charles Carroll's cousin John Carroll was a priest in the Society of Jesus until it was suppressed in 1773. In 1779, John Carroll wrote to his friend Charles Plowden that "the fullest & largest system of toleration is adopted in almost all the American states: publick protection & encouragement are extended alike to all denominations & R[oman] C[atholics] are members of Congress, assemblies, & hold civil & military posts as well as others."[31] With the establishment of the United States of America, Catholics felt a need for a bishop to lead them in the new nation, and John Carroll was seen as the leading candidate. In 1789, twenty-four of the twenty-six Catholic priests in Maryland voted for John Carroll to be their bishop, and Pope Pius VI approved this choice.

As the first Catholic bishop in the new United States, John Carroll enjoyed a level of respect that would have been hard to imagine just a short time earlier.[32] John Carroll believed that Protestants could be saved; and having suffered from anti-Catholic discrimination, he affirmed religious liberty. He repeatedly emphasized the compatibility of the Catholic faith with American patriotism and has been described as "a friend to both republican government and liberal principles."[33] While anti-Catholic bias did not disappear, it did diminish considerably for a time.

In 1789, John Carroll took the lead in founding a new academy in Georgetown (which would later become Georgetown University) that would welcome students from every religious background.[34] When other clerics objected to this policy of religious openness, John Carroll responded by pointing out that Catholics had just recently been granted equal toleration in the new nation; he thought Catholics would be making a serious mistake if they were to deny acceptance to others in the new school.[35] Many were moved by Carroll's example. His leadership in this area

---

[29] Mark S. Massa, *Anti-Catholicism in America: The Last Acceptable Prejudice* (New York: Crossroad, 2003), 20–21.

[30] Beneke, *Beyond Toleration*, 181.

[31] John Carroll, Letter February 28, 1779; John Carroll Papers I, 53; Robert Emmett Curran, *A History of Georgetown: From the Academy to University, 1789–1889* (Washington, DC: Georgetown University Press, 2010), 10.

[32] Beneke, *Beyond Toleration*, 3.

[33] Ibid., 185.

[34] Curran, *History of Georgetown*, 27.

[35] John Carroll, *The John Carroll Papers*, ed. Thomas O'Brien O'Hanley, 3 vols. (Notre

quickly attracted Protestant families to send their sons; his initiative in religious openness also contributed to the efforts of Protestants and Catholics in the new capital of Washington, DC, in resisting anti-Catholic nativists who sought to stigmatize and reject Catholics.[36]

Like Catholics, Jews in the new nation experienced an improvement in their standing in a predominantly Protestant society. In colonial times, Jews were a small community, probably fewer than three thousand in the late eighteenth century.[37] Many state constitutions required officeholders to be Christians, but the U.S. Constitution forbade this requirement for federal offices, and overall there was increasing pressure to include Jews more fully in the new republic. Beneke comments that by the 1780s, "Jews enjoyed more rights under the federal government than they did under any other national government in the world. At the same time Christians were beginning to use respectful language and sometimes even extend kind gestures towards their Jewish neighbors."[38]

The mood of the young United States of America was not hostile toward established religion in the way the French Revolution came into conflict with the Catholic Church; instead, the American Revolution established the new society as an open playing field for competition among multiple religious movements, especially those that were Protestant.[39] The new nation was born with the promise of religious freedom for all, though this was never granted to the enslaved Muslims who had been brought from Africa. By the time of the Bill of Rights of the United States Constitution, the discussion had moved from religious toleration to the right to religious liberty. The First Amendment of the Constitution forbids the establishment of any national religion and also guarantees the free exercise of religion. The Bill of Rights of the U.S. Constitution originally applied only to the federal government, whose strength vis-à-vis the states at this time was not nearly as strong as it would later become. Many states, such as Massachusetts and Connecticut, continued to have an established Protestant church for decades; but the trend toward freedom of conscience, religious liberty, and separation of church and state was clear. By 1833, every state in the union offered, at least in principle, freedom of worship and conscience.

In 1784, Hannah Adams published a survey of the religious diversity in the new nation, listing all the various religious communities from Abrahamites and Artotyrites to Servetians and Zwinglians. Adams promised to be unbiased and allow each community to represent itself; and later editions included Jews, Muslims, and "Heathens." Nonetheless, her editor clearly felt that the Christian

---

Dame, IN: University of Notre Dame Press, 1976), 1:158; William W. Warner, *At Peace with All Their Neighbors: Catholics and Catholicism in the National Capital, 1787–1860* (Washington, DC: Georgetown University Press, 1994), 15–16.

[36] Warner, *At Peace with All Their Neighbors*, 16.

[37] Beneke, *Beyond Toleration*, 186.

[38] Ibid., 186–87.

[39] Kidd, *God of Liberty*.

Bible offered a point of reference and a standard for judgment.[40] Chris Beneke explains the limits of this openness: "To the extent that Hannah Adams's brand of pluralism prevailed in late-eighteenth-century America, it would be mitigated by her editor's assumption that all legitimate faiths shared the same essential Protestant, or at least Christian, elements."[41] This assumption would shape Christian attitudes toward other religions into the twentieth century.

In 1782, the French immigrant Hector Saint John de Crèvecoeur hoped that the bitter religious conflicts of Europe would evaporate in the atmosphere of the New World; he described the mixing of religious traditions in America: "A very perceptible indifference, even in the first generation, will become apparent; and it may happen that the daughter of the Catholic will marry the son of the seceder, and settle by themselves at a distance from their parents."[42] At least among the elite of early American society, there was an acceptance of religious differences. Tragically, however, at the very time when religious openness was increasing, racial discrimination was hardening.[43]

Beneke describes the developing American acceptance of religious diversity in the late eighteenth century as equal recognition: "Equal recognition could not be denied to any group without threatening the inclusive foundation upon which all claims to recognition were made."[44] Whereas Europeans had traditionally seen religious dissent as a political danger to society's stability, the new federal government of the United States of America extended equal recognition to a wide array of religious traditions. Even though Americans' openness to accepting religious diversity had some precedents in early English attitudes, they were distinctive "in the extent to which they joined religious rights and religious civility, equal legal treatment and equal public recognition."[45] Nonetheless, the equal recognition of religious traditions required membership in what has been called "the sole Denomination of *Americans*."[46] Equal acceptance of religious diversity went hand in hand with formation of American national identity, based on shared democratic political principles; Christian morality; and civil rights, at least for European American Jews and Christians.

---

[40] Hannah Adams, *A Dictionary of All Religions and Religious Denominations, Jewish, Heathen, Mahometan, Christian, Ancient and Modern,* ed. Thomas Tweed (Atlanta, GA: Scholars Press, 1992); Beneke, *Beyond Toleration,* 157–58. See also Gary D. Schmidt, *A Passionate Usefulness: The Life and Literary Labors of Hannah Adams* (Charlottesville: University of Virginia Press, 2004).

[41] Beneke, *Beyond Toleration,* 158.

[42] J. Hector St. John de Crèvecoeur, *Letters from an American Farmer and Sketches of Eighteenth-Century America,* ed. Albert E. Stone (New York: Penguin, 1986), 75–76.

[43] Beneke, *Beyond Toleration,* 197.

[44] Ibid., 200.

[45] Ibid., 221.

[46] Ibid., 222.

Tensions in Christian America

Despite the promise of religious freedom in the Constitution and the incipient openness to religious diversity in the new American republic, there were movements opposing religious acceptance and openness. While Catholics were accepted in principle, anti-Catholic attitudes remained strong, and many Protestants questioned their loyalty to America.[47] Moreover, many Protestants felt hostility toward the religious traditions of American Indians and enslaved Africans and refused to extend toleration and civility to them.[48] The first Muslims who came to the United States in large numbers were brought as slaves from Africa,[49] but as I noted in the Introduction, enslaved Muslims would rarely be granted the free exercise of religion promised by the First Amendment of the U.S. Constitution. Some biblical interpretations buttressed the enslavement of Africans; and the nineteenth century witnessed the development of new racial theories that would justify the subordination of American Indians and African Americans; discrimination would be rationalized increasingly on racial grounds.[50]

Since the time of the First Great Awakening, significant numbers of African Americans embraced Christianity. Some churches reached out to them, but racism was rampant in American society. Most churches were racially segregated, with African Americans seated in separate sections and buried in separate graveyards. In 1794, Richard Allen, who had been born into slavery but was allowed to purchase his freedom through extra work, protested segregation and led the founding of the first black church in Philadelphia, Bethel African Methodist Episcopal Church. In 1816, he became the first bishop of the African Methodist Episcopal Church and worked tirelessly to improve the situation of African Americans and give them a dignified ecclesial home in which to worship.

Many European American Christians vilified expressions of African religious traditions brought by enslaved people across the Atlantic. Most European Americans despised American Indians and saw their "heathen" religious practices as a basis for conquering them and seizing their lands.[51] The most serious unresolved tension of the Revolutionary period was the contradiction between the Declaration of Independence's affirmation of the inalienable God-given rights of all, on the one hand, and the displacement of American Indians and the enslavement of African Americans, on the other.

---

[47] Massa, *Anti-Catholicism in America.*

[48] Beneke, *Beyond Toleration,* 198.

[49] Sylviane A. Diouf, *Servants of Allah: African Muslims Enslaved in the Americas* (New York: New York University Press, 1998).

[50] Stephen R. Haynes, *Noah's Curse: The Biblical Justification of American Slavery* (Oxford: Oxford University Press, 2002); George M. Fredrickson, *Racism: A Short History* (Princeton, NJ: Princeton University Press, 2002).

[51] Richard Slotkin, *Regeneration through Violence: The Mythology of the American Frontier, 1600–1860* (Norman: University of Oklahoma Press, 1973), 78–93.

Another ominous harbinger for the future was that from the beginning of the American republic, many Americans believed that the United States had received a divine mission to spread peace and democracy to the rest of the world, even if at times this might require using military force.[52] As the nineteenth century began, many Protestant Christians eagerly took up the project of building a Christian America, which sought to unite a wide range of American Protestants but which was less hospitable to Catholics or Jews, not to mention Muslims.[53] In 1811, the U.S. Supreme Court stated frankly that Americans are a Christian people; and this notion was repeated in various forms by later Supreme Courts, the Senate Judiciary Committee, Abraham Lincoln, and the U.S. Congress.[54] All those who did not conform to the dominant Protestant culture were not fully accepted.

The Second Great Awakening in the early nineteenth century marked a stirring revival of Protestant identity in sharp opposition to the Enlightenment Deism of the Founding Fathers. Some Protestant preachers attacked Deism as a satanic foe leading to atheism and secularism. Methodist and Presbyterian preachers, who often had little formal education, held emotional revival meetings that addressed frontier populations. The dominant tone of American culture became strongly Protestant and would remain so until the middle of the twentieth century.[55]

Catholic Immigrants

At the dawn of the nineteenth century, the population of the United States remained overwhelmingly Protestant. This changed dramatically when Catholic immigrants from Ireland and Germany began to come to the United States in large numbers, triggering a nativist anti-Catholic reaction that at times was fierce. In an atmosphere that was frequently bitterly anti-Catholic, some Catholic leaders, like Bishop John England, enthusiastically embraced the American ideal of religious liberty.[56] England was born and ordained in Cork, Ireland, worked with Daniel O'Connell for Catholic Emancipation in Ireland in the 1810s, immigrated to the United States, and became the first Catholic bishop of Charleston, South Carolina, in 1820. Quietly ignoring papal condemnations of religious liberty and freedom

---

[52] Ernest Lee Tuveson, *Redeemer Nation: The Idea of America's Millennial Role* (Chicago: University of Chicago Press, 1968); Robert Jewett and John Shelton Lawrence, *Captain America and the Crusade against Evil: The Dilemma of Zealous Nationalism* (Grand Rapids, MI: Eerdmans, 2003); Peter J. Kastor, *America's Struggle with Empire: A Documentary History* (Washington, DC: CQ Press, 2010).

[53] Robert T. Handy, *A Christian America: Protestant Hopes and Historical Realities* (2nd ed., rev. and enlarged; New York: Oxford University Press, 1984).

[54] Samuel Huntington, *Who Are We?: The National Challenges to America's National Identity* (New York: Simon & Schuster, 2005), 98.

[55] Noll, *History of Christianity*, 165–90.

[56] Patrick W. Carey, *An Immigrant Bishop: John England's Adaptation of Irish Catholicism to American Republicanism* (Yonkers, NY: U.S. Catholic Historical Society, 1982).

of the press, England forthrightly accepted American practices, including both religious liberty and, tragically, slavery. Like John Carroll, he supported religious liberty, the American practice of separating church and state, the voluntary nature of religious associations, and the American form of government.[57]

During the same years when Pope Leo XII was firmly condemning religious freedom, John England argued even more forcefully and publicly than John Carroll that the Catholic faith and the American form of government were compatible, most notably in *A Discourse before Congress,* which he delivered on January 8, 1826, in the presence of President John Quincy Adams and the U.S. Congress. England boldly rebutted Adams's earlier charge that the Catholic Church was a despotic and superstitious enemy of religious freedom.[58] England's understanding of liberty was, however, limited; tragically, he was a staunch and eloquent defender of slavery on the basis of scripture and tradition.[59] He also failed to criticize the forced transfer of American Indians from the Southeast to the West. Despite their acceptance of religious freedom, European American Catholics generally shared the racist biases of their Protestant compatriots.[60]

Many American Protestants, however, paid attention to papal teachings and were not impressed by England's interventions; and the new waves of Catholic immigrants aroused increasing anxiety and concern. Samuel F. B. Morse, the inventor of the famous Morse Code, believed that Catholic immigrants were being sent to the United States to prepare for a papal takeover. The prominent Protestant leader Lyman Beecher read Pope Gregory XVI's condemnations of religious liberty, freedom of conscience, and freedom of the press with alarm; he and other Protestants worried that Catholic immigrants would seek to implement the principles proclaimed by the nineteenth-century popes, which would mean the end of American freedom of religion and the press.[61] At times, anti-Catholicism turned violent, as when an angry mob burned an Ursuline convent near Boston in 1834, and a number of Catholic churches were burned. For the most part, American Catholics had little or no knowledge of the papal teachings condemning American practices. Generations of American Catholics grew up without hearing Catholic preachers ever mention the papal denunciations of religious liberty, freedom of the press, and separation of church and state.

American Protestants, as well as followers of other religious traditions, saw the papal position of claiming religious freedom for Catholics and denying it to

---

[57] Patrick W. Carey, ed., *American Catholic Religious Thought: The Shaping of a Theological and Social Tradition,* 2nd ed. (Milwaukee, WI: Marquette University Press, 2004), 103.

[58] Ibid., 105–41.

[59] Cyprian Davis, *The History of Black Catholics in the United States* (New York: Crossroad, 1996), 46–47.

[60] Ibid., 28–66.

[61] Lyman Beecher, *A Plea for the West* (Cincinnati, OH: Truman & Smith, 1835), 66–68; Beneke, *Beyond Toleration,* 209–10.

others as inconsistent, even hypocritical. This Catholic policy was a long-standing barrier to ecumenical and interreligious relations. The American Catholic bishops met in Baltimore in 1837 and issued a pastoral letter that declared their loyalty to the government of the United States and proclaimed that they were free from any subservience to a foreign power.[62]

During the nineteenth century, Catholic experience in the United States continued to be many sided and ambiguous. There was fierce anti-Catholic feeling, but there was also increasing Catholic integration into American life and culture. In 1831, Alexis de Tocqueville remarked upon the distinctive style of Christian practice in the United States and its strong influence on Catholics: "American priests kept away from public affairs. This is the most striking but not the only example of their self-restraint. In America, religion is a world apart where the priest is sovereign but whose bounds he takes care never to leave."[63] He observed the similarity of Catholics to other Christians in America: "Although American Christians are divided into a mass of sects, they all view their religion in this same light, which applies to Catholicism as much as to other beliefs."[64] De Tocqueville commented on the different style of Catholicism in the United States from Europe, noting that "America is the most democratic country on earth while, at the same time, the country where, according to reputable reports, the Catholic religion makes the most progress."[65]

In 1855, a Catholic priest of German origin who was active in Wisconsin commented on the different atmosphere in the United States: "All the resolutions made in Europe dissolve as soon as one feels the breezes of the American coastline; every tie, including the one with God, must be retied here and undergo the American 'probatum est' [i.e., testing] before it can be said that it is secure."[66] Patrick W. Carey comments on the challenge for American Catholics responding to the questions of religious freedom, separation of church and state, and the American republic:

> The Catholic experience of Christianity and the American experience mutually conditioned theological reflection upon these and related issues. The Catholic responses to these questions were to some extent both attempts to understand the ultimate significance of the American

[62] James Hennesey, "An American Catholic Tradition of Religious Liberty," *Journal of Ecumenical Studies* 14, no. 1 (1977): 37; see also John Pawlikowski, "Jews and Christians: Their Covenantal Relationship in the American Context," in *Two Faiths, One Covenant? Jewish and Christian Identity in the Presence of the Other*, ed. Eugene B. Korn and John T. Pawlikowski (Lanham, MD: Rowman & Littlefield, 2005), 162.

[63] Alexis de Tocqueville, *Democracy in America and Two Essays on America*, trans. Gerald E. Bevan (London: Penguin Books, 2003), 517.

[64] Ibid.

[65] Ibid., 519.

[66] Carey, *American Catholic Religious Thought*, 12.

experience from the Catholic perspective and to interpret the meaning of Catholicism from the American perspective.[67]

Papal condemnations often clashed with the realities of American life. Of particular importance, the word "liberty" could mean different things in different contexts during the nineteenth century. In 1858, an Irish immigrant, the Catholic Archbishop John Hughes of New York City, informed Vatican officials about the situation in his archdiocese:

> Liberty, in this Country, has a very clear and specific meaning. It is not understood in Europe as it is here. Here, it means the vindication of personal rights; the fair support of public laws; the maintenance, at all hazards, of public order, according to those laws; the right to change them when they are found to be absurd or oppressive. Such, in brief, is the meaning of the word liberty, as understood by the people of the United States.[68]

Isaac Hecker, the founder of the Congregation of the Missionary Priests of St. Paul the Apostle, united both the Catholic faith and American ideals in his vision of American Catholic life, stressing the harmony between Catholicism and the American value of religious freedom and spiritual fulfillment.[69] In his preface to a biography of Hecker, Archbishop John Ireland commented: "Father Hecker understood and loved the country and its institutions. . . . His favorite topic in book and lecture was, that the Constitution of the United States requires as its necessary basis, the truths of Catholic teaching regarding man's natural state."[70] When this work was translated into French, it received yet another introduction, which aroused serious concern in the Holy See and led to Pope Leo XIII's warning about Americanism.[71]

New Migrations

The nineteenth century witnessed growing migrations to the United States both from Europe and from Asia. Beginning in the 1830s, Jewish immigrants also

---

[67] Ibid., 13.

[68] "Archbishop Hughes Explains American Liberty to Rome (1858)," in *American Catholic History: A Documentary Reader,* ed. Mark Massa, SJ, with Catherine Osborne (New York: New York University Press, 2008), 52.

[69] James T. Fisher, *Communion of Immigrants: A History of Catholics in America* (Oxford: Oxford University Press, 2008), 64–65.

[70] John Ireland, "Introduction to the *Life of Father Hecker* (1891)," in Massa and Osborne, *American Catholic History*, 62.

[71] Pope Leo XIII, *Testem Benevolentiae Nostrae: Concerning New Opinions, Virtue, Nature and Grace, with Regard to Americanism,* January 22, 1899; Thomas T. McAvoy, *The Americanist Heresy in Roman Catholicism, 1895–1900* (South Bend, IN: University of Notre Dame Press, 1963).

arrived in increasing numbers. It has been estimated that between 1830 and 1860 the Jewish population in the United States grew from about 4,500 to 150,000.[72] But however remarkable this increase may have appeared at the time, it was a small fraction of the much larger numbers to come. Between 1881 and 1914, the very same decades when large numbers of Catholics were also entering the country, about two million Jews arrived from Eastern Europe. After the assassination of Tsar Alexander II in 1881 and the anti-Jewish legislation in Russia in 1882, many Jews fled the Russian Empire and immigrated to the United States. Jewish historian Oscar Handlin would later note similarities between Jewish and Catholic migrant experiences, comparing the situations of Jews fleeing pogroms in Eastern Europe and Irish Catholics who fled hunger and starvation in British-ruled Ireland.[73]

During the latter part of the nineteenth century, many of the new immigrants came from southern and eastern Europe and were Catholic, causing increasing anxiety to some Protestants. So many newcomers arrived that Catholics were frequently viewed as an immigrant church.[74] In an often-hostile Protestant milieu, Catholics created a network of institutions in which they could succeed and thrive. Catholic parishes were major social centers where new immigrants found understanding and support in a confusing new world. Catholic priests, sisters, and brothers taught in grammar schools, high schools, colleges and universities, making possible the socioeconomic success of Catholics in later generations. Catholics built large numbers of churches, shrines, hospitals, and orphanages. In a segregated world, the Knights of Columbus for whites and the Knights of Peter Claver for African American Catholics provided Catholic social groups as alternatives to the anti-Catholic Masons. Like Samuel Morse in an earlier generation, the Ku Klux Klan worried that the Knights of Columbus were preparing for a Catholic military takeover of the United States.

Most controversial of all were the followers of Joseph Smith. Smith published a text that he called an English translation of the Book of Mormon in 1830 in New York State; he and his followers, who would come to be known officially as the Church of Jesus Christ of Latter-Day Saints, aroused deep suspicions and animosity. The claim to have received a new book of divine revelation, together with the practice of plural marriage or polygamy, provoked hostility in one area after another.[75] Amid repeated controversies, an angry mob killed Smith while he was in jail in Nauvoo, Illinois, in 1844. In the aftermath, his followers moved

---

[72] John Corrigan and Lynn S. Neal, *Religious Intolerance in America: A Documentary History* (Chapel Hill: University of North Carolina Press, 2010), 148.

[73] Oscar Handlin, *The Uprooted: The Epic Story of the Migration That Made the American People* (Philadelphia: University of Pennsylvania Press, 2001); David J. O'Brien, "The Religions, or Religion, of America," *U.S. Catholic Historian* 23, no. 1 (2005): 43.

[74] Fisher, *Communion of Immigrants.*

[75] *The Book of Mormon: An Account Written by the Hand of Mormon upon Plates Taken from the Plates of Nephi,* trans. Joseph Smith (Salt Lake City, UT: Church of Jesus Christ of Latter-Day Saints, 1981).

progressively further westward until they settled in Salt Lake City, Utah. Protestant Americans were long hostile toward the community of the Latter-Day Saints, and many did not recognize them as Christians, or even as "Whites."[76]

In the middle of the nineteenth century, significant numbers of immigrants also began coming to California from China and later Japan. Large-scale migration from China to the United States began after the discovery of gold in California in 1848; at this time mainland China was convulsed by the Taiping Rebellion, with large numbers fleeing to what they thought would be the relative safety of Hong Kong. Steve Tsang comments on the large numbers of workers being shipped from Hong Kong to San Francisco:

> Much of this movement of people in fact involved the trafficking of human beings, with many Chinese going overseas as indentured labourers in appalling conditions. Whatever one may feel about the morality of this traffic, it was an important economic activity in the formative years of Hong Kong as a colony.[77]

Often coming as bonded laborers in conditions close to slavery, Chinese immigrants brought Buddhist and Chinese religious traditions that appeared threatening to many Americans who believed the country to be a Christian nation. The Chinese were the harbingers of many later Asian immigrants who brought Buddhist and other religious practices to an often-difficult new environment.[78]

To protect their jobs as well as the identity of their country, many concerned Americans took up the slogan: "The Chinese must go!"[79] In a climate of intense hostility, many Chinese were harassed and forcibly driven out of towns in California.[80] In 1882, the U.S. Congress passed the Chinese Exclusion Act, banning the Chinese from immigrating to the United States for ten years and declaring them ineligible for citizenship; the bill was signed into law by President Chester Arthur in 1882. In 1888, the Scott Act expanded this legislation by forbidding the return of Chinese who traveled outside the United States.[81] This legislation was challenged in court, but in 1889, the U.S. Supreme Court upheld its constitutionality. It was not repealed until 1943, when the United States was an ally of China in World

---

[76] Terryl L. Givens, *The Viper on the Hearth: Mormons, Myths, and the Construction of Heresy* (New York: Oxford University Press, 1997), 135.

[77] Steve Tsang, *A Modern History of Hong Kong* (London: I. B. Taurus, 2004), 58.

[78] Richard Hughes Seager, *Buddhism in America* (New York: Columbia University Press, 1999), 51–181; Rick Fields, *How the Swans Came to the Lake: A Narrative History of Buddhism in America* (Boulder, CO: Shambhala, 1981), 70–82.

[79] Beth Lew-Williams, *The Chinese Must Go: Violence, Exclusion, and the Making of the Alien in America* (Cambridge, MA: Harvard University Press, 2018).

[80] Jean Pfaelzer, *Driven Out: The Forgotten War against Chinese Americans* (New York: Random House, 2007); Roger Daniels, ed., *Anti-Chinese Violence in North America* (New York: Arno Press, 1978).

[81] Lew-Williams, *Chinese Must Go*.

War II against Japan. In the early twentieth century, there was suspicion of Japanese immigrants, which led to the immigration legislation of the 1920s that severely limited immigrants from Asian countries with large Buddhist populations.

Despite the promise of the First Amendment of the Constitution, all too often American Protestants refused to accept religious minorities, including Catholics, Jews, Hindus, Buddhists, Daoists, Confucianists, Sikhs, Mormons, and Muslims, as true Americans. Tragically, there has often been a conflict between the American value of welcoming immigrants from diverse backgrounds, symbolized by the Statue of Liberty in the New York City harbor, and the repeated suspicion and fear of immigrants who differed culturally and religiously from the dominant population in American society. Many Protestant Americans viewed followers of other religious traditions as "not like us" and thus as "not wanted" in America.[82] Racial and religious prejudices intertwined and reinforced each other.[83]

Interreligious Explorations

This suspicion and hostility toward religious diversity was not universal, however. While many Americans were wary of other religious traditions, others explored religious diversity with growing interest and curiosity. When he was young, Washington Irving, who would eventually become the first prominent American writer, lived in Spain and immersed himself in the lore of Islamic Spain, writing *Tales of the Alhambra* and later a biography of Muhammad, which brought awareness of Muhammad and Islam to a broad reading public.

During the nineteenth century, some Americans became interested in Hinduism and Buddhism, which were not yet very clearly distinguished in the general population's awareness. The young Ralph Waldo Emerson immersed himself in the study of Muhammad as well as other religious figures and texts from Asia. His writings had a major impact on American attitudes toward religious diversity.[84] But while Emerson introduced many Americans to positive values in Asian religions, his legacy on racial relations was very negative. Following the lead of Thomas Jefferson and Thomas Carlyle, Emerson praised extravagantly the so-called Saxon race, while sharply contrasting it with the despised Celtic race, which included the Irish Catholic immigrants who were coming to America in increasing numbers.[85] For Emerson, only the so-called Saxons counted as true Americans; American

---

[82] Roger Daniels, *Not Like Us: Immigrants and Minorities in America: 1890–1924* (Chicago: Ivan R. Dee, 1997).

[83] Daniel B. Lee, "A Great Racial Commission: Religion and the Construction of White America," in *Race, Nation, and Religion in the Americas,* ed. Henry Goldschmidt and Elizabeth McAlister (Oxford: Oxford University Press, 2004), 85–110.

[84] Peter Schineller, "Emerson and Contemporary Religious Attitudes," *Journal of Religious Thought* 26, no. 1 (1969): 61–69.

[85] Nell Irvin Painter, "Ralph Waldo Emerson's Saxons," *Journal of American History* 95, no. 4 (2009): 980–82.

Indians, African Americans, Asian Americans, and Celts did not truly belong to the nation.

There was renewed interest in other religions at the end of the nineteenth century. Liberal Protestant leaders John Henry Barrows and Charles Bonney organized the World's Parliament of Religions, which was held in Chicago in 1893, in conjunction with the Columbian Exposition celebrating the four-hundredth anniversary of Columbus's voyage. The Parliament was significant in introducing Muslim, Hindu, Buddhist, Parsee, Daoist, Shinto, and Confucian leaders who were intelligent and well-spoken to Americans who had for the most part never encountered such people before.

The Parliament was also a major moment symbolizing the acceptance of Catholics and Jews in American society alongside of Protestants. Because the liberal Protestant organizers were concerned about being opposed and even ridiculed by more conservative Protestants, they were very interested in gaining Catholic participation. The Catholic archbishops of the United States met in Baltimore in November 1892 to consider this invitation. There was no Catholic precedent for participating; popes had warned against the danger of indifferentism, and thus some archbishops thought it more prudent to decline the invitation. Bishop John J. Keane, the first rector of the Catholic University of America, had written a letter recommending acceptance of the invitation and addressing the concerns of those who were doubtful.[86] The result was that the archbishops decided that James Cardinal Gibbons of Baltimore, the leading Catholic churchman of the day, should direct Keane to organize a Catholic delegation. Most of the Catholic speakers at the Parliament had been either born or raised in Ireland. Acutely aware of anti-Catholic discrimination from Protestants both in British-ruled Ireland and in the United States, they decided to align themselves with the progressive Protestants and reach out to leaders of the world's religions in friendship and understanding.

In the company of Hindus, Buddhists, Jews, Muslims, Shintoists, Parsees, Daoists, Confucianists, and others, Cardinal Gibbons opened the Parliament on September 11, 1893, with the Lord's Prayer; and Chicago's Archbishop Patrick Feehan welcomed the assembly to his city. In his opening Words of Welcome, Barrows set forth the ringing challenge

> that whoever would advance the cause of his own faith must first discover and gratefully acknowledge the truths contained in other faiths. . . . Why should not Christians be glad to learn what God has wrought through Buddha and Zoroaster—through the sage of China, and the prophets of India and the prophet of Islam?[87]

---

[86] James F. Cleary, "Catholic Participation in the World's Parliament of Religions, Chicago, 1893," *Catholic Historical Review* 55, no. 4 (1970): 591.

[87] John Henry Barrows, "Words of Welcome," in *The Dawn of Religious Pluralism: Voices from the World's Parliament of Religions, 1893,* ed. Richard Hughes Seager (La Salle, IL: Open Court Press, 1993), 26.

The representatives of other religious traditions found a mixed but largely positive reception. The *Chicago Tribune* found the significance of the assembly "in the fact that those whom we have been accustomed to call heathens are not so much heathens as we imagined. Under some of the religions lies the clear idea of divinity. Under all lies the clear idea of morality."[88] The paper expressed its hope that the Parliament would lead to greater understanding and toleration as well as the end of religious fanaticism.

The Social Gospel, the Christian Century, and Fears of Immigrants

The movement sometimes known as the Third Great Awakening in the late nineteenth and early twentieth centuries continued efforts begun during the earlier revival movement, proposing the Christian Social Gospel[89] and pursuing social reform of labor conditions in industrial society.[90] Protestant social reformers sought compulsory elementary education, protection of women from exploitative labor practices, and the end of child labor. The movement also renewed efforts to establish the United States as a Protestant Christian nation, now with an expanded sense of a global calling. Many Protestants hoped that the new twentieth century would be "the Christian century," and they sent missioners throughout the world.

With increasing hopes for the worldwide triumph of Protestant Christian American civilization, there was renewed suspicion of those who did not fit this mold. Chinese and Japanese immigrants were distrusted on both racial and religious grounds, and a strong Nativist reaction led to restriction of immigration. A wave of radical anti-Japanese sentiment swept the West Coast in the early 1900s, with attacks on Japanese buildings and business. An Asiatic Exclusion League was established in San Francisco in 1905.[91] In 1908, President Theodore Roosevelt pressured the Japanese government to prevent emigration to the United States, and Congress banned immigration from other Asian countries in 1917.[92] In the 1920s, western states enacted legislation restricting Japanese from owning property, and the Oriental Exclusion Act of 1924 placed severe limits on Japanese who sought to become U.S. citizens.[93] The strict restrictions on immigration in the 1920s favored northern and western European nations that were more likely to be Protestant.

---

[88] Seager, *Dawn of Religious Pluralism*, 353.

[89] See, for example, Walter Rauschenbusch, *Christianity and the Social Crisis* (New York: Macmillan, 1907); and Walter Rauschenbusch, *A Theology for the Social Gospel* (New York: Macmillan, 1917).

[90] See William McLaughlin, *Revivals, Awakenings, and Reforms* (Chicago: University of Chicago Press, 1978); Robert William Fogel, *The Fourth Great Awakening and the Future of Egalitarianism* (Chicago: University of Chicago Press, 2000), 107–36.

[91] Seager, *Buddhism in America*, 54.

[92] Huntington, *Who Are We*, 57.

[93] Seager, *Buddhism in America*, 55.

Other areas were severely limited in the numbers of people that would be accepted into the United States.

Throughout the late nineteenth and early twentieth centuries, the Ku Klux Klan demonized Jews, African Americans, and Catholics as dangers to white American Protestant identity. When in 1928 the Democratic Party nominated the Catholic governor of New York State, Al Smith, as candidate to be president of the United States, a wave of anti-Catholic sentiment swept the nation, and Smith lost the election. In response to the challenge of the Klan and the virulent anti-Catholicism of the 1928 presidential campaign, Everett Ross Clinchy, Jane Addams, Supreme Court Justice Charles Evans Hughes, and others founded the National Conference of Jews and Christians (NCJC) in 1927, which would later be renamed the National Conference of Christians and Jews (NCCJ) in the late 1930s.[94] Clinchy believed strongly that the education of young people could combat entrenched prejudices and promote tolerance. Preaching that all are children of God, NCJC and then NCCJ actively promoted mutual acceptance among Protestants, Catholics, and Jews from the 1920s to the 1950s.[95] Amid the racial and religious tensions of the era, the collaboration of Protestants, Catholics, and Jews in America on efforts for social and economic justice prepared the way for further cooperation after World War II.

Three-Faith America: Protestant-Catholic-Jew

In the wake of the Second World War, some Catholics worked to develop more positive relations with other Christians and with Jews. Most American Catholics came to believe that their Protestant and Jewish neighbors also enjoyed God's favor and could enjoy eternal salvation. Of particular importance was the issue of religious freedom. Jesuit theologian John Courtney Murray argued for the compatibility and complementarity of Catholic views and the religious liberty promised by the U.S. Constitution.[96] Murray appealed to the principle of Pope Gelasius I (556–561) that there are two powers that God has appointed to rule the world—temporal and spiritual; the temporal power of the state is charged with care for justice and promoting the prosperity and peace of the community; the spiritual authority of the Catholic Church is responsible for the worship of God and salvation of souls. Murray focused on the interpretation of this principle by John of Paris (ca. 1255–1306) in the context of medieval struggles and its influence on Pope Leo XIII.[97]

---

[94] Harold S. Wechsler, "Making a Religion of Intergroup Education: The National Conference of Christians and Jews, 1927–1957," *Journal of Ecumenical Studies* 47, no. 1 (2012): 3–40.

[95] Ibid.

[96] John Courtney Murray, *We Hold These Truths: Catholic Reflections on the American Proposition* (New York: Sheed & Ward, 1960).

[97] John Courtney Murray, "Contemporary Orientations of Catholic Thought on Church and State in the Light of History," *Theological Studies* 10 (1949): 177–234.

Murray drew the conclusion that the U.S. system of government respects this ancient papal distinction between the two powers: "What the First Amendment fundamentally declares, as the constitutional will of the American people, is the 'lay' character of the state, its non-competence in the field of religion, the restriction of its competence to the secular and temporal."[98] Murray argued that this restriction did not in any way constitute an attack on the Catholic Church: "On the contrary, there is in the First Amendment a recognition of the primacy of the spiritual."[99] Murray maintained that the U.S. Constitution assures a network of freedoms—free exercise of religion, freedom of the press, freedom of assembly, freedom of speech: "Together they assure the autonomy of the lay state; and together too they insure the primacy of spiritual end of man, and all its exigencies, over the lay state."[100] Acknowledging that no political system is perfect or ideal, Murray insisted that the U.S. Constitution "offers a political category in which the contemporary problem of religious freedom can receive its valid theoretical statement."[101]

Murray's position aroused a storm of controversy, and the Roman authorities directed him not to publish any further on this matter.[102] Murray respected this directive, but in the fall of 1960 he published *We Hold These Truths: Catholic Reflections on the American Proposition,* which proposed a fundamental harmony between the Catholic tradition of natural law and the principles of American government. On December 12, 1960, *Time Magazine* placed a portrait of Murray on its cover, noting his prominence in reconciling Catholics with American society. Murray was not invited to the first session of the Second Vatican Council, but he was invited to the second session as an advisor to the drafting of *Dignitatis Humanae, The Declaration on Religious Liberty.*[103]

The Archbishop of Boston, Richard Cardinal Cushing, whose sister had married a Jewish man, set aside the triumphalist tone of his predecessor William O'Connell, and urged all Americans to cooperate in building a better world.[104] When Leonard Feeney, SJ, denounced Jews and insisted on a rigorous, literal application of the traditional Catholic teaching that outside the Catholic Church there is no salvation, Cardinal Cushing moved to have him silenced, reprimanded, and removed.[105] As the earlier model of Protestant Christian America waned in influ-

---

[98] Ibid., 188.

[99] Ibid.

[100] Ibid., 190.

[101] Ibid.

[102] Barry Hudock, *Struggle, Condemnation, Vindication: John Courtney Murray's Journey toward Vatican II* (Collegeville, MN: Liturgical Press, 2015), 97–100.

[103] Ibid., 111–59.

[104] Mark Massa, "On the Uses of Heresy: Leonard Feeney, Mary Douglas, and the Notre Dame Football Team," *Harvard Theological Review* 84, no. 3 (1991): 334–35.

[105] Catherine Goddard Clarke, *The Loyolas and the Cabots: The Story of the Boston Heresy Case* (Boston: Ravengate Press, 1950); Patrick Carey, "Avery Dulles, St. Benedict's Center, and No Salvation Outside the Church, 1940–1953," *Catholic Historical Review* 93, no. 3 (2007): 553–75.

ence, Catholics became more open to the emerging new paradigm of Protestants, Catholics, and Jews as accepted American citizens. Many Americans looked to the Protestant preacher Norman Vincent Peale, the Catholic priest Fulton J. Sheen, and the Jewish Rabbi Joshua Liebman for what Mark Massa calls "the interdenominational chaplaincy to a genuinely post-Protestant America."[106] This open-minded attitude set up a different relation to followers of other religious paths, which Feeney and his followers felt compelled to reject. Massa notes that Feeney understood the traditional teaching of the Catholic Church as many earlier leaders, including Pope Innocent III and Francis Xavier, had done, and comments,

> The point of the story is that Feeney, for all of the private demons that undoubtedly drove him, had changed the interpretation of that dictum far less than had the experience of North American Catholicism itself. The boundary line marking those saved from those condemned had moved (or perhaps, been moved) to include others (that is, most Americans) who had no desire, implicit or otherwise, to join the Roman Communion.[107]

Many American Catholics were quietly embracing religious pluralism.

In 1955, Jewish sociologist Will Herberg, a former Marxist, described American religious identity as *Protestant-Catholic-Jew,* arguing that the traditional Protestant character of the nation had yielded to what he called a "triple melting pot" and that Protestants in the 1950s now saw themselves as only one of three religious communities in the United States.[108] Believing that by the 1950s, Catholics and Jews had found a new level of acceptance in American culture, Herberg maintained, "It is the American Way of Life that is the shared possession of all Americans and that defines the American's convictions on those matters that count most."[109] This Way of Life demanded religious faith but was indifferent as to its form; as Herberg cited President Eisenhower's famous statement: "Our government makes no sense unless it is founded in a deeply felt religious faith—and I don't care what it is."[110] Herberg stressed the implicit assumption of Eisenhower and most Americans that the three faiths were basically "'saying the same thing' in affirming the 'spiritual ideals' and 'moral values' of the American Way of Life."[111] Herberg described the American Way of Life as "individualistic, dynamic, pragmatic . . . humanitarian, 'forward looking,' optimistic."[112] He saw it as a type of "secularized Puritanism, a Puritanism without transcendence, without sense of sin or judgment . . . [T]he

---

[106] Massa, "Uses of Heresy," 337.

[107] Ibid., 340.

[108] Will Herberg, *Protestant-Catholic-Jew: An Essay on American Religious Sociology* (New York: Doubleday, 1955), 139–40, 272.

[109] Ibid., 247.

[110] *New York Times,* December 23, 1952; see Herberg, *Protestant-Catholic-Jew,* 97.

[111] Herberg, *Protestant-Catholic-Jew,* 98.

[112] Ibid., 92.

slogan, 'deeds, not creeds,' soon became the hallmark both of American religion and of the American Way of Life."[113]

Herberg believed Catholicism and Judaism had become secularized, and he warned of the loss involved in this transformation. Herberg suggested that Americans increasingly valued "the American Way of Life" as their central point of orientation, and believed that for most Americans, "religious pluralism is thus not merely a historical and political fact; it is, in the mind of the American, the primordial condition of things, an essential aspect of the American Way of Life, and therefore in itself an aspect of religious belief."[114] The upshot is, according to Herberg, that the American Way of Life becomes the dominant religion, which gives meaning to Protestant, Catholic, and Jewish faiths. "It is but one more step, though a most fateful one, to proceed from 'the religions of democracy' to 'democracy as religion' and consciously to erect 'democracy' into a super-faith above and embracing the three recognized religions."[115]

While Herberg expanded American identity from the classic Protestant mold to include Jews and Catholics, he did not include American Indians, Mormons, Muslims, Hindus, Buddhists, or any others who did not fit his tripartite model; indeed, he sternly warned that any other religious identity was not truly American.[116] Even among Christians, Herberg also neglected the important African American, evangelical, and pentecostal forms of Christianity. One of the ominous implications of Herberg's model, which continues to influence American society, is that those who are not Protestant, Catholic, or Jewish, are expected to demonstrate that they are not a threat to American security. In effect, Herberg succeeded in establishing a certain percentage of the population as integral to American identity and excluding everyone else. Other communities, including Muslims, Sikhs, Hindus, Buddhists, and others, were viewed with suspicion and pressured to demonstrate that they could conform to life in America without danger. Today some weaponize the term "Judeo-Christian" in order to exclude Muslims from so-called American values.[117]

Another stage of Catholic integration into American society came with the election of John F. Kennedy to the presidency in 1960. During the presidential campaign, Kennedy had to address accusations of Catholic allegiance to the Vatican. Kennedy strongly distinguished between his Catholic faith and his American political role. John Winthop's image of building a city on a hill had not been publicly cited for two hundred years, but Kennedy held it up as a traditional American ideal, buttressing his own integration of American patriotism and Catholic identity.[118]

---

[113] Ibid., 94, 95.

[114] Ibid., 98–99.

[115] Ibid., 101.

[116] Ibid., 256–57.

[117] Mark Silk, "Steve Bannon and the Nationalist Roots of Trump's Judeo-Christian Vision," *Religion News Service*, August 11, 2019.

[118] Daniel T. Rodgers, *As a City on a Hill: The Story of America's Most Famous Sermon* (Princeton, NJ: Princeton University Press, 2018).

Deeply rooted in Catholicism, Kennedy warmly embraced and accepted the broader religious heritage of the United States. His victory signaled another level of acceptance of Catholics in American political life.

Religious Diversity since 1965

The restrictions on immigration established in the 1920s lasted until 1965, when revised immigrations laws opened the United States to immigrants from all over the world. This opening of immigration had a powerful impact on religious diversity and attitudes toward religious pluralism in the United States. While very influential in the 1950s, the tripartite model of American religious identity as either Protestant or Catholic or Jew faced a severe challenge when new legislation on immigration opened the United States to migrants who were followers of other religious traditions. The religious composition of traditionally white Protestant American society changed dramatically. After surveying the long history of white Protestant claims for a Christian America, Robert Handy noted, "The significance of the highly pluralistic character of American religion became more difficult to avoid, however, as the sixties unfolded."[119] As the earlier Protestant confidence in a Christian America now had to make room for a broader network of religious communities, Handy revised the tripartite model to include a broader spectrum: "[R]eligiously, American had become a Catholic-Jewish-Orthodox-Protestant-Pentecostalist-Mormon-New Thought-Humanist nation."[120] But even Handy's revised model soon proved too narrow in light of the continuing arrival of new immigrants.

Since 1965, unprecedented numbers of Muslims, Hindus, Buddhists, Sikhs, Jains, and followers of other religious traditions have come to the United States;[121] and the neighborhoods of major metropolitan areas frequently contain a wide variety of the world's religions.[122] One marker of the new situation came from Robert Bellah, who remarked of Nathan Glazer's book, *We Are All Multiculturalists Now*, that its "very title makes the point."[123]

---

[119] Handy, *Christian America,* 192.

[120] Ibid., 193.

[121] See Jane I. Smith, *Islam in America* (New York: Columbia University Press, 1999), 126–85; Seager, *Buddhism in America,* 185–248; Joseph Goldstein, *One Dharma: The Emerging Western Buddhism* (San Francisco: HarperSanFrancisco, 2002); Charles S. Prebish and Kenneth K. Tanaka, eds., *The Changing Faces of Buddhism in America* (Berkeley, CA: University of California Press, 1998); Fields, *How the Swans Came to the Lake*; Vasuda Narayanan, *Hinduism in America* (New York: Columbia University Press, 2002); and Richard Wormser, *American Islam: Growing Up Muslim in America* (New York: Walker, 2002), 34–120.

[122] Diana L. Eck, *A New Religious America: How a "Christian Country" Has Now Become the World's Most Religiously Diverse Nation* (San Francisco: HarperSanFrancisco, 2001).

[123] Robert Bellah, "Is There a Common American Culture?," in *The Robert Bellah Reader,* ed. Robert N. Bellah and Steven M. Tipton (Durham, NC: Duke University Press, 2006), 319.

In 1967, Robert Bellah explored the religious dimension of the political sphere in an article, "Civil Religion in America," which sparked a wide and vigorous debate.[124] Bellah described assumptions underlying the American republic that did not belong strictly to any one religion but that provided the basis for common moral values and principles. Major texts, such as the Declaration of Independence and Lincoln's Gettysburg Address and Second Inaugural Address, express the fundamental principles of American civil religion. According to Bellah, these convictions offer a type of foundational myth for the American republic, but they do not constitute an additional religion in competition with the established religions, and they are voluntary. Ideally, the rhetoric and rites of civil religion seek to unite the American people when they are divided, call them to moral values beyond economic and political success, challenge them to humility in light of their failings, and articulate universal principles of freedom and justice that challenge the entire human community.[125] Bellah was aware that the rhetoric of civil religion has often been abused, but insisted that American civil religion at its best is not the worship of the nation, but rather an affirmation of transcendent principles that shape the vocation of the nation and that measure its failings.

As an example of American civil religion, Bellah cited John Kennedy's invocation of God in his 1961 inaugural address, emphasizing that the new president did not refer to the God of any particular religion or to the Bible but insisted that human rights come from God, not the decision of any government. Kennedy's challenge to the nation that God's work must be our own drew upon the long American tradition of articulating an obligation to carry out God's will on earth. By invoking God's will, civil religion offers legitimation for the exercise of power, including the use of military force. Later Bellah acknowledged the ambiguity of the American venture, suggesting that the American republic both is and is not a biblical republic, asserting that the American project of civil religion has been "unprecedented, unique, and confused."[126]

American civil religion as described by Bellah offered a Catholic leader like John F. Kennedy a way to remain faithful to his Catholic heritage without imposing Catholic faith on the public order of the country he was elected to lead. Followers of other theistic religions could accept the general principles of American civil religion in their own way and be faithful to their own traditions. For Buddhists, the God of civil religion poses more of a challenge because Buddhists do not believe in God as creator of the universe. The rhetoric of American civil religion can include

---

[124] Robert N. Bellah, "Civil Religion in America," *Daedalus: Journal of the American Academy of Arts and Sciences* 96, no. 1 (1967): 1–21. See also Robert N. Bellah, *Beyond Belief: Essays on Religion in a Post-Traditionalist World* (Berkeley: University of California Press, 1991); Robert N. Bellah and Philip E. Hammond, *Varieties of Civil Religion* (1980; reprint, Eugene, OR: Wipf & Stock Publishers, 2013).

[125] John D. Carlson, "Losing Our Civil Religion," *Religion & Politics*, September 29, 2017.

[126] Bellah and Hammond, *Varieties,* 6–7.

theistic religious traditions, but it excludes those who do not believe in God. Civil religion remains a debated notion.

Recently Philip Gorski has reflected on the history of civil religion in the United States, aware of the criticisms of the term but confident that it is still useful. Gorski proposes a narrative approach: "The civil religion is a narrative that tells us where we came from and where we are headed, not just what our commitments are. It embeds our values and our commitments within particular stories of civic greatness—and collective failure."[127] He comments that those who are not religious still "worship" some element in their lives, and he hopes the language of civil religion will prod them to reflect on what they worship.[128] Gorski endorses American civil religion as superior to religious nationalism, which seeks to impose a particular religious program, and to radical secularism, which seeks to drive religious language out of the public square altogether.

The challenge of articulating values that can attract interreligious assent was taken up by the second meeting of the Parliament of Religions, this time called a Parliament of the World's Religions, which convened in Chicago from August 28 to September 5, 1993. The second meeting of the Parliament offered a striking marker of the demographic changes since the previous century.[129] At the 1893 Parliament, most Americans had never seen a Muslim, a Hindu, or a Buddhist before, let alone a Sikh, a Confucianist, or a Parsee. During the 1980s, Hindus of the Vedanta Society in Chicago, as well as other religious leaders, were mindful that the centenary of the original Parliament was approaching and took the initiative of exploring the possibility of having a second convening of the Parliament. In 1988, the Council for a Parliament of the World's Religions was established to organize this event. For the 1993 Parliament, the local communities of Muslims, Hindus, and Buddhists in Chicago played a major role in organizing the conference and in welcoming their fellow practitioners from around the world.

About eight thousand people came from all over the world to the Palmer House Hilton Hotel for a week of discussions. Physicist Gerald Barney issued a rousing challenge to the world's religious leaders to come together to care for the earth and ecological well-being. Catholic leader Thomas Berry saw this as the most important development of the 1993 Parliament:

> If the finest consequence of the First Parliament of Religions, held in 1893, was the recovery of a profound sense of the divine in the human soul through the leadership of Swami Vivekananda, the finest consequence of the second Parliament of Religions, held in 1993, should be the recovery of an exalted sense of the divine in the grandeur of the natural world.[130]

---

[127] Philip Gorski, *American Covenant: A History of Civil Religion* (Princeton, NJ: Princeton University Press, 2017), 14.

[128] Ibid., 15.

[129] For comments by leaders at the 1993 Parliament, see Michael Tobias, Jane Morrison, and Bettina Gray, *A Parliament of Souls* (San Francisco: KQED Books, 1995).

[130] Thomas Berry, "The Role of Religions in the Twenty-first Century," in *The*

Berry warned of the terrible impact of a scientific-industrial worldview that exploits and plunders nature, and he saw the 1993 Parliament as teaching "that the natural world has from its beginning been a mystical as well as a physical reality. As the primary manifestation of the divine, the natural world is the primary sacred scripture and the primary sacred community."[131]

The organizers of the 1993 Parliament convened a Council of Spiritual and Religious Leaders and presented to them a text composed by Hans Küng, "A Global Ethic."[132] This declaration sets forth basic moral principles that many religious and spiritual leaders could endorse. Running through the declaration is the Golden Rule, together with a call to cherish life, respect religious diversity, and honor freedom of conscience. After vigorous debate in a tumultuous meeting, the assembly decided to accept the text with a slight change in the title: "Toward a Global Ethic: An Initial Declaration." Joseph Cardinal Bernardin, as Archbishop of Chicago, represented the Catholic Church in this Assembly and signed the Declaration.[133]

Recent Developments and Tensions

Many observers have commented on the shift from the era of a strongly Protestant Christian America to one that is considerably more religiously diverse. As we have seen, Robert P. Jones has proclaimed "The End of Christian White America."[134] Demographically, this is increasingly true of American society. Nonetheless, the long heritage of zealous white Christian American nationalism, combined with the heritage of biblical condemnation of other religions, continues to shape some American attitudes toward other religions and the global situation. Philip E. Hammond describes "a nostalgic yearning for something that happened to be importantly Protestant."[135]

Not unlike Protestant Americans in the nineteenth century who worried about the impact of new immigrants, the late Professor Samuel Huntington of Harvard University expressed concern that continuing immigration, especially of Catholics from Latin America, in conjunction with the growing influence of transnational identities and institutions, would fundamentally change the Protestant identity of the United States for the worse.[136] He argued that historically the United States has

---

Community of Religions: Voices and Images of The Parliament of the World's Religions, ed. Wayne Teasdale and George F. Cairns (New York: Continuum, 1996), 182.

[131] Ibid., 185.

[132] Hans Küng and Karl-Josef Kuschel, *A Global Ethic: The Declaration of the Parliament of the World's Religions* (New York: Continuum, 1993).

[133] *Declaration Toward a Global Ethic,* https://parliamentofreligions.org/pwr_resources/_includes/FCKcontent/File/TowardsAGlobalEthic.pdf.

[134] Robert P. Jones, *The End of Christian White America* (New York: Simon & Schuster, 2016).

[135] Bellah and Hammond, *Varieties,* 201.

[136] Huntington, *Who Are We,* 17–20.

been an Anglo-Protestant nation with its own American creed.[137] Asserting that there is a profound chasm between Mexico's Catholic culture and the Protestant culture of the United States, Huntington worried: "The continuation of high levels of Mexican and Hispanic immigration plus the low rates of assimilation of these immigrants into American society and culture could eventually change America into a country of two languages, two cultures, and two peoples."[138] While acknowledging the resurgence of evangelical Protestant identity with its renewed sense of "a Christian America," he worried that immigrants from Latin America could dramatically weaken the Anglo-Protestant core of American identity and lead to serious divisions. He warned of a "crisis of national identity" due to the increased immigration of Catholics from Latin America, who, he believed, were not being properly assimilated into traditionally Protestant American religious culture. Rejecting any possibility of a U.S. Hispanic "Americano dream," Huntington insisted, "There is only the American dream created by an Anglo-Protestant society. Mexican-Americans will share in that dream and in that society only if they dream in English."[139]

The traditionally dominant Protestant, often Calvinist and Evangelical, influence on American society is yielding to multisided relationships in which no one party dominates. Christians find their voices among Jews, Muslims, Hindus, Buddhists, and other communities. Increasingly Americans describe themselves as "spiritual but not religious," and categorize themselves as "nones," that is, none of the standard, traditional religious identities.[140] This shift brings new challenges, with both opportunities and anxieties.

The relation between religion and society in the current situation is complex and ambiguous. The United States highly values religious freedom but has repeatedly restricted its practice and discriminated against followers of minority religious traditions. For many people, the promises of the United States of America have often been a dream cruelly deferred and denied. Nonetheless, there is much that is positive in the current situation. In the last fifty years there has been a flowering of local, regional, and national contacts and exchanges among different religious groups in the United States. On many levels there has been tremendous progress in the acceptance of religious diversity in the United States.

The tensions of the present do not mean the gains in interreligious understanding and acceptance in the past decades are not important. Sociologist Rodney Stark calls attention to the degree that Americans have learned "not merely to respect but to genuinely like others of a different faith," while maintaining confidence in their own religious path. He describes this as "the most sophisticated solidarity of all: to live in respectful harmony while maintaining profoundly

---

[137] Ibid., 59–106.

[138] Ibid., 256.

[139] Ibid.

[140] Reid B. Locklin, *Spiritual but Not Religious? An Oar Stroke Closer to the Farther Shore* (Collegeville, MN: Liturgical Press, 2005).

conflicting faiths."[141] Stark notes that societies where one religion seeks to impose a monopoly face not only greater religious violence but also greater "religious apathy and alienation"; by contrast, he concludes that the experience of religious pluralism in the United States teaches us "the key to high levels of local religious commitment *and* of religious civility, is not fewer religions, but more."[142]

---

[141] Rodney Stark, *One True God: Historical Consequences of Monotheism* (Princeton, NJ: Princeton University Press, 2001), 250.

[142] Ibid., 259.

Part II

Encounters between the Catholic Church

and Other Religious Traditions

in the United States

3

CATHOLICS AND THE INDIGENOUS
RELIGIOUS TRADITIONS OF THE AMERICAS

When European Christians first came to the Caribbean and North America, they encountered a wide variety of indigenous peoples, initiating a long series of contacts and conflicts. Despite the painful tensions of these encounters, many inhabitants of North America embraced the Christian faith, and some of the most innovative intercultural religious practices in North America have come from Native Christian communities who have accepted both traditional Native and Christian practices and perspectives. Christopher Vecsey estimates that of the more than two million self-identifying Indians in the United States, more than half are Christian, and about 350,000 are Catholic.[1] However, discussions of intercultural theology and religious pluralism have not always given adequate attention to the traditional religious heritage of American Indians, the experience of the Native Christians in the United States, and the challenge that the American Indian heritage poses to Christianity, and to the methods of study of intercultural theology and religious pluralism.

The religious traditions of these first inhabitants, as well as the religious traditions that enslaved people brought with them from Africa, profoundly shaped Catholic life and practice. U.S. Hispanic Catholics have a distinctive experience of interaction with indigenous and African traditions, which is shaped by their history of intermingling in Latin America. In each of these situations, the experience of religious diversity has all too frequently been marked by suspicion, condemnation, and hostility, but there are also aspects of integration across boundaries. This chapter will examine the relationship of Catholics to indigenous religious traditions and will listen to the experiences of American Indian Catholics, with a brief reflection on the relation of Hispanic Catholics to indigenous traditions, and the relation of African American Catholics to the religious traditions of Africa.

Conquest and the Doctrine of Discovery

The first Christians to come to the areas that are now part of the United States of America were Spanish Catholics. The context of the Portuguese and the Spanish

---

[1] Christopher Vecsey, "The Good News in Print and Image: Catholic Evangeliteracy in Native America," *U.S. Catholic Historian* 27, no. 1 (2009): 1–19.

at that time was shaped by the Reconquista, the centuries-long struggle to drive
the Muslim rulers from the Iberian Peninsula. The Portuguese had concluded their
struggle to defeat Muslim rulers a half-century before the Spanish rulers conquered
Granada in 1492, and in the mid-fifteenth century, the Portuguese commenced a
series of voyages of discovery extending south along the coast of Africa that would
eventually reach India in 1498. In light of the history of conflict with Muslims,
Spanish and Portuguese Catholics often viewed the inhabitants of the Americas on
the model of the Moors.[2]

Fifteenth-century popes strongly encouraged the Portuguese and Spanish
efforts to conquer new lands and gave authorization to enslave their peoples. In
1452, as Constantinople was increasingly in danger of falling to the Ottoman
Turkish forces, Pope Nicholas V issued the papal bull *Dum Diversas,* which authorized King Afonso V of Portugal to conquer and appropriate land and enslave
Saracens, pagans, and all others who were opposed to Jesus Christ. Willie James
Jennings notes that in this document

> the right to enslave . . . is enclosed in the actions of land appropriation. This
> is indicated by a number of verbs—"invadendi, conquerendi, expugnandi,
> et subjungandi" ["of invading, conquering, subduing, and subjugating"];
> then we find "illorumque personas in perpetuam servitutem redigendi"
> ["and of reducing those persons to perpetual servitude"].[3]

Pope Nicholas reaffirmed and expanded this authorization in 1455 in the bull
Romanus Pontifex.[4] While Pope Nicholas was probably hoping the Portuguese
would launch a Crusade against the Turks, the bull granted permission that would
effectively authorize wide-ranging conquests around the globe as well as the African
slave trade. Later Popes Callistus III, Sixtus IV, and Leo X reaffirmed the bull. After
interventions by Bartolomé de Las Casas, Pope Paul III issued the bull *Sublimis
Deus* in 1537, which affirmed the rights of indigenous peoples in the Americas
to their personal freedom and possessions, whether they were Christian or not.[5]
However, Pope Paul III's directives were never fully implemented in the Americas.

After the voyage of Christopher Columbus, Spain laid claim to territories in the Americas; and the Spanish-born Pope Alexander VI issued the papal
bull *Inter Caetera* on May 4, 1493, drawing a line on the map between the lands

---

[2] Anouar Majid, *We Are All Moors: Ending Centuries of Crusades against Muslims and
Other Minorities* (Minneapolis: University of Minnesota Press, 2009).

[3] Willie James Jennings, *The Christian Imagination: Theology and the Origins of Race*
(New Haven, CT: Yale University Press, 2010), 298n.28; citing Pope Nicholas V, *Dum
Diversas,* June 18, 1452, in *European Treaties Bearing on the History of the United States and
Its Dependencies to 1648,* vol. 1, ed. Frances Gardiner Davenport (Washington, DC: Carn-
egie Institution of Washington, 1917), 1:17.

[4] Pope Nicholas V, *Romanus Pontifex,* January 8, 1455.

[5] Pope Paul III, *Sublimis Deus,* May 29, 1537.

granted to Portugal and those granted to Spain; Pope Alexander authorized the Spanish monarchs Ferdinand and Isabella to take possession of the new islands and main lands "that hitherto had not been discovered by others" and "bring to the worship of our Redeemer and the profession of the Catholic faith their residents and inhabitants."[6] Renaissance popes assumed they had the right to divide and distribute areas not ruled by European Christians; these papal bulls shaped what would later be called the doctrine of discovery, which claimed to give European powers the supposed right to take possession of lands not already claimed by other Europeans.[7] The doctrine would provide support for the later American claims of having a "Manifest Destiny" from God to conquer North America and dispossess the original inhabitants.[8] The Supreme Court of Tennessee cited papal precedents in its 1826 ruling, *Cornet v. Winton*; the court ruled that Christians were perpetual enemies of non-Christians and had a right to subject the Americas to their rule.[9] Associate Justice Joseph Story of the U.S. Supreme Court, who was a close friend of Chief Justice John Marshall, explained the reasoning behind the momentous case *Johnson v. M'Intosh,* which in 1823 ruled that U.S. citizens could not purchase land from American Indians.[10] Story published an explanation of the ruling ten years after it had been issued, citing Pope Alexander VI's bull of 1493 as legal precedent for appropriating the land of the indigenous inhabitants of America and noting that King Henry VII of England followed the pope's lead just three years later in 1496.[11]

Luis N. Rivera notes that Spanish theorists who justified the conquest of the Americas never appealed to material gain or territorial acquisition as a legitimate basis for claiming the new lands; the stated goal was always evangelization of the indigenous peoples:

> The result was peculiar: one of the largest imperial expansions in history, by an empire that never admitted, even to itself, that such was its intention. The principal objective espoused by all the main actors in the debate was the conversion of the natives, the eternal salvation of their souls.[12]

---

[6] Pope Alexander VI, *Inter Caetera,* May 4, 1493.

[7] Steven T. Newcomb, *Pagans in the Promised Land: Decoding the Doctrine of Christian Discovery* (Golden, CO: Fulcrum, 2008).

[8] Robert J. Miller, "American Indians, the Doctrine of Discovery, and Manifest Destiny," *Wyoming Law Review* 11, no. 2 (2011): 329–49; Robert J. Miller, "The Doctrine of Discovery in American Indian Law," *Idaho Law Review* 42, no. 1 (2005): 1–122; George D. Pappas, *The Literary and Legal Genealogy of Native American Dispossession: Indigenous Peoples and the Law* (London: Routledge, 2017), 27–35.

[9] Newcomb, *Pagans,* 77–78.

[10] Pappas, *The Literary and Legal Genealogy of Native American Dispossession.*

[11] Newcomb, *Pagans,* 81–87.

[12] Luis N. Rivera, *A Violent Evangelism: The Political and Religious Conquest of the Americas* (Louisville, KY: Westminster/John Knox Press, 1992), 25.

Christopher Vecsey notes the militant theological tone employed by the Spanish when addressing the indigenous peoples:

> Indeed, the first centuries of Spanish Catholic expansion to the Americas were less about "mission": (going out to convince the Natives, leaving open a choice of acceptance or refusal), than they were about proclaiming, instructing, and baptizing, under the legal authority of the Crown, itself under the aegis of the Church.[13]

The Spanish and Portuguese coming to the Americas encountered a world they had never imagined, populated by indigenous peoples who practiced a wide range of traditions that shaped all life and thought. It is disputed whether one can apply the category of religion to these traditions. Archeologist Severin Fowles argues that "religion" is a category created by modern Europeans that does not accurately describe any reality of premodern Pueblo life, and he proposes the term "doings" as a replacement for "religions" because it is more faithful to the holistic character of precontact Pueblo society.[14] Europeans distinguished some activities of the indigenous peoples as religious and others as profane, but this was not a distinction that Native peoples themselves recognized. Spanish Catholics oscillated between viewing the indigenous peoples of the Americas as not having any religion at all and as having a false religion. Christopher Columbus thought the first indigenous people he met had little knowledge of religion and would be easy to convert to the Catholic faith;[15] for example, he viewed the Arawaks as free of any religion, while he judged the Caribs to practice a devilish false religion.[16]

From the beginning, theological perspectives on religious diversity intertwined with the insatiable drive for power and wealth. During the same period when the Catholic monarchs and their subjects were forcing Jews and Muslims to convert to Catholicism or leave the Iberian Peninsula, Spanish leaders combined a stated concern for Christian evangelization with their preoccupation with *limpieza de sangre* (purity of blood, especially regarding Jewish ancestry) and racism as well as a very harsh view of the indigenous religious traditions of the Americas. European American Christians have a long tradition of regarding their religious and intellectual traditions as the pinnacle of divine providence, which is believed to authorize their conquest of other peoples. The sixteenth-century Spanish confidence in divine providence guiding their conquests would be succeeded by the later nine-

---

[13] Vecsey, "Good News," 7.

[14] Severin M. Fowles, *An Archeology of Doings: Secularism and the Study of Pueblo Religion* (Santa Fe, NM: School for Advanced Research Press, 2013), 240–63.

[15] Stanley L. Robe, "Wild Men and Spain's Brave New World," in *The Wild Man Within: An Image in Western Thought from the Renaissance to Romanticism,* ed. Edward Dudley and Maximillian E. Novak (Pittsburgh, PA: University of Pittsburgh Press, 1972), 43.

[16] Fowles, *Archeology of Doings,* 243.

teenth-century American claim of Manifest Destiny. Many Spaniards viewed the inhabitants of the Americas as lazy idolaters who had no rights. Gonzalo de Oviedo y Valdes asserted forcefully concerning the indigenous people of the Americas:

> They are naturally lazy and vicious, melancholic, cowardly, and in general a lying, shiftless people. Their marriages are not a sacrament but a sacrilege. They are idolatrous, libidinous, and commit sodomy. Their chief desire is to eat, drink, worship heathen idols, and commit bestial obscenities.[17]

Negative images of indigenous peoples continued to shape American Catholic attitudes for centuries. Writing in 1939 about the history of the Catholic Church in Louisiana at the request of the local bishop, Roger Baudier illustrates the assumption that American Indians did not know God prior to the coming of Catholic missionaries:

> The first Christian missionaries in the southern part of what is now the United States came with the first Spanish explorers in the early part of the sixteenth century. At the time that country was the wild and untamed home of the Red Man, great spaces of mysterious swamps, woodlands, swirling rivers and sluggish bayous, where dwelt many tribes of warlike Indians.... They were tribes who knew neither God, the Creator, nor His Son, the Redeemer. They were among those nations in regard to whom Christ had said: "Go, therefore, teach ye all nations, baptizing them in the name of the Father, and of the Son, and of the Holy Ghost, teaching them to observe all things whatsoever I have commanded you." This mandate of Christ was the guiding principle of Spanish sovereigns in their exploration and colonization ventures.[18]

Hernando de Soto and his forces wrought terrible destruction when they marched through the southern region of North America from 1539 to 1543, burning crops, destroying towns and religious sites, and killing many Indians in a failed quest for gold.[19] Baudier, however, passes over the atrocities in silence and frames this expedition in terms of evangelization:

> Spain sent another expedition to her new lands along the Gulf of Mexico, a great force, completely equipped and placed under the direction of Hernando de Soto. As in the case of other Spanish expeditions, the

---

[17] Cited by Stephen Neill, *A History of Christian Missions,* revised for the second edition by Owen Chadwick (London: Penguin Books, 1990), 146.

[18] Roger Baudier, *The Catholic Church in Louisiana* (1939; reprint, New Orleans: Louisiana Library Association Public Library Section, 1972), 13.

[19] James Wilson, *The Earth Shall Weep: A History of Native America* (New York: Grove Press, 1998), 135–37.

opportunity to carry out the mandate of Christ was not forgotten in this one.... [T]his marks the first conversions among the savages.[20]

The historical memory of American Catholics has generally ignored the devastation caused to the indigenous peoples by the Spanish explorers. The terrible suffering caused by the conquest and the legal difficulties flowing from the doctrine of discovery continue to challenge Catholic awareness.

Greed, Racism, and Religious Bias

The imperial drive for power, greed, and racism developed in the same context as Christian missionary efforts. This confluence of opposing currents would dominate life in the Americas for centuries and continues to shape the context of American life today. Philip Deloria, a leading American Indian thinker of the Standing Rock Sioux Tribe, recalls that in 1773 the Boston Tea Party dressed up as Mohawk Indians in order to express their fury at Great Britain. European Americans have both appropriated Indian identity and destroyed it, oscillating between cultural fusion and violent appropriation, between assimilation and destruction. Deloria also stresses the close connection between the precarious European American construction of identity and their appropriation of land in the Americas, noting that

> the indeterminacy of American identities stems, in part, from the nation's inability to deal with Indian people. Americans wanted to feel a natural affinity with the continent, and it was Indians who could teach them such aboriginal closeness. Yet, in order to *control the landscape* they had to destroy the original inhabitants.[21]

Deloria suggests there is a similar dynamic of European Americans relating to African Americans.

For centuries European Christians from various nations appealed to religious and racial prejudices as justification for conquering and mistreating the indigenous peoples. However, from the beginning of the European conquest of the Americas, not all agreed, and there was a fierce debate over how to view the inhabitants of the area, with some Christians fiercely challenging the brutality of the conquest on theological grounds. On the last Sunday of Advent in 1511, Dominican friar Antonio de Montesinos preached a sermon in which he denounced what Spanish Catholics were doing:

> Tell me, by what right or justice do you keep these Indians in such cruel and horrible servitude? ... Why do you keep them so oppressed and

---

[20] Baudier, *Catholic Church in Louisiana,* 14.

[21] Philip Deloria, *Playing Indian* (New Haven, CT: Yale University Press, 1998), 5.

weary, not giving them enough to eat, nor taking care of them in their illnesses? For with the excessive work you demand of them, they fall ill and die, or rather you kill them with your desire to extract and acquire gold every day. . . . Are these not men? Have they not rational souls? Are you not bound to love them as you love yourselves? Be certain that in such a state as this, you can no more be saved than the Moors or Turks.[22]

Montesinos's cry for justice set an agenda that some later Catholic leaders would take up, though frequently without success. Bartolomé de Las Casas, who later forcefully advocated for the concerns of Montesinos, tells us that many were astonished at Montesinos's message but "no one, so far as I have heard, converted."[23] Las Casas, originally from Seville in Spain, came with his father to Hispaniola (present-day Haiti and the Dominican Republic), where they profited from the conquest and the labor of enslaved people. Even though Las Casas commented that no one was converted by Montesinos, the sermon prompted Las Casas himself to begin a process of conversion that would eventually lead him to become a ferocious critic of the atrocities being committed upon the indigenous peoples. Later, in 1530, the Emperor Charles V forbade the enslavement of Indians, but few in the Americas paid heed, and in 1534 the order was revoked.[24] The efforts of Las Casas contributed to the New Laws of 1542, which sought to improve the situation of Indians; but these were never fully enforced in the Americas.

Las Casas famously defended the full humanity of the indigenous peoples of the Americas in his debate with Gines de Sepúlveda in 1550–51, the first major theological debate over the humanity of the Indians of the Americas.[25] Walter D. Mignolo comments that the debate concerning "'rights of the people' was the first legal attempt (theological in nature) to write down a canon of international law, that was reformulated in a secular discourse in the eighteenth century as the 'rights of men and of the citizen.'"[26] Tragically, this debate concerned only American Indians, not enslaved Africans: "Amerindians were considered vassals of the king and servants of God; as such they, theoretically, could not be enslaved. They were supposed to be educated and converted to Christianity. African slaves were not in the same category: they were part of the Atlantic 'commerce.'"[27] Even though

---

[22] Neill, *A History of Christian Missions,* 145; see also Gustavo Gutiérrez, *Las Casas: In Search of the Poor of Jesus Christ,* trans. Robert R. Barr (Maryknoll, NY: Orbis Books, 1993), 28–31.

[23] Gutiérrez, *Las Casas,* 31.

[24] Ibid., 305.

[25] Lewis Hanke, *Aristotle and the American Indians: A Study in Race Prejudice in the Modern World* (Bloomington: Indiana University Press, 1970).

[26] Walter D. Mignolo, *Local Histories/Global Designs: Coloniality, Subaltern Knowledges, and Border Thinking* (2000; reprint, Princeton, NJ: Princeton University Press, 2012), 29.

[27] Ibid., 30.

Emperor Charles V had decreed that the debates take place, there was no formal decision. Sepúlveda's side lost support in the subsequent years. Stanley L. Robe comments on the result, "The Indian was no longer a Wild Man in the official view. No other colonial power undertook such an examination of the relationship of the conqueror to the conquered in its overseas territories."[28]

Luis Rivera notes that even though Las Casas sharply criticized the abuse of the American Indians, he did not advocate for full independence for them, but rather for a more benevolent yet still paternalistic care for them: "The relationship of these free peoples with the Crown should be similar to that of the free cities of Europe and Spain, which recognize the emperor as their ultimate sovereign, without such an authority canceling their autonomy and powers for self-determination."[29] Despite his tragic flaws and limitations, the witness of Las Casas stands as a protest against the horrors that were done to the Indian populations; Gustavo Gutiérrez interprets Las Casas as a Christian "in search of the poor of Jesus Christ."[30] The legacy of Montesinos and Las Casas helped inspire liberation theologians in their protest against oppressive systems of government and economics and offers inspiration to all working for justice in the present situation.

Tragedy and Grace:
American Indian Christian Experience

The history of the relationship between the Christian churches and the Native communities in North America is a tale of both tragedy and grace. The unbearably painful account of the horrendous mistreatment of indigenous peoples by European American Christians over many centuries has often been told.[31]

The Jesuits who came to Mexico and the southwestern part of the United States repeatedly expressed a high regard for American Indians, describing them as gentle, docile, and kind, and as capable of learning.[32] Nonetheless, they assumed the superiority of European culture and the Catholic faith, they encouraged the Indians to become more like Spaniards, and over time they sought to replace indigenous beliefs and practices with the ethos of Spanish Catholicism. The Indians were not always impressed. In response to the Penitentes, a Spanish lay brotherhood that engaged in self-flagellation to share the sufferings of Christ, one Indian in San

---

[28] Robe, "Wild Men and Spain's Brave New World," 47.

[29] Rivera, *Violent Evangelism,* 65.

[30] Gutiérrez, *Las Casas.*

[31] Wilson, *Earth Shall Weep*; Ned Blackhawk, *Violence over the Land: Indians and Empires in the Early American West* (Cambridge, MA: Harvard University Press, 2006); Ronald Takaki, *A Different Mirror: A History of Multicultural America* (Boston: Little, Brown, 1993); David Treuer, *The Heartbreak of Wounded Knee: Native America from 1890 to the Present* (New York: Riverhead Books, 2019).

[32] Nicholas P. Cushner, *Why Have You Come Here? The Jesuits and the First Evangelization of North America* (Oxford: Oxford University Press, 2006), 62.

Ildefonso, New Mexico, commented, "The Indian religion is to be happy, but the Spanish religion is to be sad. That's why they are two different people."[33]

Jesuit Joseph-François Lafitau, who worked in the eastern regions of North America in the eighteenth century, appreciated and valued much of Native American culture; but he viewed their religion as "a decadent descendent of the original religion given to our first parents before their fall from grace."[34] This judgment set up a displacement model of mission that could acknowledge values in Native American religions only to the degree that they resonated with the Catholic tradition. However, as we have seen, American Indians did not make any clear distinction between religious and secular, and thus it was often difficult or impossible for Jesuit missioners in North America to discern precisely which Native customs were acceptable and which were inspired by "demons"; nonetheless, some customs, such as sorcery, shamanism, and dream interpretation, appeared to the Jesuits to be clear contradictions of Catholic faith. Alan Greer comments on the Iroquois among whom Lafitau ministered: "Native converts may have been assiduous in their devotion to Catholic prayer and regular in their attendance at mass, but they did not necessarily abandon all their indigenous techniques for approaching the sacred."[35] Lafitau recognized that Native Catholics did not relinquish their traditional practices, as he commented, "Among christianized Iroquois, it should be regarded as a heroic act when, in illnesses, one does not have recourse to shamans [*jongleurs*], especially if there is some indication or dream which causes a suspicion of sorcery."[36] Greer notes that the eclecticism of the Iroquois was not unlike the practices of Catholic peasants in seventeenth-century Europe who resorted to primordial incantations and charms that were not approved by official Catholicism.[37]

In New England in 1833, the Methodist theologian William Apess from the Pequot nation challenged the European Americans:

> Now let me ask you, white man, if it is a disgrace for to eat, drink, and sleep with the image of God, or sit, or walk and talk with them. Or have you the folly to think that the white man, being one in fifteen or sixteen, are the only beloved images of God? Assemble all nations together in your imagination, and then let the whites be seated among them. . . . Now suppose these skins were put together, and each skin had its national

---

[33] Cited by Christopher Vecsey, *On the Padres' Trail* (Notre Dame, IN: University of Notre Dame Press, 1996), 152.

[34] Carl F. Starkloff, "Native American Catholic Experience," *Chicago Studies* 42, no. 3 (2003): 232; see also Carl F. Starkloff, *Common Testimony: Ethnology and Theology in the Customs of Joseph Lafitau* (St. Louis, MO: Institute of Jesuit Sources, 2002).

[35] Allan Greer, *Mohawk Saint: Catherine Tekakwitha and the Jesuits* (Oxford: Oxford University Press, 2005), 108.

[36] Joseph Lafitau, *Customs of the American Indians Compared with the Customs of Primitive Times*, 1:246, cited in Greer, *Mohawk Saint*, 108.

[37] Greer, *Mohawk Saint*, 109.

crimes written upon it—which skin do you think would have the greatest? I will ask one question more. Can you charge the Indians with robbing a nation almost of their whole continent, and murdering their women and children, and then depriving the remainder of their lawful rights, that nature and God require them to have?[38]

Tragically, Apess's challenge was not widely heeded, and many European American Christians continued to judge the indigenous religious practices of North America to be demonic, and sought to replace them with European-style Christian faith and practice. Even when the Cherokee Nation largely accepted Christianity and Western-style customs, this did not suffice to protect their safety; and they were forcibly expelled from their lands and driven along the Trail of Tears.[39] From the sixteenth and seventeenth centuries until the twentieth century, Catholic missioners frequently distrusted the indigenous religious traditions, usually interpreting them "as an ensemble of demonic beliefs and practices," even though in some settings they did respect certain aspects of Native American culture.[40]

Religious bias and racial prejudice flowed together in shaping attitudes toward American Indians. In 1893, nearly fifty years after the emancipation of slaves in the United States, William Pope Harrison described the basis for the white race's claim to expropriation of lands:

That the aboriginal races of men, occupying the soil for thousands of years, yet failing to accomplish the object of their creation, must give place to a higher type of mankind possessing both the genius and the energy to *subdue* the earth, and to exercise dominion over it, is a truth that is illustrated by the history of every aboriginal race.[41]

Harrison noted that the Apostle Paul contradicted abolitionists and justified slavery, which Harrison thought was better than "perpetual barbarism": "The time has been in the world's history, and the time is now in the history of many millions of human beings, that the alternative existing for these millions is either slavery

---

[38] William Apess, *On Our Own Ground: The Complete Writings of William Apess, a Pequot,* edited and with an Introduction by Barry O'Connell (Amherst: University of Massachusetts Press, 1992), xiii.

[39] John Ehle, *Trail of Tears: The Rise and Fall of the Cherokee Nation* (1988; reprint, New York: Anchor Books, 2011); Theda Perdue, *Cherokee Removal: A Brief History with Documents,* 3rd ed. (Boston: Bedford/St. Martin's, 2016); Theda Perdue and Michael D. Green, *The Cherokee Nation and the Trail of Tears* (New York: Penguin Books, 2008).

[40] Carl Starkloff, "Native American Catholic Experience," 232.

[41] W. P. Harrison, *The Gospel among the Slaves: A Short Account of Missionary Operations among the African Slaves of the Southern States* (1893; reprint, New York: AMS Press, 1973), 29.

or perpetual barbarism."[42] Unfortunately, Harrison's views were widely shared in American history.

As the United States developed and expanded across the continent and around the globe, the negative theological evaluation of traditional Native religious practices frequently merged with the American belief in Manifest Destiny, which held that God intended Euro-American culture to dominate North America.[43] In light of this belief, European American Christians often acted, as Paul VanDevelder commented, as "monsters of God."[44] Many European American Christians justified the displacement of Indians because they cherished notions of providence that valorized the special role of the United States in God's plan to spread Christianity across the continent and around the world. In 1783, in the context of the American Revolution, Congregationalist minister Ezra Stiles preached to the Connecticut General Assembly in Hartford about God's choice of the new nation as God's chosen Israel.[45] In the context of the Spanish American War, the U.S. senator and prize-winning historian Albert J. Beveridge boldly proclaimed on the floor of the U.S. Senate that the American people had been chosen by God to lead in the regeneration of the world, and he justified the colonial occupation of the Philippines as part of this mission.[46] Beveridge addressed his colleagues concerning the special racial and religious role of the "redeemer nation":

[God] made us master organizers of the world to establish system where chaos reigned. He has given us the spirit of progress to overwhelm the forces of reaction throughout the earth. He has made us adept in government that we may administer government among savage and senile peoples. . . . And of all our race He has marked the American people as His chosen nation to finally lead in the redemption of the world.[47]

When American Christians cast themselves in the role of the Israelites on an errand in the wilderness seeking the Promised Land, the American Indians were

---

[42] Ibid., 28.

[43] Amy S. Greenberg, *Manifest Destiny and Territorial Expansion: A Brief History with Documents*, 2nd ed. (Boston: Bedford/St. Martin's, 2018).

[44] Paul VanDevelder, *Savages and Scoundrels: The Untold Story of America's Road to Empire through Indian Territory* (New Haven, CT: Yale University Press, 2009), 201–43.

[45] Ezra Stiles, "The United States Elevated to Honor and Glory, May 8, 1783," http://www.christianheritagemins.org/articles/Election_sermon_Stiles.htm.

[46] Albert J. Beveridge, "Policy Regarding the Philippines," *Congressional Record*, January 9, 1900, 706–712; Robert Jewett and John Shelton Lawrence, *Captain America and the Crusade against Evil: The Dilemma of Zealous Nationalism* (Grand Rapids, MI: Eerdmans, 2003), 3–4; Justin B. Litke, *Twilight of the Republic: Empire and Exceptionalism in the American Political Tradition* (Lexington: University Press of Kentucky, 2013), 115–44.

[47] Ernest Lee Tuveson, *Redeemer Nation: The Idea of America's Millennial Role* (1968; reprint, Chicago: University of Chicago Press, 1980), vii.

cast in the roles of the biblical inhabitants of the land who had to be killed or displaced.[48] American Indian Christians have repeatedly rejected these notions of providence, but when they resisted the European American Christian onslaught, they were judged negatively on religious, racial, and cultural grounds. Despite the first amendment of the U.S. Constitution, during the nineteenth and early twentieth centuries the government of the United States repeatedly forbade performance of religious ceremonies to American Indians.[49] In 1892, Thomas J. Morgan, as Commissioner of Indian Affairs, established the "Rules for Indian Courts," which criminalized many traditional American Indian practices.[50] The U.S. government, often assisted by Christian mission schools, tried to suppress the indigenous religious practices and compel Indians to abandon their religious and cultural heritage.[51] General Philip Sheridan of the U.S. Army believed that "the only good Indian is a dead Indian"; Captain Richard Pratt, the founder of the Carlisle Indian School in Pennsylvania, disagreed, proposing instead that there was hope for Indians through forced assimilation: Americans should "kill the Indian and save the man."[52]

One of the most systematic efforts to eliminate the Native population occurred in California from 1846 to 1873. Christians have devoted tremendous energy to pondering how to do theology after the Shoah (the Holocaust), but American Christians have dedicated much less attention to what Benjamin Madley has documented as the American Genocide in California: "Individuals, private groups, state militiamen, and US Army soldiers carried out these killings, ostensibly to protect non-Indians or to punish Indians for suspected crimes. In fact, the perpetrators often sought to annihilate California's indigenous peoples between 1846 and 1873."[53] He notes that on January 7, 1851, California Governor Peter H. Burnett stated publicly that "a war of extermination will continue to be waged between the races, until the Indian race becomes extinct."[54] In 1852, U.S. Senator Weller, who would later become governor of California, also affirmed that Indians in California "will be exterminated before the onward march of the white man."[55] Madley documents that both state and federal officials, including the U.S. Army and the Office

---

[48] George E. Tinker, *Spirit and Resistance: Political Theology and American Indian Liberation* (Minneapolis: Fortress Press, 2004), 90.

[49] Tisa Wenger, *Religious Freedom: The Contested History of an American Ideal* (Chapel Hill: University of North Carolina Press, 2017), 101–42.

[50] Lee Irwin, "Freedom, Law, and Prophecy: A Brief History of Native American Religious Resistance," in *Native American Spirituality,* ed. Lee Irwin (Lincoln: University of Nebraska Press, 2000), 296.

[51] David Wallace Adams, *Education for Extinction: American Indians and the Boarding School Experience, 1875–1928* (Lawrence: University Press of Kansas, 1995).

[52] Wilson, *Earth Shall Weep,* 312.

[53] Benjamin Madley, *An American Genocide: The United States and the California Indian Catastrophe, 1846–1873* (New Haven, CT: Yale University Press, 2016), xi.

[54] Ibid., 353.

[55] Ibid.

of Indian Affairs, were aware of the deliberate extermination of Indians; while some sought to protect Indians, others fully supported the physical elimination of Indians altogether: "Elected California officials were the primary architects of annihilation. Legislators created a legal environment in which California Indians had almost no rights, thus granting those who attacked them virtual impunity. Moreover, two governors threatened annihilation, and both governors and elected officials cooperated in building a killing machine."[56] The U.S. Army played a vital role in conspiring and carrying out the genocide, and U.S. senators offered legislative support, even paying for killings of Indians by the California militia.[57]

Further east, in the northern part of the United States an Indian prophet named Wovoka instructed Indians to set aside their quarrels, live in peace with whites, refrain from lying or stealing, and perform a sacred dance; Wovoka promised that their ancestors would return in 1891 with blessings and benefits, especially the animals killed by whites.[58] The American authorities frequently viewed those who practiced the Ghost Dance as a threat and persecuted them, leading to the infamous massacre at Wounded Knee on December 29, 1890, in which between 250 and 300 Indians were killed.[59] The atrocities committed against American Indians continue to challenge the American Catholic community.

Native Catholics and Missionaries

Catholic missionaries sometimes idealized Indians as innocent, but they also frequently viewed them as savages, as children, as bloodthirsty animals, or as feathered spectacles.[60] They sought to convert the Indians both to the Catholic faith and the American Way of Life, but despite the imbalance of power, Indians exerted their own influence on the missionaries and on the practice of Catholic faith.

In light of the terrible depredations done in the name of Christianity, many American Indians both past and present rejected Christianity altogether as the "white man's religion."[61] Others accepted Christianity in its European or European

---

[56] Ibid., 354.

[57] Ibid., 354–55.

[58] Karl Markus Kreis, ed., *Lakotas, Black Robes, and Holy Women: German Reports from the Indian Missions in South Dakota (1886–1900),* trans. Corinna Dally-Starna (Lincoln: University of Nebraska Press, 2007), 39–43.

[59] Dee Brown, *Bury My Heart at Wounded Knee: An Indian History of the American West,* 30th anniversary ed. (New York: Henry Holt, 2001); Treuer, *Heartbeat of Wounded Knee.*

[60] Mark Clatterbuck, *Demons, Saints, and Patriots: Catholic Visions of Native America through the Indian Sentinel, 1902–1962* (Milwaukee, WI: Marquette University Press, 2009), 55–101.

[61] For example, Robert Allen Warrior of the Osage Nation rejects the traditional interpretation of the Bible in relation to American Indian experience. Robert Allen Warrior, "Canaanites, Cowboys, and Indians: Deliverance, Conquest, and Liberation Theology Today," in *Native and Christian: Indigenous Voices on Religious Identity in the United States and Canada,* ed. James Treat (New York: Routledge, 1996), 93–100, 101–3.

American form and abandoned traditional Native American practices; these people sometimes strongly oppose any synthesis of Christian and Native symbols. Still others, however, accepted the Christian faith while in some way continuing to practice their indigenous religious traditions. Despite the history of harsh conflicts, brutal injustice, negative prejudgments, and bitter misunderstandings, there emerged Native Christian communities marked by faith, hope, and love. American Indian Catholics have long pondered to what degree it is appropriate to incorporate aspects of their traditional religious practice into their Catholic worship, and they have differing views on this question.

In the region that is today the Southwest of the United States, many Spanish Franciscans allowed much of the Pueblo religion to continue alongside Catholic practices. In some cases, this resulted in a type of compartmentalization, which continues into the present in the Yaqui Catholic community and in many other communities. Muriel Thayer Painter describes the Yaqui patterns: "Some of the native concepts have been integrated into the Catholic way; some have been reinterpreted; some remain untouched. All are intertwined, and it is difficult and often impossible to separate them. Most of the people see no inconsistencies in their expression of religion."[62] Many Native Catholics celebrate the Catholic sacraments while continuing to perform the traditional rituals of their peoples. In contrast to earlier Catholic missionaries who forcefully rejected the use of peyote as part of a spurious religion, more recent Native Catholics combine peyote with Catholic practice.[63] The website of the Taos Pueblo in New Mexico states,

> The Pueblo Indians are about 90% Catholic. Catholicism is practiced along with ancient Indian religious rites which are an important part of Taos Pueblo life. The Pueblo religion is very complex; however, there is no conflict with the Catholic church, as evidenced by the presence of both church and kiva in the village.[64]

Often American Indians do not follow a European American, linear, logical manner of thinking but accept instead a spatial approach to thinking "that permits two very different modes of consciousness to co-exist within the same spiritual space. Or better, two different modes of observance co-exist with the traditional aboriginal consciousness."[65] Achiel Peelman, an Oblate of Mary Immaculate originally from Belgium, describes much of Native American Catholic experience

---

[62] Muriel Thayer Painter, Refugio Savala, and Ignacio Alvarez, *A Yaqui Easter Sermon* (Tucson: University of Arizona Press, 1986), 71, quoted in Christopher Vecsey, *On the Padres' Trail*, vol. I of *American Indian Catholics* (Notre Dame, IN: University of Notre Dame Press, 1996), 78.

[63] Carl Starkloff, *A Theology of the In-Between: The Value of Syncretic Process* (Milwaukee, WI: Marquette University Press, 2002), 121–26.

[64] The Pueblo: Over 1,000 Years of Tradition, http://taospueblo.com/about/.

[65] Starkloff, "Native American Catholic Experience," 234.

"as religious dimorphism: the simultaneous or successive belonging to two religious systems."[66]

There have been various ways in which Catholics have combined Native American and Catholic practices. In 1883, Francis M. Craft, a Catholic priest who was partly of Mohawk descent, opened the ceremonies of the Sun Dance at the Rosebud reservation with a prayer.[67] He reportedly wore eagle feathers and participated as fully as possible in the ceremonies.[68] Craft compared the Sun Dance with the Eucharist, launching a tradition that would stress the similarity between Catholic and Lakota practices.[69]

Black Elk

Perhaps the most famous American Indian to practice both the Catholic faith and an American Indian religious tradition was Nicholas Black Elk.[70] Born in 1863 into a family of medicine people in Dakota Territory in present-day Wyoming, Black Elk received a powerful vision when he was nine years old. Franciscan Sister Marie Therese Archambault, who is Lakota born, a member of the Teton Sioux raised on the Standing Rock and Rosebud reservations in South Dakota, describes Black Elk's experience:

> He lost consciousness for twelve days. During this twelve-day coma-like period, a great vision of the cosmic completion and fullness of his Lakota world flooded his soul. In it were the powers and directions of the earth and sky: the powerful *wakinyan* (thunder and lightning spirits of the West); the grandfathers of the Lakota cosmos; the powerful horses of the four directions; the morning star; animal and herb spirits. All spoke to him. He was never the same again and the spirit world's choice of him marked his life to his dying day.[71]

---

[66] Achiel Peelman, *Christ Is a Native American* (Ottawa, CN: Novalis-Saint Paul University, 1995), 158.

[67] A few years after this event, Craft began keeping a journal of his experiences: Francis M. Craft, *At Standing Rock and Wounded Knee: The Journals and Papers of Father Francis M. Craft, 1888–1890*, ed. and annot. Thomas W. Foley (Norman, OK: Arthur H. Clark, 2009).

[68] Letter of R. H. Pratt of November 25, 1883; Clyde Holler, *Black Elk's Religion: The Sun Dance and Lakota Catholicism* (Syracuse, NY: Syracuse University Press, 1995), 123.

[69] Thomas W. Foley, *Father Francis M. Craft: Missionary to the Sioux* (Lincoln, NE: University of Nebraska Press, 2002), 49; Damien Costello, *Black Elk: Colonialism and Lakota Catholicism* (Maryknoll, NY: Orbis Books, 2005), 35.

[70] For an overview of his life, see Raymond J. DeMallie, ed., *The Sixth Grandfather: Black Elk's Teachings Given to John G. Neihardt* (Lincoln: University of Nebraska Press, 1985), 1–74.

[71] Marie Therese Archambault, *A Retreat with Black Elk: Living in the Sacred Hoop* (Cincinnati, OH: St. Anthony Messenger Press, 1998), 17; see also Black Elk, *Black Elk Speaks: Being the Life Story of a Holy Man of the Oglala Sioux as Told through John G.*

Black Elk's experience of the spirit world calling him had a lasting impact on him. He became a leader in the Ghost Dances, and many dancers received visions when he held up the red flowering stick, as he later recalled: "I was the leader in every dance. Soon I had developed so much power that even if I would stand in the center of the circle and wave this red stick, the people would fall into swoons without dancing and see their visions."[72] In 1904, Black Elk entered the Catholic Church and was baptized by Joseph Lindebner, SJ, with the Christian name Nicholas. However, he did not entirely relinquish his Native spiritual path. For many years he served as a Catholic catechist, but brought traditional perspectives and practices to the Catholic faith. In 1922, he celebrated the Catholic feast of Corpus Christi by dressing in traditional costume and leading a sacred dance to honor the presence of Christ in the Eucharist.[73] As a Catholic, Black Elk compared the sufferings in the Sun Dance to the passion of Christ.[74] In bringing together different traditions, there can be a mutual transformation. Black Elk interpreted the incarnation of God in Jesus Christ in relation to the incarnation of God in White Buffalo Cow Woman among American Indians.[75] According to Black Elk's daughter, Lucy Looks Twice, the German Jesuit missioner Eugene Buechel taught that the Blessed Virgin Mary was the figure who brought the sacred pipe, thereby identifying her with the White Buffalo Woman; Lucy Looks Twice adds that "that was what we always thought."[76]

In 1929, Black Elk recounted his life and Indian practices to John Neihardt, who published the testimonies in 1932 as *Black Elk Speaks*. The publication caused a controversy, since many Jesuit priests were shocked by Black Elk's continuing commitment to traditional Lakota religious perspectives. In 1933, Black Elk was injured by a wagon and team of horses and asked for the last rites of the Catholic Church. Upon recovering, he signed documents that appeared to recant the remarks in *Black Elk Speaks* and that claimed Neihardt had omitted Black Elk's comments on his Catholic faith.[77] Black Elk continued to be involved in both traditional Lakota rituals and also in Catholic sacramental life. Neihardt returned in

---

Neihardt (Flaming Rainbow) (1932; reprint, Lincoln: University of Nebraska Press, 1988), 20–47.

[72] DeMallie, *Sixth Grandfather*, 266.

[73] Ibid., 25.

[74] Costello, *Black Elk*, 120.

[75] Amanda Porterfield, "Black Elk's Significance in American Culture," in *The Black Elk Reader*, ed. Clyde Holler (Syracuse, NY: Syracuse University Press, 2000), 55. See also Joseph E. Brown, *The Sacred Pipe: Black Elk's Account of the Seven Rites of the Oglala Sioux* (Norman: University of Oklahoma Press, 1974).

[76] Michael F. Steltenkamp, *Black Elk: Holy Man of the Oglala* (Norman, OK: University of Oklahoma Press, 1993), 107.

[77] The documents are published in Marie Therese Archambault, Mark G. Thiel, and Christopher Vecsey, eds., *The Crossing of Two Roads: Being Catholic and Native in the United States* (Maryknoll, NY: Orbis Books, 2003), 138–40; see also Christopher Vecsey, *Where The Two Roads Meet* (Notre Dame, IN: University of Notre Dame Press, 1999), 40.

1944 to conduct another round of interviews with Black Elk.[78] Moreover, in 1947 and 1948, Joseph Epes Brown lived with Black Elk's family and recorded many experiences, including ceremonies and rituals.[79]

Black Elk poses a challenge to interpreters, and there has been much controversy over what to make of his journey. Christopher Vecsey comments that "he interpreted some of his Catholicism through the Lakota worldview, thinking, e.g., of retreats as if they were vision quests. On the other hand, his interviews with Neihardt betrayed a Christian universalism, a peaceful moralism, that seemed to have reinterpreted Lakota traditions through Christian consciousness."[80] Vecsey concludes that "Black Elk was a 'creative theologian' who was able to understand two religious traditions in terms of the other."[81]

Damian Costello stresses the integration of the two paths: "For Black Elk, Lakota tradition and Catholicism were not the two disparate systems that [Julian] Rice and [William K.] Powers describe. Rather, as Ben Black Bear argued, they composed one way of looking at the world."[82] Citing the influential work of Jesuit scholar Walter Ong on *Orality and Literacy*, Costello stresses that in oral cultures, "Originality does not come from completely new systems of knowledge but by incorporating new ideas into the established framework of knowledge. The old formulas and themes are made to interact with new and complicated situations, 'but the formulas and themes are reshuffled rather than supplanted with new materials.'"[83] Costello sees Black Elk as applying "the internal dynamics of Lakota tradition to his understanding of Christian thought."[84]

Marie Therese Archambault has also pondered the path of Black Elk as both a practicing Lakota religious leader and a Catholic catechist: "Perhaps he was unable to totally abandon the truth and universality of either his Lakota way or his Catholic convictions, even though their expressions of this truth at times seemed contradictory. Or perhaps his philosophy was a synthesis of both that transcended these contradictions. This we will never know for sure."[85] The example of Black Elk has shaped Archambault's path, as she acknowledges,

> In maturing, I've learned that the truth, for me, lies in the union of the
> Lakota ways and the Catholic faith. . . . I write from that uncomfortable

---

[78] John G. Neihardt, *When the Tree Flowered: The Story of Eagle Voice, a Sioux Indian*, new ed. (Lincoln, NE: University of Nebraska Press, 1991).

[79] Black Elk, *The Sacred Pipe: Black Elk's Account of the Seven Rites of the Oglala Sioux*, recorded and ed. Joseph Epes Brown (1953; reprint, Norman, OK: University of Oklahoma Press, 1989).

[80] Vecsey, *Where the Two Roads Meet*, 41.

[81] Ibid., 42.

[82] Costello, *Black Elk*, 77.

[83] Ibid.; Costello is citing Walter J. Ong, *Orality and Literacy: The Technologizing of the Word* (New York: Methuen, 1982), 42.

[84] Costello, *Black Elk*, 79.

[85] Archambault, *Retreat with Black Elk*, 8.

place, where millions of the globe's inhabitants are thrust now, with no secure home, no freedom to live according to their cultural heritage.[86]

Many have found inspiration in the example of Black Elk. In August 2016, the Roman Catholic Diocese of Rapid City, South Dakota, initiated the process for the canonization of Black Elk. Many now invoke him as a Servant of God, and the diocese hopes that he will soon be declared venerable. Students at the Red Cloud Indian School on the Pine Ridge Reservation have a shrine to Black Elk where they ask him to pray for them.[87]

Traditional Practices and Catholic Life

Archambault describes how American Indian Catholic women have retrieved traditional myths, stories, and rituals for the rite of passage of a girl into womanhood. She notes especially the influence of the White Buffalo Calf Story, which Nicholas Black Elk told to Joseph Epes Brown in 1947 and which exists in many variations, upon American Indian women today. The White Buffalo Calf Woman "brings the Sacred Pipe and life-giving instructions to people who have asked God for help. . . . This story has deeply touched contemporary Native American women and moved them to take action in their lives."[88] Archambault expresses the hope: "The White Buffalo Calf Woman goes further and points to a society that lives in respect on the earth, with a balance between men and women, in awareness of one God as source of life, who nourishes our deepest hungers, even those we do not know."[89]

A number of Lakota Catholics, including Frank Fools Crow, Gilbert Bad Wound, and Lucy Looks Twice, have interpreted the Sun Dance as a Christian ceremony in which the dancers become close to God by imitating Christ's sufferings.[90] The Lakota Catholic conferences in the twentieth century celebrated the Eucharist beneath a Sun Dance pole.[91] A number of Catholic priests in the late nineteenth and early twentieth centuries allowed Indians to light their sacred pipes during the Eucharist.[92]

---

[86] Ibid., 38.

[87] "Curia Corner: Servant of God Nicholas Black Elk, Pray for Us," website of the Diocese of Rapid City, SD, https://www.rapidcitydiocese.org/curia-corner-servant-of-god-nicholas-black-elk-pray-for-us/.

[88] Marie Therese Archambault, "American Indian Women and the Power of Myth," *Chicago Studies* 42, no. 3 (2003): 244.

[89] Ibid., 250.

[90] Costello, *Black Elk,* 119–20.

[91] Ibid., 120; Ross Alexander Enochs, "Black Elk and the Jesuits," in *The Black Elk Reader,* ed. Clyde Holler (Syracuse: Syracuse University Press, 2000), 296.

[92] Ross Alexander Enochs, *The Jesuit Mission to the Lakota Sioux: Pastoral Theology and Ministry, 1886–1945* (Kansas City, MO: Sheed & Ward, 1996), 138–39.

In recent years, the Catholic Church, like many other Christian communities, has gone through a profound reassessment of its relationship to other religions and to non-European cultures. As we have seen, the Second Vatican Council also declared that the Catholic Church "is not committed to any one culture."[93] The Council recognized that the Catholic Church had long drawn on the concepts and images of many different peoples and profits from a variety of cultures.[94]

This reassessment set the stage for new developments in the Catholic Church's relation to American Indians. On a visit to the United States in 1987, Pope John Paul II addressed Native American Catholics:

> I encourage you as native people to preserve and keep alive your cultures, your languages, the values and customs which have served you well in the past and which provide a solid foundation for the future. Your encounter with the Gospel has not only enriched you; it has enriched the church. We are well aware that this has not taken place without its difficulties and, occasionally, its blunders. However . . . the Gospel does not destroy what is best in you. On the contrary, it enriches spiritual qualities and gifts that are distinctive of your cultures. . . . All consciences must be challenged. There are real injustices to be addressed and biased attitudes to be challenged.[95]

John Paul II proclaimed that "not only is Christianity relevant to the Indian peoples, but *Christ, in the members of his Body, is himself Indian.*"[96] In a similar vein, Steve Charleston, a member of the Choctaw Nation and the sixth bishop of the Episcopal Diocese of Alaska, also endorses this principle:

> In the Pauline sense, I can assert that while as a man Jesus was a Jew, as the risen Christ, he is a Navajo. Or a Kiowa. Or a Choctaw. Or any other tribe. The Christ does not violate my own Old Testament. The coming of the Christ does not erase the memory banks of Native America or force me to throw away centuries of God's revealing acts among my People.[97]

---

[93] Vatican Council II, *Pastoral Constitution on the Church in the Modern World* (*Gaudium et Spes*) # 42, in Vatican Council II, *The Conciliar and Postconciliar Documents,* vol. 1, rev. ed., ed. Austin Flannery (Northport, NY: Costello and Dublin, Ireland: Dominican Publications, 2004), 1:942.

[94] Vatican II, *Gaudium et Spes* # 44.

[95] Pope John Paul II, "Address to the Native Peoples of the Americas," Memorial Stadium, Phoenix, AZ, September 14, 1987. United States Conference of Catholic Bishops, "Time for Remembering, Reconciling and Recommitting Ourselves as a People," *Origins* 21, no. 31 (1992): 498–99.

[96] Pope John Paul II, Homily for Liturgy of the Word with the Native Peoples of Canada, Martyrs' Shrine (Huronia), September 15, 1984.

[97] Steve Charleston, "The Old Testament of Native America," in *Native and Christian: Indigenous Voices on Religious Identity in the United States and Canada,* ed. James Treat (New York: Routledge, 1996), 78.

Following the lead of Vatican II and Pope John Paul II, the Catholic bishops of the United States publicly admitted the profoundly ambiguous character of the original encounters between Catholics and Native Americans, including problems and tragedies:

> We also acknowledge that the encounter with the Europeans was often a "harsh and painful one" for native peoples, and we lament the diseases, death, destruction, injustices and disrespect for native ways and traditions which came with it. We recognize that: "Often they (European Christians) failed to distinguish between what was crucial to the Gospel and what were matters of cultural preference. That failure brought with it catastrophic consequences for the native peoples, who were at times forced to become European at the same time they became Christian."[98]

The bishops strongly affirm that "Native American Catholics are called to be both true Catholic believers and authentic Native Americans. Far from being incompatible, these two traditions—the Catholic way and the native way—enrich each other and the whole church."[99] Between 1994 and 2001, the Ad Hoc Committee on Native American Catholics of the United States Conference of Catholic Bishops asked dioceses about the lives of their Native populations, including the degree to which Native American Catholics incorporate traditional rituals and symbols into their prayer life. Fifty-one dioceses, representing a little less than 30 percent of those queried, responded affirmatively; it was more common to include traditional rituals and symbols in prayer on reservations and rural areas than in cities, where the diversity of tribes makes it difficult to find common symbols or rituals that could be used; some areas include Native symbols only on special occasions and others as a regular feature of Catholic prayer. Among the practices mentioned were

- Smudging (blessing, purifying) with cedar, sage, sweetgrass, and tobacco
- Eagle feather used in blessings
- Dance and drums used for liturgies
- Indian music in liturgy (one diocese noted that Br. Martin Fenerty, FSC, has composed five Masses based on Native American melodies)
- Indian naming ceremony in conjunction with baptism
- Native attire used in local and diocesan celebrations
- Four-directional prayer
- Sweat lodge
- Statues, relics of Blessed Kateri Tekakwitha
- Medicine wheel

---

[98] U.S. Conference of Catholic Bishops, "Time for Remembering," 495.
[99] Ibid., 497.

- Native crucifix and cross
- Sacred vessels, decorations, and vestments with Native designs
- Sacred pipe.[100]

In recent decades many European American Catholic ministers have been more open to recognizing the virtues of American Indian religious practices. William Stolzman, an American Jesuit, chaired the dialogues of the Rosebud Medicine Men and Pastors' Meeting during a six-year period of reflection on points of convergence and divergence between the Lakota religion and Christianity, beginning with ritual ceremonies. He later drew upon the summaries of these dialogues in writing *The Pipe and Christ*.[101] Stolzman had personal experiences of being called by the Holy Spirit from the time he was young; beginning in 1974, he made four Lakota vision quests under the guidance of Arthur Running Horse, who is both a traditional Lakota medicine man and also a Catholic leader. On the basis of his experiences, Stolzman compared the Lakota vision quest with Catholic experience of the Holy Spirit: "The Lakota spirits and the Christian Holy Spirit are the immediate, dynamic, spiritual elements within the Lakota and Christian religions. These spirits call and empower medicine men and priests."[102]

Stolzman further compared the *hanbleciya,* literally, "crying for a dream," which is commonly known as the vision quest, to Catholic retreats and to the sacraments of Confirmation and Holy Orders.[103] He compared the Lakota *Yuwipi* ceremony to the Catholic Mass, while in each case also respectfully noting differences: "The complementarity of these two rituals and religions can be clearly seen in the similar but different attitudes the Lakota and the Christian have toward the sacred foods of these two ceremonies."[104]

Based upon many years of discussions with Native Catholics, Stolzman notes four responses regarding Lakota and Christian religious traditions: (1) Some see no difference and stress that both traditions pray to the same God. (2) Some stress the important differences between the two traditions, variously noting the differences in external practices or the variety of social and religious values; some in this group are hostile to Christianity and yearn to return to an allegedly idyllic earlier period. (3) Another group stresses the similarities and seeks harmony. Of them Stolzman comments, "Regardless of the level of education, they are good people, bent on trying to establish harmony between religions. However, in so doing they often destroy the uniqueness of revelation that gives each religion its strength and

---

[100] *Native American Catholics at the Millennium: Report on a Survey Conducted by the United States Conference of Catholic Bishops Ad Hoc Committee on Native American Catholics* (Washington, DC: U.S. Conference of Catholic Bishops, 2002), 11–12.

[101] William Stolzman, *The Pipe and Christ*, 7th ed. (Chamberlain, SD: Tipi Press, 2002).

[102] Ibid., 74.

[103] Ibid., 77–79.

[104] Ibid., 146.

place in religious history."[105] Finally, (4) Stolzman noted a group "who are able to appreciate both the similarities and differences of both religions and keep them in their respective places. Like the pivot of a teeter-totter, these people find fulfillment by first going to one side and then to the other and back again. . . . Thus the two traditions are always in constant relationship with one another."[106] In the dialogues, leaders of each tradition expressed concern that a combination could lead to the loss of identity of one side or the other, and the vice president, Moses, commented, "We are not here to combine the two religions. We are here to understand one another and to respect one another."[107] The goal of the group was to find an explanation in which "both similarities and differences had to be simultaneously recognized. . . . Just as two people do not have to be exactly alike to marry—so too, two religions, like the Lakota and the Christian religions, need not be made equivalent to be brought together in a fruitful interrelationship."[108]

Stolzman notes that Lakota Catholics often practice both Lakota and Catholic rituals, while traditional Lakota leaders are generally resistant to any incorporation of Catholic elements into traditional rituals.[109] Stolzman acknowledges weakness and imperfections in both traditions, and he suggests that "both religions together provide a stronger ladder with which to ascend toward the Sacred. In summary, the theological legitimacy of this position is grounded in a Lakota-Christian's respect for the Unity of God and the progressive distinction of Persons in the Trinity as well as the four Sacred Powers placed by God in the Four Directions."[110] He concludes with a nuanced defense of entering into both traditions, proposing that "a person can practice the Lakota religion in a totally orthodox way and also practice the Christian religion in a totally orthodox way—each at its appropriate time—both with a faith and interrelationship that encompasses the real situation of the individual, bringing blessing from God."[111]

In a variety of ways many American Indian Catholics today draw upon both the Catholic and the Native religious traditions in their spiritual journeys. Crow Catholics in Montana perform the Sun Dance and participate in other traditional Crow ceremonies.[112] Kiowas in southwestern Oklahoma combine traditional songs and Christian hymns.[113] What concrete form this should take is a subject of intense ongoing discussion and debate. Some Native Catholics have called for

---

[105] Ibid., 208–9.

[106] Ibid., 209.

[107] Ibid.

[108] Ibid.

[109] Ibid., 213.

[110] Ibid., 214.

[111] Ibid., 218.

[112] Mark Clatterbuck, ed., *Crow Jesus: Personal Stories of Native Religious Belonging* (Norman: University of Oklahoma Press, 2017).

[113] Luke Eric Lassiter, *The Jesus Road: Kiowas, Christianity, and Indian Hymns* (Lincoln: University of Nebraska Press, 2002).

the establishment of a new rite of the Catholic Church, analogous to the Eastern rites of the Catholic Church, with a distinctive cultural form and the use of the languages of the people. Most, however, do not support this option. Paul Ojibway, a Franciscan Friar of the Atonement from the Ojibwa People of Minnesota, comments, "The vast majority of Catholic Native Americans . . . do not call for a separate life, but only the space and time in which to develop our own ecclesial sense of ourselves that is integrated and grounded both in traditional life and in post-Vatican II theological praxis."[114] He names the challenge:

> We do know that the heart and soul of the Native American has not yet been put into the language and ritual of Christian faith. This is the challenge we bring to the church—to seek out a grammar of assent together. . . . It is to learn from the vision quest, that journey into the unknown where we meet our angels and devils and find a new purpose, hope and name. It is to trust the sweat lodge, the kiva, the talking circle, the medicine wheel—all those rites of healing renewal.[115]

Some Native American Catholics engage in dual practice, celebrating their traditional rituals in one context and also the Catholic sacraments in another context. Frank Fools Crow, a nephew of Nicholas Black Elk and one of the most respected Lakota holy men of his time, became a Roman Catholic in June 1917, while continuing to practice traditional Lakota rituals. He commented in interviews with Thomas E. Mails in the 1970s:

> I am still a practicing Roman Catholic. I go to Mass once or twice a month, and I receive Holy Communion whenever I can. . . . At the same time, we live according to the traditional religious beliefs and customs of our people, and we find few problems with the differences between the two.[116]

He noted that the greatest problem was the harsh Catholic condemnations of Lakota practices, but he acknowledged this had changed: "Some of the things the new faiths said were hard to take, especially their belief that we did not know the true God and that Sioux medicine and ceremonies were things of the Devil. So we

---

[114] Paul Ojibway, "A Call to Native Americans," in *The People: Reflections of Native Peoples on the Catholic Experience in North America* (Washington, DC: National Catholic Educational Association, 1992), 47.

[115] Paul Ojibway, "A Call to the Church," in *The People: Reflections of Native Peoples on the Catholic Experience in North America* (Washington, DC: National Catholic Educational Association, 1992), 66, 67.

[116] Thomas D. Mails, *Fools Crow,* with Dallas Chief Eagle (Garden City, NY: Doubleday, 1979), 45.

rejected these views until their positions began to change."[117] He recalled his uncle Black Elk's perspective:

> When he and I were discussing it one day, Black Elk told me he had decided that the Sioux religious way of life was pretty much the same as that of the Christian churches, and there was no reason to change what the Sioux were doing. We could pick up some of the Christian ways and teachings, and just work them in with our own, so in the end both would be better. Like myself, Black Elk prayed constantly that all peoples would live as one and would cooperate with one another.[118]

Fools Crow explained the practice of piercing in the Sun Dance in relation to the sufferings of Jesus Christ: "The other Indian tribes must speak for themselves, but the Sioux feel a special closeness to God in the dance and in the piercing and flesh offerings. We even duplicate Christ's crown of thorns in the sage head wreath the pledgers wear."[119] Fools Crow also noted that some Lakota have experienced the sacred tree in the Sun Dance as becoming like warm human flesh, and he compared this experience with Jesus on the cross: "So the tree, even though its growth is stopped, becomes a living thing for us. It becomes human, and it dies for us like Jesus on the cross for everyone."[120]

The annual meetings of the Kateri Tekakwitha Conference include Native spiritual forms in Catholic prayer; there emerges a new type of pan–Native American symbolism, which may seem strange to members of some Nations. There is an intense debate going on today concerning the extent to which Catholic ceremonies should include Native American symbols and traditions; at times the disputes have been fierce over the appropriate limits for appropriating Native symbols into Catholic worship. During decades of ministry among the Arapaho and Ojibwa peoples, Carl Starkloff witnessed their discernment concerning what syncretic actions were appropriate; he comments on the acceptance of a certain form of dance:

> Thus the inclusion of native dancing at Christian worship demands extensive conversation with native leaders. During my own pastorate in the late 1970s on the Wind River Reservation, elders saw value in including a very restrained "donation dance" before the Cross on Good Friday, at which the people could place small donations of money saved through abstinence for the sake of a gift for the poor.[121]

---

117 Ibid.
118 Ibid.
119 Ibid., 136
120 Ibid., 133.
121 Starkloff, *Theology of the In-Between*, 93.

The Arapaho rejected any use of their sacred pipe during a Catholic liturgy, but other Indian Nations have found this appropriate.

Raymond A. Bucko, a Jesuit anthropologist, has studied the Lakota ritual of the sweat lodge, participated in numerous sweats, and interviewed a number of participants. He found a basic form in the ritual combined with a wide variety of practices and interpretations; he also discovered a wide variety of ways of relating the sweat lodge experience to Christianity. There was a widespread assumption "that all these systems deal with the same divine being and behavioral requirements."[122] This allowed some to incorporate Christian practices into the practice of the sweat lodge—one practitioner stated, "It doesn't matter how you pray. You can use Christ in there—in certain lodges. In my friend's lodge, he won't say nothing but it bothers him afterward if they use Christ."[123] Another person recalled a medicine man telling him,

> Jesus was the greatest of all medicine men. . . . There is no contradiction between Lakota and Christian beliefs. Jesus told a young man, in order to gain entry to heaven give up all worldly possessions and follow him. Indians by virtue of our history and beliefs are able to do that.[124]

There is no consensus on how to manage the relation between Christianity and traditional practices among the Lakota that Bucko interviewed, and often the discussions are passionate over whether to include traditional elements in Catholic worship.[125] When non-Native Catholic priests have prayed with the sacred pipe at Mass and at funeral services, some Lakota have been pleased, but others have felt resentment because they believed only the Lakota had the right to use such symbols in sacred contexts. Some Lakota oppose any appropriation of their traditions, rituals, and symbols by other communities, whether the Catholic Church or New Age movements. Bucko notes:

> There is controversy also over the often stated contention that Lakota religion and symbols are universal and therefore for everyone. This is particularly true as Lakota religion is cast more and more in the mold of an ecological spirituality. Thus some Lakotas object to ceremonies performed for and sometimes by non-Lakotas.[126]

In some cases a major part of the problem has been that some non-Native Catholic priests assumed that they knew what was best without consulting the Lakota

---

    [122] Raymond A. Bucko, *The Lakota Ritual of the Sweat Lodge: History and Contemporary Practice* (Lincoln: University of Nebraska Press, 1998), 177.

    [123] Ibid., 193.

    [124] Ibid., 194.

    [125] Ibid., 240.

    [126] Ibid.

themselves; this continued older patterns of paternalism where non-Native Catholic missioners made all the major decisions.

The Archbishop Emeritus of Philadelphia, Charles Chaput, OFM Cap, comes from the Potawatomi people. In 1995, when he was the bishop of Rapid City, South Dakota, he addressed this challenge by forming the Lakota Inculturation Task Force. The Task Force included twenty-five Lakota people, who were advised by three priests with professional expertise; the priests were, however, not to dictate any conclusions. The Lakota people themselves studied Lakota culture and tradition in relation to Catholic theology and worship, discerning what traditional Lakota symbols could be appropriately used in Catholic prayer and what aspects of Lakota life were in accord with Catholic practice. They also reflected on Lakota philosophy and theology with a view to developing an authentic Lakota form of Catholic faith.[127] The members of the Task Force made recommendations regarding the use of the drum and the sacred pipe, the sage incense blessing, and traditional songs. Some of these suggestions, especially concerning the sacred pipe, were highly controversial. The Task Force stressed that only the Lakota people themselves should use their traditional symbols and rituals and lead Lakota ceremonies. The Task Force also proposed that in each local community the Lakota decide which traditional symbols and rites would be incorporated into Catholic services; public notice would be given beforehand so that those who opposed such practices could absent themselves. The Task Force insisted that it was not proposing the creation of a new, separate Lakota rite for the Catholic liturgy.

The responses from the Lakota were varied and conflicting. Some traditional Catholics remembered that they had been taught to abandon all Lakota religious ways, and they did not want to reverse this practice. Some, on the other end of the spectrum, rejected the Catholic Church altogether and were opposed to Catholic attempts to use any Lakota symbols in Catholic worship. Some of these believed that one could not be both Lakota and Catholic. Still another group consisted of those who wanted to draw upon both the Catholic and the Lakota heritages. In contrast to both the other groups, they insist that they are both authentically Lakota and also truly Catholic. While not wanting to impose their practice of inculturation on traditional Catholics, they insist, in accordance with contemporary Catholic teaching, that the use of Lakota symbols is appropriate and beneficial and needs to become an option for regular worship. Such questions continue to be a matter for ongoing discernment among American Indians themselves.

While there continues to be tremendous diversity of perspectives on these issues, Alfretta Antone eloquently expressed the spirit and hope of Native American Catholics to Pope John Paul II during his visit to Phoenix, Arizona:

---

[127] Raymond Bucko and John Hatcher, "Principles of Inculturation and the Practice of Catholicism among the Lakota People of South Dakota," *Chicago Studies* 42, no. 3 (2003): 258–61.

We choose not only to survive, but to live fully. We want to live in harmony with all people and all creation. We choose to keep alive for all generations the ways of living carved in the stones and bones of our ancestors. We are open to share and receive whatever is good for the life of the human family with all people of good will . . . . As Catholic Natives, we have come to know Jesus as the Son of God who loves us and lives with us. The Holy Spirit works in many ways through our people.[128]

Often the most powerful expressions are in ritual. In 1984, Dominic Eshka-kogan, a Catholic deacon who is also a medicine man in the Ojibway tradition, performed a sweetgrass ceremony for Pope John Paul II at the Shrine of the Canadian Martyrs, at the same spot where the Huron mission of the seventeenth century had been established. Eshkakogan described this as "One of the greatest experiences of my native spirituality. . . . I felt real acceptance of my traditions by the Church, personified by the Pope."[129] The papal affirmation of Native Catholic experience and spirituality encourages further exploration and development of both theology and practice.

Doctrine of Discovery Revisited

Meanwhile, the so-called doctrine of discovery and its history of effects continue to be contentious issues in relations with indigenous peoples today, as the doctrine remains a factor in some national and international legal discussions concerning the lands of indigenous peoples. In 2007, the General Assembly of the United Nations overwhelmingly approved the Declaration on the Rights of Indigenous Peoples. Only four nations voted against it, each of whose histories was decisively shaped by the doctrine of discovery: the United States, Canada, Australia, and New Zealand.[130]

On May 4, 2016, American Indian leaders traveled to Rome, where they met briefly with Pope Francis and then for a more extended time with Archbishop Silvano Tomasi who was assisting Cardinal Peter Turkson, then President of the Pontifical Council for Peace and Justice, in creating the new Dicastery for Promoting Integral Human Development. In the delegation were leaders of the Haudenosaunee, the Six Nations Iroquois Confederacy, the Oglala Sioux,

---

[128] Alfretta Antone, "Address to Pope John Paul II," *Origins* 17, no. 17 (1987): 296; Marie Therese Archambault, "Native Americans and Evangelization," in *The People: Reflections of Native Peoples on the Catholic Experience in North America*, ed. Suzanne E. Hall (Washington, DC: National Catholic Educational Association, 1992, 36.

[129] Christopher Vecsey, *American Indian Catholics*, vol. 2, *The Paths of Kateri's Kin* (Notre Dame, IN: University of Notre Dame Press, 1997), 2:237.

[130] Robert J. Miller, Jacinta Ruru, Larissa Behrendt, and Tracey Lindberg, *Discovering Indigenous Lands: The Doctrine of Discovery in the English Colonies* (Oxford: Oxford University Press, 2010), 1.

the Cayuse, Shawnee, Mapuche, Navajo Diné and Apache Ndee nations.[131] The indigenous leaders urged that Pope Francis rescind the doctrine of discovery, which was promulgated in various papal bulls of the fifteenth century, notably *Inter Caetera,* issued by Pope Alexander VI on May 4, 1493. Kahnawake Mohawk Kenneth Deer, who represents the Iroquois Confederacy Council in international relations, presented the proposal to Pope Francis, who simply replied, "I will pray for you."[132] Deer described the subsequent meeting with Archbishop Tomasi. Originally the Vatican representatives appeared defensive, commenting that the bulls were issued a long time ago and had already been rescinded by other papal teachings. When Deer pointed out that governments in North America continue to rely on these bulls as legal precedents for decisions today, Tomasi shifted somewhat. Deer commented, "By the time we had done with him he was changing his position. At the end he said, 'Maybe the Vatican does have to make a statement'"; Deer added, "He didn't say rescind, he said abolish—a much stronger word—he said we have to abolish the papal bulls and that maybe there should be an apology from the pope."[133] Himko Kaps Kap (Cayuse) commented on the significance of this meeting: "There is no doubt that the mere fact of the visit to the Vatican signals a tectonic shift in relations between the Vatican and indigenous peoples. . . . Surely this is a step forward."[134] As of this writing, the Holy See has not responded publicly to this intervention.

On May 31, 2018, leaders of the Rosebud Sioux Tribe sent a letter to Pope Francis requesting that he renounce the doctrine of discovery and the papal bulls that established it.[135] During the Synod of Bishops on the Amazon in October 2019, representatives of the Rosebud Sioux Tribe traveled to Rome hoping to present a letter to Pope Francis renewing this request.[136] They did not meet with Pope Francis, but Rodney M. Bordeaux, the chairman of the tribe, spoke at an event alongside the Synod on the Amazon, comparing the situation of American Indians to the indigenous peoples of the Amazon region.[137] To date, the Holy See has not issued a public retraction of the doctrine of discovery or the papal bulls relating to it.

---

[131] Himko Kaps Kap (Cayuse), "The Creator Has Been Heard," http:// longmarchtorome.com/the-creator-has-been-heard/.

[132] Paul Barnsley, "Church Considering Request to Rescind Doctrine of Discovery," *APTN News,* June 1, 2016, http://aptn.ca/news/2016/06/01/church-considering-request-to-rescind-doctrine-of-discovery/.

[133] Ibid.

[134] Himko Kaps Kap (Cayuse), "The Creator Has Been Heard," http:// longmarchtorome.com/the-creator-has-been-heard/.

[135] Jim Kent, "Rosebud Tribe Asks Pope to Renounce Papal Bulls," *Lakota County Times,* May 31, 2018.

[136] "Indigenous People from US Arrive to Rome to Ask Pope to Revoke Ancient Bull," *Rome Reports,* October 18, 2019.

[137] Inés San Martin, "Sioux Leader Says Amazon Is Dakotas 120 Years Ago," *Crux,* October 17, 2019.

Mestizaje: Latino/a Catholic Experiences

The flowing together of American Indian and Catholic traditions is of great significance for Hispanic Catholics in the United States. Virgilio Elizondo spoke for many Latino/as in foretelling "The Future is Mestizo."[138] There is considerable variety within each of these sources, and the result is a multitextured religious experience that draws many different traditions into a new series of convergences. The popular religiosity widely practiced throughout the Latino/a world draws especially from indigenous traditions and, in many cases, from African traditions as well. Miguel De La Torre and Edwin David Aponte explain the meaning of popular religion: "The religion is 'popular' because the disenfranchised are responsible for its creation, making it a religion of the marginalized. The emphasis is on *el pueblo* as opposed to the elite. Popular religion becomes the expression of the creativity of the popular classes. It is dynamic."[139] Appearing in many different forms in many different places, popular religiosity unites the variety of traditions with the needs and aspirations of people in specific contexts. The Afro-Caribbean tradition known as *Santería* honors the African spirits in relation to Catholic saints and practices, but it is not generally considered a form of Christianity.[140]

Popular Latino/a Catholicism often centered on activities in the home (sometimes called the domestic church), where women played decisive leadership roles. The dominant Anglo Protestant culture of the United States frequently marginalized and despised Latino/a Catholics, but they found dignity in their religious practices. Orlando Espín emphasizes the particular concern of Mary for the poor as a challenge to established orders that discriminate against Latino/as:

> These Latino/a Catholics believe that Mary will hear them. Not because she is like them, but because she is *not* like those who participate in and benefit from structures that oppress and marginalize others in both church and society. The belief that Mary will (preferentially) hear the poor is, in itself, an accusation against the status quo and against those who benefit from it at the expense of the poor and marginalized.[141]

Espín notes that some forms of Marian piety are syncretic, incorporating non-Christian elements, and he cites as an example veneration of the *Virgen de la*

---

[138] Virgilio Elizondo, *The Future Is Mestizo: Life Where Cultures Meet*, rev. ed. (Boulder: University Press of Colorado, 2000).

[139] Miguel A. De La Torre and Edwin David Aponte, *Introducing Latino/a Theologies* (Maryknoll, NY: Orbis Books, 2001), 119.

[140] Joseph M. Murphy, *Santería: African Spirits in America* (Boston: Beacon Press, 1993); Joseph M. Murphy, *Santería: An African Religion in America* (Bronx, NY: Original Publications, 1989); Joseph M. Murphy, *Botánicas: Sacred Spaces of Healing and Devotion in Urban America* (Jackson: University Press of Mississippi, 2015).

[141] Orlando O. Espín, "Mary in Latino/a Catholicism: Four Types of Devotion," *New Theology Review* 23, no. 3 (2010): 19.

Caridad (Virgin of Charity) who is the patron of Cuba and who has shrines at El Cobre in Cuba and, importantly, in Miami, where many Cuban Americans venerate her. There are various versions of the founding narrative; in one account there is a young enslaved person of African descent who, together with two adult Taino brothers, discovers a statue of the Virgin floating on the water but wearing a dress that is dry. Another version presents three people, one white, one black, and one Native, who come into a storm at sea when Mary appears to them and saves them. Espín relates the latter narrative to the coming of enslaved people from the Yoruba tribe to Cuba in the nineteenth century and their practice of Lukumi religious traditions, which include veneration of Oshún, who is associated with gold, yellow, copper, and glass. Cubans venerating the Virgen de la Caridad offered the same gifts that were traditionally presented to Oshún. Espín comments,

> Many Cuban-American Catholics have invested the *Virgen de la Caridad* with stories and practices that originated in the Yoruba veneration of Oshún. They sincerely believe that they are only devoted to Caridad, and they intentionally might be, while they seem unaware that some of their devout practices came from the veneration of Oshún.[142]

The multiple strands of Hispanic popular religiosity offer opportunities for enriching the life of the entire community.

Influence of African Religious Traditions

In addition to the indigenous religious traditions of the Americas, the religious traditions of Africa contributed to the interreligious texture of Christian practice in America. There has been considerable debate over the degree to which enslaved Africans and African Americans continued to practice and be influenced by the religious traditions of Africa. Jon Butler maintains that there were three stages in which (1) "a spiritual holocaust . . . effectively destroyed traditional African traditional religious *systems*, but not all particular or discrete religious practices" (1680–1760); (2) "collective religious practice of both Christian and African sorts emerged"; and (3) there was "a collective Christian practice among slaves more fully European in its character than would ever subsequently be true, as slave and free black Christianity became increasingly Afro-American *after* 1800."[143]

Based on his study of Christianity in Africa, John Thornton stresses the importance of African Christianity for shaping the practice of Christianity among Africans in the Americas. In West Africa a number of free, powerful Africans accepted Christianity and shaped an African Christian cosmology that would be very influential on both sides of the Atlantic. Thornton criticizes scholars who

---

[142] Ibid., 23.

[143] Jon Butler, *Awash in a Sea of Faith: Christianizing the American People* (Cambridge, MA: Harvard University Press, 1990), 153.

have assumed that African cosmologies were static and fixed. He emphasizes the dynamic, changing character of African religions as the context for Africans accepting Christian revelation as complementary:

> Instead, they converted because they received "co-revelations," that is, revelations in the African tradition that dovetailed with the Christian tradition. . . . The process of conversion, therefore, was really a process of exchanging and evaluating revelations. This can explain why some Europeans accepted the revelations of African diviners and mediums, just as Africans accepted the revelations of Christianity.[144]

Thornton notes that African Christianity had a significant influence in the New World through African catechists who spread Christian faith, but the context was very different because Africans from different regions were suddenly thrown together in enslavement. "In Catholic areas of the New World, co-revelations of revelations made it easy for Africans to accept Christian revelations, at least as easy as it had been for their compatriots in Africa. Indeed, most Catholic authorities believed that Africans converted easily and indeed actively sought to be Christians."[145] In Protestant North America, however, it was not until the emotional mass meetings of the Great Awakening in the 1730s that enslaved Africans and African Americans accepted Christianity in significant numbers. Thornton notes that Baptist preaching of the Holy Spirit "provided this Christian tradition with a continuous revelation that both Euro-American Christians and the African and Afro-American slaves could share."[146]

Albert J. Raboteau has explored aspects of African religious traditions in the lives of those enslaved in America.[147] Raboteau notes that in the Catholic colonies of the Spanish, Portuguese, and French empires, enslaved people frequently combined Catholic and traditional African beliefs and practices: "Over time, some slaves did become Christian. But this did not mean that they abandoned the religious beliefs and practices of Africa. Catholic slaves continued to observe African religious customs, such as venerating ancestors and praying to African spirits."[148] Enslaved Africans often interpreted Catholic saints as different forms of the gods and spirits familiar to them in African traditions. In a similar vein, Peter Paris has argued that

---

[144] John Thornton, *Africa and Africans in the Making of the Atlantic World, 1400–1800*, 2nd ed. (Cambridge: Cambridge University Press, 1998), 255.

[145] Ibid., 268.

[146] Ibid., 270.

[147] Albert J. Raboteau, *Slave Religion: "Invisible Institution" in the Antebellum South*, updated ed. (New York: Oxford University Press, 2004), 3–150.

[148] Albert J. Raboteau, *Canaan Land: A Religious History of African Americans* (New York: Oxford University Press, 2001), 10–11.

the traditions of African peoples both on the continent and in the diaspora are diverse in cultural form yet united in their underlying spirituality. . . . I will argue that the realities of cultural diversity and the unity of African spirituality both separate and unite African and African American religious and moral traditions.[149]

As noted earlier, enslaved Muslims were generally not allowed to practice Islam openly.[150]

Anthony Pinn explores the varieties of African American religious experiences by examining the overlapping trajectories of Vodou, Santería, Islam, and Humanism in relation to each other through the years.[151] Pinn sees the black Church as empowering African Americans by drawing upon African religious trances and ecstatic behavior, such as ring shouts, in order to respond to terror:

> Ring shouts demonstrated the beauty and value of black bodies, which could do more than plow fields, in that bodies could bring people into proper relationship with God and could channel God's spirit. Such bodies had to be of profound value and worth. Through the ring shout, black bodies were redeemed in ways that fought against continuing efforts to terrorize them.[152]

Charles Joyner seeks a nuanced and balanced view of the emergence of African American religious culture:

> To underestimate the Africanity of African American Christianity is to rob the slaves of their heritage. But to overestimate the Africanity of African American Christianity is to rob the slaves of their creativity. Africans were creative in Africa; they did not cease to be creative as involuntary settlers in America. The African American Christianity that developed was neither a dark version of the Christianity preached by slaveholders nor a continuation of African religion disguised as Christianity.[153]

---

[149] Peter J. Paris, *The Spirituality of African Peoples: The Search for a Common Moral Discourse* (Minneapolis: Fortress Press, 1995), 21–22.

[150] Sylviane A. Diouf, *Servants of Allah: African Muslims Enslaved in the Americas* (New York: New York University Press, 1998).

[151] Anthony B. Pinn, *Varieties of African American Religious Experience* (Minneapolis: Fortress Press, 1998).

[152] Anthony B. Pinn, *Terror and Triumph: The Nature of Black Religion* (Minneapolis: Fortress Press, 2003), 100.

[153] Charles Joyner, "'Believer I Know': The Emergence of African American Christianity," in *Religion and American Culture: A Reader,* 2nd ed., ed. David G. Hackett (New York: Routledge, 2003), 181.

African American Catholics have chronically suffered from racial biases within the Catholic Church, and Randall Miller describes the Catholic Church in relation to African American Catholics in the Old South as a "failed mission."[154] Nonetheless, despite formidable obstacles, there emerged a thriving black Catholic community with its own leaders and identity.[155]

The many indigenous traditions of American Indians and the religious traditions coming from Africa have all contributed powerfully to shaping Catholic life as well as the broader religious landscape of the United States today. Both the American Indian and African peoples have rich traditions of wisdom that venerate the presence of God in all of nature and throughout human life. This heritage has much to teach the American Catholic community about the rhythms of creation and human life.

---

[154] Randall M. Miller, "The Failed Mission: The Catholic Church and Black Catholics in the Old South," in *Catholics in the Old South: Essays on Church and Culture,* ed. Randall M. Miller and Jon L. Wakelyn (Mascon, GA: Mercer University Press, 1999), 149–70; Gary B. Mills, "Piety and Prejudice: A Colored Catholic Community in the Antebellum South," in Miller and Wakelyn, *Catholics in the Old South,* 171–91.

[155] Cyprian Davis, *The History of Black Catholics in the United States* (New York: Crossroad, 1996).

4

JEWISH-CATHOLIC RELATIONS
IN THE UNITED STATES

Catholic relations with the Jewish community in the United States of America have witnessed both challenges and opportunities distinctive to this context. While the bitter heritage of Christian anti-Judaism in Europe influenced Jewish-Catholic relations in the New World, it did not prevail in the United States of America to the same degree as had occurred throughout most of European history; American Jews recognized that the New World offered them new opportunities usually not found in Christian-ruled Europe. In the wake of the Shoah, Catholics and other Christians devoted great energy to improving relations with Jews in the United States and elsewhere; changes in Christians' relations to Jews and Jewish religious practice are of decisive importance for all other interreligious relationships because, as Pope John Paul II commented in 1986 at the Great Synagogue in Rome, Christianity is uniquely and intrinsically related to the Jewish tradition.[1] Because the Hebrew Bible and other Jewish writings from the Septuagint form the first part of the Catholic Bible, and because Jesus and his first followers were Jews who continued Jewish practice, changes in views of Jews and Judaism have a profound effect on the self-understanding of Catholics and other Christians. The Pontifical Commission for Religious Relations with Jews comments:

> From a theological perspective, Christians need to refer to the Judaism of Jesus' time and to a degree also the Judaism that developed from it over the ages for their own self-understanding. Given Jesus' Jewish origins, coming to terms with Judaism in one way or another is indispensable for Christians.[2]

Christian relations with Jews have long been troubled by bias, but there is no agreement concerning the most appropriate language for naming prejudice against

---

[1] Pope John Paul II, "Address at the Great Synagogue of Rome," April 13, 1986.

[2] Pontifical Commission for Religious Relations with Jews, *"The Gifts and Calling Are Irrevocable" (Rom. 11:29): A Reflection on Theological Questions Pertaining to Catholic-Jewish Relations on the Occasion of the 50th Anniversary of "Nostra Aetate" (No. 4)*, December 10, 2015, #14.

Jews and Jewish religious practice. Even the word "Judaism" is itself problematic; recent scholarship indicates that this word was invented and traditionally used by people who were not Jews; Daniel Boyarin points out that traditional Jewish languages did not have a term that could be translated as Judaism, and comments that "it is used as the name of the Jewish 'religion'—itself a highly problematic term—only by writers who do not identify themselves with and by that name at all, until, it would seem, the nineteenth century."[3] David Nirenberg comments on the polemical origin of the term: "'Judaism,' then, is not only the religion of specific people with specific beliefs, but also a category, a set of ideas and attributes with which non-Jews can make sense of and criticize their world."[4] The notion that Judaism can be viewed as a religion analogous to other religions is a distinctly modern development.

Catholic leaders and many other Christians often use the term "anti-Judaism" to refer to traditional religious bias against Jews and Judaism; they often understand the terms "anti-Semitism" or "antisemitism" as referring to distinctively modern, racist biases against Jews.[5] Since some scholars accept this distinction and others question it, there is no uniform practice at the present time. Albert S. Lindemann and Richard S. Levy explain that "the modern term antisemitism came into common use in the 1880s, with a somewhat novel but hardly original notion of Jews as a material body, a race, rather than as a community of belief."[6] They note that opponents of this prejudice used the term "antisemitism" to denote unjust charges against Jews. Discussing the American context, John Corrigan and Lynn Neal comment, "Prior to 1873, the term anti-Semitism did not exist. Instead, intolerance of and hatred toward Jews came under the rubric of anti-Judaism, which denoted the ill will many American Christians held toward Judaism as a religion."[7] Mary C. Boys distinguishes "antisemitism as a cultural phenomenon" from anti-Judaism as "attitudes, arguments, polemics, and actions that distort and disparage Judaism in order to support Christian claims of superiority."[8] Some scholars make a further distinction between the terms "anti-Semitism" and "antisemitism"; in

---

[3] Daniel Boyarin, *Judaism: The Genealogy of a Modern Notion* (New Brunswick, NJ: Rutgers University Press, 2019), xi.

[4] David Nirenberg, *Anti-Judaism: The Western Tradition* (New York: W. W. Norton, 2013), 3.

[5] Pontifical Commission for Religious Relations with the Jews, *We Remember: A Reflection on the Shoah,* March 16, 1998, #4.

[6] Albert S. Lindemann and Richard S. Levy, *Antisemitism: A History* (Oxford: Oxford University Press, 2011), 6.

[7] John Corrigan and Lynn S. Neal, *Religious Intolerance in America: A Documentary History* (Chapel Hill: University of North Carolina Press, 2010), 148; see also Robert Singerman, "The Jew as Racial Alien: The Genetic Component of American Anti-Semitism," in *Anti-Semitism in American History,* ed. David A. Gerber (Urbana: University of Illinois Press, 1986), 103–28.

[8] Mary C. Boys, "Christian Feminism and Anti-Judaism," in *Seeing Judaism Anew: Christianity's Sacred Obligation,* ed. Mary C. Boys (Lanham, MD: Sheed & Ward, 2005), 71.

this usage, the term "anti-Semitism" implies there is an identifiable quality that is the target of the prejudice; in contrast, "antisemitism," without capital letter or hyphen, is seen as making no claim to any scientific status.[9] No one usage is universally accepted at the present time. The English translation of Vatican documents uses the term "anti-Semitism" as distinct from "anti-Judaism."[10] I will use the term "anti-Judaism" for the religiously based Christian attitudes and actions against Jews and their religious practice, and the term "antisemitism" for the modern cultural phenomenon of animosity toward Jews and Judaism based on a variety of grounds, including racism.

From the second century, Christians claimed to be *Verus Israel,* True Israel, appropriating the biblical promises as applying to the followers of Jesus.[11] The most serious charge of all came from Melito of Sardis in the second century, who accused all Jews of responsibility for the crucifixion of Jesus; this accusation was repeatedly endlessly in different contexts across the centuries and formed the core of traditional Christian anti-Judaism.[12] Augustine shaped papal policy for centuries with his belief that Jews were to be preserved in Christian society, though in a subaltern position because of their continuing guilt.[13] In the nineteenth century, new racial theories targeted Jews, drawing on pseudobiological categories to appear "scientific" and thereby shaping the development of modern antisemitism.[14] While modern antisemitic practices were distinctly different from earlier Christian perspectives, traditional Christian hostility nonetheless prepared the way for the modern prejudice. Leonard Dinnerstein comments, "It cannot be emphasized too strongly that all aspects of American anti-Semitism are built on this foundation of Christian hostility toward Jews."[15]

Often modern prejudices on religion against the Jews and on race against people of African descent overlapped and reinforced each other; J. Kameron Carter has studied the ways in which traditional Christian anti-Judaism set the

---

[9] Egal Feldman, "American Protestant Theologians on the Frontiers of Jewish-Christian Relations, 1922–82," in Gerber, *Anti-Semitism in American History,* 383n.67.

[10] Pontifical Commission for Religious Relations with the Jews, *We Remember: A Reflection on the Shoah.*

[11] Marcel Simon, *Verus Israel: A Study of the Relations between Jews and Christians in the Roman Empire,* 5th ed., trans. H. McKeating (Portland, OR: Littman Library of Jewish Civilization, 1996).

[12] Melito of Sardis, *On the Pascha: With the Fragments and Other Material Related to the Quartodecimans,* 2nd ed., trans. Alistair C. Steward (New York: St. Vladimir's Seminary Press, 2018); Jeremy Cohen, *Christ-Killers: The Jews and the Passion from the Bible to the Big Screen* (Oxford: Oxford University Press, 2007).

[13] Paula Fredriksen, *Augustine and the Jews: A Christian Defense of Jews and Judaism* (New Haven, CT: Yale University Press, 2010).

[14] Marvin Perry and Frederick M. Schweitzer, *Antisemitism: Myth and Hate from Antiquity to the Present* (New York: Palgrave Macmillan, 2005), 73–118.

[15] Leonard Dinnerstein, *Antisemitism in America* (Oxford: Oxford University Press, 1994), xiii.

stage for modern racial bias against people from Africa.[16] Traditional Christian anti-Jewish biblical interpretations found reinforcement in new racial theories. Moreover, anti-Judaism sometimes converged with anti-Catholic sentiments, as many American Protestants criticized both Jews and Catholics in similar terms, accusing both communities of legalism and ritualism, and of not being loyal Americans. The extremist Ku Klux Klan targeted African Americans, Jews, and Catholics as undesirable.

Early Jewish-Christian Relations in North America

Sephardic Jews and Puritans came to North America in the seventeenth century in search of freedom to practice their faith according to their consciences. Both Jews and Puritans esteemed the Hebrew Bible and language, and both thought they were the heirs to biblical Israel. However, many American Christians admired biblical Israel in ways that claimed to displace the Jews as the Chosen People.[17] Beginning with the Pilgrims in the seventeenth century, many American Protestant Christians studied the Hebrew Bible carefully, applied it to their own situation, claimed to be the true Israelites, and viewed America as their "Promised Land." Enslaved African American Christians, however, had a different perspective; since they knew they were in bondage, they concluded that they were the true Israelites suffering under Pharaoh in Egypt, not the Promised Land.[18] The Pilgrims coming to New England lamented the failure of Jews to accept Jesus Christ, saw themselves as the Israelites on an errand in the wilderness, and appropriated the identity of biblical Israel, including the promise of land for the Chosen People. The Christian embrace of Zion and the displacement of Jews by Christians would be recurrent themes in relations between the two communities in the United States throughout history to the present day.[19]

Jews played an important role in the eschatological expectations of some Puritans. In 1649, Johanna and Ebenezer Cartwright submitted a petition to the War Council of Puritan leaders in England to send Jews to Israel in order to appease God's wrath.[20] Some English Protestants hoped that Jews would convert to Christi-

---

[16] J. Kameron Carter, *Race: A Theological Account* (Oxford: Oxford University Press, 2008).

[17] Samuel Goldman, *God's Country: Christian Zionism in America* (Philadelphia: University of Pennsylvania Press, 2018); Shalom L. Goldman, *Zeal for Zion: Christians, Jews, and the Idea of the Promised Land* (Chapel Hill: University of North Carolina Press, 2009); Shalom L. Goldman, *God's Sacred Tongue: Hebrew and the American Imagination* (Chapel Hill: University of North Carolina Press, 2004).

[18] Eddie S. Glaude Jr., *Exodus!: Religion, Race, and Nation in Early Nineteenth-Century Black America* (Chicago: University of Chicago Press, 2000).

[19] Eran Shalev, *American Zion: The Old Testament as a Political Text from the Revolution to the Civil War* (New Haven, CT: Yale University Press, 2013).

[20] Robert O. Smith, "The Quest to Comprehend Christian Zionism," in *Compre-*

anity and become military fighters against the Catholics and the Turks, who formed the two heads of the Antichrist.[21] The Puritans who came to New England brought with them hopes that Jews would become allies in the great struggle, leading to

> the execution of Catholics and the extermination of Muslims. The vision would be catalyzed when the Jewish bride of Christ converted and repaired to Palestine, a Puritan army marching to reclaim God's land from the greedy grasp of the usurping Turk. These ideas were transported and more intensely nationalized by Puritan settlers in the New World that would become the United States.[22]

The long and troubled history of Jewish-Catholic relations on the Iberian Peninsula was a major factor driving the first permanent community of Jewish settlers to North America. For a brief time, from 1630 to 1654, the Netherlands governed a region of Brazil, including the city of Recife, and granted equality and religious freedom to Jews. When Catholic Portuguese forces expelled the Dutch in 1654, they promptly ordered the Jews in Recife to leave. The Jews sought refuge in the Dutch settlement of New Amsterdam, where the Dutch Reformed clergy and Director General Peter Stuyvesant wanted to ban the Jews because giving them liberty to settle would set a dangerous precedent for Lutherans and Catholics. Stuyvesant distrusted Jews because he believed them to be deceitful. However, the Dutch West India Company in Holland saw the economic advantage of welcoming Jewish settlers in the New World and overruled the local Dutch leaders. As a result, Jews were allowed to settle, trade, own real estate, work as guards, and worship in their own homes. Thus, economic ambitions played a significant role in establishing religious freedom for the first Jewish community in New Amsterdam. In 1664, England gave the Netherlands an island in present-day Indonesia in exchange for New Amsterdam, which the English renamed New York. At first the English colonial authorities allowed Jews to continue their worship in private but not in public; in 1685, they rejected a Jewish petition for public worship.

Despite the reservations of some, the Christian colonial leaders eventually allowed the Sephardic Portuguese Jewish community to open a synagogue in New York.[23] Lay synagogue leaders oversaw all aspects of Jewish life, including relations of Jews to the governing authorities; throughout the eighteenth century, the *hazan* (cantor-reader) assumed responsibility for many leadership functions.[24] As Christian authorities in many areas granted more religious freedom in the

---

hending Christian Zionism: Perspectives in Comparison, ed. Göran Gunner and Robert O. Smith (Minneapolis: Augsburg Press, 2014), 329.

[21] Ibid., 331.

[22] Ibid., 333.

[23] Jonathan D. Sarna, *American Judaism: A History* (New Haven, CT: Yale University Press, 2004), 11.

[24] Ibid., 15.

eighteenth century, Jewish communities formed in other port cities of North America, including Savannah, Georgia, in 1733; Charleston and Philadelphia in the 1740s; and Newport, Rhode Island, in the 1750s. In accordance with Roger Williams's foundation of Rhode Island with the ideal of "soul-liberty," Jews in Newport dedicated the Touro Synagogue in 1763, which is the oldest continuous synagogue in the United States. During this period Catholics suffered restrictions in most of the colonies but were gradually allowed to practice their faith in some areas. Jews and Catholics both shared a precarious minority status but benefitted from the increasing acceptance of religious pluralism.

Traditional Jewish life in Europe was an integrated whole that knew no distinction between Jewish and worldly realms. In the eighteenth century both Jews and Christians in America increasingly distinguished between worldly matters governed by civil authorities and other areas deemed religious, where freedom of worship and practice was increasingly allowed by the government. Historian Jonathan Sarna explains: "Colonial synagogue-communities did not tax commercial transactions, censor what Jews wrote on the outside, or punish members for lapses in individual or business morality, unlike synagogues in Amsterdam, London, and Recife. Instead, like the neighboring churches, they confined their activities to their own sphere."[25] Some Sephardic Jews even used different names for their worldly business activities and their life in the synagogue. "Jews led bifurcated lives, complete with rules, institutions, and customs that kept synagogue life and general life distinct."[26]

In time this distinction between religious and nonreligious matters affected American Jewish and Catholic life in ways that would have been unthinkable in Europe; the distinction became particularly important in America because Jewish social interactions with Christians continued to increase.[27] Jews recognized a public space where they interacted with Christians, and distinctively Jewish life focused on the synagogue and the home. Observance of the Sabbath and of dietary laws posed particular challenges, and many Jews made compromises. Most troubling to some Jews were romantic relations between Jews and Christians that led to marriage; it has been estimated that between 10 and 15 percent of Jewish marriages in the colonial period were to Christians.[28] While some Jews left the Jewish community altogether after an interreligious marriage, others continued to practice their ancestral faith. Protestant models for organizing religious life, especially the congregational model of governance, influenced the organization of Jewish communities, and would also have an influence on Catholic developments.

The treatment of Jews and of Christian minorities developed together, for better or for worse. While many Christians treated Jews with prejudice and discrimination, Jews were not alone in this regard because the dominant Protestant communities also treated Quakers, Huguenots, Catholics, and Baptists with

---

[25] Ibid., 20–21.

[26] Ibid., 22.

[27] Ibid., 20.

[28] Ibid., 27.

similar disdain. Jews saw themselves and were seen by others as belonging to a "Jewish Society," not a "Jewish Nation." This allowed for an analogy to the Society of Friends (Quakers) and other religious communities who would form part of the new United States.[29] Many Christian colonial leaders came to recognize a clear connection between the situation of Jews and of Christian religious minorities, and the development of the ideal of religious freedom in the eighteenth century would benefit both Jewish and minority Christian communities.

During the establishment of the new nation, American Jews enthusiastically embraced the ideals of the new republic, especially the free exercise of religious practice. Jews before the Revolutionary War had often been reluctant to comment on political matters because of their lack of power and influence; but during the Revolution they were emboldened to write more forthrightly and passionately on current events because they felt they belonged to their society, whether embracing the Loyalist or the Patriotic cause. Though affected by the sufferings of the war, Jews held great hope for a better future; with the American victory, they felt part of the new American nation.[30] Jews resembled Catholics in that they constituted a small and relatively powerless minority who had suffered discrimination in the past and who hoped for a brighter future in the new republic, and warmly embraced its ideal of religious freedom. According to one estimate, there were approximately three thousand Jews in the United States at the time of its formation amid approximately three million Protestants.[31]

With the foundation of the United States, Jews and Catholics came to enjoy religious liberty in principle, even as Protestants were vigorously shaping a "Christian nation." The declarations granting religious freedom either on a state or national level did not mention Jews explicitly, and so they received religious liberty as individuals, not as a Jewish community.[32] One dramatic symbol of the new relationship and its complexity appeared when Christians and Jews marched together in a celebratory parade in Philadelphia on July 4, 1788, honoring the newly ratified U.S. Constitution. In the parade a rabbi marched arm in arm with Christian clergy, but afterward Jews ate a separate celebratory meal so they could observe dietary regulations.

President George Washington corresponded with Jewish communities, writing to the Hebrew Congregation in Savannah, Georgia, and receiving letters from Jewish congregations in New York, Philadelphia, Charleston, and Richmond. Moses Seixas, warden of the Hebrew Congregation (now known as the Touro

---

[29] Ibid., 29.

[30] Michael Hoberman, "'How It Will End, the Blessed God Knows,' A Reading of Jewish Correspondence during the Revolutionary War," *American Jewish History* 99, no. 4 (2015): 281–313.

[31] Christine Mary Athans, "Courtesy, Confrontation, Cooperation: Jewish-Christian/Catholic Relations in the United States," *Studies in Christian Jewish Relations* 5, no. 1 (2010): 2, https://ejournals.bc.edu/index.php/scjr/article/view/1577/1430.

[32] Sarna, *American Judaism*, 37.

Synagogue) of Newport, Rhode Island, wrote a warm letter of welcome to Washington in 1790. Washington's reply letter is justly famous, affirming: "All possess alike liberty of conscience and immunities of citizenship . . . [T]he Government of the United State, which gives to bigotry no sanction, to persecution no assistance, requires only that they who live under its protection should demean themselves as good citizens."[33]

While this letter was an important marker, the realization of its ideals was not complete. Most Protestant Americans viewed the United States as a Christian nation and harbored a certain amount of bias against Jews, Catholics, Indians, African Americans, Muslims, and others deemed disreputable. The First Amendment of the U.S. Constitution did not originally apply to state governments, and most of the states in the new republic required officeholders to be Trinitarian Christians.[34]

Many American Christians viewed the foundation of the new nation as the fulfillment of the biblical promises to Israel and continued the practice of appropriating the identity of Jews for their own purposes. Many American Protestants believed, like Ezra Stiles, the president of Yale College, that the newly formed United States was in a unique way the heir to the biblical promise and given a divine mission to spread liberty and equality on earth.[35] While this perspective implied a high respect for biblical Israel, it generally also meant that Protestant Christians had displaced Jews as God's Chosen People.

Despite the challenges at the time of the foundation of the new nation, many Jews felt uniquely blessed and prayed that Jews around the world could enjoy comparable religious liberty.[36] The new blessings brought new tasks, as Jews had to wrestle with the implications of religious liberty and democracy. Synagogues drew up innovative constitutions that reflected the ideals of freedom and democracy.[37] Even though some of these changes were later revised or reversed, the constitutions marked a significant transformation of American Jewish life.

Jewish-Christian Relations in the Nineteenth Century

Despite the ideals of religious liberty, many Christians in early America did not wish to grant Jews full equality. The early nineteenth century witnessed the vigorous Christian revival movement known as the Second Great Awakening, which fostered the belief that the United States was a specially chosen Christian

---

[33] George Washington, Letter to Hebrew Congregation of Newport, 1790, in Jonathan D. Sarna and David G. Dalin, *Religion and State in the American Jewish Experience* (Notre Dame, IN: University of Notre Dame Press, 1997), 80.

[34] Chris Beneke, *Beyond Toleration: The Religious Origins of American Pluralism* (Oxford: Oxford University Press, 2006), 168–69.

[35] Ernest Lee Tuveson, *Redeemer Nation: The Idea of America's Millennial Role* (Chicago: University of Chicago Press, 1968, reprint, 1980); see also Shalev, *American Zion*.

[36] Sarna, *American Judaism*, 51.

[37] Ibid., 42–43.

nation. This belief spread throughout the nineteenth century, and in 1892, the U.S. Supreme Court formally ruled in the case *Church of the Holy Trinity v. United States* that the United States was a Christian nation. Justice David Brewer, who wrote the official decision, later published a book, *The United States—A Christian Nation,* asserting that no state charter recognized Muhammad or Confucius or the Buddha, and that Judaism was merely a tolerated creed.[38] Not all Christians embraced this perspective. In the early nineteenth century, John England, a native of Ireland who in 1820 became the first Catholic bishop of Charleston, South Carolina, remembered the mistreatment of Irish Catholics at the hands of the British rulers in Ireland; and he vigorously supported Jewish emancipation in the United States.[39]

Military chaplaincy posed a particular test for interreligious acceptance. As the Civil War began, the U.S. Army demanded that all its chaplains represent a Christian denomination, and so Jewish soldiers in combat could not receive any religious services. To remedy this situation, Arnold Fischel lobbied President Abraham Lincoln and the U.S. Congress to change the law to allow for Jewish chaplains.[40] He secured Lincoln's support, and the change in legislation was approved on July 17, 1862.[41] Later that year, however, U.S. General Ulysses S. Grant blamed all Jews generically for illegal smuggling and speculative activities, and he issued the infamous General Order #11 banning all Jews from military camps, from interactions with soldiers, and from territory under his command.[42] Jews appealed Grant's command, protesting straight to Lincoln, who directed General in Chief Henry Halleck to overturn Grant's order. While this incident reflected the strength of age-old prejudices against Jews, it also dramatically demonstrated the possibility of appeal and victory against an anti-Jewish order in America.[43] Grant later bitterly regretted his decision; and as president of the United States he appointed more Jews to government positions than had previous presidents; and he sought to defend Jewish rights abroad, especially in Russia and Romania.[44]

In the aftermath of the Civil War, southern Jews joined their Christian neighbors in mourning the Lost Cause and honoring slain Confederate soldiers. Meanwhile, in the other regions, Jews participated in unprecedented interreligious exchanges such as organizing the Free Religious Association together with Christians

---

[38] David Brewer, *The United States—A Christian Nation* (Philadelphia: Winston, 1905), 33; see also Sarna and Dalin, *Religion and State,* 13–14.

[39] Athans, "Courtesy," 3.

[40] Arnold Fischel, "Statement Submitted to the United States Senate Committee on Military Affairs," in Sarna and Dalin, *Religion and State,* 130–31; Jonathan D. Sarna and Benjamin Shapell, *Lincoln and the Jews: A History* (New York: St. Martin's Press, 2015), 103–9.

[41] Gary Philip Zola, ed., *We Called Him Rabbi Abraham: Lincoln and American Jewry: A Documentary History* (Carbondale: Southern Illinois University Press, 2014), 84–90.

[42] Jonathan D. Sarna, *When General Grant Expelled the Jews* (New York: Schocken, 2012); Zola, *We Called Him Rabbi Abraham,* 91–116.

[43] Sarna, *American Judaism,* 121–22.

[44] Ronald Chernow, *Grant* (New York: Penguin Press, 2017), 641.

and practicing exchange of pulpits.[45] Rabbi Isaac Mayer Wise, the influential leader of American Reform Judaism, believed there was an emerging consensus among Jews, liberal Christians, and many rational thinkers on common religious beliefs in God and human solidarity.[46]

The American Jewish community probably increased from about 4,500 in 1830 to 150,000 in 1860;[47] about two million Ashkenazi Jewish immigrants, mainly from Eastern Europe, arrived between 1881 and 1914. Particular stimulus came from the pogroms that swept across Russia after the assassination of Tsar Alexander II in 1881, followed by the anti-Jewish May Laws of 1882. Amid often worsening economic conditions across the region, Eastern European Jews faced extremely difficult circumstances; and many were lured to immigrate to America by the promise of freedom, equality, and seemingly unlimited opportunity. Arriving in America, Jews discovered that religious practice was considered private and voluntary, and rabbis had no governmentally recognized authority; this was in sharp contrast to European contexts where Jewish life had been sharply regulated and delimited according to religious identity.[48] Many sought a balance between tradition and adaptation to the New World, while others abandoned the practice of Judaism.

There was a marked rise in antisemitism as increasing numbers of Jews came to America from Eastern Europe. Newspapers carried negative stereotypes of Jews. The Immigrant Restriction League, organized in 1894, believed that the new immigrants, including both Jews and Catholics, were racially inferior, were bearers of poverty and crime, and posed a threat to the identity of the United States.[49] The League sought to restrict their numbers and lobbied Congress for legislation to change immigration laws to favor immigrants from Northern and Western Europe.

The World Parliament of Religions in Chicago in 1893 offered the first major public platform where Jewish and Catholics leaders could speak as equals alongside Protestants. Jews and Catholics felt a certain solidarity, which was dramatically expressed on one of the days of the Parliament when Archbishop John Ireland and Bishop John Keane were unable to make their way to the general assembly in the Hall of Columbus because of the large crowds. So, they went instead to the Jewish Assembly in the Hall of Washington, where they were spontaneously invited to preside over the day's proceedings.[50]

---

[45] Sarna, *American Judaism*, 124.

[46] Isaac M. Wise, *The Cosmic God: A Fundamental Philosophy in Popular Lectures* (Cincinnati, OH: Office American Israelite and Deborah, 1876).

[47] Corrigan and Neal, *Religious Intolerance*, 148.

[48] Sarna, *American Judaism*, 159.

[49] Maddelena Marinari, *Unwanted: Italian and Jewish Mobilization against Restrictive Immigration Laws, 1882–1965* (Chapel Hill: University of North Carolina Press, 2020), 9–12, 14, 20.

[50] James F. Cleary, "Catholic Participation in the World's Parliament of Religions, Chicago, 1893," *Catholic Historical Review* 55, no. 4 (1970): 597.

Twentieth-Century Developments

At the beginning of the twentieth century, large numbers of Jewish immigrants continued to enter the United States from Eastern Europe. Despite the principle of religious freedom and equality, the age-old tradition of Christian bias against Jews continued to influence much of American life; Jews in America faced both social discrimination and religious prejudice as well as occasional physical attacks. Nonetheless, most historians believe that the "Christian nation" of the United States provided conditions for Jews that were generally far better than in most areas of Europe, offering "unparalleled possibilities for Jewish freedom."[51] William D. Rubinstein comments that "examples of American antisemitism often consisted of individual incidents rather than broad patterns of prejudice, although these have certainly existed in America."[52]

Nonetheless, there were more systemic problems in some areas. An anti-Jewish riot occurred in 1902 in New York City, when Irish workers violently attacked Jewish mourners in the funeral procession of Rabbi Jacob Joseph; the Irish Catholic police officers who were present failed to protect the Jewish mourners. Some of the police even attacked the mourners with sticks, and Leonard Dinnerstein comments, "East Side Jews considered the behavior of the police during the riot not as an ephemeral outburst but as part of a systematic and persistent persecution."[53] During the period of widespread lynching of African Americans, Rubinstein notes there was only one case of lynching of a Jewish victim for anti-Semitic reasons: Leo Frank was lynched in Atlanta, Georgia, in 1915 for the alleged killing of a fourteen-year-old girl.[54] Henry Ford was notoriously anti-Semitic, but Rubinstein notes that successful opposition to his statements led him to publicly apologize in 1927.[55]

Protestant writers sometimes compared Jews to "Papists," because of their similar customs of fasting, pilgrimage, and honoring tombs of leaders.[56] Jews were frequently viewed as a distinct and inferior race, and thus interreligious and racial prejudices reinforced each other. Some Jews believed that anti-Jewish bias in the United States was based at least in part on ignorance; Rabbi Milton Steinberg noted that Christians had variously hated or idealized Jews without ever under-standing them. Steinberg saw Jews in America as in between an older world that they could no longer inhabit and a new American world that was reluctant to accept them.

---

[51] Corrigan and Neal, *Religious Intolerance*, 147.

[52] William D. Rubinstein, "Antisemitism in the English-Speaking World," in Lindemann and Levy, *Antisemitism: A History*, 158.

[53] Leonard Dinnerstein, "The Funeral of Rabbi Jacob Joseph," in Gerber, *Anti-Semitism in American History*, 287.

[54] Rubinstein, "Antisemitism," 159.

[55] Ibid., 160.

[56] Corrigan and Neal, *Religious Intolerance,* 55–59.

In July 1927, the newly formed National Conference of Jews and Christians (NCJC) for the Advancement of Justice, Amity, and Peace, announced a fundraising drive to support efforts "to create harmony and friendship in our national social life, through adult education in its highest form, in the place of hate, bigotry and misunderstanding."[57] The Conference worked especially through education and communication such as its initiative, Religious News Service. During the late 1930s the name was changed to the National Conference of Christians and Jews (NCCJ).[58] In 1998, the Conference changed its name to the National Conference for Community and Justice to express its broader concern beyond Jewish-Christian relations. In its early years the Conference sent teams consisting of a priest, a minister, and a rabbi throughout the country to foster understanding. Catholics, however, did not play a prominent role in the early years of NCJC or NCCJ because of the Catholic Church's reluctance to participate in ecumenical ventures.

During the First World War, Catholics, Jews, and Protestants began working together to support aid for refugees and provide chaplains for the military.[59] In a society where anti-Catholic and anti-Jewish prejudices were powerful, Catholics and Jews found common concerns regarding the plight of the working class in the United States. From 1919 through succeeding decades the National Catholic Welfare Conference and the Central Conference of American Rabbis collaborated in support of legislation for more humane working conditions. Speaking to the Jewish-Catholic International Liaison Committee in Baltimore in 1992, Joseph Cardinal Bernardin, Archbishop of Chicago, looked back on James Cardinal Gibbons's endorsement of the religious pluralism of the United States and commented on its importance for Jewish-Catholic relations:

> The spirit of religious pluralism that characterized this nation made possible the slow but steady growth of trust between Jews and Catholics. We no longer feared and distrusted each other as had so often been the case in many parts of the world. As a result we were able to build coalitions for common action on a social agenda that was unprecedented in previous centuries.[60]

Bernardin stressed the importance of Catholic efforts to improve relations with Jews in the United States as preparation for *Nostra Aetate*[61] at the Second Vatican

---

[57] "Fund for Religious Amity: Conference of Jews and Christians Plan $250,000 Drive," *New York Times*, July 2, 1927.

[58] Harold S. Wechsler, "Making a Religion of Intergroup Education: The National Conference of Christians and Jews, 1927–1957," *Journal of Ecumenical Studies* 47, no. 1 (2012): 3–40.

[59] Athans, "Courtesy," 6.

[60] Joseph Cardinal Bernardin, *A Blessing to Each Other: Cardinal Joseph Bernardin and Jewish-Catholic Dialogue* (Chicago: Liturgy Training Publications, 1996), 125–26.

[61] Pope Paul VI, *Nostra Aetate*, Declaration on the Relation of the Church to Non-Christian Religions, October 28, 1965.

Council: "The positive experience of U.S. Catholicism in working with Jews for several decades on a common social agenda solidified episcopal support for the passage of this historic document."[62] In the 1960s, some Jewish and Catholic leaders came together again in support of the African American Civil Rights movement. The shared Jewish and Catholic focus on social justice prepared the way for addressing and correcting the theological misperceptions that each side had of the other.

During the 1930s and 1940s, many Christians harbored strong sentiments against Jews in the United States, and polls taken between 1939 and 1946 revealed that American citizens feared Jews more than the Japanese or the Germans.[63] A fiery Irish American priest named Charles Coughlin became a sensation on the radio, spreading vicious accusations against Jews to audiences of up to forty million listeners during the 1930s and early 1940s until he was finally silenced.[64] However, there were also Catholic initiatives to counter antisemitism. Catholic leaders, including Msgr. John Ryan, Dorothy Day, and Archbishop John J. Mitty of San Francisco, publicly repudiated Coughlin's statements regarding Jews. On November 16, 1938, in the wake of the attacks on German Jewish synagogues on *Kristallnacht,* Maurice S. Sheehy of Catholic University of America organized a radio broadcast deploring the Nazi attacks on Jews, which implicitly rejected the antisemitism of Charles Coughlin. After Sheehy's introductory remarks, Archbishop Mitty, Bishop John Gannon of Erie, Pennsylvania, Bishop Peter L. Ireton of Richmond, Virginia, Rector Joseph M. Corrigan of the Catholic University of America, and also former Democratic presidential candidate Alfred E. Smith offered radio messages on the National Broadcasting Company and the Columbia Broadcasting Company in support of Jews and in condemnation of the Nazi actions against Jews.[65] In condemning the Nazi actions, the Catholic leaders were also affirming the ideal of religious pluralism and liberty at a time when this was not yet accepted by the Vatican authorities. Maria Mazzenga comments: "The anti-Nazi protest of 1938 can be seen as a moment of expansion of American Catholic notions of religious pluralism and liberty, transpiring as it did on behalf of a non-Catholic religious group during a period in which the Church was extremely cautious about such activities."[66]

The international rise of Fascism and the horrors of the Nazi regime in Germany prompted some Christians in the United States to reject antisemitism.

---

[62] Cardinal Bernardin, *A Blessing to Each Other,* 127.

[63] Nirenberg, *Anti-Judaism,* 457–58.

[64] Mary Christine Athans, *The Coughlin-Fahey Connection: Father Charles E. Coughlin, Father Denis Fahey, C.S.Sp., and Religious Anti-Semitism in the United States, 1938–54* (New York: Peter Lang, 1991); Robert Rockaway, "Social Justice in Detroit," *Tablet,* January 2, 2020.

[65] "Text of the Catholic Protest Broadcast," *New York Times,* November 17, 1938.

[66] Maria Mazzenga, "Toward an American Catholic Response to the Holocaust: Catholic Americanism and Kristallnacht," in *American Religious Responses to Kristallnacht,* ed. Maria Mazzenga (New York: Palgrave Macmillan, 2009), 104.

At a time when anti-Semitic European Fascists claimed to be "Christian," some Christians and Jews in America promoted the term "Judeo-Christian" to emphasize shared values underlying American society. The rhetoric of a Judeo-Christian heritage stressed the moral values shared by Protestants, Catholics, and Jews in opposition to purveyors of prejudice. Michael Hoberman explains the origin of discourse about a Judeo-Christian identity: "Invented by twentieth-century pluralists who wished to uphold America's heritage of religious heterogeneity and tolerance in the fight against European totalitarianism, 'Judeo-Christian' still evokes the idea of an alliance built upon a historical continuum, from Jewish heritage to Christian completion."[67] Some Jews demurred, affirming the distinctiveness of Jewish identity;[68] Stephen M. Feldman criticized the term for being supersessionist by suggesting that Jews should evolve into Christians.[69] Jonathan Sarna notes that international opposition to Jews during these difficult years paradoxically helped to stimulate greater integration of Jews into American life: "In the face of worldwide anti-Semitic efforts to stigmatize and destroy Judaism, influential Christians and Jews in America labored to uphold it, pushing Judaism from the margins of American religious life toward its very center."[70]

A number of American Catholics sought to improve relations with Jews; many of the most prominent Catholic leaders in the American struggle against antisemitism and anti-Judaism were either born Jewish or came from a Jewish family; many immigrated to the United States fleeing Nazi oppression.[71] For example, Johannes M. Oesterreicher was born into a Jewish family in Moravia in 1904, became a Roman Catholic priest in 1927, fled from Nazi-ruled Europe to the United States in 1940, and led efforts to overcome anti-Jewish attitudes in the Catholic Church. He founded the Institute for Judeo-Christian Relations at Seton Hall University in New Jersey in 1953, which contributed greatly to Jewish-Christian dialogue, and he participated in the process of composing *Nostra Aetate*.

As in the American Civil War, so also during World War II, military chaplaincy played an important role in building better interreligious relations. Rabbinic chaplains wore the same uniforms as Catholic priests and Protestant ministers, and chaplains from each of these traditions offered prayers at funerals for unknown soldiers. On February 3, 1943, when the USS Dorchester was sinking because of a torpedo from a German U-boat, two Protestant chaplains together with a Catholic and a Jewish chaplain gave away their life belts to other seamen and went

---

[67] Michael Hoberman, "Review of Eran Shalev," *American Zion, American Jewish History* 98, no. 1 (2014): 36.

[68] Arthur A. Cohen, *The Myth of the Judeo-Christian Tradition* (New York: Harper & Row, 1969).

[69] Stephen M. Feldman, *Please Don't Wish Me a Merry Christmas: A Critical History of the Separation of Church and State* (New York: New York University Press, 1997).

[70] Sarna, *American Judaism*, 267.

[71] John Connelly, *From Enemy to Brother: The Revolution in Catholic Teaching on the Jews, 1933–1965* (Cambridge, MA: Harvard University Press, 2012), 1–10, 63–64.

down with the ship arm and arm in prayer. This image lived on after the war as an icon of interfaith in action in what was now called "Judeo-Christian America."[72] Hoberman observes that "their unified utterance of prayers in Hebrew, Latin, and English, as their ship went down gave powerful testimony that the idea '*E Pluribus Unum*' could have a religious application."[73] After the war had ended, the four chaplains received the posthumous Distinguished Service Cross, the Post Office issued a stamp honoring their heroic generosity, and Warner Brothers made plans to produce a film about the event, but no film version was actually produced until a TV documentary appeared in 2004.[74] President Dwight Eisenhower hailed the chaplains' heroism as one of the high points of American religious history. The chaplains' united courage in the face of mortal danger demonstrated to many the futility of religious controversy, marking a symbolic end to "Protestant America" and the dawn of "Tri-Faith America."

In the postwar years, Christian attitudes toward Jews changed as American culture began to move beyond its traditional, strongly Protestant atmosphere to a broader acceptance of Catholics and Jews. The 1947 film, *Gentleman's Agreement,* starring Gregory Peck and directed by Elia Kazan, presented a forceful critique of subtle antisemitic attitudes and practices. As we have seen, Will Herberg's 1955 book, *Protestant-Catholic-Jew* marked a turning point in American religious awareness, as the dominant Protestant culture began to accept Jews and Catholics more fully as Americans.

In the changing atmosphere, many American Christians began to listen to Jewish religious leaders for guidance on life to an unprecedented degree. One example was the success of Rabbi Joshua Loth Liebman's *Peace of Mind,* published in 1946, which presented Jewish wisdom for a broad American audience, becoming the most widely read inspirational book in America prior to Norman Vincent Peale's *The Power of Positive Thinking.*[75] Liebman correlated insights from modern psychology with traditional Jewish and Christian values to offer spiritual advice to mid-century Americans, boldly calling for the construction of a new, distinctively American idea of God based on "independence and interdependence" with "a feeling of confidence" leading to "practical moral activity," and culminating in a new partnership with God.[76] Looking back nearly sixty years later, historian Jonathan Sarna commented, "In more ways than anyone at the time could have imagined, *Peace of Mind* signaled the onset of a new era in American Judaism."[77] The influence flowed in both directions. As many American Christians were consulting the writings of Rabbi Liebman for spiritual counsel, some American Jews incorporated

---

[72] Sarna, *American Judaism,* 267.

[73] Hoberman, "Review of Eran Shalev," 36.

[74] Kevin M. Schultz, *Tri-Faith America: How Catholics and Jews Held Postwar America to Its Protestant Promise* (Oxford: Oxford University Press, 2011), 4.

[75] Joshua Loth Liebman, *Peace of Mind* (New York: Simon & Schuster, 1946).

[76] Ibid., 174.

[77] Sarna, *American Judaism,* 273.

the singing of African American Christian spirituals into their celebration of Passover.[78] As American Christians became more accepting of Jews and open to learning from them, the heritage of American Protestantism loomed large in the development of American Judaism and also had an influence on Catholics accepting American religious pluralism.

Jewish-Catholic-Protestant relations continued to develop on the basis of shared values in response to common challenges such as racial discrimination against African Americans. A shared concern for economic, political, and social justice led many American Jews, Protestants, and Catholics to cooperate closely in the civil rights struggle of African Americans in the 1950s and 60s. Jews who came to the United States of America from Germany in the 1930s often recognized similarities between the mistreatment of the Jews by the Nazis and the widespread racism against African Americans in the United States. Some Jewish leaders, notably Abraham Joshua Heschel, took a prominent role in supporting the protests of Martin Luther King Jr. Nonetheless, many African Americans continued to be influenced by Christianity's traditional bias against Jews, and relations between the two communities were often tense.[79] James Baldwin sharply criticized Jewish landlords with African American tenants in New York City who did not maintain their property, accusing them of racial bias; he wrote an article in the *New York Times* in 1967 with the title, "Negroes Are Anti-Semitic because They're Anti-White."[80] Baldwin saw Jews as participating in the oppressive practices of whites against African Americans and thus as part of the problem of white racist America.

Catholics developed much better attitudes toward and relationships with Jews during the middle of the twentieth century and came to acknowledge analogous experiences. Jewish historian Oscar Handlin's influential 1951 book, *The Uprooted: The Epic Story of the Migrations That Made the American People*, studied immigration as the key to American identity and stressed the similarities between Irish Catholics who immigrated because of the great hunger in British-ruled Ireland and the Eastern European Jews who immigrated because of pogroms.[81] John Pawlikowski points out that American Catholics shared a sense of marginalization with Jews, which motivated common efforts at understanding and reconciliation.[82]

---

[78] Arnold Eisen, "Choosing Chosenness in America: The Changing Faces of Judaism," in *Immigration and Religion in America: Comparative and Historical Perspectives*, ed. Richard Alba, Albert J. Raboteau, and Josh DeWind (New York: New York University Press, 2009), 229.

[79] Dinnerstein, *Antisemitism in America,* 197–227.

[80] James Baldwin, "Negroes Are Anti-Semitic because They're Anti-White," *New York Times,* 1967.

[81] Oscar Handlin, *The Uprooted: The Epic Story of the Migration that Made the American People*, 2nd ed. (1951; Philadelphia: University of Pennsylvania Press, 2001); David J. O'Brien, "The Religions, or Religion, of America," *U.S. Catholic Historian* 23, no. 1 (2005): 43.

[82] John T. Pawlikowski, "Jews and Christians: Their Covenantal Relationship in the American Context," in *Two Faiths, One Covenant? Jewish and Christian Identity in the Presence of the Other,* ed. Eugene B. Korn and John T. Pawlikowski (Lanham, MD: Rowman & Littlefield Publishers, 2005), 156–59.

During the middle of the twentieth century, one of the pivotal figures in shaping American Christian attitudes toward Jews and Judaism was Abraham Joshua Heschel, who taught for many years at Jewish Theological Seminary in Manhattan, across the street from Union Theological Seminary, where he developed friendships and eventually received an appointment as a visiting professor. In his inaugural lecture at Union Theological Seminary, programmatically entitled, "No Religion Is an Island," he set forth the basic principle of interdependence:

> The religions of the world are no more self-sufficient, no more independent, no more isolated than individuals or nations. Energies, experiences and ideas that come to life outside the boundaries of a particular religion or all religions continue to challenge and to affect every religion. Horizons are wider, dangers are greater . . . *No religion is an island.* We are all involved with one another.[83]

He posed the question, "When engaged in a conversation with a person of different religious commitment I discover that we disagree in matters sacred to us, does the image of God I face disappear?"[84] He set forth the positive agenda: "The purpose of religious communication among human beings of different commitments is mutual enrichment and enhancement of respect and appreciation rather than the hope that the person spoken to will prove to be wrong in what he regards as sacred."[85] He noted the proximate impossibility of agreement and ventured a hope: "The prospect of all men embracing one form of religion remains an eschatological hope. . . . Is religious uniformity desirable or even possible? . . . Perhaps it is the will of God that in this aeon there should be diversity in our forms of devotion and commitment to Him. In this aeon diversity of religions is the will of God."[86] Heschel trusted that all religious paths were honoring the God of Israel, and he cited the statement from the Lord through the prophet Malachi as an acknowledgment that all religions are in relation to the God of Abraham: "From the rising of the sun to its setting My name is great among the nations, and in every place incense is offered to My name, and a pure offering; for My name is great among the nations, says the Lord of hosts (Malachi 1:11)."[87]

Heschel's famous lecture originally addressed a mostly Protestant Christian audience, and in time it would reach a wide readership among Catholics in the United States and beyond. It built upon the cooperation of Jews, Protestants, and Catholics in the United States since World War I, and it articulated

---

[83] Abraham Joshua Heschel, "No Religion Is an Island," *Union Seminary Quarterly* 21, no. 2 (1966): 119.

[84] Ibid., 121.

[85] Ibid., 125–126.

[86] Ibid.

[87] Ibid., 127.

the outlines of a broader interreligious agenda of acknowledging differences and working together. More recent scholars have noted that he quoted selectively from authoritative Jewish texts, and he passed over difficult issues in silence, preferring not to address theological differences.[88] While he was very successful in influencing Christian attitudes toward Jews and Judaism, Jon D. Levenson and Alon Goshen-Gottstein argue that Heschel did not fully address the specifically Jewish theological challenges involved in interpreting authoritative Jewish sources in relation to interreligious dialogue.[89]

Rabbi and philosopher Joseph Soloveitchik cautioned Jews not to engage in theological dialogue with Christians, especially Catholics; he warned that Jews and Catholics use the same words in very different ways and thus misunderstanding is inevitable. He cautioned that

> the *logos*, the word, in which the multifarious religious experience is expressed does not lend itself to standardization or universalization. . . . It reflects the numinous character and the strangeness of the act of faith of a particular community which is totally incomprehensible to the man of a different faith community. Hence, it is important that the religious or theological *logos* should not be employed as the medium of communication between two faith communities whose modes of expression are as unique as their apocalyptic experiences. The confrontation should occur not at a theological, but at a mundane human level.[90]

Soloveitchik believed that God's message is incommunicable because it is beyond all human categories, and the divine-human encounter is incomprehensible to any other person, even to a member of the same religious tradition.[91] Soloveitchik urged Jews and Catholics to collaborate together on social matters in the mundane sphere, but he worried that "if the debate should revolve around matters of faith, then one of the confronters will be impelled to avail himself of the

---

[88] For evaluations of Heschel's contribution, see *No Religion Is an Island: Abraham Joshua Heschel and Interreligious Dialogue,* ed. Harold Kasimow and Byron Sherwin (Maryknoll, NY: Orbis Books, 1991); and Alon Goshen-Gottstein, "No Religion Is an Island: Following the Trailblazer," *Shofar: An Interdisciplinary Journal of Jewish Studies* 26, no. 1 (2007): 72–111.

[89] Jon D. Levenson, "Religious Affirmation and Historical Criticism in Heschel's Biblical Interpretation," *Association for Jewish Studies Review* 25, no. 1 (2000–2001): 25–44; Jon D. Levenson, "The Contradictions of A. J. Heschel," *Commentary* 106, no. 1 (1998): 34–38; Goshen-Gottstein, "'No Religion Is an Island,'" 77–78.

[90] Joseph B. Soloveitchik, "Confrontation," *Tradition: A Journal of Orthodox Jewish Thought* 6, no. 2 (1964): 23–24. See also Angela West, "Soloveitchik's 'No' to Interfaith Dialogue," *European Judaism: A Journal for the New Europe* 47, no. 2 (2014): 95–106.

[91] Soloveitchik, "Confrontation," 24.

language of his opponent. This in itself would mean surrender of individuality and distinctiveness."[92] He insisted that one religious community should not recommend changes in rituals or sacred texts to another tradition: "It is not within our purview to advise or solicit."[93] Soloveitchik's view was accepted by the Rabbinical Council of America as authoritative for Orthodox Jews in the United States; many Modern Orthodox Jews followed him in viewing each religion as incommensurable and unique; interreligious discussions should focus not on religious beliefs and practices but only on economic, social, and political issues. Forty years later, Eugene Korn revisited this discussion, pointing out that Soloveitchik was writing before *Nostra Aetate* and assumed Catholics would always hold a supersessionist view of Judaism. After reviewing the many changes in Catholic-Jewish relations since 1964, Korn concluded that it was not only appropriate but imperative for Jews and Christians to engage in theological dialogue.[94]

While the discussions in the Second Vatican Council were still in process, American Catholic priests and bishops met with Jewish scholars and rabbis in January 1965 at St. Vincent's Abbey in Latrobe, Pennsylvania, to discuss ways of improving their relationships. Gerard Sloyan later commented, "It was an exhilarating week. . . . Religious dialogue that was non-defensive, with no hidden agenda, was not so readily come by in those days."[95] Shared Jewish-Christian activities in the United States had in some ways already anticipated what the Second Vatican Council would declare in October 1965 in *Nostra Aetate*. Rabbi Ira S. Youdovin, a longtime Jewish participant in Jewish-Catholic dialogue in the Chicago area, noted that after World War II, many Jews and Catholics entered mainstream U.S. society and developed cordial relationships with each other; Youdovin commented that *Nostra Aetate,* "while assuredly a revolutionary document, had the effect of accelerating and expanding a process already in motion. By adding a theological dimension to a conversation already in progress, it enabled priests and the churches they led to catch up with their parishioners."[96] After the close of the Council at the end of 1965, numerous Jewish-Catholic conversations developed, and many Protestant communities increased their efforts in Jewish-Christian dialogue.[97]

---

[92] Ibid.

[93] Ibid., 25.

[94] Eugene Korn, "The Man of Faith and Religious Dialogue: Revisiting 'Confrontation,'" *Modern Judaism* 25, no. 3 (2005): 296–97, 309.

[95] Gerard S. Sloyan, "Samuel Sandmel, Ecumenist Scholar," in *Nourished with Peace: Studies in Hellenistic Judaism in Memory of Samuel Sandmel,* ed. Frederick E. Greenspahn, Earle Hilgert, and Burton L. Mack (Chico, CA: Scholars Press, 1984), 5, 6.

[96] Ira S. Youdovin, "Jewish-Catholic Relations, *Chicago Studies* 41, no. 2 (2002): 154–55.

[97] John T. Pawlikowski, "The Ever-Deepening Understanding of Jewish-Christian Bonding: *Nostra Aetate* at Forty," *Chicago Studies* 44, no. 2 (2005): 130–43.

Christians in Conversation with Jews

The horrific events of the Shoah (the Holocaust) transformed both the Jewish and Christian communities and shaped the horizon of all recent Jewish-Christian dialogue in the United States and elsewhere. In the wake of the Second World War, most Christian leaders recognized the need to purge Christian faith and practice of the traditional anti-Jewish attitudes and actions, and numerous church bodies issued statements condemning antisemitism and rejecting supersessionism (the traditional belief that Christianity had superseded Judaism and that Jews were no longer God's beloved people). Since the statements on Jewish-Christian relations by the Second Vatican Council and many Protestant church bodies, there have been countless conversations, dialogues, and symposia on various aspects of Jewish-Christian relations in America.[98]

John Pawlikowski articulated three elements of the challenge posed by the Holocaust to Christian theology: the meaning of human liberation, the meaning of the church, and how the New Testament may have contributed to antisemitic teachings.[99] Michael McGarry pondered how to reflect on Jesus Christ after Auschwitz.[100] Joseph Cardinal Bernardin agreed with the Israeli historian Uriel Tal who had argued that the Nazis wanted to abolish all previous moral ideals and any traditional sense of moral responsibility; Bernardin summarized the challenge:

> The basic issue that now confronts all of us—Jew, Christian, Muslim, Hindu—is whether it is any longer possible to maintain a society whose public value system clearly depends on the acknowledgement of God who is the ultimate source of life. This is a premise that increasingly we cannot take for granted in the Western world.[101]

Many Jewish-Christian dialogues in the United States have focused on practical issues of overcoming bias and developing constructive relations in American society. Numerous publications appeared seeking to overcome anti-Jewish bias in Christian preaching, but the challenge of overcoming supersessionism remains formidable.[102]

After the Pontifical Commission for Religious Relations with Jews issued *We Remember: A Reflection on the Shoah* in 1998, many readers were quite

---

[98] Franklin Sherman, "Protestant Parallels to *Nostra Aetate*," *Studies in Christian-Jewish Relations* 10, no. 2 (2015), 1–13, https://ejournals.bc.edu/index.php/scjr/article/view/9226/8284; Jay Moses, Dirk Ficca, Nanette Sawyer, Robert Cathey, with Jill Folan and Katie Rains, "Why Would Presbyterians Turn to a Catholic Document?," *Studies in Christian-Jewish Relations* 10, no. 2 (2015): 1–8.

[99] John T. Pawlikowski, *The Challenge of the Holocaust for Christian Theology* (New York: Center for Studies on the Holocaust, 1978), 35.

[100] Michael B. McGarry, *Christology after Auschwitz* (New York: Paulist Press, 1977).

[101] Bernardin, *Blessing*, 130.

[102] Howard Clark Kee and Irvin J. Borowsky, eds., *Removing Anti-Judaism from the Pulpit* (Philadelphia: American Interfaith Institute/New York: Continuum, 1996).

critical.[103] Jewish and Catholic leaders gathered in Chicago to discuss the ethical issues involved in developing better interreligious relations.[104] One question that hovers in the background, which the Vatican document did not address very directly, concerns the relation between traditional Christian anti-Judaism and the horrific actions of the Nazis.[105] Some scholars, such as Daniel Goldhagen, have asserted a direct continuity between early Christian views and practices and the Shoah.[106] Rabbi Marc Saperstein, however, has challenged this view, noting that many recent regimes have demonized and massacred particular groups. He questions whether the prior Christian history of anti-Judaism was necessary for the Shoah to take place: "But, in my judgment, the claim that these [traditional Christian motifs regarding Jews] were an integral and necessary component of the development and implementation of mass murder remains to be demonstrated."[107]

The Vatican statement on the Shoah did not criticize Pope Pius XII; there has been continuing discussion of the role of Pope Pius XII during the time of the Shoah, with many Jews criticizing him sharply for not denouncing the atrocities explicitly and forcefully. In March 2019, Pope Francis announced that the Vatican archives relating to Pius XII will be fully opened to researchers in 2020. While some hope that this would shed new light on the controversy, others doubt that new documents will resolve the underlying issue. Rabbi Ron Kronish, writing in *The Times of Israel,* noted that Pius XII was not alone in not doing enough during the Second World War. Kronish commented: "Not only did the Pope perhaps not do enough, but neither did American Jewry, nor the Zionist leadership of the Yishuv (pre-state Israel). Nor did FDR and the American government of the time."[108] Kronish praised *We Remember: A Reflection on the Shoah,* and commented on the continuing controversy: "This amazing statement—a product of reflection and deep introspection—was not enough for some of the Jewish professionals and lay people."[109] David Gordis, a prominent leader of American Judaism, welcomed the statement, stressing that it "must be read in the context of the pope's acts of

---

[103] A. James Rudin, "Reflections on the Vatican's *Reflection on the Shoah,*" *Cross Currents* 48, no. 4 (Winter 1998/99): 518–29.

[104] Judith H. Banki and John T. Pawlikowski, eds., *Ethics in the Shadow of the Holocaust: Christian and Jewish Perspectives* (New York: Sheed & Ward, 2001).

[105] Steven Englund, Jon D. Levenson, Donald Senior, and John Connelly, "Getting Past Supersessionism: An Exchange on Catholic-Jewish Dialogue," *Commonweal* 141, no. 4 (February 21, 2014): 17.

[106] Daniel Jonah Goldhagen, *A Moral Reckoning: The Role of the Catholic Church in the Holocaust and Its Unfulfilled Duty of Repair* (New York: Alfred A. Knopf, 2002).

[107] Marc Saperstein, "A Jewish Response to John T. Pawlikowski and Mary C. Boys," in *Christ Jesus and the Jewish People Today: New Explorations of Theological Interrelationships,* ed. Philip A. Cunningham et al. (Grand Rapids, MI: Eerdmans, 2011), 75.

[108] Ron Kronish, "Opening the Vatican Archives: Will It Matter?," *Times of Israel,* March 10, 2019.

[109] Ibid.

reconciliation with the Jewish people, including his historic visit to the synagogue of Rome and overcoming decades of obstacles and complications."[110]

While many conversations have focused on practical issues of living together and helping the world, some dialogues have discussed the theological issues involved in this relationship. A number of issues pose ongoing challenges to Jewish-Christian conversation, including the interpretation of the Bible and Christian origins, the significance of the Jewishness of Jesus, the question of whether Christians and Jews worship the same God, the meaning of revelation and covenant in each tradition, the significance of the land of Israel for theological reflection, the significance of the Shoah for Jewish and Christian understandings of God and human existence, and the possibility of forgiveness after radical evil.

Most official Jewish-Catholic dialogues assume that Jews and Christians worship the same God, but some have questioned this assumption because of Christian belief in the Trinity. Philip Cunningham and Jan Katzew consider the question of whether Christians and Jews worship the same God; they acknowledge that "some Jews and Christians believe that our differences are unbridgeable, that dialogue is undesirable, and that the definitive answer to this question is 'No.' We do not share their view."[111] While recognizing differences in Jewish and Christian interpretations of God, they assert that "we refuse to allow these differences to distract us any longer from our common task of mending the world. We share a belief in One, Good God. That makes us ethical monotheists."[112] Miroslav Volf invited Jews, Christians, and Muslims to explore together the question: *Do We Worship One God?*[113] While many recent discussions assume an affirmative answer, some Jews and Muslims accuse Christians of idolatry for viewing Jesus as truly divine and truly human. From a very different perspective, Messianic Jews challenge the notion of a final boundary between Judaism and Christianity, accepting Jesus as Lord and Messiah while claiming to be Jews; however, their views have been rejected by a large majority of Jews in the United States.[114] There is no unanimity

---

[110] David Gordis, "Vatican Statement on Holocaust Gives Sense of Repentance, Return," *Jewish Advocate* 188, no. 14 (April 9, 1998): 15.

[111] Philip A. Cunningham and Jan Katzew, "Do Christians and Jews Worship the Same God?," in *Irreconcilable Differences? A Learning Resource for Jews and Christians,* ed. David Fox Sandmel, Rosann M. Catalano, and Christopher M. Leighton (Boulder, CO: Westview Press, 2001), 48.

[112] Ibid.

[113] *Do We Worship One God? Jews, Christians, and Muslims in Dialogue,* ed. Miroslav Volf (Grand Rapids, MI: Eerdmans, 2012); Irving Greenberg, "Do Jews and Christians Worship the Same God?" *Commonweal* 132, no. 2 (January 28, 2005): 12–13; Jon D. Levenson, "Do Jews and Christians Worship the Same God?" *Commonweal* 132, no. 2 (January 28, 2005): 13.

[114] Jewish Community Relations Council of New York, "Spiritual Deception Matters Library: Hebrew Christians," http://www.jcrcny.org/wp-content/uploads/2018/05/HEBREWCHRISTIANS.pdf.

among either Jews or Christians on these issues, and there is no one format for dialogue or debate among them.

Another central question involves how the covenant that God made with Israel should be understood today. Traditionally, Catholics and other Christians largely assumed that Jews had broken this covenant definitively by rejecting Jesus and advocating his crucifixion. As we have seen, *Nostra Aetate* firmly rejected the practice of collectively blaming Jews past or present for the death of Jesus, and in 1980, Pope John Paul II described the covenant God made with Israel as *numquam revocata* (never revoked).[115] The Christian Scholars Group issued a statement on September 1, 2002, "A Sacred Obligation: Rethinking Christian Faith in Relation to Judaism and the Jewish People."[116] The statement names the challenge: "We affirm that God is in covenant with both Jews and Christians. Tragically, the entrenched theology of supersessionism continues to influence Christian faith, worship, and practice, even though it has been repudiated by many Christian denominations and many Christians no longer accept it."[117]

Some Christian scholars have vigorously debated whether there is one covenant that includes both Jews and Christians or two covenants, one for each community.[118] Mary Boys describes the dynamic of a covenant as call and response; even though humans, including both Jews and Christians, fail, God remains ever faithful to the promise of the divine covenant.[119] Philip Cunningham describes covenant as "a sharing in life with God. Theologically, it is not so much a legal contract of alliance as a dynamic interaction."[120] Meanwhile, some Catholics involved in dialogue with other religious traditions reflect on the further question of the status of the covenant with Noah.

Jewish-Christian Relations and the State of Israel

Prior to the Second World War, some Christians were ardent supporters of Zionism, but many Christians were quite skeptical of Zionism. Zionism emerged in the nineteenth century in the context of the development of European nationalism. Yotav Eliach explains:

---

[115] Norbert Lohfink, *The Covenant Never Revoked: Biblical Reflections on Jewish-Christian Dialogue* (New York: Paulist Press, 1991).

[116] Christian Scholars Group, "A Sacred Obligation: Rethinking Christian Faith in Relation to Judaism and the Jewish People," in *Seeing Judaism Anew: Christianity's Sacred Obligation,* ed. Mary C. Boys (Lanham, MD: Sheed & Ward, 2005), xiii–xix.

[117] Ibid., xiv.

[118] John T. Pawlikowski, *Jesus and the Theology of Israel* (Wilmington, DE: Michael Glazier, 1989).

[119] Mary C. Boys, "The Enduring Covenant," in *Seeing Judaism Anew: Christianity's Sacred Obligation,* ed. Mary C. Boys (Lanham, MD: Sheed & Ward, 2005), 17.

[120] Philip A. Cunningham, "Covenant and Conversion," in Boys, *Seeing Judaism Anew,* 154.

Zionism is Jewish nationalism or the national liberation movement of the Jewish nation. Nathan Birnbaum (1864–1937), co-founder in 1882 of "Kadimah," the first organization of Jewish nationalist students in the West, coined the words *Zionist* and *Zionism* in 1890. Its general definition means the national movement for the return of the Jewish people to their homeland and the resumption of Jewish sovereignty in the Land of Israel.[121]

Michael Stanislawski defines Zionism as "the nationalist movement calling for the establishment and support of an independent state for the Jewish people in its ancient homeland."[122] He observes that the controversy surrounding this movement is extremely intense, with the result that "Objectivity has ceased to be a goal not only of popular writing on the subject but also of scholarship, and the line between intellectual engagement and political activism hardly exists today."[123] He further comments that even though many or most Zionists believe Zionism is in continuity with the historic Jewish hope to return to Israel, Zionism arose as a deliberate rejection of the traditional yearning because it was linked "inexorably to the belief in the advent of a messiah chosen and anointed by God—and by God alone—who would then initiate the 'ingathering of the exiles.'"[124]

Prior to the Second World War, as Stanislawski points out, many Orthodox Jews rejected Zionism because of a traditional Jewish view that the exile would last until God sent the Messiah. Reform Jews largely rejected Zionism because they saw Judaism as a religious community and not a national identity. Isaac Wise and other Reform rabbis formulated the Pittsburgh Platform in 1885 as a statement of the principles and values of Reform Judaism, asserting, "We consider ourselves no longer a nation, but a religious community, and therefore expect neither a return to Palestine, nor a sacrificial worship under the sons of Aaron, nor the restoration of any of the laws concerning the Jewish state."[125] Many of the early Zionists were Jews who did not believe in God and saw Zionism as a way to be Jewish without God. Some prominent American Jewish leaders, including Isaac Wise, Louis Brandeis, and Solomon Schechter, supported the movement; but in the early twentieth century Zionism remained one of the most painfully divisive issues for American Jews.[126]

Before the Second World War, most of the Christians who supported Zionism were liberal Protestants.[127] In the wake of the Shoah, most Jews and American

---

[121] Yotav Eliach, *Judaism, Zionism, and the Land of Israel: The 4,000 Year Religious, Ideological, and Historical Story of the Jewish Nation* (Washington, DC: Dialog Press, 2018), 1.

[122] Michael Stanislawski, *Zionism: A Very Short Introduction* (Oxford: Oxford University Press, 2017), 1.

[123] Ibid.

[124] Ibid., 2.

[125] Sarna, *American Judaism*, 149.

[126] Ibid., 203.

[127] Mae Elise Cannon, "Mischief Making in Palestine: American Protestant Christian Attitudes toward the Holy Land, 1917–1949," in *Comprehending Christian Zionism:*

Christians agreed that there needed to be a Jewish state that would always accept Jewish refugees who are in danger. The establishment of the state of Israel in 1948 united most American Jews and Christians in support and solidarity of the new nation. Nonetheless, some Hasidic Jews continue to the present day to reject the legitimacy of the state of Israel on traditional grounds.[128]

The Second Vatican Council expressed no view of the modern state of Israel. During the debates regarding *Nostra Aetate*, Augustin Cardinal Bea insisted that the document did not take a stand on political questions. The Holy See did not recognize the state of Israel until the Fundamental Agreement between the Holy See and Israel, which was signed on December 30, 1993, and ratified by the Israeli Knesset on February 20, 1994. There were long and complex negotiations, and the provisions of the agreement have still not been fully implemented.[129] The official leadership of the Catholic Church has not expressed a theological evaluation of the foundation of the modern state of Israel. In an informal statement, Pope Emeritus Benedict XVI/Joseph Ratzinger expressed his theological opinion that it was not possible for a Catholic to consider the modern Jewish state as "the fulfillment of the promises of Scripture."[130]

Some Christians support the establishment of Israel as a Jewish state, leading to the development of Christian Zionism, but the term "Christian Zionism" has been used in a number of different ways.[131] Robert O. Smith offers a helpful working definition of Christian Zionism: "it is political action, informed by specifically Christian commitments, to promote or preserve Jewish control over the geographic area now comprising Israel and Palestine."[132] Smith describes Christian Zionism not as a stable concept but as a meme that moves constantly and changes drastically from one context to another.

Whether support for Israel should be grounded in religious faith is a disputed question. According to the Pew Research Center, more American evangelical Christians than American Jews believe that God willed the foundation of the modern state of Israel; 82 percent of white Evangelicals believe Israel was given to the Jewish people by God; only 40 percent of American Jews believed this; 55 percent of American Jews who believe in God agreed with this view.[133] Christian Zionists in

---

Perspectives in Comparison, ed. Göran Gunner and Robert O. Smith (Minneapolis: Augsburg Press, 2014), 231–55.

[128] Sarna, *American Judaism,* 297.

[129] Marshall J. Breger, ed., *The Vatican-Israel Accords: Political, Legal, and Theological Contexts* (Notre Dame, IN: University of Notre Dame Press, 2004).

[130] Pope Benedict XVI, "Grace and Vocation without Remorse: Comments on the Treatise *De Iudaeis,*" *Communio* 45 (Spring 2018): 179.

[131] Daniel G. Hummel, *Covenant Brothers: Evangelicals, Jews, and U.S.-Israeli Relations* (Philadelphia: University of Pennsylvania Press, 2019).

[132] Smith, "Quest to Comprehend," 328.

[133] Michael Lipka, "More White Evangelicals than American Jews Say God Gave Israel to the Jewish People," Pew Research Center, October 3, 2013; http://www.pewresearch.org.

the United States today come primarily from the evangelical community, where there are differences of perspective between older Evangelicals, who are more likely to support the state of Israel without reservation, and younger Evangelicals, who are more likely to be concerned about justice for Palestinians.[134]

The conflict surrounding the foundation of the state of Israel resulted in the intractable problems of Christians and Muslims within the state of Israel and of the situation of Palestine and the Palestinian refugees, which challenge Jewish-Christian relations to the present. One of the most difficult issues in Jewish-Christian relations in the United States is the fierce debate over to what degree criticisms of the government of Israel and actions of Israeli Jews are influenced by antisemitism.[135] On the one hand, Leonard Dinnerstein notes that while criticism of the state of Israel may be appropriate, "Many Jews throughout the world believe that most criticism of Israeli policies by Christians is merely a pretense for manifesting antisemitic views."[136] On the other hand, Norman Finkelstein has protested vigorously against this attitude.[137] American Jewish scholars Marc Ellis and Mark Braverman have sharply criticized the government of Israel's actions toward Palestinians, and they have also reproached Christian scholars who do not speak out against Israeli actions on behalf of Palestinians.[138] Braverman laments that the praiseworthy desire of Christians to renounce supersessionism has become coupled with uncritical support for the state of Israel and its actions. Other American Jewish leaders, in turn, are strongly critical of Ellis and Braverman.[139]

Early in her career Rosemary Radford Ruether published a vigorous critique of Christian theology, charging that antisemitism runs throughout the historic Christian tradition.[140] Ruether later became a fierce critic of Israel's treatment of Palestinians, calling for justice for this population and sharply rebuffing any accu-

---

[134] Adam Wren, "Meet the Group Trying to Change Evangelical Minds about Israel: Telos Keeps a Low Profile, but Its Ambitions Are Biblical in Proportion," *Politico Magazine,* March 10, 2019.

[135] Mae Elise Cannon, "Anti-Semitism versus Legitimate Criticism of the State of Israel," *Religion News Service,* March 7, 2019.

[136] Dinnerstein, *Antisemitism in America,* 232.

[137] Norman G. Finkelstein, *Beyond Chutzpah: On the Misuse of Anti-Semitism and the Abuse of History* (Berkeley: University of California Press, 2008), 78.

[138] Marc Ellis, *Judaism Does Not Equal Israel: The Rebirth of the Jewish Prophetic* (New York: Free Press, 2019); Marc H. Ellis, *Future of the Prophetic: Israel's Ancient Wisdom Re-Presented* (Minneapolis: Fortress Press, 2014); Mark Braverman, *Fatal Embrace: Christians, Jews, and the Search for Peace in the Middle East* (New York: Beaufort Books, 2010); Mark Braverman, *A Wall in Jerusalem: Hope, Healing, and the Struggle for Justice in Israel and Palestine* (New York: Jericho Books, 2013).

[139] Suzanne Scholtz, "Exilic Fidelity in the Work of Post-Holocaust Theologian Marc H. Ellis," *Journal of the American Academy of Religion* 71, no. 3 (2003): 659–65.

[140] Rosemary Radford Ruether, *Faith and Fratricide: The Theological Roots of Anti-Semitism* (New York: Seabury Press, 1979).

sation that she was anti-Semitic.[141] On the other hand, Jon Levenson charges that antisemitism has been transposed into anti-Zionism. He criticizes

> the demonization of the State of Israel, the presentation of it as a moral malefactor *tout court* and the subjection of it to standards and expectations that are not applied, or applied to the same degree, to any other country. As others have pointed out, this demonization draws heavily on the historical teaching of contempt that the Roman Catholic and other churches have bravely sought to correct over the past half-century.[142]

At the present time there seems less and less possibility for two viable states to be established in Israel/Palestine and little prospect of a genuine reconciliation or peace in the near future. The issue remains highly contentious in Jewish-Christian discussions in the United States.

Continuing Challenges of Antisemitism

There is strong agreement among the official leaders of Catholics, other Christians, and Jews in the United States that all expressions of anti-Judaism and antisemitism must be strongly condemned. Many thought that much progress had been made in reducing prejudices; and by the end of the twentieth century, many American Jews felt, in Leonard Dinnerstein's phrase, "at home in America." Dinnerstein concluded his 1994 magisterial study of *Antisemitism in America* with the confident affirmation: "American Jews have never been more prosperous, more secure, and more, 'at home in America' than they are today. . . . Jews have been increasingly accepted into the American mainstream."[143] In 1999, Shaye J. D. Cohen commented in his study of Jewish identity:

> The majority of Jews of the United States, perhaps the vast majority, do not feel alienated from gentile society. . . . Antisemitism is negligible. . . . American Jews have simply become white, middle-class Americans. . . . Jewish communal leaders wonder and worry: does the disappearance of the Other portend the disappearance of the Self? Without a Them can there be an Us?[144]

---

[141] Rosemary Radford Ruether and Herman J. Ruether, *The Wrath of Jonah: The Crisis of Religious Nationalism in the Israeli-Palestinian Conflict*, 2nd ed. (Minneapolis: Fortress Press, 2002), 214, 215.

[142] Steven Englund, Jon D. Levenson, Donald Senior, and John Connelly, "Getting Past Supersessionism, 22.

[143] Dinnerstein, *Antisemitism in America*, 228.

[144] Shaye J. D. Cohen, *The Beginnings of Jewishness: Boundaries, Varieties, Uncertainties* (Berkeley: University of California Press, 1999), 347.

Nonetheless, in 2006, Rabbi James Rudin published an ominous warning, *The Baptizing of America: The Religious Right's Plans for the Rest of Us*; Rudin sees "a clear and present danger" in the efforts of Christians he calls "Christocrats" to constitute the United States as a Protestant Christian nation.[145] On May 26, 2018, Katherine Stewart in the *New York Times* described "A Christian Nationalist Blitz," consisting of widespread efforts of some Christian nationalists "to secure a privileged position in society for their version of Christianity."[146]

The Anti-Defamation League's (ADL) Center on Extremism reports that expressions of white supremacy and antisemitism have increased sharply in recent times: in 2018, the ADL counted a 182 percent rise in the incidence of anti-Semitic, racist, and Islamophobic materials compared with 2017. Targets include Jews, Muslims, the LGBTQ community, African Americans, and nonwhite immigrants.[147] The Ku Klux Klan, which the ADL describes as "declining," significantly increased its efforts, leaving white supremacist propaganda on doorsteps or in driveways around the United States. The ADL traces most of the Klan incidents to a group based in North Carolina, the Loyal White Knights.[148] The ADL counted at least fifty murders by domestic extremists in the United States in 2018. All the attackers had relationships with right-wing groups, with one of them shifting to an Islamic extremist group prior to the attack. The vast majority of attackers came from white supremacist movements.[149] From January 1 to February 17, 2019, hate crimes in New York City increased 72 percent compared to the same period in 2018, and the police classified nearly two-thirds of these crimes as anti-Semitic; anti-Semitic crimes in 2018 had been 22 percent higher than the year before.[150] In many cases, the assailants attacked people in Jewish garb without provocation and without seeking to rob them. The Crown Heights Neighborhood of Brooklyn, which is the worldwide center of the Ultra-Orthodox Chabad movement, has been particularly targeted. The increasing number of swastikas painted on buildings and of anti-Semitic attacks in recent years provoked the question for one of the largest concentrations of Jews in the world: "Is it safe to be Jewish in New York City?"[151]

In October 2018, the Tree of Life Synagogue in Pittsburgh suffered an attack during the prayers on the morning of Shabbat. The ADL reported that the assailant

---

[145] James Rudin, *The Baptizing of America: The Religious Right's Plans for the Rest of Us* (New York: Thunder's Mouth Press, 2006), 3.

[146] Katherine Stewart, *New York Times,* May 26, 2018.

[147] Anti-Defamation League, "White Supremacists Step Up Off-Campus Propaganda Efforts in 2018."

[148] Ibid.

[149] Anti-Defamation League, "Murder and Extremism in the United States in 2018." https://www.adl.org/murder-and-extremism-2018.

[150] Sharon Otterman, "Anti-Semitic Attacks Fuel Rise in Hate Crimes in New York," *New York Times,* February 18, 2019.

[151] Ginia Bellafante, "Is It Safe to be Jewish in New York?," *New York Times,* October 31, 2018.

had posted vicious anti-Semitic statements online.[152] About six months later, in May 2019, another gunman attacked the Chabad Congregation Synagogue in Powar, California. Again the ADL found a link to white supremacist and anti-Semitic rhetoric, including accusations that Jews were encouraging nonwhite immigration to the United States.[153] On December 10, 2019, two assailants attacked people in a kosher food store in Jersey City, New Jersey, killing three of them; the assault was motivated by anti-Semitic attitudes. On December 28, 2019, a man entered the home of a Hasidic rabbi in Monsey, New York, and used a machete to attack Jews who were celebrating Hanukkah. In the aftermath, Deborah Lipstadt, a professor of Holocaust history at Emory University, worried that "anti-Semitism is driving Jews underground in the West. . . . When Jews feel it is safer for them to go 'underground' as Jews, something is terribly wrong—wrong for them and, even more so, wrong for the society in which they live."[154] Leaders of many different religious communities spoke out condemning the attacks on Jews, but the issue remains of grave concern.

Collaborative Scholarship

One of the most encouraging signs of the new situation is the collaboration of Jewish and Christian scholars on common projects. To advance the conversation between Jews and Christians, in 2000, Jewish scholars Tikva Frymer-Kensky, David Novak, Peter Ochs, and Michael Signer, representing various Jewish traditions, issued a statement entitled "*Dabru Emet*: A Jewish Statement on Christians and Christianity." Many other Jewish leaders have signed the statement as well. *Dabru Emet* (Speak the Truth) begins by noting the significant changes in Christian attitudes toward Jews and Judaism in recent decades. The Jewish scholars affirm that

> we believe these changes merit a thoughtful Jewish response. Speaking only for ourselves—an interdenominational group of Jewish scholars—we believe it is time for Jews to learn about the efforts of Christians to honor Judaism. We believe it is time for Jews to reflect on what Judaism may now say about Christianity.[155]

---

[152] Anti-Defamation League, "Deadly Shooting at Pittsburgh Synagogue," October 27, 2018, https://www.adl.org/blog/deadly-shooting-at-pittsburgh-synagogue.

[153] Anti-Defamation League, "Deadly Shooting at California Chabad Highlights Threat to Jewish Houses of Worship," April 27, 2019, https://www.adl.org/blog/deadly-shooting-at-california-chabad-highlights-threat-to-jewish-houses-of-worship.

[154] Deborah Lipstadt, "Jews are Going Underground," *The Atlantic,* December 29, 2019.

[155] "*Dabru Emet*: A Jewish Statement on Christians and Christianity (2000)," in Mary C. Boys and Sara S. Lee, *Christians and Jews in Dialogue: Learning in the Presence of the Other* (Woodstock, VT: Skylight, 2006), 202.

They then propose a number of brief statements, affirming that "Jews and Christians worship the same God" and further that "Jews and Christians seek authority from the same book—the Bible."[156] They affirm that "Christians can respect the claim of the Jewish people upon the land of Israel" and also that "Jews and Christians accept the moral principles of Torah."[157] They state that "Nazism was not a Christian phenomenon,"[158] and they acknowledge, "The humanly irreconcilable difference between Jews and Christians will not be settled until God redeems the entire world as promised in Scripture."[159] They hopefully proclaim, "A new relationship between Jews and Christians will not weaken Jewish practice," and they urge, "Jews and Christians must work together for justice and peace."[160]

Other Jewish leaders and scholars took exception to the statement, and a vigorous debate ensued. Jon Levenson sharply challenges any harmonizing approach to Jewish-Christian dialogue; and in particular, he forcefully criticizes the efforts of the authors of *Dabru Emet* to harmonize Jewish and Christian faith without acknowledging profound differences.[161] More broadly, Levenson reproaches interreligious dialogue partners who "ignore, water down, or explain away their distinctive truth claims" because although this approach seeks harmony, it "does so at a great cost: it requires them to ignore the theological core of their own tradition or to take so critical a view of it that it is no longer a meaningful and productive aspect of their identities. In my experience, that cost usually does not seem very great to my fellow Jews."[162] Levenson sternly warns, "When the pursuit of good human relations and social justice is the controlling factor in the dialogue, mutual affirmation becomes the goal, and religious relativism soon takes over. The future of any religious community that accepts such a model is not bright."[163]

As a means of further developing the conversation, Tikva Frymer-Kensky and four Jewish colleagues edited a thought-provoking book, *Christianity in Jewish Terms,* in which Jewish scholars wrote essays on various Christian beliefs and perspectives; the editors then invited Christian scholars to respond to the Jewish statements about Christianity.[164] The discussion is a model of respectful dialogue that honestly notes both points of convergence and of divergence.

On December 3, 2015, a number of Orthodox rabbis from the Center for Christian-Jewish Understanding and Cooperation issued an unprecedented state-

---

[156] Ibid.

[157] Ibid., 202–3.

[158] Ibid., 203.

[159] Ibid., 204.

[160] Ibid.

[161] Jon D. Levenson, "The Agenda of Dabru Emet," *Review of Rabbinic Judaism* 7, no.1 (2004): 1–26.

[162] Steven Englund, Jon D. Levenson, Donald Senior, and John Connelly, "Getting Past Supersessionism, 20–21.

[163] Ibid., 21.

[164] Tikva Frymer-Kensky, David Novak, Peter Ochs, David Fox Sandmel, and Michael A. Signer, eds., *Christianity in Jewish Terms* (Boulder, CO: Westview Press, 2000).

ment about Christianity, "To Do the Will of Our Father in Heaven: Toward a Partnership between Jews and Christians."[165] The rabbis from Israel, the United States, and Europe affirm a historic opportunity for partnership with Christians who have reached out to Jews. The statement notes the tragic centuries of anti-Jewish bias that preceded the Shoah, and then celebrates the Second Vatican Council's *Nostra Aetate,* which fundamentally and irrevocably changed Catholic teaching about Jews and Judaism, and ushered in a new era of relationships. The rabbis agree with Moses Maimonides and Yudah Halevi in seeing the appearance of Christianity as the result of the divine will; they affirm that God wants Jews and Christians to be partners and not enemies. They acknowledge "the constructive validity of Christianity as our partner in world redemption, without any fear that this will be exploited for missionary purposes." They acknowledge significant and lasting differences but affirm that the ethical monotheism that unites Jews and Christians is far more important than what differentiates the two communities.

A number of issues command attention in the theological dialogues between Jews and Christians in the United States. Some liberation and feminist theologians have continued negative stereotypes of the Jewish leaders and people of Jesus's time. Mary Boys has challenged Christian feminists who praise Jesus by presenting him against a background of allegedly oppressive, patriarchal Judaism.[166] John Pawlikowski criticized liberation theologians for identifying contemporary oppressive structures with the negative stereotypes of the Pharisees in the New Testament.[167] Timothy Sandoval, Melody Knowles, Esther Menn, and John Pawlikowski address the difficult issue of anti-Jewish perspectives expressed by Christians who are not from powerful nations:

> The question is difficult, but perhaps one response is for first-world Christians to ensure that the educational and theological resources they produce and often pass on to other Christians are free of, and actively challenge, anti-Semitic notions. . . . Any appropriate engagement, however, will take into account, but not reproduce, the imperialistic and colonial encounters of the past while seeking to honor voices from the developing world in all their particularity.[168]

---

[165] Center for Jewish-Christian Understanding and Cooperation, "To Do the Will of Our Father in Heaven: Toward a Partnership between Jews and Christians," December 3, 2015.

[166] Boys, "Christian Feminism," 70–79.

[167] John T. Pawlikowski, *Christ in the Light of the Jewish-Christian Dialogue* (1982; reprint, Eugene, OR: Wipf and Stock Publishers, 2001).

[168] Timothy Sandoval, Melody Knowles, Esther Menn, and John Pawlikowski, "*Dabru Emet*: Jewish-Christian Dialogue, and the Bible: An Introduction to *Contesting Texts,*" in *Contesting Texts: Jews and Christians in Conversation about the Bible,* ed. Melody D. Knowles, Esther Menn, John Pawlikowski, and Timothy J. Sandoval (Minneapolis: Fortress Press, 2007), 24–25.

These authors note a new alignment among Jews and Christians along political lines: "More politically liberal Jews regularly find affinity in the views of more politically and theologically progressive Christians. Politically and theologically conservative Christians and more religiously traditional Jews, who would not be able to find much common ground in religious matters, not infrequently share perspectives on social and political questions."[169]

In the last seventy years relationships between Jews and Catholics and other Christians in the United States have improved markedly, and this has provided a level of trust to address the serious ongoing issues of concern.

---

[169] Ibid., 25–26.

5

MUSLIM-CATHOLIC RELATIONS
IN THE UNITED STATES

Muslims have been present in America since colonial times, but historically many were enslaved and denied the religious freedom to practice Islam. Through much of American history European American Christians viewed Muslims and Islam with grave suspicion, and in recent times American Muslims have become targets of widespread suspicion and animosity because of violent attacks carried out by people who claim to be acting in the name of Islam. Amid the current atmosphere of distrust toward Muslims in America, there are nonetheless numerous Muslim-Christian dialogues in the United States, and Catholics collaborate with Muslims in important ways.

As we have seen, Pope John Paul II emphasized the Catholic Church's unique relationship with Judaism because the Jewish religion is "intrinsic" to Catholic faith.[1] Though it is not as frequently highlighted, Catholics and other Christians also have a unique relationship with Muslims because Islam is the only other major religion claiming a divinely revealed interpretation of Jesus of Nazareth[2] and because many major figures of the Bible appear in the Qur'an.[3] Muslims acknowledge authentic divine revelation given to the prophets of ancient Israel and Jesus, and the Qur'an is the only major scripture other than the Bible that discusses and honors Jesus and Mary. In *Nostra Aetate* #3 the Second Vatican Council acknowledged the many elements on which Muslims and Catholics converge.[4]

Historical Context of Muslim-Christian Relations in Europe

Age-old tensions between Muslims and Christians in Europe influenced Muslim-Christian relations in the United States. Historically, the rise of Islam posed a great challenge to Christians both militarily and theologically. Following

---

[1] Pope John Paul II, "Address to the Great Synagogue of Rome," April 13, 1986.

[2] Zeki Saritoprak, *Islam's Jesus* (Gainesville: University Press of Florida, 2014), 1–22.

[3] Gabriel Said Reynolds, *The Qur'an and the Bible: Text and Commentary,* Qur'an trans. Ali Quli Qarai (New Haven, CT: Yale University Press, 2018).

[4] Second Vatican Council, *Nostra Aetate*, Declaration on the Relation of the Church to Non-Christian Religions, October 28, 1965.

the lead of John of Damascus, most European Christians viewed Islam not as a separate religion but as the last and greatest of the heresies, related to Arianism and so-called Nestorianism by the denial of the divinity of Jesus Christ.[5] Muslims and Christians in Europe and the Mediterranean world had related to each other in a variety of ways for centuries before the European settlement of North America. The medieval historian R. W. Southern noted that the major options were coexistence, conversion, commerce, and Crusade.[6] In various times and places, the Iberian Peninsula was a location for each of these options. While there was repeated fighting, there were also periods of coexistence and commercial and academic exchange; at different times people converted variously to Islam or to Christianity. During the long Reconquista in the Iberian Peninsula, Christian forces pushed back the Muslim rulers further and further south. By 1249, the Portuguese Catholics had defeated the Muslim rulers in present-day Portugal.

The fifteenth century was a period of dramatic change. The Portuguese began exploring further and further areas on the western coast of Africa and eventually sailed to India in 1498; Ottoman Turkish Muslims conquered Constantinople in 1453, opening up new threats to Christian-ruled Europe; and in 1492, the Spanish monarchs Ferdinand and Isabella defeated the last remaining Moorish rulers in Granada and promptly sponsored the expedition of Christopher Columbus to what would be called the Americas. The Portuguese and Spanish Christians had a long history of fighting Muslim forces; and some hoped Columbus's mission would allow Spain to encircle the Islamic world, recruit allies in Asia, and launch a surprise attack on the Islamic holy places in the Arabian Peninsula. When Christopher Columbus first reported on his discovery to the Spanish monarchs, he focused on Islam.[7] Columbus noted that the Spanish monarchs were "enemies to the sect of Mahoma and to all idolatries and heresies," that they had defeated the Moorish rulers in Granada, and had commissioned him to go to India "with a view that they [the Muslim princes of India] might be converted to our holy faith."[8] In his diary for December 26, 1492, Columbus wrote that he hoped to discover enough gold in the Indies to finance a further expedition to seize Jerusalem from its Muslim rulers; this would prepare for even more dramatic events, as Carol Delaney explains: "The crusade to wrest Jerusalem from the Muslims was the first step in the series of events that would make possible the return of Christ before the Last Judgment at the end of the world, and time was running out."[9]

---

[5] Norman Daniel, *Islam and the West: The Making of an Image* (1960; reprint, Oxford: Oneworld Press, 1997).

[6] R. W. Southern, *Western Views of Islam in the Middle Ages* (Cambridge, MA: Harvard University Press, 1962), 3.

[7] Timothy Marr, "'Out of This World': Islamic Irruptions in the Literary Americas," *American Literary History* 18, no. 3 (2006): 525.

[8] Christopher Columbus, "Journal of the First Voyage of Columbus," in *The Northmen, Columbus and Cabot, 985–1503, Original Narratives of Early American History,* ed. Julius E. Olson and Edward Gaylord (New York: Charles Scribner's Sons, 1906), 89–90.

[9] Carol Delaney, *Columbus and the Quest for Jerusalem* (New York: Free Press, 2011), xvi.

Catholic writers had long viewed Muslims as forerunners of the Antichrist, and Protestant writers during the Reformation usually viewed the Ottoman Turkish forces who threatened Europe as the biblical Gog and Magog, and associated them with the Antichrist. Lutheran writers developed a twofold model of the Antichrist to include both the Roman Catholic pope and the Ottoman sultan. These events and perceptions shaped the background of the early period of Muslim-Christian relations in North America.

Christian Relations with Muslims in the Colonial Period

It is not certain when the first Muslims came to North America. There has been speculation about Muslims coming as traders from Africa to North and South America even before Columbus, but this seems unlikely.[10] While there may have been Muslims in the crew of Christopher Columbus, the evidence is not conclusive. There may also have been Muslims who fled Spanish persecution after 1492 and who journeyed to the Caribbean and eventually to North America. Early Spanish settlers in the New World held traditionally negative views of Muslims and Islam based on the experience in the Iberian Peninsula.

In British America there were various Christian attitudes toward Muslims. John Smith, the leader of the English settlement in Jamestown, Virginia, had earlier fought against Ottoman Turkish forces in Hungary and was captured and enslaved for a time. After escaping and coming to Virginia, he harbored a very adversarial view of Muslims and Islam, and adopted for his coat of arms the motto *Vivere est vincere* (To live is to conquer).[11] On the other hand, the Quaker Mary Fisher displayed a more positive view of Muslims. After suffering mistreatment from the Puritans in Massachusetts in 1656, she traveled with other Quakers to the eastern Mediterranean in 1658 to preach the Gospel to the Ottoman Sultan Mehmed IV. She gained an audience with the sultan in Adrianople (present-day Edirne) and was graciously received. While he did not convert to the Quaker path of Christian faith that Fisher recommended, he offered an honor escort to protect her, but she declined. During the colonial and antebellum period, many American Christians perpetuated the earlier negative perceptions of Muslims and Islam, including misperceptions and distortions. Muslims often appeared in American perceptions as a dangerous threat of anti-Christian tyranny and despotism, with the Ottoman Turkish sultan as the prototype of absolute despotism.[12] American Protestants in the colonial period frequently viewed Muhammad and the Roman Catholic Pope as two Antichrists, or as two representatives of the Antichrist; Protestant authors

---

[10] Kambiz Ghaneabassiri, *A History of Islam in America: From the New World to the New World Order* (Cambridge: Cambridge University Press, 2010), 1.

[11] Timothy Marr, *The Cultural Roots of American Islamicism* (Cambridge: Cambridge University Press, 2006), 3.

[12] Ibid., 20.

viewed Islam and Catholicism as similar irrational superstitions that deceived people and that appealed to works righteousness.[13]

During the eighteenth century, American Protestants were horrified by reports of the Barbary pirates enslaving Europeans, and anti-Muslim attitudes converged with racial prejudices against African Muslims, especially those who enslaved white Christians.[14] The Virginia House of Burgesses even passed legislation forbidding the enslavement of white Christians by Africans, mulattos, American Indians, Muslims, Jews, or other infidels.[15]

Many white American Christians, however, believed it was legitimate for them to enslave African Muslims; the trans-Atlantic slave trade brought a significant number of Muslims to North America in bondage.[16] The precise number of enslaved African Muslims in America is not known, and some estimates range up to 20 percent.[17] Records from Carolina tell of slaves who refused to eat pork and who prayed to Allah. For the most part, Muslims were not allowed to practice their religion in the New World freely and openly but were pressured to convert to Christianity. Some slaves maintained a secret practice of Islam, but did so at the risk of severe punishment. Meanwhile, Christian preachers would remind slaves of their biblical duty to be obedient to their masters.

In this context racial and religious identities were fluid constructs. In some situations Christian slave owners sought to exempt enslaved African Muslims from the usual stereotypes of their race and religion, viewing them as semicivilized and trying to convert them, usually hoping to advance trade in Africa and to spread Christianity; as a result, enslaved African Muslims were liminal figures not fitting the usual social categories.[18] The memory of enslaved African Muslims would be a significant factor in conversions of African Americans to Islam in the twentieth and twenty-first centuries.

The accounts of the prophet Muhammad that circulated in colonial America portrayed him in extremely negative terms, usually drawn from earlier European Christian polemics. The biography published in 1697 by the Anglican dean of Norwich Cathedral Humphrey Prideaux bore the title *The True Nature of Imposture Displayed in the Life of Mahomet,* and portrayed the prophet of Islam as an

---

[13] Thomas S. Kidd, *American Christians and Islam: Evangelical Culture and Muslims from the Colonial Period to the Age of Terrorism* (Princeton, NJ: Princeton University Press, 2009), 9–18.

[14] Ibid., 4–6.

[15] Ibid., 6.

[16] Sylviane A. Diouf, *Servants of Allah: African Muslims Enslaved in the Americas* (New York: New York University Press, 1998); Richard Brent Turner, "African Muslim Slaves and Islam in Antebellum America," in *Cambridge Companion to American Islam,* ed. Juliane Hammer (Cambridge: Cambridge University Press, 2013), 28–44.

[17] Jane I. Smith, *Islam in America* (New York: Columbia University Press, 1999), 76–77.

[18] Ghaneabassiri, *History of Islam,* 27–36.

imposter, a perception that spread widely in the colonies.[19] Henri de Boulainvilliers wrote *The Life of Mahomet,* which was published in English translation in London in 1731 and was widely read in British colonial America. Boulainvilliers believed that Muhammad misunderstood Christianity, protested reasonably against the corruption of the Eastern Christians, and was used by God to punish and purify the Christian community.[20] Even though most colonial American Christians knew very little accurate information concerning Muhammad and Islam, the pejorative images of Muhammad and Islam were widely used as rhetorical devices to discredit opponents, including Roman Catholics and Quakers. For example, Roger Williams viewed Catholicism, Quakerism, and Islam as similar forms of deceit that spread quickly for a time; he contrasted them sharply to the true religion of Jesus Christ.[21] Jonathan Edwards viewed Islam as similar to Roman Catholicism and heathenism and expected all three kingdoms to be overthrown in the final apocalyptic struggle.[22]

At the time of the foundation of the United States, some of the Founding Fathers had a positive view of Islam, and Thomas Jefferson owned a copy of the Qur'an.[23] James H. Hutson, chief of the Manuscript Division of the U.S. Library of Congress, notes that in principle, the drafters of the U.S. Constitution intended the First Amendment to apply to Muslims. Hutson notes that Thomas Jefferson, Richard Henry Lee, George Washington, Massachusetts Chief Justice Theophilus Parsons, as well as the citizens of Chesterfield County, Virginia, all explicitly included Muslims in their discussions of religious liberty.[24] However, in practice those enslaved had no rights; as we have seen, when the newly established government of the United States approved the First Amendment to the Constitution, it was not usually applied to enslaved African Americans. There were a few free Muslims in the United States at this time, but their number was quite small. For example, some Muslim immigrants from Morocco who had previously been enslaved successfully petitioned the state of South Carolina in 1790 for recognition as possessing the rights of white people.[25]

Christian Relations with Muslims in the Nineteenth Century

Throughout the nineteenth century, many American Christians continued to view Muslims as the forerunners of the Antichrist and harbingers of an apocalyptic

---

[19] Kidd, *American Christians,* 6–8.

[20] Ibid., 10.

[21] Ibid., 10–11.

[22] Ibid., 15–16.

[23] Denise A. Spellberg, *Thomas Jefferson's Qur'an: Islam and the Founders* (New York: Alfred A. Knopf, 2013).

[24] James H. Hutson, "The Founding Fathers and Islam: Library Papers Show Early Tolerance for Muslim Faith," *Library of Congress Information Bulletin* 65, no. 5 (May 2002); Jennifer Williams, "A Brief History of Islam in America," *Vox,* January 17, 2017.

[25] Turner, "African Muslim Slaves," 34.

struggle, which they hoped would end in the victory of Christians over their Islamic enemies. Between 1785 and 1815, Muslim Barbary pirates repeatedly attacked the ships of the young United States of America, often taking Christians as captives; while the U.S. Navy battled the pirates on the seas, American Christians responded by interpreting this military threat in light of eschatological prophecies of the final struggle between good and evil.[26] As in the colonial period, most of the Muslims in the United States in the early nineteenth century were enslaved. While Christian slave owners generally punished the practice of Islam, there was a notable exception on Sapelo Island near the coast of Georgia, where Muhammad Bilali served as an overseer on the plantation and wrote a text on Islamic law in a West African Arabic script.[27] This document survived and is today in the library of the University of Georgia.[28] Reem M. Hilal stresses that Bilali continued to use his Islamic name and presented himself as a literate enslaved person, which was a violation of the normal expectation of the slave culture and thus an assertion of his own identity and power.[29] Some enslaved Muslims may have outwardly converted to Christianity while covertly continuing to practice Islam. Omar ibn Said was a well-educated Muslim born in present-day Senegal in 1770 who was captured and taken to the United States in 1807. While he accepted the Christian faith in 1820, his Arabic language notations on his Christian Bible suggest that he continued to believe in Islam. His 1831 autobiography praises Muhammad and includes a *sura* from the Qur'an; this is the first work written in Arabic in the United States and the only slave narrative written in Arabic in the United States.[30]

The very strong prejudices against Islam in the nineteenth century made practice of the religion difficult. When enslaved Muslims received their freedom at the end of the American Civil War, many chose to become Christian. Richard Brent Turner explains: "After slavery, white American hostility to African religions and the overwhelming Black preference for Protestantism prevented Muslims from establishing Islamic institutions and a missionary program for their religion, and their descendants did not practice Islam."[31] Membership in Protestant churches offered African Americans a certain amount of refuge during the era of Jim Crow and widespread lynching. Thus, Islam as practiced by enslaved African Americans did not survive continuously in significant measure, though its memory would be important in the twentieth and twenty-first centuries.

---

[26] Kidd, *American Christians,* 19–36.

[27] Muhammad Abdullah al-Ahari, *Muhammad Bilali's Meditations* (Chicago: Magribine Press, 2017).

[28] Smith, *Islam in America,* 77.

[29] Reem M. Hilal, "Marking the American Landscape: African Muslim Slave Writings and the Place of Islam," *Journal of the African Literature Association* 11, no. 2 (2017): 140–47.

[30] Omar ibn Said, *A Muslim American Slave: The Life of Omar ibn Said,* trans. and ed. Ala Alryyes (Madison: University of Wisconsin Press, 2011); Turner, "African Muslim Slaves," 40.

[31] Turner, "African Muslim Slaves," 42.

The American Board of Commissioners for Foreign Missions (ABCFM), founded in 1810, sent Protestant missionaries across the world, including to Muslim majority areas, to proclaim the Gospel of Jesus Christ and convert Muslims and Jews to Christian faith.[32] American Christian expectations oscillated between hopes for the destruction of Islam and the conversion of Muslims to Protestantism. Many hoped that the destruction of the Ottoman Empire would lead to the return of Jews to Palestine.[33] However, throughout the nineteenth century the Ottoman Empire forbade Christian efforts to proselytize, and very few Muslims embraced Christianity.

Setting a very different tone from traditional Christian polemics against Islam, Washington Irving, the most prominent American writer of the early nineteenth century, lived for several years in Spain, studied its history, and came to a profound respect for the Iberian Peninsula's Islamic heritage. He later served as the ambassador to Spain during the 1840s. His book, *Tales of the Alhambra*, creatively retold the lore of the Moors in a way that captivated a wide reading public. Irving also wrote a biography of Muhammad, which was a landmark for its time.[34] He sought to be sympathetic and fair minded and did find much to praise in the life of Muhammad. Nonetheless, it is an ambivalent biography, which repeats the age-old charge that Islam is a "religion of the sword." Irving believed that Muhammad's political and military activity during the Medinan phase of his life was a betrayal of his originally pure religious fervor. The result is a multifaceted portrait that both praises Muhammad lavishly and chides him harshly. Irving began writing the work during his early visit to Spain in the 1820s, but he did not publish it until 1850, after he had returned from serving as the U.S. ambassador to Spain.

The first prominent interreligious encounter of Muslims and Christians in the United States on a broad stage, including representatives of other religions, took place at the World's Parliament of Religions in Chicago in 1893, in conjunction with the Columbian Exposition celebrating the four-hundredth anniversary of Columbus's voyage. Liberal Protestant leaders John Henry Barrows and Charles Bonney invited Ottoman Sultan Abdul Hamid II to send an Islamic delegation, but the sultan did not approve of this venture and did not join in the planning or send representatives. As a result, it has been commented that Islam was underrepresented.[35]

Mohammed (Alexander Russell) Webb, a former U.S. consul to the Philippines, recounted his own journey to Islam. He had questioned Christianity in his youth and had explored Buddhism and Theosophy. Originally, he told the Parliament audience, he had viewed Islam as "altogether too corrupt for consideration."[36] But as he became more familiar with Islam and Muhammad, he became fully convinced

---

[32] Kidd, *American Christians*, 37–57.

[33] Ibid., 38.

[34] Washington Irving, *Mahomet and His Successors* (1889; reprint, New York: AMS Press, 1973).

[35] Richard Hughes Seager, "General Introduction," in *The Dawn of Religious Pluralism: Voices from the World's Parliament of Religions, 1893,* ed. Richard Hughes Seager (LaSalle, IL: Open Court, 1993), 9.

[36] Mohammed (Alexander Russell) Webb, "The Spirit of Islam," in *Dawn*, 271.

of the truth of the faith and expressed his firm confidence that "ultimately Islam will be the universal faith."[37] He recalled a conversation in which he was asked if Muslims had organized a mission in New York. Webb replied to the questioner, "I told him yes, but not in the ordinary sense; that we simply wanted people to study Islam and know what it was."[38] Webb stressed the fraternity and equality of all people among Muslims and proposed Islam as an alternative path to the racial divisions of Christianity.[39]

Webb was very aware of American Christian biases against Muslims. Responding to negative stereotypes presented by Christian missioners who had traveled to Muslim areas, Webb acknowledged differences in the way Islam was practiced, depending on class and educational background; and he pleaded with his audience to consult "the educated intelligent Moslems, and they are the safest guides. No one would expect me to go into the slums of Chicago to find a reflection of the Christian religion."[40] The *Daily Inter Ocean* described Webb's reception: "His mild defense of polygamy in the opening part of his address came near to making things lively, but as he got on to speak of the good qualities of Mohammed he won sympathy."[41] The first mosque in the United States was erected as a temporary structure as part of the Columbian Exposition, a replica of the mosque of Sultan Qayt Bey in Cairo. The call to prayer rang out five times a day, and Muslims from Egypt, Morocco, and Palestine gathered for the daily prayers. At the conclusion of the Parliament, the structure was removed.[42]

In contrast to the generally tolerant and open-minded atmosphere of the World's Parliament of Religions, the late nineteenth and early twentieth centuries also saw a militant, resurgent concern for the Protestant Christian identity of the United States, coupled with a messianic sense of the destiny of the United States in civilizing and Christianizing the world. The twentieth century was expected to be "The Christian Century," as the Third Great Awakening in the 1890s united religious zeal with the quest to reform society and politics. The sense of a divine mission to spread peace, democracy, and Protestant Christian civilization through the conquest of other lands was a significant factor leading up to the Spanish-American War. Through its conquest of the Philippines in 1898, the United States assumed responsibility for a significant Muslim population. After the rapid U.S. victory over Spain in the Spanish-American War, President William McKinley was perplexed as to what to do next, and he prayed strenuously for divine guidance on how to treat the newly conquered Philippine people. One night in prayer in the White House he received an answer:

---

[37] Ibid., 270.

[38] Ibid., 275.

[39] Ibid., 273–78.

[40] Ibid., 276.

[41] Ibid., 279.

[42] Sally Howell, "Laying the Groundwork for American Muslim Histories: 1865–1965", in Hammer, *Cambridge Companion to American Islam*, 45.

That there was nothing left for us to do but to take them all and to educate the Filipinos, and uplift and civilize and Christianize them, and by God's grace do the very best we could by them. . . . And then I went to bed and went to sleep and slept soundly.[43]

Tisa Wenger comments on American attitudes toward the Muslims in the Philippines: "While U.S. colonial officers considered the Catholic Filipinos to be relatively civilized, they classified the predominantly Muslim Moros as 'barbarians' and 'fanatics' who could not yet be trusted with the individual freedoms and responsibilities of democracy."[44] Despite the First Amendment of the U.S. Constitution, Wenger finds, "Across the Philippines, the assemblages of empire identified Christianity with the civilized modern. Many U.S. officials overtly favored Christianity, and sometimes Protestant Christianity in particular, because they viewed it as the ideal grounding for democratic freedoms."[45]

Christian Relations with Muslims in the Twentieth Century

While it is difficult to know exact figures, it is estimated that in the late nineteenth and early twentieth centuries, forty thousand Muslims, mostly males, entered the United States, often coming from the Ottoman Empire in search of better economic opportunities and intending to return to their homelands.[46] By 1920, Muslims were worshipping in a rented hall in Cedar Rapids, Iowa; and in 1921, Muslim migrants in Highland Park, Michigan, built a mosque to serve their community and to welcome Americans to the practice of Islam. However, the growing numbers of Muslim immigrants, together with Catholics and Jews, came at a time of increasing anxieties over the Protestant identity of the United States; the prejudices against immigrants at this time targeted Muslims as well. During the 1920s, new Muslim migrants suffered along with others amid the resurgence of anti-Catholicism, antisemitism, and suspicion of all those foreign to the Northern European Protestant heritage.[47] The immigration laws of the 1920s narrowly curtailed the number of Muslims who were allowed to enter the United States.[48]

During the Great Migration from the South to the North in the 1920s and '30s, many African Americans from a Christian background who were acutely aware of Christianity's racist history in the United States became aware of the legacy of enslaved Muslims from Africa and decided to embrace Islam, establishing mosques

---

[43] Howard Zinn, *A People's History of the United States, 1492–Present* (New York: Perennial Classics, 2001), 313.

[44] Tisa Wenger, *Religious Freedom: The Contested History of an American Ideal* (Chapel Hill: University of North Carolina Press, 2017), 55.

[45] Ibid., 56.

[46] Howell, "Laying the Groundwork," 47.

[47] Zinn, *People's History,* 382.

[48] Ghaneabassiri, *History of Islam,* 150–52.

in many cities across the United States. Muslims see embracing Islam not so much as "conversion" as "reversion."[49] Sometimes African Americans spoke of "reverting" to Islam, mindful of the Islamic heritage of earlier African Americans and also of the Islamic conviction that all humans are naturally in a state of submission to God, or Islam. The practice of African Americans embracing Islam continues to be a significant factor in the United States. In 2019, it is estimated that African Americans comprise 20 percent of Muslims in the United States; and of these, 49 percent, almost half, have embraced, or "converted to," Islam.[50]

A number of African Americans joined the Nation of Islam, founded by W. D. Fard and Elijah Muhammad in the 1930s, which presented a number of beliefs contrary to traditional Islam. Malcolm X followed Elijah Muhammad for a time but left the Nation of Islam and embraced traditional Sunni Islam in 1964, quickly becoming one of the most prominent spokespeople for Sunni Islam in the United States.[51] After the assassination of Malcolm X in 1965, Thomas Merton reflected on his contribution to American life, praising Malcolm X's identity as a Sunni Muslim who was becoming truly a world citizen with "an extraordinary sense of *community,* of brotherhood with other Muslim pilgrims from all parts of the world, *including many who were white.*"[52] Merton believed that Malcolm had outgrown both the ghetto underworld of his early life and the religious underworld of the Nation of Islam and "was finally attaining to the freedom and fullness of understanding that gives some (still rare) American Negroes the sense of belonging to a world movement that makes them independent, to some extent, of purely American limitations and pressures."[53] Merton saw Malcolm's assassination as the price he paid for growing too fast in a way that threatened some in both the white and black communities in the United States.

To a large degree, the national cultural atmosphere in the early and mid-twentieth century did not encourage Christians to hold cordial attitudes toward Muslims. The early twentieth century witnessed the continuing dominance of the Protestant character of American society; and during the 1950s, the religious options that were widely recognized as legitimate in the United States were limited to Protestant, Catholic, and Jew. When Catholics and Jews entered more significantly into American cultural life and society in the 1950s, Muslims were not prominent in the national consciousness and were usually not included in the vision of a Judeo-Christian heritage.

---

[49] Michael Muhammad Knight, "Converts and Conversions," in Hammer, *Cambridge Companion to American Islam*, 83.

[50] Besheer Mohamed and Jeff Diamant, "Black Muslims Account for a Fifth of All U.S. Muslims, and about Half Are Converts to Islam," *Pew Research Center,* January 17, 2019.

[51] James H. Cone, *Martin & Malcolm & America: A Dream or a Nightmare* (Maryknoll, NY: Orbis Books, 1991), 151–212.

[52] Thomas Merton, "The Meaning of Malcolm X," *Continuum* 5, no. 2 (1967): 434–35.

[53] Ibid., 435.

Since the United States changed its immigration laws in 1965, Muslims from a wide variety of different countries and traditions encounter each other in American metropolitan areas, contexts profoundly different from traditional Asian or African cultures. There are both new opportunities for both interreligious and ecumenical dialogue and also continuing challenges.

Recent Encounters

The Catholic Church's public expression of respect for Muslims in *Nostra Aetate* in October 1965 established a new framework for relations between Catholics and Muslims in the United States. *Nostra Aetate* #3 briefly acknowledges the numerous historical conflicts between Muslims and Catholics and then invites both sides "to forget the past" (*praeterita obliviscentes*—perhaps more literally, "becoming oblivious to things gone by") and "make sincere efforts for mutual understanding, and so to work together for the preservation and fostering of social justice, moral welfare, and peace and freedom for all humankind."[54]

In the wake of Vatican II, some Catholic leaders accepted this challenge and began to reach out to Muslims in America seeking better relationships. Chicago's Joseph Cardinal Bernardin declared publicly in 1995 that he hoped to develop Muslim-Catholic relations to the level of Jewish-Catholic relations. He accepted the invitation of the Chicago Muslim Community Center and the American Islamic College in Chicago to attend an *iftar* dinner. The recurrence of cancer prevented him from doing so, and he died in November 1996. His successor, Archbishop Francis George, attended an *iftar* dinner in February 1998, becoming the first archbishop of Chicago to visit a mosque in an official capacity. Shortly after this event, Cardinal-designate George invited a Muslim to be part of his delegation to attend the consistory in Rome when he was created a cardinal. In the spring of 1999 the Archdiocese of Chicago and the Muslim American Society, led by Imam W. D. Muhammad, launched a dialogue involving members of the African American community. The Catholic Theological Union on the south side of Chicago launched the Cardinal Bernardin Center for Theology and Ministry in 1997 to continue Bernardin's legacy with a focus on improving relationships with Jews and Muslims, and also with a Catholic-Muslim Studies program directed by a Catholic scholar of Islam, Scott Alexander. Georgetown University established the Center for Muslim-Christian Understanding in 1993. Beginning in the mid-1980s, there were a number of exchanges between the Christian theological schools in the Chicago area and the American Islamic College. Across the country, a number of local Muslim-Christian dialogues developed.

In October 1991, the National Conference of Catholic Bishops (NCCB), the American Muslim Council, and the Muslim World League organized the first

---

[54] Thomas F. Stransky, "Translation of *Nostra Aetate*," in *Nostra Aetate: Celebrating Fifty Years of the Catholic Church's Dialogue with Jews and Muslims,* ed. Pim Valkenberg and Anthony Cirelli (Washington, DC: Catholic University of America Press, 2016), xxi.

national Muslim-Catholic dialogue. During the 1990s, John Borelli, a representative of the NCCB, helped to organize three regional dialogues of Catholics and Muslims, which met annually.[55] I participated in the Midwest Dialogue of Catholics and Muslims, which reflected on the meaning of the Word of God for Muslims and Catholics, and which produced a joint document on Catholic and Muslim perspectives on revelation in the hope of inspiring further conversations.[56]

In the wake of the attacks of September 11, 2001, there have been countless extremely negative characterizations of Islam, and pejorative stereotypes of Muslims have circulated widely. Vilification of Muslims has continued to be prominent in American life ever since. There have been attacks on mosques and threats against Muslims, as the *Los Angeles Times* reported:

> Attacks on mosques appear to have become more frequent and threats against Muslims more menacing since the terrorist attacks in Paris and the shooting in San Bernardino. "A pigs head at a mosque in Philadelphia, a girl harassed at a school in New York, hate mail sent to a New Jersey mosque ... I can't even count the amount of hate mail and threats we have received," said Ibrahim Hooper, spokesman for the Council on American-Islamic Relations.[57]

Some people in the United States have assaulted those who are commonly mistaken for Muslims, especially Sikhs. On Sunday, December 6, 2015, vandals attacked a Sikh Gurdwara in a suburb of Los Angeles, leaving hateful graffiti directed toward ISIS. Sikh leaders expressed fear that this "hate crime" is a repercussion of the California shooting. Inderjot Singyh, president of Sikh Gurdwara in Buena Park, commented: "We are concerned about the safety and security of our community members. We are of the opinion that this is a hate crime and that this is a direct result of a possible backlash from the San Bernardino killings."[58] In March 2019, there was an arson attack on the Dar-ul-Arqam Mosque in Escondido, California, with statements linking this attack to the assault on the mosque in Christchurch, New Zealand, a short time earlier.

In 2015, the Bridge Initiative of Georgetown University published *The Super Survey: Two Decades of Americans' Views of Islam and Muslims,* which found

---

[55] John Borelli, "Christian-Muslim Relations in the United States: Reflections for the Future after Two Decades of Experience," *Muslim World* 94 (July 2004): 321–33.

[56] *Revelation: Catholic and Muslim Perspectives,* prepared by the Midwest Dialogue of Catholics and Muslims cosponsored by the Islamic Society of North America and the United States Conference of Catholic Bishops (Washington, DC: United States Conference of Catholic Bishops, 2006).

[57] Molly Hennessy-Fiske, "From a Severed Pig's Head to a Bullet-Riddled Koran, Attacks on Muslims Are Rising," *Los Angeles Times,* December 9, 2015.

[58] "Gurdwara Vandalized in Los Angeles with Anti-ISIS Graffiti," *NDTV,* December 9, 2015.

In a climate of increased suspicion and skepticism towards Islam and Muslims, polling data collected over the years reveals how Americans have come to view their country's third-largest religious group. This Super Survey, which compiles and analyzes polling questions collected by over a dozen polling organizations from 1993 to 2014, finds that *Americans remain unfamiliar with Islam; feel more coldly towards Muslims than any other religious group; and tend to see Islam as "more violent" than other religions* during national debates about military action in the Middle East. Additionally, while they have been supportive of mosques in their communities, a sizeable portion has favored various measures of religious profiling. In the twenty-first century, on average, six in ten Americans have reported that they don't know a Muslim personally. And while a plurality of Americans has reported having favorable views of Muslims since 2000, unfavorable views have persisted, with relatively little fluctuation over time.[59]

Subsequently, in 2016, the Bridge Initiative sponsored a study of Catholic attitudes in the United States toward Muslims and found that only about 30 percent of American Catholics had positive views of Muslims, while 14 percent had unfavorable views, 45 percent were neither favorable nor unfavorable, and 11 percent were unsure.[60] Catholics who knew Muslims personally were much more likely to have a favorable attitude toward Muslims in general.

Khaled A. Beydoun studies Islamophobia in the United States today as both a continuation of the age-old animosity toward Muslims and Islam and also as shaped by current events: "Islamophobia is a modern extension and articulation of an old system that branded Muslims as inherently suspicious and unassimilable and cast Islam as a rival ideology at odds with American values, society, and national identity."[61] Current difficulties with Islamophobia emerge from a long history: "The term we are familiar with today rises from a hate America has always known, a hate that helped delineate who fits within the contours of American identity and who deserves to be excluded from those contours."[62] Beydoun defines Islamophobia as "the presumption that Islam is inherently violent, alien, and unassimilable, a presumption driven by the belief that expressions of Muslim identity correlate with a propensity for terrorism."[63]

---

[59] The Bridge Initiative of Georgetown University, *The Super Survey: Two Decades of Americans' Views of Islam and Muslims* (Washington, DC: Georgetown University, November 19, 2015); emphasis in the original.

[60] Jordan Denari Duffner, *Danger and Dialogue: American Catholic Opinion and Portrayals of Islam* (Washington, DC: Georgetown University, 2016), 6.

[61] Khaled A. Beydoun, *American Islamophobia: Understanding the Roots and Rise of Fear* (Oakland: University of California Press, 2018). 18.

[62] Ibid.

[63] Ibid., 28.

In a time of widespread hostility toward Muslims and Islam, responsible religious leaders called for a deeper understanding of Islam and engagement with Muslim leaders.[64] On September 14, 2001, Bishop Tod Brown of Orange, California, the chair of the U.S. Catholic Bishops' Committee for Ecumenical and Interreligious Affairs, together with prominent Islamic leaders in America, issued a joint statement deploring terrorist acts and hate crimes: "We are fully committed to one another as friends, believers and citizens of this great land. We abhor all terrorist acts and hate crimes and implore all American citizens to refrain from sinking to the mentality and immorality of the perpetrators of Tuesday's (September 11, 2001) crimes."[65] On November 14, 2001, the United States Conference of Catholic Bishops issued *A Pastoral Message: Living with Faith and Hope After September 11.* In it the bishops deplored all acts of terrorism as crimes against humanity and added: "Regrettably, the terrorists' notion of a religious war is inadvertently reinforced by those who would attribute the extremism of a few to Islam as a whole or who suggest that religion, by its nature, is a source of conflict." The bishops urged

> A deeper appreciation of the role that religion plays in world affairs is needed, as is a deeper understanding of and engagement with Islam. The Catholic community is engaged in dialogue and common projects with Muslims at many levels and in many ways in this country and around the world. To cite just one example, in many countries Catholic Relief Services is involved in fruitful collaboration with Muslim organizations committed to peace, justice and human rights. More should be done at all levels to deepen and broaden this dialogue and common action.[66]

During this period, the West Coast Dialogue of Catholics and Muslims met under the leadership of Bishop Carlos Sevilla, SJ, bishop of Yakima, Washington; Dr. Muzammil Siddiqi of the Islamic Society of Orange County; and Imam Mustafa Al-Qazini of the Islamic Education Center of Orange County, a Shia Muslim leader. In addition to the dialogues, participants also were present for the evening prayer services of each tradition. In 2003, the West Coast Dialogue issued a statement entitled *Friends and Not Adversaries: A Catholic-Muslim Spiritual Journey,*[67] which

---

[64] John Borelli, "An Overview of Christian-Muslim Relations in a Post-9/11 World," *Origins* 32, no. 37 (February 27, 2003): 615–22.

[65] U.S. Conference of Catholic Bishops' Committee Chairman and Islamic Leaders in America, "Terrorist Acts and Hate Crimes Deplored," *Catholic New Service* 31, no. 16 (September 27, 2001).

[66] United States Conference of Catholic Bishops, *A Pastoral Message: Living with Faith and Hope After September 11,* November 14, 2001; http://www.usccb.org/sdwp/sept11.htm.

[67] The West Coast Dialogue of Catholics and Muslims, "Friends and Not Adversaries: A Catholic-Muslim Spiritual Journey," 2003, http://www.usccb.org/beliefs-and-teachings/ecumenical-and-interreligious/interreligious/islam/friends-and-not-adversaries-a-catholic-muslim-spiritual-journey.cfm.

acknowledges both the tensions in the United States after the events of September 11, 2001, and also the pluralistic character and heritage of the nation: "Our American society that absorbed the tragic blows of September 11 is pluralistic in every major way—religiously, racially, ethnically, and culturally. We enjoy a religious pluralism guaranteed by the Constitution, in that no religious group is legally superior to others."[68] In February 2002, the West Coast dialogue began by focusing on the effects of the tragic events of September 11, 2001. The report noted, "Though feeling we were swimming against a tide of ignorance, uncritical public opinion, hate, and anger, at this meeting we drew closer together as faithful Catholics and Muslims wanting to do the right thing in those difficult weeks and months." The participants affirmed principles that grounded their collaboration:

1. We, Catholics and Muslims, believe that God is the source of peace and justice, and thus we fundamentally agree on the nature of peace and justice and the essential need of all to work for peace and justice.
2. Our rich teachings and traditions of peace and justice serve as a resource and inspiration for all, however, our immediate and present actions to work together are often wanting. The need to work together for peace and justice is a pressing demand in these troubled times.[69]

Theological Explorations

A number of Catholic theologians in the United States have reflected on issues of convergence and divergence in dialogue with Muslims. Precisely because Catholics and Muslims share so much, the differences stand out starkly. Sidney Griffith has provided invaluable historic context for the early Muslim-Christian relations and has been an active participant in contemporary dialogues.[70] In one conversation, Griffith responded to Seyyed Hossein Nasr regarding Muslim-Catholic dialogue after *Nostra Aetate*. In appreciation of Nasr's careful delineation of unresolved doctrinal differences, especially concerning the Trinity and the Incarnation of God in Jesus Christ, Griffith comments on the process of interreligious dialogue:

Where this process leads to rapprochement, a blessing is received; where it leads to inevitable contradiction, it may also lead to that clarity of difference just mentioned, which on scriptural grounds might prompt Christians and Muslims peaceably to leave the judgment on this matter to God and in the meantime to respect one another's goodwill and integrity.[71]

---

[68] Ibid.

[69] Ibid.

[70] Sidney H. Griffith, *The Church in the Shadow of the Mosque: Christians and Muslims in the World of Islam* (Princeton, NJ: Princeton University Press, 2008).

[71] Sidney H. Griffith, "Thoughts on Reading Professor Nasr's 'Muslim Dialogue with the Church after *Nostra Aetate*,'" in Valkenberg and Cirelli, *Nostra Aetate*, 117. See

Griffith celebrates the fifty years of theological conversations between Catholics and Muslims but suggests that "the result has been the identification of areas and topics that require much more in-depth attention than they have yet received on the part of either Muslims or Catholics."[72]

David Burrell has reflected on the meaning of creation, divine action, and eschatology in medieval Jewish, Christian, and Muslim traditions.[73] His careful historical research demonstrates that Jewish, Christian, and Muslim theologians have been thinking comparatively in dialogue with each other since the Middle Ages, as in the relations among Ibn Sina (also known as Avicenna), Moses Maimonides, and Thomas Aquinas.[74] Ibn Sina developed a new understanding of the distinction between essence and existence that clarified the difference between God and creation; this in turn influenced Moses Maimonides and Thomas Aquinas. All three thinkers believed God to be incomprehensible, and they used philosophical resources to probe as deeply as possible into the divine mystery. The outcome, for Burrell is that "the received doctrine of God in the West was already an intercultural, interfaith achievement."[75] Burrell draws the further implication for the future that "philosophical theology must henceforth entail a comparative inquiry among major religious traditions."[76]

Burrell also considers the challenging question of how Christians should view the Islamic claim of divine revelation in the Holy Qur'an. He notes the traditional Catholic teaching that after the revelation of God in Jesus Christ and the apostolic era witnessing to him, no new public revelation is expected before the end of time.[77] Burrell cites the teaching of the Qur'an that God will make the final judgment concerning religious differences and that humans should vie with each other in doing good works until the final judgment (Q 5:48); Burrell then reflects, "The only way we have of discerning the truth (or falsity) of a religious tradition, it seems, is from its fruits. . . . Faith-claims, so-called, are so thoroughly hedged by paradoxes of this sort that it is difficult to speak of ascertaining the *truth* of a religious tradition."[78] Burrell invites dialogue partners "to bracket such questions, and grant the faith assertions of another while exploring their meaning, in an effort to

---

also Seyyed Hossein Nasr, "Muslim Dialogue with the Church after *Nostra Aetate*," in Valkenberg and Cirelli, *Nostra Aetate*, 103–15.

[72] Griffith, "Thoughts," 124.

[73] David B. Burrell, *Freedom and Creation in Three Traditions* (Notre Dame, IN: University of Notre Dame Press, 1993).

[74] David B. Burrell, *Knowing the Unknowable God: Ibn-Sina, Maimonides, Aquinas* (Notre Dame, IN: University of Notre Dame Press, 1986).

[75] Ibid., 109.

[76] Ibid., ix.

[77] David B. Burrell, *Towards a Jewish-Christian-Muslim Theology* (Malden, MA: Wiley-Blackwell, 2011), 179; see Vatican II, *Dei Verbum* (*Dogmatic Constitution on Divine Revelation*), November 18, 1965, #4.

[78] Burrell, *Towards a Jewish-Christian-Muslim Theology,* 181.

probe the coherence and illuminate the life-giving character of another tradition, all the while anticipating that the exchange will also help us better to understand and appreciate our own."[79] Acknowledging that no external scrutiny can adjudicate the faith claims of another tradition, Burrell concludes that "everything points to extending respect to Muslims' faith in the Holy Qur'an, and doing so in such a way as to facilitate a radical change of attitude towards Muslims parallel with that effected towards contemporary Jews."[80]

Hagar as Point of Contact

Despite the history of conflict, in recent years a number of Catholics and other Christians in the United States have sought to develop spiritual awareness by reflecting on central passages in the Bible and the Qur'an in respectful relation to each other, with increasing attention to the relation of the Qur'an to the biblical tradition.[81] One of the most important biblical figures for imagining the relationships among Jews, Christians, and Muslims is Hagar. American Jesuit Thomas Michel reflects on the figure of Hagar in both the biblical and Islamic traditions, proposing that she be viewed as "our common 'Mother in Faith.'"[82] Michel notes that Jews and Christians have historically paid relatively little attention to Hagar, while Muslims have long venerated Hagar as "wife of a prophet, mother of a prophet, and distant ancestress of Muhammad, the Prophet of Islam."[83] Muslims on pilgrimage to Mecca reenact her difficult time in the desert. While each tradition views Hagar from its own perspective, Michel notes that they agree in acknowledging "the compassionate care shown by God to Hagar and her child when she was alone and helpless in the desert."[84] Michel notes that Paul's Letter to the Galatians cites Hagar and Sarah in an allegorical interpretation (Gal 4:21–25). While the Qur'an does not mention Hagar directly, Hadith (reports regarding Prophet Muhammad), recorded by Ibn 'Abbas and Al-Bukhari, tell her story to Muslims. Michel recounts the two narratives in Genesis (16:1–15, 21:8–21), in which Hagar leaves Abram and Sarai twice, faces dire circumstances, and encounters God in the wilderness. Michel notes the Islamic narrative recounted by Al-Bukhari and Ibn 'Abbas, according to which Abraham entrusts Hagar to the care of God, and she is satisfied. At one point Hagar climbs the hill of Safa and then the hill of Marwa and runs back and forth looking for water. When she is on the verge of despair, she cries for help, and the angel Gabriel responds, striking the earth so that water gushes out, saving the lives of Hagar and Ishmael. Muslims on the Hajj reenact the desperate

---

[79] Ibid., 181.

[80] Ibid., 183–84.

[81] Reynolds, *Qur'an and the Bible.*

[82] Thomas F. Michel, *A Christian View of Islam: Essays on Dialogue,* ed. Irfan A. Omar (Maryknoll, NY: Orbis Books, 2010), 83.

[83] Ibid.

[84] Ibid.

running of Hagar between the hills and take water from the well of Zamzam, reenacting the gift of finding water.

Michel stresses the context for viewing Hagar in the strong biblical and Qur'anic traditions of social justice, in which God cares for the widow and the orphan and all those in need. He notes the many people today who are in vulnerable situations such as low-paid domestic workers who are subject to abuse by their employers. Michel holds up Hagar as a model and praises God's care for her. However, Michel notes only in passing the troubling moments in the narrative when God commands Hagar to go back to the dwelling of Abram and Sarai and submit to them (Gn 16:9), and later of God commanding Abram to cast Hagar and her child out into the wilderness (21:12).

Abraham, Jesus, and the Aesthetic

In a similar vein, John Renard is particularly interested in the spiritual readings of each scripture, including symbolic or allegorical forms of interpretation in each tradition. To invite both Christians and Muslims to dialogical consideration of their traditions, Renard juxtaposes two stories of hospitality. The Islamic tradition tells of Abraham meeting a Zoroastrian. According to the tale, Abraham, as the paradigm of radical hospitality, did not have his breakfast each day until he could invite a guest to join him. One day, Abraham came upon an old man whom he welcomed. As the two were preparing to eat breakfast together, Abraham prayed, and then he observed the guest praying a different prayer, distinctive of a worshipper of fire. Abraham abruptly thrust the man out, saying, "I will not share my food with one who prays thus"; however, God demonstrated more interreligious openness than the patriarch, as Renard explains: "God looked down with some irritation and chided the patriarch: I have given this man life and sustenance for a hundred years; could you not be hospitable to him for one hour? Abraham ran after the old Zoroastrian and brought him back home."[85]

Renard compares this narrative to the Johannine story of Jesus and the Samaritan woman at the well, where Jesus speaks of worshipping neither in Jerusalem nor on Gerizim but "in spirit and truth" (Jn 4:24). While Renard admits that the parallel is not exact, he hopes for "the possibility of further mutual Christian-Muslim appreciation of what our respective traditions regard as theory and practice of sanctity."[86] He offers the hopeful invitation:

We need a way to come together in an open field where at least for a time what matters is neither winning nor proving, nor even negotiating, but merely standing together in appreciation of our genuinely shared

---

[85] John Renard, *Islam and Christianity: Theological Themes in Comparative Perspective* (Berkeley: University of California Press, 2011), 228.

[86] Ibid.

theological underpinnings and resolving to find ways to prevent our disagreements from causing a meltdown.[87]

Renard places his greatest hope not in rational argumentation but in the appeal of the aesthetic: "Some of the most deeply consoling experiences of my forty-year encounter with the sources of Islamic tradition have turned on the apprehension of stunning beauty in verbal and visual expression, as well as in thought and feeling."[88] These personal experiences provide the basis for his appeal: "The aesthetic argument finally comes down to this, but unlike the other arguments it presupposes an inaugural experience: once one has had a taste of the beauty and charm of the Islamic theological tradition, one can hardly imagine not engaging it further."[89] The similarities in the values that both Michel and Renard identify in Christianity and Islam provide a basis for investigating common elements in the shared heritage.

Search for Common Ground

In *Common Ground: Islam, Christianity, and Religious Pluralism,* Paul Heck searches for what he hopes will be common ground on which Christians and Muslims can meet, but he also issues a chilling warning: "The common ground may be there one moment and gone the next."[90] Nonetheless, he ventures the hope that even in the most difficult moments, the common ground "is still there, potentially if not always actually."[91] Heck develops this wager by exploring various points of contact and convergence between Islam and Christianity, ranging from divine revelation to moral and social teachings to perspectives on God and politics. He frankly acknowledges that there are areas of disagreement and divergence but accords these relatively less significance.

Posing the intriguing question of whether the Qur'an belongs in the Bible, Heck provocatively suggests "that the Qur'an speaks at all of Jesus makes it a gospel in a certain sense even if not squaring with Christian belief."[92] Heck notes the various ways in which Jesus is described in the New Testament: "The title son of God need not suggest metaphysical stature but rather connotes agent of God's plan for humanity, namely salvation."[93]

In reading the Bible and the Qur'an in relation to each other, Heck suggests that there "are key differences in beliefs but also commonality of purpose," which he describes as "reception of the word of God in the human heart. There is, then,

---

[87] Ibid., 224.

[88] Ibid., 229.

[89] Ibid.

[90] Paul Heck, *Common Ground: Islam, Christianity, and Religious Pluralism* (Washington, DC: Georgetown University Press, 2009), 6.

[91] Ibid.

[92] Ibid., 34.

[93] Ibid., 35.

some sense in looking at these two religions through a single but refracted lens of religious plurality. It is possible to speak of Christianity and Islam, along with rabbinical Judaism, as distinct commentaries on the biblical heritage."[94] He interestingly proposes that both Christianity and Islam can be understood as "rooted in the book of Isaiah."[95] Judaism, for Heck, "stands at the heart of both Christianity and Islam. . . . The common ground is ultimately tripartite."[96] Despite this strong affirmation, Heck focuses principally on Islam and Christianity, relegating Judaism for the most part to the margins of the discussion. The silence of the unheard Jewish interlocutor provides an evocative, elusive framing of all that is said, raising further questions and challenges.

Heck's search for common ground is fundamentally an act of hope that the convergences between the two traditions will prove to be of greater and more lasting importance than the divergences and disagreements. Like Michel and Renard, he looks to spirituality for resources. After acknowledging that the understandings of God among Christians and Muslims often differ in important ways, Heck observes, "Certainly there are similarities in the spirituality of the two religions, the sense of standing in, even cleaving to, the unbounded presence of God and longing for the ubiquitous face of God. There is also similarity in the ethical potential that follows from the encounter with the face of God."[97] Amid all the divergences, Heck finds a movement of convergence: "There is a common Christian-Muslim desire to reduce the ego before the revealed presence of God with a resulting readiness to forgo self-interest for the sake of a relation with God, that is, for the sake of divine favor as ultimate goal, above any worldly standard of success."[98]

Mary as Model of Dialogue

Interpretations of Mary can play many roles in interreligious relations, not all of them helpful. Catholic historical theologian Rita George-Tvrtkovic comments that Catholic veneration of Mary as Our Lady of Victory casts her into the role of "the quintessential symbol of enmity between Christians and Muslims—a symbol that has long endured, in part thanks to strong cultural props."[99] Mary became a patron for Catholics against both Muslims and Protestants, and indeed, for one European Catholic nation against another. "Clearly, the image of Mary battling Muslims has had staying power."[100]

---

[94] Ibid., 35, 36.

[95] Ibid., 36.

[96] Ibid., 2.

[97] Ibid., 107.

[98] Ibid., 108.

[99] Rita George-Tvrtkovic, *Christians, Muslims, and Mary: A History* (New York: Paulist Press, 2018), 71.

[100] Ibid., 72.

Despite the troubled history, George-Tvrtkovic notes that many elements allow Mary to serve as a bridge between Muslims and Christians. Mary is the only woman mentioned by her own name in the Holy Qur'an, and she is the only woman for whom a *sura* (chapter) of the Qur'an is named. The Qur'an presents Mary as a model of virtues: "These include faith (66:12), obedience (66:12, 3:43), pious submission, and even *ma'rifah* (secret knowledge of the divine)."[101] Above all, the Qur'an presents Mary as one specially chosen by God above all other women (3:42). George-Tvrtkovic notes that "Islamic tradition singles out Mary and Jesus as the only human persons untouched by Satan."[102] In the Qur'an, Mary is highly praised as the virginal mother of a prophet, and some Muslims have seen Mary herself as a prophet.

In an address to an interreligious banquet sponsored by the American Muslim Council on December 8, 1995, the Feast of the Immaculate Conception, William Cardinal Keeler, Archbishop of Baltimore, suggested that Mary could serve as a bridge in Muslim-Catholic relations: "It is certainly true that in her very person there is a meeting point, or at least a stepping stone, between Christianity and Islam."[103] George-Tvrtkovic acknowledges that Catholic theologians have not yet given a great deal of attention to Mary in relation to Muslims, but she suggests "Mary's greatest promise for Christian-Muslim relations today may not be doctrinal but devotional and dialogical."[104] Mary is frequently associated with mercy in Catholic piety, and this virtue is central for the Islamic tradition as well.

As we have seen, medieval Catholic theology views our condition in this world as that of *viatores,* wayfarers. The condition of a wayfarer is in-between, on the road toward a destination that is anticipated but not yet reached. Christians since the early centuries have made pilgrimages to sacred places, often as penitents seeking God's forgiveness for the sins of the past and praying for absolution and a new start toward a better future. Muslims also have a tradition of sacred pilgrimage to holy places. Christian wayfarers today can welcome Muslims as companions for the journey. While respecting the important differences between our traditions, we can hope that our journeys bring us close enough to each other that we are within the range of conversation.

As a Franciscan, Kathleen Warren appreciates the visit of Francis of Assisi to Sultan Malek al-Kamil during the Fifth Crusade and looks to the courage of Francis as a model for Muslims and Catholics in the United States and beyond:

> In the spirit of the one who fearlessly entered the camp of the "enemy" as a friend and brother, may Francis teach us today how to "be with" those

---

[101] Ibid., 39.

[102] Ibid.

[103] Cardinal William Keeler, "How Mary Holds Christians and Muslims in Conversations," December 8, 1995.

104 George-Tvrtkovic, *Christians, Muslims,* 155.

who are different from us and those from who we are alienated. . . . Francis'
eloquent witness, which has long been unheard, can lead us into new ways
of presence and exchange.[105]

The images of Francis of Assisi and Sultan Malek al-Kamil offer a hopeful model of
interreligious presence.

---

[105] Kathleen A. Warren, *Daring to Cross the Threshold: Francis of Assisi Encounters
Sultan Malek al-Kamil* (Rochester, MN: Franciscan Institute, 2003), 113.

6

HINDU-CATHOLIC RELATIONS
IN THE UNITED STATES

While the Hindu population of the United States of America has never been extremely large, Christian awareness of Hindus and Hindu wisdom has played a significant role in shaping American thought and culture, from the Transcendentalists' reading of the Bhagavad Gita in the 1830s and '40s to the dramatic speeches of Vivekananda in Chicago in 1893, the impact of the nonviolent path of resistance of Mahatma Gandhi on the African American Civil Rights movement, and the widespread practice of yoga.

Christian relationships with Hindus in the United States have been complex and often conflicted. The term "Hinduism" was not a traditional name for a religion in India. "Hindu" was a geographical term relating to the region near the Indus River. The religious heritage of South Asia included a variety of traditions, and often religious practice was referred to as *Sanatana Dharma,* which has been translated as "the Eternal Truth" or "Eternal Law." As the British came to rule over more and more of India, they used the word "Hinduism" for a variety of forms of religious practice on the subcontinent. There is no central Hindu organization or creed. While Hindus generally accept the Vedas as revelation, there is no one way of interpreting them. Although the term "Hinduism" is problematic, contemporary Hindus in the United States accept it as a term of self-designation.

Hindu scholar Arvind Sharma explains that

> a Hindu may be identified as one who does not deny being one. The collectivity of the beliefs and practices of those who accept the designation constitutes Hinduism. It is a peculiarly Hindu phenomenon that Hinduism may be defined as the religion of the Hindus and that this definition should, however narrowly, escape tautology.[1]

Sharma plays with the semantic possibilities: "Pushed to its logical extreme, a Hindu can claim that one is most a Hindu when least a Hindu, that is, when one has dissolved one's Hindu particularity in Hinduism's all-embracing inclusiveness.

---

[1] Arvind Sharma, "Hinduism," in *Our Religions,* ed. Arvind Sharma (San Francisco: HarperSanFrancisco, 1993), 5.

Hinduism in this extreme formulation paradoxically becomes identical with its own negation!"[2] Hindus often are open to including Buddhists, Jains, and Sikhs among their number; but these communities usually do not accept this designation.

Nineteenth-Century Perceptions of Hindus and Hinduism

Christian responses to Hindus and Hinduism in the United States have gone through various stages. In the early nineteenth century, as the British East India Company extended its rule over more and more of India, growing numbers of American Protestant missioners journeyed to India to preach the Gospel and establish churches and schools. Their reports to Americans about Hindu practices were overwhelmingly negative; they criticized the worship of images and the burning of widows, and stressed the contrast between the mischievous Krishna and trustworthy Jesus Christ.[3] Many of the initial American images of Hindus and Hinduism were extremely critical.

Nonetheless, during this period, a few Americans began reading Hindu texts for themselves and discovering value in the Hindu tradition. In 1822, at the home of Reverend Elijah Parish in Byfield, Massachusetts, Mary Moody Emerson, the aunt of Ralph Waldo Emerson, made the acquaintance of a Hindu visitor from India who was a disciple of the Bengali reformer Rammohan Roy.[4] Mary wrote enthusiastically to her nephew Ralph about the encounter, suggesting a convergence between Hindu and Christian perspectives on incarnation, especially a shared sense of God's universal presence and agency.[5] Nine years later, in February 1831, Ralph's wife Ellen died prematurely. During this intense time of personal loss, Emerson turned to the Bhagavad Gita, which offered him a fresh perspective on life and death.[6] He found in the Gita a wisdom that he regarded as equal to the Christian Gospels, and he incorporated Hindu perspectives into his notion of the Oversoul. While Emerson eventually rejected Christian faith, his writings influenced many Christian readers to view Hindu perspectives positively.

Emerson's friend Henry David Thoreau pondered the wisdom he found in the Bhagavad Gita during his famous stay at Walden Pond, and the influence of the Gita runs throughout *Walden, or Life in the Woods*. Paul Friedrich comments on similarities between Thoreau and the Bhagavad Gita: "For both, the attainment

---

[2] Ibid., 4.

[3] Sushil Madhava Pathak, *American Missionaries and Hinduism: A Study of Their Contacts from 1813 to 1910* (Delhi, India: Munshiram Manoharlal, 1967), 79–81.

[4] Peter Manseau, *One Nation, Under Gods: A New American History* (New York: Little, Brown, 2015), 257–62.

[5] Mary Moody Emerson, *The Selected Letters of Mary Moody Emerson*, ed. Nancy Craig Simmons (Athens: University of Georgia Press, 1993), 152; Manseau, *One Nation*, 262.

[6] Robert D. Richardson Jr., *Emerson: The Mind on Fire* (Berkeley: University of California Press, 1995), 108–17.

of revealed truth enables the enlightened few to partly grasp the divinity of the individual self or soul and the divinity of the cosmos or oversoul: the individual spark and the great fire from which it emanated and into which it must eventually fall."[7] Each text is complex, and Friedrich notes that both Thoreau and the Gita also challenge elitism:

> In both books a second consequence of attaining revealed truth is the capacity, not only to see the universal spirit in the particular, but to see that all particulars are the same, to be indifferent to the differences between a Brahmin and a garbage collector, between a lotus and a loon. This realization of inner sameness implies an egalitarian overriding of literary elitism and is fully concurrent with the aforementioned denial of opposites.[8]

Both Thoreau and the Gita praise the path of loving devotion, and both combine perspectives that conserve the traditional social order with promises to subvert it. Friedrich concludes that "someone familiar with both texts can open the latter [Thoreau's *Walden*] at random to any page and find or at least have intimations of the underlying, directive presence of the Gita within."[9]

While Emerson and Thoreau came to appreciate Hindu and Buddhist perspectives, they did not have a clear sense of any distinction between these traditions. Emerson wrote a letter describing the enthusiastic reception given to the Bhagavad Gita as a Buddhist text in Concord, Massachusetts, in 1843: "The only other event is the arrival in Concord of the Bhagavad Gita, the renowned book of Buddhism."[10]

Some years later, another giant of American thought turned to the Hindu tradition for consolation and inspiration during a time of personal grief. In 1870, the young William James suffered trauma from the illness and death of his beloved cousin Minnie Temple. In wrestling with his personal tragedy, he came to appreciate the wisdom of the Upanishads. Thirteen days after her death, James wrote in his diary:

> Minnie, your death makes me feel the nothingness of all our egotistical fury. The inevitable release is sure: wherefore take our turn kindly, whatever it contains. Ascend to some sort of partnership with fate, and since tragedy is at the heart of us, go to meet it, work it to our ends, instead of dodging it all our days, and being run down by it at last. Use your death (or your life, it's all one meaning) *tat tvam asi*.[11]

---

[7] Paul Friedrich, *The Gita within Walden* (Albany: State University of New York Press, 2008), 146.

[8] Ibid.

[9] Ibid., 148.

[10] Ibid., 25.

[11] William James, Diary 1, March 22, 1870; Robert D. Richardson, *William James*

Years later, the mature James would return to the question of identity in his reflections on mysticism and religious experience.[12] Emerson, Thoreau, and James would have a wide influence on American Christians, paving the way for positive views of Hindus and Hinduism. With the exception of Mary Moody Emerson's personal encounter with the Hindu visitor, their contacts were largely literary; personal encounters with Hindus would shift attitudes further.

The Arrival of Vivekananda

The first Hindu to come to the United States and receive widespread attention was a thirty-year-old disciple of the mystic Ramakrishna, Swami Vivekananda, who traveled all the way from India to Chicago in 1893 without realizing that it was necessary to have credentials to be registered as a delegate at the World's Parliament of Religions. Upon arrival in Chicago, he was informed that without a letter authorizing him to represent a religious organization, he would not be recognized as an official delegate and would not be authorized to speak at the Parliament. Crestfallen, the Swami left Chicago for Boston; on the train a woman was impressed by his robes and invited him to stay with her. She introduced him to a Harvard professor of Greek, J. H. Wright, who was a friend of the organizer of the Parliament responsible for selecting the delegates. Wright wrote letters to the organizers of the Parliament commending the young Hindu and then purchased a train ticket for him to return to Chicago. However, Vivekananda lost the address of the committee responsible for delegates, arrived in a German-speaking neighborhood where no one could understand him, and spent a night in an empty railroad wagon. In the morning he walked along Lake Michigan, begged for food without success, and sat down weary and frustrated. Mrs. George W. Hale noticed him, offered him breakfast, and accompanied him to the office of her friend, John Henry Barrows, the principal organizer of the Parliament. Vivekananda's biographer commented, "Once again the Swami had been strengthened in his conviction that the Lord was guiding his footsteps, and he prayed incessantly to be a worthy instrument of His will."[13]

Through his personality and vivid style of teaching, Vivekananda powerfully introduced Hindu thought to American Christians. On the opening day of the World Parliament of Religions, Vivekananda went to the podium for an impromptu address, threw open his arms, and cried out: "My brothers and sisters in America!" The crowd went wild with applause. He was a tremendous sensation, presenting Hindu perspectives in an attractive light that impressed many American

in the Maelstrom of American Modernism: A Biography (Boston: Mariner Books, 2007), 112–13.

[12] William James, *The Varieties of Religious Experience* (1902; reprint, New York: Penguin, 1985).

[13] Swami Nikhilananda, *Vivekananda: A Biography* (Calcutta, India: Advaita Ashrama, 1982), 115.

Christians who had never seen or heard a Hindu before. He proclaimed that all religions were true revelations of God, so many different refractions of the same divine light coming into this world. He believed that Hinduism was the clearest refraction of the light but also that all religions were paths of salvation. He believed that each person is potentially divine and should work to unleash the divine power that is latent within. The organizers of the Parliament realized that when other speakers were boring the crowd, they could send Vivekananda back up to revive their interest.

Vivekananda believed that people in Western nations were in search of a religious message and would self-destruct if they did not find it. He traveled across the United States after the Parliament and founded the Vedanta Society of New York in November 1894.[14] The Hindus of the Ramakrishna Mission treasure his memory. In the Ramakrishna Museum along the Ganges River near Calcutta, there is a statue of Vivekananda with his arms folded standing in front of a model of the façade of the Art Institute of Chicago. As a result of the influence of Vivekananda, many American Christians in the twentieth century viewed Hinduism largely through the lens of the Advaita Vedanta tradition he represented. Vivekananda had a powerful influence on Indians as well, including the young Mohandas Gandhi.

The Influence of Mahatma Gandhi and *Satyagraha*

For most American Christians, the most important and influential interpreter of Hinduism of the twentieth century was the Mahatma, Mohandas Gandhi. As a young man, Gandhi was very moved by Jesus's teachings in the Sermon on the Mount, and Gandhi embraced these together with the Hindu teachings of the Bhagavad Gita as central to his life and thought.[15] Prior to Gandhi, most Christians respected the teachings of Jesus concerning loving one's enemies, turning the other cheek, and going the extra mile. But Christians generally did not believe these sayings offered practical strategies for transforming society. Gandhi developed his program of *satyagraha* (literally "grasping truth," that is, nonviolent resistance to injustice) in South Africa and then brought it to India. Reinhold Niebuhr, the most influential North American theologian of the twentieth century, watched carefully what Gandhi was doing in India in the 1920s and '30s. While he critiqued Gandhi for not acknowledging that *Satyagraha* was using forms of violence, Niebuhr nonetheless thought Gandhi's approach could be helpfully applied to the situation of African Americans. In 1932, Niebuhr suggested a path of African American nonviolent resistance inspired by Gandhi that Martin Luther King Jr. would later implement.[16]

---

[14] Carl T. Jackson, *Vedanta for the West: The Ramakrishna Movement in the United States,* Religion in North America Series (Bloomington: Indiana University Press, 1994).

[15] Mahatma Gandhi, *Gandhi on Christianity,* ed. Robert Ellsberg (Maryknoll, NY: Orbis Books, 1991).

[16] Reinhold Niebuhr, *Moral Man and Immoral Society: A Study in Ethics and Politics* (1932; reprint, New York: Charles Scribner's Sons, 1960), 254.

As African American leaders looked for strategies of resistance to the dominant racism of their society, the influence of Mahatma Gandhi's practice of *satyagraha* to seek nonviolent social innovation was of great importance. In 1936, the African American theologian Howard Thurman led a delegation of African American leaders to visit Mahatma Gandhi in India. This is arguably the most influential Hindu-Christian conversation in the history of the United States, not only for Christians but for overall influence on American life and culture.[17] Thurman learned that Gandhi, like many African Americans and American Indians, made a distinction between the religion of Jesus and what Christians were doing: "I close this section of my discussion with the rather striking words of Mahatma Gandhi to me: 'The greatest enemy that the religion of Jesus has in India is Christianity in India.'"[18] Thurman and other African Americans studied Gandhi's practice of *satyagraha,* which has been variously translated as "grasping truth," "grasping reality," or "soul-force," or simply as "stubbornness," and pondered its relevance for addressing racial discrimination in the United States. Paradoxically, it was a Hindu who opened the eyes of many Christians to the significance of Jesus's teaching for nonviolent resistance to social evil.[19]

Thurman was a close friend of Martin Luther King Sr., and the young Martin Luther King Jr. studied the writings of Niebuhr, Gandhi, and Thurman as he was formulating his own program. King traveled to India only in 1959, long after the death of Gandhi, but King commented on the impact of the Mahatma:

> Gandhi was probably the first person in history to lift the love ethic of Jesus above mere interaction between individuals to a powerful and effective force on a large scale. Love for Gandhi was a potent instrument for social and collective transformation. It was in this Gandhian emphasis on love and nonviolence that I discovered the method of social reform.[20]

King later commented that Gandhi taught him for the first time that "the Christian doctrine of love, operating through the Gandhian method of nonviolence, is one of the most potent weapons available to an oppressed people in their struggle for freedom."[21] While King disagreed with Gandhi on certain particular issues, Coretta

---

[17] Howard Thurman, *With Head and Heart: The Autobiography of Howard Thurman* (San Diego, CA: Harvest Book, 1979), 131–35.

[18] Howard Thurman, "What We May Learn from India," in *American Religions: A Documentary History,* ed. R. Marie Griffith (Oxford: Oxford University Press, 2008), 496.

[19] Terrence J. Rynne, *Gandhi and Jesus: The Saving Power of Nonviolence* (Maryknoll, NY: Orbis Books, 2008).

[20] Martin Luther King, Jr., *Stride toward Freedom* (New York: Harper & Brothers, 1958), 97–98; see also Rynne, *Gandhi and Jesus.*

[21] John J. Ansbro, *Martin Luther King, Jr.: Nonviolent Strategies and Tactics for Social Change* (Lanham, MD: Madison Books, 2000), 7.

Scott King later recalled her husband repeating the refrain "Christ gave us the goals, and Mahatma Gandhi provided the tactics."[22]

Countless Christians in many different contexts followed the lead of Gandhi in seeking new ways to implement the teaching of Jesus concerning nonviolent resistance to evil. Among many others, Walter Wink developed a thorough-going Gandhian interpretation of Jesus's "Third Way," which does not accept evil structures in society but does not use violent force to overthrow them. Instead, Wink interprets Jesus in Gandhian fashion as challenging the consciousness of oppressors and opening up the "Third Way" of nonviolent resistance to oppression, especially by transforming the consciousness of one's opponent.[23] Wink followed the lead of Gandhi in developing a hermeneutic that applied scriptural principles to concrete questions of social engagement.

Yoga in the United States

Another aspect of Hindu influence on American Christians lies in the practice of yoga. The tradition of yoga goes back to the very early period of South Asian culture, shaping many of the religious traditions in this vast subcontinent and finding classic expression in the Yoga Sutras of Patanjali and in the Bhagavad Gita. The ancient Indian tradition distinguishes four major forms of yoga: *karma yoga* focuses on proper action in accordance with one's dharma (duty); *bhakti yoga* cultivates devotion to God; *jnana yoga* seeks transformational insight into saving truth; and *raja yoga* develops concentration of the mind as a path to realizing oneness with the ultimate. *Raja yoga* draws upon the physical and mental practices of *hatha yoga*. When Christians practice yoga, often it is the discipline of *hatha yoga* that they engage most directly.

While Patanjali has been immensely influential, there is no one philosophy of yoga, and practitioners in India have long approached the practice of yoga from diverse theoretical perspectives. Christians who practice yoga may or may not be aware of the sophisticated philosophical and religious reflections of Indian thinkers. Many American Christians seek physical and emotional benefits without attending to the intellectual and religious context of yoga in Indian philosophical thought.

In 1948, a French Benedictine monk, Henri Le Saux, traveled to India to explore the resources of the Hindu tradition. He sought the guidance of the renowned guru, Sri Ramana Maharshi, and came to an experience of nonduality with ultimate reality, known in Sanskrit as *advaita*. While remaining a Catholic priest and Benedictine monk, Le Saux adopted the lifestyle of a Hindu renunciant or *sannyasi*, that is, someone who has given up all property, lives a simple, ascetic, celibate life in accordance with nonviolence (*ahimsa*) in pursuit of liberation (*moksha*). Together with another French priest, Jules Monchanin, he founded

---

[22] Coretta Scott King, "Foreword," in Martin Luther King Jr., *Strength to Love* (Minneapolis: Fortress Press, 2010), ix.

[23] Walter Wink, *Jesus and Nonviolence: A Third Way* (Minneapolis: Fortress Press, 2003).

a spiritual hermitage (*ashram*) named Shantivanam in the south of India. In accordance with Hindu practice, Le Saux received a new name and came to be known as Abhishiktananda (Bliss of the Anointed Lord).

Following in their footsteps was one of the most important mentors for American Catholics who practice yoga, Bede Griffiths, a Catholic Benedictine monk from England, who went to India in 1955 and similarly immersed himself in the way of life of a Hindu *sannyasi*, receiving the name Dayananda (Bliss of Compassion). Griffiths studied the Vedic tradition, including the philosophical perspectives of Advaita Vedanta, and integrated many aspects of Hindu practice into his life as a Catholic priest and monk. He explains how meditation in the tradition of yoga contributed to his development: "How can I get to know myself? Not by thinking, for thinking only reflects my conscious being, but by meditating. Meditation goes beyond the conscious mind into the unconscious. In meditation I can become aware of the ground of my being in matter, in life, in human consciousness."[24]

For Griffiths as a Catholic, the practice of meditation was a way of entering more deeply into the mystery of the Holy Trinity, seeking the goal of union with the ultimate that is beyond all names: "Thus the sannyasi is called to go beyond all religion, beyond every human institution, beyond every scripture and creed, till coming to that which every religion and scripture and ritual signifies but can never name."[25] For Griffiths, this did not, however, mean abandonment or rejection of Christian faith but the culmination of the spiritual journey into God: "Yet when we say that the sannyasi goes beyond religion, this does not mean that the sannyasi rejects any religion. I have not felt called to reject anything that I have learned of God or of Christ or of the Church."[26] For Griffiths, as for many other Christians, the practice of a form of meditation coming from another religious tradition did not contradict Christian faith but led to a greater depth and intensity of the experience of God.[27]

The main focus of Griffiths's attention was on the development of spiritual life in dialogue with the Vedic tradition. Some, including his long-time friend Jyoti Sahi, criticized him for neglecting the Dalit (formerly Untouchable) and Adivasi (tribal) communities of India, who had long felt alienated from the Brahmanic tradition. Griffiths believed that the Sanskrit tradition had influenced all strata of Indian society through the great epics the Ramayana and the Mahabharata. His biographer Shirley du Boulay comments, "Bede's background and temperament remained a product of the middle-class, intellectual, Oxford-educated Englishman that he was; like any man he had his limitations and he knew it. But even if the accusation of elitism stands, it never led him to fail in compassion or in love."[28]

---

[24] Bede Griffiths, *Essential Writings*, ed. with intro. Thomas Matus (Maryknoll, NY: Orbis Books, 2004), 43.

[25] Ibid., 98.

[26] Ibid.

[27] For an overview of his life and spirituality, see Shirley du Boulay, *Beyond the Darkness: A Biography of Bede Griffiths* (New York: Doubleday, 1998).

[28] Ibid, 211.

Griffiths greatly admired the Asian liberation theology of Aloysius Pieris, a Sri Lankan Jesuit engaged in Buddhist-Catholic dialogue. Malkovsky recalled that Griffiths praised Pieris as

> the best theologian in Asia. He did not say that Pieris was just the best among the liberation theologians, but the best theologian in Asia—period. And yet he felt it was a mistake that many of the liberation theologians in India had begun turning away from the rich mystical and wisdom heritage of Hinduism and Buddhism. He felt that both liberations were needed, the interior transformation as well as the social.[29]

Griffiths had a major influence on many Catholics in the United States who adopted practices and perspectives of Hinduism into their religious lives.

A number of American Catholics, including Pascaline Coff, Thomas Ryan, Bradley Malkovsky, and Thomas Matus, visited Griffiths at his ashram Shantivanam, learned about his method of interreligious spiritual integration, and then returned to the United States. Pascaline Coff, a Benedictine Sister of Perpetual Adoration, spent time with Griffiths in India in 1976 and then became a leader in monastic interreligious efforts in the United States. She participated in founding Osage Forest of Peace Monastery, which was originally a Benedictine foundation that drew upon both Hindu and American Indian resources, especially the heritage of the Osage nation, which lives in the vicinity. The Benedictines later entrusted responsibility for the community to a lay board, and today it is an interspiritual contemplative retreat center. Coff was also instrumental in establishing the North American Board for East-West dialogue, which later became Monastic Interreligious Dialogue, an organization of Catholic monastics in dialogue with their counterparts in other religions.[30] Monastic Interreligious Dialogue has played a major role in developing Buddhist-Catholic relations in the United States as well.

Thomas Ryan, a Paulist priest, also visited Bede Griffiths and spent time with him at Shantivanam. Ryan returned to the United States inspired to probe more deeply into the resources of yoga, and he received formal training at the Kripalu Yoga Center in Lenox, Massachusetts, receiving certification as a yoga instructor. Ryan notes a far-reaching irony: for Hindus and Buddhists who believe in rebirth, our current body is simply one of many in our trajectory, but they have devoted tremendous attention to the posture and movement of the body in meditation practices. Christians believe in the resurrection and thus see the body as an everlasting element in our identity, but they have traditionally devoted far less attention than Hindus or Buddhists to the posture and movement of the body in meditation.

---

[29] Bradley Malkovsky, *God's Other Children: Personal Encounters with Faith, Love, and Holiness in Sacred India* (New York: HarperOne, 2013), 159.

[30] On the history of Monastic Interreligious Dialogue, see Fabrice Blée, *The Third Desert: The Story of Monastic Interreligious Dialogue,* trans. William Skudlarek and Mary Grady (Collegeville, MN: Liturgical Press, 2011).

Many Christians have experienced an unhealthy split between their body and their spiritual life. In response, Ryan seeks to integrate heart and body together as a way of opening to God. Ryan explains the relation in yoga practice between the quest for God and the physical practice of meditation:

> Seekers of conscious union with the divine in various ancient civilizations subjected to careful study the repercussions of various bodily gestures and attitudes on the spiritual in our nature. They discovered, for example, that by keeping the body still you calm the mind; that by concentrating your attention, you settle the body; that by certain methods of breath-control, the mind becomes quiet and focused. This evolved a system of practices: physical postures (*asanas*), breath-control (*pranayama*), and mental focusing on what is happening in the body-mind when one enters into and holds the posture. Together, these things make up hatha yoga.[31]

Ryan combines practice of the physical postures (*asanas*) of yoga practice with traditional Christian prayers such as the Lord's Prayer and the Prayer of St. Francis.[32] Ryan relates the Christian practice of yoga to the central principle of the faith that God has become incarnate in Jesus of Nazareth. The incarnation reveals to Christians "All flesh is holy and the ground of all human endeavors is sacred. It is in these bodies that we work out our salvation."[33] Thus, Ryan explains, there is an inner harmony between Christian faith and yoga:

> What we are doing is discovering in yoga a concrete application of our incarnational faith. The use of bodily postures to open us to God is already well-established in our own practice. . . . Yoga is a way to help us fully inhabit our bodies and to begin using them to more fully actualize what God calls us to be.[34]

Bradley Malkovsky, who was also profoundly influenced by the example of Bede Griffiths, reflects on the benefits that yoga practice can bring Christians. Like Ryan, he commends the holistic approach of yoga while noting a paradox: "The *final goal* of yoga might be defined in dualistic terms as a separation of the body from the spirit, but the *path* to that goal involves *sustained attention to the body and mind* as vehicles or tools of liberation."[35] Malkovsky praises the "sound wisdom and practical advice" of the yogic tradition as well as the benefits of

---

[31] Thomas Ryan, *Prayer of Heart and Body: Meditation and Yoga as Christian Spiritual Practice* (New York: Paulist Press, 1995), 137.

[32] These are available on DVD: Thomas Ryan, *Yoga Prayer: An Embodied Christian Spiritual Practice* (Sounds True, 2005).

[33] Ryan, *Prayer of Heart and Body*, 145.

[34] Ibid.

[35] Malkovsky, *God's Other Children*, 146, emphasis in original.

practicing the *asanas*. Malkovsky recommends the calming power of sustained attention to the mind, and yet he also notes the limits of yoga for Christians, since he finds it to be "basically a self-help discipline. This is true in both its ancient and modern expressions."[36] While he is careful to observe that yoga itself is not prayer, he is aware that "Christian practitioners often enough use yoga as a tool to center themselves so that they may learn to pray from a deeper place within themselves."[37] Malkovsky finds a fundamental limit to what yoga can offer Christians:

> Yoga practice may help to purify the mind and heart, but it does not teach people how to give their hearts to God or to open themselves to God who is Person. In yoga there is no asking or entreaty to a personal God. . . . There is *no relationship with a God of love* here, no prayer, no abandonment to divine love or to the sovereignty of the divine will.[38]

Thomas Matus, an American Camaldolese monk, received training in Christian monastic contemplation and Kriya Yoga initiation in the lineage of Paramahansa Yogananda; he spent time with Bede Griffiths at Shantivanam[39] and reflected on the practice of yoga in relation to the Jesus prayer, especially as taught by Symeon the New Theologian (949–1022). Matus explains his approach to yoga: "I personally have no interest in the attempt to blend Christianity with Hinduism or Buddhism into some kind of higher synthesis. Nor do I see any need to adopt the outward trappings of an Asian culture (clothing, diet, etc.) along with its spiritual disciplines."[40] Matus expressed concern about how yoga can contribute to the practice of the Christian life: "What is at issue for me is the use of yoga as an aid to dedicating my whole being to Christ and in fulfilling Christ's law of loving service to my neighbor."[41] He stresses that "as a practical method (apart from the metaphysical and theological systems of Hinduism and Buddhism), yoga is no more incompatible with Christianity than is a taste for exotic foods or unconventional attire."[42] However, Matus did find that the Tantric tradition of yoga offered resources to Christians: "The most helpful insight that Tantrism offers us is the way it resolves the tension between the sacred and the profane by the positive and sacrificial value it gives to all human experience."[43] He compares this to the Letter of Titus: "to the pure all things are pure" (Ti 1:15), and he stresses the

---

[36] Ibid., 147.

[37] Ibid.

[38] Ibid., 148.

[39] Thomas Matus, *Ashram Diary: In India with Bede Griffiths* (Winchester, UK: O-Books, 2009).

[40] Thomas Matus, *Yoga and the Jesus Prayer* (1984; revised edition, Winchester, UK: O-Books, 2010), 9.

[41] Ibid.

[42] Ibid., 10.

[43] Ibid., 117.

Christian continuity between body and spirit made possible through the personal experience of God in the world: "God purifies, sanctifies, and deifies the participant in the sacraments through physical contact with these signs, which are thus called 'efficacious' in virtue of the Holy Spirit's descent into their materiality."[44] Noting both points of contact and important differences, Matus integrates the practice of yoga into Catholic spiritual life.

Some Hindus have criticized those who engage in the practice of yoga apart from the traditional context of Hinduism. While Griffiths received support and approval from many Hindu leaders, Swami Devananda and Sita Ram Goel launched a fierce critique of his practice of combining Hindu and Catholic elements in his religious life.[45] Griffiths responded in a letter to Devananda, "I have known many Hindu sannyasis, visited many ashrams and had many Hindu friends, but no one before has ever objected to anything I have done."[46] There is currently a lively debate over the relation between the modern practice of yoga and the ancient traditions of South Asia.[47] The wide variety of practices of yoga in different traditions in South Asia offers a precedent for followers of other religious paths today to take up the ancient way.

Responses to Advaita Vedanta

As we have seen, Vivekananda taught a form of Advaita Vedanta at the World Parliament of Religions in 1893; he and his followers in the Vedanta societies in the United States helped to shape American perceptions of Hinduism as focusing largely on Advaita Vedanta, radical nondualism, which has often been understood as a form of monist philosophy. A number of Catholics active in the United States have reflected on Christian experience in relation to the Vedanta. Raimon Panikkar was born in 1918 near Barcelona to a Hindu father and a Catalan mother, and grew up influenced by both traditions. He came to the United States, where he taught for many years at Harvard Divinity School and the University of California, Santa Barbara, influencing many people in the United States and beyond. As an interreligious explorer and scholar, he entered deeply into both Hindu and Buddhist perspectives, articulating a creative theology that drew from Christian, Hindu, and Buddhist wisdom while being in dialogue with contemporary nonbelievers. He perceived the cosmic Christ of the Gospel of John and the Epistle to the Colossians to be active in the Hindu tradition and trusted that the manifestations of wisdom in both the Hindu and Christian traditions ultimately converged beyond all the

---

[44] Ibid.

[45] *Catholic Ashrams: Adopting and Adapting Hindu Dharma,* ed. Sita Ram Goel (New Delhi: Voice of India Publications, 1988).

[46] Bede Griffiths, Letter to Swami Devananda; du Boulay, *Beyond the Darkness,* 212.

[47] Mark Singleton, *Yoga Body: The Origins of Modern Posture Practice* (Oxford: Oxford University Press, 2010); see also the review of this book by Wendy Doniger, "Assume the Position," *Times Literary Supplement* (March 4, 2011): 10–11.

differences: "This, then, is Christ: the reality from whom everything has come, in whom everything subsists, to whom everything that suffers the wear and veil of time shall return."[48] Panikkar believed that the Christ through whom all things are created is at the center of Hindu wisdom as well: "Hence from the point of view of Christianity, Christ is already present in Hinduism. The spirit of Christ is already at work in Hindu prayer. Christ is already present in every form of worship, to the extent that it is adoration directed to God."[49] He invited Christians to explore new dimensions of Christ in the Upanishads and other Hindu writings.

Bradley Malkovsky also studied the tradition of Advaita Vedanta, especially as taught by its most influential interpreter, Samkara. Many Western scholars have interpreted Advaita Vedanta and Samkara in particular as teaching a form of monism in which there are no distinctions whatsoever; such a doctrine would be sharply opposed to traditional Christian teaching. Malkovsky notes that most interpreters have understood Samkara to teach that "the world appears to exist only to the ignorant, to those who have not attained Self-realization."[50] Malkovsky, however, challenges this interpretation, studying differing meanings of nonduality and proposing a different perspective on Advaita Vedanta that opens up new possibilities for Hindu-Christian dialogue. In particular, he explores Samkara's nuanced views of the relation between the absolute and the human seeker.

Malkovsky emphasizes that Samkara teaches "that liberation is in some sense the outcome of divine grace," even though he does not give a systematic explanation of grace.[51] Malkovsky finds that Samkara integrates understandings of both liberation-through-grace and liberation-through-knowledge. He also finds that Samkara accepts the traditional Hindu view that "human bondage is due to *avidya* [ignorance], and that this *avidya* gives rise to desire and action, which in their turn, bring about reincarnation."[52] The resolution ultimately comes not from human effort but from God: "The final cause of the dawn of liberating knowledge is the grace of the Lord. This grace is essentially illuminative, bringing the *jiva* [embodied soul] to the state of correct awareness of its unity with the Absolute, thereby eliminating the seed of desire and action that binds it."[53] Malkovsky concludes, "Liberating knowledge is ultimately dependent on the self-disclosure of the Absolute itself, which is the *atman* [soul] of the seeker."[54] He sees Samkara as affirming the need for both divine grace and human freedom, since the Lord works through creaturely freedom, not against it.

---

[48] Raimundo Panikkar, *The Unknown Christ of Hinduism: Towards an Ecumenical Christophany*, rev. and enlarged ed. (Maryknoll, NY: Orbis Books, 1981), 49.

[49] Ibid.

[50] Bradley J. Malkovsky, *The Role of Divine Grace in the Soteriology of Samkaracarya*, Numen Book Series, Studies in the History of Religions, vol. 91 (Leiden: Brill, 2001), 46.

[51] Ibid., 377.

[52] Ibid., 381.

[53] Ibid., 381–82.

[54] Ibid., 382.

Malkovsky's interpretation means that Advaita Vedanta as taught by Samkara is much more similar to traditional Christian teachings than has often been thought. Nonetheless, Malkovsky points out that there is a type of elitism in this understanding of Samkara, since it is only the *sannyasi* who can enter liberation:

> Yet we must never forget that for Samkara it is only the renunciate who is capable of Self-realization, because only he has renounced the desire for temporal goods as well as a life in the world that serves only to perpetuate the bondage of ignorance and desire... It is only the monk who has totally prepared and opened himself to receive the grace of Self-realization.[55]

While much Western scholarship has neglected the importance of grace in Samkara's theology, Malkovsky argues that this teaching is in strong continuity with earlier teachers of Vedanta, noting a paradox: "Thus there exists the paradox in Samkara of the absolute necessity of the *jiva's* action and effort and the ultimate incapability of action and effort to attain liberation."[56] He ends his discussion with a provocative question: "May it be that, on the one hand, Samkara is compelled by his personal experience to witness to the reality of grace, but, on the other hand, he recognizes the impossibility of objectifying what is properly the *mystery* of liberation?"[57]

Comparative Theology in Dialogue with Hindu Texts

Francis X. Clooney and Daniel P. Sheridan offer essays in comparative theology based on classical Hindu texts, especially those coming from traditions that focus on love of a personal God. Clooney presents *Hindu Wisdom for All God's Children* as a resource for Christians who would like to experiment with truth in different forms:

> We gain more from this wisdom than we give in the search; we become more than we could have been before. In the end, we may find ourselves thinking and imagining God in terms we had not known previously, terms neither entirely our own nor entirely borrowed from somewhere else.[58]

Clooney stresses that this quest is self-involving, unpredictable, and transformative: "But it should be clear that there is no room for mere spectators. We must explore with open minds, mindful that even as we begin to read, we are already more involved than we quite understand."[59]

---

[55] Ibid., 391.
[56] Ibid., 401.
[57] Ibid., 402.
[58] Francis X. Clooney, *Hindu Wisdom for All God's Children* (Maryknoll, NY: Orbis Books, 1998), 15.
[59] Ibid.

Clooney notes the importance of coming to know our true selves in many Hindu traditions: "Without knowledge of myself, just as I really am, nothing more is possible; if I have self-knowledge, nothing else is really necessary for me to be fully alive, here and now."[60] From the Advaitic tradition he compares the realization of the true self of Sri Ramana Maharshi in a near-death experience to Paul's experience on the road to Damascus in the Acts of the Apostles. Then he turns to the figures of Krishna, Siva, and the Goddess, drawing lessons for Christians from each:

> Reflection on Krishna will remind us that God offers the deepest fulfillment possible for a human being; reflection on Shiva reminds us that God is always more than we can imagine, and a great surprise to us; reflection on the Goddess reminds us that to know the divine is to know everything there is to know, completely.[61]

In *Divine Mother, Blessed Mother: Hindu Goddesses and the Virgin Mary*, Clooney compares devotional hymns to Mary of Nazareth and to the Goddesses of Hindu piety. He acknowledges the limits to this enterprise: "There is no plausible way for a Christian simply to affirm the existence of goddesses or to participate easily in worship of them. Those of us who are Christian cannot simply incorporate goddess worship and theology into Christian practice."[62] Clooney stresses that Mary is "not-God," in contrast to Jesus. Beyond all the differences, Clooney suggests that praise of Mary is analogous to Hindu goddess discourse: "The goddesses and Mary serve as mirrors in which humans see their own potential for divinization and its possible fulfillment, and are thus guided toward their fulfillment as complete human and even divinized persons."[63]

In *Hindu God, Christian God: How Reason Helps Break Down the Boundaries between Religions*, Clooney wagers that attention to the use of reason in conflicting traditions can yield new insights. He brings together voices who sharply disagree with each other, Hans Urs von Balthasar and Vedanta Desika and Arul Nandi; Karl Barth and Kumarila Bhatta and Sudarana Suri. Clooney explains that

> they all think and believe deeply enough that they have much in common and much about which they disagree. My goal has been to show how even the more difficult and stubborn points of religious and theological differences remain places where the mind can willingly visit think, speak, and thus infuse new vitality and insight into believing lives.[64]

---

[60] Ibid., 50.

[61] Ibid.

[62] Francis X. Clooney, *Divine Mother, Blessed Mother: Hindu Goddesses and the Virgin Mary* (Oxford: Oxford University Press, 2005), 223.

[63] Ibid., 230.

[64] Francis X. Clooney, *Hindu God, Christian God: How Reason Helps Break Down the Boundaries between Religions* (Oxford: Oxford University Press, 2001), vi.

Clooney proposes his approach as an experiment undertaken in light of the limitations of earlier approaches. He acknowledges that at the beginning of each conversation he does not know where it may lead. The focus is resolutely on the particular—on this poem, embedded within the corpus of other poems that communicate across cultures and religions. Where John Hick seeks to identify a common denominator, generically named "the Real," behind all religions,[65] Clooney eschews such generalized quests and uses a method closer to a case study— the study of a particular strand of the Hindu tradition in relation to selected texts from the Christian tradition.

In the process of encountering the other tradition, one's understanding regarding the home tradition will become reformulated. Comparative theology differs from a general "theology of religions" in resisting premature generalizations, in being committed to the demands of a particular tradition, and in seeking a reflective retrieval of the home tradition after being immersed in a different tradition. Conclusions are to follow from the particularity of the material.

Daniel P. Sheridan is concerned that the traditional Christian command to love God has become "relatively opaque within contemporary Christianity and Catholicism," and he offers a Christian commentary on the *Narada Sutras* that invites Catholic readers "to reexamine their own tradition of Catholic reflection on the love for God and to renew their own love for God."[66] From a Catholic angle of vision, Sheridan focuses on the Vaishnava tradition, which worships a personal God, trusting that the

> two traditions are neither the same nor totally different. Profound hermeneutical problems of comparison and interpretation confront the one who would simply see similarities and thus draw the conclusion of identity. Deep differences in basis, in commitment, in cultural context, and through time may be seen to exist between the two.[67]

Sheridan proposes that there is a homology between the Vaishnava and Catholic traditions, that is, "a comparison that discerns a similarity that is based on a similar function in a different system."[68] Noting that both traditions balance apophatic and kataphatic perspectives, Sheridan discovers a lasting paradox of difference in similarity: "At times the deeper we probe the more different our similarity becomes."[69]

---

[65]   John Hick, *An Interpretation of Religion: Human Responses to the Transcendent* (New Haven, CT: Yale University Press, 1989); John Hick, *A Christian Theology of Religions: The Rainbow of Faiths* (Louisville, KY: Westminster John Knox Press, 1995).

[66]   Daniel P. Sheridan, *Loving God: Kṛṣṇa and Christ: A Christian Commentary on the Narada Sutras,* Christian Commentaries on Non-Christian Sacred Texts (Leuven, Belgium: Peeters/Grand Rapids, MI: Eerdmans, 2007), 3, 2.

[67]   Ibid., 7.

[68]   Ibid., 9.

[69]   Ibid., 10.

He compares the difficulty of speaking about God to the difficulty of speaking about human love:

> The language of love is indeed "impossible," but since the experience is real, a flight of metaphors approaching to the precipice of the literal is appropriate, even necessary. We must totter on the precipice of the literal, as dangerous as it is, in order to capture the capacity of language to reach beyond itself toward greater meaning and greater grasp.[70]

Sheridan notes that the *Narada Sutras* celebrate the beauty of God, a theme that resonates deeply with the Catholic tradition, especially as interpreted by Hans Urs von Balthasar.[71]

Sheridan centers his method on the search for homologies, especially the homology "between *bhakti,* Hindu love for God, and *caritas,* Catholic love for God. . . . A homology is a comparison that discerns a similarity that is based on a similar function in a different system."[72] Sheridan notes the tension in both traditions between the kataphatic naming of God and the apophatic awareness that God is beyond names.[73] Sheridan finds a difference in the way this dynamic appears in each tradition, since the Hindu Advaita Vedanta and Yoga traditions are far more apophatic than the Vaishnavite tradition, while the Catholic tradition embraces both kataphatic and apophatic forms in Trinitarian and Incarnational theology. He describes the result: "A catalyzation of the *Narada Sutras on Loving God* by a participant in the Catholic faith will result in the shining of an intensely and emphatically kataphatic light on the kataphatic-apophatic tension within Catholic theism's approach to loving God."[74] One of the lessons Sheridan draws from his study is: "A human love for God without measure is the only adequate response a human can make before the revelation of the mysterious personally lovable and infinite reality of God."[75]

Dalits, Adivasis, African Americans, and Native Americans

The caste traditions of India pose a particular challenge and also special possibilities, since relations among traditionally subaltern communities are of particular importance for interreligious relations. We have seen that many of the most pressing concerns regarding religious pluralism in the United States come from the American Indian and African American communities; similarly, some of the most urgent

---

[70] Ibid., 14.
[71] Ibid., 183–85.
[72] Ibid., 9.
[73] Ibid., 10.
[74] Ibid., 12.
[75] Ibid., 25.

challenges for Christians in relation to Hindus concern the situation of Dalits (formerly Untouchables) and Adivasis (Tribals or Indigenous Peoples). Relations between caste Hindus, on the one side, and Dalits and Adivasis, on the other, have long been troubled.

Dalits and Adivasis in India recount a long history of humiliation, mistreatment, and oppression, which some African Americans have recognized as not unlike their own history. At least among some leaders, there have long been relations among these communities.[76] In the nineteenth century the non-Brahman leader Jotirao Phule (1827–90) was aware of the oppression of African Americans and used the word *Gulamgiri* (slavery) to refer to the situation of Sudras and Dalits in India struggling against an oppressive social order. In the early twentieth century B. R. Ambedkar came to Columbia University to study Western social theory under John Dewey, and he became strongly aware of the relationship between the Indian caste system and American racism. Ambedkar, who not only received a doctorate from Columbia University but also became the first Dalit to be admitted to the bar in the British Empire, strenuously opposed Mahatma Gandhi on how Dalits should be treated in India. Gandhi was from an upper caste; while he wanted to end discrimination against those he called *harijan* (children of God—Gandhi's name for those formerly called Untouchables), he defended the caste system against the ferocious critiques of Ambedkar. Ambedkar famously proclaimed that although he had been born a Hindu, he would not die a Hindu. Toward the end of his life, Ambedkar became a Buddhist with a strong orientation toward social engagement.[77]

In 1937, during the time of the debate between Gandhi and Ambedkar, Benjamin Mays, the president of Morehouse College in Atlanta, visited India and was introduced by a headmaster of a Dalit or "untouchable" school to the students as an untouchable who had suffered discrimination at the hands of whites but who nonetheless had achieved success. The headmaster proudly told the untouchable students that they too could succeed. Mays later reflected,

> At first I was horrified, puzzled, and angry to be called an untouchable, but my indignation was short-lived as I realized, as never before, that I was truly an untouchable in my native land, especially in the southern United States. In my country, I was segregated almost everywhere I went, always in the south and often in the north. . . . I—just as they—through the mere accident of birth, was indeed an untouchable![78]

---

[76] For a collection of essays from India regarding this relation, see N. M. Aston, ed., *Dalit Literature and African-American Literature: Literature of Marginality* (New Delhi, India: Prestige Books, 2001).

[77] B. R. Ambedkar, *The Buddha and His Dhamma: A Critical Edition* (Oxford: Oxford University Press, 2011).

[78] Benjamin E. Mays, *Born to Rebel: An Autobiography* (1971; reprint, Athens: University of Georgia Press, 2003), 158; see also Karla McLucas and Rhonda Vonshay Sharpe,

Mays later spoke about his experience in India to the young Martin Luther King Jr., who was a student at Morehouse.

Much of the academic Catholic engagement with Hinduism has involved texts from the Vedic tradition written and studied by caste Hindus, especially Brahmins. This includes various forms of Vedanta, Yoga, and the commentary traditions on sacred texts from the bhakti tradition. However, most Christians, including most Catholics, in India today come from the marginalized communities of Dalits and Adivasis. American Christians to date have given relatively less attention to the growing movement of Dalit Christian theology in India and to the beginnings of Adivasi Christian theology. Whether Dalits and Adivasis should be numbered among Hindus is a disputed question; many of them in India often do not identify themselves as Hindus, though some Hindus want to count them as Hindu. The conversions of some Dalits and Adivasis to the Catholic Church and other Christian communions are a source of major controversy at the present time, as Hindu nationalists accuse Christians in India of seeking to force conversions.

Many Catholics and Hindus in the United States share the concern for social justice. Just as many American Christians have learned from Gandhi about how to practice Christianity, some Hindus have come to new perspectives on their tradition through contact with Christians. Anantanand Rambachan, a Hindu originally from Trinidad in the Caribbean who teaches at St. Olaf College in Minnesota, takes these concerns to heart. In light of his long-time involvement in dialogue with Christians, he proposes a Hindu liberation theology that is a fruit of dialogue:

> Although this work is rooted firmly in the theological resources of the Advaita tradition, it is informed also by my dialogue with and learning from other traditions where there is a longer history of reflection on liberation theology. Such opportunities for interreligious learning are a precious gift and opportunity of our times.[79]

Rambachan notes that Christian liberation theologians have called attention to "evil as a social phenomenon" and to the inseparability of religion and justice.[80] Interpreting the tradition of Advaita Vedanta as affirming the relative reality of the world and insisting on the importance of social justice, Rambachan maintains,

> There is an essential theological teaching in Advaita that affirms, without compromise or exception, the identity and unity of the infinite as the self of all beings and of the universe. *Brahman* is the single ontological truth of everything, allowing us to see the world as its celebrative multiplication.

"African Americans, Dalits and Tribals: A Comparative Analysis of Subaltern Communities in India and the U.S.A.," *Review of Black Political Economy* 43, no. 2 (2016): 85–86.

[79] Anantanand Rambachan, *A Hindu Theology of Liberation: Not-Two Is Not One* (Albany: State University of New York Press, 2015), 4–5.

[80] Ibid., 5.

Advaita refutes all assumptions of human inequality that are the basis for oppressive social institutions such as patriarchy, caste, and homophobia. It is on the side of justice.[81]

Rambachan interprets the principle of nonduality in Advaita Vedanta as a rejection of all social, economic, and racial forms of discrimination. Because all are ultimately one, there is no basis for making pejorative distinctions among people of different backgrounds. The pressing concern for both personal integration and also for world of justice and equity unites many Christians and Hindus in the United States today.

Experiences in Dialogue

Dialogues between Hindus and Catholics in the United States have been helpful for building relationships. In April 1997 the Ecclesiastical Faculty of Theology of the University of Saint Mary of the Lake in Mundelein, Illinois, and the Secretariat for Ecumenical and Interreligious Affairs (SEIA) of the U.S. Conference of Catholic Bishops jointly sponsored a dialogue, which included public lectures on the theme of mysticism in the bhakti traditions of medieval India and in St. Francis of Assisi as well as a private meeting of Hindu and Catholic leaders to explore possibilities for collaboration.[82] In 1998, Anuttama Dasa of the International Society for Krishna Consciousness (ISKCON), in cooperation with John Borelli from SEIA, organized the first meeting of what became an annual Christian-Vaishnavite dialogue in Potomac, Maryland.[83] Dasa explains the motivation for his participation:

I come to this dialogue in the mood of a pilgrim: "I know a little something about God from my Vaishnava tradition, and perhaps I can share some of that with you. Would you kindly help me to understand some of what you know about God from your Christian tradition(s)?"[84]

Graham M. Schweig, a scholar and practitioner of the Vaishnava bhakti tradition, believes that the one Divine Reality embraces all humans and that dialogue is essential to bhakti, as modeled in the dialogue between Krishna and Arjuna in the Bhagavad Gita. In light of this perspective, he sees that interfaith dialogue offers important opportunities for humans to return the divine embrace: "It is for both this divine embrace and the return embrace that we as humans must strive. The return embrace of humans becomes stronger and stronger as the reception of

---

[81] Ibid., 12.

[82] John Borelli, "Why Hindu-Christian Dialogue: A Catholic Reflection," *Journal of Vaishnava Studies* 20, no. 2 (2012): 15–33.

[83] Anuttama Dasa, "Thoughts on the History and Development of the Vaishnava-Christian Dialogue," *Journal of Vaishnava Studies* 20, no. 2 (2012): 35–50.

[84] Ibid., 39.

revelation from tradition and humans becomes stronger and stronger."[85] He notes that often dialogue partners seek similarities in their respective traditions, but he insists on the value of dialogue even when the differences are most apparent because "it is the dialogue itself that is the goal; it is the sharing that takes place within dialogue that is the achievement."[86]

Catholics involved in this dialogue have expressed their appreciation. Gerald Carney highlights the benefit of focusing the Christian-Vaishnava dialogue on texts: "Entering deeply into the thought and experience of the Vaishnava traditions allowed me to return with an enhanced understanding of Vaishnava faith and life, but it also allowed me to look at my Catholic Christian tradition with clearer vision."[87] Carney also stressed the importance of sharing traditions of prayer: "We tell about how we pray, how our beliefs and images in practice transform our lives. Then we pray, finding inclusive prayer forms, moving beyond explanation and observation to the deepest level of participation that is possible and appropriate, leaving freedom for each individual's comfort and conviction."[88] Carney celebrates the friendships that have emerged from the years of sharing the journey. Through the years, the dialogue has explored themes and practices in both traditions, including theodicy, prayer and worship, and veneration of the Mother of God.

The Hindu tradition provides perspectives that often shed new light on traditional Christian themes and practices. Dialogue with Hindus and exploration of the resources of the Hindu tradition have enriched the lives of many Catholics in the United States and hold promise for the future.

---

[85] Graham M. Schweig, "Vaishnava Bhakti Theology and Interfaith Dialogue," *Journal of Vaishnava Studies* 20, no. 2 (2012): 65.

[86] Ibid., 54.

[87] Gerald Carney, "Reflecting on Our Journey," *Journal of Vaishnava Studies* 20, no. 2 (2012): 233.

[88] Ibid., 233–34.

7

Buddhist-Catholic Relations
in the United States

There have been many aspects to Christian relations with Buddhists in the United States, ranging from distrust and fear to admiration and embrace. While Buddhists constitute a relatively small proportion of the population of the United States, they have played a significant role in shaping American awareness and have been prominent in a number of interreligious encounters. And though few in number, Buddhists have both fascinated and concerned many Americans. Historically, religious, racial, and national prejudices often poisoned the relations of Buddhists with American Christians.

The Reception of Early Buddhists

During the nineteenth and early twentieth centuries, Buddhists who came to the United States from East Asia endured suspicion, discrimination, violent attacks, internment, and exclusion on national and racial grounds. Racial, national, and religious prejudices intertwined in the attitudes of white Christians toward the newcomers. The first Buddhists to migrate to the United States in large numbers arrived from China in the middle of the nineteenth century because of the demand for low-cost labor in California and other western regions; many arrived under less than free conditions.[1] In the background was British racial planning for the labor needs of the Empire; in 1803 British colonial official John Sullivan worried about the ominous precedent set by the successful revolt by enslaved Africans and African Americans in Haiti; and he wrote a secret memorandum to the directors of the East India Company, recommending that they look to China as a source of inexpensive labor that would be plentiful and more reliable than enslaved Africans and African Americans. He warned of the danger of insurrection from African Americans and proposed that

> no measure would so effectually tend to provide a security against this
> danger [of insurrection], as that of introducing a free race of cultivators

---

[1] Stuart Chandler, "Chinese Buddhism in America: Identity and Practice," in *The Faces of Buddhism in America,* ed. Charles B. Prebish and Kenneth K. Tanaka (Berkeley: University of California Press, 1998), 13–30.

into our islands, who, from habits and feelings could be kept distinct from the Negroes, and who from interest would be inseparably attached to the European proprietors. . . . The Chinese people . . . unite the qualities which constitute this double recommendation.[2]

Religious and racial perceptions intersected as British officials hoped that the Chinese, many of whom were Buddhists, could provide a middle level of society between the white Christian Europeans at the top and the enslaved Africans and African Americans at the bottom. As the nineteenth century unfolded, the emancipation of slaves in both the British Empire and the United States went hand in hand with the forced importation of laborers from China.

In later decades, large numbers of Chinese workers, including many Buddhists, were pressed into service in Hong Kong and brought to the Caribbean, South America, and the western coast of North America. Some made a free decision, but many were transported to foreign lands under coercion. The term "coolie" could refer to a variety of conditions, often hovering ominously between free labor and slavery; it was applied to people from East Asia, Southeast Asia, and South Asia, and would in time become a racial slur.[3] The British viewed these Chinese workers as free, but the U.S. government viewed such workers as unfree and thus as not eligible for citizenship.

Chinese Buddhists constructed the first Buddhist temple in the United States in San Francisco's Chinatown in 1853; the following year in San Francisco Judge Charles T. Murray refused to accept Chinese testimony in court because he viewed Chinese, like American Indians, as less than human and lacking in rights.[4] Even though many Americans profited from the cheap labor of the Chinese migrants, Americans were often suspicious and ambivalent about migrants from China who were both needed and feared.[5] As we have seen, in 1882, the Chinese Exclusion Act forbade Chinese from immigrating to the United States for ten years and blocked them from citizenship. This ban was lifted only in 1943, when American hostility toward Asians had become focused primarily on wartime Japan.

American Christian theological perspectives on Buddhists and Buddhism in the nineteenth and early twentieth centuries tended to be very harsh. Protestant missionaries to China during the nineteenth century generally interpreted the religious practices of the Chinese, including Buddhists, in very negative terms. Protestants usually saw the Buddhist practice of honoring images as a form of idolatry;

---

[2] *Great Britain Colonial Office Correspondence,* CO 295, vol. 17; see Lisa Lowe, *The Intimacies of Four Continents* (Durham, NC: Duke University Press, 2015), 22–23.

[3] Lowe, *Intimacies,* 24–27.

[4] Rick Fields, "Divided Dharma: White Buddhists, Ethnic Buddhists, and Racism," in *The Faces of Buddhism in America,* ed. Charles S. Prebish and Kenneth K. Tanaka (Berkeley: University of California Press, 1998), 196, 199.

[5] Andrew Gyory, *Closing the Gate: Race, Politics, and the Chinese Exclusion Act* (Chapel Hill: University of North Carolina Press, 1998).

and they often applied the traditional Protestant criticisms of Roman Catholicism to the customs, rituals, and images of Chinese Buddhists.[6] Most Catholic and Protestant theologians in nineteenth-century America had little interest in anything approaching interreligious dialogue with Buddhists.

Appreciation and Encounter

During the nineteenth century, a number of European philosophers became interested in Buddhism, but their perceptions frequently revealed more about themselves than about the Buddhist world.[7] Despite the theological criticisms of Buddhism and widespread suspicion of Asian immigrants on the West coast, a few American writers expressed a positive regard for Buddhism on the basis of reading classic texts. As we have seen, Ralph Waldo Emerson and Henry David Thoreau admired Hinduism and Buddhism without having a detailed knowledge or a precise sense of the complex relationship between these traditions. Their example inspired some American Christians to take an interest in Buddhism in the nineteenth century, but the cultural distance was very great, and no lasting institutions emerged.[8]

The first Buddhists to present their religious perspectives to a major public forum in America spoke at the World's Parliament of Religions, held in Chicago in 1893. Because most of the first Buddhist immigrants arrived on the West Coast of the United States, most Americans from the Midwest or the East at this time had never seen or heard a Buddhist. At the Parliament, Theravada Buddhist leader Anagarika Dharmapala from Sri Lanka and Zen Buddhist Shaku Soyen from Japan, as well as other Buddhist leaders, appeared on stage with the Catholic leaders and spoke to largely sympathetic audiences.[9] The Buddhists heard the opening welcome from Archbishop Patrick Feehan of Chicago, with his invitation to cordial conversation, as well as the call of James Cardinal Gibbons to work together to relieve suffering. Dharmapala stressed that "Buddhism is a scientific religion, inasmuch as it earnestly enjoins that nothing whatever be accepted on faith."[10] Because Shaku Soyen could not speak English, his paper was read by John Henry Barrows in translation; he appealed for unity among different religions: "Let us, the true followers

[6] Eric Reinders, *Borrowed Gods and Foreign Bodies: Christian Missionaries Imagine Chinese Religion* (Berkeley: University of California Press, 2004), 8, 25.

[7] Roger-Pol Droit, *The Cult of Nothingness: The Philosophers and the Buddha,* trans. David Streight and Pamela Vohnson (New Delhi, India: Munshiram Manoharlal Publishers, 2009).

[8] Thomas A. Tweed, *The American Encounter with Buddhism, 1844–1912: Victorian Culture and the Limits of Dissent* (Bloomington: Indiana University Press, 1992).

[9] Richard Hughes Seager, ed., *The Dawn of Religious Pluralism: Voices from the World's Parliament of Religions, 1893* (LaSalle, IL: Open Court, 1993), 397–420.

[10] H. Dharmapala, "The World's Debt to Buddha," in *The World's Parliament of Religions,* 2 vols., ed. John Henry Barrows (Chicago: Parliament, 1893), 2:878.

of Buddha, the true followers of Jesus Christ, the true followers of Confucius and the followers of truth, unite ourselves for the sake of helping the helpless and living glorious lives of brotherhood under the control of truth."[11] Dharmapala and Shaku Soyen were both confident that the Buddhist tradition was a rational religion that could withstand Christian criticisms and would be persuasive to modern Westerners.[12] Dharmapala later described the Parliament as "the noblest and proudest achievement in history, and the crowning work of the nineteenth century."[13]

Kinzai R. M. Hirai criticized American Christians for excluding Japanese students from universities and public schools in San Francisco and for protesting with signs marked "Japs must go"; Kinzai commented bitterly, "If such be Christian ethics, we are perfectly satisfied to be heathen."[14] The largely American Christian audience applauded loudly, Christian leaders embraced him warmly, and many cried "Shame!" as he described the mistreatment that Japanese Buddhists had endured at Christian hands.

Many Americans were positively impressed. After the Parliament ended, Dharmapala traveled across the United States, presenting his modernist interpretation of Buddhism. In 1903, he visited Harvard University, where the influential philosopher and psychologist William James admired Buddhists' psychological perspicacity. On one occasion when James noticed Dharmapala in his lecture hall, he is reported to have stopped his lecture, invited the Buddhist leader to come forward, and publicly said to him, "You are better equipped to lecture on psychology than I. This is the psychology everybody will be studying twenty-five years from now."[15]

In the aftermath of the World Parliament of Religions, American naturalist and publisher Paul Carus invited Shaku Soyen to his home and publishing house in LaSalle, Illinois, southwest of Chicago and asked him to stay and help translate Buddhist texts for the American public. Instead, Shaku Soyen recommended his young assistant and translator, Daisetz Teitaro Suzuki, to come and undertake this work. Suzuki published *Outline of Mahayana Buddhism* in 1907, and he went on to both translate and write many works presenting Buddhism, Japanese culture,

---

[11] Shaku Soyen, "Arbitration instead of War," in Barrows, *The World's Parliament of Religions*, 2:1285.

[12] John S. Harding, *Mahayana Phoenix; Japan's Buddhists at the 1893 World's Parliament of Religions* (New York: Peter Lang), 65–74; Tessa Bartholomeusz, "Dharmapala at Chicago: Mahayana Buddhist or Sinhala Chauvinist?" in *A Museum of Faiths: Histories and Legacies of the 1893 World's Parliament of Religions,* ed. Eric J. Ziolkowski (Atlanta, GA: Scholars Press, 1993), 235–50. See also Judith Snodgrass, *Presenting Japanese Buddhism to the West: Orientalism, Occidentalism, and the Columbian Exposition* (Chapel Hill: University of North Carolina Press, 2003).

[13] Rick Fields, *How the Swans Came to the Lake: A Narrative History of Buddhism in America* (Boulder, CO: Shambhala, 1981), 120.

[14] Ibid., 124.

[15] Mark Epstein, *Thoughts without a Thinker: Psychotherapy from a Buddhist Perspective* (New York: MJF Books, 1995), 2; Fields, *How the Swans,* 134–35.

and especially the Rinzai Zen tradition to Western readers.[16] Suzuki focused primarily on the Rinzai tradition of Zen that uses koans, paradoxical sayings and stories, to evoke a dramatic moment of *kensho* (seeing clearly, intuitive insight) that puts the world in a new light. Suzuki's writings over many decades would introduce generations of Americans, including Thomas Merton, to Rinzai Zen Buddhism and other Buddhist traditions. Many American Christians accepted D. T. Suzuki's presentation of Buddhism, but more recently, some scholars have sharply criticized Suzuki's style of interpreting Buddhism for Americans and its influence on Merton and others.[17]

Tensions in the Early Twentieth Century

While D. T. Suzuki would eventually become a very influential interpreter of Mahayana Buddhism for American Christians, during the early twentieth century most American Christian theologians did not explore Buddhist perspectives in any depth, and attitudes often continued to be negative. In the wake of Pope Pius X's condemnation of Modernism in 1907, most American Catholic theologians did not express interest in interreligious explorations. After the Parliament of Religions, there was relatively little organized Buddhist-Christian dialogue prior to the middle of the twentieth century.

Even though immigration from China had been blocked in 1882, during the early twentieth century Buddhist immigrants from Japan and other parts of Asia continued to come to the United States, especially Hawaii and the areas on the West Coast. European American Christians in Hawaii perceived a particular threat from the growing numbers of Japanese, including many young women, who entered the territory. Bishop Yemyo Imamura, the leader of the Honpa Hongwanji sect of Jodo Shinshu (Pure Land) Buddhism, strove for good relations with the Christian community, but he also expanded the activities of his community across the islands. Both Christians and Buddhists built schools in competition with each other, and Japanese Buddhists invited Japanese Christians to send their children to their schools. Buddhist and Christian Sunday schools also competed. Some Christian ministers worried that Hawaii was becoming more and more Buddhist, and they felt frustration at their lack of success in converting the new Japanese migrants to Christianity. The assertive activities of the Japanese Empire challenged and aroused American nationalist sentiments. Economic and religious rivalry between white Christians and Japanese Buddhists led to growing Christian resentment and fear of

---

[16] Daisetz Teitaro Suzuki, *Outline of Mahayana Buddhism* (1907; reprint, New York: Schocken Books, 1963); *A Zen Life: D. T. Suzuki Remembered,* ed. Masao Abe (Tokyo: John Weatherhill, 1986).

[17] John P. Keenan, "The Limits of Thomas Merton's Understanding of Buddhism," in *Merton and Buddhism: Wisdom, Emptiness, and Everyday Mind,* ed. Bonnie Bowman Thurston (Louisville, KY: Fons Vitae, 2007), 118–32.

the expanding Japanese Buddhist population.[18] Some Christians accused the Japanese Buddhists of being un-American. Bishop Imamura promised to Americanize the Buddhist schools, but Louise Hunter observes that "the American community refused to believe that teacher-priests wholly unacquainted with English and out of sympathy with American ideals and institutions were either capable or desirous of educating the local-born Japanese for American citizenship."[19] Distrust between the Christian and Buddhist communities continued to increase, and some Christians insisted that the only way to be American was for the Japanese Buddhist immigrants to become Christian.[20] Imamura protested that his schools did not teach Japanese nationalism and that Buddhist ideals were fully harmonious with American values, but many Christians doubted his sincerity, and the tensions remained. As time went on, Japanese Buddhist leaders presented their faith in American fashion to appeal to the younger generation born in Hawaii, organizing Boy Scout troops, adopting the English language and Christian terminology, as well as religious hymns, pews, pulpits, and even the pipe organ.[21] Nonetheless, in practice, Hunter points out, "The Buddhism preached in Hawaii was still, in too many places, inextricably tied up with Japanese nationalism. At the same time, the Christian ministers who accused Buddhist priests of fostering a rabid nationalism were themselves indulging in a great deal of flag-waving."[22] Despite the difficulties in relations with Christians, when Imamura died of a heart attack in 1932, Christians and Buddhists joined together in mourning his passing and honoring his contributions to the religious and cultural life of Hawaiian society.[23]

During the Second World War, Japanese Buddhists were the targets of intense suspicion. From 1942–45, the U.S. government confined all Japanese and Japanese Americans residents in the United States, including many Buddhists, in camps.[24] The government targeted people of Japanese ancestry in the camps regardless of their religious affiliation, including Protestants and Catholics; of the 111,170 internees, it is estimated that 61,719 were Buddhist, mainly from the Jodo Shinshu tradition.[25] The Federal Bureau of Investigation especially targeted Buddhist and Shinto ministers because they were believed to owe special allegiance to the Japanese emperor.[26]

---

[18] Louise H. Hunter, *Buddhism in Hawaii* (Honolulu: University of Hawaii Press, 1971), 93–115.

[19] Ibid., 99.

[20] Ibid., 100.

[21] Alfred Bloom, "Shin Buddhism in America: A Social Perspective," in *The Faces of Buddhism in America,* ed. Charles B. Prebish and Kenneth K. Tanaka (Berkeley: University of California Press, 1998), 33–34; Hunter, *Buddhism in Hawaii,* 131.

[22] Hunter, *Buddhism in Hawaii,* 111.

[23] Ibid., 170–71.

[24] Richard Reeves, *Infamy: The Shocking Story of the Japanese American Internment in World War II* (New York: Henry Holt, 2015).

[25] Richard Hughes Seager, *Buddhism in America* (New York: Columbia University Press, 1999), 57.

[26] Fields, *How the Swans,* 192.

Thomas Merton

After the tragedy of the Second World War, a number of American Catholics began to explore the resources of the Buddhist tradition with greater interest and openness to genuine learning. Some of the most important Catholic responses to Buddhists in the United States have come from monastics, inspired especially by the pioneering example of Thomas Merton.[27] As a Trappist monk at Gethsemani Abbey near Louisville, Kentucky, from 1941 to 1968, Merton immersed himself in Buddhist texts and corresponded with Buddhist leaders, including D. T. Suzuki. Merton described the impact of Suzuki:

Speaking for myself, I can venture to say that in Dr. Suzuki, Buddhism finally became for me completely comprehensible, whereas before it had been a very mysterious and confusing jumble of words, images, doctrines, legends, rituals, buildings, and so forth. It seemed to me that the great and baffling cultural luxuriance which has clothed the various forms of Buddhism in different parts of Asia is the beautiful garment thrown over something quite simple.... [T]he last words I remember Dr. Suzuki saying (before the usual goodbyes) were "The most important thing is Love!" I must say that as a Christian I was profoundly moved. Truly *Prajna* and *Karuna* are one (as the Buddhist says), or *Caritas* (love) is indeed the highest knowledge.[28]

Merton recognized that there were major differences between Buddhist and Catholic views and rejected any attempt to harmonize them doctrinally.[29] Nonetheless, he believed that the Christian and Buddhist paths both seek to transform human awareness so that the illusory ego dissolves and true identity can emerge. Ideally, he hoped that Buddhist and Catholic monastics could communicate this transformation to their societies, and he trusted that there was a point of convergence and unity beyond all doctrinal differences:

In place of this self-centered ego came the Christian person, who was no longer just the individual but was Christ dwelling in each one. So in each one of us the Christian person is that which is fully open to all other persons, because ultimately all other persons are Christ.[30]

---

[27] Michael Mott, *The Seven Mountains of Thomas Merton* (Boston: Houghton Mifflin, 1984); Francis X. Clooney, "Thomas Merton's Deep Christian Learning across Religious Borders," *Buddhist-Christian Studies* 37, no. 1 (2017): 49–64.

[28] Thomas Merton, *Mystics and Zen Masters* (New York: A Delta Book, 1967), 61, 62.

[29] George Kilcourse, *Ace of Freedoms: Thomas Merton's Christ* (Notre Dame, IN: University of Notre Dame Press, 1993), 217.

[30] Thomas Merton, *The Asian Journal of Thomas Merton,* ed. Naomi Burton, Patrick Hart, and James Laughlin (New York: A New Directions Book, 1973), 334.

Merton trusted that Buddhist realization of interdependence and of nirvana in the midst of illusion came "very close to the Christian monastic view of reality. It is the view that if you once penetrate by detachment and purity of heart to the inner secret of the ground of your ordinary experience, you attain to a liberty that nobody can touch, that nobody can affect, that no political change of circumstances can do anything to."[31] Merton believed Buddhist monks had gone further than Christians in some regards and thus, he hoped, "we stand a wonderful chance of learning more about the potentiality of our own traditions, because they have gone, from the natural point of view, so much deeper into this than we have."[32]

In 1961 Merton received permission to publish *Mystics and Zen Masters,* a wide-ranging series of essays that discussed Daoism, Jesuits in China, Christian mysticism, as well as Zen Buddhist monasticism, Zen koans, and Buddhism in the modern world. Merton stressed the contribution that monastics can make to inter-religious dialogue in the area of contemplation, in the sense of "the direct intuition of reality, the *simplex intuitus veritatis,* the pure awareness which is and must be the ground not only of all genuine metaphysical speculation, but also of mature and sapiential religious experience."[33] Merton's approach harmonized with D. T. Suzu-ki's style of presenting Zen Buddhism as direct intuitive awareness. Merton noted, "This direct awareness is a gift, but it also normally presupposes the knowledge and practice of certain traditional disciplines. Thus, we can say that contemplation is both a 'gift' (a 'grace') and an 'art.'"[34] For Merton, this set the agenda for contempla-tive dialogue: "genuine ecumenism requires the communication and sharing, not only of information about doctrines which are totally and irrevocably divergent, but also of religious intuitions and truths which may turn out to have something in common, beneath surface differences."[35]

On the one hand, Merton insisted on the distinctiveness of Christian expe-rience in contrast to Asian religions; in a journal entry dated June 26, 1965, he reflected: "There is one thing more—I may be interested in Oriental religions, etc., but there can be no obscuring the essential difference—this personal commu-nion with Christ at the center and heart of all reality as a source of grace and life."[36] On the other hand, Merton trusted that all religions seek an experience analogous to the Christian union with God, "and in each case this union is described in terms which have very definite analogies with the contemplative and mystical experiences in the Christian, and particularly the Catholic, tradition."[37] Merton would retain this confidence to the end of his life, when he traveled to

---

[31] Ibid., 342.

[32] Ibid., 343.

[33] Merton, *Mystics and Zen Masters,* 203.

[34] Ibid., 203–4.

[35] Ibid., 204.

[36] Thomas Merton, *The Intimate Merton: His Life from His Journals,* ed. Patrick Hart and Jonathan Montaldo (San Francisco: HarperSanFrancisco, 1999), 250.

[37] Merton, *Mystics and Zen Masters,* 205.

India and Thailand and met a number of Hindu and Buddhist leaders, including the Fourteenth Dalai Lama.

While many Catholics and other Christians have accepted Merton's perspective as a guide to viewing Buddhists, a number of scholars have strongly criticized Merton's assumptions, including his reliance upon Suzuki's description of Zen in terms of immediate experience. John P. Keenan charges that Suzuki adapted his presentation of Zen Buddhism to the United States in the 1960s to the point that it was a "caricature."[38] Keenan challenges Suzuki's description of Zen as "just too pure and too naïve, too simplistic, for it distorts both the Chan/Zen tradition and the broader Buddhist tradition."[39] It is important to note that Merton rejected the danger of what he called "an irresponsible syncretism which, on the basis of purely superficial resemblances and without serious study of qualitative differences, proceeds to identity all religions and all religious experiences with one another."[40] Merton agreed with Suzuki's decision "to say that Zen was 'not mysticism' in order to avoid certain disastrous ambiguities."[41] Judith Simmer-Brown, a practitioner and professor of Tibetan Buddhism, is more positive on Merton's reception of Buddhism, commenting that in preparation for his journey to Asia in 1968, "it is clear that Merton had done his homework as best he could," including reading Giuseppe Tucci, Arnaud Desjardins, and T. R. V. Murti, as well as the eighth-century Shantideva.[42] She also observes that Merton's "encounters with Tibetan Buddhists in India were gradually more genuine, open, and mutually transformative than not. . . . Through his months in India, Merton's Orientalist proclivities began to noticeably melt, and he met his Tibetan counterparts with greater appreciation, humanity, and inquisitiveness."[43] James Wiseman has called attention to the importance of Merton's encounter with Theravada Buddhism.[44]

Even though Merton originally had no interest in meeting a Tibetan "pontiff," he met with the young Fourteenth Dalai Lama a number of times in 1968; and they developed a very warm friendship, which would have very important ramifications for Buddhist-Catholic monastic relations in the United States.[45] Merton was positively impressed, and the Dalai Lama later commented that this was the first time that he received a strongly favorable impression of Christianity, after many years

---

[38] Keenan, "Limits," 124.

[39] Ibid., 126.

[40] Merton, *Mystics and Zen Masters,* 206.

[41] Thomas Merton, *Zen and the Birds of Appetite* (New York: A New Directions Book, 1968), 63.

[42] Judith Simmer-Brown, "The Liberty that Nobody Can Touch: Thomas Merton Meets Tibetan Buddhism," in Bonnie Bowman Thurston, *Merton and Buddhism: Wisdom, Emptiness and Everyday Mind* (Louisville, KY: Fons Vitae, 2007), 52.

[43] Judith Simmer-Brown, "Ambivalence in Shangri-La," *Buddhist-Christian Studies* 37, no. 1 (2017): 97.

[44] James A. Wiseman, "Thomas Merton and Theravada Buddhism," in Thurston, *Merton and Buddhism,* 31–50.

[45] Simmer-Brown, "Liberty," 66.

of viewing Christians critically in light of the history of colonial conquest and oppression: "This was the first time that I had been struck by such a feeling of spirituality in anyone who professed Christianity. Since then, I have come across others with similar qualities, but it was Merton who introduced me to the real meaning of the word 'Christian.'"[46] The Dalai Lama reflected:

> The key thing I learned from Merton was his profound clarity on a point that I have thought about many times since and have come to share deeply. Merton told me, and this is something he later published in his *Asian Journal,* that we, as a community of practitioners in the world religions, "have reached a stage (long overdue) of religious maturity at which it may be possible for someone to remain perfectly faithful to a Christian and Western monastic commitment and yet to learn in depth from say a Buddhist discipline and experience." Exactly the same is true from the Buddhist side as well.[47]

Looking at the contemporary world, the Dalai Lama warns of the danger of religious polarization leading to a clash of civilizations, and he proposes a true kinship of faiths that centers on the practice of compassion:

> In particular, all the great religions stress compassion as a fundamental spiritual value. Whether it is in scriptural prescriptions for leading a good life, in the ideal of life that is admired and propagated, or in the exemplary lives of many of the remarkable individuals of different faiths, past and present (some of whom I have been privileged to meet), I have no doubt that compassion lies at the heart of all these religions. If this is true, there is a tremendous potential for the world's religions to come together in the cause of human goodness.[48]

As a contribution to this goal, the Dalai Lama has offered his personal appreciation of and reflections on the teachings of Jesus Christ.[49]

Buddhist-Catholic Monastic Dialogue

After the Second Vatican Council's expression of respect for Buddhists and Buddhism, some Catholics in the United States began relating to Buddhists in new ways. The Catholic Archdiocese of Los Angeles was a founding member of the

---

[46] Dalai Lama, *Freedom in Exile: The Autobiography of the Dalai Lama* (San Francisco: Harper & Row, 1991); see also Simmer-Brown, "Liberty," 68.

[47] Dalai Lama, *Toward a True Kinship of Faiths: How the World's Religions Can Come Together* (New York: Doubleday Religion, 2010), 10.

[48] Ibid., xiii.

[49] Dalai Lama, *The Good Heart: A Buddhist Perspective on the Teachings of Jesus*, trans. Geshe Thupten Jinpa, ed. Robert Kiely (Boston: Wisdom Publications, 1996).

Interreligious Council of Southern California beginning in 1969, with Buddhists joining in 1971. The Buddhist Sangha Council and the Catholic Office of Ecumenical and Interreligious Affairs established the Los Angeles Buddhist-Catholic Dialogue on February 16, 1989.[50] This dialogue has met repeatedly for many years exploring points of convergence and divergence in a spirit of openness.

Of particular importance for Buddhist-Catholic relations in the United States, Pope Paul VI encouraged Catholic monastics around the world to engage in dialogue with their counterparts in other traditions and develop relationships of hospitality, friendship, and understanding. In the United States, Catholic monastics formed the North American Board for East-West Dialogue, which eventually became Monastic Interreligious Dialogue (MID) and is affiliated with the international body based in Europe, Dialogue Interreligieux Monastique (DIM; together the organizations are known as DIMMID).[51] DIMMID promotes contacts with monastics and other people of other religious traditions based on traditional monastic values of hospitality, contemplation, and ethical, social, and political involvement, especially concerning peace-building and care for the earth.[52]

At the second convening of the Parliament of the World's Religions in Chicago in 1993, MID organized a dialogue with Buddhists on emptiness (*kenosis* in Greek and *shunyata* in Sanskrit), focusing on similarities and differences in Catholic and Buddhist perspectives and practices. Inspired by the memory of his conversations with Merton, the Dalai Lama participated in the Chicago dialogue, was pleased with the conversation, and suggested that there be a further discussion in a monastic setting where he could be a monk among monks. The Dalai Lama recommended that twenty-five Buddhist and twenty-five Catholic monastics come together for a week at Merton's monastery, Gethsemani Abbey, and practice and discuss various aspects of monastic and spiritual life in a common setting.[53]

MID accepted the Dalai Lama's recommendation and organized the first Gethsemani Encounter with Buddhist and Benedictine and Cistercian monastics at Thomas Merton's monastery in July 1996.[54] The initial Gethsemani Encounter opened with a ceremony outside the monastic enclosure, where the Dalai Lama and the abbot of Gethsemani planted a tree, recalling the tree of Enlightenment

---

[50] "Buddhist-Catholic Dialogue: An Early Journey," *Origins: Catholic Documentary News Service* 20, no. 44 (April 11, 1991).

[51] Pierre-François de Béthune, "Monastic Inter-Religious Dialogue," in *The Wiley-Blackwell Companion to Inter-Religious Dialogue,* ed. Catherine Cornille (Sussex, UK: John Wiley & Sons, 2013), 34–50.

[52] Fabrice Blée, *The Third Desert: The Story of Monastic Interreligious Dialogue,* trans. William Skudlarek and Mary Grady (Collegeville, MN: Liturgical Press, 2011).

[53] Pascaline Coff, "How We Reached This Point: Communication Becoming Communion," in *The Gethsemani Encounter: A Dialogue on the Spiritual Life by Buddhist and Christian Monastics,* ed. Donald W. Mitchell and James A. Wiseman (New York: Continuum, 1999), 8; Blée, *Third Desert,* 109, 141–42.

[54] Mitchell and Wiseman, *The Gethsemani Encounter,* xvii–xxiii.

of Shakyamuni Buddha and the cross of Jesus Christ. As an advisor to the Board of MID at that time, I participated in the planning and the discussions of the Encounter. The primary focus was on the structures and practices of Buddhist and Catholic monastic life, and the Catholic monks continually referred to the monastic rule of St. Benedict. Buddhist monastics are familiar with their own rules and were interested in learning more. After the first Gethsemani Encounter ended, some Buddhists read and commented on the Catholic monastic rule, producing *Benedict's Dharma: Buddhists Reflect on the Rule of St. Benedict* as a fruit of dialogue.[55]

Because of the presence of the Dalai Lama, along with Maha Ghosananda, the Patriarch of Cambodian Buddhism who was widely revered as a nonviolent leader and peace-builder, and Armand Veilleux, a Trappist leader who had recently retrieved the remains of the Trappist monks who had been killed in Algeria a few months earlier, the discussions repeatedly turned to violence and how Buddhists and Catholics can respond constructively to conflict situations. The monks of Gethsemani welcomed us to sit with them for the chanting of the Psalms, including some that are violent. Zen Buddhist poet Norman Fischer, who is of Jewish heritage, later asked Catholics,

> but there are some things in the Psalms that I would find hard to swallow if I were chanting them every day. When it says something like please, Lord, break their jawbones, and trample them under foot, I wonder how you practice with this? How do you work with it?[56]

In response Benedictine monk Julian von Duerbeck commented:

> The prayer images of God destroying the enemy are themselves martial images. Sometimes I feel that in the Psalms this gets carried away because we have there reflections by people who are being persecuted by others and are really wanting God to smash in their jaws, etc. But when we do pray those Psalms, we use something called "tropology," which means that we do not think about the individual enemy, but they become symbols of evil, of injustice, of disharmony. In 1989, a group of Tibetan monks came to our abbey where they did the Dance of the Skeleton Lords which presented a frightening destruction of evil.[57]

After the dialogue ended, Fischer wanted to probe further; and so he studied Hebrew, consulted a rabbi, explored the Psalms, and produced his own, poetic,

---

[55] Norman Fischer, Joseph Goldstein, Judith Simmer-Brown, Yifa et al., *Benedict's Dharma: Buddhists Reflect on the Rule of Saint Benedict,* ed. Patrick Henry (New York: Riverhead, 2001).

[56] Mitchell and Wiseman, *Gethsemani Encounter*, 206.

[57] Ibid., 206–7.

Zen-inspired interpretation of them, which was published just before the Second Gethsemani Encounter.[58]

In April 2002, MID convened the Second Gethsemani Encounter, which focused directly on the various forms and causes of suffering and Buddhist and Catholic practices for relieving suffering.[59] In October 2004, Buddhist and Catholic male monastics met at the City of Ten Thousand Buddhas in Ukiah, California, to explore the practice of celibacy in each tradition in reference to each tradition's spirituality, history, and values.[60] The Third Gethsemani Encounter in 2008 focused on "Green Monasticism," that is, monastic resources for ecological awareness and action.[61] The Fourth Gethsemani Encounter in 2015 focused on "Spiritual Maturation," with sharing of practice. Buddhist monastics attended the Catholic Liturgy of the Hours of the Trappist hosts, and Catholics participated in Buddhist meditation practice.[62] As interreligious encounters draw Catholics and Buddhists into closer relationships, the potential of the Buddhist tradition to illumine human existence is brought into new contexts, often giving a fresh perspective on traditional Christian or Jewish themes and practices; such encounters also bring fresh questions and challenges and possibilities to the Buddhist heritage.

Responses to the Kyoto School

Some American Catholic scholars, including Donald Mitchell and James Fredericks, have been involved in dialogue with Buddhist thinkers from the movement known as the Kyoto School *(Kyoto-ha)*, which was founded in the early twentieth century by the Japanese philosopher Kitaro Nishida (1870–1945), who was a friend of D. T. Suzuki. Nishida and the later members of the Kyoto School were Buddhist philosophers associated with the University of Kyoto who studied European and American philosophy and Christian theology, proposed creative interpretations of Buddhist and Christian themes, and evoked thoughtful Christian responses.[63] The development of the Kyoto School was part

---

[58] Norman Zoketsu Fischer, *Opening To You: Zen-Inspired Translations of the Psalms* (New York: Viking Compass, 2002).

[59] *Transforming Suffering: Reflections on Finding Peace in Troubled Times by His Holiness the Dalai Lama, His Holiness Pope John Paul II, Thomas Keating, Thubten Chodron, Joseph Goldstein, and Others*, ed. Donald W. Mitchell and James Wiseman (New York: Doubleday, 2003).

[60] William Skudlarek, *Demythologizing Celibacy: Practical Wisdom from Christian and Buddhist Monasticism* (Collegeville, MN: Liturgical Press, 2008).

[61] Donald W. Mitchell and William Skudlarek, eds., *Green Monasticism: A Buddhist-Catholic Response to an Environmental Calamity* (New York: Lantern Books, 2010).

[62] Monastic Interreligious Dialogue, "Gethsemani Encounter IV, May 27–31, 2015," http://monasticinterreligiousdialogue.com; Abbey of Gethsemani—Abbey News, "27–31 May 2015—Gethsemani Hosts the Fourth Gethsemani Encounter," http://www.monks.org.

[63] Robert E. Carter, *The Kyoto School: An Introduction* (Albany: State University of New York Press, 2013); Bret W. Davis, Brian Schroeder, and Jason M. Wirth, eds., *Japanese*

of the broader Japanese engagement with Western thought and culture that began with the Meiji Restoration in 1868 and continued in the Taisho period after 1912.[64] Notable representatives were Kitaro Nishida, Hajime Tanabe, Shizuteru Ueda, Keiji Nishitani, and Masao Abe. Some of the most creative Buddhist-Christian conversations have come from dialogue with these figures, but some scholars have strongly criticized the leaders of the Kyoto School for supporting Japanese imperialism during the 1930s and 1940s.[65]

Kitaro Nishida pondered the relation between Zen practice, Western philosophy from Plato to William James and Henri Bergson, and the Christian experience of fall and redemption. In 1911, Nishida published *An Inquiry into the Good*, responding to Western philosophical descriptions of experience and presenting the experience of Zen in Western terminology without ever mentioning the word "Zen."[66] According to Nishida, the "true features of reality" are found in pure experience: "At the time of pure experience, there is still no opposition between subject and object and no separation of knowledge, feeling, and volition; there is only an independent, self-sufficient, pure activity."[67] He strove to express the meaning of this experience throughout his career, finding analogies between Zen Buddhism and some aspects of Western thought, including the paradoxical negations and the nondual language of Christian mystics such as pseudo-Dionysius the Areopagite, Meister Eckhart, and Nicholas of Cusa.[68]

American Catholic philosopher Donald Mitchell responds appreciatively to Nishida's perspectives, but he carefully distinguishes Nishida's description of Buddhist experience from the Christian experience of spirituality:

---

and Continental Philosophy: Conversations with the Kyoto School (Bloomington: Indiana University Press, 2011); Fritz Buri, *The Buddha-Christ as the Lord of the True Self: The Religious Philosophy of the Kyoto School and Christianity,* trans. Harold H. Oliver (Macon, GA: Mercer University Press, 1997); Hans Waldenfels, *Absolute Nothingness: Foundations for a Buddhist-Christian Dialogue,* trans. J. W. Heisig (New York: Paulist Press, 1980).

[64] H. Gene Blocker and Christopher L. Starling, *Japanese Philosophy* (Albany: State University of New York Press, 2001), 111–54; S. N. Eisenstadt, *Japanese Civilization: A Comparative View* (Chicago: University of Chicago Press, 1996), 1–160.

[65] James Heisig and John Maraldo, eds., *Rude Awakenings: Zen, the Kyoto School, and the Question of Nationalism* (Honolulu: University of Hawaii Press, 1995).

[66] Kitaro Nishida, *An Inquiry into the Good,* trans. Masao Abe and Christopher Ives (New Haven, CT: Yale University Press, 1990); see also Keiji Nishitani, *Nishida Kitaro,* trans. Yamamoto Seisaku and James W. Heisig (Berkeley: University of California Press, 1991), 93–160; Robert Wilkinson, *Nishida and Western Philosophy* (Farnham: Ashgate, 2009).

[67] Nishida, *Inquiry,* 47.

[68] Ibid., 164, 169; Michiko Yusa, *Zen and Philosophy: An Intellectual Biography of Nishida Kitaro* (Honolulu: University of Hawaii Press, 2002), 39, 173; Robert E. Carter, *The Nothingness beyond God: An Introduction to the Philosophy of Nishida Kitaro,* 2nd ed. (St. Paul, MN: Paragon House, 1997), 86, 134; Masao Abe, *Zen and the Modern World: A Third Sequel to Zen and Western Thought,* ed. Steven Heine (Honolulu: University of Hawaii Press, 2003), 104.

I would propose that while the Buddhist experience of Emptiness perceives no far side apart from the near side, a Christian mystic finds that through the grace of Christ indwelling within, he or she is given a "spiritual eye," as it were, to see into the mystery of the Void.[69]

Where Nishida sees Emptiness as identified with the world just as it is in its suchness, Mitchell believes that the Catholic "finds therein a far-side dimension that is *not* absolutely identified with the near side of creation, and is *not* formless and impersonal."[70] Where Nishida finds only the Emptiness "of the absolute near side," Mitchell as a Catholic discovers also "the Void has a personal trinitarian far-side dimension. . . . If one sees through the Void itself, one finds that it is not prior to a personal God."[71] Mitchell believes that Catholic practitioners can indeed experience what Nishida describes as Emptiness or the Void, but "for the Christian, the mystery of the Void on the near side opens into the mystery of the Trinity on the far side. And what a Christian mystic beholds through this eye is that the Trinity is not a derivative reality or something less than the mystical Void."[72] Mitchell summed up the difference:

A Buddhist can speak of an absolute near side in which any far-side reality is emptied out, but a Christian cannot. The kenosis of God as a near-side reality does not fully empty out the far side since it would thereby empty out its own foundation as well as the foundation of Christian hope.[73]

Nonetheless, Mitchell acknowledges that Nishida's perspective can help Christians recognize more clearly that the kenotic Godhead is self-emptying love and that God the Father is a dynamic of self-emptying into the Son and the Spirit and through them into creation, including into our identity in the image of God.

Masao Abe developed the approach of Nishida and carefully studied the letters of Paul as a springboard for further reflection in dialogue with Christians in the United States and beyond. For many years at the end of the twentieth century, Abe was at the center of academic Buddhist-Christian dialogues in the United States. Christopher Ives recalls that "Abe has striven to practice what his main teacher, Shin'ichi Hisamatsu, termed 'the unity of study and practice.'"[74] Abe insisted that Christians could not understand Zen Buddhist language until they had faced the problem of the self in their own lives. "Self-estrangement and anxiety are *not* something

---

[69] Donald Mitchell, *Spirituality and Emptiness: The Dynamics of Spiritual Life in Buddhism and Christianity* (New York: Paulist Press, 1991), 25.

[70] Ibid.

[71] Ibid.

[72] Ibid., 25–26.

[73] Ibid., 28.

[74] Christopher Ives, "Masao Abe and His Dialogical Mission," in *Masao Abe: A Zen Life of Dialogue,* ed. Donald W. Mitchell (Boston: Charles E. Tuttle, 1998), 349.

accidental to the ego-self, but are inherent to its structure. To be human is to be a problem to oneself, regardless of one's culture, class, sex, nationality, or the era in which one lives."[75] For Abe, each person must go through a crisis that leads to a breakdown of the ego-self: "The true Self is not something attainable, but that which is unattainable. When this is *existentially* realized with our whole being, the ego-self crumbles."[76] This collapse, however, brings liberation: "Hence, the genuine realization that the 'true Self is unattainable' is not a source of desperation, but is freedom from restlessness, because in this realization it no longer matters that the true Self cannot be attained."[77] Abe interpreted Christianity in light of this perspective, and he asked Christians whether they could affirm that God is Emptiness, or Emptying: "Is it not that the kenosis of Christ, that is, the self-emptying of the Son of God, has its origin in God 'the Father,' the kenosis of God?"[78]

Mitchell collaborated closely with Abe and appreciated his contributions; but as in the case of Nishida, Mitchell saw important differences between Abe and Catholic faith. Mitchell accepted Abe's proposal that the kenosis of the Son of God reveals a kenosis of God the Father: "It does seem to me that the kenotic love seen in Christ is revelatory of the kenosis of God-Love in creation."[79] Mitchell believes there is a triple kenosis of the Father in creation, the Son in redemption, and the Holy Spirit in sanctification, but, he affirms that "all three of these depend on a more primordial kenosis within the Trinity itself."[80] The encounter with the Kyoto School helped Mitchell and many other Christians to see Christian beliefs in a new way, but there remain important differences.

Off the Map

Dialogue with Buddhists poses questions about the most fundamental assumptions of Catholic theology, including the reality of God, the creation of the world, and human identity. James Fredericks, a longtime participant in the Los Angeles Buddhist-Catholic Dialogue, describes how his encounter with Buddhists and the Buddhist tradition drove him off his theological roadmap.[81] Fredericks worked closely with Masao Abe but, like Donald Mitchell, always respected the profound

---

[75] Masao Abe, *Zen and Western Thought,* ed. William LaFleur (Honolulu: University of Hawaii Press, 1985), 6.

[76] Ibid., 7.

[77] Ibid., 9.

[78] Masao Abe, "Kenotic God and Dynamic Sunyata," in *The Emptying God: A Buddhist-Jewish-Christian Conversation,* ed. John B. Cobb Jr. and Christopher Ives (Maryknoll, NY: Orbis Books, 1990), 14.

[79] Mitchell, *Spirituality and Emptiness,* 61.

[80] Ibid.

[81] James L. Fredericks, "Off the Map: The Catholic Church and Its Dialogue with Buddhists," in *Catholicism and Interreligious Dialogue,* ed. James L. Heft (Oxford: Oxford University Press, 2011), 127–44.

difference between their perspectives.[82] Fredericks tried to find a place for God in his encounter with Abe, but he and Abe both recognized that Christian faith in God cannot be identified with Buddhist experience of Emptying. Fredericks concluded, "Neither one of us has succeeded to the degree we had hoped."[83] For Fredericks, dual belonging is not an option: "I recognize the goodness of the Buddhist path but cannot embrace that path as a believer and practitioner. I am not a Buddhist. To say so would be not only pretense, but harmful to Buddhism."[84] Fredericks tried to find a place in traditional Catholic spiritual geography for his relationship with Abe, but he concluded, "My Buddhist friend has run me off my theological roadmap."[85]

In considering how a Catholic can view Buddhists, Fredericks looks to John Paul II's theology of religions. He notes that John Paul emphasizes the centrality of the redemption offered in Jesus Christ but also teaches the universality of the work of the Holy Spirit. The pope finds goodness and saving grace in other religious traditions, but always mediated by the work of Jesus Christ and the Holy Spirit who fulfill the religious aspirations of all humans. Whatever is true and holy and good in other traditions is, for Pope John Paul II, fulfilled in Christ through the power of the Holy Spirit. Fredericks argues that admirable as John Paul's theology of the Holy Spirit is, it faces a major challenge when in dialogue with Buddhists. Any attempt to fit Buddhism into a Catholic framework risks inevitably distorting it. John Paul is faithful to the demands of the Christian tradition in Fredericks's estimation, but his effort is not helpful when encountering Buddhist perspectives, which do not fit neatly into a theistic grid. Fredericks calls this the "domestication of difference," which unfortunately prevents us from seeing our dialogue partner clearly.[86] Fredericks believes that there has been a major "sea-change" in Catholic theology regarding other religions since the Second Vatican Council, and John Paul II brings one phase of the discussion to a completion. In response to this impasse, Fredericks calls not for a new theology of religions about Buddhism but for more intense dialogue and thinking with Buddhists.[87]

Anselm Min critiques Fredericks for measuring whether a Catholic doctrine is true by the degree to which it is suitable for dialogue and also for assuming that the purpose of interreligious dialogue is to be transformed by the other.[88] As a counterposition, Min proposes that the criterion for Christian and other religions' doctrines should be "adequacy to existential and historical problems of human life

---

[82] James Fredericks, "Masao Abe: A Spiritual Friendship," *Spiritus* 3, no. 2 (2003): 219.

[83] Ibid., 222.

[84] Ibid., 223.

[85] Ibid., 224.

[86] Fredericks, "Off the Map," 136.

[87] See also James L. Fredericks, *Buddhists and Christians: Through Comparative Theology to Solidarity* (Maryknoll, NY: Orbis Books, 2004).

[88] Anselm Kyongsuk Min, "A Response to James L. Fredericks," in Heft, *Catholicism and Interreligious Dialogue*, 146.

itself."[89] Min summarizes the major points of Catholic faith as offering an adequate existential response to the challenge of sin and suffering in human life. Min forthrightly acknowledges that this is anchored in the Catholic tradition and points out that all representatives of other religious traditions do something very similar in being anchored to their own heritages. Min poses the central question to Fredericks: "I wonder whether it is theoretically legitimate and practically feasible to require that a religion put aside or abandon, for fear of domesticating difference, a central doctrine of its own."[90]

Christian Practice of Meditation with Buddhists

Across the United States, Catholics and other Christians are engaging in the practice of forms of meditation coming originally from the Buddhist tradition.[91] From the Mercy Center near San Francisco to the Maria Kannon Zen Center in Texas to the Empty Bell in Massachusetts and at many points in between, Christians are learning the postures and structures of Mahayana Zen Buddhist meditation or Theravada Buddhist *vipassana* (insight) meditation, often from other Christians, and are incorporating Buddhist meditation practice into their lives as Christians. While some who have explored the treasures of the Buddhist tradition have left the Christian tradition and have adopted a Buddhist form of practice, many others remain Christians and appropriate aspects of Buddhist meditation and devotion into their spiritual path as Christians. Some Buddhists and Christians have expressed reservations about such practice across traditions, but these developments hold much promise for the future and may well be a harbinger of new forms that will be important for future generations.

The Theravada Buddhist tradition has long taught the practice of insight (*vipassana*) meditation, together with the complementary practice of loving-kindness (*metta*) meditation. The virtues of the *brahma-viharas*, or sublime dwelling-places of the Buddha (loving-kindness, compassion, sympathetic joy, and equanimity), shape loving-kindness meditation in ways that resonate deeply with the Christian tradition. The seeking of insight into one's present situation and the extending of loving-kindness and compassion to oneself and to all creatures bear strong similarities to the values of the Christian tradition. In the early church, Evagrius Ponticus taught Christians to pray by emptying their minds of all thoughts and desires: "Strive to render your mind deaf and dumb at the time of prayer and then you will be able to pray."[92] He predicted that an emotional

---

[89] Ibid.

[90] Ibid., 147.

[91] Harold Kasimow, John P. Keenan, and Linda Klepinger Keenan, *Beside Still Waters: Jews, Christians, and the Way of the Buddha* (Boston: Wisdom Publications, 2003); Leo D. Lefebure, "The Impact of Buddhist Meditation upon Christian Prayer," *Chicago Studies* 44, no. 2 (2005): 169–85.

[92] Evagrius Ponticus, *The Praktikos; Chapters on Prayer,* trans. John Eudes Bamberger

upheaval may well ensue, but he promised that meditators would come to a state of peace and tranquility that cannot be obtained in any other way. The Hesychast tradition of Byzantine Orthodox Christianity sought *hesuchia* (rest or quiet in Greek) by following the breath and trusting in the power of the Holy Spirit. While this tradition is in many ways profoundly different from Theravada Buddhist meditation practice, there are clear similarities. These areas of shared or overlapping spiritual wisdom provide a space for Christians to encounter Buddhist meditation and appropriate it into their Christian faith and practice.

The Carmelite tradition of Catholic spirituality has long valued silent meditation and the letting go of all thoughts and ideas about God. A number of Catholics from the Carmelite tradition have probed these Theravada practices very deeply; Kevin G. Culligan, Mary Jo Meadow, and Daniel Chowning have integrated insight and loving-kindness meditation into a spiritual practice inspired by St. John of the Cross, a sixteenth-century Spanish Catholic mystical leader who called for the purification of disordered appetites, intellect, memory, and will. Culligan, Meadow, and Chowning compare the teachings and practices of John of the Cross with those of Shakyamuni Buddha for training the mind. They express the hope: "By offering an ancient Buddhist meditation practice within a Christian prayer tradition, we hope to teach our readers a process of inner purification that we believe can lead to deeper Christian faith in this world and the direct vision of God in the next."[93]

The Carmelites begin with Jesus's beatitude: "Blessed are the pure in heart, for they shall see God" (Mt 5:8). They comment, "Jesus teaches that we must purify our entire interior life if we want the happiness of seeing God."[94] They then cite the words of Shakyamuni Buddha: "When you are cleansed of all impurity and the stain of all sinful passions is gone, you can enter the blessed abode of the saints."[95] They note that the Buddha taught meditation as "the practice that cleanses the heart. It purifies the heart of disordered desires, hateful thoughts, harmful memories, fear and other negative emotions, and, in their place, engenders sharp mental awareness, clear understanding, strength of will, and attentiveness to each passing moment."[96] They observe that John of the Cross describes the painful but healing process of purification of desires, thoughts, emotions, and memories. Thus the Carmelites "bring these two venerable traditions—Buddhist meditation and the Christian spirituality of St. John of the Cross—together into an ascetical practice we call Christian insight meditation."[97] In a companion volume, Mary Jo Meadow describes the complementary practice of loving-kindness meditation, which extends loving-kindness, compassion, appreciative joy, and equanimity to oneself, to one's

(Kalamazoo, MI: Cistercian Publications, 1981), 57.

[93] Kevin G. Culligan, Mary Jo Meadow, and Daniel Chowning, *Purifying the Heart: Buddhist Insight Meditation for Christians* (New York: Crossroad, 1994), 13.

[94] Ibid., 23.

[95] Dhammapada #236; Culligan et al., *Purifying*, 29.

[96] Culligan et al., *Purifying*, 29.

[97] Ibid., 30.

neighbors and friends, to one's enemies, and to all sentient beings.[98] The ancient Buddhist practices find an important place in contemporary Christian spirituality.

Ruben L. F. Habito is one of the most prominent contributors to Buddhist-Catholic relations in the United States. He began practice of Zen meditation in Japan in 1971 and quickly came to an experience that was recognized by his Buddhist teachers Koun Yamada Roshi and Hakuun Yasutani Roshi as *kensho* (seeing clearly), that is, Zen enlightenment.[99] The experience is ineffable: "But how am I to describe this experience? Trying to describe kensho is as futile as trying to meaningfully convey the experience of tasting green tea. Most usefully I can only point to a hot cup of tea and invite others to drink and taste it themselves."[100] His Zen practice first developed the power of concentration (*samadhi* or *joriki*) and then moved through *kensho* to the experience of integration, personalization, and manifestation of Zen in everyday life (*mujodo no taigen*). The experience comes as a grace: "We cannot bring about this experience through our striving, rather we can only dispose ourselves toward the occurrence of this event of grace by means of assiduously practicing zazen, attending to our breathing, and attuning ourselves to the here and now."[101] Habito discovered that his Jesuit experience of the Spiritual Exercises of Ignatius of Loyola gave him a helpful background for practicing Zen. Sitting *zazen* offered a concrete experience of healing breath, which he identified as "the living Breath of God, which recreates the earth and makes all things new."[102]

As a Catholic, Habito interprets Zen experience in traditional Christian language. The experience of *mu* (nothing) offered a new vantage point on the Jewish and Christian teaching of creation *ex nihilo* "as a very suggestive expression of an ever-present wonderment, with every breath, every step, every smile . . . every leaf, every flower, every raindrop, realized as literally as *nothing* but the grace-filled gift from the infinite and ever-flowing divine love!"[103] He also experiences Zen enlightenment as dying to one's self: "this is an event that enables one to experience the Paschal Mystery of Christ's death and resurrection (Romans 6:3–4; Colossians 2:12; Philippians 3:10; 1 Peter 3:18–22) *in this very body.*"[104] Habito's mentor, Yamada Koun Roshi, commented that when Christians asked him if they had to give up Christianity to practice Zen,

---

[98] Mary Jo Meadow, *Gentling the Heart: Buddhist Loving-Kindness Practice for Christians* (New York: Crossroad, 1994).

[99] Ruben L. F. Habito, *Living Zen, Loving God* (Boston: Wisdom Publications, 2004), 2–3.

[100] Ibid., 2.

[101] Ibid., 3.

[102] Ibid., 5; Ruben L.F. Habito, *Healing Breath: Zen Spirituality for a Wounded Earth* (Maryknoll, NY: Orbis Books, 1993).

[103] Habito, *Living Zen,* 6.

[104] Ibid., 7.

I always answer them that they need not worry about forsaking or losing their Christianity. I tell them that Zen is not a religion and they do not have to think of it as such, in the sense of a system of beliefs and concepts and practices that demands exclusive allegiance.[105]

Roger Corless, a Catholic who was a respected scholar of Buddhism, engaged in both Roman Catholic and Tibetan Buddhist practice. Corless was very critical of Christian appropriations of Buddhist meditation that do not explicitly respect and acknowledge the contradictory conceptualizations of the two traditions. Instead, he proposed a paradoxical format of Buddhist and Christian meditation that respects the ontological differences of the two traditions while bringing their meditation practices together in an encounter that even he did not claim to fully understand.[106] Three days a week (Sunday, Tuesday, Thursday) he engaged in Catholic Morning Prayer, and three days a week (Monday, Wednesday, Friday) he performed a Tibetan form of visualization practice. When he was praying according to the Catholic tradition, he found the Buddhist worldview either wrong or irrelevant. When he was engaged in Buddhist meditation, he found the Catholic perspective similarly either wrong or irrelevant. He allowed the two traditions to intersect on the seventh day of the week, and he observed what was happening in this mutual interpenetration without seeking to control the outcome. Corless acknowledged "the simultaneous yet contradictory truths of Christianity and Buddhism: that, on the one hand, if there were no God, there would be nothing; and, on the other hand, if there were God, there could be nothing."[107] He commented: "The main purpose of the meditation is the acknowledgment of Buddhism and Christianity as two Absolute Systems coinhering on the same planet (in humanity as a whole) and in your own consciousness. What these systems will then do is not your concern."[108] Corless trusted "that the confusion that a single consciousness might feel by being a focus for such contradictions can form the basis of a new spiritual path."[109]

Another approach to dual practice is presented by Sarita Tamayo-Moraga, who describes herself as follows: "I am a life-long Roman Catholic and a dharma heir of Darlene Cohen Roshi in the lineage of Suzuki Roshi of San Francisco Zen Center."[110] In 2014, she joined with Zen Buddhists, Pure Land Buddhists, Jesuits,

---

[105] Ruben L. F. Habito, *Total Liberation: Zen Spirituality and the Social Dimension* (Maryknoll, NY: Orbis Books, 1989), 85.

[106] Roger Corless, "A Form for Buddhist-Christian Coinherent Meditation," *Buddhist-Christian Studies* 14 (1994): 139–44.

[107] Ibid., 139.

[108] Ibid.

[109] Ibid.

[110] Sarita Tamayo-Moraga, "Buddhist and Ignatian Spiritualities: Report on a Trial Run of an Interfaith Retreat Based on *Ignatius and the Buddha in Conversation: A Resource for a Religiously Plural Dialog, Juxtaposing the Spiritual Exercises of Ignatius and Buddhist Wisdom*," *Buddhist-Christian Studies* 37 (2017): 132.

and Jews in an interfaith retreat at Santa Clara University entitled "Ignatius and the Buddha in Conversation." She explains their procedure: "As a group, we went back and forth between the Ignatian Spiritual Exercises and Buddhist meditation and then we would share about the experience. . . . As a Catholic and Zen teacher, I had never done something like this."[111] Participants discovered a common focus of Ignatian and Buddhist meditation on paying attention: "Both Buddhism and the Examen have this focus on how to return to what is in front of us—as in the Ignatian Spiritual Exercises, paying attention to God all day, and in Buddhism, paying attention to the present moment all day."[112] In each tradition, focus on the present led to "discovering the suffering that gets in the way of fixing one's day on God or fixing one's day on what is actually happening rather than what we wish were happening."[113]

The retreat explored kenosis and self-emptying not as concepts but as practices: "We began to empty out that which was keeping us from doing the task in front of us."[114] The practice led to greater inner freedom and resources for responding to racism, sexism, and conflicts over financial matters. As the meditation practice deepened, practitioners entered into awareness of suffering, including the suffering of Jesus and other people and also "the place where institutional and personal wounds intersected. Entering the Passion did something to all of us. I feel like we entered each other's darkness, even though that might seem fanciful."[115] The awareness of suffering in turn led to freedom for service. This is not a matter of acquiring new ideas but of becoming free from obstacles; Tamayo-Moraga evokes the Zen ox-herding pictures, which present visual images of the path of Zen awakening. "The next to last picture has no ox or person because there is only activity and only scenery. Concepts no longer get in the way."[116] In the final scene of the Zen ox-herding pictures, the practitioner returns to the marketplace free to serve others.

The retreat included reflections on the lives of both Jesus Christ and Shakyamuni Buddha. Tamayo-Moraga emphasizes the life-transforming change in perception that both Zen and Jesuit retreats call forth, especially an awareness of being loved that empowers practitioners to express love and compassion for others. For Ignatius of Loyola, this is based on God's love for us. "In Buddhism the change in perception is one from feeling isolated and separate to feeling connected with all sentient beings and nature. Without this change in perception, suffering will not be transformed."[117] In varying ways, many American Catholics have found their practice enriched by the exploration of the wisdom of Buddhist meditation.

---

[111] Ibid., 132, 133.
[112] Ibid., 133.
[113] Ibid., 133–34.
[114] Ibid., 134.
[115] Ibid., 135.
[116] Ibid.
[117] Ibid., 136.

Social Engagement

Another major focus of Buddhist-Christian dialogue in the United States has been social engagement with the goal of relieving suffering and enhancing life. One of the most important developments in recent Buddhism has been the growth of Socially Engaged Buddhism, which includes a variety of forms of Buddhist practice seeking to interpret and live the ancient Buddhist path in light of contemporary social, political, and economic challenges.[118] This is not a single organized movement, but rather includes many different movements that began independently but share similar concerns.[119]

When Thich Nhat Hanh came to the United States in 1966 to promote American awareness of the situation in Vietnam and work for peace, he visited Gethsemani Abbey, where he met Thomas Merton, who was very impressed with him.[120] Merton later wrote a reflection called "Nhat Hanh Is My Brother," in which he comments, "More than any other he has shown us that Zen is not an esoteric and world denying cult of inner illumination, but that it has its rare and unique sense of responsibility in the modern world.[121] Merton sees his close relation to Nhat Hanh as "the bonds of a new solidarity and a new brotherhood which is beginning to be evident on all the five continents."[122] Nhat Hanh and Jesuit Daniel Berrigan also shared a concern to end the U.S. involvement in the war in Vietnam. In 1974, in the suburbs of Paris, Nhat Hanh and Berrigan had conversations on the values of their respective traditions for peace, social justice, and transforming society.[123] These friendships have inspired many more recent Buddhists and Christians in the United States to collaborate on social concerns. Charles Strain draws from both Nhat Hanh and Berrigan to shape a social ethics that seeks to avoid the danger of moral righteousness prevalent in some forms of Catholic theology.[124]

In light of Christian feminist theology, Karen Enriquez explores the relation between Jesuit liberation theologians and socially engaged Buddhists.[125] She notes

---

[118] Sallie B. King, *Socially Engaged Buddhism: Dimensions of Asian Spirituality* (Honolulu: University of Hawaii Press, 2009).

[119] Donald Rothenberg, "Responding to the Cries of the World: Socially Engaged Buddhism in North America," in *The Faces of Buddhism in America*, ed. Charles B. Prebish and Kenneth K. Tanaka (Berkeley: University of California Press, 1998), 266–86.

[120] Thomas Merton, *The Hidden Ground of Love: The Letters of Thomas Merton on Religious Experience and Social Concerns,* selected and ed. William H. Shannon (New York: Farrar, Straus, and Giroux, 1985), 197.

[121] Thomas Merton, *Faith and Violence: Christian Teaching and Christian Practice* (Notre Dame, IN: University of Notre Dame Press, 1968), 107–8.

[122] Ibid., 108.

[123] Thich Nhat Hanh and Daniel Berrigan, *The Raft Is Not the Shore: Conversations toward a Buddhist-Christian Awareness* (Maryknoll, NY: Orbis Books, 2001).

[124] Charles R. Strain, *The Prophet and the Bodhisattva: Daniel Berrigan, Thich Nhat Hanh, and the Ethics of Peace and Justice* (Eugene, OR: Wipf & Stock Publishers, 2014).

[125] Karen B. Enriquez, "Expanding the Cultivation and Practice of Love and Compas-

the suspicion often posed by engaged Buddhists that the preferential option for the poor by Christian liberation theologians "can and has led to partial, dualistic, and exclusionary language, attitudes, and actions that lead to greater suffering. Moreover, it undermines Christianity's own goal of unconditional love and obscures the potential and full humanity of the oppressor, usually seen as one's enemy."[126] In response, Enriquez stresses the need to see what affluent people usually do not want to see, viz. reality as lived by the poor: "The option for the poor shows us the boundaries of our perceptions and our blind spots, and pulls us out of comfortable places of knowing and judging who is human and worthy of our attention."[127] She compares this epistemological role of the preferential option for the poor to the role of emptiness in Buddhism, "moving us out of our limiting thoughts of self and other by undercutting our reified notions of suffering and who suffers."[128] She also notes that recent discussions of intersectionality have broadened the notion of the poor to more than issues of class. While social change may involve conflict, Enriquez stresses the need for solidarity between those viewed as oppressed and as oppressors, and she highlights the challenge of confronting one's own identity as both oppressed and oppressor in the hope of cultivating greater compassion and solidarity for all. She suggests that engaged Buddhists and Christian liberation theologians face a common challenge to attend to the suffering of the poor and marginalized in all dimensions. She finds that Buddhist analyses of subtle forms of suffering can be helpful to liberation theologians seeking to befriend those perceived as enemies. She cites Thich Nhat Hanh's poem, "Call Me by My True Names," in which he identifies with oppressed and oppressors alike and thus cannot take sides.[129]

Enriquez also stresses the interdependence of personal and social dimensions in shaping our experience for better or for worse, and she relates the analysis of social sin in liberation theology to the traditional Buddhist teaching of interdependence or dependent coarising. She points out the negative working of interdependence when "we see unenlightened beings reflecting their ignorance upon others building a tower of delusion and suffering."[130] Collective delusion envelops the world in networks of ignorance and suffering, which Buddhists call collective samsara. She draws upon both Buddhist views of the sangha and Christian perspectives on community to illumine the mutual cycle of both delusion and enlightenment, as the personal shapes the social and vice versa. Work for liberation must involve both dimensions. She notes that some Buddhists and Catholics have worried that liberation theologians focus so much on the communal, political dimension that they place no value on the contemplative path. Enriquez reviews a number of liberation

---

sion in Our Suffering World: Continuing the Dialogue between Liberation Theologians and Engaged Buddhists," *Buddhist-Christian Studies* 36 (2016): 69–86.

[126] Ibid., 70.

[127] Ibid., 71.

[128] Ibid.

[129] Ibid., 73. See also Thich Nhat Hanh, *Call Me by My True Names: The Collected Poems of Thich Nhat Hanh* (Berkeley, CA: Parallax Press, 1999), 72–73.

[130] Enriquez, "Expanding the Cultivation," 74.

and feminist theologians who have emphasized the importance of spiritual practice and contemplation in the struggle for liberation. She notes that the Jesuit spirituality of Jon Sobrino, grounded in the Spiritual Exercises of Ignatius of Loyola, is a major factor shaping his vision of liberation. Of particular importance is the "gratuitousness of God's love that allows one to work in the world as one forgiven, and thus have unconditional love for both the oppressed and the oppressor."[131] She draws upon both Jesuit and Buddhist practices to explore how, despite all our negative perceptions and expectations, people we have viewed as enemies can be sacraments and gifts to us.

In June 2015, I participated in a dialogue of Buddhists and Catholics from five major metropolitan areas of the United States who met at Castel Gandolfo and Rome, Italy, to discuss the sources of suffering in the United States today and how Buddhists and Catholics can work together to alleviate suffering.[132] The dialogue took its inspiration from the words of Pope Francis in his Message for the World Day of Peace 2014: "Fraternity is an essential human quality, for we are all relational beings. A lively awareness of our relatedness helps us to look upon and treat each person as a true sister or brother; without fraternity it is impossible to build a just society and a solid and lasting peace."[133] The dialogue was also guided by the message sent by Jean-Louis Cardinal Tauran, president of the Pontifical Council for Interreligious Dialogue, to Buddhists for the celebration of Vesakh 2014, "Buddhists and Christians: Together Fostering Fraternity."[134] The Vesakh Message expanded upon the vision of Pope Francis, inviting Buddhists and Catholics

to cooperation with other pilgrims and with people of good will to respect and defend our shared humanity . . . Drawing upon our different religious convictions we are called especially to be *outspoken* in denouncing all those social ills which damage fraternity, to be *healers* who enable others to grow in selfless generosity, and to be *reconcilers* who break down the walls of division and foster genuine brotherhood between individuals and groups in society.[135]

Each morning of the dialogue began with chanting and meditation led by Buddhist participants, followed by celebration of the Catholic Eucharist. Jean-Louis Cardinal Tauran opened the dialogue by commenting, "In a world where diversity

---

[131] Ibid., 79.

[132] Jim Fredericks, "Dialogue of Suffering, Liberation, and Fraternity: A Report on the Anniversary of *Nostra Aetate,*" *Buddhist-Christian Studies* 36, no. 1 (2016): 213–14.

[133] Pope Francis, "Fraternity: The Foundation and Pathway to Peace," Message for the World Day of Peace 2014, #1.

[134] For a reflection on the call to fraternity in relation to Buddhists, see James L. Fredericks, "Nostra Aetate and Pope Francis: Reflections on the Next Fifty Years of Catholic Dialogue with Buddhists," in *Nostra Aetate,* ed. Pim Valkenberg and Anthony Cirelli (Washington, DC: Catholic University of America Press, 2016), 43–57.

[135] Pontifical Council for Interreligious Dialogue, "Message for the Feast of Vesakh 2014: Buddhists and Christians Together: Fostering Fraternity," #4.

is seen as a threat, our coming together today in friendship and peace is a sign of our openness towards one another and our commitment to human fraternity." Cardinal Tauran elaborated: "We are all pilgrims and I see this Buddhist-Catholic dialogue as part of our ongoing quest to grasp the mystery of our lives and the ultimate Truth." He noted three stages that are important for the journey of dialogue. First is carrying less baggage, in other words, "Overcoming prejudices, wounds, fears in order to listen to one's heart and to that of one's religious neighbor." The second stage is crossing borders, journeying to know the other side while remaining firmly rooted in our beliefs. This process "can thus turn ignorance into understanding, a stranger into a friend, hostility to hospitality and divergence into convergence." The final stage is returning home "transformed by what we experienced." The Cardinal's words set a hopeful tone and direction for the encounter.

Just a few days before our dialogue began, Pope Francis had issued his encyclical *Laudato Si': On Care for Our Common Home*. Hozan Alan Senauke from the Berkeley Zen Center began his reflection on nature and the climate crisis by quoting the Canticle of the Sun of St. Francis of Assisi, which inspired Pope Francis's encyclical *Laudato Si'.* One of the ancient Buddhist precepts instructs practitioners not to take what is not given; Senauke related the contemporary application of this precept to the environment: "Driving automobiles, flying on airplanes, global production and consumerism—the Industrial Growth Society involves theft. . . . Violating the precept of not stealing is an expression of structural violence." He stressed that Buddhists resonate with the call of Pope Francis's encyclical to practice integral ecology: "'Integral ecology' is not Christian or Buddhist but truly human. We are responsible to and for the world we live in." After the dialogue, Senauke posted an online response to the presentations of Catholic social teaching at the dialogue, commenting,

> In recent decades we've seen the development of socially engaged Buddhism. But it seems to me we are still lacking a rigorous Buddhist equivalent to the "Social Gospel." We need a "Social Dharma" to care for our common home. This Social Dharma must reach across our different cultures and Buddhist traditions.[136]

The other participants strongly shared the concern for caring more effectively for the earth and the entire community of life.

Precisely because the fundamental assumptions of the Buddhist tradition are so different from those of Christian faith, dialogue with Buddhists can provide Catholics with unprecedented opportunities for rethinking traditional understandings and practices. The worldviews are enormously different, but the convergence of perspectives on virtues and the analogies of monastic practice offer many opportunities for mutual illumination and growth.

---

[136] Hozan Alan Senauke, "Towards a Social Dharma—Caring for Our Common Home, Our True Body," http://www.oneearthsangha.org/articles/towards-a-social-dharma/.

Part III

New Directions in Interreligious Dialogue
and Catholic Theology

8

New Ways of Doing Catholic Theology

Encounters with other religious traditions in the United States and beyond challenge Catholic theology in a variety of ways. Much traditional Catholic theology assumed a conflictual relationship with other religious traditions, condemning Jews for their rejection of Jesus Christ as Lord and Savior, berating Islam as a Christian heresy, and condemning Hindus, Buddhists, and followers of African and American Indian religions as idolaters. With the transformation of attitudes toward other religious traditions come new opportunities and new challenges. This chapter will survey some of the new approaches to Catholic theology that reflect on religious pluralism in light of the changed situation after the Second Vatican Council. Exploring different religious traditions can bring to light assumptions that were previously taken for granted, and questions about the interpretation of religious traditions appear in a new light. As a result, hermeneutics, the art of interpretation, has become the focus of much theological reflection; and the scope of the search for wisdom has widened.

David Tracy: Hermeneutical Theology

David Tracy has been one of the most influential American Catholic theologians in the area of hermeneutical reflections on religious pluralism and interreligious dialogue.[1] He studied philosophical theology under the guidance of Canadian theologian Bernard Lonergan in Rome and wrote his first book on his mentor's work: *The Achievement of Bernard Lonergan*.[2] Lonergan insisted on the importance of critical reflection for how we come to knowledge: "Thoroughly understand what it is to understand, and not only will you understand the broad lines of all there is to be understood but also you will possess a fixed base, an invariant pattern opening upon all further developments of understanding."[3]

---

[1] For summaries and responses to his work, see Werner G. Jeanrond and Jennifer L. Rike, eds., *Radical Pluralism and Truth: David Tracy and the Hermeneutics of Religion* (New York: Crossroad, 1991); and Stephen Okey, *A Theology of Conversation: An Introduction to David Tracy* (Collegeville, MN: Liturgical Press, 2018).

[2] David Tracy, *The Achievement of Bernard Lonergan* (New York: Herder and Herder, 1970).

[3] Bernard Lonergan, *Insight: A Study of Human Understanding*, 5th ed., *Collected*

David Tracy accepted this imperative and probed the process of understanding in dialogue with process theology inspired by philosophers Alfred North Whitehead and Charles Hartshorne and also with the hermeneutical reflections of Hans-Georg Gadamer and Paul Ricoeur. Tracy accepted Gadamer's principle that to understand is to interpret, that to interpret is to apply, and that understanding involves difference: "It is enough to say that we understand in a *different* way, *if we understand at all.*"[4] Tracy also accepted Gadamer's claim that the original author does not control the meaning of the text for later generations: "Not just occasionally but always, the meaning of a text goes beyond its author."[5] Gadamer hoped that successful interpretation could lead people from very different backgrounds to a fusion of horizons wherein they can see a broader range of experience.[6] Gadamer also advised interpreters to be open to being surprised: "Every experience worthy of the name thwarts an expectation."[7] Tracy agrees with Gadamer's admonition that we frequently learn through a process of disillusionment as we come to see that our earlier assumptions were inadequate.

Gadamer hoped that encountering classic texts from a different horizon can alert us to our own prejudices and make possible a new disclosure of truth, trusting that "when we call something classical, there is a consciousness of something enduring, of significance that cannot be lost and that is independent of all the circumstances of time—a kind of timeless present that is contemporaneous with every other present."[8] Gadamer insisted that the classics of any great tradition do not exist objectively "out there." They exist only in being appropriated, interpreted, and applied in ever-changing horizons. Even though we understand differently than the author and original audience, he would argue, the difference need not be sheer loss but can reveal further dimensions of the meaning of the work. Tracy appropriates Gadamer's discussion of the classic as a tool for systematic theology, describing the task of systematic theology as critical reflection on the significance of classic Christian texts both in their original context, in the history of their reception, and in the present situation.

The hermeneutics of Gadamer provide Tracy with resources for approaching what is perhaps the most basic question for engaging religious diversity, whether we can understand different forms of religious practice at all. Tracy acknowledges that in some discussions, the partners seem so far apart that any understanding at all is precarious: "Sometimes the initial difficulty is that the dialogue-partner seems so radically other to all our usual modes of thought and practice that dialogue is

---

Works of Bernard Lonergan, vol. 3, ed. Frederick E. Crowe and Robert M. Doran (revised and augmented, 1957; reprint, Toronto: University of Toronto Press, 1997), 3:22.

[4] Hans-Georg Gadamer, *Truth and Method,* 2nd rev. ed., trans. rev. Joel Weinsheimer and Donald G. Marshall (New York: Crossroad, 1989), 297, emphasis in the original.

[5] Ibid., 296.

[6] Ibid., 306.

[7] Ibid., 356.

[8] Ibid., 288.

difficult even to begin and, once begun, to continue with any assurance of fruitful conversation."[9] It may seem that words are being used in such different ways that the only possible result is confusion. Medieval Christians distinguished three forms of language: univocal, equivocal, and analogical. In the medieval understanding, univocal language speaks "with one voice," that is, in words that have but one meaning in whatever context, and so univocal assertions describe realities directly. Equivocal language uses words that have fundamentally different senses so that misunderstanding results; the sender of a message can intend a word in one sense only to have the receiver understand it in a totally different sense. Analogical language asserts similarity in difference; words communicate truly but in different ways in different contexts. For Tracy, as for Thomas Aquinas, human language about God is analogical. In relation to religious diversity, viewing communication among different religious languages as univocal can imply some form of the claim that all religions are, at root, saying the same thing. Viewing interreligious communication as equivocal can involve a claim of such radical particularity that there is no possibility of understanding those who are different religiously; from this angle, different religious traditions use the same words in fundamentally different ways so that only misunderstanding results. Analogical strategies for addressing religious pluralism seek similarity in difference, aware that the differences among traditions may be profound but trusting that beyond all the miscommunications, persistent dialogue can nonetheless lead to a measure of mutual understanding. Tracy proposes a contemporary form of analogical imagination as a strategy for engaging those who are religiously different.

In *The Analogical Imagination: Christian Theology and the Culture of Pluralism*, Tracy proposed a hermeneutics based on the twofold analysis of religious experience and theology derived from the work of Mircea Eliade and Ricoeur, which he hoped could be applied to all religious traditions. Following Ricoeur's seminal article, "Manifestation and Proclamation,"[10] Tracy distinguished forms of religious experience that express a radical participation in the whole (which he calls manifestation trajectories) from those that emphasize the total otherness of ultimate reality and insist on a radical nonparticipation (which he calls proclamation trajectories).[11] For Tracy, analogical theologies develop the implications of manifestation trajectories, seeking ordered relationships and looking for similarities within differences.[12] Dialectical theologies reflect on the implications of proclamation

---

[9] David Tracy, *Dialogue with the Other: The Inter-Religious Dialogue* (Leuven, Belgium: Peeters/Grand Rapids, MI: Eerdmans, 1990), 48.

[10] Paul Ricoeur, "Manifestation and Proclamation," *Blaisdell Institute Journal* 11 (1978): 13–35; reprinted in Paul Ricoeur, *Figuring the Sacred: Religion, Narrative, and Imagination,* ed. Mark I. Wallace, trans. David Pellauer (Minneapolis: Fortress Press, 1995), 48–67.

[11] David Tracy, *The Analogical Imagination: Christian Theology and the Culture of Pluralism* (New York: Crossroads, 1981), 203.

[12] David Tracy and John B. Cobb Jr., *Talking about God: Doing Theology in the Context of Modern Pluralism* (New York: Seabury Press, 1983), 17–38.

trajectories: "In the wider context of the history of religions, the alternatives are variously formulated often by the contrast between two ideal types: religions with a mystical-priestly-metaphysical-aesthetic emphasis and those religions with a prophetic-ethical-historical emphasis."[13] Tracy proposed this classification as a tool for describing patterns that run through different religions and argued that each trajectory needs to be complemented and corrected by the other: every analogical theology needs a dialectical moment, and vice versa. Tracy stresses the legitimacy of each trajectory in the hope of providing a helpful framework for ecumenical and interreligious dialogue.

Tracy notes both the opportunities and dangers of discourse in a pluralistic context. The dangers are manifold; in a culture of pluralism, it is all too easy for religion to become privatized, for art to be trivialized, and for morality to become merely a matter of personal preference. For Tracy, the path to understanding in a pluralistic world leads through the interpretation and application of the claims of competing classics; that is, it leads through dialogue. At the heart of Tracy's work has been an emphasis on both the possibilities and dangers of dialogue, from Plato to the present.[14] Tracy has turned his attention to dialogue with postmodern thinkers, reflecting on the radical plurality and ambiguity of all traditions and the radical interruption of conversation caused by the "terror of history," as represented by the mass murders of the twentieth century.[15]

Informed by Lonergan's analysis of the systemic bias known as scotosis, as well as the philosophies of Paul Ricoeur and Jürgen Habermas, Tracy warns of the dangers of systemic distortion: what we assume to be true and good and holy may be biased by prejudices that to us seem self-evident but that warp relationships with other humans and with the cosmos. He insists on addressing both the plurality and the ambiguity of other religious traditions, viewing them as ambiguous but helpful resources for resistance: "Above all, the religions are exercises in resistance. . . . To interpret the religious classics is to allow them to challenge what we presently consider possible. To interpret them is also to allow ourselves to challenge them through every hermeneutic of critique, retrieval, and suspicion we possess."[16]

Stressing that this task is not a matter for the scholarly elites alone, Tracy praises interpretations from those who have been oppressed and marginalized: "In terms of the Scriptures' own standards, the oppressed are the ones most likely to hear clearly the full religious and political demands of the prophets. Among our

---

    [13] Tracy, *Analogical Imagination*, 203.

    [14] Tracy, *Dialogue with the Other*.

    [15] David Tracy, *Plurality and Ambiguity: Hermeneutics, Religion, Hope* (San Francisco: Harper & Row, 1987); David Tracy, *On Naming the Present: Reflections on God, Hermeneutics, and Church*, Concilium Series (Maryknoll, NY: Orbis Books/London: SCM Press, 1994); and David Tracy, "Religious Values after the Holocaust: A Catholic View," in *Jews and Christians after the Holocaust*, ed. Abraham J. Peck (Philadelphia: Fortress Press, 1982), 87–107.

    [16] Tracy, *Plurality and Ambiguity*, 84.

contemporaries, their readings are those the rest of us most need to hear."[17] He is particularly interested in practitioners who seek to combine mystical awareness with political commitment. On the one hand, Tracy is suspicious of the assumptions of contemporary interpreters who bring their own biases and blind spots; on the other hand, he acknowledges the ambiguity of traditional expressions of religious faith and practice: "No classic text comes to us without the plural and ambiguous history of effects of its own production and all its former receptions."[18] A unilateral proclamation from any one religious authority of whatever religious tradition will not carry credibility in a pluralistic culture. Tracy trusts that interreligious conversations about the issues of human existence can provide a path forward. He hopes that the fruit of conversation will be solidarity: "What conversation is to the life of understanding, solidarity must be to the life of action."[19]

Robert Schreiter: Theology as Wisdom

Robert Schreiter studied under Edward Schillebeeckx at the University of Nijmegen in the Netherlands and has continued Schillebeeckx's project of a careful dialogue with contemporary culture.[20] Schreiter has paid particular attention to the plurality of cultures and religions that now shape the context of the Catholic Church in the United States and around the globe. In the past, the local theologies of Western Europe and North America too often claimed universal validity without going through the demanding work of dialogue with local theologies shaped by different cultures. Today the global context and the local situation interact in ever more intimate ways, transforming each other. No longer can theologians pay attention only to European and North American voices that pretend to speak for universal or common human experience on the basis of Euro-American, North Atlantic models alone.

Schreiter has been a pioneer in developing the notion of local theology, rooted in the dynamic interaction of gospel, church, and culture.[21] By gospel he means the central message of Jesus Christ, rooted in the scriptures and proclaimed in word and sacrament, which is always incarnated within some particular ecclesial and cultural setting. The local church always finds its identity in relation to other local churches and to the larger communion within the historic tradition as well as to the other religious traditions practiced in its society. Culture, for Schreiter, "represents a way of life for a given time and place, replete with values, symbols, and meanings,

---

[17] Ibid., 104.

[18] Ibid., 69.

[19] Ibid., 113.

[20] For his assessment of Schillebeeckx's contribution, see Robert J. Schreiter, "Introduction," in Edward Schillebeeckx, *The Schillebeeckx Reader,* ed. Robert J. Schreiter (New York: Crossroad, 1984).

[21] Robert J. Schreiter, *Constructing Local Theologies* (Maryknoll, NY: Orbis Books, 1985).

reaching out with hopes and dreams, often struggling for a better world."[22] Cultures have resources both for preserving the past and for innovating for the future, strategies of constructing and maintaining identity and of handling social change.

Local theologies seek to address the concrete challenges of a local community in its multiple relationships, including with its interreligious neighbors; local theologies search for wisdom (*sapientia*) in a particular setting, continuing the practice of the early church, in contrast to systematic academic theologies that seek certain knowledge (*scientia*) for all times. The focus on wisdom offers an especially helpful approach for interreligious exploration, since each religious tradition seeks wisdom, though often in extremely diverse ways.

Often innovative local theologies emerge because the received tradition cannot handle new circumstances and challenges. Schreiter notes that earlier local theologies present an ambiguous heritage: they "can not only be obstacles and reminders [of what a local church struggled with in the past]; they can also have revelatory aspects."[23] The frustration with earlier anti-Jewish forms of Catholic theology and practice in the wake of the Shoah (the Holocaust) offers one significant example of an inheritance from the earlier tradition that is today found to be problematic. Cultures are also ambiguous, with various forms of oppression and imbalance; at times Christian practice offered a sense of dignity to people despised by the dominant culture. In light of Vatican II, Schreiter stresses the importance of scrutinizing any particular culture for signs of the work of God outside the boundaries of the church. This has particular importance for seeking reconciliation and harmony in interreligious relations.

Schreiter sees the audiences of local theologies as including the local church and the larger church, and frequently also the broader society as well as other religious partners. Academic theology can contribute much to the development of local theologies; Schreiter insists that "the community has need of the theologian's knowledge to ground its own experience within the Christian traditions of faith. In so doing, the theologian helps to create the bonds of mutual accountability between local and world church."[24] For example, in the United States, Catholic Hispanic and African American theologians have maintained regular contact with members of grassroots communities of believers both to learn from the experience of the local communities and also to share their knowledge and expertise of scripture and the Christian tradition to inform local communities' reflections.[25] Nonetheless, the academy is not the primary target audience for most local theologies. Much academic theology has ignored popular religiosity; local theologies attend to the wisdom enshrined within folk traditions and practices.

---

[22] Ibid., 21.

[23] Ibid., 27.

[24] Ibid., 18.

[25] Orlando Espín, ed., *The Faith of the People: Theological Reflections on Popular Catholicism* (Maryknoll, NY: Orbis Books, 1997); Roberto S. Goizueta, ed., *We Are a People! Initiatives in Hispanic American Theology* (1992; reprint, Eugene, OR: Wipf & Stock Publishers, 2001).

When cultures and religions differ greatly, communication among local theologies is fraught with the danger of misunderstanding. Acutely aware of this challenge, Schreiter turns to semiotics, the study of signs, for guidance. Semiotics examines the sets of rules governing the use of signs in three ways:

> syntactics (the defined sets of relationships between signs, which govern their movement through the cultural system—something like the way in which a grammar governs the movement of words through a language), semantics (the content or meaning of the message), and pragmatics (the rules that govern the communication and ranges of intelligibility of the messages).[26]

Semiotics distinguishes descriptions of a culture by insiders (emic descriptions) from those of outsiders (etic). Often the dominant styles differ: "From an inner perspective, the description will often be characterized by narrative. Explanation (stepping out of the narrative) may occur, but usually to support the narrative rather than to translate it into another mode of discourse."[27] Emic descriptions generally seek to reinforce the identity of the community. Etic descriptions, in contrast, seek explanations in order to translate the lived reality into a different mode of discourse. This may be done in service of the local community, to help it deal with social change and adjust to new relationships, or to foster interreligious understanding. Etic descriptions may also serve the interests of outsiders in ways not beneficial to the community (e.g., to allow better control of a colonial empire). Thus, Schreiter insists on asking the question of outer descriptions: "What is the purpose of the translation of the sign system? Who is being served by this translation? And how is the translation being authenticated?"[28] Both types of description are essential: emic descriptions foster the community's identity, and etic descriptions allow communication with other communities and shape broader forms of cohesion. Interreligious communication demands awareness of both dimensions.

Semiotics also attends to the perspectives of both the speaker and the hearer. Speaker-oriented approaches look for clear transmission with minimal loss of information, while hearer-centered analyses ask to what degree the hearer is able to make sense of the message in relation to his or her particular situation. Speaker-centered approaches to theology often stress clarity of doctrine and uniformity of teaching and practice and use translation-models of communication. Hearer-oriented approaches study the impact of traditional doctrinal formulas in a particular context, asking whether they may be unintelligible or alienating. Both are important if the Church is to truly be one united around the world and also local. For Schreiter, local theologies need to be especially attentive to the hearers' perspectives; in this regard, models that attend to contextualization are more helpful.[29]

---

[26] Schreiter, *Constructing Local Theologies*, 50.

[27] Ibid., 57.

[28] Ibid., 59.

[29] Ibid., 60.

Catholic theology is traditionally understood as faith seeking understanding; according to Schreiter, local theologies teach us that every quest for understanding of Christian faith presupposes a particular cultural context, which often includes contacts with other religions. The great Christian tradition is itself a series of local theologies. Every universal claim comes from a particular cultural heritage, including its interreligious relationships. "Indeed, even the epistemological forms for understanding can have a strong cultural tint, reminding us that to start with a 'universal' anthropology means starting with a local anthropology extended beyond its cultural boundaries."[30] Semiotics can help theology understand the patterns of different cultures, relate them to the scriptures and earlier Church tradition, and develop a broader community across cultural boundaries. The most effective way to communicate a local theology will vary depending on cultural circumstances. For example, in some contexts, proverbs may be more effective in communicating the Gospel than heavily philosophical discussions. Similarly, oral and written forms of communication may have varying degrees of effectiveness in different settings. Schreiter proposes that assessing effective communication in local theologies will involve the judgment of wisdom using aesthetic criteria.[31] Schreiter offered interpretations of biblical narratives and images centering on water and blood to propose a spirituality of solidarity and hope for the global Church.[32]

Catholic Theology and American Indian Traditions

After centuries of American Indian religious traditions being rejected and despised by European American Christians, in recent decades there has been a widespread and dramatic reversal of attitudes, and many in the New Age movement have explored and appropriated aspects of Native religious practice. American Indian Christians are suspicious of both perspectives. A long history of European Americans displacing Amerindians has left a legacy of distrust. American Indians value the Native traditions of the ancestors and believe they manifest the presence of God, but they are often wary of outsiders who come to study and appropriate their practices for very different purposes; for example, in 1993 leaders of the Lakota, Nakota, and Dakota Nations issued "Declaration of War against Exploiters of Lakota Spirituality," sometimes known as the Lakota Declaration.[33] European American Christians need to respect the distinctive context of American Indian life and listen to the voices of American Indian Christians.[34]

---

[30] Ibid., 75.

[31] Ibid., 85.

[32] Robert J. Schreiter, *In Water and in Blood: A Spirituality of Solidarity and Hope* (New York: Crossroad, 1988).

[33] Ward Churchill, *Indians Are Us?: Culture and Genocide in Native North America* (Monroe, ME: Common Courage Press, 1994), 273–77.

[34] Suzanne Owen, *The Appropriation of Native American Spirituality* (New York: Continuum, 2008).

Based on a careful study of the *Indian Sentinel,* published annually from 1902 to 1962 by the Bureau of Catholic Indian Missions, Mark Clatterbuck emphasizes the reciprocal character of the relation with missionaries and the role of American Indian Catholics in transforming the missionaries who came to their communities:

> With the turn of every page, the *Sentinel's* record also reminds us Catholic Indian Missions have always been, despite the inequitable power differential in political and military terms, a two-way avenue of conversion. Indians have been making converts of missionaries for as long as zealous priests and sisters have been claiming indigenous converts for themselves.[35]

Clatterbuck draws upon the hermeneutics of Paul Ricoeur for an interpretative framework.

Jesuit theologian Carl Starkloff spent decades among the Ojibway and Arapaho peoples and developed a theology of the "in-between" to reflect on the syncretic process. Starkloff acknowledges the long history of vilification of syncretism; but he, like Robert Schreiter, insists that the syncretic process is intrinsic to human experience and is always involved in contexts of mission, inculturation, and indigenization:

> The syncretic process (the term that I prefer) seems to be a process built into human nature and a process of all human social and religious interaction. The syncretic process is a *de facto* human dynamism that is not going to be dismissed, however critical we may have to be in studying it.[36]

He uses the term "syncretism" for the unconscious and spontaneous aspects of religious mingling, and the term "synthesis" for the more conscious, deliberative aspects; he sees syncretic process as "any generic phenomenon of historical amalgamation" which is usually a combination of both syncretism and synthesis.[37]

Starkloff notes that Christians have engaged in the syncretic process in formulating doctrines and celebrating liturgies from early Christianity throughout the Middle East and North Africa to the European areas and beyond. He sees this process not as an aberration or a problem but as "part of the never-ending historical quest for wholeness."[38] Starkloff recognizes syncretic processes that become demonic, as in the case of South African apartheid or Christians supporting the Nazis; nonetheless, he insists that this process occurs regularly in cross-cultural

---

[35] Mark Clatterbuck, *Demons, Saints, and Patriots: Catholic Visions of Native America through the Indian Sentinel, 1902–1962* (Milwaukee, WI: Marquette University Press, 2009), 8.

[36] Carl F. Starkloff, *A Theology of the In-Between: The Value of Syncretic Process* (Milwaukee, WI: Marquette University Press, 2002), 11.

[37] Ibid., 16.

[38] Ibid., 11.

and interreligious relationships, involves uncertainty, and requires open-minded dialogue, patience, and critical discernment, as called for by the biblical command to test the spirits (1 Jn 4:1; 1 Thes 5:21).[39] Like many other American Catholic theologians, Starkloff also turns to the thought of Bernard Lonergan on theological method for resources in naming the various aspects and challenges of this transformative experience.[40] Starkloff relates the condition of being in-between to the lasting tensions among religions and cultures and to the provisional character of life in this world in relation to the eschaton.

M. Shawn Copeland: African American Theology

M. Shawn Copeland, a leading African American Catholic systematic theologian, has drawn on the theological method of Bernard Lonergan to reflect on the varied texture of African American Catholic experience. She notes that some scholars have tried to minimize the significance of African traditions in the religious practice of enslaved African Americans, but she rejects this view. She notes that traditional African religions are not written in texts but live in people's hearts and minds, are passed on in oral history, and are celebrated in rituals. After the horrors of enslavement and the Middle Passage, these traditional religious resources continued to nourish the lives of enslaved Africans and their descendants, including those who embraced Christianity. Copeland maintains that *"the religious sensibilities of the enslaved peoples projected a religious reality in which Christianity is sublated by the reconfigured elements of traditional West African religions."*[41]

In *Knowing Christ Crucified: The Witness of African American Religious Experience,* Copeland stresses the importance and diversity of the African religious heritage, insisting that "the Middle Passage did not completely eradicate religious practices, aspects of material culture, beliefs, and cognitive orientations toward reality or life or relationships. . . . No universal 'African' religio-cultural heritage existed (or exists)."[42] She describes what survived the brutal Middle Passage as root paradigms: "These root paradigms—cognitive and moral orientations, fragments of rite and ritual, cultural memory—emerged from the interstices of loss and pushed upward in recovery and revision, in change and transformation, in improvisation. These coalesced to ground religious consciousness."[43]

---

[39] Ibid., 15.

[40] Ibid., 61–87.

[41] M. Shawn Copeland, "Foundations for Catholic Theology in an African American Context," in *Black and Catholic: The Challenge and Gift of Black Folk: Contributions of African American Experience and Thought to Catholic Theology,* 2nd ed. rev. and corrected, ed. Jamie T. Phelps (Milwaukee, WI: Marquette University Press, 2002), 119, emphasis in original.

[42] M. Shawn Copeland, *Knowing Christ Crucified: The Witness of African American Religious Experience* (Maryknoll, NY: Orbis Books, 2018), 7.

[43] Ibid., 8.

It is difficult to document much of the life of enslaved African American Catholics, but Copeland follows earlier African American theologians Howard Thurman and James Cone in turning to the spirituals for insight into their spiritual lives. Copeland cites the testimony of one emancipated woman from Kentucky who maintained that the melodies of the spirituals were brought by her ancestors from Africa.[44] The songs express many varied aspects of life and hope, bringing traditional African themes into a Christian context: "The songs are linked to adaptations of African religious rituals, including funeral and burial ceremonies. Invariably these rites included hand clapping or the stomping of feet, which would have compensated on many plantations for the outlawed drum."[45]

Dance was one of the most powerful forms of religious expression: "Thus, in dance, the Africans remembered, preserved, and transmitted a cherished religious, aesthetic-moral, and social vision of the world that dictated a life of morality and beauty."[46] Traditional African themes took on new meaning in the context of Christian faith: "In this sublation, the fragments of traditional African religio-cultural heritages function as *root paradigms* in the emergence of a crucial stratum of African American Christianity."[47] In the faith expressed in the spirituals, Jesus Christ knows what it is to suffer terrible injustice; and he is, above all, the bringer of freedom in every sense, "political *and* social, psychic *and* spiritual, metaphysical *and* ontological, this-worldly *and* other-worldly.[48]

In light of the rich heritage of the spirituals and dance, Copeland pays special attention to artistic expressions and to the religious legacies inherited from Africa. She observes that the black Catholic theologian "becomes a blues singer, a woman or man who is willing, as Ralph Ellison once wrote, 'to keep the painful details and episodes of a brutal experience alive in one's aching consciousness, to finger its jagged grin, and to transcend it.'"[49] Using Lonergan's notion of the differentiation of consciousness, with its different patterns of experience and its relentless pursing of questions, Copeland focuses on the social, the dramatic, and the religious dimensions of African American Catholic experience, seeking to "find and catch the rhythms" of black experience, to critique and transform the meanings found in black experience, and to "nurture black human living that embraces the gospel."[50]

---

[44] Copeland, "Foundations," 121.

[45] Ibid., 122.

[46] Ibid., 123.

[47] Ibid., 125.

[48] Ibid., 131.

[49] M. Shawn Copeland, "Doing Black Catholic Theology," *Chicago Studies* 42, no. 2 (2003): 128; the quotation is from Ralph Ellison, *Living with Music: Ralph Ellison's Jazz Writings,* ed. Robert G. O'Meally (New York: Modern Library, 2001), 103. On method, see also M. Shawn Copeland, "Method in Emerging Black Catholic Theology," in *Taking Down Our Harps: Black Catholics in the United States,* ed. Diana L. Hayes and Cyprian Davis (Maryknoll, NY: Orbis Books, 1998), 120–44.

[50] Copeland, "Doing Black Catholic Theology," 128.

Copeland sees African traditions as permeated with religious values and practices, and claims that it was the religious differentiation of consciousness in this heritage that sustained Africans and African Americans through centuries of racist oppression and slavery. For her, black theology

> was born in the moans of the Middle Passage; it protected the weak, suckled the orphan, and comforted the dying. Black theology was reared in slavery and weaned in reconstruction: its first word was freedom; its first memory the rhythms of Africa . . . ; its first triumph the ecstasy of the ring-shout and the spirituals.[51]

Since most enslaved African Americans were illiterate, they were paradoxically freed from the official biblical writings with the proof-texts authorizing slavery; and they creatively developed their own style of hermeneutics instead. "Only those stories of passages that affirmed black humanity and dignity, survival and emancipation were deemed as the *true* word of God."[52] Informed by this heritage, contemporary critical biblical hermeneutics explores the original social situation of the biblical texts, with attention to both the oppressive and the liberating dynamics:

> Critical biblical hermeneutics reconstructs and accentuates the experiences of women, the poor, and the excluded as these seep through in non-dominative narratives, metaphors, stories, and practices. In this way, critical biblical hermeneutics implies that the subjugated knowledges of these "little ones" direct us toward the in-breaking of the reign of God.[53]

Copeland draws upon social analysis to understand the intertwining of issues of gender, race, culture and class, with attention to the ways in which blacks have been excluded, marginalized and stereotyped by mainstream white culture and economics. She recounts a number of listening sessions held by the Black Catholic Theological Symposium, where theologians heard painful memories "of rejection and discrimination, disrespect and indifference" from African American Catholics.[54] Copeland mines the history of African American Catholics for examples of courage and initiative. For example, in 1853 a black Catholic laywoman, Harriet Thompson, together with twenty-six other people, wrote to Pope Pius IX, complaining about the neglect of both religious and secular

---

[51] M. Shawn Copeland, "Living Stones in the Household of God," in *Living Stones in the Household of God: The Legacy and Future of Black Theology*, ed. Linda E. Thomas (Minneapolis: Fortress Press, 2004), 185.

[52] Copeland, "Doing Black Catholic Theology," 131.

[53] Ibid., 133.

[54] Ibid., 136.

education by the Archdiocese of New York, then led by Archbishop John Hughes, who stated openly that he "did not recognize the black race to be a part of his flock."[55] Historically, black Catholics in America were long denied a clergy of their own, but lay leaders and women religious emerged as major influences shaping black Catholic awareness, as exemplified by the five Black Catholic Congresses held between 1889 and 1894, organized by articulate laypeople.[56]

Copeland calls for black Catholic theology to be critical in three senses: (1) in epistemology, it "interrogates and evaluates its own presuppositions, and explicitly acknowledges an integral relation between knowing and doing"; (2) it analyzes social reality and "critiques both society and church"; and (3) through reflection on black experience, it "discloses the complex and, often, conflictual forces, interests, and motives involved in social transformation."[57]

In the wake of the attacks on September 11, 2001, and the violence against Arabs, Muslims, and Sikhs in the weeks that followed, Copeland analyzed broader forms of racism and interreligious prejudice in American culture and society, which extend not only to African Americans but to Arabs, Sikhs, East Indians, Koreans, Japanese, Vietnamese, and Native Americans. In biting, prophetic tones, she charges,

> We are all living, as Audre Lorde taught us, in the "master's house"—a stunningly accurate metaphor for the union of heterosexist white racial privilege and capitalism. This domain of sin and evil is a house of disordered love: love of God become love of money, become love of whiteness, become self-hating love of a whiter, lighter self. . . . We women and men of color have learned to use and be used by the "master's tools."[58]

In this context, Copeland challenges theologians to be truth-tellers, interpreting the word of God in relation to the concrete dilemmas and contradictions of their situation. For her, reading the signs of the times, as Vatican II urged, means attending to issues of liberty, justice, and equality amid continuing racism and inequity.

In her presidential address to the Catholic Theological Society of America in 2004, which was dedicated to the memory of her teacher, Bernard Lonergan, she warned that political theology had been on the wane in the United States in recent

---

[55] M. Shawn Copeland, "Tradition and Traditions of African American Catholicism," *Theological Studies* 61 (2000): 635n10.

[56] Ibid., 637–43.

[57] Copeland, "Doing Black Catholic Theology," 137.

[58] M. Shawn Copeland, "Racism and the Vocation of the Christian Theologian," *Spiritus* 2, no. 1 (2002): 20. The phrases quoted are from Audre Lorde, "The Master's Tools Will Never Dismantle the Master's House," in her *Sister Outsider: Essays and Speeches by Audre Lorde* (Trumansburg, NY: Crossing Press, 1984), 114–23. See also M. Shawn Copeland, "Body, Representation, and Black Religious Discourse," in *Postcolonialism, Feminism, and Religious Discourse*, ed. Laura E. Donaldson and Kwok Pui-Lan (New York: Routledge, 2002), 180–97.

decades; and she called on political theology to be interruptive in a threefold sense: first, interruptive of the "spiritual and cultural deformation" that comes from the pervasive marketing of everything and that leads to disrespect of human dignity; second, interruptive of American theology itself, insofar as it has turned away from the challenges of its own situation and academically studied theologies of liberation from Latin American and South Africa; and finally, interruptive of violence in all its forms.[59]

Roberto Goizueta:
U.S. Catholic Hispanic Theology

Roberto Goizueta, who was born in Cuba, is one of the leaders developing U.S. Catholic Hispanic theology. In developing a method for theology, he insists on popular Latino/a religiosity as an important source, including its roots in the encounter between Spanish Catholicism and the indigenous traditions of the Americas. He contrasts post-Tridentine Anglo-American Catholicism, which frequently focused on doctrines and tried to exclude the influence of American Indian traditions, with the pre-Tridentine Iberian Catholicism. Iberian Catholicism centered on ceremonies and ritual celebrations of the faith, which resonated with American Indian practices. Goizueta maintains that in spite of the violent clashes of Spanish Catholics with the indigenous inhabitants of the Americas, there was nonetheless an analogy between the worldviews of the Spanish Catholics and the Native populations because both sides shared "certain presuppositions about the inherently social nature of the human person and his or her place in an organically ordered cosmos."[60] The shared elements allowed indigenous religious traditions to flow into the emerging mestizo Latino/a Catholic popular religiosity.

One of the most powerful images for Mexican American Catholics is Our Lady of Guadalupe, known affectionately as "*La Morenita.*" Goizueta emphasizes the interreligious texture as he comments on the significance of the image of her on the *tilma* reportedly worn by Juan Diego:

The image itself is of immense significance because of the many beautiful and powerful symbols it contains. These are both Christian and Nahuatl. Many are symbols of new life, a new beginning, and a new birth: She is pregnant, she wears a "maternity band" around her waist, and she bears on her womb the symbol that, for the Nahuas, represented the "reconciliation of opposites." Perhaps the most obvious symbol, however, is the very color

---

[59] M. Shawn Copeland, "Presidential Address: Political Theology as Interruptive," in The Catholic Theological Society of America, *Proceedings of the Fifty-ninth Annual Convention*, ed. Richard C. Sparks, vol. 59 (2004): 76–79.

[60] Roberto S. Goizueta, "The Symbolic Realism of Latino/a Popular Catholicism," *Theological Studies* 65 (2004): 258.

of Our Lady's skin . . . her olive skin tells the indigenous people of Mexico that she, *La Morenita,* is one of them. It tells all Latinos and Latinas that she is one of us.[61]

Goizueta notes that this encounter reveals that God identifies with the indigenous peoples of the Americas who were despised, displaced, and marginalized. He emphasizes the mutual relationship between Mary and the indigenous man to whom she appears, Juan Diego. Juan Diego finds dignity, healing from his self-deprecation, and liberation, but not according to the paradigm of individual autonomy so prized by Western imperial modernity. What begins as an apparition becomes a genuine encounter between two actors, and this relationship brings freedom to Juan Diego: "Authentic individuality and authentic community are not contradictory but mutual. As the Lady of Tepeyac affirms Juan Diego's freedom the true community affirms the freedom and uniqueness of the individual members."[62]

Together with Timothy Matovina, Goizueta draws upon the legacy of Virgilio Elizondo regarding the divine pedagogy manifested in Jesus Christ, whereby God identifies with those who are rejected.[63] They comment that in the incarnation, God identified with a particular local culture and stress the importance of the specificity of the Jewish Galilean Jesus. This calls Christians to be attentive to the concrete details of later situations, especially where people are rejected and mistreated. Galilee, which was often looked down upon by other regions, offers a hermeneutical key for interpreting the Bible, illuminating the *mestizo* experience of Elizondo, Mexican Americans, and U.S. Hispanics in general: Elizondo formulated the Galilee principle of revelation, which states that God identifies with what humans reject.[64] As Goizueta and Matovina note, Elizondo interpreted the legend of the apparition of Mary to Juan Diego at the sacred Nahua site now known as Guadalupe as affirming that God was already dwelling among the indigenous people before the arrival of Spanish Catholic missionaries.[65] Elizondo emphasized that for the indigenous peoples of the Americas, God was known not primarily in abstract rational arguments but above all in "flor y canto"—in flower and song.

To develop a new way of doing theology, Goizueta draws upon both the methods of Bernard Lonergan and Latin American liberation theologian Enrique Dussel, finding contributions on both sides that could complement each other. Dussel analyzes the structures of injustice that imprison millions of Latin Americans in poverty, but he also presents hope of dialogue between oppressors and the oppressed, based on the recognition that dehumanization of one side brings

---

[61] Roberto S. Goizueta, "Resurrection at Tepeyac: The Guadalupan Encounter," *Theology Today* 56, no. 3(1999): 340.

[62] Ibid., 344.

[63] Roberto Goizueta and Timothy Matovina, "Divine Pedagogy: *Dei Verbum* and the Theology of Virgilio Elizondo," *Theological Studies* 78, no. 1 (2017): 7–24.

[64] Ibid., 12.

[65] Ibid.

inevitably the dehumanization of the other. Dussel also challenges North Americans to a self-critical stance. Goizueta comments on Dussel's significance: "If the prophet is the one who takes his or her stand with the oppressed over against the system, then such a North American liberative method would be the foundation for what would necessarily and intrinsically be a prophetic theology."[66] Lonergan, for his part, placed conversion at the center of his methodological reflections and offered descriptions of various forms of conversion from inauthentic to authentic existence. Goizueta hoped that a constructive dialogue could be constructed between these perspectives in the North American context.[67]

Goizueta insists on integrating both Latin American theology and Western theology, warning U.S. Hispanics that they can neither simply adopt nor simply reject either approach; rather they need to appropriate critically aspects of both trajectories in the shaping of a U.S. Hispanic theology.[68] Noting that many modern philosophies and theologies have stressed the importance of praxis, he warns that too often praxis has been identified with practice, and practice in turn has been seen as a technique for social or political control. In the background lurks "the reduction of knowledge to what can be observed, measured, quantified, and thus brought under our control."[69] To counter this danger, Goizueta turns to Aristotle's distinction between praxis, which has an end in itself (exemplified by political, moral, and aesthetic activities), and *poiesis,* making or production, which has an end outside itself. Building a house is an example of poiesis, production; building a home is an act of praxis.[70]

Goizueta accuses Karl Marx, especially as interpreted by later orthodox Marxism, of confusing what Aristotle had carefully distinguished and of reducing praxis to poiesis. This reduction shaped Marx's historical materialism: "the mode of production is the engine of history."[71] Goizueta warns, however, that production is manipulative and coercive, leading to the instrumentalization of life and the diminishment of human dignity. Goizueta is concerned that Latin American liberation theology, which has drawn upon Marxist concepts, such as praxis, shares this ambiguity. He praises Gustavo Gutiérrez's stress on transformative praxis as the foundation of theology but finds an ambiguity in his thought that runs throughout much of liberation theology:

---

[66] Roberto S. Goizueta, *Liberation, Method and Dialogue: Enrique Dussel and North American Theological Discourse,* American Academy of Religion, Academy Series, ed. Susan Thistlethwaite, no. 58 (Atlanta, GA: Scholars Press, 1988), 161.

[67] Ibid., xvi.

[68] Roberto S. Goizueta, "Rediscovering Praxis: The Significance of U.S. Hispanic Experience for Theological Method," in *We Are a People! Initiatives in Hispanic American Theology,* ed. Roberto S. Goizueta (1992; reprint, Eugene, OR: Wipf and Stock Publishers, 2001), 52–53.

[69] Ibid., 56.

[70] Ibid., 57n9.

[71] Ibid., 58.

Is liberation a concomitant or a goal of praxis? If the former is true, then praxis is its own end: one becomes free in the very act or process of transforming history. If the latter is true, then the end of praxis is external to the praxis itself: one becomes free *after* one has transformed history.[72]

Goizueta turns to U.S. Hispanic experience as a resource for addressing this challenge. While deeply influenced by the methods of liberation theology, U.S. Hispanic theology reflects upon the distinctive praxis of its own context, especially popular religiosity and its interreligious heritage as fundamental to the community's *manera de ser,* manner of being in the world.[73] In popular religiosity with its interreligious heritage, praxis is communal and aesthetic, enveloped in a world of symbol and ritual, music and dance that give meaning to life. The community thus shaped, however, is not the usual North American "voluntary society of atomic individuals," which allows for only external relations among people; the community is "an organic reality" whose principal metaphor is the family, grounded in "an essential social and cosmic solidarity."[74] U.S. Hispanic praxis flows from this rich web of relationships, which is an end in itself. In contrast to much North American thought, which sees autonomous individuals as ontologically prior to communities because they exist independently and freely choose to enter into relationships, U.S. Hispanics view the community itself as ontologically prior, "for it gives birth to subjectivity."[75] Popular religious devotions express and continue this ontological bond, with Jesus, Mary, and the saints as members of the family.

For U.S. Hispanics, ethical and political obligations flow from the social nature of human existence. To judge the value of popular religiosity by its ability to bring about some further social transformation is to instrumentalize it and misunderstand it. The celebratory and aesthetic character of popular religiosity is an end in itself, not a stepping stone to some further goal: "Beauty is an end in itself; to instrumentalize beauty is to destroy it."[76] Aesthetic activity, however, especially in its expression of memories of suffering, cannot be sentimentalized or romanticized; it gives voice to an unutterably painful history and has implications for ethics and politics. Images of the crucified Christ and of Mary at the foot of the cross identify their anguish with the suffering of the U.S. Hispanic community, and the message of the resurrection gives hope to the struggle against forms of oppression. Thus, the aesthetic praxis of popular religiosity can be profoundly supportive of those who have suffered and subversive of established structures that perpetuate injustice: "By

---

[72] Ibid., 61.

[73] Ibid., 63. Goizueta notes that some Latin American liberation theologians have studied popular religiosity, but this topic has not so far had as much influence as in U.S. Hispanic discussions.

[74] Ibid., 64.

[75] Ibid.

[76] Ibid., 67. Goizueta notes that Latin American philosophers have frequently turned to aesthetics for an alternative to Cartesian epistemological models.

affirming community in the face of oppression, and the beauty of creation in the face of de-creation and destruction, popular religious praxis becomes, indirectly, a crucial source of empowerment and liberation."[77] Goizueta repeats the warning: to see the value of popular religiosity only in its service of goals of transforming society is to destroy its character as an end in itself.

Francis X. Clooney: Comparative Theology

Francis X. Clooney has proposed a model of comparative theology that has been very influential.[78] Clooney rejects the search for a general theory of religion and refuses to begin with abstract consideration of general issues such as the religious a priori. Instead, he plunges *in medias res,* into the middle of things—for example, in a poem by the Hindu saint from southern India, Shatakopan (probably eighth-century CE), a young woman goes to a temple to honor Vishnu—Narayana.[79] People do this all the time, and they go home. They see the image of God and return to their normal lives. This young woman, however, is smitten by the power of God and falls hopelessly in love. Return to her earlier state is impossible. This concrete image serves as a warning to all who would enter temples out of curiosity—while we may think that we can enter for a brief time and then return to life as normal, we can never be sure of that outcome; we may be affected more deeply than we expect. The structure of Clooney's book, *Seeing through Texts: Doing Theology among the Srivaisnavas of South India,* plays with the form of an *antati*—the style in which one verse's ending is the beginning of the next verse. When we reach the very end of the book, we find ourselves back at the same verses with which we began. The entire journey of reading moves *in medias res,* and there is no guarantee that one can ever leave. Let the reader be warned.

After an initial view of the poem, Clooney broadens the context to include the classical Vaishnavite commentators who interpreted the woman as a persona for the male poet, who goes from delight in God's presence to depression over the inability to achieve union with God in this life. Humans yearn for a consummation that is not ordinarily available in this world. There is no immediate experience of God, except for now and then. Clooney sees the invitation of the poem as extending down to the present and stretching across religious and cultural boundary markers. The poem offers an invitation to see through the text to a life-changing religious encounter. Rather than seeking to describe an "experience," Clooney focuses on the text itself.

---

[77] Ibid., 69.

[78] Francis X. Clooney, *Theology after Vedanta: An Experiment in Comparative Theology,* SUNY Series, Toward a Comparative Philosophy of Religions, ed. Frank Reynolds and David Tracy (Albany: State University of New York Press, 1993).

[79] Francis X. Clooney, *Seeing through Texts: Doing Theology among the Srivaisnavas of South India,* SUNY Series, Toward a Comparative Philosophy of Religions, ed. Paul J. Griffiths and Laurie L. Patton (Albany: State University of New York Press, 1996), 1–4.

Clooney's method is self-involving in ways that are unpredictable. When he was an undergraduate, he went to a lecture by a Jesuit from the Philippines, who urged the audience to have "hearts as large as the world."[80] The young Clooney took the challenge seriously and went to Nepal to teach high school as part of his training as a Jesuit. He later studied Indology at the University of Chicago, where he read a single poem in Tamil and became enthralled by an entire body of literature. The possibility of being transformed by a visit or a conversation or a reading of a text runs throughout Clooney's method. This means that there is no pretense of establishing a completely objective stance. Clooney enters the conversation as a Catholic theologian open to inquiry. He is a member of a believing community with specific doctrinal and liturgical commitments, and he encounters other religious traditions from this initial stance. Unlike John Hick and Paul Knitter, who insist that Christians must surrender some traditional claims about Jesus in order to learn from another tradition,[81] Clooney brings the claims of his tradition into the project of reading and learning from another religion.

In his early work, *Theology after Vedanta: An Experiment in Comparative Theology*, Clooney calls this process "*collectio*"—the Latin term that literally means "reading together"—but until that term becomes familiar, he calls his project "comparative theology." Comparative theology is a *collectio*, a reading of two traditions together, with an openness to intellectual and personal transformation. In *Theology after Vedanta*, Clooney reads the great Hindu theologian, Shankara, together with Thomas Aquinas. Clooney follows David Tracy in seeking out analogies, neither the univocal identities of some theologies of religion nor equivocal differences of some postmodern forms of thought. Comparative theology is an act of the disciplined imagination, which seeks analogies, similarities in difference and differences in similarities.

This is not an attempt to present a neutral comparative study of religion in which one brackets one's own presuppositions in the hope of objectivity. Comparative theology studies the other tradition on its own terms, in a way that moves away from one's home base. Clooney insists on looking at *prapatti*, the Hindu practice of surrendering everything to God, even one's efforts to save oneself. In the process of encountering the other tradition, one's initial expectations will likely be transformed:

---

[80] Francis X. Clooney, *Hindu Wisdom for All God's Children*, Faith Meets Faith Series, ed. Paul F. Knitter (Maryknoll, NY: Orbis Books, 1998), ix.

[81] John Hick, "The Non-Absoluteness of Christianity," in *The Myth of Christian Uniqueness: Toward a Pluralistic Theology of Religions*, ed. John Hick and Paul F. Knitter (Maryknoll, NY: Orbis Books, 1987), 16–36; Paul F. Knitter, *Jesus and the Other Names: Christian Mission and Global Responsibility* (Maryknoll, NY: Orbis Books, 1996); Paul F. Knitter, "Is the Pluralist Model a Western Imposition?," in *The Myth of Religious Superiority: Multifaith Explorations of Religious Pluralism*, ed. Paul F. Knitter, Faith Meets Faith Series, ed. Paul F. Knitter and William R. Burrows (Maryknoll, NY: Orbis Books, 2005), 28–41; Paul F. Knitter, *No Other Name? A Critical Survey of Christian Attitudes toward the World Religions*, American Society of Missiology Series, No. 7 (Maryknoll, NY: Orbis Books, 1985).

"the neighbors are really there, they are never quite what we think them to be, they have voices of their own, and we play parts in their narratives too."[82] Clooney stresses the importance of looking at interreligious relationships from the other tradition's point of view as much as possible.[83]

In *Seeing through Texts*, Clooney focuses on poetic expressions of beauty, questions of genre and literary interpretation, and the response of readers, especially those from another tradition. The initial reading of the poem about the young woman will likely prove disorienting for those not initiated in the Srivaisnavaite tradition. The names are long and unfamiliar, the allusions unclear, the background strange. Comparative theology is an incrementally progressive discipline. We start from a state of disorientation and gradually learn to orient ourselves. The understanding of both traditions is integral to the practice of reading the traditions together. As we understand something of one tradition, our understanding of both begins to shift. The discipline is neither simply theory nor simply practice. Lonergan used the image of the two blades of the scissors: the upper blade is the set of concepts used, the lower blade comprises the data being studied.[84] In comparative theology, both the upper blade and the lower blade undergo development and transformation. One's theoretical position is transformed and developed through the practice of the careful reading of texts in dialogue. Comparative theology involves the act of including as a practice rather than inclusivism as a theological theory.

The project is radically temporal, with change being expected as part of the method itself. There is no expectation of a final point of arrival. When we finish the book, *Seeing through Texts,* we find ourselves back at the beginning—reading the same poem about the young woman. In the journey, Clooney calls attention to the shifting relationships and procedures, the tensions between what is said and what is implicit, between the ordered and the disordered. To understand another religious tradition involves becoming the type of person who can see in a new way and make distinctions in new ways, and this transforms all one's relationships.

Clooney is influenced by Gadamer's and Tracy's accounts of genuine conversation: we risk our self-understanding by allowing the questions of the text to address us, even if they are different from our own questions. Clooney also borrows Jacques Derrida's method of collage—taking texts that are very different from each other and pasting them together and prodding the reader to allow them to interpret each in the act of reading. Derrida decomposes texts into "clippings" in order to release them from their controlling contexts. Some of Derrida's most exciting and bewildering readings come from excising texts from their original contexts, recomposing them, and juxtaposing them with other texts. The collage selects and combines, calls attention to certain relationships and a certain way of framing. In doing comparative theology, Clooney takes texts and images from one tradition and inserts them

---

[82] Clooney, *Seeing through Texts,* 300.

[83] Francis X. Clooney, "Hindu Views of Religious Others: Implications for Christian Theology," *Theological Studies* 64, no. 2 (2003): 306–33.

[84] Lonergan, *Insight,* 337.

into a new context, where they reveal new possibilities. The text that he writes is biblio-biographical, largely about texts, but also about how his biography has been changed by his reading of these texts. The approach is modest and incremental, not seeking bold novelties but exploring what is old in both traditions in the hope that new awareness will unfold.

Peter C. Phan: Asian American Theology

Peter Phan, who moved from his native Vietnam to the United States in 1975, notes, "By any measure Asian American Christian theology, as distinct from studies in Asian religions, is still in its infancy, compared with Black and Hispanic (Latino/a) theologies, for instance."[85] Nonetheless, the increasing numbers of Asian American Christians, including Catholics, makes it likely that this will be a significant area of future growth.[86]

Phan has taken pioneering steps toward developing an Asian American theology, beginning with theological reflection on the experience of migration, especially from non-European countries to the United States, and including dialogue with the religious traditions of Asia.[87] After being displaced, immigrants find themselves "betwixt-and-between." Belonging fully to neither their home culture nor their new culture, they nonetheless participate in both. For migrants, culture appears not as a coherent whole but as "a ground of contest in relations."[88] Phan suggests that this predicament offers creative possibilities for reflection on both cultures. Given the multicultural character of the United States, he calls for an "inter-multicultural theology" to do justice in this context.[89] Its vantage point will be multiperspectival, looking to several cultures for resources and support. Interreligious dialogue will play an integral role in shaping it.[90] In his presidential address to the American Theological Society, he reflected on the Holy Mystery: "Deus Migrator est"—God is a migrant.[91]

Phan stresses that Vietnamese American Catholic theology "is not simply a different theology but also a new way of doing theology."[92] Phan applies the model of David Tracy of theology as a mutually critical correlation between the Christian

---

[85] Peter C. Phan, *Vietnamese-American Catholics*. (New York: Paulist Press, 2005).

[86] Jonathan Y. Tan, *Introducing Asian American Theologies* (Maryknoll, NY: Orbis Books, 2008).

[87] Peter C. Phan, *Christianity with an Asian Face: Asian American Theology in the Making* (Maryknoll, NY: Orbis Books, 2003).

[88] Ibid., 12.

[89] Ibid., 8–12.

[90] Peter C. Phan, *Being Religious Interreligiously: Asian Perspectives on Interfaith Dialogue* (Maryknoll, NY: Orbis Books, 2004).

[91] Peter C. Phan, "*Deus Migrator*—God the Migrant: Migration of Theology and Theology of Migration," *Theological Studies* 77, no. 4 (2016): 845–68.

[92] Phan, *Vietnamese-American Catholics*, 101.

sources of the Bible and Christian tradition, on the one side, and the particular contexts of Vietnamese Catholic experience, on the other. This involves close attention to the context of Vietnamese American Catholics, including the history of struggles in Vietnam plus the experiences of Vietnamese expatriates, drawing upon the scriptures, Christian tradition with a special concern for the poor and marginalized.

Phan relates the Vietnamese *tam tai* philosophy to the doctrine of the Trinity, relating God the Father to Heaven, which gives birth; and God the Son with Humanity, which harmonizes, and the Holy Spirit with the earth, which nurtures.[93] Phan reflects on Jesus as the firstborn son and eldest brother, on Jesus as ancestor, and on Jesus as the immigrant par excellence, the border-crosser and the dweller at the Margins.[94] He explains traditional Christological language in relation to crossing the border between divine and human:

> In this divine crossing over to the human, the border between the divine nature and the human nature functions as the marker constituting the distinct identity of each. One is not transmuted into the other, nor confused with it. . . On the other hand, the same border is no longer a barrier preventing God and the human from joining together.[95]

The final border crossing is eschatological: "By his resurrection he crossed the borders of death into a new life, thus bringing hope where was despair. . . . In this way, the borders of death become frontiers to life in abundance."[96]

From a variety of perspectives Catholic theologians in the United States are exploring ancient teachings and values in relation to the multireligious and multitextured context of American life today. Schreiter approaches theology as a form of wisdom that attends to the scriptures, the Christian tradition, other religious traditions, and the contemporary experience of local churches. This offers a framework for viewing each of these ways of doing theology, all of which stress the importance of hermeneutics, including fresh interpretations of traditional themes in light of interreligious and intercultural experiences. Many of the theologians, especially Schreiter, Starkloff, Copeland, Goizueta, and Phan, devote considerable attention to the wisdom found in popular devotions and religion. Theology emerges not as a final achievement but as a form of dialogue attentive to multiple sources of wisdom.

---

[93] Ibid., 103–4.
[94] Ibid., 105–11.
[95] Ibid., 109.
[96] Ibid., 111.

9

New Ways of Reading Sacred Scriptures

One of the most important aspects of responding to religious diversity is the interpretation of scripture. Catholics and other Christians interpret religious pluralism in light of their understanding of the Bible, but their understanding of the Bible shifts and develops in conjunction with their changing relations with other religious traditions. When Catholics have viewed other religions as enemies and threats, they regularly looked to the Bible for images and arguments to critique other religious communities. When Catholics view others as interreligious partners and spiritual companions, they can explore points of convergence or divergence in an atmosphere shaped by interreligious respect and generosity toward the other.

Christians can draw varying lessons from the biblical traditions because the Bible offers a variety of conflicting precedents for relating to followers of other religious paths. On the one hand, Moses issued a command on behalf of God to the Israelites to kill all the inhabitants of the Promised Land because they were viewed as idolaters who would threaten Israelite worship of God (Dt 20:16–18); Elijah ordered that the prophets of Baal be slaughtered (1 Kgs 18:40). In situations of conflict, hostile interpretations of the Bible against other religious traditions can provide encouragement and justification for the use of physical violence. On the other hand, Solomon had a friendly conversation concerning wisdom with the Queen of Sheba (1 Kgs 10:1–13), and the wisdom teachers of ancient Israel were open to learning from the wisdom of their counterparts in other cultures. Biblical writers vigorously rejected idolatry but they repeatedly appropriated aspects of other religious traditions to present their vision of God's activity in human life.

Traditionally, Catholics and other Christians largely interpreted the Bible in opposition to other religious traditions, emphasizing what was best in the Christian tradition and often focusing on what was deficient in their neighbors' paths. Jesus, however, taught his followers two principles for reflecting on evil:

> Why do you see the speck in your neighbor's eye, but do not notice the log in your own eye? Or how can you say to your neighbor, "Let me take the speck out of your eye," while the log is in your own eye? You hypocrite, first take the log out of your own eye, and then you will see clearly to take the speck out of your neighbor's eye. (Mt 7:3–4)

Through most of Christian history, Catholics and many other Christians interpreted the Bible in ways that judged Jews and Muslims very harshly while neglecting their own sins and failings;[1] thus, the command of Jesus in the Sermon on the Mount directly challenges much of traditional Christian practice in interpreting the Bible against the Jews and the Muslims. Jesus also instructed his disciples: "When you are offering your gift at the altar, if you remember that your brother or sister has something against you, leave your gift there before the altar and go; first be reconciled to your brother or sister, and then come and offer your gift" (Mt 5:23–24). Christians who wish to approach God in worship need to ask the forgiveness of those brothers and sisters whom they have offended. These sayings have particular importance in offering guidance for Christian interpretations of the Bible in relation to other religious traditions.

This chapter will explore some aspects of the problematic history of Christian biblical interpretations that regarded other religious traditions with hostility and will propose a strategy to shape healthier relations by consulting the biblical writings, especially the wisdom tradition, as a guide to interpreting scriptures. Traditionally Christian theologians read the Hebrew Bible as the Old Testament, with Catholics, Byzantine Orthodox, and Oriental Orthodox theologians including other ancient Jewish writings as also included in the First Testament of their Bibles. However, Catholics and other Christians rarely took seriously the history of postbiblical Jewish interpretations of Tanakh and insisted that the First Testament could only be truly interpreted as referring to Jesus Christ. Until recently, the Qur'an was not usually taken into serious consideration in relation to the two Testaments of the Christian Bible. Today there is increasing attention to interpreting the Bible in relation to the sacred texts of other religious traditions.

The ambiguity of interpretations of the Bible has great importance in shaping relations with followers of other religious paths. Hostile interpretations can foster misunderstanding and hatred; respectful, generous interpretations can be occasions for mutual understanding; reconciliation; and commitment to social, political, and economic justice.

The prophetic and apocalyptic traditions of the Bible offer strong condemnations of injustice, which offer powerful resources in fighting social evil in every context. However, these trajectories can also be understood as condemning all followers of another religious tradition. Historically, Christians often viewed Jews and Muslims as supporters of the anti-Christ. They repeatedly condemned American Indians, Africans, Hindus, and Buddhists for worshipping idols and performing superstitious rituals that the Bible described as bowing down to graven images. A major aspect of the transformation of Christian attitudes and actions involves new ways of reading the Bible.

---

[1] Leo D. Lefebure, *True and Holy: Christian Scripture and Other Religions* (Maryknoll, NY: Orbis Books, 2014), 50–135.

From the first European Christian settlers in North America to the present United States, the interpretation of the Bible has been a battleground.[2] Catholics and other Christians in the Americas have interpreted passages in the Bible to justify conquest, expulsion, and killing of American Indians, and to rationalize the enslavement of Africans and African Americans.[3] Even though the Bible does not speak of race in the modern sense of the term, American Christians too often engaged in racist interpretations of their sacred scripture.[4] American Christians have also interpreted the Bible to challenge these oppressive practices and to find hope in hopeless situations.[5]

Reading the Bible with Jews

Many traditional problems in Jewish-Christian relations came from the Christian practice of interpreting the Bible in ways hostile to Jews and postbiblical Judaism, and one of the most important developments in positively transforming Jewish-Christian relations in America came in the area of biblical interpretation. Jews and Christians find both points of convergence and divergence in their relations to the scripture of ancient Israel, but what constitutes the Bible is disputed.[6] The First Testament of the Protestant Bible consists of the same books as Tanakh, the Jewish Bible, but the books are usually arranged in a different order. The First Testaments of the Catholic Church, the Byzantine Orthodox Churches, the Oriental Orthodox Churches, and the Assyrian Church of the East include Tanakh as well as various additional Jewish texts from the Septuagint that are not found in Tanakh. One of the most important development of recent years is the emergence of Jewish scholarship on the New Testament, which often emphasizes its Jewish character.[7] Traditionally, Catholics and other Christians generally ignored

---

[2] Mark A. Noll, *In the Beginning Was the Word: The Bible in American Public Life, 1492–1783* (Oxford: Oxford University Press, 2016).

[3] Stephen R. Haynes, *Noah's Curse: The Biblical Justification of American Slavery* (Oxford: Oxford University Press, 2002); Luis N. Rivera, *A Violent Evangelism: The Political and Religious Conquest of the Americas* (Louisville, KY: Westminster John Knox Press, 1992).

[4] Willie James Jennings, *The Christian Imagination: Theology and the Origins of Race* (New Haven, CT: Yale University Press, 2010).

[5] Cain Hope Felder, ed., *Stony the Road We Trod: African American Biblical Interpretation* (Minneapolis: Fortress Press, 1991); Eddie S. Glaude Jr., *Exodus!: Religion, Race, and Nation in Early Nineteenth-Century Black America* (Chicago: University of Chicago Press, 2000).

[6] Amy Grossblat Pessah, Kenneth J. Meyers, and Christopher J. Leighton, "How Do Jews and Christians Read the Bible?" in *Irreconcilable Differences? A Learning Resource for Jews and Christians,* ed. David Fox Sandmel, Rosann M. Catalano, and Christopher M. Leighton (Boulder, CO: Westview Press, 2001).

[7] Amy-Jill Levine and Marc Zvi Brettler, eds., *The Jewish Annotated New Testament,* 2nd ed. (Oxford: Oxford University Press, 2017).

or dismissed the Jewish tradition of interpreting Tanakh; in 2001 the Pontifical Biblical Commission proposed that

> Christians can and ought to admit that the Jewish reading of the Bible is a possible one, in continuity with the Jewish Sacred Scriptures from the Second Temple period . . . On the practical level of exegesis, Christians can, nonetheless, learn much from Jewish exegesis practiced for more than two thousand years.[8]

Conflicts described in the Christian scriptures would have a long and harmful influence on later Christian intolerance toward Jews. The Christian scriptures present both John the Baptist and Jesus as sharply criticizing Jewish leaders of the time. In the Gospel of Matthew, John the Baptist excoriates the scribes and Pharisees as "a brood of vipers" (Mt 3:7), and later in the same Gospel Jesus attacks the scribes and the Pharisees as hypocrites, blind guides, and murderers (Mt 23:13). John the Baptist and Jesus himself were, of course, Jews; and these criticisms of other Jewish leaders in their original context continue the tradition of the Hebrew prophets, who repeatedly challenged the religious and political leaders of their day. This prophetic heritage is one of the great contributions of Judaism to the world's religious history. On the lips of John the Baptist or Jesus, these charges were not anti-Jewish or anti-Semitic; John and Jesus were Jews calling other Jews to fidelity to the covenant. However, Christians who were not Jewish would later interpret the harsh language of John the Baptist and Jesus as indicting all Jews at every time and place. The polemical language in the Christian Gospels prepared the way for centuries of anti-Jewish attitudes and practices.[9]

After the death of Jesus, some Jews persecuted some early followers of Jesus, who were themselves also Jews. According to the Acts of the Apostles, a Jewish crowd stoned the deacon Stephen to death (Acts 7:1–60), and shortly afterward the young Saul sought out followers of Jesus with murderous intent, reportedly with authorization of the high priest in Jerusalem (Acts 9:1–2). Later Christians interpreted these incidents not as part of an inner-Jewish dispute, but rather as signs of the perfidy of all Jews. In later centuries, when most Christians were not Jewish, they often understood the New Testament's criticisms of Jewish leaders and the violent acts of some Jews against followers of Jesus to justify a wholesale condemnation of all Jews at all times and places.

---

[8] Pontifical Biblical Commission, *The Jewish People and Their Sacred Scriptures in the Christian Bible,* May 24, 2001, #22.

[9] Rosemary Radford Ruether, *Faith and Fratricide: The Theological Roots of Anti-Semitism* (New York: Seabury Press, 1979), 64–225; Mary C. Boys, *Redeeming Our Sacred Story: The Death of Jesus and Relations between Jews and Christians* (New York: Paulist Press, 2013), 9–24; David Nirenberg, *Anti-Judaism: The Western Tradition* (New York: W. W. Norton, 2013), 48–134.

In the second century, some Christians sharply criticized Jewish worship and practice. The Epistle to Barnabas, written about 130–140 CE, charges that the Jewish people were not worthy to understand the revelation given through Moses (14:4) and claims they were seduced by an evil spirit into their legal observances. According to the Epistle of Barnabas, Moses gave the commandments of the Mosaic Law in a spiritual sense, but the Jews misunderstood them and took them literally. The Epistle of Barnabas further claims that the covenant made at Mt. Sinai now belongs to Christians because the Jews broke it as soon as they had received it (4:7). Another second-century Christian document, the Epistle to Diognetus, views Jewish sacrifices as being on the same level as pagan worship of idols (3:5) and rejects the observance of the Sabbath as being a ridiculous superstition.

The early hostile attitudes of Christians toward Jews set a pattern for later centuries and influenced the way Christians viewed other religions as well.[10] The rise of Islam in the seventh century posed new challenges for Christians. For over a millennium most Christian images of Muhammad and Islam were overwhelmingly negative. While a few Christians in the Middle Ages had a reasonably accurate understanding of the teachings of Islam, most Christians received only an extremely biased and distorted caricature.[11] Often Christians followed John of Damascus in viewing Islam as a dangerous Christian heresy, related to early Christians who denied the full divinity of Jesus.

During the age of discovery in the fifteenth and sixteenth centuries, Catholics who came to new lands in the Americas, Africa, and Asia often viewed the religious traditions of these areas in a very harsh light, applying to them the biblical condemnations of idolatry and superstition. In the seventeenth century, Christians in New England saw themselves as on a divinely commanded errand in the wilderness on the model of the Israelites coming out of Egypt to a new land; they interpreted the indigenous inhabitants as lacking humanity and thus having little claim to the land in which they had always lived.[12] The Native Americans' supposed backward state and different religious practices were thought to deprive them of all rights. Remembering that the ancient Israelites were instructed to destroy other tribes lest they tempt them to worship other gods (e.g., Dt 20), so Christian settlers viewed Native Americans as temptations to sin and sought to exterminate them or, at least, contain them in separate areas.[13]

Even though modern historical criticism of the Bible pretended to offer a neutral objective account of ancient Israel, its Christian practitioners generally

---

[10] Edward H. Flannery, *The Anguish of the Jews: Twenty-Three Centuries of Anti-Semitism* (New York: Macmillan, 1965); William Nicholls, *Christian Antisemitism: A History of Hate* (Northvale, NJ: Jason Aronson, 1993).

[11] Norman Daniel, *Islam and the West: The Making of an Image* (1960; reprint, Oxford: Oneworld, 2000).

[12] Richard Slotkin: *Regeneration through Violence: The Mythology of the American Frontier, 1600–1860* (Tulsa: University of Oklahoma Press, 2000), 38.

[13] Ibid., 40–42.

continued to be shaped by age-old biases against Judaism. In the nineteenth century, Julius Wellhausen set the tone for much modern Protestant biblical scholarship by criticizing Judaism as a legalistic religion and praising the biblical prophets for their allegedly "pure" biblical faith. Judaism of the time of Jesus was dismissed as *Spätjudentum,* an allegedly corrupt form of religion, all too similar to Roman Catholicism, with a focus on commandments and rituals.[14]

One of the earliest and most influential American Christians to challenge the negative stereotype of Judaism as "Pharisaical" was George Foot Moore, who taught first at Andover Seminary until 1902 and thereafter at Harvard University. Based on his extensive studies of the ancient rabbis, Moore forcefully rejected negative images of the Pharisees and charged that the inherited Christian views about Jews were polemical and inaccurate.[15] He criticized the view of Judaism as legalistic, and he valued rabbinic literature on a par with the New Testament.[16] Above all, he urged Christians not to see Judaism as merely background to Christianity, but rather to allow Jewish voices to speak for themselves with their own integrity. Moore presented Judaism and Christianity as legitimate paths to God rooted in the religion of ancient Israel.

In the wake of the Shoah (the Holocaust), many Christians in Europe and the United States realized that this age-old pattern of hostile biblical interpretation against the Jewish people had poisoned the atmosphere in Europe and prepared the way for the Nazi atrocities. Some Catholic refugees from Nazi oppression in Europe played a crucial role in developing American Catholic awareness of this issue. Johannes M. Oesterreicher, who was born into a Jewish family in Moravia (then part of Austria) in 1904 and who became a Catholic priest in 1927, struggled against antisemitism in Europe in the 1930s and came from Europe to the United States in 1940 during the Second World War. After the war ended, he remained in the United States, founding the Institute for Judeo-Christian Studies at Seton Hall University in New Jersey in 1953. He collaborated with other Catholics from a Jewish background, especially Gregory Baum, who was active in both the United States and Canada, in the discussions at Vatican II that led to *Nostra Aetate.*[17] Oesterreicher and Baum were pioneers in transforming Catholic ways of interpreting the Bible in relation to Jews and Judaism. One of the most pressing concerns in recent Christian biblical interpretation has been to improve relations with the Jewish community and to banish anti-Judaism from Christian preaching and teaching.[18]

---

[14] Julius Wellhausen, *Prolegomena to the History of Israel: With a Reprint of the Article 'Israel from the Encyclopedia Britannica,'* trans. J. Sutherland Black and Allan Menzies (1885; reprint, Cambridge: Cambridge University Press, 2013).

[15] George Foot Moore, "Christian Writers on Judaism," *Harvard Theological Review* 14, no. 3 (1921): 197–254.

[16] George Foot Moore, *Judaism in the First Centuries of the Christian Era* (1927–30; reprint, Peabody, MA: Hendrickson, 1997).

[17] John Connelly, *From Enemy to Brother: The Revolution in Catholic Teaching on the Jews, 1933–1965* (Cambridge, MA: Harvard University Press, 2012), 4–7.

[18] Howard Clark Kee and Irvin J. Borowsky, eds., *Removing Anti-Judaism from the*

In the 1950s, Jews and Christians increasingly collaborated in new ways on biblical scholarship and theological discussions. In 1956, Jewish scholar Samuel Sandmel, who praised the pioneering work of Moore for shaping new and positive Christian views of Judaism, published *A Jewish Understanding of the New Testament*, sparking serious scholarly interest in investigating the origins of Christianity in dialogue with the Jewish tradition.[19] A number of Christians reciprocated, including the distinguished Lutheran New Testament scholar Bishop Krister Stendahl, who praised Sandmel's important contribution: "Samuel Sandmel was a gift of God to both Jews and Christians. It was given to him to help change the climate and even the agenda of Jewish-Christian conversations."[20]

Many other scholars, both Jewish and Christian, picked up the agenda of improving relations through better biblical interpretations, drawing on contemporary biblical scholarship to end the long history of hostile Christian biblical interpretation regarding Jews and Judaism; Jewish scholars Paula Fredriksen and Adele Reinhartz have led a team of Jewish and Christian scholars seeking to reject Christian anti-Judaism in the interpretation of the New Testament.[21] Mary Boys reinterprets New Testament passages that have been used to historically impugn all Jews of all times and places; she offers revised interpretations on the basis of dialogue with Jews.[22] She notes the personal impact of her study of Catholic interpretations of the passion and death of Jesus Christ:

Pulpit (Philadelphia: American Interfaith Institute/New York: Continuum, 1996); Philip A. Cunningham, *Sharing the Scriptures*, vol. 1, *The Word Set Free* (New York: A Stimulus Book, 2003); Bishops' Committee for Ecumenical and Interreligious Affairs of the United States Conference of Catholic Bishops, *The Bible, the Jews, and the Death of Jesus: A Collection of Catholic Documents* (Washington, DC: United States Conference of Catholic Bishops, 2004); Philip A. Cunningham, *A Story of Shalom: The Calling of Christians and Jews by a Covenanting God* (New York: A Stimulus Book, 2001).

[19] Samuel Sandmel, *A Jewish Understanding of the New Testament*, 3rd ed. (1956; reprint, Woodstock, VT: Jewish Lights and Skylight Paths, 2005); see also Samuel Sandmel, *We Jews and Jesus: Exploring Theological Differences for Mutual Understanding* (1965; reprint, Woodstock, VT: Jewish Lights and Skylight Paths, 2006).

[20] Krister Stendahl, "A Friend and His Philo-Connection," in *Nourished with Peace: Studies in Hellenistic Judaism in Memory of Samuel Sandmel*, ed. Frederick E. Greenspahn et al. (Chico, CA: Scholars Press, 1984), 13.

[21] *Jesus, Judaism, and Christian Anti-Judaism: Reading the New Testament after the Holocaust*, ed. Paula Fredriksen and Adele Reinhartz (Louisville, KY: Westminster John Knox Press, 2002); *Removing Anti-Judaism from the Pulpit*, ed. Howard Clark Kee and Irvin J. Borowsky (New York: Continuum/Philadelphia: American Interfaith Institute, 1996); United States Conference of Catholic Bishops' Committee for Ecumenical and Interreligious Affairs, *The Bible, the Jews, and the Death of Jesus: A Collection of Catholic Documents* (Washington, DC: United States Conference of Catholic Bishops, 2004).

[22] Mary C. Boys, *Redeeming Our Sacred Story: The Death of Jesus and Relations between Jews and Christians* (New York: Paulist Press, 2013).

Not that I am innocent of the shadow side of my Catholic tradition, but confronting the extent of its hostility to Judaism over the ages has been overwhelming. I have long been interested in questions about interpreting troubling biblical texts. . . . But what struck me with new force was the way in which a dominant Christianity, particularly my own Roman Catholic Church, has again and again exercised its power over against Jews, its quintessential "other."[23]

Boys calls for Catholics and all Christians to learn "just how deep and broad has been their tradition's disparagement of Jews as 'Christ killers,'" and to learn to interpret the New Testament accounts in new ways that respect and honor the Jewish people.[24]

Arguably the most dramatic revision of traditional biblical interpretation has come in relation to the Jewish community and the origins of the Christian movement. As we have seen, Jesus and his first followers were Jews, and Christianity emerged from a Jewish matrix.[25] In contrast to the earlier Christian tradition's view of Jesus in opposition to Judaism, today there is intense research on the relation of Jesus to the diverse forms of Judaism in his context.[26] Daniel Harrington writes of "Matthew's Christian-Jewish Community,"[27] and Paula Fredriksen studies Paul as a Torah observant Jew who founded subgroup Jewish communities.[28] The earliest followers of Jesus were Jews who came to believe that he was the Messiah; this belief did not by itself mean that they were no longer Jews.[29] It did set the stage for vigorous debates with other Jews who rejected this claim.

For many generations, there was a process of intermingling, intertwining, and mutual belonging that is not accounted for by the earlier model of a clear, decisive

---

[23] Ibid., 259, 260.

[24] Ibid., 16.

[25] On the Jewish character of Jesus, see Paula Fredriksen, *Jesus of Nazareth, King of the Jews: A Jewish Life and the Emergence of Christianity* (New York: Alfred A. Knopf, 1999); Amy Jill-Levine, *The Misunderstood Jew: The Church and the Scandal of the Jewish Jesus* (San Francisco: HarperOne, 2007).

[26] Sean Freyne, *Jesus, A Jewish Galilean: A New Reading of the Jesus Story* (London: T & T Clark, 2005); John P. Meier, *A Marginal Jew: Rethinking the Historical Jesus*, vol. 3, *Companions and Competitors,* Anchor Bible Reference Library (New York: Doubleday, 2001).

[27] Daniel J. Harrington, "Matthew's Christian-Jewish Community," in *Introduction to Messianic Judaism: Its Ecclesial Context and Biblical Foundations,* ed. David Rudolph and Joel Willitts (Grand Rapids, MI: Zondervan, 2013), 159–67.

[28] Paula Frederiksen, *Paul: The Pagans' Apostle* (New Haven, CT: Yale University Press, 2017).

[29] Fabian E. Udoh, Susannah Heschel, Mark Chancey, and Gregory Tatum, eds., *Redefining First-Century Jewish and Christian Identities: Essays in Honor of Ed Parish Sanders* (Notre Dame, IN: University of Notre Dame Press, 2008).

"parting of the ways" in the first and second centuries CE.[30] It was not the case that two clearly defined religions, Jewish and Christian, confronted each other by the end of the first century CE or even the second. Rather, these religious traditions both emerged from a multifarious, conflicted milieu in a process that has been called "the partition of Judaeo-Christianity."[31] Some recent scholarship suggests that what we view as Jewish and Christian communities overlapped for centuries, even into the fourth and fifth centuries CE.[32]

Given the long, difficult history of Jewish-Christian relations, it is of the greatest importance for Christian dialogues with Jews and also with other religious traditions that contemporary scholarship view Jesus as a Jew who was deeply rooted in the Jewish tradition. Many scholars have pointed out that in their original context, the disputes reflected in the New Testament writings constitute a family quarrel that has become extremely heated. Interpreting this polemical language remains a disputed area of scholarship. The Gospel of John presents Jesus in strong disagreement with other Jews, telling his Jewish interlocutors at one point: "You are from your father the devil, and you choose to do your father's desires. He was a murderer from the beginning and does not stand in the truth, because there is no truth in him" (Jn 8:44). Francis Moloney argues that "the Jews" in the Gospel of John "are those characters in the story who have made up their minds about Jesus. They are one side of a Christological debate . . . at the end of the first century."[33] Moloney concludes that "Jewish people as such are not represented by the term 'the Jews,' and the Fourth Gospel must not be read as if they were."[34] Other scholars, however, see serious problems in the Gospel of John. Adele Reinhartz is more critical and forcefully argues that the gospel of John is anti-Jewish.[35]

In a lecture at Hebrew University in 1995, Joseph Cardinal Bernardin, Archbishop of Chicago, accepted the judgment of Raymond Brown that Catholics today cannot endorse the teaching of the Gospel of John regarding "the Jews," especially the claim that they are children of the devil: "Father Brown maintains that this teaching of John about the Jews, which resulted from the historical

---

[30] Daniel Boyarin, *Dying for God: Martyrdom and the Making of Judaism and Christianity* (Stanford, CA: Stanford University Press, 1999).

[31] Daniel Boyarin, *Border Lines: The Partition of Judaeo-Christianity* (Philadelphia: University of Pennsylvania Press, 2010), 1.

[32] Oskar Skarsaune and Reidar Hvalvik, eds., *Jewish Believers in Jesus: The Early Centuries* (Peabody, MA: Hendrickson Publishers, 2007); Matt Jackson-McCabe, ed., *Jewish Christianity Reconsidered: Rethinking Ancient Groups and Texts* (Minneapolis: Fortress Press, 2007); Daniel Boyarin, "Rethinking Jewish Christianity: An Argument for Dismantling a Dubious Category (to which Is Appended a Correction of My Border Lines)," *Jewish Quarterly Review* 99, no. 1 (2009): 7–36.

[33] Francis J. Moloney, *The Gospel of John* (Collegeville, MN: Liturgical Press, 1998), 10.

[34] Ibid., 11.

[35] Adele Reinhartz, *Cast Out of the Covenant: Jews and Anti-Judaism in the Gospel of John* (Lanham, MD: Lexington Books/Fortress Press, 2018).

conflict between Church and synagogue in the latter part of the first century CE, can no longer be taught as authentic doctrine or used as catechesis by contemporary Christianity."[36] As the framework for interpreting the Bible, Bernardin appealed to the Second Vatican Council's affirmation that "the Jews remain a covenanted people, revered by God. The teaching of recent Popes has also emphasized this."[37] Regarding the negative statements about "the Jews" in the Fourth Gospel, Bernardin drew the remarkable conclusion: "Christians today must come to see that such teachings, while an acknowledged part of their biblical heritage, can no longer be regarded as definitive teaching in light of our improved understanding of developments in the relationship between early Christianity and the Jewish community of the time."[38] While scholarly debates continue unabated over reconstructing the developments of the first century and much remains uncertain, Bernardin's hermeneutical principle of critique of biblical teachings in light of the Second Vatican Council sets an important precedent for Catholics interpreting the Bible in relation to the Jewish community.

The difficulty with interpreting problematic biblical texts is not unique to Christians. Jon Levenson compared New Testament passages that are critical of Jews to the criticism of the religions of the peoples of the land in the Hebrew Bible, including commands of mass slaughter.[39] Amy-Jill Levine states that as a Jew, she is appalled "by the sanctioned genocide suggested by passages in Deuteronomy and Joshua."[40] Rabbi Jonathan Sacks suggests that all scriptures contain passages that can be understood as a narrow particularism and others that stress openness to the stranger: "The choice is ours. Will the generous texts of our tradition serve as interpretive keys to the rest, or will the abrasive passages determine our ideas of what we are and what we are called on to do?"[41] Jews and Catholics and all Christians face the challenge of interpreting and critiquing the biblical texts in light of current values and perspectives.

David Sandmel, Rosann Catalano, and Christopher Leighton organized a series of theological conversations that invited Jews and Christians to read texts together:

Ask any long-term participant of the dialogue, and they will tell you that interfaith text study works an intoxicating magic. It teaches Jews and Christians what they can learn in no other setting: that the other brings to

---

[36] Joseph Cardinal Bernardin, *Antisemitism: The Historical Legacy and the Continuing Challenge for Christians* (Chicago: J. S. Paluch, 1995), 13.

[37] Ibid.

[38] Ibid.

[39] Jon D. Levenson, "Is There a Counterpart in the Hebrew Bible to New Testament Antisemitism?" *Journal of Ecumenical Studies* 22, no. 2 (1985): 242–60.

[40] Levine, *Misunderstood Jew*, 14.

[41] Jonathan Sacks, *The Dignity of Difference: How to Avoid the Clash of Civilizations*, rev. ed. (London: Continuum, 2003), 207–8.

the study of a particular text ways of seeing and hearing, ways of listening and learning that illumine portions of the textual terrain that otherwise remain in darkness.[42]

These organizers emphasize that every reading of a sacred text brings at least implicit assumptions, which involve theology: "If they cannot speak theologically, neither Jews nor Christians can access their respective traditions. Deprived of the wisdom borne by synagogue and church, Jews and Christians become disconnected from a particular way of living in the world."[43] In response to this challenge, Sandmel, Catalano, and Leighton call for theological dialogue that is "*self-conscious* ... *self-critical,* and ... *modest.*"[44] They note the ability of interlocutors from another tradition to elicit the unspoken assumptions that lurk behind familiar theological perspectives. Presbyterian theologian Christopher M. Leighton and Jewish scholar Daniel Lehmann express the hope that

> Christians who dare to learn about the dynamics of Judaism become better and more knowledgeable Christians. Jews who risk engagement with Christianity develop deeper and firmer grounding in Judaism. The Christian-Jewish entanglement runs far deeper than most of us have acknowledged, and the tangled interplay of our communities requires unraveling.[45]

In light of the important research on the historical intertwining of Judaism and nascent Christianity and the history of the development of the two traditions, Leighton and Lehmann challenge the traditional view of Christian origins of both Jews and Christians and propose a new model that sees ancient Israelite religion as the ancestor of both rabbinic Judaism and Christianity, which emerge in the wake of the destruction of the Second Temple in 70 CE.

Cosmopolitan Wisdom: A Sapiential Hermeneutic

If the long history of Christian violence and disrespect toward members of other religious traditions were the final word, there would be little hope for future Christian interreligious relations. Fortunately, this is not all there is in the Christian tradition. Followers of Jesus read the history of the Christian tradition critically in light of the teaching of Jesus himself that challenge his disciples to seek out more

---

[42] David Fox Sandmel, Rosann M. Catalano, and Christopher M. Leighton, *Irreconcilable Differences? A Learning Resource for Jews and Christians* (Boulder, CO: Westview Press, 2001), 5.

[43] Ibid., 6.

[44] Ibid., 7.

[45] Christopher M. Leighton and Daniel Lehmann, "Jewish-Christian Relations in Historical Perspective," in Sandmel, Catalano, and Leighton, *Irreconcilable Differences,* 16.

constructive ways of relating to members of other traditions. The parable of the Samaritan who helps the injured traveler makes clear that Jesus called his followers to view all people, including specifically members of different religious and ethnic traditions who were commonly despised at the time, as their neighbors. To love our neighbor requires that we know our neighbor. If our neighbor practices a different religion than our own, the command to love our neighbor includes the responsibility of getting to know our neighbor's religious practices.

The Bible contains numerous examples of positive contacts with people from different religious backgrounds. According to the First Book of Kings, the Queen of Sheba came to examine the wisdom of Solomon, and was favorably impressed (1 Kgs 10:1–11). In the Gospel of Luke, Jewish elders ask Jesus to cure the servant of a Roman centurion "because he loves our people and even built our synagogue for us"; after receiving a message from the centurion that humbly acknowledges Jesus's authority and power, Jesus praises the Roman lavishly for his faith (Lk 7:1–10). Of ten lepers who are healed, the one who returns to give thanks to God is a Samaritan (Lk 17:11–19). Jesus himself learns from his encounter with the Syro-Phoenician woman who challenges him to heal her daughter and include her and her daughter in the community of salvation as well (Mt 15:21–28; Mk 7:24–30). The Prologue of the Gospel of John tells us that the Word of God through whom all things were created enlightens all people throughout the world, prior to the Word becoming flesh in Jesus of Nazareth (Jn 1:9).

Ancient Israel produced a wisdom tradition that is found in the books of Proverbs, Job, and Ecclesiastes, as well as in various Psalms and wisdom narratives like that of Joseph in Genesis. As part of a broad, cosmopolitan culture of sages that extended throughout the Middle East, the wisdom trajectory of the Bible offers analogies to other religious traditions and resources for the community of religions today.[46] The wisdom teachers of ancient Israel were actively engaged in conversation with the wisdom traditions of other ancient religions, thus offering a precedent for dialogue with other religious traditions.

The Hebrew word *chokmah,* usually translated as "wisdom," refers to skills for living, especially the art of navigating the challenges of life. In the Bible, wisdom is the practical virtue of how to live with integrity and humility, in right relationships with God, other humans, and all creation; wisdom guides one to be virtuous and successful. The tradition places a high value on finding the proper understanding of wisdom, which will in turn lead to proper conduct. There may have been royal schools to teach wisdom to the children of the aristocracy in ancient Israel, to instill in them principles of virtue and discernment to prepare them for leadership in

---

[46] Roland E. Murphy, *The Tree of Life: An Exploration of Biblical Wisdom Literature,* Anchor Bible Reference Library (New York: Doubleday, 1992); James L. Crenshaw, *Old Testament Wisdom: An Introduction* (Atlanta, GA: John Knox Press, 1981); Leo G. Perdue, Bernard Brandon Scott, and William Johnston Wiseman, *In Search of Wisdom: Essays in Memory of John G. Gammie* (Louisville, KY: Westminster John Knox Press, 1993); Richard J. Clifford, *The Wisdom Literature* (Nashville: Abingdon Press, 1998).

society. A concern for justice runs throughout the wisdom tradition. The biblical wisdom tradition asserts that there is a principle of justice embedded in creation itself, universal and summoning all to live in accord with her. Proverbs 1:20–33 is a fierce prophetic attack on those who spurn the call of Wisdom who is personified as a forceful woman.

The quest for justice of ancient Israel emerged from the international search for wisdom across the Ancient Near East. Prior to the biblical writings, Egypt produced its own wisdom tradition, which taught that there is a principle of justice embedded in the cosmos that supports the poor who are mistreated by corrupt rulers. James Henry Breasted describes the early Egyptian developments as "The Dawn of Conscience,"[47] and John Wilson calls attention to the protodemocratic context of this text in the history of Egypt: "It is significant that so sweeping a statement of the ultimate opportunity of every man is known only from that period which came closest to democratic realization."[48]

During the Old Kingdom in the middle of the third millennium BCE, Egyptian writings present a figure of cosmic justice in *Maat,* "truth, justice, righteousness, right dealing, order."[49] Maat is instrumental in creating the cosmos; she is the cosmic source for justice in human society, judging people after death to determine their fate. Wilson claims this was "ancient Egypt's democratic age" in

> the secondary but common meaning of social equalitarianism, the disregard of political or economic barriers in the belief that all men have equal rights and opportunities—or should have such. It seems clear from the texts which we have cited that there was a belief in social justice for everybody at this time and that even the poorest man had rights to the gifts of the gods because the creator-god "made every man like his fellow."[50]

Jan Assmann describes Maat as "the very principle of embedment, of creating connectivity in the social, temporal, and cosmic dimensions, establishing social bonds between humans and temporal connections between yesterday, today, and tomorrow ensuring memory, success, stability, and even immortality."[51] A concern for social and political justice runs through all the wisdom traditions of the ancient

---

[47] James Henry Breasted, *The Dawn of Conscience* (New York: Charles Scribner's Sons, 1933, 1968). See also H. and H. A. Frankfort, John A. Wilson, Thorkild Jacobsen, and William A. Irwin, *The Intellectual Adventure of Ancient Man: An Essay on Speculative Thought in the Ancient Near East* (Chicago: University of Chicago Press, 1946, 1972).

[48] John A. Wilson, *The Burden of Egypt: An Interpretation of Ancient Egyptian Culture* (Chicago: University of Chicago Press, 1951, 1967), 118.

[49] Ibid., 119.

[50] Ibid., 123.

[51] Jan Assmann, "Cultural Memory and the Myth of the Axial Age," in *The Axial Age and Its Consequences,* ed. Robert N. Bellah and Hans Joas (Cambridge, MA: Belknap Press of Harvard University Press, 2012), 396–96.

Near East, and it continues to speak to later ages through the biblical writings; it was a sermon on a text from the book of Sirach that first prompted Bartolomé de Las Casas to question his participation in the Spanish encomienda system.

At some point in the history of Israel, the sages began to use the word *chokmah* as a poetic image, a symbolic personification. It is difficult to date the early biblical wisdom texts, and we do not know the exact context in which the poetic, symbolic connotation of personified Wisdom first emerged. The sages of Israel expressed the dynamic activity of God in creation through the personification of *Chokmah*, today variously called Lady Wisdom or Woman Wisdom or, by her Greek name, *Sophia*. In Latin she is *Sapientia*. Personified Wisdom is a cosmic figure, playing in creation, inviting humans to seek true treasure in her, warning of chastisement if they reject her, guiding kings and promising that all who find her find life and favor from YHWH (Prov 8:1–36). She makes her first appearance in the book of Proverbs as an angry prophet condemning injustice (Prv 1:20–31). The relation of Lady Wisdom to YHWH in the book of Proverbs remains somewhat ambiguous and has been interpreted in various ways. For Leo Perdue, she is "the incarnate voice of God who provides insight into both the Creator and the reality he has made and rules. Woman Wisdom is also the queen of heaven who dispenses wisdom and life to her devotees and chooses kings to rule in justice."[52] For Roland E. Murphy, personified Wisdom "is, then, the revelation of God, not merely the self-revelation of creation."[53] By contrast, Michael Fox sees Lady Wisdom in Proverbs 8:22 as "an accidental attribute of godhead, not an essential or inherent one."[54]

It is significant for current interreligious interpretation of the Bible that the sages of ancient Israel were in close contact with their neighbors' religions, accepting and appropriating some ideas and practices, while rejecting others. For ancient Israelites, religious and cultural boundaries were porous and fluid.[55] When the Queen of Sheba visited King Solomon, they shared a common horizon of sapiential exploration, culminating in an exchange of gifts symbolic of the cordial relationship established (1 Kgs 10:1–13). The legend of the encounter of the Queen of Sheba and Solomon would live on in the Ethiopian Orthodox tradition, which would later claim that the rulers of Ethiopia were descended from the union of Solomon and the Queen of Sheba.

---

[52] Leo G. Perdue, *Wisdom Literature: A Theological History* (Louisville, KY: Westminster John Knox Press, 2007), 74–75.

[53] Roland E. Murphy, "Wisdom and Creation," *Journal of Biblical Literature* 104, no. 1 (1985): 9.

[54] Michael V. Fox, *Proverbs 1–9: A New Translation with Introduction and Commentary*, Anchor Yale Bible (New Haven, CT: Yale University Press, 2000), 279.

[55] Mark S. Smith, *The Early History of God: Yahweh and the Other Divinities in Ancient Israel*, 2nd ed. (Grand Rapids, MI: Eerdmans, 2002); Mark S. Smith, *The Origins of Biblical Monotheism: Israel's Polytheistic Background and the Ugaritic Texts* (New York: Oxford University Press, 2003).

From Egypt to Mesopotamia, teachers of wisdom reflected on the order of justice embedded in the universe and formulated precepts for humans to flourish in virtue.[56] Sages in Israel recognized the wisdom of their counterparts in Egypt and Mesopotamia, and drew freely upon their perspectives. Open to the truth and discernment of other religious traditions, the wisdom teachers of the Bible acknowledged an international, interreligious, and intercultural community of discourse: since the wisdom implanted in creation is universal and universally accessible, sages from different religious backgrounds could find points of contact and exchange.[57]

The sages of ancient Israel reflected on the patterns in ordinary human experience and expressed their insights in proverbs, poems, and riddles. Rather than claiming any special prophetic call or apocalyptic vision, they sought discernment and understanding in everyday life. In ancient Israel, as in cultures around the world, wisdom sayings express the insights of past ages for each new generation, advising what attitudes and actions lead to lasting joy or to needless suffering. Proverbs, aphorisms, and gnomic sayings name what is important to take into account; they instruct humans regarding patterns of discernment, counsel responses to difficulties, and summon hearers to wakefulness and vigilance. Often, they point out paradoxes or make comparisons. Frequently, they make promises of future benefit to those who follow their counsel. In principle, wisdom is open to all those who seek diligently for understanding through discipline. Michael Fox notes the Israelite sages did not claim exclusive wisdom but saw themselves sharing in a cosmopolitan wisdom with their colleagues elsewhere.[58]

Because the ancient search for wisdom crossed cultural and religious boundaries, biblical wisdom literature could incorporate contributions from non-Israelites. Proverbs 22:17–24:22 draws material from the Egyptian *Wisdom of Amenemope*.[59] The book of Ahiqar inspired a number of the sayings in Proverbs.[60] The book of Proverbs also presents sayings of Agur ben Jakeh and Lemuel, who may be understood as coming from Massa, an Ishmaelite tribe in the north of Arabia (Prv 30:1, 31:1).[61] Leo Perdue comments on the international influences on Proverbs:

---

[56] William McKane, *Proverbs: A New Approach* (Philadelphia: Westminster Press, 1970), 51–210; Leo G. Perdue, *The Sword and the Stylus: An Introduction to Wisdom in the Age of the Empires* (Grand Rapids. MI: Eerdmans, 2008); Perdue, *Wisdom Literature*.

[57] Jon Levenson, *The Universal Horizon of Jewish Particularism* (New York: American Jewish Committee, 1985). See also G. E. Bryce, *A Legacy of Wisdom: The Egyptian Contribution to the Wisdom of Israel* (Lewisburg, PA; London: Associated University, 1979).

[58] Fox, *Proverbs 1–9*, 358.

[59] John L. McLaughlin, *An Introduction to Israel's Wisdom Traditions* (Grand Rapids, MI: Eerdmans, 2018), 59; Michael V. Fox, *Proverbs 10–31: A New Translation with Introduction and Commentary,* Anchor Yale Bible (New Haven, CT: Yale University Press, 2009), 753–67.

[60] Ibid., 767.

[61] The word "*Massa*" in Proverbs 30:1 and 31:1 could be understood as a proper name referring to a north Arabian tribe, or it could be taken as a common noun meaning "pronouncement" or "oracle." Fox argues that in Proverbs 30:1, it is a common noun, and in

The Israelites held Egyptian wisdom in high regard (1 Kgs 5:10) and borrowed freely from their sapiential traditions, in particular those of the schools in the court and temples. . . . "The Instruction of Lemuel" [Prv 31:1–9] is an Arabic teaching offered by the queen mother to her son who has just assumed the position of chief.[62]

Job, who is not an Israelite, lived in Uz, which was probably in the south of Edom; he is described as "the most prosperous of all the Sons of the East" (Jb 1:3), a phrase used to describe "all who lived east of Palestine, more particularly in Edomite or Arab territory."[63]

The figure of cosmic Lady Wisdom personified as a woman in the Hebrew Bible may have been inspired by the model of Maat in Egypt. John McLaughlin comments: "Both Maat and Wisdom existed before creation, are the effective agent in the king's rule, and they love and are loved by Yahweh or the gods. . . . There is probably some influence from Maat to Wisdom."[64] Nonetheless, McLaughlin insists on an important difference in that "the gods must live in accordance with Maat, but Wisdom is subordinate to Yahweh, serving as the medium through which he creates."[65] While scholars differ on this issue, it is quite likely that the ancient Israelite personification of Wisdom emerged from interreligious contacts.

Elsewhere in the ancient world, there were comparable developments. In ancient Israel, Greece, India, and China, the search for wisdom contributed to the religious and philosophical transformations that would influence later developments so decisively that the German philosopher Karl Jaspers spoke of an Axial Age in the first millennium BCE that formulated basic assumptions that still shape cultures today.[66] While the theory of an Axial Age remains controversial, Robert Bellah and Karen Armstrong have recently argued that the results of this epochal change in different regions around the globe continue to affect our world.[67]

In the biblical tradition, the earliest sources for understanding wisdom and the cosmos in interreligious encounter lie not in the abstract theories of philosophical theology but in the proverbs, narratives, hymns, wisdom teachings, apocalyptic visions, Gospels, and epistles of the Bible.[68] The concrete biblical language about

---

Proverbs 31:1 it is a proper name. Fox, *Proverbs 10–31,* 852, 882–84.

[62] Perdue, *Wisdom Literature,* 42, 44.

[63] *New Jerusalem Bible,* 757.

[64] McLaughlin, *Introduction,* 51.

[65] Ibid.

[66] Karl Jaspers, *The Origin and Goal of History* (New Haven, CT: Yale University Press, 1953).

[67] Robert Bellah, *Religion in Human Evolution: From the Paleolithic to the Axial Age* (Cambridge, MA: Belknap Press of Harvard University Press, 2011); Karen Armstrong, *The Great Transformation: The Beginning of Our Religious Traditions* (New York: Alfred A. Knopf, 2006); Steven G. Smith, *Appeal and Attitude: Prospects for Ultimate Meaning* (Bloomington: Indiana University Press, 2005).

[68] Walter Brueggemann, *An Introduction to the Old Testament: The Canon and Chris-*

Sophia presents transformative encounters with wisdom and refigures the possibilities of human life in light of them.[69] The context of the biblical wisdom tradition changed dramatically with the conquests of Alexander the Great.

Wisdom and Philosophy in Hellenistic Judaism

The origins of the Christian movement and early Christian literature were decisively influenced by the Jewish relations with the Hellenistic world. Greek-speaking Jews honored Chokmah as Sophia and interpreted her in relation to their new Greek-speaking environment, including Greek philosophy. In the centuries after Alexander the Great, Sophia gained greater significance as Jews faced both new opportunities and new dangers. On the one hand, the cultural and intellectual horizon broadened to include Greek philosophy in the circle of conversation, but on the other hand, in the early second century BCE King Antiochus IV Epiphanes tried to destroy the Jewish tradition altogether and impose Hellenism. In this changed world, some representatives of the Jewish wisdom tradition began a creative dialogue with the Greek philosophical pursuit of wisdom, shaping a vibrant Hellenistic Jewish community that focused much attention on Sophia as the primary way to name the experience of God.[70] In response to the threats of Antiochus IV and other hostile pagan rulers, the apocalyptic tradition continued and developed the theology of holy war in a context of interreligious conflict and persecution. In apocalyptic writings, *Chokmah* or Sophia appears as an exclusive revelation from God, a mantic wisdom not of this world that is not available except through special divine intervention.[71] During this period, the wisdom trajectory from the Hebrew Bible intersected and merged in some respects with apocalyptic wisdom, so that a clear line cannot always be drawn between wisdom and apocalyptic.[72]

The book of Jesus ben Sira (commonly known as Sirach) was composed in Hebrew in the early second century BCE, when Hellenistic culture was dramatically reshaping the Mediterranean world and challenging the traditional values of Jews; but for centuries it was known only in its Greek translation, which was included in the Septuagint and the Catholic and Eastern Christian Bibles. To Jews

---

tian Imagination (Louisville, KY: Westminster John Knox Press, 2003).

[69] See Paul Ricoeur, *Figuring the Sacred: Religion, Narrative, and Imagination,* ed. Mark I. Wallace, trans. David Pellauer (Minneapolis: Fortress Press, 1995).

[70] John J. Collins, *Jewish Wisdom in the Hellenistic Age* (Louisville, KY: Westminster John Knox Press, 1997).

[71] John J. Collins, *Daniel: A Commentary on the Book of Daniel,* ed. Frank Moore Cross (Minneapolis: Fortress Press, 1993).

[72] John J. Collins, "Wisdom, Apocalypticism, and Generic Compatibility," in *In Search of Wisdom: Essays in Memory of John G. Gammie,* ed. Leo G. Perdue, Bernard Brandon Scott, and William Johnston Wiseman (Louisville, KY: Westminster John Knox Press, 1993), 165–85.

who were tempted to abandon their faith in favor of Hellenistic customs, Ben Sira presented the Torah as the manifestation of Sophia: Lady Wisdom, who rules the entire cosmos, dwells in Israel in the form of the Torah (Sir 24:1–9).[73] Ben Sira correlated Israel's specific experience of the Torah with the universal sway of Lady Wisdom: Sophia, the primeval world, order "pitches her tent" in Israel as the Torah.[74] This image provided Jews, and later Christians, with a way of affirming both the universal sway of Sophia and also her particular dwelling in Israel.

While Ben Sira insisted that loyal Jews need not become Greek to find Wisdom, he also praised the ideal scribe in what is likely a self-portrait: "He seeks out the wisdom of all the ancients, and is concerned with prophecies. . . . [H]e travels in foreign lands and learns what is good and evil in the human lot" (Sir 39:1, 4b). The reader may assume that this scribe pondered the wisdom found in the foreign proverbs of international courts and countries and incorporated these experiences and insights into his own reflections.[75] The journeys of Ben Sira's exemplary scribe invite further exploration of the wisdom of foreign countries in relation to the biblical tradition.

Over a century later, a sophisticated Jew writing in Alexandria between 50 BCE and 50 CE took up this challenge. Using the pseudonym of King Solomon, the author of the book known as the Wisdom of Solomon (called simply the Book of Wisdom in Catholic and Orthodox Bibles) employed Greek philosophical concepts to present Sophia as the dynamic presence of God in the world.[76] The Wisdom of Solomon opens with a call to the international rulers of the earth to love justice (1:1) and pursue Sophia.[77] David Winston comments, "The author is clearly addressing the pagan world-rulers. The fiction of Solomonic authorship requires that that renowned monarch address his pagan colleagues."[78]

According to the First Book of Kings, the newly enthroned Solomon had ardently pursued and prayed for Wisdom (1 Kgs 3:4–14; cf. Ws 7:7); in the Wisdom of Solomon the pseudonymous author recalls his quest for Sophia (7:7–10), celebrates his reception of her gifts (7:11–22), and shares Sophia's treasures with his readers from various religious traditions. The Wisdom of Solomon opens with a forceful command: "Love righteousness, you rulers of the earth," and it warns rulers who think they can get away with murder that the Spirit of God hears all things, and Wisdom will bring about justice (Ws 1:6–10). The tale of the persecu-

---

[73] Patrick W. Skehan and Alexander A. Di Lella, *The Wisdom of Ben Sira*, Anchor Bible 39 (New York: Doubleday, 1987), 40.

[74] John J. Collins, "The Biblical Precedent for Natural Theology," *Journal of the American Academy of Religion* 45, Suppl. (1977): 35–67; Gerhard von Rad, *Wisdom in Israel*, trans. James D. Martin (Nashville; Abingdon Press, 1972), 245–46.

[75] Skehan and Di Lella, *Wisdom of Ben Sira*, 46–47.

[76] Collins, *Jewish Wisdom*, 196–22; Perdue, *Wisdom Literature*, 267–324.

[77] David Winston, *The Wisdom of Solomon: A New Translation with Introduction and Commentary*, Anchor Bible 43 (Garden City, NY: Doubleday, 1979).

[78] Ibid., 101.

tion of the righteous man is presented as a parable against government corruption of all times and places (Ws 2:10–3:10).

The Wisdom of Solomon is nuanced in its attitude toward other gods. On the one hand, it clearly rejects the worship of idols (13:10–15:13), since the knowledge of God is available to all humanity through the beauty of creation (13:1–5); on the other the author judges that idolaters' blame is slight "for perhaps they go astray while seeking God and desiring to find him" (13:6). The Wisdom of Solomon fiercely critiques religious persecution, describing the just, wise man who is unjustly accused by pagan rulers and put to death, only to be vindicated in the final judgment beyond the grave, while the unrighteous will be humiliated and punished (Ws 2–5).

The Wisdom of Solomon employs the abstract language of Greek philosophy to develop and expand the understanding of Sophia. David Winston argues that the thought-world of the Wisdom of Solomon is Middle-Platonism, even though the author never mentions the Platonic doctrine of *anamnesis* (knowledge as recollection) or metempsychosis.[79] In this regard, there are very strong similarities between the Wisdom of Solomon and Philo of Alexandria (ca. 20 BCE–50 CE): both interpreted Sophia in light of Hellenistic philosophy, which was not simply a theory about the universe but was a religious practice and way of life. David Winston comments that the Wisdom of Solomon "implies that Sophia contains the paradigmatic patterns of all things (9:9; cf. 9:8), a basic principle in Philo's cosmology."[80] Furthermore, Winston notes that the Wisdom of Solomon and Philo

also have virtually identical theories of creation. God created the world out of primordial matter . . . , and Sophia, the agent of creation, pervades it through and through. . . . She is, however, both immanent and transcendent, and while pervading all things, yet remains in unbroken union with God.[81]

Philo sees philosophy as "devotion to wisdom" and views wisdom as "the knowledge of things divine and human and their causes."[82] Sophia, for Philo, is identical with both the Torah given through Moses and with the best of Greek philosophy.[83] Philo closely associates Logos and Sophia, using the terms Logos and Sophia almost interchangeably.[84] While many scholars have argued that Philo was dependent upon Middle Platonic philosophy,[85] Daniel Boyarin rejects this claim,

---

[79] Ibid., 28–29.

[80] Ibid., 59.

[81] Ibid., 60.

[82] David Winston, "Introduction," in *Philo of Alexandria, The Contemplative Life, the Giants, and Selections,* trans. David Winston (Mahwah, NJ: Paulist Press, 1981), 25.

[83] Ibid.

[84] David Winston, *Logos and Mystical Theology in Philo of Alexandria* (Cincinnati, OH: Hebrew Union College Press, 1985).

[85] John Dillon has demonstrated the dependence of Philo upon Middle Platonism:

stressing the originality of Philo and the role of the Bible in shaping his under-
standing of Logos, which includes Sophia in a synthesis of numerous elements;
Boyarin insists, "Notions of the second god as the personified Word or Wisdom
of God were present among Semitic-speaking Jews as well. This point is important
because it further disturbs the dichotomies that have been promulgated between
Hellenistic Judaism and rabbinic (by which is usually meant 'authentic,' 'really real')
Judaism."[86] Boyarin sees Philo's notion of Sophia/Logos as very similar to Justin
Martyr's notion of the Logos; Boyarin even affirms that Philo "is surely on a way that
leads to Nicaea and the controversies over the second person of the Trinity."[87]

Sophia was the gateway for Jews to dialogue with the religious philosophy of
the Hellenistic world. However, the modern view of philosophy as an academic
discipline practiced by intellectuals in universities is misleading for the Hellenistic
period. Pierre Hadot comments that in this period

> philosophy was a mode of existing-in-the-world, which had to be practiced
> at each instant, and the goal of which was to transform the whole of the
> individual's life. For the ancients, the mere word, *philo-sophia*—the love of
> wisdom—was enough to express this conception of philosophy. . . . For real
> wisdom does not merely cause us to know: it makes us "be" in a different
> way.[88]

For Jewish Hellenistic sages, as well as pagan philosophers, to follow Sophia
truly one must change one's life and follow a religious practice. Spiritual exercises
were essential to pursuing Sophia for Jews and pagan philosophers as well as later on
for Christians in antiquity.[89] Loving Sophia was not a merely theoretical endeavor but
demanded that one align one's life with the patterns of God embedded in the universe.
The encounter of Jews with Middle Platonic, Stoic, and Pythagorean thought was
a religious event; the synthesis of Judaism and Hellenism that emerged would shape
Christian understanding of Sophia for centuries. Hellenistic Judaism was an extremely
influential matrix for early Christian reflection on Sophia in dialogue with Hellenistic
thought. Sophia and the closely related term, Logos, would be central to Hellenistic
Jewish theology, to early Christian thought on the Trinity, and to the eventual
differentiation of rabbinic Judaism and orthodox Christianity.

To note similarities is not to claim that the different traditions are saying the
same thing. There are profound differences in the cosmologies and anthropologies

---

The Middle Platonists: 80 B.C. to 220 A.D. (Ithaca, NY: Cornell University Press, 1977),
139–83. See also Winston, *Philo of Alexandria*, 1–37. Perdue adds influences on Philo from
Stoicism, mysticism, and Pythagorean numerology as well. Perdue, *Wisdom Literature,* 279.

[86] Boyarin, *Border Lines*, 115, 116.

[87] Ibid., 114.

[88] Pierre Hadot, *Philosophy as a Way of Life: Spiritual Exercises from Socrates to
Foucault,* ed. Arnold I. Davidson, trans. Michael Chase (Oxford: Blackwell, 1995), 265.

[89] Ibid., 126–44.

of the world's wisdom traditions, but they share a focus on healing the unnecessary suffering of the human condition by integrating humans into the order of the universe. The Hellenistic philosophy from which Hellenistic Jews and early Christians drew so heavily offered what Martha Nussbaum has called a "therapy of desire,"[90] a description that could also be applied to the teachings of Shakyamuni Buddha or Confucius. Like the Buddha, Hellenistic philosophers and early church fathers saw their reflections as a form of medicine, a therapy that had to be adapted to various illnesses.[91] The early church father Gregory of Nyssa similarly sought to adapt the therapy of Jesus Christ to the particular form of disease of the audience.[92] In their search for wisdom, Hellenistic Jews and Christians pondered and learned from the teachings of Greek philosophers, whose worldview differed in significant ways from their own. For Christians to reflect on Sophia in an interreligious context is to continue this age-old conversation on wisdom as a practical form of healing.

Interpreting Wisdom as a Point of Contact with Other Religious Traditions

There is no one understanding of the figure of personified Wisdom in the biblical or the later Christian traditions. Most early church writers identified Sophia with the Logos, the Son of God (Athenagoras, *Supplication for the Christians* 10.2; Hippolytus, *On Heresies* 6.14.3; Origen, *On First Principles* 1.2.1–2).[93] Not all early Christian writers accepted this identification, however, because the Spirit is also closely identified with Wisdom in the Wisdom of Solomon. Irenaeus of Lyons followed this lead and identified Sophia with the Holy Spirit (*Against the Heresies* 4.20.3). In the Trinitarian debates of the fourth century, many, including both Arius and Athanasius of Alexandria, identified Sophia with the Second Person of the Trinity. However, Sophia could also be identified with the essence of God, the divine *ousia,* and thus with each of the divine hypostases. Thus, Augustine could on the one hand identify Wisdom (Sapientia) as the Logos (*On the Trinity* 4.5.27), while on the other hand, he could also view the Father as Wisdom and the Son and the Holy Spirit as each being "Wisdom from Wisdom" (*On the Trinity* 7.1.2; 15.7.12).[94] Augustine and later Latin medieval theologians, especially the mystical writers, continued the biblical wisdom tradition, reflecting at length on *sapientia,*

---

[90] Martha Nussbaum, *The Therapy of Desire: Theory and Practice in Hellenistic Ethics* (Princeton, NJ: Princeton University Press, 1994).

[91] Ibid., 87.

[92] Hans Dieter Betz, *The Sermon on the Mount: A Commentary on the Sermon on the Mount, Including the Sermon on the Plain (Matthew 5:3–7:27 and Luke 6:20–49),* ed. Adela Yarbro Collins (Minneapolis: Fortress Press, 1995), 87.

[93] Lewis Ayres, *Nicaea and Its Legacy: An Approach to Fourth-Century Trinitarian Theology* (Oxford: Oxford University Press, 2009), 23–25.

[94] Ibid., 377–79.

the Latin translation of the term. Augustine focused especially on the concrete horizon of the mind, whether corrupted by sin or illumined by divine Wisdom.

The interpretation of wisdom and the universe in light of Logos or Sophia in Christology and Christian Trinitarian theology may appear to be a barrier to dialogue with other religious traditions precisely because of the strong claims it makes for the Christian understanding of Sophia in Jesus Christ and in the Holy Spirit. If we look to other religions for an exact parallel to the place of Wisdom in Christian Trinitarian discourse, we will of course be disappointed. However, if we view Wisdom as God's loving presence and our transformation in it, and if we accept the biblical testimony to the universal embrace of Wisdom, we should not be surprised to find analogies to her in other religious traditions. The Russian Sophiologist, Vladimir Solovyov, believed that Sophia guided a wide variety of religious traditions through mystical experiences;[95] Raimon Panikkar assumed Wisdom was active in all religious traditions.[96]

Biblical wisdom played a major role in the Jewish and Christian mystical traditions, often being interpreted in light of Neoplatonic perspectives that were influential in other traditions as well.[97] Frequently, the mystical trajectories of different religions share analogous concerns and hermeneutical strategies while remaining very divergent in other respects.

The book of Proverbs warns that those who think they are wise have even less hope than fools (Prv 26:12). We have seen that Paul acknowledges that he knows only imperfectly (1 Cor 13:12). Christians can interpret the Bible in relation to other religions in light of the tradition of the openness of the wisdom tradition and the humility of apophatic theology, acknowledging, with Nicholas of Cusa, that our knowledge of God is at best a "learned ignorance,"[98] and recognizing, with Thomas Aquinas, that our supreme knowledge of God is that we do not know God insofar as we know that what God is surpasses all we can possibly understand.[99] The biblical wisdom tradition flowed into the later Christian mystical tradition, which insisted that words are inadequate to describe the immediate experience of God. The biblical trajectory of sapiential dialogue continues into the present. Even though Christian encounters with other religions in later periods were frequently inspired by the perspectives of the holy war, nonetheless, the ideal of dialogue based upon the sapiential trajectory offers possibilities for the future.

---

[95] Judith Deutsch Kornblatt, *Divine Sophia: The Wisdom Writings of Vladimir Solovyov* (Ithaca, NY: Cornell University Press, 2009), 86.

[96] Raimon Panikkar, *A Dwelling Pace for Wisdom*, trans. Annemarie S. Kidder (Louisville, KY: Westminster John Knox Press, 1993), 2.

[97] Michael A. Sells, *Mystical Languages of Unsaying* (Chicago: University of Chicago Press, 1994).

[98] Nicholas of Cusa, *Selected Spiritual Writings*, trans. H. Lawrence Bond (New York: Paulist Press, 1997), 85–206.

[99] Thomas Aquinas, *De Potentia* 7.5; see Karl Rahner, "Thomas Aquinas on the Incomprehensibility of God," *Journal of Religion* 58, Suppl. (1978): S107–125.

Interpreting Difference: Paul Ricoeur

Different religious traditions seek wisdom, but they do so in radically different contexts and horizons. The profound differences among the traditions, however, need not be a barrier to conversation but can serve as an invitation to further exploration and dialogue.

Paul Ricoeur hoped that differences can be productive by stimulating awareness of different aspects of experience previously unnoticed:

> For what would be the use of comparative religion if it did not aim at producing an echo in the midst of our own experience, and if, at the price of some painful tensions and conflicts, it did not enlarge our own self-understanding, by contrasting what we understand with what we do not understand of the religions of the others?[100]

The work of Paul Ricoeur offers helpful resources for analyzing the dynamics of language in various religious traditions that differ. Ricoeur understands religious language as referring to limit-experiences of human existence. Religious language, like poetic language, has the power to redescribe human experience through what Ricoeur, following Ian Ramsey, calls a "disclosure model" of language. A disclosure model, according to Ricoeur, employs the sequence "orient—disorient—reorient," without ever perhaps allowing us to make a 'whole,' a system of our experience."[101] Such a model views truth not as adequate correspondence to external reality but as manifestation. A religious text opens up visions of possible ways of being in the world. Ricoeur calls this vision of new possibilities "the world of the text."[102] This world is a metamorphosis of the world of everyday reality, a redescription of the possibilities of human existence.

Ricoeur notes that in an age of suspicion, there is no direct way to explain the human subject. Our immediate self-understanding is suspect, and we can only find a more appropriate self-understanding through the interpretation of language and actions. Silence itself demands interpretation, for genuine silence must be understood in relation to the words that precede it and that it envelops. Otherwise, we have no way of distinguishing the silence of the wise from that of fools.

While Christian and other religions' perspectives on wisdom and ultimate reality are clearly different, even to describe the difference is to establish a relationship between the differing perspectives. Viewing religious perspectives on wisdom not as objective descriptions of external reality as but as redescriptions of the

---

[100] Paul Ricoeur, "The History of Religions and the Phenomenology of Time Consciousness," in *The History of Religions: Retrospect and Prospect,* ed. Joseph M. Kitagawa (New York: Macmillan/London: Collier Macmillan, 1985), 28–29.

[101] Paul Ricoeur, "Biblical Hermeneutics," *Semeia* 4 (1975): 126.

[102] Ricoeur, *Figuring the Sacred,* 41–47.

possibilities of human existence invites a genuine conversation among all seekers. In settings that are systemically distorted by bias and prejudice and long-standing oppressive practices, redescriptions of the possibilities of human existence are among the most precious gifts we can receive from our religious traditions.

Aware of the limitations of all claims of religious knowledge, Christians can interpret the Bible while remaining open to wisdom coming from other sources. In different ways, Jesus Christ and many other traditions propose humble paths that renounce the quest for domination through the power of knowledge and teach paths of wisdom and compassion that can transform life for the better. In a world of massive, unjust, and unnecessary suffering that threatens the entire community of life, Jesus Christ and the teachers of many other religious traditions come as physicians offering healing and wisdom.

10

THE HOLY SPIRIT IN
INTERRELIGIOUS PERSPECTIVE

Christian belief in the Holy Spirit emerged from descriptions of the Spirit of God in the First Testament of the Bible, received decisive points of orientation in the concrete images of the Spirit in the New Testament, and became the focus of theological reflection in the early Church in figures such as Basil of Caesarea. Irenaeus of Lyons viewed the Holy Spirit as identical with the biblical figure of personified Wisdom or Sophia: "But that Wisdom, which is the Spirit, was with him [God the Father] before all creation, it says through Solomon: 'God by Wisdom founded the earth, he prepared the heaven by understanding; by his knowledge the abysses burst forth, and the clouds dropped down the dew' (Prov 3:19–20)."[1] Biblical attention to the work of Wisdom in other religions offers support for a broad view of the activity of the Holy Spirit in other religious traditions.

Catholic faith in the Holy Spirit offers both an important contrast and also a variety of points of contact with other religious traditions. After a history that often neglected the role of the Holy Spirit, recent Catholic understandings of the Holy Spirit in the United States and elsewhere have gone through significant developments in light of interreligious discussions. Traditionally, Catholic theologians emphasized the supernatural action of the Holy Spirit guiding the Catholic Church; they usually rejected claims of spiritual guidance or inspiration outside of the Christian community, or sometimes even in Christian communities other than their own. In Catholic theology the Magisterium claimed the role of interpreting the work of the Holy Spirit; often Catholic leaders viewed anything contrary to the Magisterium's directives as a rejection of the Holy Spirit. For the most part, there was little or no attention to the life-giving, salvific work of the Holy Spirit in other religious traditions and even in other Christian communities.

The transformation of Catholic attitudes and actions in relation to other religions has profound implications for the interpretation of the activity of the Holy Spirit. In *Gaudium et Spes*,[2] the Second Vatican Council affirmed that the Holy

---

[1] Irenaeus of Lyons, *Against the Heresies* 4.20.3; Robert M. Grant, *Irenaeus of Lyons* (London: Routledge, 1997), 151.

[2] Pope Paul VI, *Gaudium et Spes,* Pastoral Constitution on the Church in the Modern World, December 7, 1965.

Spirit is active in all human life, offering salvation to everyone (#22). *Nostra Aetate*[3] affirmed that the Catholic Church rejects nothing that is true and holy in other religions; while Catholics had long recognized the possibility of a partial, natural knowledge of God for all people, *Nostra Aetate* implies that there is holiness, which is the fruit of the supernatural gift of grace, of God's loving presence and human transformation in it (#2).

In his first encyclical, *Redemptor Hominis,* John Paul II affirmed that religious belief in traditions other than Christianity is the work of the Holy Spirit: "Does it not sometimes happen that the firm belief of the followers of the non-Christian religions—a belief that is also an effect of the Spirit of truth operating outside the visible confines of the Mystical Body [*quae et ipsa procedit a Spiritu veritatis, extra fines aspectabiles Corporis mystici operante*]—can make Christians ashamed at being themselves so often disposed to doubt?"[4] John Paul II affirmed the universal presence of the Holy Spirit inspiring authentic prayers in followers of other religious paths. In his encyclical on the Holy Spirit, he writes,

> We cannot limit ourselves to the two thousand years which have passed since the birth of Christ. We *need to go further back,* to embrace the whole of the action of the Holy Spirit even before Christ—*from the beginning,* throughout the world, and especially in the economy of the Old Covenant. For this action has been exercised, in every place and every time, indeed in every individual, according to the eternal plan of salvation. . . Grace, therefore, bears within itself both a Christological aspect and a pneumatological one.[5]

John Paul II continued: "The Spirit, therefore, is at the very source of man's existential and religious questioning, a questioning which is occasioned not only by contingent situations but by the very structure of his being."[6] According to Pope Francis, the Holy Spirit whom Christians experience in Jesus Christ can nurture and shape the lives of followers of other religious paths as well. Christians do not have a monopoly on grace and can learn from other traditions: "The same Spirit everywhere brings forth various forms of practical wisdom which help people to bear suffering and to live in greater peace and harmony. As Christians, we can also benefit from these treasures built up over many centuries, which can help us better to live our own beliefs."[7]

From the perspective of study of ancient Egypt, Jan Assmann comments on words in various languages relating to the English word "spirit": "As far as the

---

[3] Pope Paul VI, *Nostra Aetate,* Declaration on the Relation of the Church to Non-Christian Religions, October 28, 1965.

[4] Pope John Paul II, *Redemptor Hominis,* March 4, 1979, #6.

[5] Pope John Paul II, *Dominum et Vivificante,* May 18, 1986, #53.

[6] Pope John Paul II, *Redemptoris Missio,* December 7, 1990, #54.

[7] Pope Francis, *Evangelii Gaudium,* November 24, 2013, #254.

Western part of the Axial hemisphere is concerned, the concept of *Geist* (*ruach,*
neshamah, pneuma, logos, nous, psyche, animus, spiritus) plays in fact an enor-
mous and ever-increasing role in the cultural texts of the ancient, especially (neo-)
Platonic, Jewish, Christian, and, above all, Gnostic worlds."[8]

Catholics and other Christians today are challenged to discern the working of
the Holy Spirit in all human life, with particular attention to other religious traditions. While the ontological beliefs often differ in profound ways, the working of
the Holy Spirit in Christian life often bears analogies to the movement of the Spirit
of God or spirits in other religious traditions. The descriptions of the Spirit found
in the Bible can serve as a point of orientation for Christians approaching other religions. The Spirit of God demands justice, condemns oppression. The Spirit of God
empowers people to pray. The Spirit blows where it will. Where these signs appear,
Christians can trust that the Spirit of God is at work.

Traditional Catholic theology distinguished the immanent Trinity from the
economic Trinity. The immanent Trinity consists of the internal, eternal relationships, which are the divine persons; the economic Trinity involves the activity of
the divine persons in the world, creating, redeeming, sanctifying, and leading to
ultimate fulfillment. Discussions of the economic Trinity concern the activities
of the divine persons with regard to creation and the salvific missions of the Holy
Spirit and the Word to heal, elevate, and unite humans and all creation to God. In
the economic Trinity, the Spirit is the driving force in creation, in redemption, in
sanctification, in transforming human life, and in opening up hope in seemingly
hopeless situations. Regarding the immanent Trinity, there is a long-standing debate
between the Byzantine Orthodox tradition and Catholic traditions over how to
view the procession of the Holy Spirit. The Catholic and Byzantine Orthodox
traditions insist on appropriate language to describe the relationships in the Trinity,
but they also maintain the incomprehensibility of the Trinity. The words are not
literal descriptions but pointers to a mystery that invites us to a process of transformation that we cannot define but that we can display in a way of life.

While there are triads in various religious traditions, no other religion has a
precise equivalent to the doctrine of the immanent Trinity of traditional Christianity. In exploring analogies in other religious traditions, my focus will be on
analogies in other religions to the movement of the Holy Spirit in shaping and
reshaping the created world. Catholics may be able to learn more about the movement of God in other people's lives by listening to their witness.

Biblical Images

The Hebrew Bible presents the Spirit (*ruach*) of God in various manifestations. In Hebrew, *ruach* refers to air in motion, including both breath and wind.

---

[8] Jan Assmann, "Cultural Memory and the Myth of the Axial Age," in *The Axial Age
and Its Consequences,* ed. Robert N. Bellah and Hans Joas (Cambridge, MA: Belknap Press
of Harvard University Press, 2012), 373.

Ruach is also the word used to describe the unpredictable power of God moving in creation and transforming human life. The Greek word *pneuma* also refers to air in motion and was used to translate the Hebrew *ruach*. Similarly, in Latin, *spiritus* denotes air in motion and was used to translate both *ruach* and *pneuma*. The book of Genesis describes *ruach*, the wind or Spirit of God, shaping creation from the beginning (1:2) and giving life to the first human (2:7). In the book of Numbers, the Spirit of God comes upon Joshua (27:18); and in the book of Judges, the Spirit of God comes upon Othniel (3:10), Gideon (6:34), and Samson (13:25, 14:6), empowering them for leadership. The Spirit seizes Saul (1 Sm 10:10), though it later departs from him (1 Sm 16:14). The prophet Isaiah describes the characteristics that the Spirit of the Lord will bestow upon the hoped-for just ruler or Messiah, associating the Spirit of God with wisdom: "The spirit of the Lord shall rest on him, the spirit of wisdom and understanding" (Is 11:2). In time, Catholics would interpret these as the seven gifts of the Holy Spirit: wisdom, understanding, counsel, fortitude, knowledge, piety, and fear of the Lord. The later sections of the book of Isaiah describe the Spirit of God inspiring people with a prophetic mission (Is 42:1, 61:1, 63:10, 11). Ezekiel describes the Spirit entering him and preparing him to hear the word of God (Ez 2:2). In the Psalms, the Spirit of God gives life (Ps 104:30) and inspires holiness (Ps 143:10). According to the prophet Joel, God promises to send the Spirit on all human beings so that they may prophesy (Jl 3:1). Like Isaiah, 1 Enoch also relates wisdom to the spirit in describing the Chosen One: "And in him dwell the spirit of wisdom and the spirit of insight" (49:3).[9]

The Wisdom of Solomon relates Wisdom (Sophia) very closely to Spirit (*pneuma*) and probably identifies them.[10] The immortal Spirit of God is in everything (Ws 12:1) and is what holds all things together and serves as the ultimate accountability for human rulers tempted to abuse power: "For wisdom is a kindly spirit, but will not free blasphemers from the guilt of their words. . . . Because the spirit of the Lord has filled the world. And that which holds all things together (*to synekon ta panta*) knows what is said" (Ws 1:6, 7). In this context personified Wisdom is intimate with God and manifests God in the world; she guides all creation and orders all things in number, measure, and weight (Ws 11:20). In chapters 10–12 the Wisdom of Solomon presents the universal activity of Wisdom to a Hellenistic audience by retelling the formative historical events of ancient Israel without mentioning any proper names. At first the text presents Wisdom as leading the people out of slavery, but then shifts to speaking directly to God with no apparent change in referent (Ws 11:26, 12:2). Wisdom appears to be the way God relates to the world.[11] The stories of divine guidance in the Torah illustrate the presence of Wisdom throughout human life and the cosmos.

---

[9] George W. E. Nickelsburg and James C. VanderKam, *1 Enoch: A New Translation Based on the Hermeneia Commentary* (Minneapolis: Fortress Press, 2004), 63.

[10] David Winston, *The Wisdom of Solomon: A New Translation with Introduction and Commentary,* Anchor Bible (Garden City, NY: Doubleday, 1979), 99–100.

[11] Ibid., 226.

The New Testament presents numerous descriptions of the Holy Spirit transforming people's lives. The Apostle Paul describes the work of the Spirit as building up the community and endowing different people with varying gifts (1 Cor 12:4–13); the fruit of the Spirit for Paul is "love, joy, peace, patience, kindness, generosity, faithfulness, gentleness, and self-control" (Gal 5:22). Paul views the Spirit as a pledge given by God to support us in times of difficulty (2 Cor 5:5), and he proclaims that the Spirit of God who raised Jesus from the dead is at work in the followers of Jesus (Rom 8:11), pouring the love of God into our hearts (Rom 5:5). Paul trusts that all who accept guidance from the Spirit are children of God (Rom 8:14). Paul describes all creation as groaning and subjected to futility because of human sin and hopes for liberation coming through the Spirit and believes that followers of Jesus already enjoy the first fruits of the Spirit (Rom 8:19–24). He acknowledges that we do not know how to pray properly but is confident that the Spirit intercedes for us in groans without words (Rom 8:26). Noting that some have seen the experience of the Holy Spirit as a unifying thread that unites the diverse books of the New Testament, Robert Morgan comments that Christians reading the New Testament

> will learn that the Spirit is from God and that God is Spirit. The fourth-century church was to argue about the divinity of the Holy Spirit and the shape of trinitarian theology, but such arguments are not found in the New Testament. Its writers inherited spirit-language from their mainly Jewish tradition and interpreted their own and their co-religionists' experience in the light of biblical prophecies.[12]

In the synoptic Gospels, Jesus warns that those who blaspheme against the Holy Spirit will not be forgiven (Mk 3:29; Mt 12:31–32; Lk 12:10). In the Gospel of Mark, Jesus promises that the Holy Spirit will speak through the disciples when they are placed on trial (Mk 13:11). However, the Bible warns that not all spirits are from God, and in the Gospel of Matthew, Jesus advises his followers that they can discern good and bad religious practitioners by their fruits (7:16).

In the Gospel of Luke, the Holy Spirit comes upon Mary in the Incarnation (1:35) and has a special relationship to her. When Mary encounters Elizabeth, the Holy Spirit fills Elizabeth so that she can pronounce Mary blessed (Lk 1:41). According to Luke, the Holy Spirit descends upon Jesus at his baptism in the form of a dove (3:22), leads Jesus into the desert where he is tempted (4:1–2), and then accompanies him back to Galilee (4:14). In Luke, Jesus launches his public ministry in the synagogue in Nazareth by reading from the prophet Isaiah about the Spirit of the Lord coming upon him to proclaim a year of favor from the Lord (Lk 4:17–21);

---

[12] Robert Morgan, "Unity and Diversity in New Testament Talk of the Spirit," in *The Holy Spirit and Christian Origins: Essays in Honor of James D. G. Dunn*, ed. Graham N. Stanton, Bruce W. Longenecker, and Stephen C. Barton (Grand Rapids, MI: Eerdmans, 2004), 12.

this quotation from Isaiah frames the vocation of Jesus in light of a strong message of social justice, proclaiming liberty to captives.

The Acts of the Apostles begins with a brief reflection on Jesus's ministry as inspired by the Holy Spirit and the Risen Lord Jesus's promise that his followers will receive the power of the Holy Spirit so they can be witnesses to him (1:2–8). The Holy Spirit then comes upon the small group of followers of Jesus in Jerusalem with the sound of loud wind; the Spirit gives them courage and energy to proclaim good news at the risk of imprisonment or death; and Peter proclaims the resurrection of the Christ and the promise of God to send the Spirit (Acts 2:1–38). Throughout the narrative, when followers of Jesus meet obstacles, the Spirit offers them tremendous resilience. The Spirit comes upon the deacon Stephen as he is dying, allowing him to see the glory of God and Jesus at the right hand of God (Acts 7:55). The disciples pray and lay hands upon people who have been baptized so that they may receive the Holy Spirit (Acts 8:12–17, 19:6). The Spirit opens up new possibilities and shapes new relationships, bidding Philip to meet the Ethiopian court official and explain a scripture passage to him (Acts 8:29–39). When Peter preaches to the Roman centurion Cornelius and other Gentiles, the Holy Spirit comes upon his listeners, to the amazement of his Jewish followers (Acts 10:44–45, 11:15).

In the Gospel of John, Jesus tells Nicodemus that the Spirit blows where it will and brings people to a new birth (Jn 3:5–8). At the Last Supper, Jesus prays that the Father will send his disciples another Paraclete who is described as the Spirit of truth (Jn 14:16–17). A little later he promises that the Father will send the Paraclete, the Holy Spirit, who will teach the disciples everything they need to know (Jn 14:26, 15:26). The Spirit is usually identified with the Paraclete, the advocate or defense attorney. Jesus promises that the Spirit of truth will guide the disciples to complete truth and will glorify Jesus (Jn 16:13).

The First Letter of John advises: "Beloved, do not believe every spirit, but test the spirits to see whether they are from God; for many false prophets have gone out into the world" (1 Jn 4:16). The Letter of John then presents various criteria for discerning the Spirit, and the Letter can be interpreted in different ways. On the one hand, 1 John presents confessing Jesus in the flesh as the criterion for knowing the true Spirit of God (4:2–3); any spirit failing to acknowledge Jesus as coming from God is the spirit of Antichrist (4:3). This could be interpreted as restricting the Spirit to those who explicitly confess Jesus as Lord, and there is a long history of Catholics and other Christians viewing Jews and Muslims as allies of the Antichrist.[13] On the other hand, the First Letter of John affirms that God is love and that anyone who loves is of God: "God is love, and whoever abides in love abides in God, and God abides in them" (4:16). Love of God is demonstrated practically in love of one's sibling (1 Jn 4:20–21). This could establish a broader interpretation of the Spirit as present wherever love is found. R. W. L. Moberly comments on the perspective of the author of the Letter: "His point is that the visible and

---

[13] Bernard McGinn, *Antichrist: Two Thousand Years of Fascination with Evil* (New York: Columbia University Press, 2000).

accessible (and 'moral') practice of love for brother (and, no doubt, sister) is what enables one to rebut, or confirm, claims to knowledge/love with regard to the invisible and otherwise inaccessible ('spiritual') reality of God."[14] The ambiguity of the text allows opposite conclusions to be drawn from it, with some claiming that only those with the correct view of Jesus can truly love, and others concluding that all those who truly love are inspired by the Spirit and thus are one with God, whether they verbally confess Jesus in the flesh or not.

The Spirit in Theological Reflection

Christians reflecting on these passages came to see the Holy Spirit as offering the power of transformation in their lives, the driving force in creation, redemption, and sanctification. The Holy Spirit condemns injustice but also offers comfort in times of distress. When we come to an impasse and find ourselves in hopeless situations, the Spirit appears with new energy to open up new possibilities.

The activities of the Holy Spirit in Christian theology overlap with those of personified Wisdom in the biblical tradition. Irenaeus of Lyons viewed the Holy Spirit as identical with Sophia (*Against the Heresies* 4.20.3). Basil the Great wrote the first major treatise on the Holy Spirit, focusing primarily on the economic role of the Trinity in salvation, especially in baptism.[15] Basil sees the human dilemma as fundamentally caused by ignorance and thus stresses the role of the Spirit in granting wisdom. As Stephen Hildebrand comments, "So for Basil, salvation is a salvation from sin unto righteousness but only as a corollary and prerequisite to salvation from ignorance unto wisdom."[16] In baptism, water brings about death, and the Spirit gives life and light in Christ. Basil compares the Holy Spirit to light; we do not see light itself but see all things in the light: "When a sunbeam falls on a transparent substance, the substance itself becomes brilliant, and radiates light from itself. So too Spirit-bearing souls, illumined by Him, finally become spiritual themselves, and their grace is sent forth to others."[17] Basil elaborates: "To worship in the Spirit implies that our intelligence has been enlightened."[18] Theologically, the Spirit offers the illumination that allows believers to see Jesus Christ as the revelation of the glory of God the Father. Basil sees the activity of the Holy Spirit as universal: "In the same way the Spirit is given to each one who receives Him as if He were the possession of that person alone, yet He sends forth sufficient grace to fill all

---

[14] R. W. L. Moberly, "'Test the Spirits': God, Love, and Critical Discernment in 1 John 4," in Stanton, Longenecker, and Barton, *The Holy Spirit and Christian Origins*, 305.

[15] Basil the Great, *On the Holy Spirit*, translated by Stephen Hildebrand (Yonkers, NY: St. Vladimir's Press, 2011).

[16] Stephen Hildebrand, *The Trinitarian Theology of Basil of Caesarea: A Synthesis of Greek Thought and Biblical Truth* (Washington, DC: Catholic University of America Press, 2011), 175.

[17] Basil, *On the Holy Spirit*, 44.

[18] Ibid., 97.

the universe."[19] Basil emphasizes the incomprehensibility of God: "The supreme eminence of the Father is inconceivable; thought and reflection are utterly unable to penetrate the begetting of the Lord."[20] Basil distinguishes between the incomprehensible nature of God and the divine energies which affect all creation: "These titles do not describe His nature, but, as I have already said, are concerned with his manifold energies, by which He satisfies the needs of each in His tenderheartedness to His own creation."[21] The implication of Basil's description is that the Holy Spirit is always present throughout all creation, but we have no adequate way to describe the Holy Spirit in concepts or images. Nonetheless, we can reflect on the effects of the Holy Spirit in human life and the cosmos as a whole.

Gifts of the Spirit

The gifts of the Holy Spirit are the manifestations of the power of the Spirit transforming human life. Interpreting the text of Isaiah 1:2, Augustine of Hippo correlates the gifts of the Holy Spirit mentioned by Isaiah with the Beatitudes taught by Jesus in the Gospel of Matthew. Augustine sees Isaiah as beginning from the highest stage (wisdom) and Jesus as beginning from the lowest (poverty of spirit). Augustine then proposes a series of correspondences between the two lists: humility and fear of the Lord (which is the beginning of wisdom) correspond to poverty of spirit; piety corresponds to meekness; knowledge corresponds to mourning (Augustine notes that the Spirit as Paraclete comforts those who mourn); fortitude corresponds to hunger and thirst for justice; counsel corresponds to being merciful; understanding corresponds to being pure of heart; and wisdom corresponds to peacemaking.[22]

Thomas Aquinas views the Spirit as love and gift and interprets the work of the Spirit as seeking a good that does not yet exist.[23] Aquinas views the gifts of the Holy Spirit as coming from the direct impetus of the Spirit, and so they are ways we experience the movement of the Spirit from within.[24] Aquinas relates the seven gifts to the principal virtues: wisdom relates to charity; understanding and knowledge relate to faith; counsel relates to prudence; fortitude relates to courage; fear of the Lord relates to hope and can also express itself in temperance; piety or reverence relates to justice.

In his Apostolic Exhortation *Gaudete et Exsultate,* Pope Francis develops the thought of Aquinas by stressing the Holy Spirit's gift of joy: "The Christian life is 'joy in the Holy Spirit' (Rom 14:7)," for "the necessary result of the love of charity is

---

[19] Ibid., 43–44.

[20] Ibid., 30.

[21] Ibid., 35.

[22] Augustine, *On the Sermon on the Mount,* ed. and trans. Denis J. Kavanagh (Washington, DC: Catholic University of America Press, 2010), 1:27–30.

[23] Thomas Aquinas, *Summa Theologiae* 1.36, 1.37.

[24] Ibid., 1–2:68.1.

joy; since every lover rejoices at being united to the beloved . . . the effect of charity is joy."[25] Francis reiterates the point: "The path of holiness is a path of peace and joy, given to us by the Spirit. At the same time it demands that we 'keep our lamps lit' (Lk 12:35) and be attentive."[26]

In medieval Roman Catholic theology the word *spiritus* could refer to the deepest point of the human person, the point of contact that opens to the divine; it could also refer to the Holy Spirit, the power of God moving within the person, overcoming sin, healing wounds, and uniting to God in an intimate union. While other religious traditions do not have doctrines of the immanent Trinity, they do frequently describe the movement of the divine power within and among humans, overcoming resistance and inviting to union.

The Spirit among American Indians

Although there is no precise equivalent to Christian Trinitarian theology among American Indian religions, nonetheless images of spiritual agents pervade Native religious life and spirituality, and various indigenous words, including "Wakan Tanka" and "Gitche Manitou," have been translated as "Spirit" or "Great Spirit" in English.[27] Manitou is a life force pervading the universe, and some traditions describe the Great Spirit as creating men and women and other creatures.[28] From the time of early contacts with Europeans, Christians noted similarities.[29] A seventeenth-century Jesuit missionary to Illinois, Claude Allouez, commented that Illinois Indians "honor our Lord in their own way," though Christopher Bilodeau points out that later scholars have understood this claim in directly conflicting ways; some think that the Jesuits completely misunderstood the indigenous people, others that there was a relatively smooth process of conversion.[30] Bilodeau goes on to comment that manitou "meant, in various contexts, 'power,' 'mystery,' and 'medicine,' but its most important definition to the Illinois religion was 'spirit.'"[31]

---

[25] Pope Francis, *Gaudete et Exsultate,* March 19, 2018, #122; Pope Francis is quoting Thomas Aquinas, *Summa Theologiae* 1–2.70.3.

[26] Pope Francis, *Gaudete et Exsultate* #164.

[27] For a critical reflection on the process of translation in the nineteenth century, see J. H. Trumbull, "On the Algonkin Name 'Manit' (or 'Manitou') Sometimes Translated as 'Great Spirit' and 'God,'" *Old and New,* 1, no. 3 (March, 1870): 337–42.

[28] John C. Wright, *The Crooked Tree: Indian Legends of Northern Michigan* (1917; reprint, San Diego, CA: Thunder Bay Press, 1996), 131–32.

[29] R. Murray Thomas, *Manitou and God: North-American Indian Religions and Christian Culture* (Westport, CT: Praeger, 2007).

[30] Christopher Bilodeau, "'They Honor Our Lord among Themselves in Their Own Way': Colonial Christianity and the Illinois Indians," *American Indian Quarterly* 25, no. 3 (2001): 352–77.

[31] Ibid., 356.

While some missionaries found nothing good in Indian religious practices, others emphasized positive and promising points of contact with Christian faith. In violation of the First Amendment of the U.S. Constitution, European American Christian leaders in some settings refused to see anything of the Holy Spirit in Native religious practices, forbade the practice of traditional Indian religion, and instituted Christianity as a form of state religion. As Charles Trimble comments about the post–Civil War period:

> To the well-meaning "reformers" who held great influence over the formation of Indian policy following the Civil War, "civilizing" the Indians demanded that they be brought into Christianity and that their pagan beliefs and practices be destroyed. Thus Christianity became the state religion as it applied to the tribes, and a zero tolerance became official policy as it applied to Native religions.[32]

As we have seen, according to the Wisdom of Solomon, the Spirit holds all things together (1:7); in Christian theology the Holy Spirit pervades creation, giving life and breath and creativity. Joseph Epes Brown articulates the Lakota worldview as resonating with the Christian vision of the Spirit:

> The Lakota have a wide base of pragmatic knowledge about how to utilize animals. Yet deeply interrelated with the pragmatic dimension is an inner world of belief and values derived from the animals that gives overall meaning and cohesion to society. The presence of the Great Mysterious is within every being, and even the smallest being, a little ant, for example, can communicate something of the Great Mystery.[33]

Brown also cites the testimony of Siya'ka of the Teton Lakota people on relying on Wakan Tanka:

> All classes of people know that when human power fails they must look for a higher power for fulfillment of their desires. No man can succeed in life alone, and he cannot get the help he needs from men; therefore he seeks help through some bird or animal which Wakan Tanka sends for his assistance.[34]

---

[32] Charles Trimble, "Introduction," in Esther Black Elk DeSersa, Olivia Black Elk Pourier, Aaron DeSersa Jr., and Clifton DeSersa, *Black Elk Lives: Conversations with the Black Elk Family,* ed. Hilda Neihardt and Lori Utecht (Lincoln: University of Nebraska Press, 2000), xiv.

[33] Joseph Epes Brown with Emily Cousins, *Teaching Spirits: Understanding Native American Religious Traditions* (Oxford: Oxford University Press, 2001), 71.

[34] Frances Densmore, "Teton Sioux Music," *Bureau of American Ethnology Bulletin* 61

We have seen that Nicholas Black Elk served as a Catholic catechist while continuing Native religious practices. Joseph Epes Brown listened to Nicholas Black Elk, hoping to hear metaphysical teachings, but his mentor continually spoke about animals and birds, the winds and the four directions. Brown finally realized that Black Elk was speaking about ultimate reality in terms of direct, immediate experience, without dichotomies between the natural and the supernatural. Brown recalled Black Elk praying, "Wakan-Tanka, you are everything and above everything."[35] Reflecting on the Native sense of the relatedness of all realities, Brown comments: "For most Native American culture, the relatedness is rooted in the perception of a shared spiritual reality that transcends physical differences. Some believe that this common essence is the life breath; others refer to it as the presence of the Great Spirit."[36]

Ronald Niezen comments, "The willing conversion to various denominations of Christianity by many Native people throughout North America has coexisted with a variety of surprisingly resilient forms of traditional spirituality, despite concerted efforts at suppression and cultural assimilation."[37] Niezen notes that traditional American Indian culture is pervaded by spiritual agency; hunting and agriculture are both shaped by spiritual agencies; he further notes analogies to practices and beliefs in Protestant and Catholic circles in the sixteenth and seventeenth centuries.[38] Where many earlier missionaries usually saw indigenous beliefs and practices regarding spirits as misguided, even evil, contemporary Christians often explore points of convergence between the Holy Spirit and Native American Indian experience of the Great Spirit.

Since the Spirit blows where it wills (Jn 3:8), it is, above all, important to listen to Native Christian voices about their experience of drawing upon both traditional indigenous practices and perspectives and Christian faith. There is no agreement among American Indians today concerning religious diversity. Some practice traditional religion and strongly reject any harmonizing with Christianity. Some practice Christianity and do not wish to continue Native practices. There are also many American Indians who live with a hybrid identity, integrating Native practices and perspectives into Christian life.[39] In Chapter 3 we noted Black Elk's experience of the world of the spirits that changed his life. In his mature identity he integrated both traditional Lakota and Catholic understandings of Spirit. Even though some charged that this represented a betrayal of one tradition or the other, nonetheless, the

---

(1918): 184; Brown, *Teaching Spirits,* 71.

[35] Brown, *Teaching Spirits,* 84.

[36] Ibid., 87.

[37] Ronald A. Niezen, *Spirit Wars: Native North American Religions in the Age of Nation Building* (Berkeley: University of California Press, 2000), 2.

[38] Ibid., 12–14.

[39] Michael D. McNally, "The Practice of Native American Christianity," *Church History* 69, no. 4 (2000): 834–59.

Roman Catholic Diocese of Rapid City, South Dakota, has introduced the cause for his beatification, and this was endorsed by the U.S. Conference of Catholic Bishops in November 2017.

Benjamin Black Elk, who translated the remarks of his father, Nicholas Black Elk, for John Neihardt, speaks of the guidance of his people by the Great Spirit, and he describes his own dual identity:

> I have led two lives—one as a Christian and one as a believer of the Indian religion. So when I lecture on Indian religion, I feel that I am trying to tear down Christianity, but that isn't so. Today it has all merged together, and I feel that I live the one life now, which is our modern religion.[40]

Benjamin Black Elk was born nine years after the massacre at Wounded Knee on December 29, 1890. He reflected afterward: "In the old days the Indian taught that we must love each other. Our belief is that this love was established here on earth by the Great Spirit."[41] Even though the U.S. government forbade continuation of Native practices, for Benjamin Black Elk and his family, the Great Spirit of the Indians was identical with the Holy Spirit of Christians. Benjamin Black Elk recalls,

> We became Christians. We wanted to keep some of our old ceremonies. When we pray, we don't read from a book. It comes from our hearts. But the government outlawed some of our worship, like the sun dance, so we had to do our ceremonies secretly—where we would not be caught. That made us feel bad. It was like the early Christians who had to worship secretly.[42]

For a while, it seemed to Benjamin Black Elk that there was a conflict between the Indian sacred pipe and Christianity, but later he came to accept them both, using the sacred pipe in Christian ceremonies: "We see there is no clash. After these years it comes together. Now I live only one way. I can be free in what I tell and what I do."[43] He added, "There is only one prayer the Indian uses: 'Oh Great Spirit, be merciful to me, that my people may live.' When we say 'my people' in the Sioux, we say *oiyáte*. *Oiyáte* means the whole universe that God created."[44] Benjamin Black Elk describes creation not as an event in the distant past but as a continual process renewed every day: "And the creation of the universe happens every morning, but we never realize it. Then the light comes, and that's the light of the eternal light from the Great Spirit. It will never end, never end."[45] He reflected on his father,

---

[40] Benjamin Black Elk, "The Legacy," in DeSersa et al., *Black Elk Lives*, 5.
[41] Ibid., 8.
[42] Ibid., 8–9.
[43] Ibid., 9.
[44] Ibid., 16.
[45] Ibid., 17.

Black Elk: "My father was a Christian. He died a Catholic; he is buried in a Catholic cemetery. But he still believed in the Indian religion."[46]

As we have seen, in the biblical traditions Spirit and breath are intimately related; and the Apostle Paul warned the community in Rome that because we do not know how to pray as we ought, the Spirit prays for us in wordless groans (Rom 8:26–27). Orpingalik, an Eskimo shaman of the Netsilik people, described a similar experience of receiving words:

> Songs are thoughts, sung out with the breath when people are moved by great forces and ordinary speech no longer suffices. Man is moved just like the ice floe sailing here and there in the current. His thoughts are driven by a flowing force when he feels joy, when he feels fear, when he feels sorrow. Thoughts can wash over him like a flood, making his breath come in gasps and his heart throb. Something, like an abatement in the weather, will keep him thawed up. And then it will happen that we, who always think we are small, will feel still smaller. And we will fear to use words. But it will happen that the words we need will come of themselves. When the words we want to use shoot up of themselves, we get a new song.[47]

Joseph Epes Brown cites Orpingalik's words as representative of a legacy in all the surviving Native American languages. In a similar vein, Robert Williamson comments on the experience of Eskimos:

> *Sila* is the word for air, without air there is no life; air is in all people and all creatures; anything deprived of air ceases to live. In that air therefore is life and without air there is no life, that Eskimos believed that they are part of the Life-Giving Spirit, that each individual is animated by the Life-Giving Spirit, and that they are part of his soul, that part which is the essence of all things living, is part of the ultimate deity of *Sila*.[48]

Like *ruach* in the Bible, wind has multiple resonances for the Navajo people both physical and spiritual. Trudy Griffin-Pierce explains:

> Wind—swirling gusts and fresh breezes, blustery gales and turbulent air—more than any other natural force, embodies the energy of change and a sense of dynamic force. The Navajo view of the world, which is based on movement, change, and flux, is most evident in a central concept of Navajo philosophy—the Holy Wind.[49]

---

[46] Ibid., 18.

[47] Brown, *Teaching Spirits,* 41.

[48] Robert Williamson, *Eskimo Underground: Socio-Cultural Change in the Central Canadian Arctic* (Uppsala, Sweden: Almquist and Wiksell, 1974), 13; see Brown, *Teaching Spirits,* 43.

[49] Trudy Griffin-Pierce, "The Continuous Renewal of Sacred Relations: Navajo Reli-

The Navajo universe is in constant change with ever-changing dynamic relationships constituting the whole. The Holy Wind seeks harmony amid diversity:

> The Holy Wind—the vital energy that animates the universe—unites all forms of life by virtue of its omnipresence inside and outside all life forms. . . . The act of breathing is a sacred act that unites all beings and phenomena—humans, deer, mountains, stars, and the Holy People.[50]

As we saw in Chapter 3, William Stolzman relates his experience of the Lakota vision quests to his Catholic faith in the experiences of the Holy Spirit. While he is careful to note significant differences between Lakota and Catholic practice, he nonetheless suggests analogies between the Power of the East in Lakota tradition and the Holy Spirit, especially as sources of wisdom:

> Like the Power of the East, the Holy Spirit is associated with the obtaining of wisdom. . . . Both spirits are related to "enlightenment." Charisms and the exercise of spiritual power, however, are received according to the religious and cultural tradition to which one belongs, for wisdom perfects and unites that which has already been given by God.[51]

Stolzman notes a similarity in perspective that bonds the traditions: "Both the Lakota and Christian religions maintain that there is continual contact with the spirit world, at least in a materially supportive way, even though ordinary people are little conscious of it."[52]

The Spirit among Africans and African American Christians

While the African religions whose legacy influenced African American Christians offer no exact equivalent of the Holy Spirit as third person of the Trinity, there are, nonetheless, in African traditional religions many expressions of spirits and of divine power active in human life. African traditional religions had a widespread belief in God as the source and sustainer of all life and the ultimate power permeating the universe. Spirits are believed to have access to this source as well as a few humans (medicine men, witches, priests, rainmakers), for good or for ill. In African American religion, there is a powerful belief in the Spirit of God sustaining people in times of difficulty and transforming situations.

---

gion," in *Native Religions and Cultures of North America: Anthropology of the Sacred*, ed. Lawrence A. Sullivan (New York: Continuum, 2000), 123.

[50] Ibid., 126.

[51] William Stolzman, *The Pipe and Christ*, 7th ed. (Chamberlain, SD: Tipi Press, 2002), 203.

[52] Ibid., 74.

E. Bolaji Idowu notes the Nuer belief in a transcendent Spirit: "Kwoth is the Creator and Mover of all things. He is the very Spirit of the universe. The universe is his: this fact occurs frequently in their thought and prayers and determines their attitude to life and all its issues."[53] Idowu explains,

> Thus, although Kwoth is in the sky, he is at the same time on earth and this resolves for the Nuer the paradox of his transcendence-immanence as one who is far away and at the same time actively and effectively rules the universe and governs human affairs. He is the giver and, naturally, the sustainer of life. He instituted the social order and is its guardian. Kwoth is always and every good.[54]

Idowu stresses the distinction between the Spirit or Deity and subordinate spirits, insisting that "the divinities owe their being and divine authority to Deity and that they are not to be confused with him in any way."[55] God is transcendent as well as immanent, creating and also caring for creatures and enforcing divine justice without favoritism. There are also spirits everywhere throughout the created universe, and their importance and significance vary from one people to another, but they should not be confused with the supreme Spirit. These subordinate spirits are not always benevolent and can often work harm.

Peter Paris emphasizes the importance for African American Christian spirituality of the African "realm of the spirit (inclusive of the Supreme Deity, the sub-divinities, the ancestral spirits), which is the source and preserver of all life."[56] Paris finds that this fundamental African belief assumed many different forms but continued to shape life in the African diaspora, including African American Christians: "Africans in the diaspora were able to preserve the structural dimensions of their spirituality: belief in a spirit-filled cosmos and acceptance of a moral obligation to build a community in harmony with all the various powers in the cosmos."[57] The structural similarity between belief in God and spirits in African religions and Christianity facilitated an amalgamation of the traditions even under the conditions of enslavement. Paris argues that there was a mutual transformation of Christianity and African religions, producing a new form of spiritual life, expressed most powerfully in the African American spirituals.

Anthony Pinn sees African American Christians drawing upon African traditions of shouting and dancing in order to respond to the context of terror and affirm black bodies as valuable: "As the music plays, people sing, shout, and dance

---

[53] E. Bolaji Idowu, *African Traditional Religion: A Definition* (London: SCM Press, 1973), 157.

[54] Ibid., 157–58.

[55] Ibid., 159.

[56] Peter J. Paris, *The Spirituality of African Peoples: The Search for a Common Moral Discourse* (Minneapolis: Fortress Press, 1995), 25.

[57] Ibid., 35.

the 'holy dance.' The Holy Spirit fills believers and often provides messages, at times in special languages interpreted by others, that respond to the pressing issues faced by blacks living in a hostile land."[58]

Recently Jemar Tisby has offered a searching critique of the white racism that has dominated American Christian practice, closing with an invocation of faith in the power of Jesus to overcome all divisions and stressing the presence of the Holy Spirit today in the people:

> Jesus crossed every barrier between people, including the greatest barrier of all—the division between God and humankind. He is our peace, and because of his life, death, and resurrection, and coming return, those who believe in Jesus not only have God's presence *with* us but *in* us in the Holy Spirit.[59]

African American Christians have drawn strength from the hopes of both the African traditional religions and Christianity, as the power of the Spirit establishes connections and continuities.

The Holy Spirit in Hispanic Catholic Piety

The power of the Holy Spirit coming upon Mary has played a vital role in Catholic Marian veneration, including in Spanish and Latin American traditions. Orlando Espín has studied the impact of the presentation of Catholic faith in sixteenth-century Mexico upon popular Catholicism in the United States today. He notes that the European philosophical categories that had long been used to interpret Trinitarian doctrine were completely foreign to the Amerindian populations of the Americas. The first Catholic evangelizers in the Americas were orthodox in doctrine concerning the Holy Spirit, but they did not succeed in making Trinitarian faith accessible to new Amerindian Catholics who had suffered devastating conquest and displacement. The missionaries placed a very strong emphasis on the suffering and death of Jesus Christ but relatively little on the power of the Holy Spirit. Espín notes, "In this context the mother of Jesus became a necessary religious symbol of compassion and care in an otherwise cruel world."[60] He emphasizes the close relationship between Mary and the Holy Spirit in Hispanic Catholic devotion, but he carefully notes in response to Protestant criticisms that Mary is not worshipped as divine. He recalls that Hispanic Catholics accept the fundamental Catholic teaching about the Holy Spirit:

---

[58] Anthony B. Pinn, *Terror and Triumph: The Nature of Black Religion* (Minneapolis: Fortress Press, 2003), 101.

[59] Jemar Tisby, *The Color of Compromise: The Truth about the American Church's Complicity in Racism* (Grand Rapids, MI: Zondervan, 2019), 215.

[60] Orlando O. Espín, "Trinitarian Monotheism and the Birth of Popular Catholicism: The Case of Sixteenth-Century Mexico," *Missiology* 20, no. 2 (1992): 201.

Simply put, the Holy Spirit is one of the three ways in which God is God, in the Mystery of Godself, throughout eternity. God—the Holy Spirit—is loving, accepting, sustaining, guiding, enthusing, and correcting. God—the Holy Spirit—leads and comforts, teaches, counsels and enlightens, gives courage, makes possible faith, hope and love, and in every best way is and acts maternally.[61]

Espín poses the question based on the intimate relation of Mary to the Spirit: "Why can't we understand the 'Mary' categories of Latino Catholicism as *orthodox popular pneumatology?*"[62]

Carmen Nanko-Fernández develops this perspective, noting the relation of Mary to various indigenous female figures and reflecting on how Latino/a Catholics experience the Holy Spirit in and through veneration of Mary under her many Hispanic forms. Carefully distinguishing Mary from God, she proposes that "to come to an appreciation of Mary as one filled with the Holy Spirit will refocus our attention on the Trinity. In that sense, to speak of Mary is to speak of God."[63] Rejecting any identification of Mary with God, Nanko-Fernández poses the question, "But is there a way to appreciate Mary, 'full of grace,' as a sacrament of God? As the Spirit-filled one who gives concrete expression to animation by the Holy Spirit? Is there wisdom in popular Marian devotion for which our theologizing has not provided a sufficient vocabulary?"[64] Nanko-Fernández endorses Elizabeth Johnson's presentation of Mary as filled with the Holy Spirit and offering a model of discipleship in the Magnificat.

This song of the lowly ones raised up by a merciful God has ethical implications for those who are filled by the Spirit.... The retrieval of Mary as one filled with the Spirit of God perhaps makes Mary more accessible to some Protestant sensibilities; at the same time, it also makes the Holy Spirit accessible to Catholics in a church that has not warmly embraced Spirit-led movements.[65]

Locating Mary within the communion of saints invites exploration of the role of the Holy Spirit in *lo cotidiano,* the everyday life of communities. "The spirit is made known in the company the Spirit keeps. Therefore, to know Mary is to know, in some way, the Spirit of God."[66]

---

[61] Orlando O. Espín, "Mary in Latino/a Catholicism: Four Types of Devotion, *New Theology Review* 23, no. 3 (2010): 24 (16–25).

[62] Orlando O. Espín, *The Faith of the People: Theological Reflections on Popular Catholicism* (Maryknoll, NY: Orbis, 1997), 9.

[63] Carmen M. Nanko-Fernández, "From *Pájaro* to Paraclete: Retrieving the Spirit of God in the Company of Mary," in *Building Bridges, Doing Justice: Constructing a Latino/a Ecumenical Theology,* ed. Orlando O. Espín (Maryknoll, NY: Orbis Books, 2009), 16.

[64] Ibid., 17–18.

[65] Ibid., 22.

[66] Ibid.

Ruach Hakodesh, Shekhinah, Chokmah in Jewish Life

Christian understandings of the Holy Spirit developed from the Jewish context of ancient Israel, Hellenistic Judaism, and the early followers of Jesus; and so, there is considerable convergence in the ancient period. As the two traditions eventually separated and defined their identities in contrast to each other, Jews firmly rejected Christian formulations of belief in the Holy Trinity, and Christian understandings of the Holy Spirit often became polemical against Jewish understandings. Traditionally Christians claimed that the Holy Spirit empowered them to see the revelation of God in Jesus Christ, while they charged that Jews remained blind and bereft of the gifts of the Holy Spirit. In contrast, in today's post–Vatican II climate, Christians can approach the Jewish tradition with humility and openness to learning.

In the rabbinic tradition Jews use the term *ruach hakodesh* (holy spirit) to name God's inspiring individuals to a prophetic vocation. In postbiblical Judaism, the Holy Spirit was closely associated with and could be identified with *Shekhinah,* the divine presence;[67] she was also related to Sophia in Hellenistic Judaism.[68] The noun *Shekhinah* does not appear in the Hebrew Bible, which uses forms of the related verb *shakhan* for the visible appearances of God or dwelling of God among the people of Israel. *Shekhinah* literally means "the act of dwelling" or "settling." While Jews vigorously rejected Christian formulations of the immanent Trinity as violating the oneness of God, nonetheless the presentation of Shekinah as God's dwelling presence among the people of Israel bears many similarities to Christian understandings of the role of the Holy Spirit in the economic Trinity. One of the most important aspects of the traditional Christian experience of the Holy Spirit is the indwelling of the Spirit in the hearts of the faithful. Arthur Green comments on the indwelling of Shekhinah: "*Shekhinah* is the presence of the One amid the many, the palpable reality of divinity within the here-and-now."[69]

Raphael Patai has studied interpretations of Shekhinah in rabbinic literature, describing her as "the manifestation of God's presence . . . the loving, rejoicing, motherly, suffering, mourning, and, in general, emotion-charged aspect of deity."[70] Shekhinah is "the direct heir of the biblical Cloud of Glory which had dwelt in the sanctuary and had been visible in Yahweh's manifestation of His presence in His House."[71] During the same period when Christians were debating how to understand the Spirit and Sophia in relation to God, Patai finds that Shekinah in Midrashic literature appears as distinct from God but also as manifesting the presence of God:

---

[67] Michael E. Lodahl, *Shekhinah/Spirit: Divine Presence in Jewish and Christian Religion* (New York: Paulist Press, 1992).

[68] Winston, *Wisdom of Solomon,* 103.

[69] Arthur Green, *Ehyeh: A Kabbalah for Tomorrow* (Woodstock, VT: Jewish Lights, 2004), 55.

[70] Raphael Patai, *The Hebrew Goddess,* 3rd ed. (Detroit, MI: Wayne State University Press, 1990), 32.

[71] Ibid., 105.

"it appears that in the late Midrashic literature the Shekhinah concept stood for an independent feminine divine entity prompted by her compassionate nature to argue with God in defense of man."[72] In the Hebrew Bible, the cloud or glory of God comes to dwell in the tabernacle in the desert and later in the Temple in Jerusalem built by Solomon. The tent sanctuary was called the dwelling (*mishkan*), which contains the root for Shekhinah. Patai sees the role of Chokmah in the Hebrew Bible and the Wisdom of Solomon as also contributing to the development of Shekhinah, who first appears in the Targum Onkelos, an Aramaic translation and paraphrase of the Bible.[73] Where the Hebrew Bible describes God dwelling among the people of Israel, the Targum Onkelos inserts the noun Shekhinah (*Shekhinta* in Aramaic) to name the presence of God.[74] As the rabbinic tradition developed, some authors describe Shekhinah as possessing physical characteristics apparent to humans, in contrast to God who transcends all sense perception. For example, the container of the tablets of the covenant is described as the casket of Shekhinah.[75]

Some rabbis believed that Shekhinah moved to a more remote location and eventually into exile because of the repeated sins of the Jewish people; sometimes the rabbis saw her as withdrawing in order to await the repentance of the people, when she would graciously return with forgiveness. The rabbinic tradition viewed Shekhinah as dwelling continuously in the First Temple built by Solomon, but some rabbis believed that she dwelled only intermittently or not at all in the Second Temple erected after the exile. However, the general belief was that Shekhinah accompanied the Jewish people wherever they went in exile and would always dwell among them until their redemption.[76] Patai's description of her activity corresponds closely to the Christian Holy Spirit: "The Shekhina joins the sick to comfort them, and helps those who are in need. Moreover, she has a special concern for the repentant sinners of Israel."[77] She also cares for those who worship in different ways: "Good deeds, even if performed by idolaters, attract the Shekhina; when the prophets of Baal practiced hospitality, the Shekhina descended and rested upon them."[78] Shekhinah is present throughout the cosmos but she can contract herself to dwell in a small space in the Temple or in the ark next to the basket containing the infant Moses.

Originally there was no distinction between Shekhinah and God in Jewish thought, but in later traditions she sometimes opposes God in order to defend humans.[79] In this regard, rabbis speak of the Holy Spirit and Shekhinah interchangeably. Patai explains:

---

[72] Ibid., 96.

[73] Ibid., 97–98.

[74] Luke Devine, "*Shekhinah* as 'Shield' to Israel: Refiguring the Role of Divine Presence in the Jewish Tradition and *Shoah*," *Feminist Theology* 25, no. 1 (2016): 64.

[75] Patai, *Hebrew Goddess,* 100.

[76] Ibid., 101–3.

[77] Ibid., 103.

[78] Ibid.

[79] Devine, "Shekinah as 'Shield,'" 66–69.

When, therefore, a Talmudic teacher speaks of the Holy Spirit, he may as well have used the term Shekhinah. With this in mind, let us quote a saying of Rabbi Aha, a Galilean teacher who lived ca. 300: "The Holy Spirit comes to the defense [of sinful Israel by] saying first to Israel: "Be not a witness against thy neighbor without a cause," and thereafter saying to God, "Say not: I will do to him as he has done to me."[80]

In the Gospel of John, Jesus promises to send a *parakletos,* which can be understood as a defense attorney or an advocate or a comforter (14:16). He speaks of "the Paraclete, the Holy Spirit" (Jn 14:26), and the later Christian tradition has usually identified the Paraclete with the Spirit. As we have seen, Paul tells the Romans that when we do not know how to pray, the Holy Spirit intercedes for us (Rom 8:26). In the Jewish tradition Shekhinah identifies so closely with the people of Israel that she suffers with them.

Shekhinah is the presence of God but at times advocates for humans in a manner that seems to distinguish her from God. Patai notes the disparity of views among the rabbis concerning the relation of Shekhinah and God; some saw them as distinct entities, while others rejected any notion of plurality. After viewing Shekhinah as distinct from God, Patai goes on to acknowledge she is one with God:

> Yet the Shekhina, with her feminine gender, comes quite close in the Talmudic sources to being regarded as a feminine manifestation of the deity.... That the Shekhina is the love aspect of God is clearly stated in a parable which compares the Temple to Solomon's palanquin: just as the latter was inlaid with love so did the Shekhina fill the sanctuary. But she also represents the divine punitive power.[81]

Like the Holy Spirit in Christian theology, Shekhinah can bring mercy but also just punishment for sin.

Where Jews pondered the ambiguity of the identity or relation of Shekhinah and God, Christians in a very different theological context sought to articulate both distinction and oneness in God, asserting that the Holy Spirit is one in essence with God the Father while also a distinct person. Patai comes close to language used by Christians when he comments that after Shekhinah was viewed as speaking to humans and to God, "there was no longer any doubt that the deity was considered as comprised of two persons: God and the Shekhina."[82]

The Book of Zohar and the later Kabbalistic tradition would continue this trajectory, viewing Shekhinah as a manifestation of God who was simultaneously

---

[80] Patai, *Hebrew Goddess,* 105; Luke Devine questions Patai's interpretation, "How *Shekhinah* Became the God(dess) of Jewish Feminism," *Feminist Theology* 23, no. 1 (2014): 74.

[81] Patai, *Hebrew Goddess,* 108, 109.

[82] Ibid., 110.

distinct from and one with God.[83] Patai comments on the later development that seemed to transgress the divine unity: "Especially to popular imagination, the Shekhina was no mere symbol or emanation, but a great heavenly reality whose shining countenance shoved the theoretical doctrine of the Oneness of God into the background."[84] The Kabbalistic tradition explored the mysterious *sefirot* (enumerations or emanations), aspects of the divine life that overflow and affect the world. *Ruach* was not usually listed among the ten sefirot, but Shekhinah played the role of intermediary and mediator between the infinite, incomprehensible God and the creation, including the Jewish people.[85]

Analogies to the Experience of the Holy Spirit among Muslims

Thomas Michel sets forth a principle to guide Catholic reflections on the Holy Spirit, Wisdom, and Islam:

The early Fathers of the Christian community were well aware that the divine wisdom that God had so bountifully distributed among men and women should be understood as the effect of the work of God's own Spirit. In a beautiful observation attributed to St. Ambrose, it is said: "Every truth, by whomever it is expressed, comes from the Holy Spirit."[86]

The Holy Qur'an speaks of the spirit (*ruh*) of God, as well as of the presence (*sakinah*) and the wisdom (*hikmah*) of God. The Arabic word *ruh* ("spirit") is related to the Hebrew *ruach,* as *sakinah* (presence) is to Shekhinah, and *hikmah* (wisdom) is to chokmah. Both *ruh* and *ruach* can mean breath or blowing; both can refer to created spirits; both can name an experience of God transforming human life.[87] The Islamic tradition speaks of *ruh al-qudus* ("the holy spirit") as the source of prophetic inspiration.[88] Sometimes Muslims identify the Holy Spirit with the angel Gabriel or another created spirit who breathes life into Adam and who comes upon Mary when she conceives Jesus; the Qur'an describes Jesus as *ruh* (4:171).

Like Christianity, Islam has a strong sense of the presence of God pervading human life in creation, prophecy, and the guidance of humanity; but Islam does not

---

[83] Moshe Idel, *The Privileged Divine Feminine in Kabbalah,* ed. Vivian Liska (Berlin: Walter de Gruyter, 2019).

[84] Patai, *Hebrew Goddess,* 116.

[85] Devine, "How *Shekhinah* Became," 76–77.

[86] Thomas Michel, *A Christian View of Islam: Essays on Dialogue,* ed. Irfan A. Omar (Maryknoll, NY: Orbis Books, 2010), 167.

[87] Michael Sells, "Spirit," in *The Encyclopaedia of the Qur'an,* 6 vols., ed. Jane McAuliffe (Boston: Brill, 2004), 5:114–17.

[88] Sidney H. Griffith, "Holy Spirit," in McAuliffe, *Encyclopaedia of the Qur'an,* 2:442–44.

recognize any distinctions within God and strongly rejects Christian belief in the immanent Trinity. Despite the rejection of belief in the Trinity, Islam offers analogies to the Christian tradition's view of the Holy Spirit in creation and transforming human life. Sidney Griffith notes that in its references to the holy spirit, the Qur'an may be responding to and correcting Christian uses of the term "Holy Spirit."[89] It is important to remember that when the Qur'an uses the term "holy spirit," the meaning is very different than the Christian Trinitarian usage. When the Qur'an speaks of God giving Jesus clear proofs and strengthening him with the holy spirit (2:87; see also 2:253 and 5:110), some commentators have understood the holy spirit here as a reference to the angel Gabriel or to a name Jesus used to revive the dead or to the Gospel itself:

> The word *Holy, qudus,* is defined by some as "blessing" (*berakah'*) or "purity" (*tubr*), while others say *qudus* is synonymous with the Divine Name *al-Quddus the Holy*; see 59:23; 62:1). In this latter sense *the Holy Spirit* means "the spirit of (God) the Holy" and refers to the same Spirit that was breathed into Adam in 15:29.... Jesus was *strengthened* in the sense of being supported, helped, and reinforced.[90]

The Qur'an describes the holy spirit as bringing down the revelation of God (16:102), and most commentators understand this as a reference to Gabriel.[91] Concerning those who query the Prophet, the Qur'an comments: "They ask thee about the Spirit. Say, 'The Spirit is from the Command of my Lord, and you have not been given knowledge, save a little'" (17:85), and commentators have interpreted this as referring variously to the archangel Gabriel or to "the Spirit that is the source of human life" or to the Qur'an itself.[92] The Qur'an also states concerning the Day of Resurrection: "That Day the Spirit and the angels stand in rows, none speaking, save one whom the Compassionate permits and who speaks aright" (78:28). Here again commentators have differed, with some seeing this as a reference to Gabriel or to another angelic figure.[93]

However, it would be misleading to focus too much on the meaning of the word *ruh,* since it is not used in the same sense as the Holy Spirit in Christianity. In other linguistic expressions Muslims offer numerous testimonies to the movement of God within and among them, healing them, overcoming estrangement, and inviting them to intimate union with God, especially in the Sufi tradition. The Sufi tradition has a strong sense of God's power moving within people to endow them with a unitive mystical experience of God. Sufis speak of the "Breath of the

---

[89] Ibid., 443–44.

[90] *The Study Quran: A New Translation and Commentary,* ed. Seyyed Hossein Nasr et al. (New York: HarperOne, 2015), 42.

[91] Ibid., 685.

[92] Ibid., 720.

[93] Ibid., 1466–67.

Compassionate" as the basis of cosmic existence. Seyyed Hossein Nasr explains the role of God's Breath in creation and revelation:

God breathed upon the archetypal realities of this world, and the consequence of this action was the realm of separative existence we call the world. It is most significant that this "Breath" (*nafas*) is associated with the goodness and compassion of God and not some other quality. Compassion is therefore at the root of our very existence, the gate through which both revelation and creation were brought forth.[94]

Central to the Sufi tradition is *ma ʾrifa* (the experiential knowledge of God), which is distinguished from ordinary discursive, conceptual knowledge often called ʾilm; John Renard explains that *ma ʾrifa* "means access to the divine presence, perhaps even an invasion or being overcome by the reality of God. It includes both the experiential dimension and knowing in a way that 'gnosis' cannot quite convey. Aquinas's *cognitio experimentalis* more closely approximates the meaning of *ma ʾrifa* as the Sufis developed it."[95] Islamic experiential knowledge of God is not an autonomous act of the intellect; it involves a surrender of the entire person to the power of God moving within. Abu Bakr al-Kalabadhi (d. ca. 994–95 CE) tells us that "there is no cause of experiential knowledge other than God's self-disclosure to the mystic so that he experiences God intimately by means of that disclosure."[96] He explains that "the innermost self experiences the grandeur of God, the magnification of His reality, and the glorification of His power in a way that eludes articulation."[97]

The Wisdom of Solomon described Sophia as passing into human beings and rendering them "friends of God and prophets" (7:27); the Sufi tradition highly valued "friends of God" and has a similar understanding of the Wisdom of God passing into human lives and transforming them into friends of God and prophets. Farid ad-Din ʿAttar (d. ca. 1230) wrote *Memorials of God's Friends: Lives and Sayings of the Sufis,* which can be compared to Christian lives of the saints that bear witness to the movement of the Holy Spirit in their lives.[98]

---

[94] Seyyed Hossein Nasr, *The Heart of Islam: Enduring Values for Humanity* (New York: HarperOne, 2002), 204.

[95] John Renard, "Introduction," in *Knowledge of God in Classical Sufism: Foundations of Islamic Mystical Theology,* trans. John Renard (New York: Paulist Press, 2004), 11.

[96] Abu Bakr al-Kalabadhi, "The Exploration of Sufi Teachings," in *Knowledge of God in Classical Sufism: Foundations of Islamic Mystical Theology,* trans. (New York: Paulist Press, 2004), 103.

[97] Al-Kalabadhi, "Exploration," 105.

[98] Farid ad-Din Attar, *Memorial of God's Friends: Lives and Sayings of Sufis,* trans. Paul Losensky (New York: Paulist Press, 2009); John Renard, *Friends of God: Islamic Images of Piety, Commitment, and Servanthood* (Berkeley: University of California Press, 2008).

Analogies to the Experience of the
Holy Spirit among Hindus

Hindus have no exact equivalent of Christian faith in the Trinity, including the Holy Spirit. What is sometimes called the Trinity of Hinduism consists of three divinities: Brahma the Creator, Vishnu the Sustainer, and Shiva the Destroyer. Devotion to Brahma is relatively limited in India today. Many Hindus are Vaishnavites, devotees of Vishnu, who often see all the myriad deities of the Hindu tradition as expressions of the one God, Vishnu. Many others are Shaivites, devotees of Shiva who believe that Shiva is revealed in all the various deities. Devotees of the Goddess, meanwhile, view all the deities as expressions of the underlying female divinity, variously named Devi or Kali. Interpreters of Vedanta speak of Brahma without qualities, which is beyond any characteristics, manifesting itself in Ishvara, the Lord, who is manifested in avataras and various divine interventions.

The Upanishads have long given rise to multiple and conflicting traditions of interpretation. While there is no exact equivalent of the Holy Spirit in Hindu terminology, various scholars have used the English word "Spirit" for aspects of the Hindu worldview. John G. Arapura proposes an interpretation of the Upanishads as presenting

> a unique conception of the Spirit and spiritual knowledge—and hence of salvation as well. It consists in speaking in identical ways about the supreme Being, that is, as Spirit in the objective sense (Brahman) and as the supreme Self, Spirit in the subjective sense (Atman), the latter having its ultimate conceptual base in what we know as our own self. Further, what we know as our own self goes all the way to the point of absolute identity with the supreme Being, or supreme Spirit, resulting in a vision of the human being and its destiny which has no parallel in the world. The purpose of spiritual knowledge is to realize the human being's oneness with the supreme Spirit.[99]

In contrast to those who stress the immanence and oneness of the ultimate in the Upanishads, Arapura stresses the transcendence of Spirit in the Upanishads: "This is clearly the distinctiveness of the Upanishads, that they declare, embody, and, in fact, *are* the devoted posture of proximity to the absolutely transcendent Spirit, in its pure *transcendence*."[100] For Arapura, the Upanishads are not simply the expression of a revelation; they make the revelation possible: "Thus, they go much deeper than speculative thought and mystical experience; rather, they can generate these perpetually and without end."[101] Spiritual knowing is not a human

---

[99] John G. Arapura, "Spirit and Spiritual Knowledge in the Upanishads," in *Hindu Spirituality: Vedas through Vedanta,* ed. Krishna Sivaraman (New York: Crossroad, 1989), 64.

[100] Ibid., 66.

[101] Ibid.

accomplishment but the activity of Spirit in humans: "This spiritual knowledge is gathered directly from the supreme Spirit (i.e., Brahman/Atman) and not from even the highest of human activities."[102] This experience is not merely intellectual, for it involves eros moving humans to the highest experience and moving all beings in humans. Arapura describes the dynamic: "We *contemplate* the supreme Spirit, but we do so by *meditating* on the revelatory statements (*vaky*(*a*)s), which constitute what are called by the word *Upanishad* and as such are stations of proximity to the supreme Spirit."[103] The initiative does not come from humans:

> This spirituality is, so to say, suspended from above, from the Spirit (Brahman/Atman) itself, and not something projected by human efforts upward. . . . In fact, insofar as it is not a description of something that a human being does, it cannot be spoken of as a "way" (*marga*) at all . . . [I] t is truly the actualization of what man is capable of doing with himself spiritually (though not *by* himself) provided he is set on the course of knowing the Spirit.[104]

Sarvepalli Radhakrishnan, who studied the biblical and Western philosophical traditions, used the word "Spirit" to correlate Hindu terminology with biblical images of Logos and Sophia. For Radhakrishnan, the word "Spirit" can name the second and third of the four "poises or statuses of reality, (1) the Absolute, Brahman, (2) the Creative Spirit, *Ishvara*, (3) the World-Spirit, *Hiranya-garbha*, and (4) the World. This is the way in which the Hindu thinkers interpret the integral nature of the Supreme Reality."[105] Citing the Taittiriya Upanishad, Radhakrishnan compares the Absolute to the nest from which the three birds emerge. In itself, the Absolute is perfectly one and is ineffable, beyond all thought. When the Absolute is viewed as "the spirit moving everywhere in the universe, it is called *Hiranya-garbha*" (the golden germ, the world-soul); when viewed as the personal God, the Absolute is named *Ishvara,* which includes both wisdom and power, Shiva and Shakti. Noting the importance of the Logos for Plato, the Stoics, and Philo of Alexandria, Radhakrishnan compares the Platonic Logos to *Vac,* word or wisdom, which appears in the Rig Veda as "the all knowing. The first-born of Rta [cosmic order] is vac. . . . The Logos is conceived as personal like *Hiranya-garbha.* 'The Light was the light of men.' 'The Logos became flesh.'"[106] In this framework, the biblical figure of Sophia, especially as interpreted by Philo and by Christian Neoplatonists, resembles both Ishvara and Hiranya-garbha, mediating between the ultimate source of all reality and the world in which we live.

---

[102] Ibid., 69.
[103] Ibid., 71.
[104] Ibid., 81.
[105] S. Radhakrishnan, *The Basic Writings of Radhakrishnan,* ed. Robert A. McDermott (Mumbai, India: Jaico, 2007), 126.
[106] Ibid., 123.

Radhakrishnan reconciles the differing views within the Hindu family as focusing primarily on one aspect or another of Brahman as it manifests itself in the world. Thus, he affirms, "Both the Absolute and the Personal God are real. . . . The soul when it rises to full attention knows itself to be related to the single universal consciousness, but when it turns outward it sees the objective universe as a manifestation of this single consciousness."[107] Because he viewed each perspective as possessing its own validity, Radhakrishnan found a basis for relating Hindu perspectives with all other wisdom traditions, including Sophia and the Holy Spirit in Christianity.

While acknowledging varieties in expression, Radhakrishnan emphasized the common elements in the articulations of religious experience in the world's traditions, ranging from the Upanishads to the Buddha, to Plato, Jesus Christ, Dante, Teresa of Avila, Spinoza, and William Blake: "All being is consciousness and all consciousness being. Thought and reality coalesce and a creative merging of subject and object results. Life grows conscious of its incredible depths. In this fullness of felt life and freedom, the distinction of the knower and the known disappears."[108] For Radhakrishnan, this wisdom gives birth to the world's mystical traditions.

Despite the similarities that he points out, it is important to note that when Radhakrishnan writes of the divine Spirit, he does so from a framework very different than Christian Trinitarian theology. While Radhakrishnan acknowledges a relation with a personal God as legitimate, he does not believe this is the highest level of realization:

A "Personal God" has meaning only for the practical religious conscious-ness and not for the highest insight. To the finite individual blinded by the veils, the Absolute seems to be determinate and exclusive of himself. . . . God is no God if he is not the All; if he be the All, then religious experience is not the highest.[109]

Radhakrishnan admits that "there are features of our religious experience which require us to look upon God as a self-determining principle manifested in a temporal development, with wisdom, love and goodness as his attributes. From this point of view God is a personal being with whom we can enter into personal relationship."[110] On the highest level, Radhakrishnan affirms that "the Absolute represents the totality of being and there is nothing other than it. The Absolute is in this world in the sense that the world is only an actualisation of one possibility of the Absolute."[111]

---

[107] Ibid., 139.

[108] Sarvepalli Radhakrishnan, *An Idealist View of Life* (London: Unwin Paperbacks, 1988), 72.

[109] Sarvepalli Radhakrishnan, *An Anthology*, ed. A. N. Marlow (London: George Allen and Unwin, 1952), 30–31.

[110] Ibid., 33.

[111] Ibid., 31.

Analogies to the Holy Spirit and
Wisdom among Buddhists

The Buddhist tradition differs profoundly from Christianity in not relying on a transcendent God who creates the universe. The contrast between Buddhist cosmologies and Christian views of the Holy Spirit as creator, giver of life, guide of prophets, and sanctifier is profound. Nonetheless, Peter Phan notes that a Christian can recognize the movement of the Holy Spirit in central Buddhist teachings and practices: "To put it in Christian terms, the experience of Divine Spirit, or the Holy Spirit, can be obtained in the experience of the Four Noble Truths."[112] Some Mahayana Buddhist texts present the power of the Buddha extending through the entire cosmos in ways that resemble Christian faith in the Holy Spirit. For example, The *Flower Ornament* (*Avatamsaka*) *Sutra* presents a vision of the cosmic Buddha sending forth illumination and relieving suffering:

> The Buddha's body emanates great light
> With physical forms boundless and totally pure
> Filling all lands like clouds,
> Everywhere extolling the Buddha's virtues.

> All illumined by the light rejoice,
> Beings in distress are all relieved:
> This is the work of the Buddha's power.[113]

Ruben Habito compares the practice of following one's breath in Zen Buddhist meditation to the advice of St. John of the Cross on breathing:

> The breathing of the air is properly of the Holy Spirit, for which the soul here prays, so that she may love God perfectly. She calls it the breathing of the air, because it is a most delicate touch and feeling of love which habitually in this state is caused in the soul by the communion of the Holy Spirit.[114]

The Shin or Pure Land Buddhist tradition offers another analogy. This tradition views humans as imprisoned in ignorance and self-seeking and unable to find the path to enlightenment on our own. Nonetheless, Shin Buddhists trust in the Primal Vow of Amida Buddha to illumine and guide us. The bodhisattva

---

[112] Peter C. Phan, *The Joy of Religious Pluralism: A Personal Journey* (Maryknoll, NY: Orbis Books, 2017), 61.

[113] *The Flower Ornament Sutra: A Translation of the Avatamsaka Sutra,* trans. Thomas Cleary (Boulder, CO: Shambhala, 1984), 264.

[114] Ruben L. F. Habito, *Healing Breath: Zen Spirituality for a Wounded Earth* (Maryknoll, NY: Orbis Books, 1993), 43.

Dharmakara performed meritorious actions for eons and eons of time, and made a series of vows that those who called on his name in trust would receive enlightenment despite their unworthiness. While Christian belief in the Holy Spirit as a divine person is quite different from anything in the Buddhist tradition, the movement of the Holy Spirit in human lives invites comparison to the action of the Primal Vow of Amida Buddha. According to the thirteenth-century Japanese leader Shinran, when we are powerless, Amida Buddha comes to our aid, offering wisdom in the Holy Name, *namu-amida-butsu* (I take refuge in Amida Buddha).[115] Shinran writes, "Namu-amida-butsu is the Name embodying wisdom; hence, when a person accepts and entrusts himself to this Name of the Buddha of inconceivable wisdom-light, holding it in mindfulness, Avalokiteshvara and Mahasthamaprapta accompany him constantly, as shadows do things. . . . Together they bring forth wisdom in all beings."[116] Ultimately, it is the power of the Name that makes possible the practitioner's entrustment (*shinjin*, the entrusting to the Primal Vow) in an experience that Shinran and later Shin Buddhists describe as Other Power: "The power of the Buddha's wisdom-compassion bringing all beings to enlightenment through the Primal Vow."[117] However, the word "Other" has to be understood in a particular context:

> "Other," however, should not be understood as a relative term used in simple contrast with "self" to describe a different origin of practice, for Other Power refers to great compassion that transcends the duality of self and other. . . . Other Power, then, is the power of the Vow that becomes the power of the practice in his or her realization of shinjin.[118]

Shin Buddhists experience Other Power as the Great Compassion (*daihi*):

> in Buddhism compassion goes beyond any division or dichotomy between self and other into the world of complete identity. . . . the misery, suffering, or personal tragedy of another is none other than one's very own. Such a nondichotomous compassion is guided by *prajna*, a wisdom that surpasses conventional thinking and feeling and moves in nondichotomous perception.[119]

---

[115] Shinran, *The Essential Shinran: A Buddhist Path of True Entrusting,* comp. and ed. Alfred Bloom (Bloomington, IN: World Wisdom), 2007.

[116] Shinran, *Notes on "Essentials of Faith Alone": A Translation of Shinran's Yuishinsho-mon'i,* trans. Dennis Hirota et al. (Tokyo: Hongwanji Center, 1979), 31–32.

[117] *The Collected Works of Shinran,* vol. 2, *Introduction, Glossaries, and Reading Aids,* trans. with intro., glossaries, and reading aids, by Dennis Hirota, Hisato Inagaki, Michio Tokunaga, and Tyushin Uryzy (Kyoto: Jodo Shinshu Hongwanji-ha, 1997), 2:198.

[118] Ibid.

[119] Ibid., 2:188.

This perspective can be compared to, though not identified with, Catholic theology's view that the Holy Spirit dwells in the hearts of the faithful so that their acts are actions of the Spirit but also truly their own.

For Shinran, wisdom is inaccessible to humans through our own efforts, but it has been made available to us only because of the great practice of the bodhisattva Dharmakara, which culminated in his great vows.[120] According to Shinran, the holy Name, namu-amida-butsu, is an active force throughout the cosmos, for it

> spreads universally throughout the worlds in the ten quarters, countless as minute particles, and guides all to the practice of the Buddha's teaching. This means that, since there is no one—whether among the wise of the Mahayana or the Hinayana, or the ignorant, good or evil—who can attain supreme nirvana through his or her own self-cultivated wisdom, we are encouraged to enter the ocean of the wisdom-Vow of the Buddha of unhindered light, for the Buddha's form is the light of wisdom. This form comprehends the wisdom of all the Buddhas. It should be understood that light is none other than wisdom.[121]

Shinran interprets the great Vow as the manifestation of dharmakaya-as-compassion. As Yoshifuma Ueda points out, usually Mahayana Buddhists use the term "dharmakaya" "only to refer to the formless and nameless Tathagata," who pervades the countless worlds.[122] Shinran, however, follows the Chinese Pure Land Buddhist leader T'an-luan in distinguishing two forms of dharmakaya: dharmakaya-as-suchness, which has no form or conceptualization and dharmakaya as compassion, which does possess form and characteristics. Dharmakaya as compassion appears as Amida Buddha and thus makes itself accessible and comprehensible to humans.

These two forms of dharmakaya are inseparable but distinct. In the *Kyogyo-shinsho,* Shinran quotes T'an-luan: "Dharmakaya-as-compassion arises out of dharmakaya-as-suchness, and dharmakaya-as-suchness emerges into human consciousness through dharmakaya-as-compassion. These two aspects of dharmakaya differ but are not separate; they are one but not identical."[123] The formless, incomprehensible oneness of dharmakaya-as-suchness manifests itself in the form of dharmakaya-as-compassion in Dharmakara. The result of the Shin Buddhist path is compassion and service to others. The fundamental cosmological and anthropological assumptions of Shin Buddhists and Catholics are very different, but there are similarities between the movement of the Holy Spirit in Catholic experience and

---

[120] Shinran, *Essential Shinran,* 124–82; Alfred Bloom, *Shinran's Gospel of Pure Grace* (Tucson: University of Arizona Press, 1981), 27–36.

[121] Shinran, *Notes on "Essentials of Faith Alone,"* 31.

[122] Yoshifuma Ueda, "Introduction," in Shinran, *Notes on "Essentials of Faith Alone." A Translation of Shinran's Yuishinsho-mon'i,* trans. Dennis Hirota et al. (Tokyo: Hongwanji Center, 1979), 4.

[123] Ibid., 5.

the Shin Buddhist experience of dharmakaya-as-compassion healing and opening up new possibilities in human life.

During the middle of the twentieth century Hajime Tanabe, a member of the Kyoto School, reflected on the Shin or Pure Land Buddhist tradition in dialogue with Christianity and in light of the catastrophe of Japan's involvement in the Second World War.[124] Drawing upon both the earlier Pure Land tradition, especially Shinran, and Christian perspectives in the context of contemporary Japanese experience, Tanabe insists that humans come into a dilemma of radical evil from which they cannot free themselves; Other Power allows them to go through a process of conversion that he calls metanoesis. This transformation mediates the Great Compassion, opening up new possibilities for humans that would not otherwise be available.

Donald Mitchell compares the Catholic experience of the Holy Spirit to Hajime Tanabe's understanding of the process of transformation through Other Power.[125] Mitchell notes that Tanabe's view of Other Power is different from Catholic faith in the Holy Spirit but nonetheless proposes that "if one looks at the phenomenon of transformation brought about by Other-Power, then we find many similarities. It is from this phenomenological viewpoint of metanoesis that I can affirm many of the insights of Tanabe concerning spiritual transformation."[126] In Catholic belief, the Holy Spirit does not act at the beckoning of the human will but comes freely to transform human life. Where Tanabe tends to identify Other Power with the transformation process itself, Mitchell distinguishes, "That is, in Christian sanctification, one is opened up to something more than the transformation process itself. One is aware of the mediation of the absolute as being a trinitarian mediation of God-Love that is an activity of the Trinity itself."[127]

While Trinitarian belief in the Holy Spirit is unique to Christians, in widely different ways many religious traditions bear witness to a Power greater than ourselves who assists us in our weakness, heals and reorients us, and offers us opportunities for new life and hope. Exploring these traditions can broaden and deepen Catholic understanding of the Holy Spirit's transformative effects.

---

[124] *The Religious Philosophy of Tanabe Hajime: The Metanoetic Imperative,* ed. Taitetsu Unno and James W. Heisig (Berkeley, CA: Asian Humanities Press, 1990).

[125] Donald W. Mitchell, *Spirituality and Emptiness: The Dynamics of Spiritual Life in Buddhism and Christianity* (New York: Paulist Press, 1991), 79–108.

126 Ibid., 94.

[127] Ibid.

11

JESUS CHRIST IN
INTERRELIGIOUS PERSPECTIVE

Jesus of Nazareth offers both a point of contact among the world's religious communities and also many ongoing points of contrast and controversy. The significance of Jesus is not confined to his original context, for he has both encouraged and challenged people of widely differing religious and cultural contexts across the centuries. In the Gospel of John, Jesus promises his followers: "Peace I leave with you; my peace I give to you. I do not give to you as the world gives. Do not let your hearts be troubled, and do not let them be afraid" (14:27). In the Gospels of Matthew and Luke, Jesus warns his followers that he has come not to bring peace but a sword and that he will divide people against each other (Mt 10:34–36; cf. Lk 12:51–53). Vigorous debates over the identity, ministry, and significance of Jesus of Nazareth from his lifetime to the present have long divided followers of Jesus among themselves and from other communities. In interreligious relations, conflicting views of Jesus have also been the source of much controversy, often contributing to animosity among religions. In the United States, white racists claiming to be followers of Jesus have deployed images of him to reinforce white Christian nationalism, but African Americans and American Indians and Hispanics have also turned to images of Jesus to rebut such claims.[1]

Modern scholars using the tools of biblical criticism have long claimed to be neutral arbiters of Jesus's historical identity, but questers for the historical Jesus have repeatedly discovered their own values in Jesus.[2] Catholics and other Christians have frequently posited a sharp contrast between Jesus and the Jews of his time, variously presenting Jesus as an ethical prophet against the ritualism of the Temple or as a feminist against patriarchal Judaism or as a liberator against oppressive Jewish structures. Jewish scholars of the New Testament have regularly protested

---

[1] Edward J. Blum and Paul Harvey, *The Color of Christ: The Son of God and the Saga of Race in America* (Chapel Hill: University of North Carolina Press, 2012); Douglas Kelly Brown, *The Black Christ* (Maryknoll, NY: Orbis Books, 1994); William Stolzman, *The Pipe and Christ*, 7th ed., (Chamberlain, SD: Tipi Press, 2002).

[2] Paula Fredriksen, *Jesus of Nazareth, King of the Jews: A Jewish Life and the Emergence of Christianity* (New York: Alfred A. Knopf, 1999), 34–41.

against the anti-Jewish bias in many such presentations.[3] As scholars of differing religious commitments or of no religious background continue to investigate the historical Jesus in his original context, there remain strong differences of judgment, and no consensus is in sight.

There are both points of contrast and of contact between Catholic understandings of Jesus and those of other religious traditions, and present-day discussions often bear a relationship to the long legacy of interreligious conflict. Through most of Christian history, Christians largely interpreted Jesus in opposition to other religious leaders and claims of revelation in other religions. Even though in one sense Catholics have always known that Jesus and his first followers were Jews, they often separated Jesus and his disciples from the Jewish tradition; David Nirenberg comments on the rhetorical legacy of the Gospel of John against "the Jews":

> Just as he [the evangelist of the Fourth Gospel] denies the flesh any significance in the history of salvation ("It is the spirit that gives life. The flesh has nothing to offer" [6:63]), he strips the Jews of their lineage, assigns to them a demonic spiritual paternity, and insists on their eternal role as enemies of God. From within such a polarity, the "believing Jew" becomes something of a genetic impossibility.[4]

From Melito of Sardis in the second century to recent times, many Christians have blamed Jews of every generation for the death of Jesus.[5] One notorious expression of this tradition was the Oberammergau Passion Play, which is presented every ten years in a town near Munich, Germany; traditionally this drama portrayed Jews in a very negative light; the version written by a Benedictine monk, Ferdinand Rosner, in 1750, presented the Devil as bearing much of the responsibility of Jesus's death:

> But by identifying the Devil with the Jews, Rosner raised the specter of another, and no less pernicious, form of stereotyping. Moreover, Rosner had introduced into the play the blood curse that first appears in the Gospel of Matthew, in which the Jews willingly accept collective guilt in perpetuity for Jesus' death.[6]

---

[3] Fredriksen, *Jesus of Nazareth*; Amy-Jill Levine, "Introduction," in *The Historical Jesus in Context*, ed. Amy-Jill Levine, Dale C. Allison, and John Dominic Crossan (Princeton, NJ: Princeton University Press, 2006), 1–39; Amy-Jill Levine, *The Misunderstood Jew: The Church and the Scandal of the Jewish Jesus* (New York: HarperOne, 2006).

[4] David Nirenberg, *Anti-Judaism: The Western Tradition* (New York: W. W. Norton, 2013), 81.

[5] Jeremy Cohen, *Christ Killers: The Jews and the Passion from the Bible to the Silver Screen* (Oxford: Oxford University Press, 2007).

[6] James Shapiro, *Oberammergau: The Troubling Story of the World's Most Famous Passion Play* (New York: Pantheon Books, 2000), 65.

After the Second World War many voices called for reform of the play. In 1990, Christian Stückl became the director of the Passion Play and worked to eliminate the anti-Jewish characteristics of the traditional drama and make it an occasion for interreligious understanding. In January 2020, Rabbi Walter Homolka, rector of Abraham Geiger College in Potsdam, announced that Stückl was the recipient of the Abraham Geiger Prize, which recognizes outstanding contributions to Judaism.

Traditionally, Catholics often viewed Jews, in general, as like Judas, as Jeremy Cohen notes: "Above all else, Judas Iscariot epitomizes the Jewish Christ killer, illuminating the monstrosity of the crime against Jesus on the one hand, and the guilt of the Jews on the other hand."[7] Despite the teaching of the Second Vatican Council concerning the Jewish people, this tradition has not completely died; for the celebration of Easter in 2019, a crowd in the town of Pruchnik, Poland, beat and burned an eighteen-foot doll "dressed to look like a bearded hassid—complete with a long, hooked nose, 'peyot' (sidelocks) and a black hat," and cast it into the river as an image of Judas: "The doll was supposed to symbolize Judas who, according to the Christian Bible, betrayed Jesus. Emblazoned on the front of the shirt worn by the doll was the name 'Judas' and '2019.'"[8] Catholic officials as well as Polish government officials condemned the incident, which reflects the age-old tradition of viewing all Jews as like Judas.

Christians historically interpreted Jesus's criticisms of the Jewish leaders of his day as applying to all Jews of all times and places; they viewed Jews of every generation as personally responsible for the crucifixion of Jesus unless they converted to Christianity; the statement of the Jerusalem crowd in the Matthean passion narrative was thought to apply to all Jews throughout the centuries: "His blood be on us and on our children!" (Mt 27:25). My friend the late Rabbi Herman Schaalman, who was born in Germany in 1916, told me that one day in Munich when he was seven years old, many of his Catholic playmates joined together to beat him up. They had never done anything like this before; and when they finished fighting him, he asked them why they did it. They replied that they had just come from catechism class, where they had learned that he had killed Christ; and so, they were mad at him. At age seven, Herman did not remember killing anyone and went home where his father tried to explain this age-old accusation, telling him, "The children do not know what they are talking about."[9]

Anti-Jewish interpretations of Jesus poisoned Catholic-Jewish relations for centuries. In an influential historical survey, Rosemary Radford Ruether called Christian anti-Judaism "the left hand of Christology."[10] In response to Christian

---

[7] Cohen, *Christ Killers,* 257; see also Peter Stanford, *Judas: The Most Hated Name in History* (Berkeley, CA: Counterpoint, 2015).

[8] Micah D. Halpern, "Above the Fold: Jews as Judas in 2019," *Jerusalem Post,* April 30, 2019.

[9] Richard Damashek, *A Brand Plucked from the Fire: The Life of Herman E. Schaalman* (Jersey City, NJ: KTAV, 2013), 21

[10] Rosemary Radford Ruether, *Faith and Fratricide: The Theological Roots of Anti-Semitism* (New York: Seabury, 1974).

accusations, Jews often viewed Jesus in harshly negative terms.[11] The transformation of interreligious relationships in recent decades has had a major impact on both Jewish and Christian perceptions of Jesus as a Jew, with many Jews viewing Jesus positively in Jewish terms, and increasing numbers of Jews participating in professional New Testament studies.[12]

Catholics have traditionally believed that Jesus Christ established the fundamental structures of the Catholic Church, appointing Peter as the first pope,[13] and instituting the sacraments of the Eucharist and Holy Orders at the Last Supper.[14] Catholics have often viewed Mary less as a Jewish woman than as the mother of the Catholic Church.[15] Today scholars view Jesus, his mother, and his first followers as faithful Jews.[16] As part of an exhaustive study of the historical Jesus, Catholic biblical scholar John P. Meier concludes that "Jesus the eschatological prophet did not intend to form an elite group or esoteric sect within or apart from Israel. He intended instead to address, challenge, and regather the whole of God's people, the whole of Israel, in expectation of the coming kingdom of God."[17] The eventual distinction and separation of Jewish and Christian communities was a long and gradual process, with some Jews following Jesus into the fourth and fifth centuries.

There was no one set of expectations for the Messiah among first-century Jews, and Jews who did look for a Messianic figure generally expected him to bring the Messianic Age of justice and peace.[18] Jesus did not usher in an age when the

---

[11] Peter Schäfer, *Jesus in the Talmud* (Princeton, NJ: Princeton University Press, 2007).

[12] Amy-Jill Levine and Marc Zvi Brettler, eds., *The Jewish Annotated New Testament*, 2nd ed. rev. (New York: Oxford University Press, 2017). For two differing Jewish views of Jesus as a Jew, see Amy-Jill Levine, "Reflections on Reflections: Jesus, Judaism, and Jewish-Christian Relations," *Studies in Jewish-Christian Relations* 8, no. 1 (2013); Arthur J. Dewey, "What Difference Does a Life Make: Reflections on Jesus as a Jew," *Studies in Jewish-Christian Relations* 8, no. 1 (2013): 1–13. For a Christian perspective, see Joseph B. Tyson, "Jesus—A Faithful Jew," in *Seeing Judaism Anew: Christianity's Sacred Obligation,* ed. Mary C. Boys (Lanham, MD: Sheed & Ward, 2005), 29–37.

[13] First Vatican Council, *First Dogmatic Constitution on the Church of Christ,* July 18, 1870; Roger Collins, *Keepers of the Keys of Heaven: A History of the Papacy* (New York: Basic Books, 2009), 6–21; Richard P. McBrien, *Lives of the Popes: The Pontiffs from St. Peter to John Paul II* (San Francisco: HarperSanFranciso, 1997), 25–33. *Catechism of the Catholic Church* (Chicago: Loyola University Press, 1994), 231–37.

[14] Council of Trent, *Decree on the Sacraments,* March 3, 1547; *Decree on the Most Holy Sacrament of the Eucharist,* October 11, 1551.

[15] Second Vatican Council, *Lumen Gentium,* November 21, 1964, ##63–68; Mary Christine Athans, *In Quest of the Jewish Mary: The Mother of Jesus in History, Theology, and Spirituality* (Maryknoll, NY: Orbis Books, 2013).

[16] Paula Fredriksen, *When Christians Were Jews: The First Generation* (New Haven, CT: Yale University Press, 2018).

[17] John P. Meier, *A Marginal Jew: Rethinking the Historical Jesus,* vol. 3, *Companions and Competitors* (New York: Doubleday, 2001), 3:289.

[18] David B. Levenson, "Messianic Movements," in Levine and Brettler, *The Jewish Annotated New Testament,* 622–28.

lion would lie down with the lamb and all would beat their swords into plough-shares; thus, many Christian scholars today acknowledge that Jesus did not fulfill the concrete expectations of the Jewish Messiah, and some challenge Christians to recognize a positive significance in the Jewish people's rejection of Christian Messianic claims.[19] This does not require abandoning traditional Christian doctrines concerning Jesus Christ, but it does open up a framework where respectful dialogue becomes more possible.

Because Muslims honor Jesus as a prophet but not as divine, Catholics and other Christians traditionally saw the Qur'an and Islam as variations of the early Christian heresies of Arius or Nestorius; and they dismissed Muslims' perceptions of Jesus out of hand. Muslims, in turn, often accused Christians of being idolaters because of their view of Jesus as divine.[20] Historically, Christians condemned both Jews and Muslims for not accepting the Christian interpretations of Jesus as fully divine and fully human, as the incarnation of the second person of the Holy Trinity. Christians often assumed that their claims were perfectly clear to all who had an open mind; thus they believed Jews and Muslims were culpable for rejecting them. John Chrysostom charged, "although these Jews had been called to the adoption of sons, they fell to kinship with dogs. . . . Nothing is more miserable than those people who never failed to attack their own salvation."[21]

Research on the historical Jesus and the origins of the Christian movement challenges Christian theologians to acknowledge that from a historical point of view there is nothing necessary about the development of the later Christian views, and that Jews and Muslims can view the historical evidence regarding Jesus in good conscience from their respective perspectives.

Catholics and other Christians also generally interpreted Jesus in opposition to what they perceived to be the superstitions and idolatry of Hinduism and Buddhism, and the indigenous religions of the Americas, Asia, and Africa. In each of these relationships, improvements in interreligious relations have opened new horizons for reflection on the meaning and identity of Jesus. Differences in interpretations of Jesus will most likely continue unabated, but interreligious dialogues have sought to frame the differences in more respectful ways that allow for enhanced relationships rather than unending acrimony.

In many interreligious dialogues in the United States and beyond, Christians and their partners are not simply discussing a figure from the past, but rather a religious leader important for people's practice today, though viewed from

---

[19] John T. Pawlikowski, "Christology and the Jewish-Christian Dialogue," *Irish Theological Quarterly* 72 (2007): 156.

[20] Mustafa Aykol, *The Islamic Jesus: How the King of the Jews Became a Prophet of the Muslims* (New York: St. Martin's Press, 2017); Zeki Saritoprak, *Islam's Jesus* (Gainesville: University Press of Florida, 2014); Tarif Khalidi, *The Muslim Jesus: Sayings and Stories in Islamic Literature* (Cambridge, MA: Harvard University Press, 2001).

[21] John Chrysostom, *Discourses against Judaizing Christians,* trans. Paul W. Harkins (Washington, DC: Catholic University of America Press, 1979), 5, 7.

different perspectives. In considering the significance of Jesus Christ in interreligious perspectives, it is crucial to remember that for all Muslims, many Hindus, and some Buddhists, Jesus of Nazareth is a religious figure in their practice. Reform Jews in the nineteenth century interpreted Jesus as a Reform rabbi in opposition to Orthodox Judaism. Muslims believe that Jesus is a prophet teaching the same divinely sent message as Muhammad. Some Hindus view Jesus in Hindu categories as a manifestation of God in light of Hindu mysticism.[22] Some Buddhists see Jesus in Buddhist terms as a manifestation of *dharmakaya* (ultimate reality) to the Jewish people of his context.[23] African Americans were confident that Jesus was one of them and suffered their kind of cruel death, recognizing the homology of the cross and the lynching tree, while almost all European American Christians, including highly educated theologians, missed this connection altogether.[24]

There is a constant danger of people from differing vantage points simply projecting their own ideals onto Jesus without relating him to his original immediate context. To avoid another recurrence of the long, bitter history of anti-Jewish interpretations, it is crucial to locate Jesus in his original context as a Torah-observant Jew who vigorously debated *halakhah* with his contemporaries in Jewish fashion. Nonetheless, Jesus's identity is not completely limited or controlled by his original context. As a classic religious figure, Jesus emerges from his original context to challenge successive generations of people in many different religious and cultural contexts around the world, including the United States.

Catholics view Jesus Christ as the incarnation of the Word of God, fully divine and fully human; most of the early Church writers identified the biblical Lady Wisdom with the Word of God. As the Word and Wisdom of God, Christ is a cosmic figure holding all things together and offering reconciliation to all things in heaven and on earth (Col 1:15–20). Jews and Muslims generally resist the language of the incarnation of God in a human person, though Arthur Green and Daniel Boyarin have explored incarnational dimensions of Jewish spirituality.[25] Hindus often accept an incarnational claim for Jesus while not seeing him as a unique incarnation. Buddhists do not speak of an incarnation of God, but many Mahayana Buddhists have long viewed the earthly life of Shakyamuni Buddha as a manifestation of ultimate reality, dharmakaya. In commenting on the Lotus Sutra, Thich Nhat Hanh speaks of the historical dimension of the Buddha in the human life of

---

[22] Ravi Ravindra, *The Gospel of John in the Light of Indian Mysticism* (Rochester, VT: Inner Traditions, 2004).

[23] Daisetz Teitaro Suzuki, *Outlines of Mahayana Buddhism* (1907; reprint, New York: Schocken Books, 1967), 259.

[24] Kelly Brown Douglas, *The Black Christ* (Maryknoll, NY: Orbis Books, 1993); James Cone, *The Cross and the Lynching Tree* (Maryknoll, NY: Orbis Books, 2011), 94.

[25] Arthur Green, *Radical Judaism: Rethinking God and Tradition* (New Haven, CT: Yale University Press, 2010); Daniel Boyarin, *Border Lines: The Partition of Judaeo-Christianity* (Philadelphia: University of Pennsylvania Press, 2010).

Shakyamuni, and he also speaks of the eternal dimension of the Buddha.[26] After pondering the significance of the historical Jesus as a Jew, Jewish biblical scholar Arthur Dewey comments on the broader dynamic:

> The reality is that Jesus has leaked out. He is no longer the sole property of the churches, nor of the synagogues. Indeed, he, along with Moses, Mohammad, Buddha, and other religious figures, has become available to all. This does not mean that we can bleach Jesus of his particularity. Rather it means that even greater critical focus must be made along with a reappraisal of the consequences of bringing this difficult Jew into the global arena.[27]

In her study of the anonymous characters in the Bible, Adele Reinhartz comments that "the variety of readings proposed for biblical characters, both named and unnamed, suggests that identity hovers in the encounter between character and reader and is demanding of both."[28] This principle applies to religious interpretations of Jesus in interreligious contexts whether in the United States or elsewhere. If it is true that in interpreting the anonymous characters in the Bible, "identity hovers in the encounter between character and reader and is demanding of both," we can also say that in interreligious dialogue the identity of Jesus hovers in the encounter between religious practitioners and is demanding of each partner. This means that Jews and Christians cannot predict or control what importance the Jewishness of Jesus will have for dialogues with followers of other religious paths. They often bring very different horizons of expectation, and they may well see different implications of both Jewishness and of Jesus than Jews or Christians.[29]

Reflection on Terminology

A number of terms are often used in discussing Jesus, and usage can be confusing. I understand the Jesus of history to be the actual person who lived in Galilee in the first century and who did and said many, many things, the vast majority of which we have no record whatsoever. I understand the term "the historical Jesus" to refer to the result of modern historical critical scholarship, applying the academic tools of critical research to investigate what is historically likely to have been the actions and teachings of Jesus. The understanding of the historical Jesus is necessarily tentative and open to revision in light of ongoing research and

---

[26] Thich Nhat Hanh, *Opening the Heart of the Cosmos: Insights on the Lotus Sutra* (Berkeley, CA: Parallax Press, 2003).

[27] Dewey, "What Difference," 12–13.

[28] Adele Reinhartz, *"Why Ask My Name?" Anonymity and Identity in Biblical Narratives* (New York: Oxford University Press, 1998), 4.

[29] For a survey of Asian religious views of Jesus, see R. S. Sugirtharajah, *Jesus in Asia* (Cambridge, MA: Harvard University Press, 2018).

new discoveries.[30] There have been endless debates both on the proper methods for investigating the historical Jesus and also on the results. This research is very important for developing Christian understandings of Jesus, but I do not believe that Christian faith is founded upon the latest historical reconstruction of what Jesus said and did and suffered. I believe that Christian faith is founded upon the proclamation of Jesus Christ by the Christian tradition in Word and Sacrament. Nonetheless, for me as a Catholic, historical research on Jesus is very important for developing my understanding of him, especially where such research has challenged many traditional Catholic views of Jews and Judaism that were quite pejorative. I also acknowledge that Muslims accept as authoritative the Qur'anic presentation of Jesus (known in Arabic as Isa). Muslim-Christian dialogue concerning Jesus involves conversation concerning Jesus as presented in our varying scriptures and contexts of faith; research on the historical Jesus can inform the participation of all involved in this conversation.

Jesus Christ in Jewish-Catholic Dialogue

Much recent Jewish-Catholic discussion has focused on the significance of the Jewishness of Jesus. It may seem odd to focus on the Jewishness of Jesus, since in one sense almost everyone has always known this—except for some theologians supporting the Nazis who insisted Jesus was an Aryan and was not Jewish at all. The Institute for the Study and Eradication of Jewish Influence on German Church Life, founded in 1939, sought to dejudaize Christianity altogether. Walter Grundmann argued that Jesus was from the non-Jewish population of Galilee and opposed Judaism; one "German Christian" catechism issued in 1940 stated, "Was Christ a Jew? It is the greatest lie that the Jews have brought into the world, that Jesus is a Jew."[31] Similar ideas have circulated among other religious communities. Writing in 1939, Sarvepalli Radhakrishnan cited Rudolph Otto's 1938 claim that Jesus's preaching of the Kingdom of God contained aspects that were not Palestinian, but rather Aryan or Iranian.[32] There continues to be a danger of removing Jesus from his Jewish context and interpreting him only in relation to a different tradition. The resurgence of antisemitism today makes it important to refute any such ideas and keep in mind the Jewishness of Jesus. While thoroughly discredited by historical scholarship, claims that Jesus was not Jewish continue to circulate in some anti-Semitic circles.

---

[30] Sarah J. Tanzer, "The Historical Jesus," in Levine and Brettler, *The Jewish Annotated New Testament*, 628–33.

[31] Susannah Heschel, *The Aryan Jesus: Christian Theologians and the Bible in Nazi Germany* (Princeton, NJ: Princeton University Press, 2008), 127.

[32] S. Radhakrishnan, *Eastern Religions and Western Thought* (New York: Oxford University Press, 1959), 171; Radhakrishnan cites Rudolph Otto, *The Kingdom of God and the Son of Man: A Study in the History of Religion*, (London: Lutterworth Press, 1938), 16.

While there have been numerous discussions of Jesus as a Jew in recent decades, the use of the terms "Jew" and "Jewishness" and "Judaism" can be understood in various ways and can be problematic for both past and present contexts.[33] As Amy-Jill Levine comments, "The question 'who is a Jew' was a problem in antiquity, and it remains a problem today. Scholars have sometimes set up constructs of what Jews think and do, and then checked to see whether Jesus fit the predetermined definitions."[34] Recent research has shown how fluid and multisided first-century Jewish practice was, and many earlier generalizations about Jews of that era are now discredited.[35] Even the terms "Judaism" and "Jew" did not have their later meanings.[36] Researchers have stressed the dominance of Roman rule in shaping the colonial situation in which Jesus lived and preached and died.[37] The criterion of dissimilarity proposed by many scholars holds that if sayings of Jesus are to be recognized as authentic, their perspectives must be dissimilar to the Judaism of his time and to the early Christianity of the Church. This principle risks separating Jesus from his Jewish context and presumes certain constructs of Jewish life at that time, constructs that recent scholarship has often found to be problematic.[38]

Scholars have also demonstrated how Jewish life in the time of Jesus was permeated by Hellenistic culture with a variety of religious practices. Jesus's Sermon on the Mount is rooted in Jewish sapiential tradition and also bears numerous analogies to Hellenistic wisdom teachings.[39] From the beginning, Jesus was interpreted in relation to other religious models and practices. Dennis MacDonald argues that Greek literary tradition permeated Jewish culture at the time of Jesus and decisively influenced the presentation of Jesus in the Gospels.[40] Lawrence M. Wills finds numerous similarities between the Gospels and *The Life of Aesop*, which is roughly contemporary.[41] Marianne Palmer Bonz compares Luke-Acts to Virgil's *Aeneid*.[42]

---

[33] Daniel Boyarin, *Judaism: The Genealogy of a Modern Notion* (New Brunswick, NJ: Rutgers University Press, 2018).

[34] Levine, "Reflections on Reflections," 9.

[35] E.g., Mary Rose D'Angelo, "Abba and Father: Imperial Theology in the Contexts of Jesus and the Gospels," in Levine, Allison, and Crossan, eds., *The Historical Jesus in Context*, 64–78.

[36] Boyarin, *Judaism*.

[37] Richard A. Horsley, *Jesus and Empire: The Kingdom of God and the New World Disorder* (Minneapolis: Fortress Press, 2002); John Dominic Crossan, *The Historical Jesus: The Life of a Mediterranean Jewish Peasant* (San Francisco: HarperSanFranciso, 1991).

[38] Levine, "Introduction," 9–10.

[39] Hans Dieter Betz, *The Sermon on the Mount: A Commentary on the Sermon on the Mount, including the Sermon on the Plain (Matthew 5:3–7:27 and Luke 6:20–49)*, ed. Adele Yarbro Collins (Minneapolis: Fortress Press, 1995).

[40] Dennis R. MacDonald, *Mythologizing Jesus: From Jewish Teacher to Epic Hero* (Lanham, MD: Rowman & Littlefield Publishers, 2015); Dennis R. MacDonald, *The Dionysian Gospel: The Fourth Gospel and Euripedes* (Minneapolis: Fortress Press, 2017).

[41] Lawrence M. Wills, "The Aesop Tradition," in Levine, Allison, and Crossan, eds., *The Historical Jesus in Context*, 222–37.

[42] Marianne Palmer Bonz, *The Past as Legacy: Luke-Acts and Ancient Epic* (Minneapolis: Fortress Press, 2000).

Jesus and his first interpreters lived in a multicultural, multireligious milieu and variously accepted or rejected different aspects of it.

It was a long-standing practice of Catholic and other Christian scholars to present Jesus as critiquing the practice of the Law of Moses by Jews of his day.[43] However, the New Testament writings present Jesus as a Torah-observant Jew who proclaimed the reign of God, worked healing miracles, and debated and disagreed with various contemporary Jews about following *halakha* (Jewish law).[44] Recent scholars have explored both similarities and differences between Jesus and the developing rabbinic tradition, challenging many of the traditional generalizations.[45] In contrast to some traditional interpretations of the Last Supper that viewed Jesus as rejecting the Jewish Temple and its sacrificial practice and instituting the Catholic Mass, Jewish scholar Jonathan Klawans views the Last Supper in light of the Jewish practice of channeling the holiness of the Temple into other practices like eating and praying.[46]

In the New Testament Jesus appears in many of the traditional Jewish roles of leadership and is described as exceeding them; he appears as a prophet but is said to be greater than Jonah; he is presented as a teacher of wisdom but is said to be greater than Solomon (Mt 12:41–42; Lk 11:31–32); Paul proclaims Jesus to be the Wisdom of God through whom all things are (1 Cor 1:24; 8:6).[47] Jesus utters apocalyptic statements in the Gospels, but it is highly debated whether the historical Jesus expressed apocalyptic expectations; in the book of Revelation he appears as an apocalyptic figure. Though Jesus was not from a priestly family, the Letter to the Hebrews interprets him as a priest who understands our weaknesses (4:14–15).[48] The Jewish prophetic, sapiential, priestly, and apocalyptic trajectories intertwine in the New Testament, offering a variety of points of contrast and contact with other religious traditions. The view of Jesus as prophet provides a strong link to Islam, though the meaning of prophecy varies in important ways in the different traditions. The perspective of Jesus as teacher of wisdom and incarnation of Lady

---

[43] On the variety of perspectives on Jesus and the Law of Moses, see John P. Meier, *A Marginal Jew: Rethinking the Historical Jesus,* vol. 4, *Law and Love,* Anchor Yale Bible Reference Library (New Haven, CT: Yale University Press, 2009), 1–25.

[44] E. P. Sanders, *The Historical Figure of Jesus* (London: Allen Lane Penguin Press, 1993); Meier, *Law and Love.*

[45] Jonathan Klawans, "Morality and Purity," in Levine, Allison, and Crossan, eds., *The Historical Jesus in Context,* 266–84; Herbert W. Basser, "Gospel and Talmud," in Levine, Allison, and Crossan, eds., *The Historical Jesus in Context,* 285–95; Alan J. Avery-Peck, "The Galilean Charismatic and Rabbinic Piety: The Holy Man in the Talmudic Literature," in Levine, Allison, and Crossan, eds., *The Historical Jesus in Context,* 149–65.

[46] Jonathan Klawans, "Interpreting the Last Supper: Sacrifice, Spiritualization, and Anti-Sacrifice," *New Testament Studies* 48, no. 1 (2002): 1–17.

[47] James D. G. Dunn, "Jesus: Teacher of Wisdom or Wisdom Incarnate?" in *Where Shall Wisdom Be Found? Wisdom in the Bible, the Church and the Contemporary World,* ed, Stephen C. Barton (Edinburgh: T & T Clark, 1999), 75–92.

[48] Alan C. Mitchell, *Hebrews* (Collegeville, MN: Liturgical Press, 2007), 104–15.

Wisdom offers points of both contact and contrast with Jewish views of Jesus, a line of continuity to later Christian views of Jesus, as well as important resources for a number of interreligious dialogues with Hindus and Buddhists.[49]

In the New Testament, Jesus is a sage who teaches in the style and content of the wisdom tradition, as well as in prophetic and apocalyptic modes of discourse, and he may have used humor in his teaching; Arthur Dewey sees him as

> one of the earliest in a long line of Jewish stand-up comics. Jesus envisioned an atmosphere where one could fall into the hands of the enemy and come out the better for it. His is a curious God who delivers benefits without distinction or discrimination. It is a God in whom the nobodies of the land can trust.[50]

The Sermon on the Mount is filled with wisdom sayings regarding classic themes such as the proper use of wealth, donations to the poor, upright character, humility, choosing the right treasure, living one day at a time, not judging others, and following one master. Many parables of Jesus present the consequences of wise and foolish behavior. In Luke 7:32–35, Jesus describes Lady Wisdom sending envoys, her children, into the world; even though they are rejected, Wisdom is nonetheless vindicated by them. Jesus here appears to be a child of Wisdom.[51] In a variation of this passage, the Gospel of Matthew tells us that Wisdom is vindicated by her own deeds, suggesting to some scholars that Matthew identifies Jesus and Wisdom.[52] Jesus's prayer of thanksgiving to God for revealing wisdom to infants also evokes Wisdom (Mt 11:25–27). Jesus's invitation, "Take my yoke upon you" (Mt 11:29), echoes the invitation of Ben Sira to accept the yoke of Wisdom (Sir 51:26). The teachings of Jesus in the Sermon on the Mount and the Sermon on the Plain develop and challenge many of the perspectives about wisdom in the Jewish and Greco-Roman Hellenistic world, including the concern with reflection as "preventive ethical therapy."[53]

Stephen C. Barton points out that Jesus's wisdom teachings involve not only content:

> It is also a *way of seeing* which attends to what lies hidden as well as to what lies on the surface. Insofar as it attends to what is hidden, wisdom is a way of seeing which has the potential for being innovative, paradoxical, ironic

---

[49] James D. G. Dunn, *Christology in the Making: A New Testament Inquiry into the Origins of the Doctrine of the Incarnation*, 2nd ed. (Grand Rapids, MI: Eerdmans, 1996).

[50] Dewey, "What Difference?" 6.

[51] Joseph A. Fitzmyer, *The Gospel According to Luke (I–IX): Introduction, Translation, and Notes,* Anchor Bible (New York: Doubleday, 1981), 681.

[52] Jack Suggs, *Wisdom, Christology, and Law in Matthew's Gospel* (Cambridge, MA: Harvard University Press, 1970), 57–60.

[53] Betz, *Sermon on the Mount*, 86.

and subversive. Here, the place of the wise is taken by the fool, the place of the strong by the weak, the place of the mature by the child.[54]

This way of seeing continues the warning of the book of Proverbs that those who think themselves wise are worse off than fools (26:12).

Jesus the Wisdom of God

A number of New Testament writings present Jesus as the incarnation of personified Wisdom. Paul proclaims Christ crucified as "the power of God and the wisdom [Sophia] of God" (1 Cor 1:24). In this context, wisdom is God's plan of salvation, which is fulfilled in Christ. Later in the same letter, Paul comments,

> Indeed, even though there may be so-called gods in heaven or on earth—
> as in fact there are many gods and many lords—yet for us there is one
> God, the Father, from whom are all things and for whom we exist, and
> one Lord, Jesus Christ, through whom are all things and through whom
> we exist. (1 Cor 8:5–6)

Paul makes this provocative assertion in the context of a dispute in Corinth over the practice of eating meat sacrificed to idols; his language poses many questions regarding the apparently crowded environment of "many gods and many lords." The claim that all things are "from" (*ek*) and "for" (*eis*) God the Father and that all things exist "through" (*dia*) the Lord Jesus Christ reaches far beyond the original context in Corinth, challenging other visions of the universe and inviting philosophical reflection.

Lest we think we understand too easily the meaning of this assertion, Paul prefaces the statement with a sharp warning that pretensions to knowledge can be foolish: "Knowledge puffs up, but love builds up. Anyone who claims to know something does not yet have the necessary knowledge; but anyone who loves God is known by him" (1 Cor 8:1b–3). For Paul, the belief that all things are from and for God the Father and exist in Jesus Christ evidently is not the type of knowledge that "puffs up" but involves the love that "builds up." Wisdom demands recognition and acceptance of one's limits, and Paul rejects claims to absolute knowledge, confessing later in the same letter: "Now we see only reflections in a mirror, mere riddles. . . . Now I can know only imperfectly" (1 Cor 13:12). These passages in 1 Corinthians together with other New Testament passages (Jn 1:1–5; Col 1:15–20; Heb 1:3), provide a decisive precedent for recognizing the limits of religious knowledge and a challenge to discern whether religious perspectives "puff up" or "build up." Both of these views provide important guidance for comparative theological reflection today.

---

[54] Stephen C. Barton, "Gospel Wisdom," in Barton, *Where Shall Wisdom Be Found*, 94.

Many scholars believe that the background of Paul's statement about Jesus Christ lies in the role of Sophia in creation and salvation in the Hellenistic Jewish wisdom tradition, as represented by the Wisdom of Solomon. For example, the editors of *The New Oxford Annotated Bible* comment on these verses: "Paul must be replacing Wisdom with Christ in formulas borrowed from the Corinthian theological knowledge, just as he argued that the real wisdom of God is the crucified Christ in 1.24."[55] Paul attributes to Jesus Christ the mediating role in creation of personified Wisdom or Sophia. The long and influential tradition of cosmic Christology arises from this identification.[56] To acclaim Jesus Christ as Wisdom means to find in him the power through whom the entire universe was created and holds together in being. The Wisdom of God, who plays in creation and unites the natural world, has taken flesh and entered the world in Jesus Christ.

The Letter to the Colossians develops the presentation of Jesus as Wisdom incarnate to include cosmic reconciliation: "For in him the fullness of God was pleased to dwell, and through him God was pleased to reconcile to himself all things, whether on earth or in heaven, by making peace through the blood of his cross" (Col 1:19–20). It is noteworthy that the scope of the reconciliation offered through Christ extends to everything in heaven and earth. The Letter to the Hebrews also uses the traditional language of Wisdom to describe Christ: "He is the reflection of God's glory and the exact imprint of God's very being, and he sustains all things by his powerful word" (Heb 1:3). Most influential was the Prologue of the Gospel of John presenting Jesus as the incarnation of the Logos, which was very closely related to Sophia in Hellenistic Jewish thought: Logos/Sophia comes to dwell in Jesus. As James Dunn comments, "In that Gospel [John], there is no doubt that Jesus is presented as Wisdom Incarnate. In particular, it is generally agreed that the prologue to the Gospel (Jn 1:1–18) is shot through with language and imagery attributed to divine wisdom in earlier Jewish traditions."[57] Dunn also argues that there is a strong continuity in the proclamation of Jesus as Wisdom Incarnate and the earliest memories of Jesus's teaching.[58]

Earlier scholars frequently understood these affirmations to mark a final separation from the Jewish tradition, but today scholars recognize that throughout the first century, the conflicts over the identity and mission of Jesus were not yet a question of two completely separate religions.[59] While many Jews would reject the claim

---

[55] Michael D. Coogan et al., eds., *The New Oxford Annotated Bible: Augmented Third Edition with the Apocryphal/Deuterocanonical Books* (Oxford: Oxford University Press, 2007), 279 New Testament.

[56] For recent articulations of this tradition, see Rowan Williams, *Christ the Heart of Creation* (London: Bloomsbury Continuum, 2018); and Richard Rohr, *The Universal Christ: How a Forgotten Reality Can Change Everything We See, Hope For, and Believe* (New York: Convergent Books, 2019).

[57] Dunn, "Jesus," 77.

[58] Ibid., 92.

[59] Boyarin, *Border Lines*.

that Jesus is to be seen as Wisdom Incarnate, Jewish scholar Daniel Boyarin interprets the prologue of John as typically Jewish midrash, a homily based on Genesis
1:1–5 that interprets the text of creation in Genesis in light of the presentation of
personified Wisdom in Proverbs 8.[60] Boyarin sees the Fourth Gospel as applying a
thoroughly Jewish view of Logos/Sophia to Jesus Christ.[61]

During the period of the early Church, the interpretation of Sophia or Logos
was central to Jewish-Christian debates. Boyarin argues that it was the Logos
theology of Justin Martyr and his colleagues that would eventually become the
fundamental point of differentiation between rabbinic Judaism and orthodox
Christianity. Many Jews, like Philo of Alexandria, viewed Logos or Sophia as a way
to affirm both the transcendence and the immanence of God in the world. Boyarin
comments,

> The idea that the Logos or Sophia (Wisdom, and other variants as well) is
> the site of God's presence in the world—indeed, the notion of God's Word
> or Wisdom as a mediator figure—was a very widespread one in the world
> of first- and even second-century Judaic thought. Rather than treating
> Logos theology as the specific product of "Christianity," with Philo a
> sort of Christian avant la lettre, I wish to explore the evidence for Logos
> theology as a common element in Jewish, including Christian Jewish, reli-
> gious imagination.[62]

In contrast to earlier Hellenistic Jews who had readily embraced belief in the
Logos, the later rabbis of the second through fourth centuries CE came to reject
it. Boyarin comments that even as Justin was making acceptance of Logos theology
the touchstone of orthodox Christian faith, "the Rabbis agree, as it were, to cede
traditional Jewish Logos theology to Christianity, declaring it and its once orthodox
holders (symbolized by no less than Rabbi Akiva) as members of an imagined
heretical group, 'Two Powers in Heaven.'"[63] In the fourth century and later, belief
in Sophia or the Logos would eventually become the cornerstone of Christian
Trinitarian theology; rejection of the Logos would become a fundamental point of
identity for rabbinic Judaism.

The interpretation of Jesus that would be a major factor in the eventual parting
of Jews and Christians emerges from Jewish styles of belief. The implications of
a Wisdom Christology for interreligious dialogue are multifaceted.[64] If Christ is
the power through whom all things exist and are reconciled, then Christ is present

---

[60] Daniel Boyarin, "*Logos,* a Jewish Word: John's Prologue as Midrash," in Levine and
Brettler, *The Jewish Annotated New Testament,* 546–49.

[61] Boyarin, *Border Lines,* 104.

[62] Ibid., 112.

[63] Ibid., 31.

[64] Gerald O'Collins, *A Christology of Religions* (Maryknoll, NY: Orbis Books, 2018).

throughout the entire cosmos, including in other religious traditions. As the early Christian community developed the doctrine of the Trinity, this perspective on Jesus would become a major factor in the uniqueness of Christian faith, a point of divergence from all other religious traditions. Jews and Muslims reject the claim that Jesus can be seen as the incarnation of the Wisdom of God; Hindus may accept it in their own fashion but understand it very differently, while some Buddhists see Jesus as a manifestation of cosmic Wisdom, though without belief in a divine Creator. As Robert Schreiter comments, "To see Christ as the Wisdom of God—certainly no new representation of the Lord—is a way of reading the divine presence in a culture that is already working out the saving activity."[65]

A Wisdom Christology views the incarnation as central to Christian faith. John Pawlikowski believes "that a focus on the incarnation offers the best option for developing a Christology that allows for continued covenantal inclusion of the Jewish People."[66] He proposes that "what ultimately came to be recognized with clarity for the first time through the ministry and person of Jesus was profoundly how integral humanity was to divine biography. This in turn implied that each person somehow shares in divinity."[67] Pawlikowski insists that humanity is not identical with divinity since there remains an unbridgeable gulf between them. He argues that humans could never have come to the realization of its link with divinity without the Christ event; he does not note that many Hindus find a similar affirmation of divine-human unity in the Upanishads, which date from hundreds of years before the time of Jesus.

Death and Resurrection of Jesus Christ

Perhaps the greatest contrast with other religious traditions is found in the accounts of Jesus's death and resurrection. No other tradition has a narrative that is precisely the same, and some followers of other religious traditions have firmly rejected Christian views of death and resurrection. Nonetheless, there may be resonances with certain aspects of other traditions that offer an opening to dialogue; from a Jewish perspective, Arthur Dewey notes that in the Gospel of Mark Jesus's death is "not envisioned as an exclusive event but as a death in solidarity with all those innocent sufferers."[68] The crucifixion of Jesus was central to Paul's proclamation of Christ crucified as the wisdom of God, a wisdom not of this world that seems foolish to the Greeks and poses a stumbling block to Jews (1 Cor 1:23). Paul came to see that a new glory was coming through the shame of the cross; as Barton comments, "In short, Paul's understanding of Christ and the life of faith is indebted to wisdom both as a body of thought and as a way of seeing. The converse is even

---

[65] Robert J. Schreiter, *Constructing Local Theologies* (London: SCM Press, 1985), 39.

[66] Pawlikowski, "Christology and the Jewish-Christian Dialogue," 150.

[67] Ibid., 160.

[68] Dewey, "What Difference?," 7.

more true: wisdom for Paul is now wisdom understood in relation to Christ and the cross."[69]

Perhaps most surprising is the proclamation of reconciliation in and through the death and resurrection of Jesus Christ. Often reconciliation in interreligious relationships seems to be difficult, if not impossible. The New Testament authors present reconciliation not as a human accomplishment but as a gift from God coming through Jesus Christ and extending to the entire cosmos. The resurrection is not more of the same old cycle—it is a new chance for the entire human race, both in this world and the next. The resurrection of Jesus is the sheer power of absolute love bringing forth life from amidst the ruins of history. In the Acts of the Apostles, Peter tells the people that they have put to death the author of life, but God raised him from the dead (Acts 3:15). The author of life will not stay dead. He bursts back into history and reaches out to each of his followers with an invitation. The old cycle of sin and death, of violence and shame, has been defeated. After sin comes forgiveness, after domination comes freedom, after violence comes healing, after shame comes acceptance, after death comes life. Even from the cross Jesus prayed to God to forgive his executioners because they did not know what they were doing (Lk 23:34). According to the Gospel of John, Jesus's first word to the group of disciples after the Resurrection was "Peace" (Jn 20:20).

In dying, Jesus entered into the cycle of violence that dominates so much of world history and broke through its power. The powers and principalities that rule this world through violence have been overcome, even though in practice their might is still great.[70] Often we believe that we either have to flee the power of violence and evil or we have to fight it with its own weapons. Either way we lose. By fleeing, we abandon the field to evil; by resisting with the same tools of violence, we become like the powers we are opposing. Jesus opens up a third way, neither passive acceptance nor violent resistance.[71]

In this world of brutality and violence, Christians proclaim the resurrection and all that it brings: the forgiveness of sins, the healing of the soul, peace, a season of refreshment. And yet the cycles of violence obviously continue. Jesus gave Christians an example of facing oppression in his own meeting with Pontius Pilate. He did not fight violently; he did not summon legions of angels to destroy Pilate. Neither did he simply accept Pilate's authority. He quietly undermined the assumptions of the whole Roman system, calling Pilate himself into question (Jn 19:11). This set a model for Christian resistance to the Roman Empire and all other oppressive systems.

Aware of the limitations of all claims of religious knowledge, Christians can be open to wisdom coming from other sources. In different ways, Jesus Christ and many other traditions propose humble paths that renounce the quest for domina-

---

[69] Barton, "Gospel Wisdom," 94.

[70] Walter Wink, *Engaging the Powers: Discernment and Resistance in a World of Domination* (Minneapolis: Fortress, 1992).

[71] Ibid.

tion through the power of knowledge, and teach paths of wisdom and compassion that can transform life for the better. In a world of massive, unjust, and unnecessary suffering, Jesus Christ and the teachers of many other religious traditions come as physicians offering healing and wisdom.

Jesus as Prophet and Messenger in Islam

While it may seem tempting to compare the place of Jesus Christ in Catholic faith with Muhammad in Islam, the more fitting analogy is between Jesus Christ as the final revelation of God for Catholics and the Qur'an as the final revelation of God for Muslims. John Renard, a Catholic scholar who has long studied the Islamic tradition, stresses the difference in the status of the Bible and the Qur'an in their respective traditions and the similarity between Jesus and the Qur'an:

> As the presence of the word of God in book form, or "inlibration," the Qur'an functions more as a theological counterpart to the Christian understanding of Jesus as God's Word made flesh in the "incarnation." The New Testament, as the words of Jesus, could then be paralleled with the Hadith, the authoritative gatherings of the words and deeds of Muhammad.[72]

For Christians, the fullest revelation of God is the person of Jesus Christ, and the Bible bears witness to how to follow him; for traditional Muslims, the final revelation of God is the Qur'an (i.e., the Arabic text), and the reports of the life of Muhammad bear witness to how to follow the Qur'an. Renard offers his comparisons as suggestions for further reflection: "All comparisons and analogies, implicit or forthright, I suggest only as possible ways of making links between two very different families of religious traditions."[73] He suggests that in each tradition the earliest form of theological discourse was narrative theology.

With the possible exception of the crucifixion of Jesus, Muslims can accept most of the findings of scholars seeking the historical Jesus. Some years ago, I spoke on themes of the New Testament to American Muslim leaders at the Islamic Society of North America in Indianapolis. I began by summarizing contemporary research on the historical Jesus, and then I presented an overview of interpretations of Jesus by New Testament authors. The Muslim leaders completely accepted the material on the historical Jesus, with the important exception of his death by crucifixion. There is a long Islamic debate over how to interpret the Qur'an concerning the end of Jesus's earthly existence, and most Muslims believe that God protected Jesus from death.[74] After my presentation, one Muslim scholar commented to me, "First you

---

[72] John Renard, *Islam and Christianity: Theological Themes in Comparative Perspective* (Berkeley: University of California Press, 2011), x.

[73] Ibid., xi.

[74] See A. H. Matthias Zahniser, *The Mission and Death of Jesus in Islam and Chris-*

gave me a very Muslim Jesus, and then you added all that Christian stuff." Another responded that he could accept 80 percent of what I had said; when questioned on the percentage, he responded enthusiastically, "They're Shi'ite numbers!" Presenting Jesus as a Jew in his original context allows Muslims to accept him quite easily in relation to the view of Jesus in traditional Islam.

The prophetic identity of Jesus relates him to the Islamic tradition, but it is also important to note differences in the understanding of prophecy. While Muslims believe aspects of *Injil*, the message brought by Jesus, can be found in the New Testament, they generally do not believe that the New Testament is a faithful record of *Injil*. Similarly, they generally do not believe that the current text of the Hebrew Bible accurately preserves *Tawrah* (Torah) and *Zabur* (the Psalms) the message Muslims believe was given through David. Many Muslims understand Jesus's promise in the Gospel of John to send a *Parakletos* to be a prophecy of Muhammad; this association is facilitated by the fact that changing one vowel in the Greek word "Parakletos" gives "Paraklytos," which can be translated as "Ahmed" in Arabic, which is one of the names given to Muhammad.

Muslims can readily acknowledge that Jesus as a Jewish prophet proclaimed the rule of God, that he healed people through the power of God, that he challenged people to repent for their sins and accept God's will. Muslims are pleased to know that biblical scholarship indicates that the historical Jesus never proclaimed a doctrine of the Trinity and never explicitly claimed to be the eternal, only-begotten Son of God. The teaching of the historical Jesus resonates deeply with the early suras of the Qur'an, which stress the oneness of God, the necessity for justice in society, and the coming judgment of all people by God. Muslim scholar Neal Robinson points out that Muslims are impressed that in the Gospel of Mark, Jesus "thought of himself as a prophet, objected when someone called him good, and stressed the oneness of God (Mark 6:4; 10:17; 12:29)."[75] Muslims rejoice that the hallmark of Jesus's teaching is "radical obedience to God," which they identify with true *islam*.[76] Concerning the Lord's Prayer, Muslims can accept that Jesus as a Jew prayed to God as Father without any implication of a divine Trinity, and they can endorse all the petitions in the prayer.[77]

---

 [75] Neal Robinson, "Which Islam, Which Jesus?" in *Jesus in the World's Faiths: Leading Thinkers from Five Religions Reflect on His Meaning*, ed. Gregory A. Barker (Maryknoll, NY: Orbis Books, 2007), 139.

 [76] Ibid., 140.

 [77] In this sense Hasan Askari accepts the Lord's Prayer, explaining, "The immanence of the Lord's Prayer (God as 'Father') is immediately balanced by transcendence (God is holy). Both the intimacy and the awe concerning God, as found so beautifully placed side by side in the Lord's Prayer, is also part and parcel found in Islam." Hasan Askari, "The Real Presence of Jesus in Islam," in Barker, *Jesus in the World's Faiths*, 145.

The initial sura of the Qur'an, known as *Surat Al-Fatihah* ("The Opening") is at the center of Islamic prayer and plays a role in Islamic piety analogous to that of the Lord's Prayer in Christian worship:

> In the name of God,
> the Benevolent,
> the Merciful.
> Praise is proper to God,
> Lord of the universe,
> the Benevolent,
> the Merciful,
> Ruler of the Day of Requital.
> It is You we serve.
> to you we turn for help.
> Show us the straight path,
> the path of those You have favored
> not of those who are objects of anger,
> nor of those who wander astray. (Q 1:1–7)[78]

The themes of *Al-Fatihah* coincide, overlap, and resonate with the Lord's Prayer. The opening invocation, also translated as "In the Name of God, the All-Merciful, the All-Compassionate,"[79] sanctifies the name of God, as Jesus urged, and seeks God's forgiving mercy. Offering praise (*hamd*) to God is a way of sanctifying God's name and offering gratitude. The term "Lord" (*Rabb*) specifies God's relationship to the universe and has multiple overtones, as Ali Unal explains: "(i) Upbringer, Trainer, Sustainer, Nourisher; (ii) Lord and Master; (iii) He Who directs and controls."[80] All of these meanings resonate with the prayer of Jesus and its Jewish context. By calling God "Ruler of the Day of Requital" (also translated as "The Master of the Day of Judgment"[81]), *Al-Fatihah* acknowledges that the kingship of God will come to completion on the Day of Judgment. The term *malik* is cognate with the Hebrew word *melek,* king, and is variously translated as "master," "ruler" or "sovereign." The *Fatihah* prays that God's will be done by pledging to serve or worship God alone and seek assistance only from God. The request for guidance on the straight path seeks help in doing God's will, noting the danger of the alternate paths that go astray and incur God's wrath.

---

[78] *The Qur'an: A New Translation by Thomas Cleary* (n.p.: Starlatch Press, 2004), 1.

[79] *The Qur'an with Annotated Interpretation in Modern English,* by Ali Unal (Somerset, NJ: Light, 2006), 2.

[80] Ibid., 5.

[81] Ibid., 2; so also 'Abdullah Yusu 'Ali, *The Meaning of The Holy Qur'an: New Edition with Qur'anic Text (Arabic), Revised Translation, Commentary and Newly Compiled Comprehensive Index* (Beltsville, MD: Amana Publications, 1989), 14.

The Qur'an presents Jesus as confirming the Torah; the Qur'anic Jesus says, "And [I come] confirming that which was before me, the Torah, and to make lawful unto you part of that which was forbidden unto you. And I have come to you with a sign from your Lord" (Q 3:50).[82] Muslim commentators have offered varying views on precisely what Jesus made lawful. Some have thought it involved dietary restrictions in Torah, while others have thought it refers to things that the Israelites had forbidden but that were not in Torah itself.[83] Recent research on the observance of Torah by Jesus coheres with a traditional Islamic perspective.

The Qur'an identifies Jesus as emerging from and participating in the line of prophets and leaders in ancient Israel:

> Say, "We believe in God and what has been sent down upon us, and in what was sent down upon Abraham, Ishmael, Isaac, Jacob, and the Tribes, and in what Moses, Jesus, and the prophets were given from their Lord. We make no distinction among any of them, and unto Him we submit." (Q 3:84)

According to the Qur'an, the message brought by Jesus is in its core identical with that of Moses and the other prophets of ancient Israel as well as with that of Muhammad. Muslims see the message brought by Jesus, which they call *Injil*, as a complement to the message brought by Moses, *Tawra*, and that brought by David, *Zabur*.[84] According to Amin Ahsan Islahi, Jesus may be said to fulfill the Mosaic Law in that he brings it back to its original purity and wisdom, which had been lost sight of.[85] Muslims view Jesus as the last of the prophets of Israel, and thus they can call him the seal of the prophets of Israel. Muslims note that the Qur'an does not present Muhammad as bringing a new message from God; the Qur'an says, "Naught is said to thee (Muhammad) but what already was said to the Messengers before thee" (41:43).

As a result of these developments, Christian scholars today see the historical Jesus in a manner that bears strong similarity to some aspects of the Qur'anic Jesus. To be sure, there are Qur'anic statements concerning Jesus that would not be accepted by researchers seeking the historical Jesus, such as him speaking from the cradle (3:46, 5:110, 19:29–30) or fashioning a clay bird into a real bird (3:49, 5:110); but the findings of researchers on the teachings of the historical Jesus are largely consistent with Qur'anic perspectives, including the oneness of God, the necessity for justice in society, and the coming judgment of all people by God. The

---

[82] *The Study Quran: A New Translation and Commentary,* ed. Seyyed Hossein Nasr et al. (New York: HarperOne, 2015), 145; unless otherwise noted, all quotations from the Qur'an will be from this edition.

[83] Ibid.

[84] Mustansir Mir, "Islamic Views of Jesus," in Barker, *Jesus in the World's Faiths,* 121.

[85] Ibid.

Qur'anic titles for Jesus could all be applied to Jesus as understood in historical research today: Messiah or Christ, Son of Mary, Messenger, Prophet, Servant, allowing for differences in usage, Word and Spirit of God.[86] Christian affirmation of Jesus as divine Wisdom and Son of God will continue to be a major point of divergence between them, but this need not be a source of animosity as in the past.

American Indians and Jesus

American Indians have responded to Jesus in a variety of ways; some reject Christian faith and follow traditional religious paths. Others, however, have embraced Christian faith and combine traditional Native religious practices with faith in Jesus Christ. In the early twentieth century, Charles Alexander Eastman, also known by his Indian name as Ohiyesa, of the clan of the Wah'petons of the Sioux nation, met an elderly Indian man who commented,

> I have come to the conclusion that this Jesus was an Indian. He was opposed to material acquirement and to great possessions. He was inclined to peace. He was as unpractical as any Indian and set no price upon his labor of love. These are not the principles upon which the white man has founded his civilization. It is strange that he could not rise to these simple principles which were commonly observed among our people.[87]

Eastman himself argued in similar fashion that the aggressive Euro-American conquest and humiliation of American Indians was not inspired by the example of Jesus Christ; he concluded that "there is no such thing as 'Christian civilization.' I believe that Christianity and modern civilization are opposed and irreconcilable, and that the spirit of Christianity and our ancient religion is essentially the same."[88]

Lamenting the tragic history of disrespect toward Indian peoples, Marie Therese Archambault, a Franciscan sister from the Hunkpapa Lakota nation, movingly expresses the significance of Jesus Christ for her community today:

> When we read the Gospel, we must read it as *Native people*, for this is who we are. We can no longer try to be what we think the dominant society wants us to be. . . . We have to go beyond the *white gospel* in order to perceive its truth. When we do this, we shall meet Jesus as our brother and recognize him as one who has been with us all along as the quiet servant, the one who has strengthened us through these centuries. Then

---

[86] See Geoffrey Parrinder, *Jesus in the Qur'an* (1965; reprint, London: Oneworld, 2013), 16.

[87] Charles Alexander Eastman (Ohiyesa), *From the Deep Woods to Civilization* (1916; reprint, Mineola, NY: Dover Publications, 2003), 81.

[88] Charles Alexander Eastman (Ohiyesa), *The Soul of the Indian* (1911; reprint, Mineola, NY: Dover Publications, 2003), 6.

we will know that the cry of Jesus from the cross was the cry of our people at Wounded Knee, Sand Creek and other places of the mass death of our people. He was our companion during these years of our invisibility in this society. This same Jesus is the one who challenges us to grow beyond ourselves. . . . this is the heart and core meaning of the Gospel.[89]

Archambault movingly laments the horrific events of the past and describes the exigency of the current situation:

In the past the church has obscured the face of Christ through ignorance of or outright dismissal of Native cultures. It has attempted to enter the reality of Native people at superficial levels, almost always from the European viewpoint and perspectives. . . . Through this manner of teaching, many Indian people were placed in the profoundly impossible situation of accepting the Gospel for their own good on the one hand while, on the other, having to devalue their culture and thus themselves. . . . Now, we must undo this attitude and do all we can to reveal the face of Christ, who goes beyond all cultures. This means we must "de-evangelize" Native people.[90]

Michael Galvan, a Catholic priest from the Ohlone Indian Nation in California, notes that Native traditions view time in cyclic fashion and thus interpret the hope of the Second Coming of Jesus as a possibility even today: "For Natives, the Second Coming is accessible at the present time and not only at the end of time. One does not simply look forward to heaven through the passage of time but one sees the beginnings of heaven here in a life lived harmoniously with all of creation."[91] Galvan stresses the importance of land for Native identity; he recalls his grandmother warning him when he was young: "When I lost touch with Mother Earth, I misbehaved. When I attended to the land, however, my behavior improved. In other words, the land itself can heal."[92] Galvan finds a resonance between the preaching of Jesus and Native solidarity with all creation: "In Scripture, we find that Jesus utilizes such an approach: look at the clouds, see the mustard seed, observe the birds of the sky. Creation reveals God to us. For Native peoples, one lives as part of the created order and not as ruler of it."[93] Galvan challenges the dominant Western culture to become more familiar with and respectful of the variety of Native traditions, and he also issues a challenge to Native peoples "to appreciate the beauty and

---

[89] Marie Therese Archambault, "Native Americans and Evangelization," in *The People: Reflections of Native Peoples on the Catholic Experience in North America* (Washington, DC: National Catholic Educational Association, 1992), 23.

[90] Ibid., 26.

[91] Ibid.

[92] Ibid., 210–11.

[93] Ibid., 211.

giftedness of Western Tradition. In dialogue with one another, each will grow and develop."[94] Galvan articulates an agenda of care for Mother Earth that many Native Catholics in the United States are taking up.

African American Perceptions of Jesus

The center of African American celebration of salvific action is Jesus Christ. The Gospel of Matthew interprets the birth of Jesus in light of the prophet Isaiah (7:14): "'[T]hey shall name him Emmanuel,' which means 'God is with us'" (Mt 1:23). The African American spirituals sing that in Jesus, God is with us, drawing traditional African religious perceptions of God into the interpretation of Jesus Christ.[95] James Cone notes that in the spirituals "statements about God are not theologically distinct from statements about Jesus Christ. Jesus is understood as the King, the deliverer of humanity from unjust suffering."[96] Howard Thurman comments on the spirituals' expression of the incarnation of God:

He was able to particularize Himself in the man Jesus, the anointed. Thus all believers feel in this Man the achievement supreme—at last God had been able to speak Himself into time and space. Thus Jesus becomes the object of religious devotion, while he himself remains always the subject of religious experience. But here again even the believers continue to try to say who Jesus is; and no explanation is the final explanation.[97]

In a world of overwhelming trouble, a spiritual advises us to seek refuge in Jesus: "Steal away, steal away, steal away to Jesus!"

Howard Thurman and James Cone both conjecture that slave owners did not highlight Christmas because they did not want enslaved people to realize its concrete implications for the political liberation of the oppressed. Thurman comments on the delicate position of the slave owner:

It was dangerous to let the slave understand that the life and teachings of Jesus meant freedom for the captive and release for those held in economic, social, and political bondage. . . . What limitless release would have been available to the slave if the introduction to Jesus had been on the basis of his role as the hope of the disinherited and the captive.[98]

---

[94] Ibid.

[95] Peter J. Paris, *The Spirituality of African Peoples: The Search for a Common Moral Discourse* (Minneapolis: Fortress Press, 1995), 27–49.

[96] James Cone, *Spirituals and the Blues: An Interpretation*, 2nd rev. ed. (Maryknoll, NY: Orbis Books, 1992), 43.

[97] Howard Thurman, *Deep River and Negro Spiritual Speaks of Life and Death* (Richmond, IN: Friends United Press, 1975), 82.

[98] Ibid., 16; see also Cone, *Spirituals*, 46.

Even though white racist Christians did not emphasize this side of the Gospel message, African Americans heard it nonetheless. They trusted that God in Jesus Christ was with them in the midst of their suffering, and so Jesus understood what no one else could: "Nobody knows the trouble I've seen, nobody knows but Jesus." Even though suffering threatens to isolate us from sources of support, Jesus has known the worst suffering, and so the presence of Jesus opens up a way where there is no way. This was particularly important for the moment that seem most God forsaken: being lynched.

African American Christians understood Jesus's crucifixion as a lynching, and so they knew that in some way God knows what it is to be lynched, just as African Americans knew what it meant to be crucified. Thurman comments, "In the spirituals the death of Jesus took on a deep and personal poignancy.... They knew what He suffered; it was a cry of the heart that found a response and an echo in their own woes. They entered into the fellowship of His suffering."[99] When Howard Thurman and other African Americans visited Mohandas Gandhi in India in 1936, the Mahatma asked them to sing the hymn, "Were you there when they crucified my Lord?" For African Americans singing this hymn, the word "you" would include other African Americans, while the word "they" included the white racists involved in lynching. Thurman explains that the singer expresses a sense of being there, "an experimental grasping of the quality of Jesus' experience, by virtue of the racial frustration of the singers."[100] The final hope of African American Christians lay in the resurrection of Jesus and the prospect of heaven. At some point in its development, the hymn about being present at the cross received two additional questions: "Were you there when he rose up from the dead? Were you there when they rolled the stone away?"[101]

Japanese Buddhist D. T. Suzuki looked at an image of Jesus on the cross and worried, "The crucified Christ is a terrible sight and I cannot help associating it with the sadistic impulse of a physically affected brain."[102] For African Americans, the sadism came not from God but from earthly oppressors, whether the Romans or the slave masters or, more generally, white racists. Karen Baker-Fletcher comments, "God does not *cause* Jesus' death, because God is good. Evil, which is God's adversary, causes Jesus's death... Accompanied by the risen Christ, in the power of the Holy Spirit, men, women, and children are to overcome suffering and evil."[103] She explains this theology of accompaniment: "Christ as cosufferer accompanies us through our pain and suffering to help us overcome it and to help us live into resurrected life in the power of the Holy Spirit."[104]

---

[99] Thurman, *Deep River*, 22.

[100] Ibid., 23.

[101] Bruno Chenu, *The Trouble I've Seen: The Big Book of Negro Spirituals* (King of Prussia, PA: Judson Press, 2003), 191, 282.

[102] Daisetsu Teitaro Suzuki, *Mysticism; Christian and Buddhist* (London: Unwin Paperbacks, 1988), 99.

[103] Karen Baker-Fletcher, *Dancing with God: The Trinity from a Womanist Perspective* (St. Louis, MO: Chalice Press, 2006), 137.

[104] Ibid., 143.

In the spirituals, heaven is not only a future hope but also a present reality that enabled hearers to live in a new way. Hope of heaven assured their ultimate worth before God, which was secure from all white degradation. Often the spirituals sang of crossing the River Jordan as a multilayered image for passing to freedom in this world and also for passing to heaven in the next. Cone comments that

> the spirituals employ eschatological language to express transcendence in the slaves' present existence. "I've *started* to make heaven my home," "Marching up the heavenly road, I'm bound to fight till I die"—such lines make clear that black slaves were not passively waiting for the future; they were actively living as if the future were already present in their community.[105]

They found in the death and resurrection of Jesus Christ a freedom and a dignity that the white racist Christian establishment could not take from them and that empowered them to act in new ways with hope and courage. Howard Thurman concluded his classic study of the spirituals by noting how the salvific action of God empowered people to act with new courage: "This is the message of the spiritual. Do not shrink from moving confidently out into choppy seas. Wade in the water, because God is troubling the water."[106]

Jesus in Relation to Hindus

Many Hindus during the last two centuries have honored and worshipped Jesus Christ as a divine manifestation.[107] In dialogue with Hindus, Christians face a paradox: many Hindus fully accept Jesus Christ as divine, but many are very distrustful of Christian missionaries and the modern Western academic study of religion, which entered India with the British colonizers.[108] Hindu religious acceptance of Jesus developed about two hundred years ago in the context of the British dominating more and more of India, together with Protestant missioners from Britain and the United States challenging Hindu practices like child marriage, sati, and the caste system. In response to both Christian missionaries and British colonial officials, some educated Hindus began rethinking the meaning of Hinduism and launched what has been variously called the Bengali Renaissance or Neo-Hinduism. They accepted Jesus, frequently claiming that Christians do not understand Jesus,

---

[105] Cone, *Spirituals*, 83.

[106] Thurman, *Deep River*, 94.

[107] Sandy Bharat, *Christ across the Ganges* (Winchester, WA: O Books, 2007).

[108] In 1784, Warren Hastings, the governor-general for Bengal of the East India Company, promoted the publication of an English translation of the Bhagavad Gita to the Company directors by explaining, "Every accumulation of knowledge, and especially such as is obtained by social communication with people over whom we exercise a dominion founded on the right of conquest, is useful to the state." Richard H. Davis, *The Bhagavad Gita: A Biography* (Princeton, NJ: Princeton University Press, 2015), 83.

but Hindus do. From Ram Mohan Roy through Keshub Chandra Sen, Ramakrishna, Swami Vivekananda,[109] Mahatma Gandhi, Sarvepalli Radhakrishnan to
contemporary scholar Ravi Ravindra in Halifax, many Hindus have accepted Jesus
as a significant religious leader and divine manifestation.[110] Radhakrishnan speaks
for many in this lineage: "Suppose a Christian approaches a Hindu teacher for
spiritual guidance, he would not ask his Christian pupil to discard his allegiance to
Christ but would tell him his idea of Christ was not adequate, and would lead him
to a knowledge of the real Christ, the incorporate Supreme."[111]

Mahatma Gandhi was the most successful and influential in claiming to understand Jesus better than Christians. When criticized for his activities against the
British Empire, he pointed out that Jesus died opposing a mighty empire through
nonviolent means, and he was simply following the example of Jesus and the
Buddha.[112] Gandhi convinced many Christians that Jesus's teachings on nonviolent
resistance to evil could be put into practice on an unprecedented level to transform
societies.[113]

Some Hindus have emphasized Jesus's ethical teaching, but some have also
viewed him as fully divine, an *avatara,* a descent of God into this world bringing
eternal wisdom. From this perspective, the Jewishness of Jesus would be the effect
of *Ishvara,* the manifestation of the ultimate *Brahman,* graciously adapting itself
to communicate with Jewish culture. Advaita Hindus such as Vivekananda,
Radhakrishnan, or Ravindra, generally assume that they understand the ultimate
truth of Jesus's identity as nondual much better than most Jews or Christians; many
Hindus would see historical, contextual research as of little import. The great nineteenth-century leader Ramakrishna, who worshipped Jesus, commented, "Whether
Christ or Krishna lived or not is immaterial; the people from whose brain the
Christ ideal, or Krishna ideal, has emanated did actually live as Christ or Krishna
for the time being."[114]

Ramakrishna's disciple Vivekananda interpreted Jesus's teaching on three levels:
Dvaitic or dual for the noneducated, exemplified by the Lord's Prayer; Vishtad-
vaitic or modified nondual for the higher circle, exemplified by Jesus saying "I am
in my Father, and ye in me, and I in you."[115] Finally, for the most highly advanced,
Jesus teaches Advaita Vedanta when he claims to be one with the Father, but he was

[109] Vivekananda, "Christ, the Messenger," in *Christianity through Non-Christian Eyes,*
ed. Paul J. Griffiths (Maryknoll, NY: Orbis Books, 1990), 204–214.

[110] *Neo-Hindu Views of Christianity,* ed. Arvind Sharma (Leiden: E. J. Brill, 1988);
Bharat, *Christ across the Ganges.*

[111] Radhakrishnan, *The Hindu View of Life* (New York: Macmillan, 1973), 34.

[112] Mohandas K. Gandhi, *Gandhi on Christianity,* ed. Robert Ellsberg (Maryknoll,
NY: Orbis Books, 1991), 28.

[113] Terrence J. Rynne, *Gandhi and Jesus: The Saving Power of Nonviolence* (Maryknoll,
NY: Orbis Books, 2008).

[114] M. M. Thomas, *The Acknowledged Christ of the Indian Renaissance* (London: SCM
Press, 1969), 129.

[115] Ibid., 125.

misunderstood by Jews and Christians alike. Vivekananda does not believe Jesus was really crucified: "Christ was God incarnate; they could not kill him. That which was crucified was only a semblance, a mirage."[116] Vivekananda was very aware of the disagreements over the historical Jesus in the late nineteenth century, and he thought that this opened the door for Hindus to explain Jesus's teaching freed from the worries of historical evidence.[117]

Among contemporary Hindu scholars, Ravi Ravindra, who is based in Halifax, Nova Scotia, has written a Hindu interpretation of the Gospel of John in which he presents Jesus as a guru in light of Hindu mysticism.[118] He proposes a spiritual elitism where mystics of all traditions can communicate with each other, but all others cannot. Positing an allegedly universal mystical spirituality, Ravi Ravindra assumes that Hindu categories can adequately interpret the significance of figures and events in the Fourth Gospel. He recontextualizes Jesus so radically that the original Jewish context plays little to no role in his interpretation of the Gospel of John. I think it is a legitimate hermeneutical wager to interpret one tradition in light of the categories of another, but to read in the categories of one tradition into a text without any attention to the original context is to my mind problematic and unconvincing.

K. R. Sundararajan, a Hindu scholar long based in the United States, has criticized other Hindus for reading Hindu ideas into Jesus, and he challenges Hindus to broaden their horizons and open themselves in dialogue with Christians to "the possibility of a 'suffering God.'"[119] Similarly, Anantanand Rambachan, a Hindu scholar originally from Trinidad now teaching at St. Olaf's College in Minnesota, strenuously objects to the long history of Hindus reading their own ideas into Jesus.[120] Regarding the implications for Christian theology, the Indian

---

[116] Ibid., 126.

[117] Westerners tend to assume that what is historical is real. The encounter with South Asian religions and cultures poses questions about our most fundamental assumptions, including the meaning and importance of history and historical research. In India "the historical Jesus" can mean "the unreal Jesus." Moreover, Hindu avatars are not necessarily fully human, and they do not suffer and die for the salvation of the world. Hindu scholar K. R. Sundararajan, who was involved in dialogue with Christians for many years, noted that in Hinduism "theologically speaking, the divine incarnations cannot suffer and die. So a sort of 'docetist' understanding of Hindu *avataras* and Christ came to be stressed." K. R. Sundararajan, "Responses," Appendix in *Christ across the Ganges*, 180. See also Bradley Malkovsky, "Christ in Hinduism: Traditional Views and Recent Developments," in *Alternative Christs*, ed. Olav Hammer (Cambridge: Cambridge University Press, 2009), 179.

[118] Ravi Ravindra, *The Gospel of John*.

[119] Sundararajan, "Responses," 181.

[120] "As a Hindu, one has to resist the inclination to see and interpret Jesus in the categories of Hinduism. This approach was very common in the nineteenth and early twentieth centuries and it is not unusual today. The attempt is often made to see his life and teachings in the categories of the Hindu tradition of *advaita* (non-dualism). This, however, is only possible through a very selective use of the records of his sayings, and the dismissal of

Christian theologian M. Thomas Thangaraj expresses concern that many Indians, both Hindu and Christian, have accepted Jesus as divine but have not seen him as fully human.[121] Thangaraj himself stresses the issue of suffering and interprets Jesus as "The Crucified Guru."

Hindus reject the Christian claim that Jesus is in a unique sense the only-begotten Son of God. Many Hindus have seen Jesus as revealing the innate divine-human oneness that is the birthright of all humans.[122] While Advaitic Hindus would likely view most Jews and Christians as either Dvaitic or Vishishtadvaitic, aspects of Jewish and Christian mysticism offer interesting analogues to Hindu teachings on nonduality. Advaitic Hindu scholars with their sophisticated educational backgrounds have generally come from upper castes. Many of those involved in the Bengali Renaissance and Neo-Hinduism worked to reform or abolish the caste system and the status of untouchability, but this remains a highly contested issue in India today.

Raimon Panikkar, who was born in 1918 to a Hindu-Catholic family in Barcelona, taught for many years at Harvard University and the University of California, Santa Barbara, and had wide influence on Catholic interreligious life in the United States and beyond. Guided by the biblical figure of Sophia, Panikkar sought to enter deeply into both Hindu and Buddhist traditions, and see the world from each one's perspective. Lady Wisdom offered Panikkar the guiding thread that runs throughout his writings.[123] She comes to us from the ancient sages of the Bible, but Panikkar believed he found her dwelling also in ancient India; his life's work was to explore the play of wisdom in and through the biblical and the Indian traditions. The wisdom tradition, especially the identification of Jesus and Wisdom, lies behind Panikkar's discussion of *The Unknown Christ of Hinduism*. Panikkar insists that Jesus is more than a remarkable Jewish teacher: "Any Christ who is less than a Cosmic, Human and Divine Manifestation will not do. . . . Christ is still a living symbol for the totality of reality: human, divine and cosmic."[124] Panikkar explains:

---

the way in which he has been traditionally understood by most Christians." Anantanand Rambachan, *The Hindu Vision* (Delhi, India: Motilal Banarsidass, 1994), 45.

[121] "The humanity of Jesus has always been a problem to the Indian people. They find it easier to accept the divinity of Jesus in docetic terms than the humanity of Jesus in historical terms." M. Thomas Thangaraj, *The Crucified Guru: An Experiment in Cross-Cultural Christology* (Nashville: Abingdon Press, 1994), 122.

[122] In the background is the tradition of *ishtadeva*, the ability to choose one's deity, as Anantanand Rambachan explains: "Within a certain framework, we have the freedom to choose concepts and representations of God with which we can most easily identify, and with whom we can enter into a relationship." Rambachan, *The Hindu Vision*, 3.

[123] Leo D. Lefebure, "Who's Playing with Whom? The Many Dwelling Places of Wisdom in the Theology of Raimon Panikkar," in *Raimon Panikkar: A Companion to His Life and Thought*, ed. Peter C. Phan and Young-chan Ro (Cambridge: James Clarke, 2018), 131–51.

[124] Raimon Panikkar, *The Unkown Christ of Hinduism: Towards an Ecumenical Christophany*, rev. ed. (Maryknoll, NY: Orbis Books, 1981), 27.

"Christ stands for that centre or reality, that crystallization-point around which the human, the divine and the material can grow."[125] If Christ is present throughout the entire cosmos, then Christ is present in Hindus: "Hence from the point of view of Christianity, Christ is already present in Hinduism. The spirit of Christ is already at work in Hindu prayer. Christ is already present in every form of worship, to the extent that it is adoration directed to God."[126] Panikkar urges Christians to explore new dimensions of Christ as the cosmic Wisdom within Hindu traditions. There are clearly profound differences of language and philosophical perspective, but Panikkar trusts that the *Upanishads* and the *Bhagavad Gita* and other Hindu texts express in their own way the cosmic wisdom incarnate Christians find in Jesus Christ. He related Christ to Ishvara in the *Brahma Sutra* I, 1, 2, concluding, "Ultimately, we have but one comment to make: *that from which this World comes forth and to which it returns and by which it is sustained, that is Ishvara, the Christ.*"[127] Many in the Hindu tradition have a similar view, believing all those who seek God in truth are seeking Krishna.

Jesus in Relation to Buddhists

Buddhists have distinctive teachings on nonduality, differing from Jews and Christians and some Hindus in that they do not believe in a God who creates the universe. For Buddhists, there is no God; and there is no substantial, enduring self. Dialoguing with Buddhists on questions of identity can be challenging and instructive because they identify clinging to any fixed identity as the primary source of unnecessary suffering. For Buddhists, a fundamental error is to identify ourselves wrongly as substantial, enduring entities. Mahayana Buddhists in particular warn that only when we see ourselves, our religious traditions, and all reality as empty will we be free from the cycle of the three poisons: ignorance, craving, and anger. The Buddhist perspectives on no-God and no-self pose questions to the fundamental assumptions of theistic traditions.

There is no widespread traditional history of Buddhist acceptance of Jesus as a religious figure on the scale of Muslim or Hindu responses. Because many Buddhists first came to know about Jesus in the context of European Christian missionaries who arrived in Asia together with the European colonial empires, they have often had extremely negative impressions of Jesus and the Christian message; and these suspicions linger today in many Asian Buddhist communities. Nonetheless, in many contexts there have been very fruitful Buddhist-Christian dialogues, and a number of prominent Buddhist leaders have embraced Jesus in light of Buddhist perspectives. In the early twentieth century, the influential Japanese Buddhist scholar D. T. Suzuki commented that many Buddhists view Jesus "as a manifestation of the Dharmakaya [ultimate reality] in human form. He is a Buddha and as such not

---

[125] Ibid.
[126] Ibid., 49.
[127] Ibid., 162; emphasis in the original.

essentially different from Shakyamuni [Buddha]. . . . The Dharmakaya appeared in the person of Christ on the Semitic stage, because it suited their taste best in this way."[128] From Suzuki's perspective, the Jewishness of Jesus reflects the compassion (*karuna*) and skillful means (*upaya*) of Dharmakaya manifesting and adapting the truth to Jews and others in this particular context, but there can be no essential difference between Jesus as a Buddha and the teaching of Shakyamuni Buddha.

One of the most influential Buddhists inviting Christians to dialogue was Masao Abe, who spent a number of years in the United States at various universities and was very influential in Buddhist-Christian discussions. He interpreted the emptying of Jesus Christ in Paul's Letter to the Philippians in relation to emptying in Zen Buddhism. For Abe, Christ "is a kind of *bodhisattva*,"[129] and the death of Christ was an existential event that every authentic practitioner must go through; to view it simply as an external, objective event in past history meant one had not realized its significance.[130] Abe engaged in dialogue with Jewish scholars, but the specifically Jewish identity and context of Jesus played relatively little role in his thought.

Abe returned again and again to the words of Paul in his Letter to the Philippians: "Let the same mind be in you that was in Christ Jesus, who, though he was in the form of God, did not deem equality with God as something to be exploited [or grasped at], but emptied himself" (Phil 2:5–7a). Abe interpreted this in light of Mahayana Buddhism, and he used to ask Christians if they can affirm that God is emptiness. Abe applies his Mahayana Buddhist perspective on nonduality to the Son of God:

> There can be no Son of God existing merely as "the Son of God" apart from us. Without encountering it, one can talk about the preexistence of Logos only theoretically or theologically. The "preexisting" Son of God must be realized right here, right now, at the depth of our present existence, as the self-emptying Son of God.[131]

In accordance with his existential hermeneutic, Abe insists that interpreters can understand the hymn in the Letter to the Philippians only by relating it to their own existential crisis:

---

[128] Daisetz Teitaro Suzuki, *Outlines of Mahayana Buddhism* (1907; reprint, New York; Schocken Books, 1967), 259.

[129] James L. Fredericks, "Masao Abe: A Spiritual Friendship," in *Interreligious Friendship after Nostra Aetate,* ed. James L. Fredericks and Tracy Sayuki Tiemeier (New York: Palgrave Macmillan, 2015), 162.

[130] Masao Abe, "God, Emptiness, and the True Self," in *The Buddha Eye: An Anthology of the Kyoto School,* ed. Frederick Franck (New York: Crossroad, 1982), 67.

[131] Masao Abe, "The Kenotic God and Dynamic Sunyata," in *The Emptying God: A Buddhist-Jewish-Christian Conversation,* ed. John B. Cobb, Jr., and Christopher Ives (Maryknoll, NY: Orbis Books, 1990), 10.

All discussion of Christ as the Son of God will be religiously meaningless if engaged in apart from the problem of human ego, our own existential problem of the self. The notion of Christ's kenosis or his self-emptying can be properly understood only through the realization of our own sinfulness and our own existential self-denying.[132]

Abe notes a major difference between the traditions in that Christians see the incarnation of God in Jesus Christ as a unique event, even though others are called to share in it analogically. Where Christians live "in Christ" and become in some way one with him, Abe finds a more radical identity of the practitioner and ultimate reality in Zen, where there are no traces of distinction.[133]

Donald Mitchell, who worked closely with Abe for many years, offers a very thoughtful response to Abe's view of Jesus Christ: "I greatly appreciate Abe's study of the Christian notion of kenosis. It does seem to me that the kenotic love seen in Christ is revelatory of the kenosis of God-Love in creation."[134] While Mitchell praises Abe for extraordinary insight into the kenosis of God, he differs from Abe by noting Abe's neglect of the primordial kenosis within the Holy Trinity; he accuses Abe of reducing kenosis simply to God in creation. As a Catholic, Mitchell insists that

the persons of the Trinity are different in kind from the forms of creation. The persons of the Trinity are God by their eternal kenosis, and the created forms of this world are what they are by God's creative kenosis in space and time. Further, the kenosis of the incarnation and cross of Jesus Christ is a unique redemptive kenotic act of the divine *hypostasis* of the Son.[135]

Mitchell believes that Abe's Buddhist perspective can help Christians to understand implications of kenosis, but for Mitchell, the kenosis of God and the kenosis of creation are not identical.

Thomas Merton

Immersing himself in dialogues with Jews, Muslims, Hindus, Daoists, and Buddhists, as well as Russian Orthodox theologians, Thomas Merton developed a vision of Christ as Sophia, Wisdom, who is found in every religious tradition.[136] In a commonly cited passage, Merton experienced an epiphany of wisdom at the

---

[132] Ibid., 11.

[133] Ibid., 15–19.

[134] Donald W. Mitchell, *Spirituality and Emptiness: The Dynamics of Spiritual Life in Buddhism and Christianity* (New York: Paulist Press, 1991), 61.

[135] Ibid., 63.

[136] Christopher Pramuk, *Sophia: The Hidden Christ of Thomas Merton* (Collegeville, MN: Michael Glazier, 2009), 133.

corner of Fourth and Walnut Streets in Louisville, Kentucky, which awoke him from his dream of separateness:

> I was suddenly overwhelmed with the realization that I loved all those people, that they were mine and I theirs, that we could not be alien to one another even though we were total strangers. It was like waking from a dream of separateness, of spurious self-isolation in a special world, the world of renunciation and supposed holiness. The whole illusion of a separate holy existence is a dream.[137]

Meditating on the Wisdom hymn in Colossians 1, Merton saw Christ as the one in whom all beings hold together, the one who unites all reality to God: "At the center of our souls we meet together, spiritually, in the infinite source of all our different created lives."[138] As the cosmic Sophia, Christ is present as the source of unity throughout religious experience in all traditions, and so Merton identifies Sophia with the Dao of Chinese traditions.[139] Merton finds the primordial light that enlightens all people (Jn 1:9) to be active in the wisdom and illumination of Zen Master Hui Neng.[140] Merton explored the Hasidic tradition of Judaism, the Sufi tradition of Islam, and a variety of Hindu and Buddhist traditions. Redemption, for Merton, is a recovery of the primordial unity that we have lost.[141] Citing the Sufi tradition, Merton viewed the divine mercy as the ground for all beings, not an external event coming from outside but a deep unity beyond all the differences among different religions.[142] As Christopher Pramuk comments, "Above all Sophia is unfathomable *mercy*, made manifest in the world by means of the incarnation, death, and resurrection of Jesus Christ."[143] Pramuk believes that it was the Sophia Christology of Merton that allowed him "to affirm the other *as* other, to say yes to the other, to say yes to everyone."[144] Pramuk believes that "Russian sophiology seems to have carved out something rather new and unexpected in Merton, a space

---

[137] Thomas Merton, *Conjectures of a Guilty Bystander* (Garden City, NY: Doubleday, 1966), 140.

[138] Thomas Merton, *The New Man* (New York: Farrar, Straus & Giroux, 1961), 142–43.

[139] Donald P. St. John, "Ecological Wisdom in Merton's *Chuang Tzu*," in *Merton & the Tao: Dialogues with John Wu and the Ancient Sages,* ed. Cristóbal Serrán-Pagán y Fuentes (Louisville, KY: Fons Vitae, 2013), 103.

[140] Thomas Merton, *Mystics & Zen Masters* (New York: Delta, 1967), 24–25.

[141] George Kilcourse, *The Ace of Freedoms: Thomas Merton's Christ* (Notre Dame, IN: University of Notre Dame Press, 1993), 53.

[142] Bernadette Dieker, "Merton's Sufi Lectures to Cistercian Novices, 1966–68," in *Merton & Sufism: The Untold Story: A Complete Compendium,* ed. Rob Baker and Gray Henry (Louisville, KY: Fons Vitae, 1999), 144–45.

[143] Pramuk, *Sophia,* 194.

[144] Christopher Pramuk, "*Hagia Sophia:* The Unknown and Unseen Christ of Thomas Merton," *Cistercian Studies Quarterly* 41 (2006): 167.

and a language in which there was enough room, both conceptually and imaginatively to envision God's unbounded freedom, love, and presence to peoples and cultures everywhere."[145]

Merton's meditation, "Hagia Sophia," presents Wisdom as his sister who plays in the entire world, who summons him to awaken from the dream of separateness and who flows with him throughout the rhythmic hours of the monastic day, bringing about the great work of pardon, until at the end of the day "a homeless God, lost in the night, without papers, without identification, without even a number, a frail expendable exile lies down in desolation under the sweet stars of the world and entrusts Himself to sleep."[146]

Concluding Reflections

Various aspects of the Jewish biblical traditions intertwine in the identity of Jesus, including the prophetic, apocalyptic, and sapiential trajectories. While all three are important and interrelated, in one dialogical context or another, each tradition may have a particular contribution to make. In contexts where systemic evil is dominant, the apocalyptic tradition offers resources with its demand for justice. In dialogue with Muslims, the shared prophetic heritage is often in the forefront of the discussion. In discussions with Hindus and Buddhists, Christians find helpful resources in the wisdom tradition of ancient Israel, which prized the paradoxical, which acknowledged the importance of recognizing the proper time for action or nonaction, which personified *Chokmah* as a way of naming the way humans encounter God in the world (Prv 8), and which was open to finding wisdom in other traditions.

Jesus can appear in unexpected ways. Some years ago, I met with Robert Aitken, one of the great leaders of American Zen Buddhism. He told me that he had been so bored in the Christian churches of his youth that he thought he had left all that behind him when he became a Zen Buddhist as an adult. Yet as a respected Zen teacher interacting with his students, he again and again found Jesus rising up before him, and he had to admit to his surprise, "I'm still a Christian." When I asked him who Jesus was for him, he answered simply, "elusive." In each of these interreligious dialogues, the identity of Jesus hovers in the encounter, making demands on each partner.

---

[145] Pramuk, *Sophia,* 173.
[146] Thomas Merton, "Hagia Sophia," in Pramuk, *Sophia,* 305.

12

CATHOLIC IDENTITY AND
INTERRELIGIOUS RELATIONS

Interreligious Pilgrims in "This Sacred Communion"

Speaking to an interreligious assembly in December 1964, on the historic first papal journey to India for the International Eucharistic Congress in Bombay, Pope Paul VI invited Hindus, Muslims, Sikhs, Jains, Parsis, and leaders of many other religions to come closer together in what he called "this sacred communion." Quietly reversing a long history of hostile Catholic attitudes toward other religions, he spoke as a pilgrim and expressed a cordial desire for sacred communion with other religious leaders for the sake of the entire human community:

> Therefore we must come closer together, not only through the modern means of communication, through press and radio, through steamships and jet planes,—we must come together with our hearts, in mutual understanding, esteem and love. We must meet not merely as tourists, but as pilgrims who set out to find God—not in buildings of stone but in human hearts. Man must meet man, nation meet nation, as brothers and sisters, as children of God. In this mutual understanding and friendship, in this sacred communion, we must also begin to work together to build the common future of the human race. We must find the concrete and practical ways of organisation and cooperation, so that all resources be pooled, and all efforts united towards achieving a true communion among all nations. Such a union cannot be built on a universal terror or fear of mutual destruction; it must be built on the common love that embraces all and has its roots in God, who is love.[1]

Pope Paul VI's invitation came in the middle of the process of the Second Vatican Council's profound transformation of the Catholic Church's relationship with every other religious community. The change in attitude toward other religions was closely related to a renewed self-understanding of the Catholic

---

[1] Pope Paul VI, "Address to the Members of Non-Christian Religions," Journey to India, December 3, 1964.

Church. Promulgated in November 1964, just before Pope Paul's visit to India, *Lumen Gentium, The Dogmatic Constitution on the Church,*[2] describes the Catholic Church as a sacrament, sign, and instrument of communion with God and of unity among all humans (#1); a sacrament is a concrete sign and action communicating God's transforming presence. *Lumen Gentium* presents the Catholic Church as the pilgrim People of God (#48), which implies that the Church is in process and has not arrived at its final identity; Pope Paul developed one highly significant implication of this image by inviting leaders of other traditions to meet as "pilgrims who set out to find God." Above all, *Lumen Gentium* presents the Catholic Church as the People of God. If the Holy Spirit and the cosmic Christ are active among all people offering salvation and union with God, then all who respond positively have a claim to be among the People of God. Citing the Acts of the Apostles, *Lumen Gentium* affirms: "At all times and in every nation whoever fears God and does what is right is acceptable to God (Acts 10:35)" (#9).

In October 1965, Pope Paul VI and the Second Vatican Council issued *Nostra Aetate,*[3] which made the daring claim: "For all peoples are one community" ("*Una enim communitas sunt omnes gentes,*" #2). This statement could easily be contradicted in light of the multiple divisions and conflicts that plague humanity, but the Council looked beyond the struggles of the present to the common origin and final end of humanity in God, "whose providence, manifestation of goodness and plans for salvation are extended to all" (#1). As we have seen, *Nostra Aetate* speaks respectfully of Hindus, Buddhists, Muslims, and Jews, seeking to move beyond the problems of past history toward dialogue and cooperation and a sharing in sociocultural values. The Declaration affirms the rights and dignity of all humans, condemning all harassment or discrimination based on nationality, race, color of skin, class, or religion (#5). Shaping the one community of all peoples demands respect for all and the condemnation of racism and religious bias of all forms.

In December 1965, as the Council came to its conclusion, Pope Paul VI and the Second Vatican Council promulgated *Gaudium et Spes, The Pastoral Constitution on the Church in the Modern World,*[4] a document unlike any other earlier conciliar document in the history of the Catholic Church. Its opening sentence expresses the solidarity of Catholics with the joys and hopes, the sorrows and anxieties of all people everywhere, "especially those who are poor and afflicted."[5] The Constitution affirms that all humans are "called to communion with God" and

---

[2] Pope Paul VI, *Lumen Gentium,* The Dogmatic Constitution on the Church, November 21, 1964.

[3] Pope Paul VI, *Nostra Aetate,* Declaration on the Relation of the Church to Non-Christian Religions, October 28, 1965.

[4] Pope Paul VI, *Gaudium et Spes,* Pastoral Constitution on the Church in the Modern World, December 7, 1965.

[5] "The joys and hopes and the sorrows and anxieties of people today, especially of those who are poor and afflicted, are also the joys and hopes, sorrows and anxieties of the disciples of Christ, and there is nothing truly human which does not also affect them" (#1).

describe this as the outstanding feature for human dignity (#19) The document also frankly acknowledges that Catholics have fallen short of their vocation and have at times concealed the true features of God and religion (#19). *Gaudium et Spes* also affirms the universal significance of the incarnation of God in Jesus Christ and the universal offer of salvation through the Holy Spirit (#22). The Second Vatican Council articulates a vision of the Catholic Church marked by humility, openness, and service to the world, and dialogue for the sake of shared values and the common good.

Instead of the traditional condemnations, Pope Paul VI and the leaders of the Council were inviting religious leaders to a very different type of relationship than Catholics had previously established with other religions. Building on the legacy of Pope John XXIII, Pope Paul VI hoped that interreligious dialogue could create new types of interreligious relationships that would help transform the world. Pope Paul was transforming the Catholic Church's self-image by inviting the world's religious leaders to share forms of friendship across religious boundaries and to participate in a new reality that he called "this sacred communion" and that Vatican II called "one community." Karl Rahner wrote an influential essay on the importance of the Second Vatican Council as the beginning of the age of the truly global Church; by focusing solely on the Mediterranean and Europe, Rahner unfortunately neglected the growth of Christian communities in the first millennium in Ethiopia, the Middle East, and across much of Asia; nonetheless, he expressed the dynamic globalization of Catholic awareness in the 1960s.[6] Developing a transformed and widened sense of community with other religious traditions is one of the most important elements of a sacred communion with other religious practitioners.

The Second Vatican Council set in motion a new series of reflections on Catholic identity in relation to other religious traditions and traditional forms of discrimination. Traditional Catholic identity had been shaped largely through a process of oppositional bonding whereby Catholics defined their identity in sharp opposition to Jews, Muslims, Hindus, Buddhists, and followers of indigenous religions. For most of its history, the official leaders of the Catholic Church did not listen receptively to the voices of other religious leaders; all too often Catholic leaders issued condemnations that left little openness for any serious dialogue. Catholic theologians traditionally presented an ideal vision of the Church as the spotless Bride of Christ or as the Mystical Body of Christ endowed with the Holy Spirit, while firmly rejecting followers of other paths, often accusing Jews and Muslims of being allies of the Antichrist.[7] Catholic leaders regularly offered interreligious comparisons that focused on the highest ideals of Catholic identity and contrasted

---

⁶ Karl Rahner, "A Basic Theological Interpretation of the Second Vatican Council," in *Theological Investigations,* vol. 20 (New York: Crossroad, 1981), 20:77–89; Philip Jenkins, *The Lost History of Christianity: The Thousand-Year Golden Age of the Church in the Middle East, Africa, and Asia—And How It Died* (New York: Harper Collins, 2008).

⁷ Bernard McGinn, *Antichrist: Two Thousand Years of the Human Fascination with Evil* (San Francisco: HarperSanFrancisco, 1994).

these with the failings in the practice of followers of other religious paths. From the time of the early Church, Christian polemicists often used the words "Jewish" or "Judaizing" to target heretics.[8] The traditional harsh condemnations of other religions powerfully shaped the form of the Catholic Church's identity around the world. The Catholic Church in the modern world claimed to be a *societas perfecta* (a complete society) that needed nothing from any other body.[9] The Catholic Church often drew strict boundary lines and enforced them with harsh legal penalties for those who violated certain practices and obligations. This seemed to leave little room for dialogue with those following other religious paths.[10]

In the aftermath of the Second Vatican Council, Thomas Merton warned against the danger of establishing Catholic identity by saying "no" to other religions and sought another avenue: "The true way is just the opposite: the more I am able to affirm others, to say 'yes' to them in myself, by discovering them in myself and myself in them, the more real I am. I am fully real if my own heart says *yes to everyone*."[11] Merton was aware that this meant a major shift in Catholic identity formation:

I will be a better Catholic, not if I can *refute* every shade of Protestantism, but if I can affirm the truth in it and still go further. So, too, with the Muslims, the Hindus, the Buddhists, etc. This does not mean syncretism, indifferentism, the vapid and careless friendliness that accepts everything by thinking of nothing.[12]

He issued a stern warning to himself and others:

If I affirm myself as a Catholic merely by denying all that is Muslim, Jewish, Protestant, Hindu, Buddhist, etc., in the end I will find that there is not much left for me to affirm as a Catholic: and certainly no breath of the Spirit with which to affirm it.[13]

Merton enjoyed a wide readership among American Catholics, and his example of interreligious openness influenced many.[14]

---

[8] Daniel Boyarin, "Rethinking Jewish Christianity: An Argument for Dismantling a Dubious Category (to Which Is Appended a Correction of *My Border Lines*)," *Jewish Quarterly Review* 99, no. 1 (2009): 7–36.

[9] Pope Leo XIII, *Immortale Dei*, November 1, 1885, #3.

[10] William L. Portier, *Divided Friends: Portraits of the Roman Catholic Modernist Crisis in the United States* (Washington, DC: Catholic University of America Press, 2013).

[11] Thomas Merton, *Conjectures of a Guilty Bystander* (Garden City, NY: Doubleday, 1966), 129.

[12] Ibid.

[13] Ibid.

[14] Jaechan Anselmo Park, *Thomas Merton's Encounter with Buddhism and Beyond: His Interreligious Dialogues, Inter-Monastic Exchanges, and Their Legacy* (Collegeville, MN:

Living in Covenant

Central to traditional Catholic self-understanding was the claim to have replaced the Jewish people in God's covenant. In a visit to the Jewish community in Mainz, Germany, in 1980, Pope John Paul II clarified that the covenant of God with Abraham and the people of Israel has never been revoked.[15] The Pontifical Commission for Religious Relations with the Jews comments, "The Church does not replace the people of God of Israel."[16] John Pawlikowski and other Catholics involved in dialogue with Jews have reflected on the implications of this development for Catholic theology, insisting that the changes in Catholic views of Jews be incorporated into all understandings of ecclesial identity.[17]

While the Catholic Church's relationship with the Jewish community is unique, the transformation of this relationship has implications for every other interreligious relationship.[18] The covenant with Abraham was preceded by the cosmic covenant that God made not only with Noah and his descendants (i.e., all humans) but also with all forms of life on this planet and with the earth itself (Gn 9:8–17). If the covenant with Abraham has not been revoked, the question arises of the status of the earlier covenant with all humanity, all living beings, and the earth through Noah. The Pontifical Biblical Commission notes that in the covenant with Noah, God makes an everlasting promise without conditions: "No obligation is imposed on Noah or on his descendants. God commits himself without reserve. This unconditional commitment on God's part towards creation is the basis of all life."[19] The Pontifical Commission for Religious Relations with the Jews notes the trajectory of covenants with Noah, Abraham, and Moses, the biblical prophets' promises of a covenant, and the New Covenant in Jesus Christ, commenting, "Each of these covenants incorporates the previous covenant and interprets it in a new way."[20] This means that the covenant with Noah and all life and the earth is still in effect.

Peter Phan has reflected on the implications of the universal primordial covenant for Catholic relations with other religions; he points out that Irenaeus

---

Liturgical Press, 2019).

[15] Pope John Paul II, "Address to Representatives of the Jewish Community in Mainz, West Germany," November 17, 1980.

[16] Pontifical Commission for Religious Relations with the Jews, *"The Gifts and the Calling of God Are Irrevocable" (Rom 11:29: A Reflection on Theological Questions Pertaining to Catholic-Jewish Relations on the Occasion of the 50th Anniversary of "Nostra Aetate" (No. 4)*, December 10, 2015, #23.

[17] John T. Pawlikowski, "Christology and the Jewish-Christian Dialogue: A Personal Journey," *Irish Theological Quarterly* 72, no. 2 (2007): 164.

[18] John T. Pawlikowski, "The Uniqueness of the Christian-Jewish Dialogue: A Yes and a No," *Studies in Christian-Jewish Relations* 12, no. 1 (2017): 1–14.

[19] Pontifical Biblical Commission, *The Jewish People and Their Sacred Scriptures in the Christian Bible*, May 24, 2001, #41.

[20] Pontifical Commission for Religious Relations with the Jews, *"The Gifts and the Calling,"* #32.

of Lyons believed that God made four covenants, beginning with Adam and then with Noah, Abraham, and Jesus:

> If God's covenant with Abraham, and in him with his descendants, has not been abolished, nor even *aufgehoben* in the Hegelian sense, the same must be said of God's other covenants with all peoples. In particular, the so-called Noachic covenant, which is embodied primarily in peoples' religions, has never been revoked, and remains eternally valid.[21]

Just as Catholics renounced the traditional teaching of contempt against the Jewish people, so Phan calls for a rejection of the age-old teaching of contempt against the religious traditions of Asia.

Pope Francis

Building on the earlier developments, Pope Francis in his programmatic Apostolic Exhortation, *Evangelii Gaudium*, cites and develops the teaching of the Second Vatican Council that the Church is "the sacrament of the salvation offered by God."[22] Pope Francis makes clear that the Church is not the exclusive locus of grace and salvation: "The salvation which God has wrought, and the Church joyfully proclaims, is for everyone. God has found a way to unite himself to every human being in every age. He has chosen to call them together as a people and not as isolated individuals" (#113). God offers salvation to all humans in and through relationships; Pope Francis proclaims: "Jesus did not tell the apostles to form an exclusive and elite group" (#113). Francis calls Catholics to be signs of this transforming grace to the world. "This means we are to be God's leaven in the midst of humanity.... [T]he Church must be a place of mercy freely given, where everyone can feel welcomed, loved, forgiven and encouraged to live the good life of the Gospel" (#114).

Pope Francis stresses the importance and the transformative power of listening in shaping one's identity: "Efforts made in dealing with a specific theme can become a process in which, by mutual listening, both parts can be purified and enriched. These efforts, therefore, can also express love for truth" (#250). Francis is aware of the important differences among various religious traditions and does not wish to ignore or minimize them: "A facile syncretism would ultimately be a totalitarian gesture on the part of those who would ignore greater values of which they are not the masters. True openness involves remaining steadfast in one's deepest convictions, clear and joyful in one's own identity, while at the same time being 'open to understanding those of the other party' and 'knowing that dialogue can enrich each

---

[21] Peter C. Phan, "Reading *Nostra Aetate* in Reverse: A Different Way of Looking at the Relationships among Religions," *Studies in Christian-Jewish Relations* 10, no. 2 (2015): 1–14.

[22] Pope Francis, *Evangelii Gaudium*, November 24, 2013, #112.

side'" (#250; quoting Pope John Paul II). Regarding how to handle the disagreements among different religious traditions, Francis stresses honesty, mutual respect, and trust.

The covenant with Noah has important implications for care for the earth and ecological awareness. Pope Francis has emphasized the link between care for the earth and interreligious relationships, calling Catholics together with all religious people and all people of good will to care for the community of life on this planet and to attend to the values of religious traditions with regard to the earth. Following the lead of his namesake Francis of Assisi, Pope Francis calls for fraternity with all creation:

> Care for nature is part of a lifestyle which includes the capacity for living together and communion... Fraternal love can only be gratuitous; it can never be a means of repaying others for what they have done or will do for us. That is why it is possible to love our enemies. This same gratuitousness inspires us to love and accept the wind, the sun and the clouds, even though we cannot control them. In this sense, we can speak of a "universal fraternity."[23]

Enlarging the sense of community, Pope Francis draws upon mystical visions of the universe manifesting the presence of God: "The universe unfolds in God, who fills it completely. Hence, there is a mystical meaning to be found in a leaf, in a mountain trail, in a dewdrop, in a poor person's face."[24] Pope Francis adds a note to this passage that quotes an Islamic mystical writer, Ali al-Khawas, who praises those who seek ecstasy in music or poetry: "There is a subtle mystery in each of the movements and sounds of this world. The initiate will capture what is being said when the wind blows, the trees sway, water flows, flies buzz, doors creak, birds sing, or in the sound of strings of flutes, the sighs of the sick, the groans of the afflicted."[25] Pope Francis also cites the wisdom of the Jewish Sabbath, "a day which heals our relationships with God, with ourselves, with others and with the world."[26]

American Catholic Identity Transformed

The identity of Catholics in the United States has long been contested, as many Protestants accused Catholics of having a foreign loyalty to the papacy. A number of Catholics sought ways to be both Catholic and American while developing improved relations with followers of other religious traditions.[27] As a result, the

---

[23] Pope Francis, *Praise Be to You: Laudato Si': On Care for Our Common Home* (Vatican City: Libreria Editrice/San Francisco: St. Ignatius Press, 2015), # 228.

[24] Ibid., #233.

[25] Ibid.

[26] Ibid., #237.

[27] James Cardinal Gibbons, "Patriotism and Politics," *North American Review* 154, no. 425 (April 1892): 385–400.

Catholic Church in the United States has been both a leader in developing interreligious relations and at times an object of suspicion. During the World Parliament of Religions in Chicago in 1893, the Apostolic Legate, Archbishop Francesco Satolli was concerned that Catholic participation meant that the one true Church was perceived to be simply one among many religions, and so he wrote a negative report to Pope Leo XIII. Pope Leo, in turn, wrote to James Cardinal Gibbons directing that if there should be another interreligious event that was not organized by the Catholic Church, Catholics were not to participate. Pope Leo did allow that Catholics could hold their own assemblies and invite "dissenters" from other religions to attend.[28]

The papal directive concerning interreligious gatherings has been seen as a prelude to the condemnation of Americanism a few years later. In 1895, Pope Leo issued an encyclical to the Catholic Church relating to the situation in the United States. He noted approvingly that the Catholic Church was allowed to flourish "unopposed by the Constitution and government of your nation, fettered by no hostile legislation"; but he very pointedly warned:

> Yet, though all this is true, it would be very erroneous to draw the conclusion that in America is to be sought the type of the most desirable status of the Church or that it would be universally lawful or expedient for State and Church to be, as in America, dissevered and divorced.[29]

In 1899, Leo XIII issued a papal letter to Cardinal Gibbons, *Testem Benevolentiae,* which warned of the danger of thinking that the Catholic Church must adapt to any form of modern civilization in doctrine or discipline. Leo rejected the placing of religious liberty above papal authority, as if people did not need infallible papal external authority to guide them. Archbishop Ireland, Cardinal Gibbons, and all others involved denied that they held any such ideas, but the rebuke caused tremendous pain and forced the leading Americanists to be much more careful in their rhetoric.[30] The later condemnation of Modernism by Pope Pius X cast a suspicion on those who would be too open to other religions.

At the Second Vatican Council American Catholic leaders, including Francis Cardinal Spellman, Albert Cardinal Meyer, and John Courtney Murray, played a leading role in the development of *Dignitatis Humanae.*[31] When the second Parliament of the World's Religions was held in Chicago in 1993, the directive of

---

[28] James F. Cleary, "Catholic Participation in the World's Parliament of Religions, Chicago, 1893," *Catholic Historical Review* 55 (1970): 605.

[29] Pope Leo XIII, *Longinqua,* Encyclical of Pope Leo XIII on Catholicism in the United States, January 6, 1895, #6.

[30] Thomas T. McAvoy, *The Americanist Heresy in Roman Catholicism, 1895–1900* (South Bend, IN: University of Notre Dame Press, 1963), 231–35, 259–99.

[31] Pope Paul VI, *Dignitatis Humanae,* Declaration on Religious Freedom on the Right of the Person and of Communities to Social and Civil Freedom in Matters of Religious Promulgated by His Holiness, December 7, 1965.

Pope Leo XIII that Catholics should not participate was quietly ignored. Joseph Cardinal Bernardin, the Archbishop of Chicago, attended, served as a member of the Council of Spiritual and Religious Leaders, and signed the declaration *Toward a Global Ethic.*[32] Instead of protesting against Catholic participation in the Parliament of the World's Religions, the Holy See sent Archbishop Francesco Gioia, who delivered one of the presentations on behalf of the Pontifical Council for Interreligious Dialogue. In 1893, Catholics and Jews were appearing for the first time on a major public stage as equals of Protestants; in 1993, Catholics were among the long-established religious communities in Chicago who played an important role in preparing for the Parliament. The shift was one signal of the transformation of the Catholic Church's relationship to the modern world and to other religions. Many saw the 1993 Parliament of the World's Religions as offering a vision of what the community of religions could look like.[33]

In a changed interreligious situation, the process of shaping Catholic ecclesial identity involves repentance for histories of oppression, cooperation, and even intermingling with other religious traditions, and living with often porous boundaries. Self-critical reflection can facilitate better relations with other religions, and another important result of interreligious relationships and dialogue can be the formation of new forms of fellowship and communion that cross traditional boundaries and that reshape each community's identity. Listening with an open mind and heart, as Pope Francis urges, can be profoundly transformative.

Chaos theory warns us that boundaries that are too rigid stifle growth and can lead to death; on the other hand, not to have boundaries is not to have an identity and to merge into the general environmental flow.[34] For a religious community to lack boundaries is to lack identity; the community is likely to flow into the general religious and cultural currents of its milieu without remainder. If the community is too open to borrowing and learning from others, it lacks an identity of its own. If boundaries are too rigid, the community risks ossification and death. As Robert Schreiter observes, "Consciousness of boundaries is tied up with consciousness of identity. They interact, causing the one to bring about a change in the other."[35]

Despite the image of an unchanging Church, the ongoing dynamic of establishing firm boundaries and then modifying them runs throughout the history of the Catholic Church.[36] While Catholic leaders have repeatedly drawn a sharp contrast between Catholic identity and all other religions, there is precedent in

---

[32] Parliament of the World's Religions, *Declaration Toward a Global Ethic*, Chicago, September 4, 1993.

[33] Wayne Teasdale and George F. Cairns, eds., *The Community of Religions: Voices and Images of the Parliament of the World's Religions* (New York: Continuum, 1996).

[34] James Gleick, *Chaos*, rev. ed. (New York: Open Road, 2011); John Briggs, *Turbulent Mirror: An Illustrated Guide to Chaos Theory and the Science of Wholeness* (New York: Harper & Row, 1990).

[35] Robert J. Schreiter, *Constructing Local Theologies* (London: SCM Press, 1985), 72.

[36] W. C. Smith, *Towards a World Theology: Faith and the Comparative History of Religions* (Philadelphia: Westminster Press, 1981), 15.

the biblical traditions for borrowing and incorporating aspects of other traditions. Biblical prophets condemned idolatry, but scholars have shown that the religion of ancient Israel developed by adapting and incorporating elements from other religious traditions.[37] Mark S. Smith views the emergence of monolatry in ancient Israel as a product of movements of convergence and differentiation: "Convergence involved the coalescence of various deities and/or some of their features into the figure of Yahweh. . . . Features belonging to deities such as El, Asherah, and Baal were absorbed into the Yahwistic religion of Israel."[38] Early Christians distinguished themselves from other religious options, but they also drew from multiple sources in developing their identity, including the philosophical religions of the Hellenistic world. Christian thinkers rejected worship of pagan deities, but they drew heavily from the resources of Stoicism, Pythagoreanism, Middle Platonism, and the Neoplatonism of Plotinus and Porphyry.[39] From ancient times it was recognized that the Christian Church combined various elements into its life. The pagan Emperor Julian the Apostate viewed Hellenism and Judaism as two contradictory religions, and he accused Christianity of trying to be an impure hybrid of both, which he viewed incompatible.[40] The historic process of appropriation from other religious traditions offers a precedent for contemporary learning from other religions.

Both global and local developments shape the dynamic of American Catholic identity in relation to religious pluralism; the distinctiveness of the American situation is in intimate relation with worldwide processes such as migration and the sharing of ideas and practices. Seeking to shape a worldwide community of religious traditions presents both opportunities and challenges for the identity of the Catholic Church both in the United States and elsewhere. In reflecting on *The New Catholicity*, Schreiter explores what catholicity means in light of globalization.[41] He notes the problem: "Globalization has created a certain homogenization of the world in its wake, but has at the same time unleashed new particularisms."[42] Globalization has resulted in cultural and religious contexts becoming increasingly distinct from geographical boundaries, as migrations bring millions of people to new settings, where borders are not primarily territorial. As we have seen, migra-

---

[37] Mark S. Smith, *The Early History of God: Yahweh and the Other Divinities in Ancient Israel*, 2nd ed. (Grand Rapids, MI: Eerdmans, 2002); Mark S. Smith, *The Origins of Biblical Monotheism: Israel's Polytheistic Background and the Ugaritic Texts* (New York: Oxford University Press, 2003).

[38] Smith, *Early History of God*, xxiii.

[39] Robin Lane Fox, *Pagans and Christians* (San Francisco: Harper & Row, 1986).

[40] Julian, "Against the Galileans," in *The Works of the Emperor Julian*, trans. W. C. F. Wright (London: Heineman, 1913), 313–433; see also Boyarin, "Rethinking Jewish Christianity," 21–22.

[41] Robert J. Schreiter, *The New Catholicity: Theology between the Global and the Local*, Faith and Culture Series (Maryknoll, NY: Orbis Books, 1997).

[42] Ibid., ix.

tions have repeatedly reshaped the religious composition of the United States of America, and the process continues.[43]

Relations with many different religious and ethnic traditions comprise American Catholic identity today, and one significant development is that more and more people have multiple sources of religious belonging. Many contexts are hybridized, as some people and communities draw on a variety of sources for shaping their identity and practice.[44] This has particular importance for the U.S. Hispanic community, where theologians point out that more and more people are in one sense or other mestizo.[45]

Schreiter notes the ambiguity of the word "syncretism": the term is usually used in an accusatory sense to reject certain options as a betrayal of fidelity, but he observes that the process of incorporating aspects of other religious traditions often continues nonetheless. He is very alert to the historic dangers of trying to impose unity through imperialism and hegemony. In a world where there is constant interaction between the local context and the worldwide identity of the Church, Schreiter calls for a new theological anthropology developed in light of intercultural and interreligious dialogue, centering on reconciliation and leading to a sense of a new catholicity. Schreiter accepts the understanding of catholicity as "wholeness and fullness through exchange and communication," and reflects on what each element of this definition means in the present global context.[46] The wholeness of the Church requires both a trust in the commensurability of cultures and a willingness to allow fresh experiments in the inculturation of Christian faith in different contexts. Wholeness also demands recognition of the imbalances of power brought about by globalization: "Most important, a new catholicity must be present at the boundaries between those who profit and enjoy the fruits of the globalization process and those who are excluded and oppressed by it."[47]

In order to better understand the fullness of faith in the new catholicity, Schreiter calls for attention to the process of reception of messages sent across cultural and religious boundaries, a process that occurs both within the United States and around the world. He notes that the narratives of the gospel message can be communicated through a variety of means in different cultures and in relation to different audiences, resulting in a certain indeterminacy. While this may appear to be a problem to some, he stresses that this can be a positive value: "Indeterminacy, rather than being a defect, is rather an important aspect of the message's fullness,

---

[43] Peter C. Phan and Diana Hayes, eds., *Many Faces, One Church: Cultural Diversity and the American Catholic Experience* (Lanham, MD: Sheed & Ward, 2005).

[44] Catherine Cornille, ed., *Many Mansions? Multiple Religious Belonging and Christian Identity* (Maryknoll, NY: Orbis Books, 2002).

[45] Arturo Banuelos, ed., *Mestizo Christianity: Theology from the Latino Perspective* (Maryknoll, NY: Orbis Books, 1995).

[46] Schreiter, *New Catholicity*, 128.

[47] Ibid., 130.

for without it the message might not be able to be expressed in some cultures."[48] To communicate effectively in a diverse world, we need to reflect on the dynamics of intercultural and interreligious hermeneutics. We need to be aware not only of referential notions of truth but also of the existential understandings of truth embodied in the orthopraxis of the community. Navigating this process calls for "the constant negotiation of the relations between samenesss and difference" and for "an emphasis on agency in both speaker and hearer."[49]

One of the great challenges for Catholic identity in a pluralistic situation is to keep in mind both the local Church and the global Church community. Schreiter sees the audiences of local theologies as primarily the local Church but also as including the larger Church, and frequently including the broader society as well as followers of other religious traditions. Academic theology can contribute much to the development of local theologies, but the academy is not the primary target audience for most local theologies. While much academic theology has ignored popular religiosity, local theologies attend to the wisdom enshrined within folk traditions and practices.

To avoid the danger of a unity that is imposed on unwilling subjects, Schreiter cites the experience of the World Council of Churches "that unity will not come about simply through doctrinal agreement, but when an ecclesiology can be found in which the three hundred or so member churches can all find a home."[50] Analogously, we can say that the sacred communion of religions that Pope Paul VI sought will not come about through doctrinal agreement but only through all participants coming to find a home in a community of religions. While this may seem unrealistic given the massive tensions among religious traditions, it stands as an eschatological ideal and as a challenge and call to present efforts to improve interreligious relationships. From the encounter with other traditions there can emerge a level of interfaith learning that is not usually included in academic curricula but that can be a profound form of learning. This involves entering not only into the ideas of another religion but into its religious and spiritual practices as well.

American Indian Catholic Identity

The tragic history of intrusion and violence against American Indian religious practitioners has shaped an atmosphere marked by suspicion toward the Catholic Church today. Some American Indians are understandably wary of any outsider attempts to interpret their traditions, and some are extremely critical of so-called "New Age" appropriations of Native practices.[51] Anthropologists have been criticized for disrupting Native religious practices and appropriating artifacts for

---

[48]   Ibid., 131.

[49]   Ibid., 132.

[50]   Schreiter, *Constructing Local Theologies*, 38.

[51]   Philip Jenkins, *Dream Catchers: How Mainstream America Discovered Native Spirituality* (Oxford: Oxford University Press, 2004).

museums, treating Indians as a supposedly disappearing culture; there are currently efforts to restore human remains and artifacts to the Indian communities from which they were taken.[52] Despite the painful history of displacement by European Christian settlers and soldiers, many American Indian Catholics draw upon and participate in traditional Native rituals and customs, establishing a mixed identity as Catholic and Native.

Michael Galvan, a Catholic priest from the Ohlone Indian Nation in California, reflects on how Black Elk and other American Indians have wrestled with the challenge of a dual identity: "How does one be Native and Catholic at the same time?"[53] Galvan recalls that his grandmother "spoke in very few and short sentences. The multiplication of words destroyed the beauty and the sacredness of words."[54] For her, as for Indians in general, words do not express only concepts but become stories that express "the very life of a people. As a result, Native peoples tend to express themselves more in stories, in symbolic language. Such an approach is not counter to the Gospels but is rather similar to the manner of the New Testament."[55] For Native Catholics, Galvan notes, it is vital to tell their stories together with those of Jesus:

> For Native peoples, not to tell our stories, not to live our lives out of our tribal stories, means that we experience a death to our full identity. We are both Native and Roman Catholic. . . . A method I have found useful is to parallel the Gospel stories to tribal stories. These stories enrich one another and empower a person to live by both stories: Native and Christian.[56]

William Stolzman relates the four winds of the Lakota tradition to Catholic perspectives. He suggests analogies between the Lakota spirit of the West, the North wind, and the power of the East, and the three persons of the Trinity. He proposes that the Mystical Body of Christ eschatologically united to the Trinity can be compared to the South in the Lakota tradition:

> The south was different from the others in that it was more corporate and dealt with the after-life more than with the present. Comparatively, the

---

[52] Chip Colwell, *Plundered Skulls and Stolen Spirits: Inside the Fight to Reclaim Native America's Culture* (Chicago: University of Chicago Press, 2017). See also Severin M. Fowles, *An Archaeology of Doings: Secularism and the Study of Pueblo Religion* (Santa Fe, NM: School for Advanced Research Press, 2013).

[53] P. Michael Galvan, "Native Catechesis and the Ministry of the Word," in *The Crossing of Two Roads: Being Catholic and Native in the United States,* ed. Marie Therese Archambault, Mark G. Thiel, and Christopher Vecsey (Maryknoll, NY: Orbis Books, 2003), 209.

[54] Ibid.

[55] Ibid.

[56] Ibid., 210.

question arose immediately: Is there any divine Christian reality that will be universally corporate in the after-life? The immediate answer was. Yes, the Mystical Body of Christ![57]

Black Catholic Identity and Religious Pluralism

We have seen that racial and interreligious prejudices have intertwined and reinforced each other throughout history, posing one of the most intractable obstacles to shaping a healthy community of the world's religions. With a few exceptions, most European American Catholic theologians have not paid a great deal of attention to the implicit racism of much white theology.[58] African Americans share a history marked by various religious traditions coming from Africa and the Caribbean as well as Islam. In 1984, the African American Catholic bishops published *"What We Have Seen and Heard": A Pastoral Letter on Evangelization from the Black Bishops of the United States.*[59] They lament and condemn the history of racism in the United States and celebrate "the gifts we share, gifts rooted in our African heritage."[60] They describe the black Church, without a formal structure but nonetheless a reality based in common experience and history of African Americans and transcending the usual ecclesiastical boundaries. As Catholics, they endorse this sense of the black Church and propose it as a basis for Catholic ecumenical openness and also for interreligious relationships with Jews, Christians, and others.[61] Bryan Massingale endorses the 1979 Pastoral Letter on Racism of the United States Catholic Bishops, *Brothers and Sister to Us*;[62] but he sharply criticizes the lack of implementation and action on this issue, charging that "despite the bold words of *Brothers and Sisters to Us,* we must conclude that racial justice is not now—and never has been—a passionate matter for most American Catholics."[63]

M. Shawn Copeland has reflected on Catholic identity and salvific action in the wake of the terrible damage inflicted on black bodies through racist practices of enslavement, lynching, rape, and humiliation. She indicts white American Catholic

---

[57] William Stolzman, *The Pipe and Christ*, 7th ed. (Chamberlain, SD: Tipi Press, 2002), 204.

[58] Jon Nilson, *Hearing Past the Pain: Why White Catholic Theologians Need Black Theology* (New York: Paulist Pres, 2007); Jeannine Hill Fletcher, *The Sin of White Supremacy: Christianity, Racism, and Religious Diversity in America* (Maryknoll, NY: Orbis Books, 2017); *Interrupting White Privilege: Catholic Theologians Break the Silence,* ed. Laurie M. Cassidy and Alex Mikulich (Maryknoll, NY: Orbis Books, 2007).

[59] Joseph L. Howze et al., *"What We Have Seen and Heard": A Pastoral Letter on Evangelization from the Black Bishops of the United States* (Cincinnati, OH: St. Anthony Messenger Press, 1984).

[60] Ibid., 3.

[61] Ibid., 16.

[62] U.S. Catholic Bishops, *Brothers and Sisters to Us: Pastoral Letter on Racism,* 1979.

[63] Bryan N. Massingale, *Racial Justice and the Catholic Church* (Maryknoll, NY: Orbis Books, 2010), 77.

leaders for historic complicity with white supremacy,[64] and she warns ominously that the current process of globalization marks a reracialization of the world with new forms of bias against people of color.[65] She celebrates aesthetic experience and the turn toward the beautiful as major resources for Christian theology inspired by African American Catholic experience.[66] She turns not only to interpretation of the Bible but above all to the celebration of the Eucharist as the place where Catholics experience salvific action and a call to share with others in a practice of remembrance, racial healing, and hope.

U.S. Hispanic Catholic Identity

Latino/a Catholic theologians exploring the many dimensions of *mestizaje* recognize that interreligious relations have long played an important but often neglected role in shaping Catholic identity. Summarizing the discussions of a Latino/a ecumenical theological gathering, Neomi De Anda and Néstor Medina note the painful history of colonization, conflict, and discrimination that has shaped the Latino/a community, and they call attention to the indigenous and African religious traditions that have influenced this heritage. They call for a broadening of the notion of who constitutes the People of God:

> The challenge, which will require much careful reflection, is the recognition of an existence among Latino/a communities of a matrix of many peoples who belong to different traditions within Christianity (Jehovah Witnesses, Mormons) and outside Christianity (Buddhists, Hare Krishnas, Jews, Muslims, and others), and who cannot be excluded from a broader understanding of the people of God.[67]

De Anda and Medina reflect on the challenge of dislocation that comes with broadening one's sense of community:

> Ecumenical conversations require a sense of displacement and dislocation, but that was not perceived as necessarily bad. At the same time, denominational and cultural boundaries were not perceived as

---

[64] M. Shawn Copeland, "White Supremacy and Anti-Black Logics in the Making of U.S. Catholicism," in *Anti-Blackness and Christian Ethics*, ed. Vincent W. Lloyd and Andrew Prevot (Maryknoll, NY: Orbis Books, 2017), 61–74.

[65] M. Shawn Copeland, *Enfleshing Freedom: Body, Race, and Being* (Minneapolis: Fortress Press, 2010), 66.

[66] M. Shawn Copeland, "Doing Black Catholic Theology: Rhythm, Structure, and Aesthetics," *Chicago Studies* 42, no. 3 (2003): 127–41.

[67] Neomi De Anda and Néstor Medina, "*Convivencias*: What Have We Learned? Toward a Latino/a Ecumenical Theology," in *Building Bridges, Doing Justice: Constructing a Latino/a Ecumenical Theology*, ed, Orlando O. Espín (Maryknoll, NY: Orbis, 2009), 187.

hermetically sealed, but rather fluid and porous as open new spaces are created where the *rostros distintos de Dios* [distinct faces of God] (Elsa Tamez) can all exist.[68]

Participants in this consultation acknowledge: "There is no point of neutrality or neutral space from which to depart."[69] Regarding Christian ecumenical relations, which are fraught with historical memories of conflict, participants were justifiably suspicious of "any facile move toward unity, for it can easily turn into homogeneity and uniformity."[70] The consultation recognized the interlacing of ecumenical and interreligious relations, not only with Jews and Muslims but with indigenous and African traditions that survived in the heart of Christian practice: "Latino/a religious faith expressions are syncretistic, which means that when we are talking about different Christian traditions we are also talking about different non-Christian traditions."[71] De Anda and Medina also problematize the use of language of Latino/a and *mestizaje*. They question what set of characteristics would allegedly distinguish Latinos/as from other groups, and they challenge the notion that there is one meaning of being *mestizo*, noting some that of those identifying as *mestizo* have perpetrated violence against others.[72]

Roberto Goizueta reflects on the ecclesial identity of the People of God in light of the Latino/a Catholic experience of living in a borderland as marginalized and despised persons.[73] Reviewing the medieval development of the understanding of the Church as the Mystical Body of Christ, Goizueta reinterprets this classical image in light of contemporary globalization and migration, stressing the resources of popular religiosity. The Latino/a Catholic religion of the people, which brought the vibrant Iberian medieval tradition into contact with American Native religions, has traditionally had porous boundaries and has been open to receiving religious and cultural influences from indigenous religious traditions in the Americas on many levels. He laments that in the United States, Latino/a popular Catholicism has often been despised and calls attention to its multidiscursive and pluriconfessional resources for the future:

> If Latino/as can continue to appreciate (or, perhaps, learn to appreciate) the richness of our diverse religious history rather than fall prey to reductionist ecclesiologies that seek to erect barriers where historically there have been porous borders, we will have much to offer all the Christian churches of our adopted land.[74]

---

[68] Ibid., 189.

[69] Ibid., 190.

[70] Ibid., 192.

[71] Ibid.

[72] Ibid., 192–95.

[73] Roberto Goizueta, "*Corpus Verum*: Toward a Borderland Ecclesiology," in Espín, *Building Bridges*, 152–55.

[74] Ibid., 163.

Jewish-Catholic Relationships
in the United States Today

After centuries of claiming to have displaced Jews in God's covenant, Catholics today face the challenge of rethinking and re-forming relationships with Jews in a manner that acknowledges the rich heritage we share with them while also respecting the identity and boundaries of the Jewish community. Given the long history of abuse and the current resurgence of anti-Jewish attitudes, many Jews are understandably wary of Catholic efforts about forming a new relationship. While acknowledging continuing Jewish suspicions, Rabbi Irving Greenberg speaks for many Jews in the United States in articulating a cautious openness to establishing a covenantal partnership:

> To grow into a genuine partnership will require a higher level of dialogue than ever before. Only the love that grows out of deep encounter—out of knowing the value, equality, and uniqueness of the other as an image of God nurtured by their religious system—can overcome entrenched barriers to understanding. Only sufficient encounter with the vitality and holiness of the other's religious life can give us the courage to build a future that incorporates the other's contribution to the world and to my own renewal.[75]

Greenberg frames the Catholic-Jewish partnership as a challenge to give a joint witness, responding to secular culture, critiquing economic injustice, and identifying with God in the marginalized: "Our joint task is to identify with our Lord who dwells with the humble and 'seeks to revive the heart of the depressed' (Is 57:5) to imitate God 'who renders justice to the oppressed and feeds those who are hungry, who sets the captives free, opens the eyes of the blind, raises up those who are bowed down' (Ps 146:7–8)."[76]

Catholics have a long history of appropriating Jewish themes and putting them to the service of Catholic perspectives, often in ways that disrespected the original Jewish context. Michele Saracino looks at the complex experiences of boundaries in families and expresses sensitivity to the danger of Catholic trespassing in Jewish-Catholic relations: "I contend that in being about borders Catholics are elected to respect the feelings of the other to the point of surrendering and mourning any entitled attachment to their own religious story."[77] She stresses the importance for Catholics of allowing Jewish memories to contest their

---

[75] Irving Greenberg, "From Enemy to Partner: Toward the Realization of a Partnership between Judaism and Christianity," in *Nostra Aetate,* ed. Pim Valkenberg and Anthony Cirelli (Washington, DC: Catholic University of America Press, 2016), 196.

[76] Ibid., 204.

[77] Michele Saracino, *Being about Borders: A Christian Anthropology of Difference* (Collegeville, MN: Liturgical Press, 2011), 71.

own; and "when heeding another's memories it becomes imperative that we begin to open up, as difficult as it may seem, to the possibility of relinquishing our story in order to honor that of another."[78] This also means Catholics must let go of feelings of entitlement regarding the Jewish tradition. She challenges Catholics "to reflect on porous boundaries between the Jewish and Christian traditions," and "to realize how those leaky borders have led to enmeshed stories and contested memories—a hybridized existence."[79]

Much of Catholic ritual arises from the Jewish tradition; precisely because the two traditions share so much, there are many questions about what are appropriate levels of sharing. One form of interfaith sharing that emerged in the United States after the Second Vatican Council involves Catholics celebrating a Seder service as an aspect of the heritage shared by Christians and Jews. Some Jews fully approved of this practice; and Rabbi Leon Klenicki and Gabe Huck developed a format of the traditional Seder service, celebrating Passover, designed for Catholics and other Christians to celebrate; this was jointly published by The Anti-Defamation League of B'nai B'rith and The Liturgy Training Publications of the Archdiocese of Chicago.[80] For a time, a number of Catholic communities in the United States celebrated the Seder service, often seeking to understand the Jewish tradition and the roots of the Eucharist better. More recently, some Jews and Catholics have questioned the appropriateness of this practice, and today it is more common for Catholics to celebrate the Seder service together with Jewish friends.

There is a wide diversity of Jewish views of interfaith sharing; some Jewish-Christian families raise their children practicing both traditions, and some American Jews practice Zen, while other Jews warn against practices that could lead to syncretism. Jon D. Levenson notes the growth of syncretistic practices among Jews and Christians, including Unitarians who unite these and other traditions such as Hindu yoga or Zen Buddhism or Native American practices. He cites the example of Jews who enter the Unitarian Universalist tradition and combine aspects of Jewish practice with customs from a variety of other religions. He also notes that many Christian congregations began to practice Seder services, and Jews who marry Christians often combine aspects of both traditions in raising their children in what is often called hyphenated identity. While this may appear to be open and welcoming, Levenson poses a challenge to claims of hyphenated identity:

> The belief in the legitimacy of hyphenation is not itself hyphenated, but pure, not some pragmatic compromise (like the Unitarian attempt at a compromise between Judaism and Christianity), but a substantive position in its own right. And the foundation of that position is the claim

---

[78] Ibid., 78.

[79] Ibid., 80.

[80] *The Passover Celebration: A Haggadah for the Seder,* prepared by Rabbi Leon Klenicki and Myra Cohen Klenicki, introduction by Gabe Huck (1980; revised edition, Chicago: Liturgy Training Publications, 2001).

that, in matters of religious belief and practice, personal preference is supreme, not only empirically, but also normatively.[81]

Levenson does not accept hyphenated identities as appropriate for Jews. From a Jewish perspective, Karl A. Plank worries that Thomas Merton inadvertently eclipsed Jewish identity in his efforts at dialogue. He worries that Merton's attempts to identify with Jewish experience, especially suffering, led to a confusion of boundaries that does not help Jews: "Merton intends no harm in pursuing Jewish relations; on the contrary, he desires to diminish suffering and affirm kinship. Yet the consequences of displacing Jewish difference, even and especially in ecumenical conversation, are serious."[82] Plank cites with approval Merton's description of the vocation to charity requiring us not only to love but also to be loved; Plank takes this statement of Merton as a basis for critiquing Merton's own attempt to enter into Jewish identity, insisting that Catholics respect the otherness of Jews with a distinct identity: "Accordingly, Jewish difference challenges Christians not first to speak but to hear speech not their own, not simply to love but to consent to the prospect of being loved by an other."[83] Merton himself in other passages expresses reservations about mixing traditions. During his visit to India, he discussed this issue with Sonam Kazi, a Tibetan lay Nyingmapa monk, and agreed with him:

Sonam Kazi is against the mixing of traditions, even Tibetan ones. Let the Kagyudpa keep to itself. He suggests that if I edit a book of Tibetan texts, let them all be *one* tradition. A fortiori, we should not try to set up a pseudocommunity of people from different traditions, Asian and Western.[84]

Abraham Joshua Heschel insisted that "No Religion Is an Island," but many Jews have expressed concerns about persons claiming a dual identity of Jewish and Christian. For many Jews, if someone accepts the traditional Christian belief in Jesus as Lord and Savior, it is not possible for that person to continue to practice Judaism. Nonetheless, the second half of the twentieth century witnessed the development of Messianic Judaism, which challenges the assumption of a clear and unending boundary between Jews and Christians. Jennifer Rosner comments on the challenge Messianic Judaism poses for both Jews and Christians involved in dialogue: "Both sides have had a difficult time mapping Messianic Jews on the religious landscape, as Messianic Judaism categorically blurs the lines that the

---

[81] Jon D. Levenson, "The Problem with Salad Bowl Religion," *First Things* 78(1997): 11.

[82] Karl A. Plank, "The Eclipse of Difference: Merton's Encounter with Judaism," in Thomas Merton, *Merton & Judaism: Recognition, Repentance, and Renewal—Holiness in Words*, comp. and ed. Beatrice Bruteau (Louisville, KY: Fons Vitae, 2003), 79.

[83] Ibid., 82.

[84] Thomas Merton, *The Asian Journal of Thomas Merton*, ed. Naomi Burton, Patrick Hart, and James Laughlin (New York: New Directions Book, 1973), 85.

dialogue has come to depend upon."[85] A Messianic Jewish delegation met with Vatican representatives in 2000; the Jewish Community Relations Council of New York issued a very critical statement rejecting Hebrew Christianity and Messianic Judaism in 1993, and most Jews in the United States reject the movement of Messianic Judaism.[86]

Amy-Jill Levine, a distinguished Jewish scholar of the New Testament, urges Jews and Christians to frankly acknowledge and accept disagreements: "The day that Jews and Christians agree on everything is the day the messiah comes, or comes back. The point of interfaith conversation is not to convert the person across the table, but it is also not to abdicate one's own theology for the sake of reaching agreement."[87] Especially in relationship to Jews, with whom Catholics share so much, it is especially important to be respectful of interreligious boundaries and honor the distinct identity of the Jewish tradition.

Muslim-Catholic Relationships in the United States Today

In many historic contexts relationships between Catholics and Muslims have been fraught with tension; and the attacks of September 11, 2001, led to an increase in Islamophobia in the United States. Nonetheless, a number of recent developments encourage warmer relations. Catholics and Muslims were already meeting regularly in three regional dialogues, and Catholic and Muslim leaders responded together in a statement issued a few days after the attacks of September 11, 2001, condemning the attacks and calling on both Catholics and Muslims to acknowledge the positive relationships of dialogue and not to overgeneralize about the other community. On December 23, 2003, the West Coast Dialogue of Catholics and Muslims in the United States issued a programmatic statement on the relationships that they have formed in dialogue: "Friends and Not Adversaries: A Catholic-Muslim Spiritual Journey."[88] The dialogue partners lament that most Catholics and Muslims in the United States do not know a great deal about each other's tradition. In their meetings, each side presents aspects of its tradition's faith

---

[85] Jennifer M. Rosner, "Messianic Jews and Jewish-Christian Dialogue," in *Introduction to Messianic Judaism: Its Ecclesial Context and Biblical Foundations*, ed. David Rudolph and Joel Willitts (Grand Rapids, MI: Zondervan, 2013), 145; for a Jewish rejection of Messianic Judaism, see Jewish Community Relations Council of New York, "Spiritual Deception Matters Library: Hebrew Christians," http://www.jcrcny.org/wp-content/uploads/2018/05/HEBREWCHRISTIANS.pdf.

[86] Jewish Community Relations Council of New York, "Spiritual Deception Matters Library: Hebrew Christians."

[87] Amy-Jill Levine, *The Misunderstood Jew: The Church and the Scandal of the Jewish Jesus* (New York: HarperOne, 2007), 6.

[88] The West Coast Dialogue of Catholics and Muslims, "Friends and Not Adversaries: A Catholic-Muslim Spiritual Journey," December 23, 2003.

and practice; members of each side are respectfully present at the prayer services of their partners.

In February 2019, Pope Francis traveled to Abu Dhabi in the United Arab Emirates and met with Muslim leaders, especially Ahmad al-Tayyeb, the Grand Imam of Al-Azhar University. They issued a joint declaration and appeal: "Human Fraternity for World Peace and Living Together."[89] The leaders call for developing a culture of mutual respect and acceptance; they forcefully condemn all violence, especially that done in the name of religion, noting that God does not need to be defended and does not want the Divine Name to be used to terrorize people. They affirm,

> The pluralism and the diversity of religions, colour, sex, race and language are willed by God in His wisdom, through which He created human beings. This divine wisdom is the source from which the right to freedom of belief and the freedom to be different derives. Therefore, the fact that people are forced to adhere to a certain religion or culture must be rejected, as too the imposition of a cultural way of life that others do not accept.[90]

In the United States, despite considerable Islamophobia, a 2017 Pew study found that 89 percent of American Muslims express pride in being both American and Muslim, but in recent years they have found it more difficult to be Muslim in the United States because of Muslim extremists in other countries and misconceptions about Islam among Americans.[91] In 2018, a study of Muslims in the United States conducted by the Institute for Social Policy and Understanding found that American Muslims often felt stigmatized for their faith, but nonetheless, 81 percent of American Muslims said they value their American identity.[92]

In American metropolitan areas, Muslims from a wide variety of different countries and traditions encounter Catholics as well as other Muslims in settings profoundly different from traditional Asian or African cultures, and they are going through a process of inculturation of Islam in North America.[93] In December 2009, I participated in a delegation of American Muslims visiting Thailand to talk about Islamic life in the United States. I was invited as a non-Muslim who has been involved in dialogue. Often the young Thai Muslims believed that Muslims could

---

[89] Pope Francis and the Grand Imam of Al Azhar, Ahmad al-Tayyeb, "Human Fraternity for World Peace and Living Together," Abu Dhabi, February 4, 2019.

[90] Ibid.

[91] "U.S. Muslims Concerned about Their Place in Society, but Continue to Believe in the American Dream: Finds from Pew Research Center's 2017 Survey of U.S. Muslims," July 16, 2017.

[92] Institute for Social Policy and Understanding, *American Muslim Poll 2018: Pride and Prejudice.*

[93] Jane I. Smith, *Islam in America* (New York: Columbia University Press, 1999).

not live freely in the United States. The leader of the delegation, Kareem Irfan, an American Muslim, was very forthright in insisting that American Muslims are free to practice their faith, often freer than in Muslim-majority countries where the government intervenes in Islamic affairs. He also affirmed that Muslims in the United States often have cordial relationships with their Christian neighbors, which I was happy to confirm.

In the many areas where American Catholics and other Christians live in close contact with Muslims, they know Muslims as neighbors, colleagues, classmates, and often become friends. One of the most powerful ways to express communion and shape a new community is to share meals together. In recent years Muslims in the United States have regularly invited Jewish and Christian friends to share an *iftar* meal with them, breaking their fast at the end of the day during the month of Ramadan.

In the United States today, there is a national Catholic-Muslim dialogue chaired by Shaykh Abdool Rahman Khan of Charlotte, North Carolina, and Blase Cardinal Cupich, Archbishop of Chicago, as well as a number of local Muslim-Christian dialogues. Georgetown University has a Center for Muslim-Christian Understanding and has sponsored a summer Institute on Islam and Christianity, bringing together Muslim and Christian pastoral leaders so they can get to know each other, learn about each other's traditions in respect, ask questions in confidence, and develop trust. In one place after another around the world, memories of past injuries poison the present. Coming to know people in situations of safety and respect can do much to improve relations.

A New Sangha: Buddhist-Catholic Relations in the United States

In addition to issuing his invitation to a sacred interreligious communion in Bombay in 1964, Pope Paul VI had an intuition that monastics of different religious traditions could communicate with each other on a deep level, an intuition that led eventually to the formation of the Dialogue Interreligieux Monastique/ Monastic Interreligious Dialogue.[94] In the United States, the leaders of Monastic Interreligious Dialogue have been very creative in shaping new approaches to interreligious monastic solidarity and communion. Catholic monasteries in the United States have hosted Buddhist monastics, and a number of Catholic monastics have visited Buddhist monasteries and have practiced Buddhist forms of meditation. One outcome is that, in traditional Christian language, new forms of community, *koinonia,* have emerged, or in Buddhist language, a new type of *sangha* has been shaped. William Skudlarek, secretary-general of Dialogue Interreligieux Monastique/Monastic Interreligious Dialogue, explains the new application of the traditional monastic virtue of hospitality:

---

[94] Fabrice Blée, *The Third Desert: The Story of Monastic Interreligious Dialogue,* trans. William Skudlarek with Mary Grady (Collegeville, MN: Liturgical Press, 2011).

If the quest for oneness, the heart of the monastic vocation, predisposes the monk for dialogue with the followers of other religious traditions, the monastic practice of hospitality, so strongly emphasized by Saint Benedict in Chap. 53 of his *Rule,* is the pre-eminent monastic way of entering into relationship with the followers of other religions.[95]

The Gethsemani Encounters at Gethsemani Abbey in Kentucky are among the most significant of these events. Buddhist and Catholics monks were present at each other's meditations and liturgies. As an advisor to the board of Monastic Interreligious Dialogue, I attended the first two Gethsemani Encounters, and together with Zoketsu Norman Fischer I offered a closing personal reflection at the conclusion of the second Gethsemani Encounter in April 2002.[96] Fischer and I both agreed that the most important outcome of the weeklong dialogue was that a new form of community had been shaped, uniting Buddhists and Catholics in a new way.[97] He suggested: "I think that the virtue of interfaith dialogue is that the more we dialogue together, the more we come to some unity in living our religious lives while also recognizing the real differences in flavor."[98] I mentioned the Buddhist teaching that we are all intimately interconnected and compared this to the affirmation of the Letter to the Colossians that all things hold together in Christ, and Christ has reconciled all things in heaven and on earth; I suggested: "We can realize the truth of these teachings in the twofold sense of becoming conscious of them in a new way and of making real the connections among us."[99] Skudlarek offers a Catholic perspective on this dynamic: "The secret joy of the Holy Spirit of God is the establishment of communion within the created universe. In so doing, the Spirit of God is subtly but steadfastly at work, bringing into being new ways of imaging the perfect communion that exists within the Godhead itself."[100] Buddhists, of course, would not use the language of the Holy Spirit but can well delight in the establishment of communion.

In addition to the sense of communion among Buddhist and Catholic monastics, there are communities of Catholics and other Christians who gather to engage in Buddhist meditation with their Buddhist friends. The Jesuit priest and Zen

---

[95] William Skudlarek, "Monastic Interreligious Dialogue: Dialogue at the Level of Spiritual Practice and Experience," in *Catholicism Engaging Other Faiths: Vatican II and Its Impact,* ed. Vladimir Latinovic, Gerard Mannion, and Jason Welle (Cham, Switzerland: Palgrave Macmillan, 2018), 234–35.

[96] Donald W. Mitchell and James Wiseman, eds., *Transforming Suffering: Reflections on Finding Peace in Troubled Times* (New York: Doubleday, 2003), 233–38.

[97] Leo Lefebure, "Reflection," https://www.urbandharma.org/buca/Geth2/ge2-38.pdf; Leo Lefebure and Zoketsu Norman Fischer, "Discussion," https://www.urbandharma.org/buca/Geth2/ge2-39.pdf.

[98] Mitchell and Wiseman, *Transforming Suffering,* 233.

[99] Ibid., 235–36.

[100] Skudlarek, "Monastic Interreligious Dialogue," 240.

Roshi, Robert Kennedy, and the Zen master and former Jesuit, Ruben Habito, are among the Catholics who have embraced the practice of Buddhist meditation and lead communities of practitioners who draw from both traditions.[101]

Conclusion: A Wisdom Community

We have seen that the search for wisdom flows through many different traditions, offering points of contact and convergence. One way to imagine the sacred communion to which Pope Paul VI invited the leaders of other religions is as a wisdom community. Bishop Edward Braxton has reflected on the Catholic Church as a wisdom community.[102] This image offers a path for reimagining the relationship of the People of God in the Catholic Church to all those in other religious traditions whose lives are shaped by what Catholics see as the movement of the Holy Spirit and the reconciling power of the cosmic Christ.

Braxton notes that the Catholic Church "is more than the sum of its parts. The Church moves through history as the bearer of an ever developing self-understanding."[103] The self-understanding is not the same as the doctrines or ceremonies: "This wisdom cannot be completely equated with teachings, dogmas, and intellectual theories. It is more elusive. Many people are gifted with great intelligence and learning, but wisdom eludes them."[104] The wisdom is not secret or esoteric. "This wisdom comes from the telling and retelling of the story of Jesus of Nazareth through the centuries. . . . It is not 'possessed' by the priests, or the laypeople, or the scholars, or the bishops, or the artists, in an independent or exclusive way."[105]

Braxton notes that we live in many worlds, including the encounter with other cultures and religions and often have trouble finding our way. To suggest what a wisdom community can look like, he draws upon the theological method of Bernard Lonergan to describe a self-correcting process of learning for the Catholic Church to develop its identity by seeking ever broader experience; fashioning more reliable interpretive tools; making more accurate judgments leading to more responsible decisions and eventually a metanoia, a conversion on intellectual, moral, emotional, and spiritual levels.[106] Lonergan made an important distinction between classical understandings of culture, which believed one culture was normative and to be emulated, and contemporary empirical understandings of culture, in

---

[101] Robert Kennedy, *Zen Gifts to Christians* (New York: Continuum, 2000); Ruben L. F. Habito, *Living Zen, Loving God* (Boston: Wisdom Publications, 2004).

[102] Edward K. Braxton, *The Wisdom Community* (New York: Paulist Press, 1980).

[103] Ibid., 1.

[104] Ibid.

[105] Ibid., 2.

[106] Bernard J. F. Lonergan, *Method in Theology*, vol. 14, *Collected Works of Bernard Lonergan*, 2nd ed., rev. and augmented, ed. Robert Doran and John D. Dadosky (Toronto: University of Toronto Press, 2017).

which a plurality of cultures offer resources and values of different kinds. Lonergan's articulation of a theological method is designed to guide a community through the discernment of how to understand and judge its past and present experience, act responsibly in the present, and go through intellectual, moral, and religious conversions when necessary. Braxton describes the call to intellectual conversion as the search for a holistic way of knowing, which can have a purifying and integrating effect.[107] Moral conversion involves a turn to values, which requires constant scrutiny and vigilance in a self-correcting process in community with others. Religious conversion can come in various forms, including an ecclesial conversion or turn to community. If individuals and communities successfully navigate the passage through conversion, then the second side of Lonergan's program articulates the steps of clarifying and sharing the wisdom learned with others. While this process can be envisioned in primarily an intraecclesial manner, the current encounter of other religious traditions in the United States and elsewhere presents both formidable challenges and also unprecedented opportunities for interreligious and intercultural learning and collaboration.

Citing both Pope Paul VI's call to dialogue in *Ecclesiam Suam* and also Paulo Freire's *Pedagogy of the Oppressed,* Braxton comments: "The attitude of heart and the style of thought desired for the wisdom community can be characterized by a certain understanding of human communication or dialogue, and an appreciation of, and a fidelity to, the dictates of authentic human knowing, loving, and doing."[108] While Braxton does not apply his ecclesiological model to the challenge of shaping an interreligious community, his appropriation of the methodology of Lonergan for ecclesiological reflection has much to offer to Catholics seeking deeper communion with followers of other religious paths. The further challenge is to develop a healthy sense of the community of religious traditions living in harmony with the earth and the entire community of life on this planet. The ringing invitation of Pope Paul VI to representatives of all the world's religions to meet as pilgrims in a new form of sacred communion echoes still.

---

[107] Braxton, *Wisdom Community,* 91.
[108] Ibid., 172.

13

CATHOLIC SPIRITUALITY AND
INTERRELIGIOUS RELATIONS

Despite their ambiguous history of shaping or misshaping interreligious relationships, the biblical traditions and the principles of Christian spirituality can provide guidance for fostering interfaith relations. One classical approach to Catholic spirituality involves three stages: *via purgativa* (the way of purgation), *via illuminativa* (the way of illumination), and *via unitiva* (the way of union).[1] Developing the perspectives of Dionysius the Areopagite and other early Christian writers, Bonaventure explains: "For purgation leads one to peace; illumination draws one to truth; perfection is the same as charity. When these three are in your possession, then indeed your soul will be beatified and from these three it will receive increasing merit."[2] Bonaventure continues: "If you wish to undergo purgation, let conscience play its role; if you wish to ascend to the illuminative way, let the ray of intelligence guide you; if you still desire union in perfection, then may the fire of wisdom consume you and bring forth your love!"[3] According to Bonaventure, the purgative way purifies the memory, leading to peace; the illuminative way opens the intellect to truth; and the unitive way transforms and perfects the will, leading to love. Thomas Aquinas describes the development of charity in terms of these three stages:

> For at first it is incumbent on man to occupy himself chiefly with avoiding sin and resisting his concupiscences, which move him in opposition to charity: this concerns beginners, in whom charity has to be fed or fostered lest it be destroyed; in the second place man's chief pursuit is to aim at progress in good, and this is the pursuit of the proficient, whose chief aim is to strengthen their charity by adding to it: while man's third pursuit is

---

[1] Bonaventure of Bagnoregio, *The Triple Way or The Kindling of Love,* trans. and ed. Peter Damien M. Fehlner (New Bedford, MA: Academy of the Immaculate, 2012).

[2] Bonaventure, *The Enkindling of Love, also called The Triple Way,* adapted from the original, ed. and arranged by William I. Joffe (Paterson, NJ: Saint Anthony Guild Press, 1956), xiv.

[3] Ibid., 3.

to aim chiefly at union with and enjoyment of God: this belongs to the perfect who *desire to be dissolved and to be with Christ*.[4]

While traditional spiritual writers did not usually apply these principles to interreligious relations, these dimensions of the spiritual journey provide a helpful framework for relating Catholic spirituality to the challenges and opportunities of interfaith encounters. They are not strictly sequential stages that succeed one another; they are aspects of the spiritual journey that intertwine and overlap; development in one area will deepen the experience of the other dimensions. The first and often the most formidable challenge in the spirituality of interreligious relations involves turning away from sin, that is, acknowledging wrongdoing, forgiving, asking forgiveness for whatever evil troubles the relationship, seeking reconciliation, healing the wounds of sin, and moving toward mutual respect and trust. The ancient purgative way finds new relevance and urgency in addressing and reconciling interreligious and interracial injuries.

In mutual confidence interreligious partners can develop their relationship by pursuing reciprocal illumination by exploring the wisdom of their respective religious paths. The illuminative way can serve as an interreligious path to seeing others clearly, to mutually sharing faith and practice, and to cultivating charity. Frequently, participants in interreligious exchanges gain not only new familiarity with another religious tradition but also fresh ability to interpret the spiritual resources of their own tradition in new ways.

In exploring the traditional unitive way, interreligious participants can hope for a deeper experience of unity and oneness with their partners in dialogue, with all forms of life, with the entire universe, and with ultimate reality. On this level, human identity is profoundly transformed in ways that surpass ordinary comprehension; Dionysius the Areopagite describes Moses entering the divine presence on Mt. Sinai: "Here, being neither oneself nor someone else, one is supremely united by a completely unknowing inactivity of all knowledge, and knows beyond the mind by knowing nothing."[5] In presenting the unitive way, Bonaventure evokes the fire of divine wisdom and love; Thomas Aquinas speaks of enjoying God and being dissolved in Christ. The mystical paths of other religious traditions often present analogies amid important differences.[6]

Religious practitioners approach the challenges of their respective spiritual paths in distinctive ways; while there are profound dissimilarities, the traditional

---

[4] Thomas Aquinas, *Summa Theologica,* trans. Fathers of the English Dominican Province (New York: Benzinger Brothers, 1947), 2:2.24.9.

[5] Dionysius the Areopagite, *Pseudo-Dionysius: The Complete Works,* trans. Colm Luibheid (New York: Paulist Press, 1987), 137.

[6] Michael A. Sells. *Mystical Languages of Unsaying* (Chicago: University of Chicago Press, 1994); Leo D. Lefebure, "Christian Mysticism in Interreligious Perspective," in *The Wiley-Blackwell Companion to Christian Mysticism,* ed. Julia A. Lamm (Malden, MA: Wiley-Blackwell, 2013), 610–25.

Catholic images of turning away from sin, of learning to see more clearly, and becoming one with God often resonate with themes in other religious traditions. Unity can mean various things in interreligious relationships and is not always a positive outcome. One danger in history is that many religious and political leaders sought to impose unity through force by suppressing difference; one of the most important goals of interreligious dialogue is to shape a healthy community of the world's religions that respects and appreciates diversity. We can explore the unitive way in interreligious perspective, considering experiences of union with God in various traditions, as well as the significance of nonduality in nontheistic traditions.

Via Purgativa: Healing Wounds, Purifying Memory, Seeking Reconciliation

Biases and prejudices frequently warp the identities of religious communities. We see this more easily in historical communities or in other contexts around the world, but it is much more difficult to acknowledge our own biases and prejudices, whether personal or collective. In situations of conflict, religious communities can foster a distorted sense of identity based on oppositional bonding—we know who we are because we are opposed to other people whom we stereotype in pejorative fashion. Then religious identities can fuel struggles over power, wealth, and social status. One vital role of interreligious dialogue is to challenge our inherited prejudices with new understandings that reject the old models.

Interreligious bias and hatred can become long-standing prejudices, shaping generation after generation to think and feel harshly toward followers of other religions, often culminating in violent physical attacks. Catholics inherit a history of offending virtually every other religious tradition, and many followers of other religious paths view Catholics with suspicion because of the earlier history. Anti-Jewish and anti-Islamic invective runs throughout much of the earlier Catholic tradition; and many Catholic missionaries harshly condemned the images of other religions, including Hinduism, Buddhism and indigenous religions, as idols, without fully understanding their significance.[7] In many settings today, the first and often the greatest difficulty for interreligious relationships is the heritage of bitter memories of injuries past and present. Anger and resentment can poison relationships, if these issues are not addressed and processed in a healthy manner.

Jews and Christians hear from the book of Leviticus that God instructed the people of Israel: "You will not exact vengeance on, or bear any sort of grudge against, the members of your race, but will love your neighbor as yourself. I am the Lord" (Lv 19:18). In the Gospel of Matthew, Jesus instructs his followers: "So when you are offering your gift at the altar, if you remember that your brother or sister has something against you, leave your gift there before the altar and go; first be reconciled to your brother or sister, and then come and offer your gift" (Mt 5:23–24).

---

[7] Leo D. Lefebure, *True and Holy: Christian Scripture and Other Religions* (Maryknoll, NY: Orbis Books, 2014).

Even though present-day Catholics are not personally guilty of the sins of past generations, it is important to be aware of how the injuries inflicted by earlier Catholics have lingering effects on interfaith relationships today and to work for healing in these relationships. While much progress has been made in recent decades, intractable clashes continue to shape the interreligious landscape today. Catholic spirituality tells us that it is important to be honest in admitting faults and failings. As long as we deny sin, it has power over us. When we acknowledge sin and entrust ourselves and our companions to God's loving forgiveness, we can begin anew.

In his Apostolic Letter in 1994, *Tertio Millennio Adveniente*, Pope John Paul II acknowledged the need for Catholics to acknowledge sins and crimes committed by earlier generations of Catholics against followers of other religious paths; he challenged Catholics to go through a frank and honest purification of memory in order to prepare for the year 2000 and the third millennium of Christian faith:

> Hence it is appropriate that, as the Second Millennium of Christianity draws to a close, the Church should become more fully conscious of the sinfulness of her children, recalling all those times in history when they departed from the spirit of Christ and his Gospel and, instead of offering to the world the witness of a life inspired by the values of faith, indulged in ways of thinking and acting which were truly *forms of counter-witness and scandal*. . . . She cannot cross the threshold of the new millennium without encouraging her children to purify themselves, through repentance, of past errors and instances of infidelity, inconsistency, and slowness to act.[8]

During the season of Lent in 2000, Pope John Paul II presided at an unprecedented prayer service in the Vatican in which cardinals read petitions asking God's forgiveness for such sins, and one prayer asked God's forgiveness for all the harm done to the Jewish people throughout the ages. Later that spring, John Paul II journeyed to Jerusalem and prayed at the Western Wall, the most sacred site for the Jewish people to pray. Following the Jewish custom, he inserted a piece of paper into a crack in the wall containing the prayer from the Lenten prayer service. Today that prayer is in Yad Vashem, the World Holocaust Remembrance Center in Jerusalem. The pope's prayer had a tremendous healing impact on Jewish-Catholic relations. Aharon Lopez, ambassador of Israel to the Holy See, commented, "By following the Jewish tradition, he won the hearts of Israelis."[9]

The tragic history of interreligious relations is so fraught with suffering that in many contexts, reconciliation may seem to be difficult, if not impossible. Robert Schreiter recalls the New Testament teaching that reconciliation is not a human

---

[8] Pope John Paul II, *Tertio Millennio Adveniente*, November 10, 1994, #33.

[9] Anthony J. Cernera, "The Center for Christian-Jewish Understanding of Sacred Heart University: An Example of Fostering Dialogue and Understanding," in *Examining Nostra Aetate after 40 Years: Catholic-Jewish Relations in Our Time*, ed. Anthony J. Cernera (Fairfield, CT: Sacred Heart University Press, 2007), 154.

achievement but a gift from God, and poses the question: "*How can I discover the mercy of God welling up in my own life, and where does that lead me?* Reconciliation, then, is not a process that we initiate or achieve. We discover it already active in God through Christ."[10] The activity of the Holy Spirit presents this offer of reconciliation to those in each religious tradition and to those outside religious practice. This perspective invites seekers of reconciliation to be alert to elements in a situation that may be moving toward reconciliation.

Schreiter notes that among the resources of religious and indigenous traditions around the world are rituals for reconciliation:

> Some cultures have a very distinct concept of reconciliation that is expressed ritually: an accusation of wrongdoing is leveled at someone, that person acknowledges the wrongdoing and apologizes in some formal way, the apology is accepted by the community, and the wrongdoer is ritually reintegrated into the community, signifying forgiveness. Sometimes a probationary period marked by ritual punishment (such as a fine or a continuing partial exclusion from the community) precedes full reintegration. This pattern is reenacted in myriad variations throughout the world.[11]

In addition to the challenges inherited from the past, it is understandable for there to be difficulties in present-day interreligious relationships. While interreligious experiences can offer many benefits, relationships with those dissimilar to us can also be occasions for misunderstanding and irritation. We often unconsciously assume that our manner of thinking and living is universally valid. Often, we come to realize how much we take for granted only when we encounter people who do not share the same worldview as ourselves. Frequently, followers of other religious paths do not share our tacit assumptions, and so misunderstandings can arise without our fully understanding what went wrong. Conflicts need not sabotage relationships and can even lead to deeper understanding. However, if not properly handled, they can fester and poison contacts. Mercy, forgiveness, the renunciation of vengeance, and the healing of memory are teachings and practices shared by many of the world's religions.[12]

European American theologians have usually interpreted Jesus's proclamation of the reign of God and repentance in terms of time, pondering to what degree it is already present and to what degree it is imminent in the future. George Tinker of the Osage Nation responds to Jesus's call to repent (*metanoiete*) in light of American

---

[10] Robert J. Schreiter, *Reconciliation: Mission and Ministry in a Changing Social Order* (Maryknoll, NY: Orbis Books/Cambridge, MA: Boston Institute of Theology, 1992), 43.

[11] Robert J. Schreiter, *The Ministry of Reconciliation: Spirituality and Strategies* (Maryknoll, NY: Orbis Books, 2004), 13; see also ibid., 92–93.

[12] *Memory and Hope: Forgiveness, Healing, and Interfaith Relations,* ed. Alon Goshen-Gottstein (2015; reprint, Eugene, OR: Wipf and Stock, 2018).

Indian spatial understandings of returning, which resonate with the spatial meaning of the Hebrew word *shub,* "to return":

> to return to the ideal relationship between Creator and the created, to live in the spatiality of creation fully cognizant of God's hegemony. . . . In the Native American world, we recognize that interrelatedness as a peer relationship between the two-leggeds and all others: four-leggeds, wingeds, and living-moving things.[13]

The *via purgativa* involves reconciliation with all creation, and it has particular importance for the Catholic Church and indigenous peoples. At the Second World Meeting of Popular Movements in Bolivia in July 2017, Pope Francis apologized to indigenous peoples across the Americas for the crimes committed against them by Catholics in the name of God. "I wish to be quite clear, as was Saint John Paul II: I humbly ask forgiveness, not only for the offenses of the Church herself, but also for crimes committed against the native peoples during the so-called conquest of America."[14]

After the Holy See's Commission for Religious Relations with the Jews issued the statement, *We Remember: A Reflection on the Shoah,* in March 1998, American Catholics and Jews met to discuss the statement's effort to remember the victims, condemn anti-Semitism, and improve Jewish-Catholic relations. John Pawlikowski and other American Catholics criticized the document for not going further in acknowledging the damage caused by traditional Catholic attitudes toward Jews; he labeled traditional Catholic anti-Judaism the "seedbed" for Nazism.[15] Jewish leader David Gordis welcomed the statement and noted that Jews do not have a concept of repentance: "We have no 'repentance' in Judaism; we have 'teshuvah,' or 'return.' The difference is important. As Jews reflect on the past, we look to a positive reshaping of our behavior and our relationship with God and with our fellow human beings." Gordis noted John Paul II's hope that this document would help to heal wounds, and he concluded that "the document, if read in the context of history, represents both a true act of Christian repentance and an act of teshuvah."[16]

In the United States, many Catholic scholars, including Mary Boys, have studied and critiqued the anti-Jewish biases of the historical Catholic tradition,

---

[13] George E. Tinker, *Spirit and Resistance: Political Theology and American Indian Liberation* (Minneapolis: Fortress Press, 2004), 98.

[14] Pope Francis, "Address of the Holy Father," Second World Meeting of Popular Movements, Santa Cruz de la Sierra, Bolivia, July 9, 2015.

[15] John T. Pawlikowski, "The Vatican and the Holocaust: Putting *We Remember* in Context," in *Ethics in the Shadow of the Holocaust: Christian and Jewish Perspectives,* ed. Judith H. Banki and John T. Pawlikowski (Franklin, WI: Sheed & Ward, 2001), 223.

[16] David Gordis, "Vatican Statement on Holocaust Gives Sense of Repentance, Return," *Jewish Advocate* 188, no. 14 (April 9, 1998): 15.

seeking to purge Catholic life of the traditional anti-Jewish biases, and reshape our understanding of Jews and Judaism.[17] Boys challenges Catholic and other Christian leaders to acknowledge and mourn their traditions' role in fostering anti-Jewish bias through the centuries: "Christians need more frank acknowledgment of how the cross also became a symbol of our violence toward the 'other,' particularly Jews. I suspect that many in the leadership of our churches—Catholic, Orthodox, and Protestant—have never truly *grieved* for Christianity's role in antisemitism."[18] Similarly, Philip Cunningham seeks to heal relations with Jews by proposing how to tell the Christian story in a new way to promote Shalom.[19]

Because of the long history of animosity and conflict, there is also much need for reconciliation and healing in relations between Catholics and Muslims, and *Nostra Aetate*[20] urged both parties to forget the past and work toward mutual understanding (#3). Sidney Griffith interprets *Nostra Aetate*'s appeal to Catholics and Muslims as a quest for reconciliation: "One might take this statement as a confession and an expression of the Catholic Church's act of contrition for past sins, coupled with a firm purpose of amendment, made concrete by the call for and encouragement of interreligious dialogue."[21] The theme of mercy runs throughout the Holy Qur'an and the entire Islamic tradition; *al-Fatihah*, the opening sura of the Qur'an, which is regularly recited by Muslims, proclaims: "In the Name of God, the Compassionate, the Merciful. Praise be to God, Lord of the worlds, the Compassionate, the Merciful, Master of the Day of Judgment" (1:1–3).[22] The Qur'an sets the tone for all Islamic life by describing God as the Compassionate (*al-Rahman*) and the Merciful (*al-Rahim*); both words come from *Ramah*, which can be translated as "Mercy" or "Loving-Mercy."[23]

The theme of mercy shapes both Islamic and Catholic spirituality, and Thomas Michel has compared "the ethics of pardon and peace" in the thought of John Paul II and the influential twentieth-century Muslim theologian Bediuzzaman Said Nursi.[24]

---

[17] Mary C. Boys, *Has God Only One Blessing? Judaism as a Source of Christian Self-Understanding* (New York: Paulist Press, 2000).

[18] Mary C. Boys, *Redeeming Our Sacred Story: The Death of Jesus and Relations between Jews and Christians* (New York: Paulist Press, 2013), 261.

[19] Philip A. Cunningham, *A Story of Shalom: The Calling of Christians and Jews by a Covenanting God* (New York: Paulist Press, 2001).

[20] Pope Paul VI, *Nostra Aetate*, Declaration on the Relation of the Church to Non-Christian Religions, October 28, 1965.

[21] Sidney H. Griffith, "Thoughts on Reading Professor Nasr's 'Muslim Dialogue with the Church after *Nostra Aetate*,'" in *Nostra Aetate,* ed. Pim Valkenberg and Anthony Cirelli (Washington, DC: Catholic University of America Press, 2016), 120.

[22] *The Study Quran: A New Translation and Commentary,* ed. Seyyed Hossein Nasr et al. (New York: HarperOne, 2015), 5.

[23] Ibid., 6.

[24] Thomas Michel, *A Christian View of Islam: Essays on Dialogue,* ed. Irfan A. Omar (Maryknoll, NY: Orbis Books, 2010).

Michel notes John Paul II's insight that justice by itself does not lead to reconciliation, and Michel compares the command of Jesus to love one's enemies and pray for one's persecutors (Mt 5:43–44) to the holy Qur'an: "But it is better to forgive" (42:40).[25] Pope John Paul II and Michel find that the common value placed on forgiveness and pardon unites Muslims and Christians in relating to God and to each other. Michel summarizes Nursi's point: "God manifests Himself to those who believe in terms of truth, love, and mercy and they respond to God with faith, worship, and thanksgiving."[26] For Michel, this text offers

> a succinct statement of Nursi's understanding of human existence. As humans, we exist in order to learn the truth of this world and the next from the Word of God, to worship the loving God who is himself eminently worthy of our love, and to thank and praise God continually for the great mercy that God has always shown to us.[27]

In the United States, the West Coast Dialogue of Catholics and Muslims considered the difficult atmosphere after the terrorist attacks of September 11, 2001. In December 2003, they issued a public statement, "Friends and Not Adversaries: A Catholic-Muslim Spiritual Journey," which included the following points of consensus on forgiveness, mutual respect, and trust:

1. We, Catholics and Muslims, believe that God is the source of peace and justice, and thus we fundamentally agree on the nature of peace and justice and the essential need of all to work for peace and justice.
2. Our rich teachings and traditions of peace and justice serve as a resource and inspiration for all; however, our immediate and present actions to work together are often wanting. The need to work together for peace and justice is a pressing demand in these troubled times.
3. We believe that it is God who forgives and that as Catholics and Muslims we are called by God to offer forgiveness. Forgiveness is an important step to moving beyond our past history if we are to preserve human dignity, to effect justice, and to work for peace.
4. We may disagree on certain points of doctrine, even as we respect the others' rights to a fundamental integrity of their teachings and affirm all their human and religious rights. With love and in the pursuit of truth, we will offer or criticisms of one another when we believe there is a violation of integrity of faith in God. We must avoid demonizing one another and misrepresenting one another's teachings and traditions.
5. When we meet in dialogue and discuss matters of peace, justice, and forgiveness, while being faithful to our traditions, we have experienced a

---

[25] Ibid., 110.
[26] Michel, "Is a God-Centered Life an Antidote," 338–39.
[27] Ibid., 339.

profound and moving connection on the deepest level of our faith, which must take effect in our lives.[28]

Thomas Ryan has found that the traditional Hindu practice of yoga offers resources for purification and integration of body, mind, and heart. Practice of the yogic exercises and breathing techniques can result in "an experience of equilibrium, peace, and interior harmony. Stretching and lengthening muscles that are chronically contracted helps to rebalance both body and mind. What happens in the body affects the mind, just as the mind affects the body."[29] He also notes that the practice of fasting, shared by Catholics and many other traditions, can have both physical and spiritual benefits of healing: "A fast day is an opportunity for the body to 'clean house.' When it is given a day off from its normal process of digestion, assimilation, and elimination, the body will use the occasion to cleanse itself of toxins, throw off old cells, and tend to a general refurbishing."[30]

Similarly, Casey Rock has discovered that yoga practice can help to acknowledge and heal physical injuries: "Every body bears scars and wounds, from scrapes and accidents, from the slight to the serious. . . . All such experience is still carried in the body. The yoga class is a place where we come up against those memories once again."[31] Rock finds that a skilled instructor can be a "gentle guide into our meeting this layered self in the present. A wise yoga teacher negotiates these precarious waters by speaking always of tolerance."[32] At best, the yoga class can offer "the re-creation of a childlike state, even if only that of our dreams."[33] Rock recalls that traditional Catholic theology viewed age seven as the time when a child becomes morally responsible; she adds that after about age seven, children learn to see their body "as if it were alien and a liar"; and she recommends yoga practice as a path of healing and integration where people of all ages "are provided the space, encouragement, and motivation to meet themselves as they are and to develop attitudes of compassion, patience, and gratitude."[34]

The Buddhist tradition also has resources for the *via purgativa*. From different angles of vision, both the Buddhist and the Catholic traditions warn us of the danger of primordial ignorance. Primordial ignorance involves a systemic warping of our most fundamental assumptions about ourselves, our relationships, and our world. When we are entrapped by ignorance, we identify with our anxious,

---

[28] The West Coast Dialogue of Catholics and Muslims, "Friends and Not Adversaries: A Catholic-Muslim Spiritual Journey," December 23, 2003.

[29] Thomas Ryan, "The Body Language of Faith," in *Reclaiming the Body in Christian Spirituality,* ed. Thomas Ryan (New York: Paulist Press, 2004), 90.

[30] Ibid., 61–62.

[31] Casey Rock, "Voices from the Mat," in *Reclaiming the Body in Christian Spirituality,* ed. Thomas Ryan (New York: Paulist Press, 2004), 104.

[32] Ibid., 105.

[33] Ibid.

[34] Ibid., 106.

frightened ego; we crave certain outcomes and think that these are necessary for our well-being. If our demands and cravings do not find satisfaction in the way we expect, we frequently become frustrated and angry, and can easily move into conflicts with others and ourselves. Fundamental ignorance is not innocent. It involves a systemic distortion of our true identity, but it is never total.

The warnings of the Buddhist tradition about the three poisons—ignorance, craving, and anger—resound deeply within the Catholic tradition, which speaks of ignorance, concupiscence, and malice as the roots of sin. As long as we are operating within a horizon shaped by fundamental ignorance, we can exert great efforts only to encounter more and more frustration. The traditional Buddhist teaching offers a vantage point for challenging the prejudices of racism, sexism, homophobia, virulent nationalism, and religious intolerance that trouble our present world.

The wisdom of the Buddha converges with the teaching of Jesus in challenging us not to hold grudges and to seek reconciliation. In the Dhammapada, the Buddha teaches us the vital importance of seeking conciliation:

> Conquer anger with conciliation,
> Evil with good
> Stinginess with giving,
> And a liar with the truth.[35]

Moreover, the Buddha advised his followers not to cling to past injuries:

> He insulted me; he struck me; he defeated me; he robbed me.
> For those who dwell on such resentments, enmity never ceases.
> He insulted me; he struck me; he defeated me; he robbed me.
> For those who do not dwell on such resentments, enmity subsides.
> Enmities are never appeased by enmity.
> They are appeased by peace. This is an eternal law.
> Many do not realize that we must die.
> Those who do realize this appease their quarrels.[36]

The traditions of Buddhist meditation offer helpful practices for purifying the mind and heart. Carmelites Mary Jo Meadow, Kevin Culligan, and Daniel Chowning compare the journeys of purification of John of the Cross and the Theravada practice of *vipassana* or insight meditation; they describe the classical Carmelite path of purification:

> The journey to union with God in love is thus a dark journey because we travel always in purifying faith. . . . The journey is dark also because

---

[35] Leo D. Lefebure and Peter Feldmeier, *The Path of Wisdom: A Christian Commentary on the Dhammapada* (Leuven, Belgium: Peeters/Grand Rapids, MI: Eerdmans, 2011), 231.
[36] Ibid., 30.

we voluntarily undertake, to purify and empty sense and spirit of every disordered attachment that hinders God's purifying and transforming self-communication.[37]

They turn to the traditional Theravada practice of insight meditation as a practical path to purify our mental contents: "Right concentration, right mindfulness, and right effort are spiritual disciplines that purify the mind and heart. . . . Right mindfulness purifies the intellect by keeping us aware of our inner world, and keeping us from investing energy needlessly in thoughts, concepts, and ideas."[38] This offers a practical path to ending unnecessary suffering: "We realize that we do not practice for comfort or pleasure, but for purgation. We understand that purifying conduct and mind is the only way out of the human dilemma—that no magic, hard wishing, or other maneuver does the job."[39]

In a similar vein, Peter Feldmeier draws on both Buddhaghosa and John of Cross to find resources for the path of purification and the dark night of the soul, proposing that the wisdom and practices of the Carmelite and Theravada traditions can flow together.[40] In a world filled by conflicts and misunderstandings, the practice of mindfulness calls us to attend to the full reality of the present moment without judgment, allowing all factors of our experience to emerge into our awareness in an atmosphere of wisdom and compassion. The transformed awareness can lead to both personal and social healing and growth. When we try to force experience in certain ways, we risk distorting our perceptions, ignoring important factors, and creating needless problems. Buddhist meditation can converge with Christian values offering a constructive path forward.

In the *via purgativa*, we travel on a path of conversion away from sin toward interreligious reconciliation, respect, and understanding. While many issues in interreligious relationships remain unresolved at the present time, much has happened in this regard to heal Catholic relations with other religious communities in the United States in the last generation.

Via Illuminativa: Learning to See Anew, Growing in Charity

Because the history of interreligious relations has often been marred by biases and distortions, learning to see others clearly in the light of charity is of urgent importance today. Even though the task of purification and reconciliation may not

---

[37] Mary Jo Meadow, Kevin Culligan, and Daniel Chowning, *Christian Insight Meditation: Following in the Footsteps of John of the Cross,* ed. Mary Jo Meadow (Boston: Wisdom Publications, 2007), 114.

[38] Ibid., 151.

[39] Ibid., 142.

[40] Peter Feldmeier, *Experiments in Buddhist-Christian Encounter: From Buddha-Nature to the Divine Nature* (Maryknoll, NY: Orbis Books, 2019), 39–67.

ever be fully accomplished in this world, with a sufficient level of trust and healing interreligious partners can travel on the illuminative way, seeking mutual insight concerning their respective religious paths. In the path of illumination, partners in dialogue can look for what is true and holy in other traditions and develop friendly relations. Often Catholics in dialogue with other traditions have learned that many traditions share important values even though they may be viewed and practiced in very different ways. Efforts at mutual illumination today need to address the challenge of our past, understand more clearly our present situations, and move toward greater harmony by shaping a healthy community of the world's religions.

In traditional Catholic theology, one of the effects of our primal warping through original sin is the distortion of our ability to see what is good and pursue it; the path of illumination seeks the power of vision offered by God. Illumination is a central value in the Augustinian tradition. In a dialogue with his son Adeodatus, Augustine warned that no human being can genuinely teach another human being about the lasting virtues, since Christ is the unseen teacher.[41] According to Augustine, all humans need the assistance of divine light in order to see clearly. Karl Rahner taught that love is the lamp of knowledge and concluded that all genuine interpersonal knowledge involves an act of love empowered by God.[42]

In the Catholic tradition, grace can be understood as God's loving presence and our transformation in it. By healing our relationships with God and other humans and all creation, grace makes possible new forms of seeing and sharing. Grace in Catholic theology both heals human life and elevates it to another dimension, making possible new types of relationships. God's loving presence was known as uncreated grace in traditional theology and our transformation in it was known as created grace.[43] In earlier times, Catholics were often skeptical that grace could be found in other religious traditions; today in light of a renewed theology of the Holy Spirit's universal activity, Catholics and other Christians can look for the presence of God in all the world's religious traditions and be alert to recognize signs of transformation.

Given the long history of Catholic biases toward other religious traditions, the traditional *via illuminativa* finds new significance in seeing other religious traditions with respect and appreciation, and cultivating relationships of charity and friendship. This has profound implications for Catholic views of Jews and the Jewish tradition. Mary C. Boys reflects together with her Jewish colleague Sara S. Lee on the process of *Learning in the Presence of the Other* as mutually transformative.[44] Boys gathered another group of colleagues to reflect together on *Seeing*

---

[41] Augustine, *Against the Academicians; On the Teacher,* trans. Peter King (Indianapolis, IN: Hackett, 1995).

[42] Karl Rahner, *Hearer of the Word: Laying the Foundation for a Philosophy of Religion,* trans. from the first edition by Joseph Donceel, ed. Andrew Tallon (New York: Continuum, 1994), 81.

[43] Charles R. Meyer, *A Contemporary Theology of Grace* (Staten Island, NY: Alba House, 1971).

[44] Mary C. Boys and Sara S. Lee, *Christians and Jews in Dialogue: Learning in the Pres-*

Judaism Anew: Christianity's Sacred Obligation.[45] Often there will be misunderstandings because of different assumptions and perspectives; these need not be a major problem but can offer opportunities for new learning if they can be handled with trust and honesty.

There is a particular need for illumination in relations with American Indians, and in recent years many American Indians have explored ways of drawing upon both Native and Christian traditions in their faith and practice.[46] Some seek a new vision of both Catholic faith and Native American spirituality in relation to each other, so that each transforms the other and is transformed in turn. This process develops the interreligious and intercultural openness of the Second Vatican Council. Raymond A. Bucko notes the shift in Catholic perceptions of the sweat lodge experiences in the 1980s: "The most salient shift in this modern literature is that it not only ceases to condemn Lakota traditional religious practice; it even documents missionaries' participation in these ceremonies and their appreciation of Lakota rites."[47]

Marie Therese Archambault offers an example of what a Native style of Catholic spirituality can look like in her reflections on Black Elk, who, as we have seen, engaged devoutly in Catholic practice while continuing traditional Indian religious practices. Archambault comments that Black Elk "was able to transfer his understanding of the *wakan* [the sacred, the incomprehensible] from his Lakota religion to what it meant in biblical, literate terms."[48] Black Elk interprets Paul's famous hymn of charity in 1 Corinthians 13 in light of his Native experience, even though there is no exact word in Lakota that corresponds to *agape*.[49] Black Elk resonates with Paul's boasting only of his weakness (2 Cor 11:30), and he speaks of communicating with the sacred by "sending a pitiful voice"; Archambault notes that Black Elk's prayer "always accentuates his own existential weakness and that of human beings who are *ushica* (in a miserable state of being, either spiritually or materially)."[50] Archambault notes that Black Elk practiced both traditions:

> It appears from the witness of his life that Black Elk embraced two religious traditions whole-heartedly; he gave himself to both and lived them fully. Not a contradiction or a paradox this, but the blessing of the [sacred

ence of the Other (Woodstock, VT: Skylights Paths, 2006).

[45] *Seeing Judaism Anew: Christianity's Sacred Obligation,* ed. Mary C. Boys (Lanham, MD: Sheed & Ward, 2005).

[46] Steven Charleston and Elaine A. Robinson, eds., *Coming Full Circle: Constructing Native Christian Theology* (Minneapolis: Fortress Press, 2015).

[47] Raymond A. Bucko, *The Lakota Ritual of the Sweat Lodge: History and Contemporary Practice* (Lincoln: University of Nebraska Press, 1999), 81.

[48] Marie Therese Archambault, *A Retreat with Black Elk* (Cincinnati, OH: St. Anthony Messenger Press, 1998), 20.

[49] Ibid., 21.

[50] Ibid., 22.

direction of] East in Black Elk's life. At its heart, it was the gifted intuition that *all being is one. Mitakuye Oyasin* [All my relatives]![51]

Ben Black Bear Jr., a member of the Lakota nation and a Catholic deacon, shared his experience of Catholic and Lakota spirituality with Marie Therese Archambault.[52] He recalled that his mother's ancestors had become Catholic in the 1850s and 1860s during the time of Fr. Pierre-Jean de Smet, SJ, and described Ironwood, the town of his childhood, as both traditional Lakota and also overwhelmingly Catholic. He recalled, "So this early Catholic activity was tied into traditional Lakota ways."[53] An uncle was a medicine man, and he described his experience:

> So the sense of spirituality that I had—sort of meshed traditional Lakota spirituality with Christian/Catholic spirituality—was done in Lakota. . . . It helped me to see Catholicism in Lakota and then a lot of the traditional teachings and beliefs that I learned in Lakota became a part of me.[54]

His father was a Catholic who continued to participate in traditional Lakota ceremonies. Ben Black Bear speculated that Catholic missionaries who rejected the ceremonies did not truly understand them. Marie Therese Archambault, a member of the Lakota people who studied Ben Black Bear's experience, relates the societies established by Catholic missionaries to the traditional Lakota practice of communicating with the spirit world:

> Crucial in this context, the societies were a means of being in and communicating with the spirit world of which dreams and visions were the main communication. This is important to note because the matrix of all Lakota spiritual leanings and aspirations was through encounters with the spirit world, through dreams and visions during ceremonies.[55]

Prejudices against Muslims continue to challenge Catholic relations with Muslims in the United States and many other areas. In this context, Pim Valkenberg, who is originally from the Netherlands and who is a professor of theology at the Catholic University of America in Washington, DC, seeks mutual illumination in dialogue with Bediüzzaman Said Nursi as part of an ambitious and thoughtful project in comparative theology, *Sharing Lights on the Way to God: Muslim-Christian*

---

[51] Ibid., 65.
[52] Marie Therese Archambault, "Ben Black Bear, Jr.: A Lakota Deacon and a 'Radical Catholic' Tells His Own Story," *U.S. Catholic Historian* 16, no. 2 (1998): 90–106.
[53] Ibid., 92.
[54] Ibid., 94.
[55] Ibid., 104.

Dialogue and Theology in the Context of Abrahamic Partnership.[56] To orient the project of sharing lights, Valkenberg turns to the shared virtue of hospitality, which challenges both parties to receive the stranger and to respect the manners of friendship. Valkenberg, noting that interpretations of classic texts can move through multiple dimensions and can lead to a variety of results, advises us that "a Christian interpretation of a Muslim text may contribute not only to a rereading of the Christian tradition enriched with Muslim ideas but also to the dialogue between Christians and Muslims on the ideas embodied in the text and their practical consequences."[57] Valkenberg notes that Nursi was empowered to journey from estrangement (*ghurba*) to companionship (*uns*) by relying on the Islamic virtues of faith, trust, and patience; and he cites the traditional Catholic hymn, *Te Deum*: "O Lord, let Thy mercy lighten upon us as our trust is in Thee. O Lord, in Thee have I trusted; let me never be confounded."[58] Valkenberg finds that Nursi's patience, endurance, and trusting in God resonate with the poem of Teresa of Avila that invites us to let nothing upset us and reminds us that all things pass and that God alone suffices.[59]

Reid Locklin seeks mutual illumination with Hindus by juxtaposing teachings from Shankara's *Upadesasahasri* in the Advaita tradition with texts that have influenced the Christian tradition, beginning with the Apostle Paul and ranging widely through later figures. Locklin attends especially to Paul as the first Christian writer and one of the most authoritative voices in the entire Christian tradition, and also as a dialogical author who is always in communication with a particular audience.[60] Locklin considers a variety of ways of framing the relationship between Christian faith and Advaita, including the claims of Jacques Dupuis and Peggy Starkey that the Hindu scriptures satisfy the Christian criterion of agape; however, he prefers more modest claims: "Such a conclusion overreaches the evidence. It may, in any case, be quite beside the point to search for this Christian teaching in these Advaita scripts."[61] Rather than trying to assess one tradition by a criterion from the other, he proposes a rather different goal: "By identifying points of resonance around the notion of *agape*, we are attempting something more modest: namely, to assist in the ongoing articulation of merely one of many bases for ongoing conversations about human rights, social justice and one's fundamental moral disposition in the world."[62]

---

[56] Pim Valkenberg, *Sharing Lights on the Way to God: Muslim-Christian Dialogue and Theology in the Context of Abrahamic Partnership,* Currents of Encounter 26 (Amsterdam: Rodopi, 2006).

[57] Ibid., 209.

[58] Ibid., 291.

[59] Ibid., 304.

[60] Reid B. Locklin, *Liturgy of Liberation: A Christian Commentary on Shankara's Updasasahasti,* Christian Commentaries on Non-Christian Sacred Texts (Leuven, Belgium: Peeters/Grand Rapids, MI: Eerdmans, 2011), 42–43.

[61] Ibid., 317.

[62] Ibid., 318.

Locklin proposes that each tradition can offer "friendly amendments" to the other in a process of mutual correction. In contrast to those who seek common ground, Locklin suggests a slightly different metaphor: "*Agape* may not represent a common ground, in other words, but the ground it does provide can and has become *shared ground*."[63] Locklin hopes that the process of mutual correction can lead Christians to discover the "'ever greater meaning' (*sensus plenior*) of the Christian scriptures and indeed of God's love in Christ. More than this, we will have discovered a fuller meaning [of] this same Christ himself."[64]

Francis Clooney has sought mutual illumination in his two volumes reflecting on Catholic spirituality in dialogue with the fourteenth-century Hindu theologian Sri Vedanta Desika. *The Truth, the Way, the Life: Christian Commentary on the Three Holy Mantras of the Srivaisnava Hindus* explores three Indian mantras both in the context of the fourteenth-century Hindu theologian Sri Vedanta Desika and also in light of Christian perspectives.[65] The other volume, *Beyond Compare: St. Francis de Sales and Sri Vedanta Desika on Loving Surrender to God*, builds on the first and explores the meaning of "loving surrender to God" in Francis de Sales' *Treatise on the Love of God* and Desika's *Essence of the Auspicious Three Mysteries*.[66] In the latter work Clooney rejects any pretense of having an "outside higher viewpoint" and writes explicitly from within the Roman Catholic tradition that he shares with Francis de Sales, the seventeenth-century Catholic bishop of Geneva, Switzerland, who wrote spiritual works for lay Catholics.[67] Clooney integrates personal, imaginative, and affective dimensions into his intellectual work, hoping for "a 'post-objective' empathy and engagement."[68] Clooney's central wager is that a religious insider's perspective on reading these two works in tandem offers advantages not accessible either through allegedly neutral, objective scholarship or through the study of a single text by itself.

Clooney notes several paradoxes that affect both authors. Both de Sales and Desika use words to do what words by themselves cannot do, that is, lead the reader to the deeply personal act of surrendering to God. Both authors employ the resources of reason and language while remaining ambivalent about the efficacy of reasoning and of language. Both root themselves firmly in their respective traditions while also being highly creative. Desika denied any originality, claiming simply to hand on his heritage without any innovation; nonetheless, he creatively developed the Srivaisnava tradition of South India by stressing the importance of complete

---

[63] Ibid.

[64] Ibid.

[65] Francis X. Clooney, *The Truth, the Way, the Life: Christian Commentary on the Three Holy Mantras of the Srivaisnava Hindus,* Christian Commentaries on Non-Christian Sacred Texts (Leuven, Belgium: Peeters/Grand Rapids, MI: Eerdmans, 2008).

[66] Francis X. Clooney, *Beyond Compare: St. Francis de Sales and Sri Vedanta Desika on Loving Surrender to God* (Washington, DC: Georgetown University Press, 2008).

[67] Ibid., 187.

[68] Ibid., 5.

human dependence on God as expressed in three mantras. There is also the paradox of loving surrender itself: is it the action of God or of the human person? In Desika, as in Francis de Sales, both divine grace and free will are necessary for the act of submission. Both authors offer a type of resolution to the paradoxes by placing theoretical perspectives in service of the practical goal of transforming lives. Clooney stresses the similarities in their strategies of addressing these issues.

In his Christian commentary on three mantras from the Vaishnavite tradition, Clooney juxtaposes various pairs of short sayings such as the prayer of Jesus on the cross in the Gospel of Luke, "Father, into your hands I commend my spirit" (Lk 23:46), with the Dvaya Mantra: "I approach for refuge the feet of Narayana with Shri, obeisance to Narayana with Shri."[69] Clooney stresses the complementarity to the point that he accepts the Dvaya Mantra as possible for a Christian to pray: "While a Christian utterance of the Dvaya Mantra may remain incomplete, it none-theless becomes for the Christian a real prayer that merits utterance."[70] The result for the Christian is "a still richer site for prayer."[71]

Clooney similarly juxtaposes Jesus's command to the rich young man, "If you would be perfect, go, sell your possessions and give the proceeds to the poor" (Mt 19:28), with "Having completely given up all *dharmas*, to Me alone come for refuge. . . "(Bhagavad Gita 18:66a, first line of Carama Sloka).[72] According to Clooney, both sayings advise us "before we make our choice and act, we need also to recognize that at our best, we are responding to a gracious invitation from God who is always before us, first"; Clooney points out that in both traditions God "asks us to make a radical choice to risk everything, depending on nothing but God alone."[73] Clooney stresses the similarity of "[r]enunciation, intimacy with the Lord, and service" in both sayings, and he trusts that the juxtaposition enhances the significance of each saying as he draws the hopeful conclusion: "Insofar as the texts differ, they can be taken as complementary, each enriching the way the other is read and pondered."[74]

Clooney's project of reading the two authors in relation to each other faces its own paradoxes; and the conclusions he draws are careful, cautious, and modest. On the one hand, Clooney presents the experience of reading these texts together as unsettling and undermining any exclusivist self-confidence.[75] The dual reading is said to disorient readers in both traditions. On the other hand, Clooney mitigates the impact of this disorientation by stressing the complementary character of the differences between de Sales and Desika.[76] While acknowledging genuine

---

[69] Clooney, *Truth,* 143, 189.
[70] Ibid., 145.
[71] Ibid.
[72] Ibid., 75, 107.
[73] Ibid., 75.
[74] Ibid., 106, 107.
[75] Ibid., 186.
[76] Ibid., 185.

divergences, Clooney nonetheless concludes that on balance, the God of de Sales and the God of Desika are more similar than different, "with most of the same characteristic features, including compassion, proximity, and the willingness and intention to protect."[77] Comparative readings are often like looking at a Gestalt that can be viewed in completely different ways. Clooney foregrounds the similarities while relegating differences to the background. One could imagine sharply different readings that accentuate points of divergence. For example, Clooney mentions the issue of caste only in passing.[78]

Clooney places the rhetoric of loving surrender at the service of comparative theology, eschewing the options of exclusivism or pluralism or the "comforts" of knowing only one tradition; in this strange new world Clooney hopes that comparative reading itself can bring the reader "closer to the precipice of a real act of loving surrender."[79] Interreligious reading becomes a new way to seek the goals of both de Sales and Desika. For Clooney, the effect of reading them together is primarily mutual reinforcement, as "each text intensifies and magnifies the other."[80]

As Peter Phan, following the lead of the Federation of Asian Bishops Conferences, has noted, the central virtues of the Buddhist tradition resonate deeply with Catholic values.[81] The Brahma-viharas (the noble dwelling places) teach loving-kindness (*metta*) and compassion (*karuna*) not only for all humans but for all sentient beings; they also include the virtue of appreciative joy (*muditha*). Mary Jo Meadow, Kevin Culligan, and Daniel Chowning have found that Theravada Buddhist meditation practice is extremely helpful for learning to see clearly without distortions: "Right understanding means clear-seeing, seeing-reality as it truly is, without the blinders of desires, aversions, or delusions. It is seeing the truth of things unclouded by any smoke screens that self-sense throws up in self-projection."[82] Learning to see is not simply grasping a new concept but a "deep, direct seeing that produces life-changing learning."[83]

Both the Buddhist and the Christian traditions warn us that our ordinary sight is clouded by desire, fear, and anger. Seeing clearly (*kensho*) is a prime value of the Japanese Zen tradition. Ruben Habito notes that the practice of *zazen*, sitting in silent meditation, can be a powerful aid to calming the mind and seeing clearly. He compares the practice of Buddhist meditation to the *Philokalia,* a collection of texts on prayer and meditation, and also to the wisdom of St. John of the Cross.[84] He presents the traditional Jesuit Spiritual Exercises of Ignatius of Loyola in relation to

---

[77] Ibid., 187.

[78] Ibid., 190.

[79] Ibid., 186.

[80] Ibid., 183.

[81] Peter C. Phan, *The Joy of Religious Pluralism: A Personal Journey* (Maryknoll, NY: Orbis Books, 2017), 61.

[82] Meadow, Culligan, and Chowning, *Christian Insight Meditation,* 140.

[83] Ibid.

[84] Ruben L. F. Habito, *Healing Breath: Zen Spirituality for a Wounded Earth* (Maryknoll, NY: Orbis Books, 1993), 42–43.

Zen Buddhist practices. Noting that the second week of the Spiritual Exercises is devoted to "illuminating our path with [Jesus's] own life in his words and actions,"[85] Habito relates the Jesuit practice of contemplating the life of Jesus to a Zen koan that invites us to attend to the present moment: "This koan brings the seeker back down to earth and calls attention to the fact that the ultimate Way is right here, closer than we can imagine, right in the midst of the ordinary events of our day-to-day life."[86] For Habito, the Zen and Jesuit traditions flow together in calling to us to acknowledge that "Each moment can be the gateway to a realm that is beyond the linear flow of time from past to present to future, as it opens up and gives us a glimpse of the eternal, right *here, now,* in the very mundane and ordinary tasks of daily life."[87] The mutual illumination and understanding found in interreligious relationships can in turn invite us into a deeper communion with the entire community of life on this planet and with the earth, as in the Buddhist-Catholic monastic dialogue on "Green Monasticism."[88]

Via Unitiva: The Way of Union

The traditional Catholic *via unitiva* seeks union, a state of oneness with God and other creatures. The language of oneness can function in very different ways and is not without danger. On the one hand, the One can serve as a name for the ultimate starting point and goal of the journey of the entire universe: the Neoplatonic philosopher Plotinus portrayed all things flowing forth from the One and returning to it.[89] Jewish, Christian, and Muslim mystical authors drew upon Plotinus's vocabulary to articulate their spiritual journeys, while insisting that the journey and its goal remain incomprehensible, ineffable, and indescribable.[90] The tradition of seeking oneness with all reality lives on in various forms among American Catholics today—for example, John S. Dunne takes inspiration from Native American vision quests to explore the path of union. He seeks to unite American Indian wisdom with the ancient view of all things emanating from the One and also with Teilhard de Chardin's view of evolution where all things converge in the end; the result is a new form of the Neoplatonic vision of all things coming from God and returning to God.[91] Hindus and Buddhists

---

    [85] Ruben L. F. Habito, *Zen and the Spiritual Exercises: Paths of Awakening and Transformation* (Maryknoll, NY: Orbis Books, 2013), 81.
    [86] Ibid., 102–3.
    [87] Ibid., 104.
    [88] Donald W. Mitchell and William Skudlarek, eds., *Green Monasticism: A Buddhist-Catholic Response to an Environmental Calamity* (New York: Lantern Books, 2010).
    [89] Plotinus, *The Enneads,* ed. Lloyd P. Gerson, trans. George Boys-Stones et al. (Cambridge: Cambridge University Press, 2019).
    [90] Sells, *Mystical Languages of Unsaying.*
    [91] John S. Dunne, *A Vision Quest* (Notre Dame, IN: University of Notre Dame Press, 2006), vii.

offer a variety of perspectives on nonduality, stressing the importance of realizing oneness with ultimate reality.[92]

On the other hand, religious actors can seek to impose oneness by force, and attempts to force union are oppressive. This ambiguity haunts the motto of the United States: *e pluribus unum* (out of many, one). The phrase can be taken in many different ways. Unity can be an oppressive experience when religious empires impose a type of oneness. This has long been a temptation for Christian imperial ambitions in the Americas, including the Spanish Catholic Empire that dominated others while claiming to impose the unity of the Catholic faith, and also the Protestant American Empire that conquered the Philippines in the name of civilization and religion.[93] White Catholic educators tried to force Native American children into a type of oneness with American identity in ways that violated their dignity and culture.[94]

Nonetheless, if taken in conjunction with the First Amendment of the Constitution of the United States and the ideal of religious liberty, the phrase *e pluribus unum* can set forth a challenge of shaping a genuine community that does not impose any one religious identity but seeks union precisely in respectful diversity. The path of union can encourage the formation of a harmonious community out of many diverse constituencies, as in George Washington's visit to the Touro Synagogue in Newport, Rhode Island, and his famous letter promising that the United States allows no place for religious bigotry. The project of shaping a United States with equal respect for all religious communities has long been conflicted and fragile, but it remains an ideal of unity in diversity.

Respect for interreligious partners requires acknowledgment of their distinctive identity and the boundaries between religious traditions. Nonetheless, in different ways, practitioners discover that boundaries can be porous, and the unitive path can be understood as identifying with various religious paths. Thomas Merton claimed a type of oneness with other traditions in a letter to Czeslaw Milosz on January 18, 1962:

> I cannot be Catholic unless it is made quite clear to the world that I am a Jew and a Moslem, unless I am execrated as a Buddhist and denounced for having undermined all that this comfortable and social Catholicism stands for: this lining up of cassocks, this regimenting of birettas.[95]

---

[92] Anantanand Rambachan, *The Advaita Worldview; God, World, Humanity* (Albany: State University of New York Press, 2006); Akira Sadakata, *Buddhist Cosmology: Philosophy and Origins,* trans. Gaynor Sekimori (Tokyo: Kosei, 2004), 79–89.

[93] Stuart Creighton Miller, *Benevolent Assimilation: The American Conquest of the Philippines, 1899–1903* (New Haven, CT: Yale University Press, 1982).

[94] David Wallace Adams, *Education for Extinction: American Indians and the Boarding School Experience, 1875–1928* (Lawrence: University Press of Kansas, 1995).

[95] Thomas Merton, *The Courage for Truth: Letters to Writers,* ed. C. M. Bochen (New York: Farrar, Straus & Giroux, 1993), 79.

For Merton, unity with other religions was not a question of abandoning his own vocation as a Catholic monk; it came through the deepening of his search for God through his exchanges with followers of other paths.[96]

One of most important manifestations of the unitive path is spiritual friendship, a classical virtue that the twelfth-century Cistercian monk Aelred of Rievaulx explored in his writings.[97] Aelred begins his discussion of *Spiritual Friendship* by invoking Christ as the third between two friends: "Here we are, you and I, and I hope a third, Christ is in our midst."[98] Aelred links friendship with wisdom so closely that he concludes, "I might almost say friendship is nothing else but wisdom."[99] Based on the Johannine identification of God with love (1 Jn 4:16), Aelred affirms, "God is friendship."[100] He concludes his discussion with an eschatological hope of universal friendship, trusting that "we shall rejoice in the eternal possession of Supreme Goodness; and this friendship, to which here we admit but few, will be outpoured upon all and by all outpoured upon God, and God shall be all in all."[101]

Even though Aelred was not thinking of interreligious relationships, his perspectives find fresh applications when in recent years many interreligious explorers in the United States and beyond have invoked the virtue of friendship. Buddhist leader, Ven. Thubten Chodron and Catholic Sister Donald Corcoran have shared their journey and friendship as "Spiritual Sisters."[102] Thomas Michel edited a series of Jesuit reflections on encountering Jews: *Friends on the Way*.[103] James Fredericks has written of the virtue of spiritual friendship, noting the importance of respecting the otherness of one's friend: "Ideally, friendships foster a sense of community between persons, in that similarity can be recognized without loss of separate identity and in that enduring differences can be faced as real and yet honored."[104] He warns, "Interreligious friendships are no longer healthy when they are no longer relationships wherein religious differences are honored and recognized

---

[96] Sidney H. Griffith, "Mystics and Sufi Masters: Thomas Merton and Dialogue between Christians and Muslims," *Islam and Christian-Muslim Relations* 15, no. 3 (2004): 299–316.

[97] Aelred Squire, *Aelred of Rievaulx: A Study* (Kalamazoo, MI: Cistercian Publications, 1981), 98–111.

[98] Aelred of Rievaulx, *Spiritual Friendship*, trans. Mary Eugenia Laker (Kalamazoo, MI: Cistercian Publications, 1977), 51.

[99] Ibid., 65.

[100] Ibid., 65–66.

[101] Ibid., 132.

[102] Ven. Thubten Chodron, ed., *Spiritual Sisters* (Seattle, WA: Dharma Friendship Foundation, n.d.).

[103] Thomas Michel, ed., *Friends on the Way: Jesuits Encounter Contemporary Judaism* (New York: Fordham University Press, 2007).

[104] James L. Fredericks, "Interreligious Friendship: A New Theological Virtue," *Journal of Ecumenical Studies* 35, no. 2 (1998): 172.

as possible resources for deepening our own religious self-understanding."[105] James Fredericks has reflected in particular on his spiritual interreligious friendship with Masao Abe, emphasizing, "In no small way, our strangeness to one another is the bond that holds our friendship together."[106] Fredericks emphasizes the crossing of boundaries that can enlarge our sensibility: "Welcoming a stranger entails a de-centering of the self. We are moved off our home ground. The sovereignty of the ego is undermined. In welcoming a stranger, we have to make room for another way of imagining the world and acting within it."[107]

At the second Gethsemani Encounter, a Buddhist monk, Ajahn Amaro, commented, "In Christianity, since God is love and unity, loving communion between persons can be considered a living out of Ultimate Reality. For Buddhists, community is also a deeply significant center of our lives."[108] He went on to recall a conversation between Shakyamuni Buddha and his disciple Ananda in which the disciple asked about the principle that "spiritual friendship is half of the holy life"; the Buddha reportedly answered, "Not so, Ananda. It is not half of the holy life. It's the whole of the holy life."[109] Ajahn Amaro explained that in spiritual friendship one relates to goodness and beauty: "And externally this goodness and beauty one finds in a spiritual relation manifests as unity or harmony in unselfish and compassionate relationships with other beings."[110] I recalled the view of Aelred of Rievaulx that God is friendship and that Christ is the third between two friends. Zoketsu Norman Fischer commented, "Friendship is a tremendously powerful source of healing. When friends share about their suffering, hearts fall open, people connect, and communion happens. A listening heart, a caring heart soothes our anxieties."[111] Buddhists would not use the language of God; but from a Catholic perspective, encountering Buddhists as friends is a way of meeting God in Christ. In developing interreligious relations, the ancient value of spiritual friendship takes on new importance.

The traditional Catholic *via unitiva* invites sharing with Jewish and Islamic paths that lead to mystical union, becoming one or realizing oneness with God.[112] The term "mysticism" is controversial; it has been defined and appraised in many different ways, with some seeing it as the most valuable aspect of all religious experience and others decrying it as a distortion of religion. Often mystical experi-

---

[105] Ibid.

[106] James Fredericks, "Masao Abe: A Spiritual Friendship," *Spiritus* 3, no. 2 (2003): 223–24; James Fredericks, ed., *Interreligious Friendship after Nostra Aetate* (New York: Palgrave Macmillan, 2015).

[107] Ibid., 220.

[108] Donald W. Mitchell and James Wiseman, eds., *Transforming Suffering: Reflections on Finding Peace in Troubled Times* (New York: Doubleday, 2003), 80.

[109] Ibid.

[110] Ibid., 81.

[111] Ibid., 233.

[112] Moshe Idel and Bernard McGinn, eds., *Mystical Union in Judaism, Christianity, and Islam: An Ecumenical Dialogue* (London: Bloomsbury, 1999).

ence involves a sense of the immediate presence of ultimate reality leading to an experience of union and oneness. Bernard McGinn views the mystical element in Christianity as "that part of its belief and practices that concerns the preparation for, the consciousness of, and the reaction to what can be described as the immediate or direct presence of God."[113] Based on his extensive study of Kabbalah, Gershom Scholem accepts the phrase of Thomas Aquinas, "the experimental knowledge of God" (*cognitio dei experimentalis*) as applicable to Jewish mystics.[114] According to John Renard, Islamic mystics seek and probe the experiential knowledge of God (*m'arifa*).[115] Annemarie Schimmel describes the mystical path in Islam and other religions: "In its widest sense [mysticism] may be defined as the consciousness of the One Reality—be it called Wisdom, Light, Love, or Nothing."[116]

The Qur'an and the entire Islamic tradition proclaim *Tawhid*—the oneness of God. Sufis describe a process of the human subject going through *fana*—annihilation that brings oneness with God—followed by *baqa*—survival in a transformed state. In a wide variety of ways Hindus and Buddhists speak of oneness and nonduality.[117] The variety of perspectives on oneness invites reflection on nonduality as a theme in multiple traditions. While the language of nonduality may sound strange to some Catholics, Cardinal Nicholas of Cusa in the fifteenth century insisted that God is not other than the world because God is infinite and thus not limited by the world.[118]

Thomas Ryan finds that Christian practice of yoga is a concrete path to realizing union:

The meaning of yoga—union—says it all. This union, or harmonious integration of spirit and body, is not about uniting separate things. Rather, the practice of yoga fosters realization of the union which is already present. Union with parts of ourselves, with others, with all of creation, and with God.[119]

Thomas Merton explored Jewish, Islamic, Hindu, and Buddhist paths with a view to realizing more consciously the oneness that he believed already

---

[113] Bernard McGinn, *The Presence of God: A History of Western Christian Mysticism*, vol. 1, *The Foundations of Mysticism* (New York: Crossroad, 1991), 1:xvii.

[114] Gershom G. Scholem, *Kabbalah* (New York: Dorset Press, 1987), 4.

[115] John Renard, *Knowledge of God in Classical Sufism: Foundations of Islamic Mystical Theology*, trans. John Renard (New York: Paulist Press, 2004), 19.

[116] Annemarie Schimmel, *Mystical Dimensions of Islam* (Chapel Hill: University of North Carolina Press, 1975), 4.

[117] David Loy, *Nonduality in Buddhism and Beyond* (1988; reprint, Boston: Wisdom Publications, 2018).

[118] Nicholas of Cusa, *Nicholas of Cusa on God as Not-Other: A Translation and Appraisal of De Li Non Aliud,* ed. and trans. Jasper Hopkins (Minneapolis: A. J. Banning Press, 1987).

[119] Thomas Ryan, *Prayer of Heart and Body: Meditation and Yoga as Christian Spiritual Practice* (New York: Paulist Press, 1995), 211.

united practitioners; but as we have seen, he also disapproved of the mixing of traditions. He deeply respected the otherness of his interreligious dialogue partners. Nonetheless, in an informal talk in Calcutta, India, in October 1968, just two months before his death, he commented,

> And the deepest level of communication is not communication, but communion. It is wordless. It is beyond words, and it is beyond speech, and it is beyond concept. Not that we discover a new unity. We discover an older unity. My dear brothers, we are already one. But we imagine that we are not. And what we have to recover is our original unity. What we have to be is what we are.[120]

Many Catholics in the United States have discovered points of both convergence and divergence in walking spiritual paths with followers of other religious traditions. In some settings, there are openings toward the original unity and communion that Merton evoked. The call of Bonaventure to allow conscience to guide us on the path of purification, to accept the guidance of intelligence on the path of illumination, and to follow the fire of wisdom on the path of union finds new importance and application in developing interreligious relations.

---

[120] Thomas Merton, *The Asian Journal of Thomas Merton*, ed., Naomi Burton, Patrick Hart, and James Laughlin (New York: New Directions Book, 1973), 308.

Epilogue

A Blessing to the World

In his 1980 address to the Jewish community in Mainz, Germany, Pope John Paul II invoked God's promise to Abram in Genesis 12:2–3, and challenged Jews and Christians to be together a blessing to the world (Gn 12:2ff.) by working for peace and justice.[1] In 2015, Rabbi Jonathan Sacks repeated this call: "It is not our task to conquer or convert the world or enforce uniformity of belief. It is our task to be a blessing to the world."[2] The most urgent challenge that emerges from all the trials and struggles of living with religious pluralism in the United States is how followers of different religious paths can be a blessing to each other and to the world. In light of today's ecological crisis, followers of all religious paths are called to be a blessing for the world, that is, a blessing not only for human communities but for all forms of life and the earth.

In the Lotus Sutra, Shakyamuni Buddha presents a moving parable of children in a house on fire who are fascinated by their toys and oblivious to the flames that are threatening their lives. They are so preoccupied by their play that they fail to heed their father's shouts warning them to leave their toys behind and flee. At a time when fires rage through much of the Amazon rainforest, Siberia, Australia, and Indonesia, the vivid warning of the Buddha poignantly expresses the present dilemma of humans preoccupied with our toys and failing to heed the warnings of a planet increasingly on fire because of global climate change.[3] The repeated warnings of scientists regarding the condition of the earth have so far not brought about the necessary changes on a global scale to respond to this crisis. The ecological crisis threatening the community of life on earth is among the most urgent demands on the interreligious community.

Among the most important recent developments in the long history of religious pluralism in the United States is the channeling of interreligious

---

[1] John Paul II, "Address to Representatives of the Jewish Community, Mainz, Germany," November 17, 1980.

[2] Jonathan Sacks, *Not in God's Name: Confronting Religious Violence* (New York: Schocken Books, 2015), 4–5.

[3] *The Lotus Sutra,* trans. Burton Watson (New York: Columbia University Press, 1993), 56–57; Kendra Pierre-Louis, "The Amazon, Siberia, Indonesia: A World on Fire," *New York Times,* August 29, 2019; Keith Bradsher and Isabella Kwai, "Australia's Fires Test Its Winning Growth Formula," *New York Times,* January 14, 2020.

conversations toward care for the earth and the entire community of life on this planet. One prominent moment came in 1993 at the second convening of the Parliament of the World's Religions in Chicago, when physicist Gerald Barney delivered a moving evocation of the multiple threats to life on this planet in the lifetime of a child born on that day.[4] After Barney presented a series of very somber scientific predictions based on current trends, he challenged the leaders of all the world's religious traditions to marshal their moral authority in service of care for the earth. Rabbi Herman Schaalman was chairing the session and spoke immediately afterward: "Now we know why we have come. We have heard from the soul of a man for whom the universe is his soul."

Thomas Berry, who had already seen a connection between the comparative study of religious traditions and ecological concerns, was present and took Barney's plea to heart.[5] Earlier in his life Berry had studied the Confucian heritage, as well as Hinduism, Buddhism, and American Indian religious traditions, and he had founded the doctoral program in the history of religions at Fordham University, which trained many of the significant leaders in Catholic interreligious involvement for the next generation. As he became increasingly aware of ecological concerns, Berry came to see more and more that the trajectory of interreligious encounter must move toward addressing the crisis of all life on earth. Berry summed up the significance of the first two Parliaments:

> If the finest consequence of the First Parliament of Religions, held in 1893, was the recovery of a profound sense of the divine in the human soul through the leadership of Swami Vivekananda, the finest consequence of the second Parliament of Religions, held in 1993, should be the recovery of an exalted sense of the divine in the grandeur of the natural world. Vivekananda himself recognized that the locus for the meeting of the divine and the human must take place in the natural world if it is to survive in the human soul.[6]

Berry issued a forceful programmatic statement of what he called "The Great Work" as the current generation's primary challenge.[7] Berry warned of the dire consequences of a scientific-industrial worldview that views nature simply as resources to

---

[4] Gerald O. Barney, "What Shall We Do?," in *The Community of Religions: Voices and Images of the Parliament of the World's Religions*, ed. Wayne Teasdale and George F. Cairns (New York: Continuum, 1996), 77–82.

[5] Mary Evelyn Tucker, John Grim, and Andrew Angyal, *Thomas Berry: A Biography* (New York: Columbia University Press, 2019).

[6] Thomas Berry, "The Role of Religions in the Twenty-First Century," in *The Community of Religions: Voices and Images of the Parliament of the World's Religions*, ed. Wayne Teasdale and George F. Cairns (New York: Continuum, 1996), 182.

[7] Thomas Berry, *The Great Work: Our Way into the Future* (New York: Bell Tower, 1999); Thomas Berry, *Evening Thoughts: Reflecting on Earth as Sacred Community*, ed. Mary Evelyn Tucker (San Francisco: Sierra Club Books, 2006).

be exploited and plundered. Berry saw the 1993 Parliament as contributing to the awareness "that the natural world has from its beginning been a mystical as well as a physical reality. As the primary manifestation of the divine, the natural world is the primary sacred scripture and the primary sacred community."[8] Today, countless inter-religious discussions around the world include concern for ecology.

Because the ecological crisis is global, the response needs to be global, drawing upon the resources of all the world's religious traditions. Addressing the challenge calls for creativity and openness to insights from all sources. Across the United States, interreligious neighbors work together to shape a sustainable future that will be "really green."[9] Many religious leaders ponder how their traditions can enter their ecological phase.[10] American Indians come together to resist the devastation of the earth and explore their spiritual traditions for resources.[11] Buddhist ecologist Stephanie Kaza comments on how to develop whole-earth mindfulness: "The wisdom-seeking process is not a single path nor a predictable path."[12] The urgent teachings of the Buddha resonate with those of Jesus in the Gospels as well as with many other religious leaders in calling us to awaken to our current situation with all its peril, to seek wisdom and act resourcefully with compassion for all forms of life. With a similar sense of urgency, Pope Francis describes the contemporary world as caught in a type of Third World War and summons the Catholic community to serve as a field hospital for all who suffer.[13] Pope Francis laments the devastation of the earth and stresses the intrinsic relationship between care for the earth, care for the world's poor, and interreligious learning.[14] In his "Address to the Members of the Diplomatic Corps Accredited to the Holy See for the Traditional Exchange of New Year Greetings," on January 9, 2020, Pope Francis emphasized the importance of an ecological conversion in how humans relate to each other, other forms of life, and the earth; and he mourned: "Sadly, the urgency of this ecological conversion seems not to have been grasped by international politics, where the response to the problems raised by global issues such as climate change remains very weak and a source of grave concern."[15]

---

[8] Berry, "Role of Religions," 185.

[9] Erin Lothes Biviano, *Inspired Sustainability: Planting Seeds for Action* (Maryknoll, NY: Orbis Books, 2016).

[10] Mary Evelyn Tucker, *Worldly Wonder: Religions Enter Their Ecological Phase* (Chicago: Open Court, 2003).

[11] Jace Weaver, ed., *Defending Mother Earth: Native American Perspectives on Environmental Justice* (Maryknoll, NY: Orbis Books, 2001).

[12] Stephanie Kaza, *Mindfully Green: A Personal and Spiritual Guide to Whole Earth Thinking* (Boston: Shambhala, 2008), 95.

[13] Pope Francis, *The Name of God Is Mercy: A Conversation with Andrea Tornielli*, trans. Oonagh Stransky (New York: Random House, 2016), 8.

[14] Pope Francis, *Praise Be to You: Laudato Si': On Care for Our Common Home* (Vatican City: Libreria Editrice/San Francisco: Ignatius Press), 25–30.

[15] Pope Francis, "Address to the Members of the Diplomatic Corps Accredited to the Holy See for the Traditional Exchange of New Year Greetings," January 9, 2020.

Catholics who understand themselves to be serving in a field hospital can benefit from the cosmological visions and the practical wisdom of all the world's religious traditions and learn to collaborate with all people of good will. The invitation to be a blessing to each other calls us to walk with the practitioners of all religious paths in accepting the ecological challenge of becoming a blessing to the earth and the entire community of life on this planet.

Index

Abraham
  covenant with God, 22, 317–18, 363
  in Islam, 14, 15, 147–48, 298
Act of Toleration, 38
Adam, 269, 270, 318
Adams, Hannah, 41–42
Adams, John Quincy, 45
Adivasis (tribal communities of India),
    170, 171
Aelred of Rievaulx, 359, 360
Afonso V of Portugal, 66
African Americans
  African American Christianity, lack of
    respect for, 56
  African American theology, 212–16
  Black Catholic identity and religious
    pluralism, 326–27
  Chinese considered a level above,
    175–76
  First Amendment not applying to,
    135
  grassroots communities, importance to,
    208
  Great Awakening, accepting Christianity
    during, 38, 43
  Holy Spirit among Black Christians,
    262–64
  Jesus, perceptions of, 279, 284, 301–3
  Knights of Peter Claver, Black Catholics
    belonging to, 48
  Ku Klux Klan, as the target of, 53
  National Museum of African American
    History and Culture, xxii
  satyagraha concept, influence on civil
    rights movement, 157–59
  subordination of, Protestant
    justification for, 43

U.S. nation, not truly belonging to, 51
What We Have Seen and Heard pastoral
    letter, 326
African Methodist Episcopal Church, 43
African traditional religions
  aspects of, African American
    Christians retaining, 38
  Assisi World Day of Prayer,
    representation at, 20
  influence of, 94–97, 327
  melodies of spirituals as derived from,
    213, 301
  Middle Passage, root paradigms as
    surviving, 212
  Santería, honoring the spirits of, 93
  Spirit among, 262–64
  traditional practices considered as
    heathenish, 43
Against the Heresies (Irenaeus), 255
agape (unconditional love), 351, 353–54
Aitken, Robert, 311
Ajacán Mission, 34
Akiva, Rabbi, 292
Alexander, Scott, 141
Alexander II, Tsar, 48, 108
Alexander VI, Pope, 67, 92
Allen, Richard, 43
Allouez, Claude, 257
Amaro, Ajahn, 360
Ambedkar, B. R., 170
Ambrose, Saint, 269
American Indians
  American Indian Christian experience,
    65, 72–77
  Catholic identity, 324–26
  children, attempts to keep Native
    culture from, 358